PHYSICAL ANTHROPOLOGY AND ARCHAEOLOGY

Carol R. Ember
Human Relations Area Files

Melvin Ember
Human Relations Area Files

Peter N. Peregrine
Lawrence University

Prentice Hall

Upper Saddle River, New Jersey 07458

Library of Congress Cataloging-in-Publication Data

EMBER, CAROL R.
    Physical anthropology and archaeology/Carol R. Ember, Melvin Ember, Peter N.
Peregrine.—1st ed.
      p. cm.
    Includes bibliographical references and index.
    ISBN 0-13-092944-1 (pbk.)
    1. Physical anthropology.   2. Archaeology.   I. Ember, Melvin.   II. Peregrine, Peter N.
(Peter Neal).   III. Title.

GN60 .E45 1995
599.9—dc21

                                      2001033929

VP, Editorial Director: Laura Pearson
AVP, Publisher: Nancy Roberts
Managing Editor: Sharon Chambliss
Marketing Manager: Chris Barker
VP, Director of Production and Manufacturing: Barbara Kittle
Project Manager: Joan Stone
Prepress and Manufacturing Manager: Nick Sklitsis
Prepress and Manufacturing Buyer: Ben Smith
Creative Design Director: Leslie Osher
Art Director: Kathryn Foot
Interior and Cover Design: Eve Siegel
Asst. Manager, New Media: Lynn Pearlman
Media Project Manager: Kate Ramunda
Director, Image Resource Center: Melinda Reo
Manager, Rights and Permissions: Kay Dellosa
Interior Image Specialist: Beth Boyd
Photo Researcher: Sheila Norman
Cover Art (left to right): FBI Federal Bureau of Investigation; Joe Cornish/Stone;
Silver Burdett Ginn; John Reader/Science Photo Library/Photo Researchers, Inc.

This book was set in 10/11.5 Minion by ElectraGraphics
and was printed and bound by Courier Companies, Inc.
The cover was printed by Phoenix Color Corp.

© 2002 by Pearson Education, Inc.
Upper Saddle River, New Jersey 07458

Printed in the United States of America
10 9 8 7 6 5 4 3 2 1

ISBN 0-13-092944-1

Pearson Education LTD., London
Pearson Education Australia PTY, Limited, Sydney
Pearson Education Singapore, Pte. Ltd
Pearson Education North Asia Ltd, Hong Kong
Pearson Education Canada, Ltd., Toronto
Pearson Educación de Mexico, S.A. de C.V.
Pearson Education—Japan, Tokyo
Pearson Education Malaysia, Pte. Ltd
Pearson Education, Upper Saddle River, New Jersey

BRIEF CONTENTS

CONTENTS

BOXES

CURRENT ISSUES

NEW PERSPECTIVES ON GENDER

RESEARCH FRONTIERS

APPLIED ANTHROPOLOGY

The challenge of writing a textbook for an introductory course in physical anthropology and archaeology is finding the right balance between the details of human evolution and prehistory and conveying the larger picture so that students can understand where humans came from, where we might be going, and how knowledge about the past may be useful. This first edition of *Physical Anthropology and Archaeology* is a much expanded and revised version of the physical and archaeology sections of Ember and Ember's *Anthropology*. As always, we try to go beyond descriptions. We are interested not only in *what* humans are and were like; we are also interested in *why* they got to be that way, in all their variety. When there are alternative explanations, we try to communicate the necessity to evaluate them both logically and on the basis of the available evidence. Throughout the book, we try to communicate that no idea, including ideas put forward in textbooks, should be accepted even tentatively without supporting tests that could have gone the other way.

This book has four foci. First, we focus on the physical evidence of human evolution—not only the fossils but also the genetics and evolutionary processes that help us make sense of the fossils. Second, we focus on the major "revolutions" in human cultural evolution—the emergence of patterned stone tools, the elaboration of complex culture, the development of domesticated plants and animals, and the rise of cities and states. Third, we explore contemporary variation in humans, and particularly the concept of "race." Finally, we consider how physical anthropologists and archaeologists apply their knowledge to problems and issues of practical importance today.

Part I: Introduction

CHAPTER 1: WHAT IS ANTHROPOLOGY?

Chapter 1 introduces the student to anthropology. We discuss what we think is special and distinctive about anthropology in general, and about each of its subfields in particular. We outline how each of the subfields is related to other disciplines such as biology, psychology, and sociology. We direct attention to the increasing importance of applied anthropology. There are four boxes, each focusing on an individual anthropologist and her or his work.

CHAPTER 2: HOW WE DISCOVER THE PAST

Chapter 2 gives an overview of archaeological research. We discuss the types of evidence archaeologists and paleoanthropologists use to reconstruct the past, the methods they use to collect the evidence, and how they go about analyzing and interpreting the evidence of the past. We also describe the many techniques used by archaeologists and paleoanthropologists to determine the age of archaeological materials and fossils. There are two boxes, one examining

evidence for unilinear trends in cultural evolution, the other considering how gender is studied by archaeologists.

Part II: Human Evolution: Biological and Cultural

CHAPTER 3: GENETICS AND EVOLUTION

Chapter 3 discusses evolutionary theory as it applies to all forms of life, including humans. Following an extensive review of genetics and the processes of evolution, including natural selection and what it means, we discuss how natural selection may operate on behavioral traits and how cultural evolution differs from biological evolution. We consider ethical issues posed by the possibility of genetic engineering. The first box examines the evidence suggesting that evolution proceeds abruptly rather than slowly and steadily. The second box discusses whether genetic engineering should be feared.

CHAPTER 4: THE LIVING PRIMATES

Chapter 4 describes the living nonhuman primates and their variable adaptations as background for understanding the evolution of primates in general and humans in particular. After describing the various kinds of primate, we discuss some possible explanations of how the primates differ—in body and brain size, size of social group, and female sexuality. The chapter ends with a discussion of the distinctive features of humans in comparison with the other primates. The first box deals with how and why many primates are endangered and how they might be protected. The second box describes a primatologist and some of her work.

CHAPTER 5: PRIMATE EVOLUTION: FROM EARLY PRIMATES TO HOMINOIDS

Chapter 5 begins with the emergence of the early primates and ends with what we know or suspect about the Miocene apes, one of whom (known or unknown) was ancestral to bipedal hominids. We link major trends in primate evolution to broader environmental changes that may have caused natural selection to favor new traits. To highlight how theory is generated and revised, the first box explains how a paleoanthropologist has reexamined his own theory of primate origins. The second box describes a giant ape that lived at the same time as the first humans, and why that ape became extinct.

CHAPTER 6: THE FIRST HOMINIDS

Chapter 6 discusses the evolution of bipedal locomotion—the most distinctive feature of the group that includes our genus and those of our direct ancestors, the australopithecines. We discuss the various types of australopithecines and how they might have evolved. The first two boxes discuss new australopithecine finds and how they appear to fit into our current understanding of human evolution. The third box describes the technique of cladistic analysis, widely used by paleoanthropologists to chart evolutionary relationships.

CHAPTER 7: THE ORIGINS OF CULTURE AND THE EMERGENCE OF HOMO

Chapter 7 examines the first clear evidences of cultural behavior—stone tools—and other clues suggesting that early hominids had begun to develop culture about 2.5 million years ago. We discuss what culture is and how it may have evolved. We then discuss the hominids—the first members of our genus, *Homo*—who are most likely responsible for the early signs of cultural behavior. The first box discusses hunting behavior by chimpanzees as a model for early human hunting. The second box examines the evolution of the brain and the physical changes in early humans that allowed the brain to increase in size. The third box explains how archaeologists and paleoanthropologists distinguish stone tools from ordinary rocks.

CHAPTER 8: HOMO ERECTUS AND THE ORIGINS OF LANGUAGE

This chapter focuses on *Homo erectus*, the first hominid to leave Africa and the first to demonstrate complex cultural behavior. We examine *Homo erectus* culture through stone tools, hunting and butchering of large game, and campsites. We then consider whether *Homo erectus* may have developed language. After describing language and its evolution, we conclude that *Homo erectus* did not likely have language as we know it today. The first box discusses research evaluating the claim that *Homo erectus* should be divided into two species. The second box describes how paleoanthropologists and artists work together to reconstruct the faces of early humans. The third box considers whether mother-infant communication may have led to the development of language.

 Part III: Modern Humans

CHAPTER 9: THE EMERGENCE OF HOMO SAPIENS

Chapter 9 examines the transition between *Homo erectus* and *Homo sapiens* and the emergence of modern-looking humans. In keeping with our global orientation, we discuss fossil and archaeological evidence from many areas of the world, not just from Europe and the Near East. We give special consideration to the Neandertals and the question of their relationship to modern humans. One box feature examines patterns of growth and development among Neandertals as a way of evaluating how long their period of infancy was. The other box describes the evidence from mitochondrial DNA regarding the "Out-of-Africa" theory of modern human origins.

CHAPTER 10: THE UPPER PALEOLITHIC WORLD

Chapter 10 considers the cultures of modern humans in the period before agriculture developed, roughly 40,000 to 10,000 years ago. We examine their tools, their economies, and their art—the first art made by humans. We also discuss human colonization of North and South America and the impact of humans on the new environments they encountered. The first box examines the possible routes humans may have taken to enter the Americas. The second box considers how women are depicted in Upper Paleolithic art.

CHAPTER 11: ORIGINS OF FOOD PRODUCTION AND SETTLED LIFE

Chapter 11 deals with the emergence of broad-spectrum collecting and settled life, and then the domestication of plants and animals in various parts of the world. Our discussion focuses mainly on the possible causes and consequences of these developments in Mesoamerica and the Near East, but we also consider Southeast Asia, Africa, North and South America, and Europe. The first box examines the domestication of dogs and cats; the second box describes how researchers are finding out about ancient diets from chemical analysis of bones and teeth.

CHAPTER 12: ORIGINS OF CITIES AND STATES

Chapter 12 deals with the rise of civilizations in various parts of the world and the theories that have been offered to explain the development of state-type political systems. Our focus is on the evolution of cities and states in Mesoamerica and the Near East, but we also discuss the rise of cities and states in South America, South Asia, China, and Africa. How states affect people living in them and their environments is examined. We conclude with a discussion of the decline and collapse of states. One box considers the links between imperialism, colonialism, and the state. The other box discusses the consequences of ancient imperialism for women's status.

CHAPTER 13: HUMAN VARIATION AND ADAPTATION

Chapter 13 brings the discussion of human biological and cultural evolution into the present by dealing with physical variation in living human populations and how physical anthropologists study and explain such variation. We examine how both the physical environment and the cultural environment play important roles in human physical variation. In a section on race and racism we discuss why many anthropologists think the concept of "race" as applied to humans is not scientifically useful. We talk about the myths of racism and how "race" is largely a social category in humans. The first box deals with biological factors affecting the capacity to have offspring; the second box reviews differences in average I.Q. scores and what they mean; and the third box explores African American versus European American disparities in death.

 Part IV: Using Anthropology

CHAPTER 14: APPLIED AND PRACTICING ANTHROPOLOGY

This chapter discusses the types of jobs outside of academia, the history and types of applied anthropology in the United States, the ethical issues involved in trying to improve people's lives, the difficulties in evaluating whether a program is beneficial, and ways of implementing planned changes. We point out how applied anthropologists are playing more of a role in planning change rather than just advising programs already in place. The two boxes show how anthropologists have been able to help in business and in reforestation.

CHAPTER 15: MEDICAL ANTHROPOLOGY

This chapter discusses cultural understandings of health and illness, the treatment of illness (particularly from a biocultural rather than just a biomedical point of view), political and economic influences on health, and the contributions of medical anthropologists to the study of various health conditions and diseases. Those conditions and diseases include AIDS, mental and emotional disorders, the folk illness *susto*, depression, and undernutrition. The first box deals with why an applied medical project didn't work; the second box considers eating disorders and the cultural construction of "beauty." The third box examines the effects of modernization on health and nutrition.

 Other Features

BOXES IN EACH CHAPTER

Current Issues These boxes deal with topics students may have heard about in the news or topics that are currently the subject of debate in the profession.

Research Frontiers These boxes look at researchers at work or take an in-depth look at new research or a research controversy.

New Perspectives on Gender These boxes involve issues pertaining to sex and gender, both in anthropology and everyday life.

Applied Anthropology These boxes deal with some of the ways anthropologists have applied their knowledge to practical problems.

READABILITY

We derive a lot of pleasure from trying to describe research findings, especially complicated ones, in ways that introductory students can understand. Thus, we try to minimize technical jargon, using only those terms students must know to appreciate the achievements of anthropology and to take advanced courses. We think readability is important, not only because it may enhance the reader's understanding of what we write, but also because it should make learning about anthropology more enjoyable! When new terms are introduced, which of course must happen sometimes, they are set off in boldface type and defined right away.

GLOSSARY TERMS

At the end of each chapter we list the new terms that have been introduced; these terms were identified by boldface type and defined in the text. We deliberately do not repeat the definitions at the end of the chapter to allow students to test themselves against the definitions provided in the Glossary at the end of the book.

CRITICAL QUESTIONS

We also provide three or four questions at the end of each chapter that may stimulate thinking about the implications of the chapter. The questions do not ask for repetition of what is in the text. We want students to imagine, to go beyond what we know or think we know.

INTERNET EXERCISES

Internet exercises have been developed to provide students with Web-based resources on topics covered in each chapter. Students are encouraged to use the Internet addresses (URLs) to discover more about the changes that are occurring in the field of anthropology.

SUMMARIES AND SUGGESTED READING

In addition to the outline provided at the beginning of each chapter, there is a detailed summary at the end of each chapter that will help the student review the major concepts and findings discussed. Suggested Reading provides general or more extensive references on the subject matter of the chapter.

A COMPLETE GLOSSARY AT THE END OF THE BOOK

Important glossary terms for each chapter are listed (without definitions) at the end of each chapter, so students can readily check their understanding after they have read the chapter. A complete Glossary is provided at the back of the book to review all terms in the book and serve as a convenient reference for the student.

NOTES AT THE END OF THE BOOK

Because we believe firmly in the importance of documentation, we think it essential to tell our readers, both professional and student, what our conclusions are based on. Usually the basis is published research. References to the relevant studies are provided in complete notes by chapter at the end of the book.

BIBLIOGRAPHY AT THE END OF THE BOOK

All of the references cited throughout the book are collected and listed at the end of the book.

Supplements

The supplement package for this textbook has been carefully crafted to amplify and illuminate materials in the text itself.

FOR THE PROFESSOR

Instructor's Resource Manual This essential instructor's tool includes chapter outlines, resources for discussion, discussion questions, paper topics and research projects, web resources, and film resources. The instructor's manual is available in an electronic version on the faculty CD-ROM.

Test Item File This carefully prepared manual includes over 1,600 questions in multiple-choice, true/false, and essay formats. All test questions are page-referenced to the text. The test questions are available in both **Windows** and **Macintosh** computerized formats. Contact your Prentice Hall representative for more details.

Interactive CD-ROM, Faculty Version Available with every new copy of the text, this CD-ROM provides an exciting learning experience for students. Interactive simulations and exercises, a complete map atlas, and reference resources all help to illustrate the concepts described in the book. Included on the faculty version are the instructor's manual, PowerPoint™ slides, and other materials designed to enhance the classroom learning environment.

Distance Learning Solutions Prentice Hall is committed to providing our anthropology content to the growing number of courses being delivered over the Internet by developing relationships with the leading vendors. Please see your Prentice Hall sales representative for more information.

Transparency Acetates Taken from graphs, diagrams, and tables in this text and other sources, these full-color transparencies offer an effective means of amplifying lecture topics.

Videos Prentice Hall is pleased to offer two new video series: *The Changing American Indian in a Changing America: Videocases of American Indian Peoples,* and *Rites of Passage: Videocases of Traditional African Peoples.* In addition, a selection of high quality, award-winning videos from the Filmmakers Library collection is available upon adoption. Please see your Prentice Hall sales representative for more information.

FOR THE STUDENT

Study Guide Designed to reinforce information in the text, the study guide includes chapter outlines and summaries, glossary term definition exercises, and self-test questions keyed to the text.

Companion Website™ In tandem with the text, students can now take full advantage of the World Wide Web to enrich their study of anthropology through the Ember Website. This resource correlates the text with related material available on the Internet. Features of the Website include chapter objectives, study questions, and links to interesting material and information from other sites on the Web that can reinforce and enhance the content of each chapter. Address: **www.prenhall.com/ember**

Interactive CD-ROM Available with every new copy of the text, this CD-ROM provides an exciting learning experience for students. Interactive simulations and exercises, a complete map atlas, and reference resources all help to illustrate the concepts described in the book.

Anthropology on the Internet: Evaluating Online Resources, 2001 This guide focuses on developing the critical thinking skills necessary to evaluate and use online sources effectively. The guide also provides a brief introduction to navigating the Internet, along with complete references related specifically to the anthropology discipline and how to use the *Companion Websites™* available for many Prentice Hall textbooks. This brief supplementary book is free to students when shrinkwrapped as a package with *any anthropology title.*

The New York Times/*Prentice Hall Themes of the Times*
The New York Times and Prentice Hall are sponsoring *Themes of the Times,* a program designed to enhance student access to current information relevant to the classroom.  Through this program, the core subject matter provided in the text is supplemented by a collection of timely articles from one of the world's most distinguished newspapers, *The New York Times.* These articles demonstrate the vital, ongoing connection between what is learned in the classroom and what is happening in the world around us. To enjoy a wealth of information provided by *The New York Times* daily, a reduced subscription rate is available. For information, call toll-free: 1–800–631–1222.

Prentice Hall and *The New York Times* are proud to co-sponsor *Themes of the Times.* We hope it will make the reading of both textbooks and newspapers a more dynamic, involving process.

Acknowledgments

We thank the people at Prentice Hall for all their help: Nancy Roberts, Publisher for the Social Sciences; Sharon

Chambliss, Managing Editor; Joan Stone for seeing the manuscript through the production process; and Sheila Norman for photo research.

We could not include all the suggestions they made, but we are grateful to the following people for their suggestions about what to include in the new chapter on medical anthropology: Carole Browner, William Dressler, Alan Goodman, W. Penn Handwerker, Leslie Sue Lieberman, Shirley Lindenbaum, Margaret Lock, and Arthur Rubel.

We want to thank the following for reviewing our other chapters and making suggestions about them:

Marie Boutté, University of Nevada, Reno
I. Randolph Daniel, Jr., East Carolina University
Meini Deng, Edmonds Community College
Jeffrey R. Hanson, University of Texas–Arlington
S. Homes Hogue, Mississippi State University
Lucy Jayne Kamau, Northeastern Illinois University
Timothy J. Kloberdanz, North Dakota State University
Michael C. Robbins, University of Missouri

Thank you all, named and unnamed, who gave us advice.

Carol R. Ember, Melvin Ember, and Peter N. Peregrine

Carol R. Ember started at Antioch College as a chemistry major. She began taking social science courses because some were required, but she soon found herself intrigued. There were lots of questions without answers, and she became excited about the possibility of a research career in social science. She spent a year in graduate school at Cornell studying sociology before continuing on to Harvard, where she studied anthropology primarily with John and Beatrice Whiting.

For her Ph.D. dissertation she worked among the Luo of Kenya. While there she noticed that many boys were assigned "girls' work," such as babysitting and household chores, because their mothers (who did most of the agriculture) did not have enough girls to help out. She decided to study the possible effects of task assignment on the social behavior of boys. Using systematic behavior observations, she compared girls, boys who did a great deal of girls' work, and boys who did little such work. She found that boys assigned girls' work were intermediate in many social behaviors, compared with the other boys and girls. Later, she did cross-cultural research on variation in marriage, family, descent groups, and war and peace, mainly in collaboration with Melvin Ember, whom she married in 1970. All of these cross-cultural studies tested theories on data for worldwide samples of societies.

From 1970 to 1996, she taught at Hunter College of the City University of New York. She has also served as president of the Society of Cross-Cultural Research and was one of the directors of the Summer Institutes in Comparative Anthropological Research, which were funded by the National Science Foundation. She is now executive director at the Human Relations Area Files, Inc., a nonprofit research agency at Yale University.

After graduating from Columbia College, Melvin Ember went to Yale University for his Ph.D. His mentor at Yale was George Peter Murdock, an anthropologist who was instrumental in promoting cross-cultural research and building a full-text database on the cultures of the world to facilitate cross-cultural hypothesis testing. This database came to be known as the Human Relations Area Files (HRAF) because it was originally sponsored by the Insti-

tute of Human Relations at Yale. Growing in annual installments and now distributed in electronic format, the HRAF database currently covers more than 370 cultures, past and present, all over the world.

Melvin Ember did fieldwork for his dissertation in American Samoa, where he conducted a comparison of three villages to study the effects of commercialization on political life. In addition, he did research on descent groups and how they changed with the increase of buying and selling. His cross-cultural studies focused originally on variation in marital residence and descent groups. He has also done cross-cultural research on the relationship between economic and political development, the origin and extension of the incest taboo, the causes of polygyny, and how archaeological correlates of social customs can help us draw inferences about the past.

After four years of research at the National Institute of Mental Health, he taught at Antioch College and then Hunter College of the City University of New York. He has served as president of the Society for Cross-Cultural Research and has been president since 1987 of the Human Relations Area Files, Inc., a nonprofit research agency of Yale University.

Peter N. Peregrine came to anthropology after completing an undergraduate degree in English. He found anthropology's social scientific approach to understanding humans more appealing than the humanistic approach he had learned as an English major. He undertook an ethnohistorical study of the relationship between Jesuit missionaries and Native American peoples for his master's degree and realized that he needed to study archaeology to understand the cultural interactions experienced by Native Americans prior to contact with the Jesuits.

While working on his Ph.D. at Purdue University, Peter Peregrine did research on the prehistoric Mississippian cultures of the eastern United States. He found that interactions between groups were common and had been shaping Native American cultures for centuries. Native Americans approached contact with the Jesuits simply as another in a long string of intercultural exchanges. He also found that relatively little research had been done on

Native American interactions and decided that comparative research was a good place to begin examining the topic. In 1990 he participated in the Summer Institute in Comparative Anthropological Research, where he met Carol R. Ember and Melvin Ember.

Peter Peregrine taught at Juniata College and is currently Associate Professor and Chair of the anthropology department at Lawrence University in Appleton, Wiscon-

sin. He serves as research associate for the HRAF Collection of Archaeology and is co-editor with Melvin Ember of the *Encyclopedia of Prehistory*. He continues to do archaeological research, and he recently celebrated his first decade of teaching anthropology and archaeology to undergraduate students.

1

What Is Anthropology?

Anthropology, by definition, is a discipline of infinite curiosity about human beings. The term comes from the Greek *anthropos* for "man, human" and *logos* for "study." Anthropologists seek answers to an enormous variety of questions about humans. They are interested in discovering when, where, and why humans appeared on the earth, how and why they have changed since then, and how and why modern human populations vary in certain physical features. Anthropologists are also interested in how and why societies in the past and present have varied in their customary ideas and practices. There is a practical side to anthropology too. Applied and practicing anthropologists put anthropological methods, information, and results to use, in efforts to solve practical problems.

But defining anthropology as the study of human beings is not complete, for such a definition would appear to incorporate a whole catalog of disciplines: sociology, psychology, political science, economics, history, human biology, and perhaps even the humanistic disciplines of philosophy and literature. Needless to say, practitioners of the many other disciplines concerned with humans would not be happy to be regarded as being in subbranches of anthropology. After all, most of those disciplines have existed longer than anthropology, and each is somewhat distinctive. There must, then, be something unique about anthropology—a reason for its having developed as a separate discipline and for its having retained a separate identity over the last 100 years.

The Scope of Anthropology

Anthropologists are generally thought of as individuals who travel to little-known corners of the world to study exotic peoples or who dig deep into the earth to uncover the fossil remains or the tools and pots of people who lived long ago. These views, though clearly stereotyped, do indicate how anthropology differs from other disciplines concerned with humans. Anthropology is broader in scope, both geographically and historically. Anthropology is concerned explicitly and directly with all varieties of people throughout the world, not just those close at hand or within a limited area. It is also interested in people of all periods. Beginning with the immediate ancestors of humans, who lived a few million years ago, anthropology traces the development of humans until the present. Every part of the world that has ever contained a human population is of interest to anthropologists.

Anthropologists have not always been as global and comprehensive in their concerns as they are today. Traditionally, they concentrated on non-Western cultures and left the study of Western civilization and similarly complex societies, with their recorded histories, to other disciplines. In recent years, however, this division of labor among the disciplines has begun to disappear. Now anthropologists work in their own and other complex societies.

What induces anthropologists to choose so broad a subject for study? In part, they are motivated by the belief that any suggested generalization about human beings, any possible explanation of some characteristic of human culture or biology, should be shown to apply to many times and places of human existence. If a generalization or explanation does not prove to apply widely, we are entitled or even obliged to be skeptical about it. The skeptical attitude, in the absence of persuasive evidence, is our best protection against accepting invalid ideas about humans.

For example, when American educators discovered in the 1960s that African American schoolchildren rarely drank milk, they assumed that lack of money or education was the cause. But evidence from anthropology suggested a different explanation. Anthropologists had known for years that in many parts of the world where milking animals are kept, people do not drink fresh milk; rather, they sour it before they drink it, or they make it into cheese. Why they do so is now clear. Many people lack an enzyme, lactase, that is necessary for breaking down lactose, the sugar in milk. When such people drink regular milk, it actually interferes with digestion. Not only is the lactose in milk not digested but other nutrients are less likely to be digested as well; in many cases, drinking milk will cause cramps, stomach gas, diarrhea, and nausea. Studies indicate that milk intolerance is found in many parts of the world.[1] The condition is common in adulthood among Asians, southern Europeans, Arabs and Jews, West Africans, Inuit (Eskimos), and North and South American Indians, as well as African Americans. Because anthropologists are acquainted with human life in an enormous variety of geographic and historical settings, they are often able to correct mistaken beliefs about different groups of people.

The Holistic Approach

In addition to the worldwide as well as historical scope of anthropology, another distinguishing feature of the discipline is its **holistic**, or multifaceted, approach to the study of human beings. Anthropologists study not only all varieties of people but many aspects of human experience as well. For example, when describing a group of people, an anthropologist might discuss the history of the area in which the people live, the physical environment, the organization of family life, the general features of their language, the group's settlement patterns, political and economic systems, religion, and styles of art and dress.

In the past, individual anthropologists tried to be holistic and cover many subjects. Today, as in many other disciplines, so much information has been accumulated that anthropologists tend to specialize in one topic or area. Thus, one anthropologist may investigate the physical characteristics of some of our prehistoric ancestors. Another may study the biological effect of the environment on a human population over time. Still another will concentrate on the customs of a particular group of people.

Despite this specialization, however, the discipline of anthropology retains its holistic orientation in that its many different specialties, taken together, describe many aspects of human existence, both past and present.

The Anthropological Curiosity

Thus far we have described anthropology as being broader in scope, both historically and geographically, and more holistic in approach than other disciplines concerned with human beings. But this statement again implies that anthropology is the all-inclusive human science. How, then, is anthropology really different from those other disciplines? We suggest that anthropology's distinctiveness lies principally in the kind of curiosity it arouses.

Anthropologists are concerned with many types of questions: Where, when, and why did people first begin living in cities? Why do some peoples have darker skin than others? Why do some languages contain more terms for color than other languages? Why do women have more of a voice in politics in some societies than in others? Why do populations differ in their acceptance of birth control? Although these questions deal with very different aspects of human existence, they have at least one thing in common: They all deal with *typical characteristics* (traits, customs) of particular populations. The typical characteristic of a people might be relatively dark skin, a language with many color terms, female participation in politics, or ac-

ceptance of birth control. This concern with typical characteristics of populations is perhaps the most distinguishing feature of anthropology. For example, whereas economists take a monetary system for granted and study how it operates, anthropologists ask why only some societies during the last few thousand years used money. In short, anthropologists are curious about the typical characteristics of human populations—how and why such populations and their characteristics have varied throughout the ages.

Fields of Anthropology

Different anthropologists concentrate on different typical characteristics of societies. Some are concerned primarily with *physical,* or *biological, characteristics* of human populations; others are interested principally in what we call *cultural characteristics.* Hence there are two broad classifications of subject matter in anthropology: **physical anthropology** (sometimes called biological anthropology) and **cultural anthropology.** Physical anthropology is one major field of anthropology. Cultural anthropology is divided into three major subfields—archaeology, linguistics, and ethnology. Ethnology, the study of recent cultures, is now usually referred to by the parent name, cultural anthropology (see Figure 1–1). Cross-cutting these four fields is a fifth, **applied** or **practicing anthropology.**

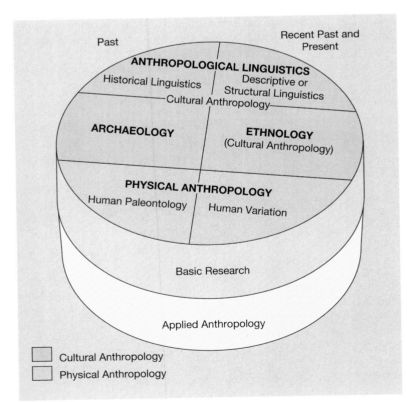

Figure 1–1
The Subdivisions of Anthropology

The four major subdisciplines of anthropology (in bold letters) may be classified according to subject matter (physical or cultural) and according to the period with which each is concerned (distant past versus recent past and present). There are applications of anthropology in all four subdisciplines.

CD-ROM Exercise I-1

PHYSICAL ANTHROPOLOGY

Physical anthropology (sometimes called biological anthropology) seeks to answer two distinct sets of questions. The first set includes questions about the emergence of humans and their later evolution (this focus is called **human paleontology** or **paleoanthropology**). The second set includes questions about how and why contemporary human populations vary biologically (this focus is called **human variation**).

In order to reconstruct human evolution, human paleontologists search for and study the buried, hardened remains or impressions—known as **fossils**—of humans, prehumans, and related animals. Paleontologists working in East Africa, for instance, have excavated the fossil remains of humanlike beings who lived more than 3 million years ago. These findings have suggested the approximate dates when our ancestors began to develop two-legged walking, very flexible hands, and a larger brain.

In attempting to clarify evolutionary relationships, human paleontologists may use not only the fossil record but also geological information on the succession of climates, environments, and plant and animal populations. Moreover, when reconstructing the past of humans, paleontologists are also interested in the behavior and evolution of our closest relatives among the mammals—the prosimians, monkeys, and apes, which, like ourselves, are members of the order of **Primates**. Anthropologists, psychologists, and biologists who specialize in the study of primates are called **primatologists**. The various species of primates are observed in the wild and in the laboratory. One especially popular subject of study is the chimpanzee,

which bears a close resemblance to humans in behavior and physical appearance, has a similar blood chemistry, and is susceptible to many of the same diseases. It now appears that chimpanzees share 99 percent of their genes with humans.[2]

From primate studies, physical anthropologists try to discover characteristics that are distinctly human, as opposed to those that might be part of the primate heritage. With this information, they may be able to infer what our prehistoric ancestors were like. The inferences from primate studies are checked against the fossil record. The evidence from the earth, collected in bits and pieces, is correlated with scientific observations of our closest living relatives. In short, physical anthropologists piece together bits of information obtained from different sources. They construct theories that explain the changes observed in the fossil record and then attempt to evaluate their theories by checking one kind of evidence against another. Human paleontology thus overlaps disciplines such as geology, general vertebrate (and particularly primate) paleontology, comparative anatomy, and the study of comparative primate behavior.

The second major focus of physical anthropology, the study of human variation, investigates how and why contemporary human populations differ in biological or physical characteristics. All living people belong to one species, ***Homo sapiens sapiens,*** for all can successfully interbreed. Yet there is much that varies among human populations. Investigators of human variation ask such questions as: Why are some peoples taller than others? How have human populations adapted physically to their environmental conditions? Are some peoples, such as Inuit (Eskimos), better equipped than other peoples to endure cold? Does darker skin pigmentation offer special protection against the tropical sun?

To understand better the biological variations observ-

Nadine Peacock, a biological anthropologist, studying reproduction and health among the Efe-Ituri Pygmies of Zaire.

RESEARCH FRONTIERS

Researcher at Work: Timothy G. Bromage

When Timothy Bromage was young, his parents took him to hear a lecture by the legendary paleoanthropologist Louis Leakey. He isn't sure why his parents had driven so far and paid so much to hear this lecture, nor why they had dragged him along. But he does know that it started him on the way to becoming a paleoanthropologist himself. Three decades ago, he was brought to hear a lecture on paleoanthropology. Now he gives such lectures regularly at Hunter College of the City University of New York, where he is a professor of anthropology.

Bromage specializes in studies of growth and development in the earliest members of the human family, the australopithecines, dating back over 2 million years ago. He is particularly interested in how the face grows. Ever since graduate school, he was aware that humans, both ancient and modern, physically change over their lifetimes. Traditional studies of fossils treated organisms as static, as if maturity didn't make a difference. Bromage wondered if it would be possible to study fossils to learn how ancient humans had physically changed as they grew up. Working with researchers at University College London, Bromage found that with modern skulls one can determine how bones change as an organism matures by looking at patterns of tissue deposition and resorption using a scanning electron microscope. Could the same technique be used to study growth and development in fossil skulls? After several years of collecting and studying fossils and perfecting techniques, Bromage was able to answer that question with a yes.

Bromage found that specimens commonly referred to as gracile australopithecines grew to adulthood in a very ape-like manner—the front parts of the skull built up tissue that grew into very forward-jutting faces and jaws. Thus, by looking at fossil faces and how they changed with age, Bromage developed an entirely new way to study how our ancient ancestors had evolved. He found that experimental techniques using electron microscopy can tell us things about fossils that surface inspection of the bones cannot tell us. For example, he discovered that the later, robust australopithecine had a pattern of facial growth that resulted in a flatter face than in the gracile australopithecine, a flatter face more like the face in modern humans.

Tim Bromage examining a stone tool made by an early human.

Source: Timothy G. Bromage, "Paleoanthropology and Life History, and Life History of a Paleoanthropologist," in Carol R. Ember, Melvin Ember, and Peter N. Peregrine, eds, *Research Frontiers in Anthropology,* vol. 1 (Upper Saddle River, NJ: Prentice Hall, 1998). Prentice Hall/ Simon & Schuster Custom Publishing.

able among contemporary human populations, physical anthropologists use the principles, concepts, and techniques of at least three other disciplines: human genetics (the study of human traits that are inherited), population biology (the study of environmental effects on, and interaction with, population characteristics), and epidemiology (the study of how and why diseases affect different populations in different ways). Research on human variation, therefore, overlaps research in other fields. Physical anthropologists, however, are concerned most with human populations and how they vary biologically.

CULTURAL ANTHROPOLOGY

Cultural anthropologists are interested in how populations or societies vary in their cultural features. But what is culture? To an anthropologist, the term **culture** refers to the customary ways of thinking and behaving of a particular population or society. The culture of a social group includes many things—its language, religious beliefs, food preferences, music, work habits, gender roles, how they rear their children, how they construct their houses, and many other learned behaviors and ideas that have come to be widely shared or customary among the group. The three main branches of cultural anthropology are **archaeology** (the study of past cultures, primarily through their material remains), **anthropological linguistics** (the anthropological study of languages), and **ethnology** (the study of existing and recent cultures), now usually referred to by the parent name, cultural anthropology.

ARCHAEOLOGY The archaeologist seeks not only to reconstruct the daily life and customs of peoples who lived in the past but also to trace cultural changes and to offer possible explanations for those changes. This concern is similar to that of the historian, but the archaeologist reaches much farther back in time. The historian deals only with societies that left written records and is therefore limited to the last 5,000 years of human history. Human societies, however, have existed for more than a million years, and only a small proportion in the last 5,000 years had writing. For all those past societies lacking a written record, the archaeologist serves as historian. Lacking written records for study, archaeologists must try to reconstruct history from the remains of human cultures. Some of these remains are as grand as the Mayan temples discovered at Chichén Itzá in Yucatán, Mexico. More often they are as ordinary as bits of broken pottery, stone tools, and garbage heaps.

Most archaeologists deal with **prehistory,** the time before written records. But there is a specialty within archaeology, called **historical archaeology,** that studies the remains of recent peoples who left written records. This specialty, as its name implies, employs the methods of both archaeologists and historians to study recent societies for which there is both archaeological and historical information.

In trying to understand how and why ways of life have changed through time in different parts of the world, archaeologists collect materials from sites of human occupation. Usually, these sites must be unearthed. On the basis of materials they have excavated and otherwise collected, they then ask various questions: Where, when, and why did the distinctive human characteristic of toolmaking first emerge? Where, when, and why did agriculture first develop? Where, when, and why did people first begin to live in cities?

To collect the data they need in order to suggest answers to these and other questions, archaeologists use techniques and findings borrowed from other disciplines, as well as what they can infer from anthropological studies of recent and contemporary cultures. For example, to guess where to dig for evidence of early toolmaking, archaeologists rely on geology to tell them where sites of early human occupation are likely to be found, because of erosion and uplifting, near the surface of the earth. To infer when agriculture first developed, archaeologists date the relevant excavated materials by a process originally developed by chemists. And to try to understand why cities first emerged, archaeologists may use information from historians, geographers, and others about how recent and contemporary cities are related economically and politically to their hinterlands. If we can discover what recent and contemporary cities have in common, we can speculate on why cities developed originally. Thus, archaeologists use information from the present and recent past in trying to understand the distant past.

ANTHROPOLOGICAL LINGUISTICS Anthropological linguistics is another branch of cultural anthropology. *Linguistics,* or the study of languages, is a somewhat older discipline than anthropology, but the early linguists concentrated on the study of languages that had been written for a long time—languages such as English that had been written for nearly a thousand years. Anthropological linguists began to do fieldwork in places where the language was not yet written. This meant that anthropologists could not consult a dictionary or grammar to help them learn the language. Instead, they first had to construct a dictionary and grammar. Then they could study the structure and history of the language.

Like physical anthropologists, linguists study changes that have taken place over time, as well as contemporary variation. Some anthropological linguists are concerned with the emergence of language and also with the divergence of languages over thousands of years. The study of how languages change over time and how they may be related is known as **historical linguistics.** Anthropological linguists are also interested in how contemporary languages differ, especially in their construction. This focus of linguistics is generally called **descriptive** or **structural linguistics.** The study of how language is used in social contexts is called **sociolinguistics.**

In contrast with the human paleontologist and archaeologist, who have physical remains to help them reconstruct change over time, the historical linguist deals only with languages—and usually unwritten ones at that. (Remember that writing is only about 5,000 years old, and most languages since then have not been written.) Because an unwritten language must be heard in order to be studied, it does not leave any trace once its speakers have died. Linguists interested in reconstructing the history of unwritten languages must begin in the present, with comparisons of contemporary languages. On the basis of these comparisons, they draw inferences about the kinds of

NEW PERSPECTIVES ON GENDER

Researcher at Work: **Elizabeth M. Brumfiel**

Now a professor of anthropology at Albion College, Elizabeth Brumfiel became interested in the origins of social inequality when she was an undergraduate. Archaeologists had known for some time that substantial wealth differences between families developed only recently (archaeologically speaking), that is, only after about 6,000 years ago. The archaeological indicators of inequality are fairly clear—elaborate burials with valuable goods for some families and large differences in houses and possessions. But why the transformation occurred was not so clear. When she was in graduate school at the University of Michigan, Brumfiel says, she didn't accept the then-current explanation, that inequality provided benefits to the society (for example, the standard of living of most people improved as the leaders got richer). Consequently, for her Ph.D. research in central Mexico, she began to test the "benefit" explanation in an area that had been independent politically at first and then became part of the Aztec Empire. She studied the surface material remains in the area and historical documents written by Europeans and Aztec nobility. Her findings contradicted the benefit explanation of social inequality; she found little improvement in the standard of living of the local people after the Aztec Empire had absorbed them.

Another important part of her research agenda was understanding the lives of women. How were they affected by the expansion of the Aztec Empire? Did their work change? How were women portrayed in art? In the Aztec capital of Tenochtitlán, images of militarism and masculinity became increasingly important with the growth of the empire, and sculptures showed women in subordinate positions (for example, kneeling). But the images of women in the area of Brumfiel's fieldwork did not change. For example, most of the sculptures after the Aztecs had taken over still showed women standing, not kneeling.

Like many anthropologists, Brumfiel asked herself how she could contribute to the community in which she did her fieldwork. She decided to design an exhibit to display the successes of the people who had lived in the area for 1,200 years. The exhibit tells the people of Xaltocan what she found out from her studies.

As she continues to explore is-

Elizabeth Brumfiel.

sues about the origins of inequality and the position of women, Brumfiel is quite comfortable with knowing that someone will think that she has "gotten it wrong, and will set out on a lifetime of archaeological research to find her own answers."

Source: Elizabeth M. Brumfiel, "Origins of Social Inequality," in Carol R. Ember, Melvin Ember, and Peter N. Peregrine, eds., *Research Frontiers in Anthropology* (Upper Saddle River, NJ: Prentice Hall, 1998). Prentice Hall/Simon & Schuster Custom Publishing.

change in language that may have occurred in the past and that may account for similarities and differences observed in the present. The historical linguist typically asks such questions as these: Did two or more contemporary languages diverge from a common ancestral language? If they are related, how far back in time did they begin to differ?

Unlike the historical linguist, the descriptive (or structural) linguist is typically concerned with discovering and recording the principles that determine how sounds and words are put together in speech. For example, a structural description of a particular language might tell us that the sounds *t* and *k* are interchangeable in a word without causing a difference in meaning. In American Samoa, one could say *Tutuila* or *Kukuila* as the name of the largest island, and everyone, except perhaps the newly arrived anthropologist, would understand that the same island was being mentioned.

The sociolinguist is interested in the social aspects of

language, including what people speak about and how they interact conversationally, their attitudes toward speakers of other dialects or languages, and how people speak differently in different social contexts. In English, for example, we do not address everyone we meet in the same way. "Hi, Sandy" may be the customary way a person greets a friend. But we would probably feel uncomfortable addressing a doctor by first name; instead, we would probably say, "Good morning, Dr. Brown." Such variations in language use, which are determined by the social status of the persons being addressed, are significant for the sociolinguist.

ETHNOLOGY   Ethnologists seek to understand how and why peoples today and in the recent past differ in their customary ways of thinking and acting. Ethnology—usually now called *cultural anthropology*—is concerned with patterns of thought and behavior, such as marriage customs, kinship organization, political and economic systems, religion, folk art, and music, and with the ways in which these patterns differ in contemporary societies. Ethnologists also study the dynamics of culture—that is, how various cultures develop and change. In addition, they are interested in the relationship between beliefs and practices within a culture. Thus, the aim of ethnologists is largely the same as that of archaeologists. Ethnologists, however, generally use data collected through observation and interviewing of living peoples. Archaeologists, on the other hand, must work with fragmentary remains of past cultures, on the basis of which they can only make inferences about the customs of prehistoric peoples.

One type of ethnologist, the **ethnographer,** usually spends a year or so living with, talking to, and observing the people whose customs he or she is studying. This fieldwork provides the data for a detailed description (an **ethnography**) of many aspects of the customary behavior and thought of those people. The ethnographer not only tries to describe the general patterns of their life but also may suggest answers to such questions as: How are economic and political behavior related? How may the customs of people be adapted to environmental conditions? Is there any relationship between beliefs about the supernatural and beliefs or practices about the natural world? In other words, the ethnographer depicts the way of life of a particular group of people and may suggest explanations for some of the customs observed.

Because so many cultures have undergone extensive change in the recent past, it is fortunate that another type of ethnologist, the **ethnohistorian,** is prepared to study how the ways of life of a particular group of people have changed over time. Ethnohistorians investigate written documents (which may or may not have been produced by anthropologists). They may spend many years going through documents, such as missionary accounts, reports by traders and explorers, and government records, to try to establish the cultural changes that have occurred. Unlike ethnographers, who rely mostly on their own observations, ethnohistorians rely on the reports of others. Often, they must attempt to piece together and make sense of widely scattered, and even apparently contradictory, information. Thus, the ethnohistorian's research is very much like that of the historian, except that the ethnohistorian is usually concerned with the history of a people who did not themselves leave written records. The ethnohistorian tries to reconstruct the recent history of a people and may also suggest why certain changes in their way of life took place.

With the data collected and analyzed by the ethnographer and ethnohistorian, the work of a third type of ethnologist, the **cross-cultural researcher,** can be done. The cross-cultural researcher is interested in discovering why certain cultural characteristics may be found in some societies but not in others. Why, for example, do some societies have social stratification (classes and castes) and others have more egalitarian systems? Why do some religions have a high god or supreme being? Why do some societies have large, extended families? In testing possible answers to such questions, cross-cultural researchers use data from samples of cultures to try to arrive at general explanations of cultural variation. Archaeologists may find the results of cross-cultural research useful for making inferences about the past, particularly if they find material indicators of cultural variation.

Because ethnologists may be interested in many aspects of customary behavior and thought—from economic behavior to political behavior to styles of art, music, and religion—ethnology overlaps with disciplines that concentrate on some particular aspect of human existence, such as sociology, psychology, economics, political science, art, music, and comparative religion. But the distinctive feature of cultural anthropology is its interest in how all these aspects of human existence vary from society to society, in all historical periods, and in all parts of the world.

Applied Anthropology

All knowledge may turn out to be useful. In the physical and biological sciences it is well understood that technological breakthroughs like DNA splicing, spacecraft docking in outer space, and the development of miniscule computer chips could not have taken place without an enormous amount of basic research to uncover the laws of nature in the physical and biological worlds. If we did not understand fundamental principles, the technological achievements we are so proud of would not be possible. Researchers are often simply driven by curiosity, with no thought to where the research might lead, which is why such research is sometimes called *basic research*. The same is true of the social sciences. If a researcher finds out that societies with combative sports tend to have more wars, it may lead to other inquiries about the relationships between one kind of aggression and another. The knowledge acquired may ultimately lead to discovering ways to correct social problems, such as family violence and war.

RESEARCH FRONTIERS

Researcher at Work: Terence E. Hays

Books and articles often report research in a straightforward manner: Here's the problem; here's the answer—that kind of thing. But many researchers know from experience that knowledge does not always come in a straightforward manner. Now a professor at Rhode Island College, Terence Hays has reflected on the twists and turns in his fieldwork among the Ndumba in the Eastern Highlands Province of Papua New Guinea. He first started out studying whether different types of people (for example, women and men) had different types of plant knowledge and whether they classified plants differently. (The interest in plant and animal classification, *ethnobiology,* is closely connected with linguistic research.) In the course of his first fieldwork, in 1972, he witnessed an initiation ceremony for 10- to 12-year-old males—a dramatic and traumatic rite of passage ceremony that included the physical trauma of nose-bleeding as well as the social traumas of "attacks" by women and seclusion in the forest. The ceremony was full of symbolism of why the sexes needed to avoid each other. And while he collected stories and myths about plants for his research on ethnobiology, he kept uncovering themes in the stories about the danger of men's associating with women.

Terence Hays.

Hays's curiosity was aroused about these ceremonies and myths. How important are myths in perpetuating cultural themes? Do other societies that have separate men's houses have similar myths? He realized when he returned home from the field that many societies have similar stories. Are these stories generally linked to initiation rites and to physical segregation of the sexes? Answering these questions required comparison, so he embarked on collecting myths and folktales from colleagues who worked in other New Guinea Highland societies. In the course of collecting these comparative materials, he realized he didn't have all the ethnographic information he needed, so he went

back to the field to get it. As Hays remarked, "As an ethnographer I was continually faced with the question, How do you know it's true? But even when I could reach a (hard-won) conviction that something was true for the Ndumba, the second question awaited: How do you know it's generally true, which you can't know without comparison?"

Source: Terence E. Hays, "From Ethnographer to Comparativist and Back Again," in Carol R. Ember, Melvin Ember, and Peter N. Peregrine, eds., *Research Frontiers in Anthropology* (Upper Saddle River, NJ: Prentice Hall, 1998). Prentice Hall/ Simon & Schuster Custom Publishing.

Whereas basic research may ultimately help to solve practical problems, applied research is more explicit in its practical goals. Today about half of all professional anthropologists are applied, or practicing, anthropologists. **Applied** or **practicing anthropology** is explicit in its concern with making anthropological knowledge useful.[3] Applied anthropologists may be trained in any or all of the subfields of anthropology. In contrast to basic researchers, who are almost always employed in colleges, universities, and museums, applied anthropologists are usually

APPLIED ANTHROPOLOGY

Getting Development Programs to Notice Women's Contributions to Agriculture

When Anita Spring first did fieldwork in Zambia in the 1970s, she was not particularly interested in agriculture. Rather, medical anthropology was her interest. Her work focused on customary healing practices, particularly involving women and children. She was surprised at the end of the year when a delegation of women came to tell her that she didn't understand what it meant to be a woman. "To be a woman is to be a farmer," they said. She admits that it took her a while to pay attention to women as farmers, but then she began to participate in efforts to provide technical assistance to them. Like many others interested in women in development, Spring realized that all too often development agents downplay women's contributions to agriculture.

How does one bring about change in male-centered attitudes and practices? One way is to document how much women actually contribute to agricul-

ture. Beginning with the influential writing of Ester Boserup in *Woman's Role in Economic Development* (1970), scholars began to report that in Africa south of the Sahara, in the Caribbean, and in parts of Southeast Asia, women were the principal farmers or agricultural laborers. Moreover, as agriculture became more complex, it required more work time in the fields, so the women's contribution to agriculture increased. In addition, men increasingly went away to work, so women had to do much of what used to be men's work on the farms.

In the 1980s, Spring designed and directed the Women in Agricultural Development Project in Malawi, funded by the Office of Women in the U.S. Agency for International Development. Rather than focusing just on women, the project aimed to collect data on both women and men agriculturalists and how they were treated by develop-

ment agents. The project did more than collect information; mini-projects were set up and evaluated so that successful training techniques could be passed on to development agents in other regions. Spring points out that the success of the program was due not just to the design of the project. Much of the success depended on the interest and willingness of Malawi itself to change. And it didn't hurt that the United Nations and other donor organizations increasingly focused attention on women. It takes the efforts of many to bring about change. Increasingly, applied anthropologists like Anita Spring are involved in these efforts from beginning to end, from the design stage to implementation and evaluation.

Source: Anita Spring, *Agricultural Development and Gender Issues in Malawi* (Lanham, MD: University Press of America, 1995).

---

employed in settings outside of traditional academia, including government agencies, international development agencies, private consulting firms, businesses, public health organizations, medical schools, law offices, community development agencies, and charitable foundations.

Physical anthropologists may be called upon to give forensic evidence in court, or they may work in public health, or design clothes and equipment to fit human anatomy. Archaeologists may be involved in preserving and exhibiting artifacts for museums and in doing contract work to find and preserve cultural sites that might be damaged by construction or excavation. Linguists may work in bilingual educational training programs or may work on ways to improve communication. Ethnologists may work in a wide variety of applied projects ranging from community development, urban planning, health

care, and agricultural improvement to personnel and organizational management and assessment of the impact of change programs on people's lives.[4] We discuss applied anthropology more fully in the section of the book on "Using Anthropology."

SPECIALIZATION

As disciplines grow, they tend to develop more and more specialties. This trend is probably inevitable because, as knowledge accumulates and methods become more advanced, there is a limit to what any one person can reasonably keep track of. So, in addition to the general divisions we have outlined already, particular anthropologists tend to identify themselves with a variety of specializations. It is common for anthropologists to have a geographic specialty, which may be as broad as Old World or

Archaeologists working at a site in Siberia.

New World or as narrow as the southwestern United States. And those who study the past (archaeologists or human paleontologists) may also specialize in different time periods. Ethnologists often specialize in more specific subject matters in addition to one or two cultural areas. Just as most of the chapters in this book refer to broad subject specialties, so some ethnologists identify themselves as *economic anthropologists,* or *political anthropologists,* or *psychological anthropologists.* Others may identify themselves by theoretical orientations, such as *cultural ecologists,* who are concerned with the relationship between culture and the physical and social environments. These specialties are not mutually exclusive, however. A cultural ecologist, for example, might be interested in the effects of the environment on economic behavior, or political behavior, or how people bring up their children.

Does specialization isolate an anthropologist from other kinds of research? Not necessarily. Some specialties have to draw on information from several fields, inside and outside anthropology. For example, *medical anthropologists* study the cultural and biological contexts of human health and illness. Thus, they need to understand the economy, diet, and patterns of social interaction, as well as attitudes and beliefs regarding illness and health. In addition, they may need to draw on research in human genetics, public health, and medicine.

The Relevance of Anthropology

Anthropology is a comparatively young discipline. It was only in the late 1800s that anthropologists began to go to live with people in far-away places. Compared to our knowledge of the physical laws of nature, we know much less about people, about how and why they behave as they do. That anthropology and other sciences dealing with hu-

mans began to develop only relatively recently is not in itself a sufficient reason for our knowing less than in the physical sciences. Why, in our quest for knowledge of all kinds, did we wait so long to study ourselves? Leslie White suggests that those phenomena most remote from us and least significant as determinants of human behavior were the first to be studied. The reason, he surmises, is that humans like to think of themselves as citadels of free will, subject to no laws of nature. Hence, there is no need to see ourselves as objects to be explained.[5]

The idea that it is impossible to account for human behavior scientifically, either because our actions and beliefs are too individualistic and complex or because human beings are understandable only in otherworldly terms, is a self-fulfilling notion. We cannot discover principles explaining human behavior if we neither believe such principles exist nor bother to look for them. The result is assured from the beginning. Persons who do not believe in principles of human behavior will be reinforced by their finding none. If we are to increase our understanding of human beings, we first have to believe it is possible to do so.

If we aim to understand humans, it is essential that we study humans in all times and places. We must study ancient humans and modern humans. We must study their cultures and their biology. How else can we understand what is true of humans generally or how they are capable of varying? If we study just our own society, we may come up only with explanations that are culture-bound, not general or applicable to most or all humans. Anthropology is useful, then, to the degree that it contributes to our understanding of human beings everywhere.

In addition, anthropology is relevant because it helps us avoid misunderstandings between peoples. If we can understand why other groups are different from ourselves, we might have less reason to condemn them for behavior that appears strange to us. We may then come to realize that many differences between peoples are products of physical and cultural adaptations to different environments. For example, someone who first finds out about the !Kung as they lived in the Kalahari Desert of southern Africa in the 1950s might think that the !Kung were savages.[6] The !Kung wore little clothing, had few possessions, lived in meager shelters, and enjoyed none of our technological niceties. But let us reflect on how a typical North American community might react if it awoke to find itself in an environment similar to that in which the !Kung lived. The people would find that the arid land makes both agriculture and animal husbandry impossible, and they might have to think about adopting a nomadic existence. They might then discard many of their material possessions so that they could travel easily, in order to take advantage of changing water and food supplies. Because of the extreme heat and the lack of extra water for laundry, they might find it more practical to be almost naked than to wear clothes. They would undoubtedly find it impossible to build elaborate homes. For social security, they might start to share the food brought into the group. Thus, if they survived at all, they might end up looking and acting far more like the !Kung looked than like typical North Americans.

Physical differences, too, may be seen as results of adaptations to the environment. For example, in our society we admire people who are tall and slim. If these same individuals were forced to live above the Arctic Circle, however, they might wish they could trade their tall, slim bodies for short, compact ones, because stocky physiques conserve body heat more effectively and may therefore be more adaptive in cold climates.

Exposure to anthropology might help to alleviate some of the misunderstandings that arise between people of different cultural groups from subtle causes operating below the level of consciousness. For example, different cultures have different conceptions of the gestures and interpersonal distances that are appropriate under various circumstances. Arabs consider it proper to stand close enough to other people to smell them.[7] On the basis of the popularity of deodorants in our culture, we can deduce that Americans prefer to keep the olfactory dimension out of interpersonal relations. We may feel that a person who comes too close is being too intimate. We should remember, however, that this person may only be acting according to a culturally conditioned conception of what is proper in a given situation. If our intolerance for others results in part from a lack of understanding of why peoples vary, then the knowledge accumulated by anthropologists may help lessen that intolerance.

Knowledge of our past may also bring both a feeling of humility and a sense of accomplishment. If we are to attempt to deal with the problems of our world, we must be aware of our vulnerability so that we do not think that our problems will solve themselves. But we also have to think enough of our accomplishments to believe that we can find solutions to our problems. Much of the trouble we get

Simplicity of technology should not be taken to imply backwardness. The Inuit have very ingenious ways of dealing with their extremely difficult environment. Constructing an igloo out of specially shaped blocks of ice, as shown here in the Canadian Arctic, is not easy.

into may be a result of feelings of self-importance and invulnerability—in short, our lack of humility. Knowing something about our evolutionary past may help us to understand and accept our place in the biological world. Just as for any other form of life, there is no guarantee that any particular human population, or even the entire human species, will perpetuate itself indefinitely. The earth changes, the environment changes, and humanity itself changes. What survives and flourishes in the present might not do so in the future.

Yet our vulnerability should not make us feel powerless. There are many reasons to feel confident about the future. Consider what we have accomplished so far. By means of tools and weapons fashioned from sticks and stones, we were able to hunt animals larger and more powerful than ourselves. We discovered how to make fire, and we learned to use it to keep ourselves warm and to cook our food. As we domesticated plants and animals, we gained greater control over our food supply and were able to establish more permanent settlements. We mined and smelted ores to fashion more durable tools. We built cities and irrigation systems, monuments and ships. We made it possible to travel from one continent to another in a single day. We conquered some illnesses and prolonged human life.

In short, human beings and their cultures have changed considerably over the course of history. Human populations have often been able to adapt to changing circumstances. Let us hope that humans continue to adapt to the challenges of the present and future.

Summary

1. Anthropology is literally the study of human beings. It differs from other disciplines concerned with people in that it is broader in scope. It is concerned with hu-

mans in all places of the world (not simply those places close to us), and it traces human evolution and cultural development from millions of years ago to the present day.

2. Another distinguishing feature of anthropology is its holistic approach to the study of human beings. Anthropologists study not only all varieties of people but also all aspects of those peoples' experiences.

3. Anthropologists are concerned with identifying and explaining typical characteristics (traits, customs) of particular human populations.

4. Physical or biological anthropology is one of the major fields of the discipline. Physical anthropology studies the emergence of humans and their later physical evolution (the focus called human paleontology). It also studies how and why contemporary human populations vary biologically (the focus called human variation).

5. Another broad area of concern to anthropology is cultural anthropology. Its three subfields—archaeology, anthropological linguistics, and ethnology (now usually referred to by the parent name, cultural anthropology)—all deal with aspects of human culture, that is, with the customary ways of thinking and behaving of particular societies.

6. Archaeologists seek not only to reconstruct the daily life and customs of prehistoric peoples but also to trace cultural changes and offer possible explanations for those changes. Therefore, archaeologists try to reconstruct history from the remains of human cultures.

7. Anthropological linguists are concerned with the emergence of language and with the divergence of languages over time (a subject known as historical linguistics). They also study how contemporary languages differ, both in construction (descriptive or structural linguistics) and in actual speech (sociolinguistics).

8. The ethnologist (now often called simply a cultural anthropologist) seeks to understand how and why peoples of today and the recent past differ in their customary ways of thinking and acting. One type of ethnologist, the ethnographer, usually spends a year or so living with and talking to a particular population and observing their customs. Later, she or he may prepare a detailed report of the group's behavior, which is called an ethnography. Another type of ethnologist, the ethnohistorian, investigates written documents to determine how the ways of life of a particular group of people have changed over time. A third type of ethnologist, the cross-cultural researcher, studies data collected by ethnographers and ethnohistorians for a sample of cultures and attempts to discover which explanations of particular customs may be generally applicable.

9. In all four major subdisciplines of anthropology, there are applied anthropologists, people who apply anthropological knowledge to achieve more practical goals, usually in the service of an agency outside the traditional academic setting.

10. Anthropology may help people to be more tolerant. Anthropological studies can show us why other people are the way they are, both culturally and physically. Customs or actions that appear improper or offensive to us may be other people's adaptations to particular environmental and social conditions.

11. Anthropology is also valuable in that knowledge of our past may bring us both a feeling of humility and a sense of accomplishment. Like any other form of life, we have no guarantee that any particular human population will perpetuate itself indefinitely. Yet knowledge of our achievements in the past may give us confidence in our ability to solve the problems of the future.

Glossary Terms

anthropological linguistics
anthropology
applied (practicing) anthropology
archaeology
biological anthropology
cross-cultural researcher
cultural anthropology
culture
descriptive (or structural) linguistics
ethnographer
ethnography
ethnohistorian
ethnology
fossils
historical archaeology
historical linguistics
holistic
Homo sapiens sapiens
human paleontology
human variation
paleoanthropology
physical anthropology
prehistory
Primates
primatologists
sociolinguistics

Critical Questions

1. Why study anthropology?
2. How does anthropology differ from other fields of study you've encountered?
3. What do you think about the suggestion that anthropology is the fundamental discipline concerned with humans?

Internet Exercises

1. Many of you may keep up with the news and weather on the Internet. But have you ever tried to keep up with the latest news in anthropology? Check out the latest on what is happening in anthropology at **http://www.tamu.edu/anthropology/news.html**. What are the two latest news items?

2. Have you ever gone to a virtual museum? Check out one of these virtual museums. In a visit to the Canadian Museum of Civilization (**http://www.civilization.ca/cmc/cmceng/plan1eng.html**), explore the lower-level exhibits, which are devoted to the First Peoples. For a virtual museum experience whose content is created by students, visit the Minnesota State University, Mankato's EMuseum at **http://www.anthro.mankato.msus.edu/**. Other museums can be accessed from **http://archnet.asu.edu/museums**. Write a brief summary of your findings.

3. Anthropology is an interdisciplinary subject. Researchers in the field of anthropology employ various tools and techniques to learn about the interaction of humans and their environments. Explore one such study in which robots are used in anthropology. Learn all about the use of the latest techniques to study anthropology at **http://www.usc.edu/dept/raiders/story/fmi.html**. What are your thoughts on the application of these techniques?

Suggested Reading

BOAZ, N. T., AND ALMQUIST, A. J. *Biological Anthropology: A Synthetic Approach to Human Evolution.* Upper Saddle River, NJ: Prentice Hall, 1997. After briefly reviewing the principles and sequences of biological evolution, the authors review human evolution from earliest times to the present. The book also includes chapters on human variation, human growth and adaptability, and applied physical anthropology.

EMBER, C. R., EMBER, M., AND PEREGRINE, P. N., EDS. *Research Frontiers in Anthropology.* Upper Saddle River, NJ: Prentice Hall, 1998. Prentice Hall/Simon & Schuster Custom Publishing. Particularly appropriate to this chapter are pieces written by 10 researchers from different subfields of anthropology about their careers and personal research experiences ("Researchers at Work"). They are physical anthropologists Timothy Bromage and Katharine Milton, archaeologists Richard Blanton and Elizabeth Brumfiel, linguists Benjamin Blount and Susan Philips, ethnologists Carol Ember and Terence Hays, and applied anthropologists Andrew Miracle and Susan Weller.

FAGAN, B. M. *People of the Earth: An Introduction to World Prehistory*, 9th ed. New York: HarperCollins, 1997. A survey of world prehistory, describing what we know from archaeology about hunters and gatherers, farmers, and cities and civilizations in all areas of the world.

FOLEY, W. A. *Anthropological Linguistics: An Introduction.* Malden, MA: Blackwell, 1997. An overview of anthropological linguistics, including the evolution of language, linguistic universals, linguistic relativism, and the ethnography of speaking.

HOWELLS, W. *Getting Here: The Story of Human Evolution*, 2nd ed. Washington, DC: Compass Press, 1997. An accessible introduction to the study of human evolution.

SELIG, R. O., AND LONDON, M. R., EDS. *Anthropology Explored: The Best of Smithsonian AnthroNotes.* Washington, DC: Smithsonian Institution Press, 1998. A collection of nontechnical articles on the work of anthropologists in different subfields.

VAN WILLIGEN, J. *Applied Anthropology: An Introduction*, rev. ed. Westport, CT: Bergin and Garvey, 1993. A survey of applied anthropology that includes a history of the discipline, research techniques, examples of applied projects, and a discussion of ethics.

2

How We Discover the Past

ow can archaeologists and **paleoanthropologists** (anthropologists who study human evolution) know about what may have happened thousands or even millions of years ago? There are no written records from those periods from which to draw inferences. But we do have other kinds of evidence from the past, and we have ways of "reading" this evidence that allow us to know quite a lot about how our human ancestors evolved and how they lived long ago.

The Evidence of the Past

Archaeologists and paleoanthropologists rely on four kinds of evidence to learn about the past: *artifacts, ecofacts, fossils,* and *features*. As we will see, each provides unique information about the past. Together, artifacts, ecofacts, fossils, and features provide a detailed story about human life long ago. However, we need to be trained to "read" this story.

ARTIFACTS

Anything made or modified by humans is an **artifact.** The book you are reading now, the chair you are sitting in, the pen you are taking notes with are all artifacts. In fact, we are surrounded by artifacts, most of which we will lose or throw away. And that is exactly how things enter the archaeological record. Think about it: How much garbage do you produce in a day? What kinds of things do you throw away? Mostly paper, probably, but also wood (from the ice cream bar you had at lunch), plastic (like the pen that ran out of ink last night), and even metal (the dull blade on your razor). Into the garbage they go and out to the dump or landfill. Under the right conditions many of those items will survive for future archaeologists to find. Most of the artifacts that make up the archaeological record are just this kind of mundane waste—the accumulated garbage of daily life that archaeologists may recover and examine to reconstruct daily life long ago.

By far the most common artifacts from the past are stone tools, which archaeologists call **lithics**. Indeed, lithics are the only artifact available for 99 percent of human history. Humans first started using stone tools more than two and a half million years ago, and some tools of stone (grinding and polishing stones, for example) are still used today. Stone has been used for almost any purpose you can think of, from cutting tools to oil lamps, although their most common use has probably been as hunting, butchering, and hide-processing tools. Another common kind of artifact is **ceramics** (pots and other items made from baked clay). Humans first started making ceramics about 10,000 years ago, and ceramic objects such as storage and cooking vessels quickly came to be widely used. Because they are both fragile and relatively easy to make, ceramics show up frequently in the garbage that makes up the archaeological record. Wood and bone artifacts are common too, and were used to make hide-working, cooking, hunting, and even butchering tools. Wood and bone

A ceramic pot from China, dating to the period when agriculture first developed there—some 6,000 years ago.

tools have been used by humans at least as long as stone tools, but unlike stone tools, they tend not to survive well in the archaeological record. In some places metals and glass are common artifacts. These survive well in the archaeological record, and hence they are often found where they were used.

ECOFACTS

Ecofacts are natural objects that have been used or affected by humans. A good example are the bones of animals that people have eaten. These bones are somewhat like artifacts, but they haven't been made or modified by humans, just used and discarded by them. Another example is pollen found at archaeological sites. Because humans bring plants back to their houses to use, pollens from many plants are commonly found. These pollens may not have come from the same location. The only reason they are together is that they have been brought together by human use. Yet another example are the remains of insect and animal pests that associate with humans, such as cockroaches and mice. Their remains are found in sites because they associate with humans and survive by taking advantage of the conditions that humans create. Their presence is in part caused by the human presence, and thus they are considered ecofacts too.

FOSSILS

And then there are fossils, which are rare but particularly informative about human biological evolution. A **fossil**

The fossil of a trilobite from the Cambrian period, 500 million years ago.

may be an impression of an insect or leaf on a muddy surface that now is stone. Or it may consist of the actual hardened remains of an animal's skeletal structure. When an animal dies, the organic matter that made up its body begins to deteriorate. The teeth and skeletal structure are composed largely of inorganic mineral salts, and soon they are all that remains. Under most conditions, these parts eventually deteriorate too. But once in a great while conditions are favorable for preservation—for instance, when volcanic ash, limestone, or highly mineralized groundwater is present to form a high-mineral environment. If the remains are buried under such circumstances, the minerals in the ground may become bound into the structure of the teeth or bone, hardening the remains and thus making them less likely to deteriorate.

But we don't have fossil remains of everything that lived in the past, and sometimes we only have fragments from one or a few individuals. So the fossil record is very incomplete. For example, Robert Martin estimates that the earth has probably seen 6,000 primate species; and remains of only 3 percent of those species have been found. It is hardly surprising that primate paleontologists cannot identify most of the evolutionary connections between early and later forms. The task is particularly difficult with small mammals, such as the early primates, which are less likely than large animals to be preserved in the fossil record.[1]

FEATURES

Features are a kind of artifact, but archaeologists distinguish them from other artifacts because they cannot be easily removed from an archaeological site. Hearths are a good example. When humans build a fire on bare ground the soil becomes heated and is changed—all the water is driven out of it and its crystalline structure is broken down and re-formed. It becomes hard, redder, and even slightly magnetic (as we discuss later). When an archaeologist finds a hearth, what exactly is found? An area of hard, reddish soil, often surrounded by charcoal and ash. Here, then, is an artifact—an object of human manufac-

ture. But it would be very hard, if not impossible, for the archaeologist to pick the hearth up and take it back to the lab for study like a lithic or ceramic. A hearth is really an intrinsic feature of a site—hence the name *feature*.

Hearths are common features, but by far the most common features are called *pits*. Pits are simply holes dug by humans that are later filled with garbage or eroded soil. They are usually fairly easy to distinguish because the garbage or soil they are filled with is often different in color and texture from the soil the pit was dug into. *Living floors* are another common type of feature. These are the places where humans lived and worked. The soils in these locations are often compacted through human activity and are full of minute pieces of garbage—seeds, small stone flakes, beads, and the like—that became embedded in the floor. Finally, *buildings* are a common feature on archaeological sites. These can range from the remains of stone rings that once held down the sides of tents to palaces built of stones that had been shaped and fitted together. Even the remains of wooden houses (or parts of them) have been preserved under some conditions. Features are a diverse array of things that can provide lots of information about the past.

Finding the Evidence

Evidence of the past is all around us, but finding it is not always easy or productive. Archaeologists and paleoanthropologists usually restrict their search to what are called *sites*. **Sites** are known or suspected locations of human activity in the past that contain a record of that activity. Sites can range from places where humans camped for perhaps only one night to entire ancient cities. Regardless of their size or complexity, sites can reveal many things about life in the past.

HOW ARE SITES CREATED?

Sites are created when the remnants of human activity are covered or buried by some natural process. The most dramatic one is volcanic activity; the record of human behavior (and even the humans themselves) can be totally buried within seconds. The most impressive example of this must be Pompeii, an entire city that was buried in the eruption of Mount Vesuvius in A.D. 79. Today archaeologists are digging out the city and finding the remains of ancient life just as it was left in the moments before the eruption.[2] Less dramatic means of burying the record of human behavior are the natural processes of dirt accumulation and erosion. Wind- or water-borne soil and debris can cover a site either quickly (as in a flood) or over a long period of time, preserving intact the artifacts, ecofacts, fossils, and features left by humans. Finally, the processes through which soils are built up can also bury artifacts, ecofacts, fossils, and features in a way that allows archaeologists to uncover them later. In forests, for example, falling leaves cover the locations where humans camped.

Over time the leaves decay and build up soil, covering the remains of the human encampment slowly but completely over many years.

Since good locations to live and work in are often reused by humans, many sites contain the remains of numerous human occupations. The most valuable sites to archaeologists and paleoanthropologists are those in which the burial processes worked quickly enough that each use of the site is clearly separated from the previous one. Such sites are called **stratified;** each layer, or *stratum*, of human occupation is separate like a layer in a layer cake. Not only do stratified sites allow the archaeologist or paleoanthropologist to distinguish easily the sequence of site occupations, but the strata themselves provide a way to know the relative ages of the occupations—earlier occupations will always be below later ones.

 CD-ROM Stratigraphy Simulation II-1

TAPHONOMY

It is important to note that the very processes that create sites can often damage or destroy them. The study of the processes of site disturbance and destruction is called **taphonomy.** Some archaeologists and paleoanthropologists argue that natural processes such as wind and water erosion not only bury the materials left by humans but may affect them so significantly that we need to be very cautious when interpreting what is found in an archaeological site. For example, Harold Dibble and his colleagues have argued that the Lower Paleolithic site of Cagny-L'Epinette in France does not actually contain locations where Lower Paleolithic peoples lived and worked, as previous excavators suggested. Rather, Dibble and his colleagues argue that what looks like locations of human activity were created by water running across the site and accumulating artifacts in low-lying places.[3] This doesn't mean that nothing can be learned from such a site, even one that has been subjected to considerable disturbance, but rather that archaeologists and paleoanthropologists must use caution when interpreting them. An understanding of site taphonomy can help an archaeologist make an informed and cautious interpretation of the past.[4]

HOW ARE SITES FOUND?

There is no single method of finding sites, and indeed many sites are found by happenstance—someone digs into the ground and discovers a lot of artifacts or perhaps a feature. But when archaeologists and paleoanthropologists want to go out and find sites, they typically employ one of two basic methods: pedestrian survey and remote sensing.

Pedestrian survey is what the name suggests—walking around and looking for sites. But there are a number of techniques that archaeologists and paleoanthropologists use to enhance the effectiveness of pedestrian survey beyond simply walking around. These include the use of sampling and systematic surveying methods to reduce the area to be covered on foot. Another way archaeologists reduce the area to be examined is by focusing their search on places humans are likely to have occupied. Paleoanthropologists, for example, typically focus only on those locations where there are exposed fossil beds dating to the time period of the early humans or apes they are interested in finding. Pedestrian survey, while very low tech, can be an extremely effective way of finding sites.

Remote sensing is a much more high-tech way of finding sites. With remote sensing techniques, archaeologists and paleoanthropologists find archaeological deposits by sensing their presence from a remote location, usually the current surface of the ground beneath which the archaeological deposits are buried. Most remote sensing techniques are borrowed from exploration geology, and are the same ones geologists use to find mineral or oil de-

A site is a location where archaeological materials are found in context. Even a site as large as the ancient city of Nippur, Iraq, shown here, can be buried and preserved by wind- and water-borne soil.

posits. They typically involve the measurement of minute variations in phenomena like the earth's magnetic or gravitational field, or changes in an electric current or pulse of energy directed into the ground. When these subtle changes, called *anomalies*, are located, more detailed exploration can be done to map the extent and depth of the buried archaeological deposits.

One of the most common remote sensing techniques used in archaeology is *geomagnetics*. Geomagnetic sensing is based on the fact the earth has a strong magnetic field that varies locally depending on what is beneath the ground. Features such as hearths, stone walls, and pits filled with organic material can alter the earth's magnetic field, as can metal and ceramic artifacts. By carefully measuring the earth's magnetic field, an archaeologist can often locate these features and artifacts. The archaeologist uses a highly sensitive instrument called a magnetometer to map the earth's magnetic field over a large area. When the map is complete, areas with anomalously high or low readings point to locations where buried features or artifacts may be present. In many cases, these anomalies form patterns that can be easily interpreted.

Geomagnetic sensing is called a "passive" technique because the archaeologist simply measures the existing magnetic field. There are also "active" remote sensing techniques by which the archaeologist sends a pulse of energy into the ground and records how it is affected by whatever is buried. One of the most commonly used active techniques is *soil interface radar (SIR)*, sometimes also called *ground penetrating radar (GPR)*. This technique is based on the fact that different soils reflect radar energy differently. By sending a radar pulse into the ground and recording how the soils reflect it, the archaeologist can map the various soils below the ground. More importantly, if there are features such as walls and pits below the ground, those can be mapped as well. To conduct a radar survey, the archaeologist pulls an antenna along the ground, the size of which depends on the depth of pene-

tration the archaeologist wants and the features expected. The antenna both sends and receives the radar pulses, and the received radar reflections are recorded on a paper strip or in a computer file. These recordings give the archaeologist a picture of what is below the ground.

HOW ARE ARTIFACTS, ECOFACTS, AND FEATURES RECOVERED FROM SITES?

Whether they are identified by pedestrian survey or remote sensing, once archaeological deposits are found there is only one way to recover them—by excavation. *Excavation* itself is a complex process with two goals: (1) to find every scrap of evidence (or a statistically representative sample) about the past that a given site holds, and (2) to record the horizontal and vertical location of that evidence with precision. Archaeologists and paleoanthropologists have developed many excavation strategies and techniques to accomplish these goals, but all of them involve the careful removal of the archaeological deposits, the recovery of artifacts, ecofacts, fossils, and features from the soil those deposits have been buried in, and the detailed recording of where each artifact, ecofact, fossil, and feature was located on the site.

Excavation does not mean simply digging holes, not even neat square ones. Because few sites can ever be fully excavated (the cost involved would be tremendous, and most archaeologists feel it is important to leave some archaeological deposits undisturbed in case new techniques are developed that might be employed on the site), archaeological excavations must be carefully planned, usually using some method of sampling. Sampling allows archaeologists to recover a full range of artifacts, ecofacts, fossils, and features while excavating only a small portion of a site. Sampling, however, requires that the archaeologist carefully plan where excavations will be conducted so that all areas of the site have an equal likelihood of being examined.

Paleoanthropologists excavating an early human site in northwestern Kenya. The exposed fossils are those of an elephant that may have been butchered by humans.

To date, no one has figured out a way to recover artifacts, ecofacts, fossils, and features from a site without destroying the site in the process, and this is one of the strange ironies of archaeological research. As we discuss shortly, it is the relationships between and among artifacts, ecofacts, fossils, and features that are of most interest to archaeologists, and it is precisely these relationships that are destroyed when archaeologists remove them from a site. For this reason most excavation by professional archaeologists today is done only when a site is threatened with destruction, and then only by highly trained personnel using rigorous techniques.

Archaeologists and paleoanthropologists collect data in basically the same ways, with one important difference. Archaeologists tend to be most concerned with recovering intact features, whereas paleoanthropologists tend to be most concerned with recovering intact fossils. This leads to some differences in approaches to collecting data, particularly where to look.

Archaeologists tend to seek out undisturbed sites where intact features can be found. Paleoanthropologists, on the other hand, seek sites dating to the time period when the species of interest lived and might have been fossilized. In many cases, disturbances are a plus for paleoanthropologists, because disturbed sites may make finding fossils easier—they may be eroding out of the surface of the ground and be easily visible without digging. This doesn't mean archaeologists never excavate disturbed sites, because they do. And paleoanthropologists have sometimes made important discoveries by excavating undisturbed sites.[5]

A conservator applying preservative to a decaying Alaskan totem pole.

Analyzing the Evidence

Once archaeologists and paleoanthropologists have found a site and recovered artifacts and other materials from it, they are ready to begin "reading" what they've found to learn the story of the past. This "reading" of the archaeological record is called *analysis*. Like excavation, archaeological analysis is a varied and sophisticated process that we will touch on only briefly here.

It should be obvious from our discussion of the archaeological record that much of what is lost or discarded by humans never survives. It is also the case that much of what does survive comes to us in fragments and in a fragile, deteriorated state. Before doing analysis, then, archaeologists and paleoanthropologists must first conserve and reconstruct the materials they have found.

CONSERVATION AND RECONSTRUCTION

Conservation is the process of treating artifacts, ecofacts, and in some cases even features, to stop decay and, if possible, even reverse the deterioration process. Some conservation is very simple, involving only cleaning and drying the item. Some conservation is highly complex, involving long-term chemical treatments and, in some cases, long-term storage under controlled conditions. The so-called

"Ice Man," for example, the 5,000-year-old individual found in 1993 in the Italian Alps, is kept in permanently glacial-like conditions after investigators found to their dismay that warming the remains for study induced the growth of mold. The archaeologists removed the mold, but decided that his remains would have to be kept under the same conditions that preserved them in the first place, and so a complex storage facility had to be built to recreate the glacial environment in which he was originally found.[6]

Reconstruction is like building a puzzle—but a three-dimensional puzzle where you're not sure which pieces belong and you know not all of the pieces are there. First, materials have to be sorted into similar types. For example, to reconstruct ceramics from a site, all the ceramics have to be sorted into types with similar color, decoration, and shapes. Then the similar pieces are compared to see if any seem to come from the same vessel. Once all the pieces thought to be from the same vessel are located, they can be assembled. Reconstruction is clearly a long, difficult process—in some cases taking years.

WHAT CAN WE LEARN FROM ARTIFACTS?

Once conservation and reconstruction are complete, the archaeologist or paleoanthropologist can begin to analyze

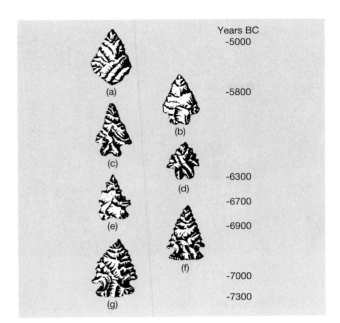

Figure 2–1 *A Projectile Point Chronology from the Icehouse Bottom Site in Tennessee*

Source: Jefferson Chapman, *Tellico Archaeology* (Knoxville: Tennessee Valley Authority, 1985), Fig. 1.15.

the artifacts they've found. Archaeologists have developed specific and often unique ways to analyze the many different types of artifacts. Stone tools are examined in different ways from ceramics, and both are examined differently from bone. But there are some commonalities in the way artifacts are analyzed, regardless of what they are made of.

First, archaeologists typically examine the *form* of an artifact—how it is shaped. For most common artifacts, such as lithics and ceramics, forms are known well enough to be grouped into typologies. Placing artifacts into a **typology** is often the primary purpose of *formal analysis,* because typologies allow archaeologists to place a particular artifact into context with other artifacts found at the site or even at other sites. Typologies often provide a lot of information about an artifact, including its age, the species or culture with which it is affiliated, and in some cases even how it was made, used, or exchanged in the past. Figure 2–1 shows a projectile point typology for a site in Tennessee and the time period between about 7,300 and 5,000 B.C. Over time the forms of the projectile points changed. The bases of points (*f*) and (*g*) are very different in their form from those of (*c*), (*d*), and (*e*), and all of them are different from (*a*). With this sort of typology, an archaeologist can estimate the age of a projectile point just by looking at the form of its base.

Second, archaeologists often measure artifacts, recording their size in various, often strictly defined, dimensions. Such *metric analysis,* as this activity is called, is used much like formal analysis to group artifacts into a typology. Figure 2–2 shows the standard measurements taken from

projectile points. With these measurements one can create a typology similar to that in Figure 2–1. Instead of looking at the form of the projectile points, one looks at their sizes. Clearly, the base widths of points (*a*), (*d*), and (*f*) in Figure 2–1 are going to differ in a manner similar to the way their base forms differ. The value of metric analysis, however, is that the typology created is less subjective than a typology using forms. In addition, many measurements can be taken from broken or partial artifacts that might not be classifiable by formal analysis.

Third, archaeologists often attempt to understand how an artifact was made. By examining the material the artifact is made from and how that material was manipulated, archaeologists can learn about the technology, economy, and exchange systems of the peoples who made the artifact. For example, if the material is not locally available, that means the people traded for it. Archaeologists can also study present-day peoples and how they make similar artifacts in order to understand how ancient artifacts were made. Anne Underhill was interested in understanding how ceramics were produced during the Longshan period in China—a time known for its elegant, thin-walled pottery. In addition to studying the Longshan ceramics and the sites they came from, Underhill also visited living potters who make similar vessels today. She found that both full-time and part-time potters produce ceramics today, but was this the case in the past? Underhill measured ceramics being produced by these potters and performed a metric analysis. She found, to her surprise, that both full-time and part-time potters produce high-quality and highly uniform ceramics, difficult to tell apart from one another.[7]

Finally, archaeologists attempt to understand how an

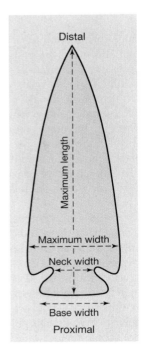

Figure 2–2
Standard Metrical Measurements of Chipped Stone Tools

Archaeologists examining the wall of an excavation at Nippur, Iraq. The thick white line in the wall is the plastered floor of a building. Items found on the floor can all be assumed to date from the same time, while items found below it can be assumed to date from an earlier time. This is a simple example of using stratigraphy for relative dating.

artifact was used. Knowing how an artifact was used allows the archaeologist a direct window onto ancient life. Because this information is so important, a number of sophisticated techniques have been developed to determine how artifacts were used. For stone, bone, and wood tools, a technique called *use-wear analysis* has been developed, which can determine how a tool was used by the careful examination of the wear on its edges. We discuss use-wear analysis in more detail in later chapters. For ceramic vessels, techniques have been developed to extract residues trapped in the clay and determine what the vessel held. Archaeologist Patrick McGovern and chemist Rudolf Michel, for example, took samples of a pale yellow residue found in grooves inside ceramic vessels from Grodin Tepe in Turkey. Their analysis determined that the residue was from barley beer, providing the earliest evidence of brewing in the world (the ceramics date from 3500 to 3100 B.C.).[8]

But what can archaeologists really learn by placing artifacts in typologies through formal and metric analysis, or by learning how an artifact was manufactured and used? A lot. Typologies allow archaeologists to use relative dating (which we discuss below) to determine the age of an artifact or site by locating it in a sequence involving other artifacts and sites with known ages. Typologies thus allow archaeologists to determine which groups were related to one another in the distant past, how information was shared among those groups, and in some cases even what social behavior was like (how labor was organized, who traded with whom).

For example Carla Sinopoli examined the ceramics from the Iron Age site of Vijayanagara, in southern India. Previous excavations had identified distinct residential areas of the site, including a "Noblemen's Quarter," composed of elite residences of high-caste Hindus, the "East Valley," which was thought to contain residences of lower-caste Hindus, and the "Islamic Quarter," which was thought to house Muslim mercenaries. When Sinopoli compared ceramics across the three areas, she found distinct differences: The "Islamic Quarter" had significantly more eating vessels than either of the two other areas, a difference which Sinopoli interpreted as being related to Hindu restrictions on the use of ceramics for holding food (some Hindus will not reuse food containers, so they are often made of disposable materials, such as leaves). Ceramics not only can inform the archaeologist about the social organization of a site, they can also reveal religious beliefs![9] Even gender roles can be revealed archaeologically (see the box "Women in the Shell Mound Archaic").

Knowing how an artifact was made allows the archaeologist to understand the technology and technical abilities of peoples in the past. For example, Thomas Wynn analyzed both the final forms and the methods used by early humans—*Homo erectus*—to make stone tools roughly 300,000 years ago. He found that manufacturing these tools was a multistage process, involving several distinct steps and several distinct stone-working techniques to arrive at the finished product. He then took this information

An early Acheulian hand axe from Olduvai Gorge, Tanzania. Lawrence Keeley examined the edge wear on this and later types of hand axes to determine how they were used.

NEW PERSPECTIVES ON GENDER
Women in the Shell Mound Archaic

One of the main issues addressed by archaeologists interested in gender is how we can learn about and understand gender roles in prehistoric cultures. Gender roles might seem impossible to study in archaeological contexts. How is gender preserved in the archaeological record? How can knowledge about gender roles be recovered? Information about gender roles can be recovered if one maintains an awareness of how material culture that is associated ethnographically with particular gender roles changes over time. Archaeologists argue that such an awareness leads not only to a better understanding of gender in prehistory but can also lead to a fuller understanding of prehistoric cultures overall.

An example is Cheryl Claassen's work on the Shell Mound Archaic culture of the Tennessee River valley. The Shell Mound Archaic represents the remains of people who lived in Tennessee and Kentucky between about 5,500 and 3,000 years ago. They were hunters and gatherers who lived in small villages, and probably moved seasonally between summer and winter communities. The most distinctive feature of the Shell Mound Archaic is the large mounds of mollusk shells they constructed for burying their dead. Tens of thousands of shells were piled together to create these mounds. Yet, around 3,000 years ago, shellfishing and thus the creation of shell burial mounds stopped abruptly. Claassen wondered why.

Suggested explanations include climate change, overexploitation of shellfish themselves, and emigration of shellfishing peoples from the area. None has proven wholly satisfactory. In contemporary cultures shellfishing is typically done by women and children, and Claassen wondered whether an approach that considered gender roles might be more productive. She decided to approach the problem through the perspective of women's workloads, since it would have been women who would have most likely been the ones shellfishing. The end of shellfishing would have meant that women would have had a lot of free time—free time that could have been put to use in some other way. What might have changed to lead women to stop shellfishing? Would something else have perhaps become more important, so that women's labor was needed more for those other tasks?

Women's labor might have been redirected toward domesticated crops. There is archaeological evidence that about 3,000 years ago several productive but highly labor-intensive crops became widely used. For example, chenopodium, one of the more plentiful and nutritious of these new crops, has tiny seeds that require considerable labor to harvest, clean, and process. Women were likely the ones burdened with such work. They not only would have harvested these crops but also would have been the ones to process and prepare meals from them. Thus the emergence of agricultural economies would have required women to undertake new labor in food production and processing that may well have forced them to stop other tasks, like shellfishing.

The development of agricultural activities might also have brought about changes in ritual and ceremonialism. The shell burial mounds were clearly central to Shell Mound Archaic death ceremonies. Considerable labor, mostly by women, would have been required to collect the shells and to build these mounds. Later societies in the region buried their dead in earthen mounds. Could this be a reflection of the new importance earth had in an emerging agricultural economy? If so, what role did women play in ceremonies of death and burial? If they were no longer the providers of the raw materials needed for burial, does that mean their status in society as a whole changed?

We may never know exactly why the Shell Mound Archaic disappeared, or how women's work and women's roles in society changed. But as Claassen points out, taking a gender perspective provides new avenues along which to pursue answers to these questions, and interesting new questions to pursue.

Sources: Cheryl Claassen, "Gender and Archaeology," in P. N. Peregrine, C. R. Ember, and M. Ember, eds., *Archaeology: Original Readings in Method and Practice* (Upper Saddle River, NJ: Prentice Hall, 2002); Cheryl Claassen, "Gender, Shellfishing, and the Shell Mound Archaic," in J. Gero and M. Conkey, eds., *Engendering Archaeology: Women and Prehistory* (Oxford: Blackwell, 1991), pp. 276–300.

and evaluated it in terms of a measure of human cognitive ability developed by Jean Piaget, and concluded that the people who made these tools probably had organizational abilities similar to those of modern humans.[10]

Finally, knowing how an artifact was used allows the archaeologist to know something of people's behavior and activities. Lawrence Keeley conducted detailed use-wear analyses on Acheulian hand axes made by *Homo erectus* peoples and found that they had a variety of uses. Some were apparently used to cut meat, others to cut wood, and others to dig in the ground (probably for edible roots). On some hand axes, one edge was apparently used for one activity and the other for a different activity. Thus hand axes appear to have been multipurpose tools for our *Homo erectus* ancestors—something like a Swiss Army knife that they carried along with them. This knowledge gives us an interesting picture of these people: They used a fairly sophisticated manufacturing technique to make multipurpose tools that they carried with them and used for whatever job was at hand. This is a picture of the behavior of our ancient ancestors that is unavailable from any other source.[11]

WHAT CAN WE LEARN FROM ECOFACTS AND FOSSILS?

Ecofacts are diverse, and what archaeologists and paleoanthropologists can learn from them is highly diverse as well. Here we'll focus on fossils, but in a later chapter on the Upper Paleolithic world we'll discuss how archaeologists use ecofacts to reconstruct ancient environments; and in a still later chapter on the origins of domesticated plants and animals we'll learn how archaeologists use ecofacts to distinguish wild from domestic plants and animals and to reconstruct how these plants and animals were domesticated.

Paleontologists can tell a great deal about an extinct animal from its fossilized bones or teeth, but that knowledge is based on much more than just the fossil record itself. Paleontologists rely on comparative anatomy to help reconstruct missing skeletal pieces, as well as the soft tissues attached to bone. New techniques, such as electron microscopy, CAT scans, and computer-assisted biomechanical modeling, provide much information about how the organism may have moved about, the microstructure of bone and teeth, and how the organism developed. Chemical analysis of fossilized bone can suggest what the animal typically ate. Paleontologists are also interested in the surroundings of the fossil finds. With methods developed in geology, chemistry, and physics, paleontologists use the surrounding rocks to identify the time period in which the organism died. In addition, the study of associated fauna and flora can suggest what the ancient climate and habitat were like.[12]

Much of the evidence for primate evolution comes from teeth, which are the most common animal parts (along with jaws) to be preserved as fossils. Animals vary in *dentition*—the number and kinds of teeth they have, their size, and their arrangement in the mouth. Dentition provides clues to evolutionary relationships because animals with similar evolutionary histories often have similar teeth. For example, no primate, living or extinct, has more than two incisors in each quarter of the jaw. That feature, along with others, distinguishes the primates from earlier mammals, which had three incisors in each quarter. Dentition also suggests the relative size of an animal and often offers clues about its diet. For example, comparisons of living primates suggest that fruit-eaters have flattened, rounded tooth cusps, unlike leaf- and insect-eaters, which have more pointed cusps.[13] CAT scan methodology has helped paleontologists image the internal parts of teeth, such as the thickness of enamel, which can also suggest the diet (seed and nut eaters have thicker enamel). Electron microscopy has revealed different patterns of growth in bones and teeth; different species have different patterns.[14]

Paleontologists can tell much about an animal's posture and locomotion from fragments of its skeleton. Arboreal quadrupeds have front and back limbs of about the same length; because their limbs tend to be short, their center of gravity is close to the branches on which they move. They also tend to have long grasping fingers and toes. Terrestrial quadrupeds are more adapted for speed, so they have longer limbs and shorter fingers and toes. Disproportionate limbs are more characteristic of vertical clingers and leapers and *brachiators* (species that swing through the branches). Vertical clingers and leapers have longer, more powerful hind limbs; brachiators have longer forelimbs.[15] Even though soft tissues are not preserved, much can be inferred from the fossils themselves. For example, the form and size of muscles can be estimated by marks found on the bones to which the muscles were attached. And the underside of the cranium may provide information about the proportions of the brain devoted to vision, smell, or memory. The skull also reveals information about characteristics of smell and vision. For example, animals that rely more on smell than on vision tend to have large snouts. Nocturnal animals tend to have large eye sockets.

WHAT CAN WE LEARN FROM FEATURES?

The analysis of features is a little bit different from the analysis of artifacts, ecofacts, and fossils. Because features cannot be removed to the lab (see our earlier discussion of hearths), they cannot be subjected to the same range of analyses as artifacts, ecofacts, and fossils. However, archaeologists have developed a number of powerful tools to analyze features in the field. The primary one is detailed mapping, usually using a surveyor's transit. Extensive records are made about each feature, explaining not only what the feature is but also what archaeological materials were found associated with it. This information can be brought together using a *geographic information system (GIS)*. A GIS allows the archaeologist to produce a map of the features on a site and combine that map with information about the archaeological materials that were also found. Combining these kinds of information can reveal patterns in the archaeological record that tell us about human behaviors in the past.

A good example of how patterns of features can reveal past human behavior comes from the Range Site in west-central Illinois. Humans lived on the Range Site for over a thousand years, and during that time the ways they organized their settlement changed. About 2,300 years ago the people at the Range Site lived in small houses arranged around a circular courtyard. This pattern continued and was elaborated upon for almost 700 years; the courtyard area was a focus of activity and perhaps ritual. About 1,000 years ago the pattern changed. Houses became more substantial and were arranged linearly, in rows. This change suggests a radical alteration in social organization. From cross-cultural research (comparative studies using ethnographic data), we know that where circular communities are found, the communities commonly function as a single political and economic unit, whereas communities arranged linearly often do not function as one political and economic unit. What the changes in the Range Site seem to show is an attenuation or reduction of the basic social and economic unit, from the community to the individual household. This change seems to be related to the evolution of a large, centralized polity located at Cahokia, only 15 kilometers from the Range Site, whose impact on surrounding communities like the one at the Range Site may have been dramatic, transforming a socioeconomic structure that had persisted for almost a millennium.[16]

PUTTING IT ALL IN CONTEXT

You might have gained the impression from our discussion that archaeologists and paleoanthropologists analyze artifacts, ecofacts, fossils, and features as individual objects, separate from one another. Nothing could be farther from the truth. In fact, the analysis of the Range Site just described is much more like a typical archaeological analysis. It combined information about features across time to come to a generalization about how the social and economic organization of the people living there changed. We call this putting the material in context. **Context** is the relationship between and among artifacts and other materials. The analysis of context is really what archaeology and paleoanthropology are all about. Artifacts, ecofacts, fossils, and features in isolation may be beautiful or interesting by themselves, but it is only when they are placed in context with the other materials found on a site that we are able to "read" and tell the story of the past.

To illustrate this point, let's consider a set of letters that were found separately: *A E G I M N N*. They are arranged here in alphabetical order, the way a set of beautiful artifacts might be arranged in a display case in order of size. But do these arrangements tell us anything? No. What if we knew something about the relationships between and among these letters—their context? What if, for example, we knew that the *M* was the first letter found, and that the *A* and *E* were found next to the *M*, but in reverse order,

that one *N* was found between the *E* and *I*, and that the other *N* was found between the *I* and the *G*? Knowing in what context the letters were found would tell us that the letters should be arranged like this: *M E A N I N G*. And meaning is exactly what context gives to artifacts, ecofacts, fossils, and features.

 Dating the Evidence

An important, indeed vital, part of putting artifacts and other materials into context is putting them in chronological order. To reconstruct the evolutionary history of the primates, for example, one must know how old primate fossils are. For some time, relative dating methods were the only methods available. The last 45 years have seen important advances in absolute dating, including techniques that allow the dating of the earliest phases of primate evolution.[17] **Relative dating** is used to determine the age of a specimen or deposit relative to another specimen or deposit. **Absolute dating,** or chronometric dating, is used to measure how old a specimen or deposit is in years.

RELATIVE DATING METHODS

The earliest, and still the most commonly used method of relative dating, is based on *stratigraphy,* the study of how different rock formations are laid down in successive layers or strata. Older layers are generally deeper or lower than more recent layers. Indicator fossils are used to establish a stratigraphic sequence for the relative dating of new finds. These **indicator fossils** are from animals (fauna) and plants (flora) that spread widely over short periods of time, or that died out fairly rapidly, or that evolved rapidly. Different animals and plants are used as indicators of relative age in different areas of the world. In Africa, elephants, pigs, and horses have been particularly important in establishing stratigraphic sequences. Once the stratigraphy of an area is established, the relative ages of two different fossils in the same or different sites are indicated by the associated flora and fauna.[18] Major transitions in flora and fauna define the epochs and larger units of geologic time. The dates of the boundaries between such units are estimated by absolute dating, described in the next section.

If a site has been disturbed, stratigraphy will not be a satisfactory way to determine relative age. As noted earlier, remains from different periods may be washed or blown together by water or wind. Or a landslide may superimpose an earlier on a later layer. Still, it may be possible using chemical methods to estimate the relative age of the different fossils found together in a disturbed site.

Three of the chemical methods used to date fossil bones relatively are the fluorine, uranium, and nitrogen tests, sometimes known as the **F-U-N trio.**[19] All are based on the same general principle: Bones and teeth undergo a slow transformation in chemical composition when they remain buried for long periods, and this transformation reflects the mineral content of the groundwater in the area in which they are buried. Fluorine is one mineral present in groundwater; therefore, the older a fossil is, the higher its fluorine content will be. Uranium, like fluorine, is also present in groundwater, so the longer bones or teeth remain in the ground, the greater their uranium content. The proportions are reversed for nitrogen: The older the fossil is, the smaller the amount of nitrogen present in it. Thus, older bones have relatively higher concentrations of fluorine and uranium and less nitrogen than recent bones do.

But a problem can arise with the F-U-N tests because the mineral content of bones reflects the mineral content of the groundwater in the area. A 30-million-year-old fossil from a high-mineral area may have the same fluorine content as a 50-million-year-old fossil from a low-mineral site. So these chemical relative dating methods cannot be used to find the relative ages of specimens from widely separated sites. The F-U-N tests are restricted, then, to specimens from the same site or from neighboring sites.

Each of the chemical relative dating methods, used alone, can give only tentative evidence. But when the three methods are combined and confirm—that is, corroborate—one another, they are very effective. Of the three methods, the uranium test is by far the most reliable when used alone. It is not strictly a relative dating method. There seems to be some consistency in the increase in radioactivity with age, even in bones from different deposits. The uranium test has another distinct advantage over the other tests. Because uranium is radioactive, measuring the radioactivity does not require the destruction of any part of the sample in testing.

ABSOLUTE, OR CHRONOMETRIC, DATING METHODS

Many of the absolute dating methods are based on the decay of a radioactive isotope. Because the rate of decay is known, the age of the specimen can be estimated, within a range of possible error.

RADIOCARBON DATING   Radiocarbon, or **carbon-14** (^{14}C), **dating** is perhaps the most popularly known method of determining the absolute age of a specimen. It is based on the principle that all living matter possesses a certain amount of a radioactive form of carbon (carbon-14, or ^{14}C). Radioactive carbon, produced when nitrogen-14 is bombarded by cosmic rays, is absorbed from the air by plants and then ingested by animals that eat the plants (see Figure 2–3). After an organism dies, it no longer takes in any of the radioactive carbon. Carbon-14 decays at a slow but steady pace and reverts to nitrogen-14. (By *decays*, we mean that the ^{14}C gives off a certain number of beta radiations per minute.) The rate at which the carbon decays—its **half-life**—is known: ^{14}C has a half-life of 5,730 years. In other words, half of the original amount of ^{14}C in organic matter will have disintegrated 5,730 years after the organism's death; half of the remaining ^{14}C will have dis-

integrated after another 5,730 years; and so on. After about 50,000 years, the amount of ^{14}C remaining in the organic matter is too small to permit reliable dating.

To discover how long an organism has been dead—that is, to determine how much ^{14}C is left in the organism and therefore how old it is—we count the number of beta radiations given off per minute per gram of material. Modern ^{14}C emits about 15 beta radiations per minute per gram of material, but ^{14}C that is 5,730 years old emits only half that amount (the half-life of ^{14}C) per minute per gram. So if a sample of some organism gives off 7.5 radiations a minute per gram, which is only half the amount given off by modern ^{14}C, the organism must be 5,730 years old.[20] Because the ^{14}C method is not accurate for samples more than 50,000 years old, a particle accelerator is used to allow researchers to assess the actual amount of ^{14}C, not just its radioactive emissions, in some material; this new method provides a way to date specimens that are up to 80,000 years old.[21]

The accuracy of radiocarbon dating was tested by using it to judge the age of parts of the Dead Sea Scrolls and some wood from an Egyptian tomb, the dates of which were already known from historical records. The results based on ^{14}C analysis agreed very well with the historical information.

THERMOLUMINESCENCE DATING   Many minerals emit light when they are heated (*thermoluminescence*), even before they become red hot. This cold light comes from the release, under heat, of "outside" electrons trapped in the crystal structure. **Thermoluminescence dating** makes use of the principle that if an object is heated at some point to a high temperature, as when clay is baked to form a pot, it will release all the trapped electrons it held previously.[22] Over time, the object will continue to trap electrons from radioactive elements (potassium, thorium, uranium) around it. The amount of thermoluminescence emitted when the object is heated during testing allows researchers to calculate the age of the object, if it is known what kind of radiation the object has been exposed to in its surroundings (for example, the surrounding soil in which a clay pot is found).

Thermoluminescence dating is well suited to samples of ancient pottery, brick, tile, terra cotta, and other objects that are made at high temperatures. This method can also be applied to burnt flint tools, hearth stones, lava or lava-covered objects, meteorites, and meteor craters.[23]

ELECTRON SPIN RESONANCE DATING   Electron spin resonance dating is a technique that, like thermoluminescence dating, measures trapped electrons from surrounding radioactive material. But the method in this case is different. The material to be dated is exposed to varying magnetic fields, and a spectrum of the microwaves absorbed by the tested material is obtained. Because no heating is required for this technique, electron spin resonance is especially useful for dating organic material such as bone and shell, which decompose if heated.[24]

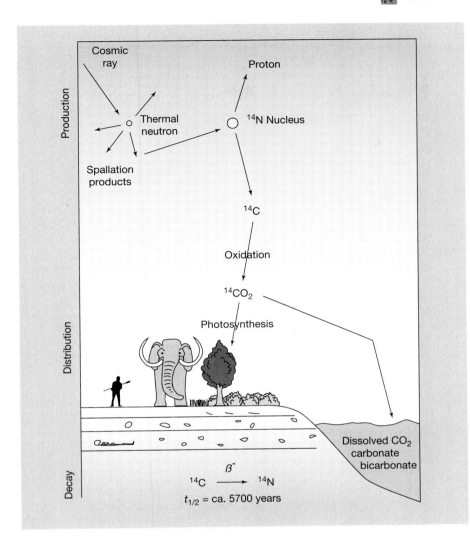

Figure 2–3 *The Carbon-14 Cycle*

Source: "The Carbon-14 Cycle" from "Radiocarbon Dating" by R. E. Taylor, from *Chronometric Dating in Archaeology* by R. E. Taylor and M. J. Aitken, eds. Copyright © 1997 by Plenum Publishing. Reprinted by permission of the publisher.

PALEOMAGNETIC DATING When rock of any kind forms, it records the ancient magnetic field of the earth. When this knowledge is put together with the fact that the earth's magnetic field has reversed itself many times, the geomagnetic patterns in rocks can be used to date the fossils within those rocks. **Paleomagnetic dating** dates rocks in terms of the sequence of geomagnetic patterns in them. Strictly speaking, paleomagnetic dating is not an absolute dating method, but geomagnetic time periods have been dated absolutely in conjunction with potassium-argon dating (described below). Paleomagnetic dating has dated primate finds from the Eocene through the Miocene, from 55 million to 5 million years ago.[25]

Not only does the earth's magnetic field reverse itself, but the locations of its poles move constantly (albeit very slowly) over time. The wanderings of the North Pole have been determined for the recent past, and this knowledge allows archaeologists to date some archaeological features. When soil, rock, or metal is heated to a high temperature, it liquifies and its constituent molecules align themselves to the earth's magnetic field. When cooled, the molecules

retain their alignment, and thus create something of an arrow pointing to the earth's magnetic poles. When an archaeologist finds a hearth, pottery kiln, metal workshop, or something else in which earth, rock, or metal was heated to its melting point and cooled in place, the archaeologist can take a sample of that material, carefully recording its location in terms of the earth's present-day magnetic field, and then measure the material's magnetic field in the laboratory. The difference between the direction of the earth's current magnetic field and that recorded in the material can be used to date when the material was melted and cooled.

POTASSIUM-ARGON DATING AND ARGON-ARGON DATING Potassium-40 (^{40}K), a radioactive form of potassium, decays at an established rate and forms argon-40 (^{40}Ar). The half-life of ^{40}K is a known quantity, so the age of a material containing potassium can be measured by the amount of ^{40}K compared with the amount of ^{40}Ar it contains.[26] Radioactive potassium's (^{40}K's) half-life is

CURRENT ISSUES

Are There Unilinear Trends in Cultural Evolution?

Late in the 1800s, in the early days of anthropology, the prevailing view of theorists like Edward Tylor and Lewis Henry Morgan was that culture generally develops or evolves in a uniform or progressive manner. It was thought that most societies pass through similar stages, to arrive ultimately at a common end. The early evolutionists believed that European and European-derived cultures were at the highest stages of evolution. Other cultures were still in the lower stages. The school of historical particularism associated with Franz Boas rejected the idea that there were universal laws governing all human cultures. Instead, the historical particularalists proposed that culture traits had to be studied in the context of the society in which they appeared. Boas stressed the need to collect data on as many societies as possible, an activity that became a central part of the anthropological enterprise.

Evolutionism did not die with the early evolutionists, however. For example, in the 1960s, Marshall Sahlins and Elman Service discussed two kinds of evolutionary processes—specific evolution, which refers to the particular changes of a particular society, and general evolution. General evolution refers to the general tendency of "higher" forms to surpass "lower" forms, but it does not insist that every society goes through exactly the same stages or progresses toward the "higher" stages. Nonetheless, anthropologists are not particularly keen on the idea of *unilinear* (one-directional) evolution, perhaps because the idea is still associated with the assumption of European superiority by the early evolutionists. But looking at the long stretch of human history, we see that some things seem to have changed in a fairly consistent way. For example, human populations have grown, technology has become more sophisticated, and most people on earth have come to live in state societies. Surely there are some unilinear trends in cultural evolution—or are there? How can we tell?

The third author (Peter Peregrine) of this textbook approached the question through cross-cultural research. He decided to test whether overall cultural complexity has increased over time. To do so he needed a measure of cultural complexity, and he needed a group of cultures to measure that represented all the cultures on earth over a long period of time. Happily, both exist. The measure of cultural complexity he used was developed by anthropologist George Peter Murdock to examine variation in cultural complexity among ethnographically known cultures. The measure looks at 10 different features of the culture, including its technology, economy, political system, and population density. Peregrine simplified this measure to make it easier to use with archaeologically known cultures, and he limited himself to Old World cultures dating to the last 15,000 years listed in the *Outline of Archaeological Traditions*. He measured cultural complexity for these cultures using the information about them given in the *Encyclopedia of Prehistory*.

Peregrine found strong evidence that cultural complexity has increased in a fairly regular manner over the last 15,000

very long—1,330 million years. This means that **potassium-argon (K-Ar) dating** may be used to date samples from 5,000 years up to 3 billion years old.

The K-Ar method is used to date potassium-rich minerals in rock, not the fossils that may be found in the rock. A very high temperature, such as occurs in a volcanic event, drives off any original argon in the material. Therefore, the amount of argon that accumulates afterward from the decay of radioactive potassium is directly related to the amount of time since the volcanic event. This type of dating has been extremely useful in East Africa, where volcanic events have occurred frequently since the Miocene, which began 24 million years ago.[27] If the material to be dated is not rich in potassium, or the area did not experience any high-temperature events, other methods of absolute dating are required.

One problem with the K-Ar method is that the amounts of potassium and argon must be measured on different rock samples; researchers must assume that the potassium and argon are evenly distributed in all the rock samples from a particular stratum. Researchers got around this problem by developing the **^{40}Ar-^{39}Ar dating method.** After measuring the amount of ^{40}Ar, a nuclear reactor is used to convert another kind of argon, ^{39}Ar, to

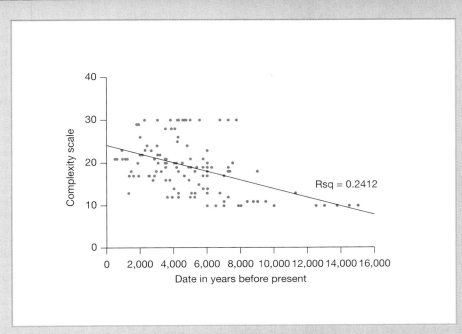

The Relationship between Cultural Complexity and Time

In general, cultural complexity has increased over time.

years. The figure in this box displays this trend graphically. The horizontal scale is the date of the culture, starting with today at the left and going back into the past as you move to the right. The vertical scale is the culture's cultural complexity score. It's clear from the figure that cultural complexity scores have tended to increase over time. Indeed the increase is statistically significant (unlikely to be due to chance). However, it is also clear that the increase is not universal: Some cultures scored low in the past while others scored higher, and some score low today while others score higher. Thus not all cultures have undergone change in the same way. But the figure suggests that human cultures generally have tended to become more complex over time. Why? We offer no answer, but we suggest it is an excellent question to ponder as you read through this book.

Sources: Peter N. Peregrine, *Outline of Archaeological Traditions* (New Haven, CT: HRAF, 2001); Peter N. Peregrine and Melvin Ember, eds., *Encyclopedia of Prehistory* (New York: Kluwer Academic/Plenum, 2001); Peter N. Peregrine, "Cross-Cultural Approaches in Archaeology," *Annual Review of Anthropology*, 30 (2001).

potassium so that the potassium-argon ratio can be measured from the same sample.[28]

URANIUM-SERIES DATING   The decay of two kinds of uranium, [235]U and [238]U, into other isotopes (such as [230]Th, thorium) has also proved useful for dating sites with remains of *Homo sapiens* (modern-looking humans), particularly in caves where stalagmites and other calcite formations form. Because water that seeps into caves usually contains uranium but not thorium, the calcite formations trap uranium. Uranium starts decaying at a known rate into other isotopes (such as thorium-230, or [230]Th),

and the ratio of those isotopes to uranium isotopes can be used to estimate the time elapsed. The thorium-uranium ratio is useful for dating cave sites less than 300,000 years old where there are no volcanic rocks suitable for the potassium-argon method. Early *Homo sapiens* from European cave sites in Germany, Hungary, and Wales were dated this way.[29] There are different varieties of **uranium-series dating,** depending on the specific isotope ratios used.

FISSION-TRACK DATING   Fission-track dating is another way to determine the absolute age of fossil deposits.[30] Like the K-Ar method, it dates minerals contemporaneous with the deposit in which fossils are found and it also requires the prior occurrence of a high-temperature event, as a volcanic eruption. But the kinds of samples it can be used to date, such as crystal, glass, and many uranium-rich minerals, include a much wider variety than those that can be dated by the K-Ar method. The age range of fission-track dating, like that of K-Ar dating, is extensive—20 years to 5 billion years.[31]

How does fission-track dating work? This method is basically the simplest of all the methods discussed here. It entails counting the number of paths or tracks etched in the sample by the fission—explosive division—of uranium atoms as they disintegrate. Scientists know that ^{238}U, the most common uranium isotope, decays at a slow, steady rate. This decay takes the form of spontaneous fission, and each separate fission leaves a scar or track on the sample, which can be seen when chemically treated through a microscope. To find out how old a sample is, one counts the tracks, then measures their ratio to the uranium content of the sample.

The fission-track method was used to date Bed I at Olduvai Gorge in Tanzania, East Africa, where some early human ancestors were found.[32] It was able to corroborate earlier K-Ar estimates that the site dated back close to 2 million years. That the K-Ar and fission-track methods use different techniques and have different sources of error makes them effective as checks on each other. When the two methods support each other, they provide very reliable evidence.

The Results of Archaeological Research

When archaeologists and paleoanthropologists finish a research project, what is the result? What are the goals of archaeological research? There are several distinct answers.

One goal of archaeological research is the description or reconstruction of what happened in the past. Much of what archaeologists do, and much of what we do in this book, fall under this goal. Archaeologists attempt to determine how people lived in a particular place at a particular time, and when and how their life-styles changed. Also of interest, of course, is whether new cultures arrived or established cultures moved out of a given area. Creating histories of cultures and their changes over time is called, simply enough, **culture history.** Doing culture history was the primary goal of archaeology until the 1950s.[33]

A second major goal of archaeological research, and one that has become the primary goal since the 1950s, is testing specific theories and hypotheses about human evolution and behavior. In part this change in focus is due to the growth in our knowledge about the past—the culture history of many areas is today well known. But this change is also due to changes going on in anthropology as a

whole. Until the 1950s a school of thought called *historical particularism* was dominant in American anthropology. It suggested that variation in human cultures was best explained by considering the specific historical developments of particular cultures. Like the purpose of historical particularism, the purpose of culture history was to trace historical developments.

After the 1950s a variety of new approaches became prominent in anthropology, most of them sharing the idea that the environment and the way humans use it actively shape cultures and mostly explain cultural variability. Archaeology became a key tool for anthropologists attempting to understand how changes in the ways humans used the environment explained variation in human cultures. One of the outgrowths of this focus on hypothesis testing and human use of the environment was research on agricultural origins, which we discuss in the chapter on the origins of food production and settled life. Another was a concern with the rise of cities and states, which appears to have radically transformed human use of the environment. We devote a separate chapter to that subject.

In addition to testing hypotheses, archaeology has a primary role within anthropology in its attempt to identify and understand general trends and patterns in human biological and cultural evolution. As we discussed in the last chapter, cross-cultural research has this as a goal as well. But only archaeology is able to look through time and directly examine evolutionary trends. In the box "Are There Unilinear Trends in Cultural Evolution?" we consider one way archaeology is able to elucidate long-term trends. In later chapters in this book we trace the evolution of humans and human cultures from their beginnings. As we shall see, a major emphasis in paleoanthropology is demonstrating long-term trends and patterns that help us understand how and why we have come to be the way we are. In this pursuit, archaeology and paleoanthropology come together to help answer what may be the fundamental question of anthropology: What does it mean to be human?

Summary

1. Archaeologists and paleoanthropologists have four basic sources of evidence about the past: artifacts, ecofacts, fossils, and features.

2. Sites are locations where the evidence of the past has been buried and preserved. Sites are found through pedestrian survey or remote sensing, and artifacts, ecofacts, fossils, and features are recovered from sites through excavation.

3. Information about the past is obtained by analyzing the evidence recovered from sites. Much information can be gained through the analysis of the forms, sizes, and composition of archaeological materials, but the materials themselves are not the primary focus of analysis. Rather it

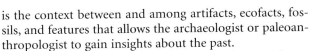

is the context between and among artifacts, ecofacts, fossils, and features that allows the archaeologist or paleoanthropologist to gain insights about the past.

4. A key aspect of putting archaeological material into context is being able to date material accurately. A wide variety of dating techniques are used. Relative dating techniques determine the age of archaeological materials relative to other materials of known ages. Absolute dating techniques determine the age of the archaeological deposits or materials themselves.

5. Archaeology allows for cultural histories to be developed and hypotheses about cultural change to be tested. Its primary goal is to provide insights into human physical and cultural evolution—the central concern of this book.

Glossary Terms

absolute dating	lithics
^{40}Ar-^{39}Ar dating	paleoanthropologists
artifact	paleomagnetic dating
ceramics	potassium-argon (K-Ar)
conservation	dating
context	radiocarbon, or carbon-14
culture history	(^{14}C), dating
ecofacts	relative dating
electron spin resonance	sites
dating	stratified
features	taphonomy
fission-track dating	thermoluminescence
fossils	dating
F-U-N trio	typology
half-life	uranium-series dating
indicator fossils	

Critical Questions

1. Why is context so important in archaeological research?

2. What kinds of information can be learned from a stone projectile point?

3. What factors have to be considered when choosing a dating technique?

 Internet Exercises

1. Visit **http://archnet.asu.edu** and explore one or more of the subject areas concerning archaeological methods. Write a brief essay describing a new method or technique you learned about.

2. Learn about archaeological sampling at **http://archnet.asu.edu/archnet/topical/theory/sampling/sampling.html**. Try the various techniques and determine which gives the best results.

3. Visit the carbon-14 dating Web site at **http://www.c14dating.com/**. Read about the method's history, and how carbon-14 samples are collected, prepared, and analyzed. Summarize what you learned.

4. Take the seriation test at **http://emuseum.mankato.msus.edu/archaeology/dating/seriate.html** and determine your potential as an archaeologist.

 Suggested Reading

BAHN, P. *Archaeology: A Very Short Introduction.* New York: Oxford University Press, 1996. Just what the name says— a short, well-written introduction to archaeology.

BINFORD, L. *In Pursuit of the Past: Decoding the Archaeological Record.* New York: Thames and Hudson, 1983. One of the most influential archaeologists of our time uses his own research to explain how archaeological research is carried out.

FAGAN, B. *In the Beginning: An Introduction to Archaeology,* 9th ed. New York: Longman, 1997. A classic introduction to archaeological research.

GIBBON, G. *Anthropological Archaeology.* New York: Columbia University Press, 1984. Perhaps the single best introduction to archaeology ever written.

PEREGRINE, P. *Archaeological Research: A Brief Introduction.* Upper Saddle River, NJ: Prentice Hall, 2001. An overview of the purposes, practices, and results of archaeological research, written for a general audience.

PURDY, B. *How to Do Archaeology the Right Way.* Gainesville: University Press of Florida, 1996. An introduction to archaeological excavation and field methods.

RENFREW, C., AND BAHN, P. *Archaeology: Theories, Methods, and Practice.* New York: Thames and Hudson, 1996. A comprehensive and detailed overview of archaeology.

3

Genetics and Evolution

CAROLI LINNÆI
EQUITIS DE STELLA POLARI,
ARCHIATRI REGII, MED. & BOTAN. PROFESS. UPSAL.;
ACAD. UPSAL. HOLMENS. PETROPOL. BEROL. IMPER.
LOND. MONSPEL. TOLOS. FLORENT. SOC.

SYSTEMA
NATURÆ

PER
REGNA TRIA NATURÆ,

SECUNDUM

CLASSES, ORDINES,
GENERA, SPECIES,

CUM

CHARACTERIBUS, DIFFERENTIIS,
SYNONYMIS, LOCIS.

TOMUS I.

EDITIO DECIMA, REFORMATA.

Cum Privilegio S:æ R:æ M:tis Sveciæ.

HOLMIÆ,
IMPENSIS DIRECT. LAURENTII SALVII,
1758

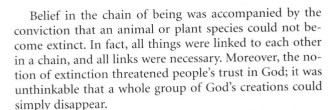
strionomers estimate that the universe has been in existence for some 15 billion years, plus or minus a few billion. To make this awesome history more understandable, Carl Sagan devised a calendar that condenses this span into a single year.[1] Using as a scale 24 days for every billion years and 1 second for every 475 years, Sagan moves from the "Big Bang," or beginning of the universe, on January 1 to the origin of the Milky Way on May 1. September 9 marks the beginning of our solar system, and September 25 the origin of life on earth. At 10:30 in the evening of December 31, the first humanlike primates appear. Sagan's compression of history provides us with a manageable way to compare the short span of human existence with the total time span of the universe. Humanlike beings have been around for only about 90 minutes out of a 12-month period! In this book we are concerned with what has happened in the last few hours of that year.

Some 55 million to 65 million years ago, the first primates appeared. They were ancestral to all living primates, including monkeys, apes, and humans. The early primates may or may not have lived in trees, but they had flexible digits and could grasp things. Later, about 35 million years ago, the first monkeys and apes appeared. About 15 million years ago, some 20 million years after the appearance of monkeys and apes, the immediate apelike ancestors of humans probably emerged. About 4 million years ago the first humanlike beings appeared. Modern-looking humans evolved only about 100,000 years ago.

How do we account for the biological and cultural evolution of humans? The details of the emergence of primates and the evolution of humans and their cultures are covered in subsequent chapters. In this chapter we focus on how the modern theory of evolution developed and how it accounts for change over time.

The Evolution of Evolution

Traditional Western ideas about nature's creatures were very different from Charles Darwin's theory of *evolution,* which suggested that different species developed, one from another, over long periods of time. In the fifth millennium B.C., the Greek philosophers Plato and Aristotle believed that animals and plants form a single, graded continuum going from more perfection to less perfection. Humans, of course, were at the top of this scale. Later Greek philosophers added the idea that the creator gave life or "radiance" first to humans, but at each subsequent creation some of that essence was lost.[2] Macrobius, summarizing the thinking of Plotinus, used an image that was to persist for centuries, the image of what came to be called the "chain of being": "The attentive observer will discover a connection of parts, from the Supreme God down to the last dregs of things, mutually linked together and without a break. And this is Homer's golden chain, which God, he says, bade hand down from heaven to earth."[3]

Belief in the chain of being was accompanied by the conviction that an animal or plant species could not become extinct. In fact, all things were linked to each other in a chain, and all links were necessary. Moreover, the notion of extinction threatened people's trust in God; it was unthinkable that a whole group of God's creations could simply disappear.

The idea of the chain of being persisted through the years, but it was not discussed extensively by philosophers, scientists, poets, and theologians until the eighteenth century.[4] Those discussions prepared the way for evolutionary theory. It is ironic that, although the chain of being did not allow for evolution, its idea that there was an order of things in nature encouraged studies of natural history and comparative anatomical studies, which stimulated the development of the idea of evolution. People were also now motivated to look for previously unknown creatures. Moreover, humans were not shocked when naturalists suggested that humans were close to apes. This notion was perfectly consistent with the idea of a chain of being; apes were simply thought to have been created with less perfection.

Early in the eighteenth century, an influential scientist, Carolus Linnaeus (1707–1778), classified plants and animals in a *systema naturae,* which placed humans in the same order (Primates) as apes and monkeys. Linnaeus did not suggest an evolutionary relationship between humans and apes; he mostly accepted the notion that all species were created by God and fixed in their form. Not surprisingly, then, Linnaeus is often viewed as an anti-evolutionist. But Linnaeus's hierarchical classification scheme, in descending order going from kingdom to class, order, genus, and species, provided a framework for the idea that humans, apes, and monkeys had a common ancestor.[5] See Figure 3–1.

Others did not believe that species were fixed in their form. According to Jean Baptiste Lamarck (1744–1829), acquired characteristics could be inherited and therefore species could evolve; individuals who in their lifetime developed characteristics helpful to survival would pass those characteristics on to future generations, thereby changing the physical makeup of the species. For example, Lamarck explained the long neck of the giraffe as the result of successive generations of giraffes stretching their necks to reach the high leaves of trees. The stretched muscles and bones of the necks were somehow transmitted to the offspring of the neck-stretching giraffes, and eventually all giraffes came to have long necks. But because Lamarck and later biologists failed to produce evidence to support the hypothesis that acquired characteristics can be inherited, this explanation of evolution is now generally dismissed.[6]

By the nineteenth century, some thinkers were beginning to accept evolution while others were trying to refute it.[7] For example, Georges Cuvier (1769–1832) was a leading opponent of evolution. Cuvier's theory of *catastrophism* proposed that a quick series of catastrophes accounted for changes in the earth and the fossil record.

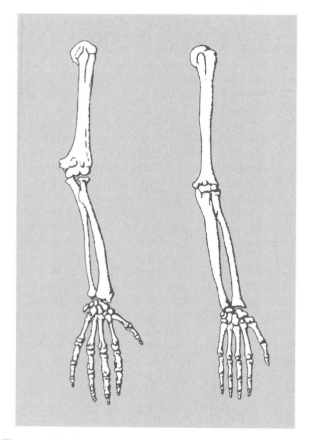

Figure 3–1

The idea that chimpanzees and humans descend from a common ancestor is suggested by anatomical similarities, such as in their forelimbs. Chimpanzee forelimb skeleton (left); human forelimb skeleton (right).

Cataclysms and upheavals such as Noah's flood had killed off previous sets of living creatures, which each time were replaced by new creations.

Major changes in geological thinking occurred in the nineteenth century. Earlier, the geologist James Hutton (1726–1797) had questioned catastrophism, but his work was largely ignored. In contrast, Sir Charles Lyell's (1797–1875) volumes of the *Principles of Geology* (1830–1833), which built on Hutton's earlier work, received immediate acclaim. Their concept of *uniformitarianism* suggested that the earth is constantly being shaped and reshaped by natural forces that have operated over a vast stretch of time. Lyell also discussed the formation of geological strata and paleontology. He used fossilized fauna to define different geological epochs. Lyell's works were read avidly by Charles Darwin before and during Darwin's now-famous voyage on the *Beagle*. The two corresponded and subsequently became friends.

After studying changes in plants, fossil animals, and varieties of domestic and wild pigeons, Charles Darwin (1809–1882) rejected the notion that each species was created at one time in a fixed form. The results of his investigations pointed clearly, he thought, to the evolution of

species through the mechanism of natural selection. While Darwin was completing his book on the subject, Lyell sent him a manuscript by Alfred Russel Wallace (1823–1913), a naturalist who had independently reached conclusions about the evolution of species that matched Darwin's own.[8] In 1858, the two men presented the astonishing theory of *natural selection* to their colleagues at a meeting of the Linnaean Society of London.[9]

In 1859, when Darwin published *The Origin of Species by Means of Natural Selection,*[10] he wrote, "I am fully convinced that species are not immutable; but that those belonging to what are called the same genera are lineal descendants of some other and generally extinct species, in the same manner as the acknowledged varieties of any one species."[11] His conclusions outraged those who believed in the biblical account of creation, and the result was bitter controversy that continues to this day.[12]

Until 1871, when his *The Descent of Man* was published, Darwin avoided stating categorically that humans were descended from nonhuman forms, but the implications of his theory were clear. People immediately began to take sides. In June 1860, at the annual meeting of the British Association for the Advancement of Science, Bishop Wilberforce saw an opportunity to attack the Darwinists. Concluding his speech, he faced Thomas Huxley, one of the Darwinists' chief advocates, and inquired, "Was

Charles Darwin. (*Source:* Gemalde von John Collier, 1883, "Charles Robert Darwin." Ol auf Leinwand. 125.7 x 96.5 cm. London, National Portrait Gallery/1024. Bildarchiv Preussischer Kulturbesitz. Photo: Jochen Remmer.)

it through his grandfather or his grandmother that he claimed descent from a monkey?" Huxley responded,

> If . . . the question is put to me would I rather have a miserable ape for a grandfather than a man highly endowed by nature and possessing great means and influence and yet who employs those faculties and that influence for the mere purpose of introducing ridicule into a grave scientific discussion—I unhesitatingly affirm my preference for the ape.[13]

The Principles of Natural Selection

Darwin was not the first person to view the creation of new species in evolutionary terms, but he was the first to provide a comprehensive, well-documented explanation —natural selection—for the way evolution had occurred. **Natural selection** is the main process that increases the frequency of adaptive traits through time. The operation of natural selection involves three conditions or principles.[14] The first is *variation:* Every species is composed of a great variety of individuals, some of which are better adapted to their environment than others. The existence of variety is important. Without it, natural selection has nothing on which to operate; without variation, one kind of characteristic could not be favored over another. The second principle of natural selection is *heritability:* Offspring inherit traits from their parents, at least to some degree and in some way. The third principle of natural selection is *differential reproductive success:* Since better adapted individuals generally produce more offspring over the generations than the poorer adapted, the frequency of adaptive traits gradually increases in subsequent generations. A new species emerges when changes in traits or geographic barriers result in the reproductive isolation of the population.

When we say that certain traits are adaptive or advantageous, we mean that they result in greater reproductive success in a particular environment. The phrase *particular environment* is very important. Even though a species may become more adapted to a particular environment over time, we cannot say that one species adapted to its environment is "better" than another species adapted to a different environment. For example, we may like to think of ourselves as "better" than other animals, but humans are clearly less adapted than fish for living under water, than bats for catching flying insects, than raccoons for living on suburban garbage.

Although the theory of natural selection suggests that disadvantageous or maladaptive traits will generally decline in frequency or even disappear eventually, it does not necessarily follow that all such traits will do so. After all, species derive from prior forms that have certain structures. This means that not all changes are possible; it also means that some traits are linked to others that might have advantages that outweigh the disadvantages. Choking may be very maladaptive for any animal, yet all vertebrates are capable of choking because their digestive and respiratory systems cross in the throat. This trait is a genetic legacy, probably from the time when the respiratory system developed from tissue in the digestive system of some ancestral organism. Apparently, the propensity to choke has not been correctable evolutionarily.[15]

Changes in a species can be expected to occur as the environment changes or as some members of the species move into a new environment. With environmental change, different traits become adaptive. The forms of the species that possess the more adaptive traits will become more frequent, whereas those forms whose characteristics make continued existence more difficult or impossible in the modified environment will eventually become extinct.

Consider how the theory of natural selection would explain why giraffes became long-necked. Originally, the necks of giraffes varied in length, as happens with virtually any physical characteristic in a population. During a period when food was scarce, those giraffes with longer necks, who could reach higher tree leaves, might be better able to survive and suckle their offspring, and thus they would leave more offspring than shorter-necked giraffes. Because of heredity, the offspring of long-necked giraffes are more likely to have long necks. Eventually, the shorter-necked giraffes would diminish in number and the longer-

The giraffe's long neck is adaptive for eating tree leaves high off the ground. When food is scarce, longer-necked giraffes would get more food and reproduce more successfully than shorter-necked giraffes; in this environment, natural selection would favor giraffes with longer necks.

CURRENT ISSUES

Is Evolution Slow and Steady or Fast and Abrupt?

Darwin's evolutionary theory suggested that new species emerge gradually over time. Through the process of natural selection, frequencies of traits would slowly change, and eventually a new species would appear. But Darwin did not explain why so much speciation has occurred. If trait frequencies change only gradually over time, wouldn't descendant populations retain their ability to interbreed and wouldn't they, therefore, continue to belong to the same species?

In the 1930s and 1940s, Theodosius Dobzhansky, Julian Huxley, Ernst Mayr, George Simpson, and others advanced what came to be called the "modern synthesis" in evolutionary theory, adding what was known from genetics about heredity. Mutation and the recombination of genes now provided for genetic variety. The driving force of change was still adaptation to environments through natural selection; gene frequencies of a population presumably changed slowly as adaptive traits (because of existing genes or mutations) increased in prevalence and maladaptive traits decreased. As for speciation, the development and divergence of different species, the modern synthesis postulated that it would occur when subpopulations became isolated by geographic barriers or when different subpopulations encountered different climatic conditions or moved into new ecological niches; those environmental isolating processes would eventually result in the development of re-

productive isolation and therefore new species.

This gradualist view of evolution was challenged in 1972 by Niles Eldredge and Stephen Jay Gould. Their alternative model of evolution is referred to as "punctuated equilibrium." They still assume that natural selection is the primary mechanism of evolutionary change, but they see the pace of evolution quite differently. In their view, new species evolve quickly; but once a successful species emerges, its characteristics are likely to change very little over long periods of time. Thus, in contrast to the modern synthesis, Eldredge and Gould do not think it is common for the world's species to change gradually into descendant species. Rather, species are born more or less abruptly, they have lifetimes during which they do not change much, and they become extinct. As examples, Eldredge and Gould cite the history of North American trilobites and Bermudan land snails. In both groups of animals, it looks as if the different species did not change for a long period of time—millions of years for some species—but then certain species seem to have been quickly replaced by related species from nearby areas. In short, Eldredge and Gould believe that the succession of one species after another involves replacement from outside more often than gradual change over time.

Evolution may or may not occur as the model of punctuated equilibrium specifies, but most

evolutionists today agree that change could occur relatively quickly. Recent research suggests that some relatively quick climate changes in the earth's history helped bring about massive extinctions of species and families of species and exponential increases in the subsequent number of new families. For example, there is considerable evidence that a large meteorite collided with the earth at the end of the Cretaceous geological period, about 65 million years ago. Louis Alvarez and his colleagues proposed that so much dust was sent into the atmosphere by the collision that the earth was shrouded in darkness for months, if not longer. Some investigators now think that the meteorite impact may have also triggered a great deal of volcanic activity, even on the opposite side of the world, which would also have reduced solar radiation to the earth's surface. Not only the dinosaurs disappeared about 65 million years ago, so also did many sea animals and plants. Afterward, the earth saw the proliferation of many other kinds of animals, such as fish, lizards, birds, and mammals, as well as flowering trees. As we shall see in the chapter on primate evolution, our own biological order, the Primates, is believed to have emerged around that time.

Peter Grant recently studied the same finches on the Galápagos Islands that partially inspired Darwin's theory. But, unlike Darwin, Grant had the chance to see natural selection in action. And it was surprisingly quick. Central

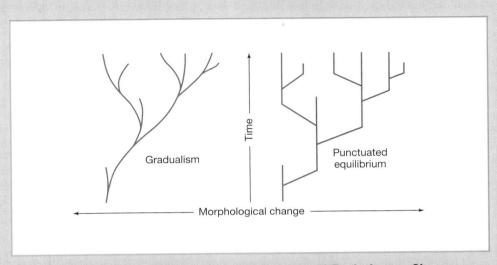

Gradualism

Time

Punctuated equilibrium

Morphological change

A Graphical Depiction of Gradual versus Punctuated Evolutionary Change

to the project was the attachment of colored bands to each individual bird, which allowed each bird to be identified at a distance. In the midst of the project, in 1977, when half the birds had been banded, there was a serious drought. Of the two main species of finch on one island, the cactus finch and the medium finch, only the cactus finches were able to breed, but they had no surviving offspring. During the next 18 months, 85 percent of the adult medium finches disappeared. Those finches that survived tended to be larger and to have larger beaks than the ones that died. Why larger beaks? Both species of finch eat seeds, but small seeds produced by grasses and herbs are scarce in a drought; bigger seeds are more available. So it seems that natural selection under conditions of drought favored finches with

bigger beaks, which are better at cracking the husks of large seeds.

If it were not for the fact that wet years, which favor smaller finches, occur between years of drought, we might see the quick evolution of new finch species. It is estimated that 20 drought episodes would be sufficient to produce a new species of finch. Darwin's (and Grant's) finches do not really provide an example of punctuated equilibrium (no replacement from outside occurred), but they do suggest that evolutionary change could be a lot quicker than Darwin imagined.

Controversy continues over whether evolution is slow and steady or fast and abrupt. But many scholars, including Gould, point out that there is no need to pit one model against the other. Both may be correct in different instances. In any case much more

investigation of evolutionary sequences is needed to help us evaluate the competing theoretical models.

Sources: Ian Tattersall, "Paleoanthropology and Evolutionary Theory," in Peter N. Peregrine, Carol R. Ember, and Melvin Ember, eds., *Physical Anthropology: Original Readings in Method and Practice* (Upper Saddle River, NJ: Prentice Hall, 2002); Charles Devillers and Jean Chaline, *Evolution: An Evolving Theory* (New York: Springer-Verlag, 1993); Peter R. Grant, "Natural Selection and Darwin's Finches," *Scientific American*, October 1991, 82–87; Jonathan Weiner, *Beak of the Finch* (New York: Vintage, 1994).

necked giraffes would increase. The resultant population of giraffes would still have variation in neck length but on the average would be longer-necked than earlier forms.

Natural selection does not account for all variation in the frequencies of traits. In particular, it does not account for variation in the frequencies of neutral traits—that is, those traits that do not seem to confer any advantages or disadvantages on their carriers. Changes in the frequencies of neutral traits may result rather from random processes that affect gene frequencies in isolated populations—*genetic drift*—or from matings between populations—*gene flow*. We discuss these other processes later in the chapter.

OBSERVED EXAMPLES OF EVOLUTION

Because the process of evolution may involve nearly imperceptible gradations over generations, it is usually difficult to observe directly. Nevertheless, because some life forms reproduce rapidly, some examples of natural selection have been observed over relatively short periods in changing environments.

For example, scientists think they have observed natural selection in action in British moths. In 1850, an almost black moth was spotted for the first time in Manchester. That was quite unusual, for most of the moths were speckled gray. A century later, 95 percent of the moths in industrial parts of Britain were black; only in the rural areas were the moths mostly gray. How is this to be explained? It seems that in the rural areas, the gray-speckled moth is hard to spot by bird predators against the lichen growing

on the bark of trees. But in industrial areas, lichen is killed by pollution. The gray-speckled moths, formerly well adapted to blend into their environment, became clearly visible against the darker background of the lichen-free trees and were easier prey for birds. In contrast, the black moths, which previously would have had a disadvantage against the lighter bark, were now better adapted for survival. Their dark color was an advantage, and subsequently the darker moths became the predominant variety in industrial regions.

How can we be sure that natural selection was the mechanism accounting for the change? Consistent evidence comes from a series of experiments performed by H.B.D. Kettlewell. He deliberately released specially marked moths, black and gray, into two areas of England—one urban industrial and one rural—and then set light traps to recapture them subsequently. The proportions of the two kinds of moths recovered tell us about differential survival. Kettlewell found that proportionately more black moths compared with gray moths were recovered in the urban industrial area. Just the reverse happened in the rural area; proportionately more gray-speckled moths were recovered.[16] The same transformation—the switch to darker color—occurred in 70 other species of moth, as well as in a beetle and a millipede. It did not occur just in Britain; it also happened in other highly polluted areas, the Ruhr area of Germany and in the Pittsburgh area of the United States. Moreover, in the Pittsburgh area, antipollution measures in the last 40 years have apparently caused the black moth to dwindle in number once again.[17]

The type of natural selection in the moth example is called **directional selection** because a particular trait seems to be positively favored and the average value shifts over time toward the adaptive trait. But there can also be **normalizing selection.** In this type of selection the average value does not change, but natural selection removes the extremes.[18] An example is the birthweight of babies. Both very low birthweights and very high birthweights are disadvantageous and would be selected against. Directional and normalizing selection both assume that natural selection will either favor or disfavor genes, but there is a third possibility—balancing selection.[19] **Balancing selection** occurs when a *heterozygous* (varied) combination of *alleles* (genes) is positively favored even though a *homozygous* (genes in the pairs are the same) combination is disfavored. In the chapter on human variation, we discuss a trait that apparently involves balancing selection—sickle-cell anemia—which is found in persons of West African ancestry, among other populations.

Another well-known example of observed natural selection is the acquired resistance of houseflies to the insecticide DDT. When DDT was first used to kill insects, beginning in the 1940s, several new, DDT-resistant strains of housefly evolved. In the early DDT environment, many houseflies were killed, but the few that survived were the ones that reproduced, and their resistant characteristics became common to the housefly populations. To the cha-

The changes that occurred in the moth population in different areas of England show natural selection in action. Before industrialization, tree trunks were lighter and light-colored moths predominated. (Rural areas today, with little or no industrial air pollution, show that natural selection in unpolluted areas still favors light-colored moths.) But with industrial pollution and the darkening of tree trunks, light-colored moths became more visible to predators. Darker-colored moths quickly increased in number in the new industrial environment.

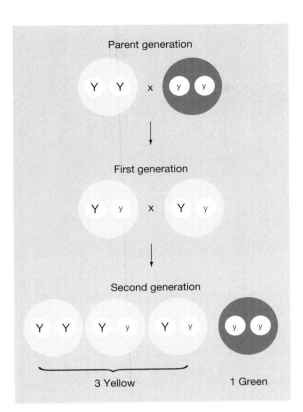

Parent generation

Y Y x y y

First generation

Y y x Y y

Second generation

Y Y   Y y   Y y   y y

3 Yellow   1 Green

Figure 3–2

When Mendel crossed a plant having two genes for yellow peas (YY) with a plant having two genes for green peas (yy), each offspring pea was yellow but carried one gene for yellow and one gene for green (Yy). The peas were yellow because the gene for yellow is dominant over the recessive gene for green. Crossing the first generation yielded three yellow pea plants for each green pea plant.

Gregor Mendel's pioneering studies in the science of genetics provided the foundation for such a model, but his discoveries did not become widely known until 1900.

Heredity

GREGOR MENDEL'S EXPERIMENTS

Mendel (1822–1884), a monk and amateur botanist who lived in what is now the Czech Republic, bred several varieties of pea plants and made detailed observations of their offspring. He chose as breeding partners plants that differed by only one observable trait. Tall plants were crossed with short ones, and yellow ones with green, for example.

When the pollen from a yellow pea plant was transferred to a green pea plant, Mendel observed a curious phenomenon: All of the first-generation offspring bore yellow peas. It seemed that the green trait had disappeared. But when seeds from this first generation were crossed, they produced both yellow and green pea plants in a ratio of three yellow to one green pea plant (see Figure 3–2). Apparently, Mendel reasoned, the green trait had not been lost or altered; the yellow trait was simply **dominant** and the green trait was **recessive**. Mendel observed similar results with other traits. Tallness dominated shortness, and the factor for smooth-skinned peas dominated the factor for wrinkled ones. In each cross, the 3-to-1

Gregor Mendel.

grin of medical practitioners, similar resistances develop in bacteria. A particular antibiotic may lose its effectiveness after it comes into wide use because new, resistant bacterial strains emerge. These new strains will become more frequent than the original ones because of natural selection. In the United States now, a few strains are resistant to *all* antibiotics on the market, a fact that worries medical practitioners. One possible way to deal with the problem is to stop using antibiotics for a few years, so resistance to those antibiotics might not develop or develop only slowly.

The theory of natural selection answered many questions, but it also raised at least one whose answer eluded Darwin and others. The appearance of a beneficial trait may assist the survival of an organism, but what happens when the organism reproduces by mating with members that do not possess this new variation? Will not the new adaptive trait eventually disappear if subsequent generations mate with individuals that lack this trait? Darwin knew variations were transmitted through heredity, but he did not have a clear model of the mode of inheritance.

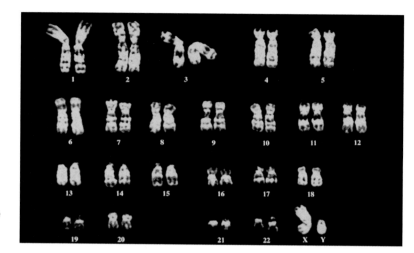

This karyotype shows the 23 paired chromosomes in a normal human male. Note the small Y chromosome at the bottom right that makes this individual male.

ratio appeared in the second generation. Self-fertilization, however, produced different results. Green pea plants always yielded green pea plants, and short plants always produced short plants.

From his numerical results, Mendel concluded that some yellow pea plants were pure (homozygous) for that trait, whereas others also possessed a green factor (the plants were heterozygous). That is, although two plants might both have yellow peas, one of them might produce offspring with green peas. In such cases, the genetic makeup, the **genotype,** differed from the observable appearance, or **phenotype.**

GENES: THE CONVEYORS OF INHERITED TRAITS

Mendel's units of heredity were what we now call **genes.** He concluded that these units occurred in pairs for each trait and that offspring inherited one unit of the pair from each parent. Each member of a gene pair or group is called an **allele.** If the two genes, or alleles, for a trait are the same, the organism is **homozygous** for that trait; if the two genes for a characteristic differ, the organism is **heterozygous** for that trait. A pea plant that contains a pair of genes for yellow is homozygous for the trait. A yellow pea plant with a dominant gene for yellow and a recessive gene for green, although phenotypically yellow, has a heterozygous genotype. As Mendel demonstrated, the recessive green gene can reappear in subsequent generations. But Mendel knew nothing of the composition of genes or the processes that transmit them from parent to offspring. Many years of scientific research have yielded much of the missing information.

The genes of higher organisms (not including bacteria and primitive plants such as green-blue algae) are located on ropelike bodies called **chromosomes** within the nucleus of every one of the organism's cells. Chromosomes, like genes, usually occur in pairs. Each allele for a given trait is carried in the identical position on corresponding chromosomes. The two genes that determined the color of

Mendel's peas, for example, were opposite each other on a pair of chromosomes.

MITOSIS AND MEIOSIS The body cells of every plant or animal carry chromosome pairs in a number appropriate for its species. Humans have 23 pairs, or a total of 46 chromosomes, each carrying many times that number of genes. Each new body cell receives this number of chromosomes during cellular reproduction, or **mitosis,** as each pair of chromosomes duplicates itself.

  CD-ROM Simulation II-2

But what happens when a sperm cell and an egg cell unite to form a new organism? What prevents the human baby from receiving twice the number of chromosomes characteristic of its species—23 pairs from the sperm and 23 pairs from the egg? The process by which the reproductive cells are formed, **meiosis,** ensures that this will not happen (see Figure 3–3). Each reproductive cell contains *half* the number of chromosomes appropriate for the species. Only one member of each chromosome pair is carried in every egg or sperm. At fertilization, the human embryo normally receives 23 *separate* chromosomes from its mother and the same number from its father, which add up to the 23 pairs.

DNA As we have said, genes are located on chromosomes. Each gene carries a set of instructions encoded in its chemical structure. It is from this coded information carried in genes that a cell makes all the rest of its structural parts and chemical machinery. It appears that in most living organisms, heredity is controlled by the same chemical substance, **DNA**—deoxyribonucleic acid. An enormous amount of research has been directed toward understanding DNA—what its structure is, how it duplicates itself in reproduction, and how it conveys or instructs the formation of a complete organism.

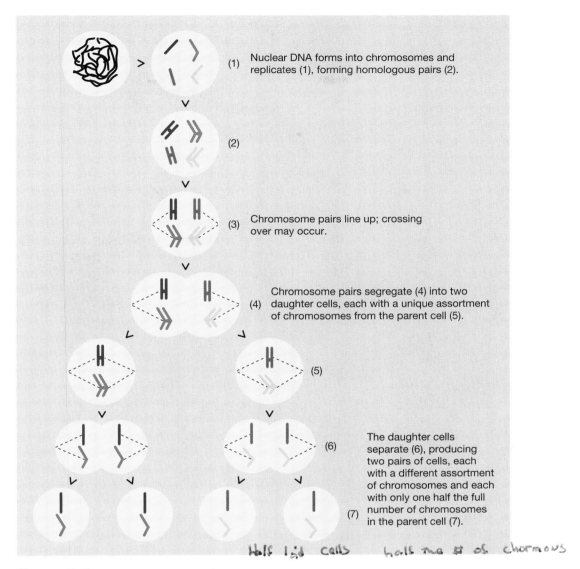

(1) Nuclear DNA forms into chromosomes and replicates (1), forming homologous pairs (2).

(2)

(3) Chromosome pairs line up; crossing over may occur.

(4) Chromosome pairs segregate (4) into two daughter cells, each with a unique assortment of chromosomes from the parent cell (5).

(5)

(6) The daughter cells separate (6), producing two pairs of cells, each with a different assortment of chromosomes and each with only one half the full number of chromosomes in the parent cell (7).

(7)

Half 1;d cells   half the # of chromous

Figure 3–3   *Meiosis (sex cells)*

CD-ROM Simulation II-3

One of the most important keys to understanding human development and genetics is the structure and function of DNA. In 1953, the American biologist James Watson, with the British molecular biologist Francis Crick, proposed that DNA is a long, two-stranded molecule shaped like a double helix[20] (see Figure 3–4). Genetic information is stored in the linear sequences of the bases; different species have different sequences, and every individual is slightly different from every other individual. Notice that in the DNA molecule each base always has the same opposite base; adenine and thymine are paired, as are cytosine and guanine. The importance of this pattern

is that the two strands carry the same information, so that when the double helix unwinds each strand can form a template for a new strand of complementary bases.[21] Because DNA stores the information required to make up the cells of an organism, it has been called the language of life. As George and Muriel Beadle put it,

> the deciphering of the DNA code has revealed our possession of a language much older than hieroglyphics, a language as old as life itself, a language that is the most living language of all—even if its letters are invisible and its words are buried deep in the cells of our bodies.[22]

Once it was understood that genes are made of DNA, concerted efforts were begun to map DNA sequences and their locations on the chromosomes of different organisms. A project known as the human genome project set out to assemble a complete genetic map for humans. In July 2000, the initial mapping of the human genome was

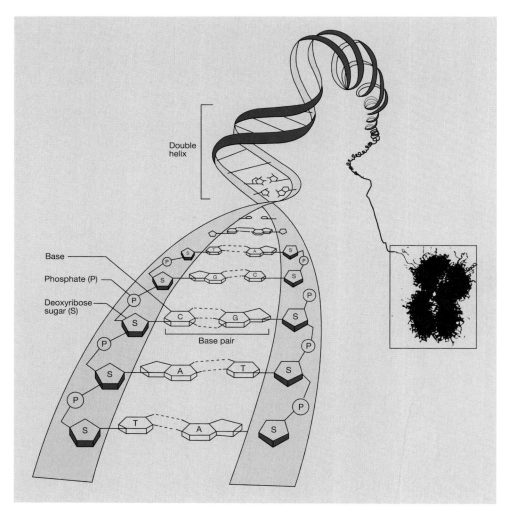

Figure 3–4 *The DNA molecule consists of two spiral sugar-phosphate strands. The strands are linked by the nitrogenous bases adenine (A), guanine (G), thymine (T), and cytosine (C). When the DNA molecule reproduces, the bases separate and the spiral strands unwind. Each original strand serves as a mold along which a new complementary chain is formed. Source:* From *The Language of Heredity* by Paul Berg and Maxine Singer. Reprinted by permission of University Science Books, 55D Gate Five Road, Sausalito, Ca 94965.

completed. While much work remains, this is a significant achievement and will certainly lead to breakthroughs in our understanding of how the genetic code functions.[23]

  CD-ROM Simulation II-4

MESSENGER RNA DNA stores the information to make cells, but it does not directly affect the formation of cells. One type of ribonucleic acid (RNA), **messenger RNA (mRNA),** is copied from a portion of DNA and moves outside the cell nucleus to direct the formation of proteins.[24] Proteins have so many functions that they are considered to be responsible for most of the characteristics of an organism. They act as catalysts for synthesizing

DNA and RNA and for the activities of cells; they also contribute many structural elements that determine the shape and movement of cells.[25] Messenger RNA is like DNA in that it has a linear sequence of bases attached to a sugar-phosphate backbone, but it is slightly different chemically. One difference is that messenger RNA has the base uracil instead of the base thymine. Messenger RNA also has a different sugar-phosphate backbone and is single- rather than double-stranded. Messenger RNA is formed when a double-stranded DNA molecule unwinds and forms a template for the mRNA. After a section of DNA is copied, the mRNA releases from the DNA and leaves the nucleus, and the double helix of the DNA is re-formed.[26]

PROTEIN SYNTHESIS Once the mRNA is released from the DNA, it travels out of the cell nucleus and into the body of the cell. There it attaches to a structure in the cell called a **ribosome,** which uses the information on the mRNA to make proteins. The ribosome essentially "reads" the chemical bases on the mRNA in commands that tell the ribosome the specific amino acids to join together to form a protein (see Figure 3–5). For example, the mRNA sequence adenine, adenine, guanine (AAG) tells the ribosome to place the amino acid lysine in that location, whereas the sequence adenine, adenine, cytosine (AAC) calls for the amino acid histidine. There are also mRNA commands that tell the ribosome when to begin and when to stop constructing a protein. Thus, the DNA code copied onto mRNA provides all the information necessary for ribosomes to build the proteins that make up the structures of organisms and drive the processes of life.

 CD-ROM Simulation II-5

Sources of Variability

Natural selection proceeds only when individuals within a population vary. There are two genetic sources of variation: genetic recombination and mutation.

GENETIC RECOMBINATION

The distribution of traits from parents to children varies from one offspring to another. Brothers and sisters, after all, do not look exactly alike, nor does each child resemble 50 percent of the mother and 50 percent of the father. This variation occurs because when a sperm cell or an egg is formed, the single member of each chromosome pair it receives is a matter of chance. Each reproductive cell, then, carries a random assortment of chromosomes and their respective genes. At fertilization, the egg and sperm that unite are different from every other egg carried by the mother and every other sperm carried by the father. A unique offspring is thus produced by a shuffling of the parents' genes. One cause of this shuffling is the random **segregation,** or sorting, of chromosomes in meiosis. Conceivably, an individual could get any of the possible assortments of the paternal and maternal chromosomes. Another cause of the shuffling of parental genes is **crossing-over,** the exchange of sections of chromosomes between one chromosome and another (Figure 3–6).[27] Thus, after meiosis, the egg and sperm do not receive just a random mixture of complete paternal and maternal chromosomes; because of crossing-over they also receive chromosomes in which some of the sections may have been replaced.

 CD-ROM Simulation II-6

The traits displayed by each organism are not simply the result of combinations of dominant and recessive genes, as Mendel had hypothesized. In humans, most traits are influenced by the activity of many genes. Skin color, for example, is the result of several inherited characteristics. A brownish shade results from the presence of a pigment known as *melanin;* the degree of darkness in the hue depends largely on the amount of melanin present and how it is distributed in the layers of the skin. Another factor contributing to the color of all human skin is the blood that flows in blood vessels located in the outer layers of the skin. Humans carry at least five different genes for the manufacture of melanin and many other genes for the other components of skin hue. In fact, almost all physical characteristics in humans are the result of the concerted action of many genes. Some traits are sex-linked. The X chromosome, which together with the presence or absence of a Y chromosome determines sex, may also carry the gene for hemophilia or the gene for color blindness. The expression of these two characteristics depends on the sex of the organism.

Genetic recombination produces variety, which is essential for the operation of natural selection. Ultimately, however, the major source of variability is mutation. This is because mutation replenishes the supply of variability, which is constantly being reduced by the selective elimination of less fit variants. Mutation also produces variety in organisms that reproduce asexually.

MUTATION

A **mutation** is a change in the DNA sequence. Such a change produces an altered gene. The majority of mutations are thought to occur because of occasional mismating of the chemical bases that make up DNA. Just as a typist will make errors in copying a manuscript, so will DNA, in duplicating itself, occasionally change its code.[28] A mutation will result from such an error. Some mutations have more drastic consequences than others. Suppose the error is in one base on a DNA strand. The effect depends on what that portion of the DNA controls. The effect may be minimal if the product hardly affects the organism. On the other hand, if the change occurs at a place where the DNA regulates the production of many proteins, the effect on the organism can be serious.[29]

Although it is very difficult to estimate the proportions of mutations that are harmful, neutral, or beneficial, there is no doubt that some mutations have lethal consequences. We can discuss the relative merits or disadvantages of a mutant gene only in terms of the physical, cultural, and genetic environment of that gene.[30] Galactosemia, for example, is caused by a recessive mutant gene and usually results in mental retardation and blindness. But it can be prevented by dietary restrictions begun at an early age. In this instance, the intervention of human culture counteracts the mutant gene and allows the afflicted individual to lead a normal life. Thus, some cultural factors can modify the effects of natural selection by helping

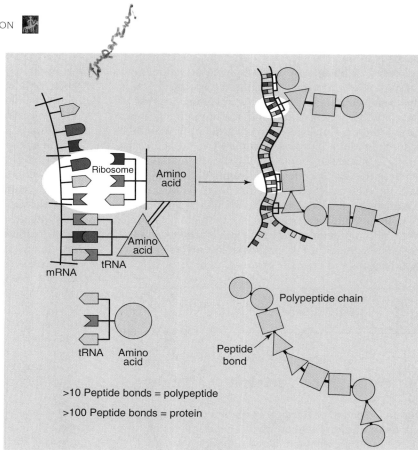

Figure 3–5 *Translation and Protein Synthesis*

The mRNA copy of the cellular DNA is "read" by a ribosome that attaches the amino acid with the corresponding transfer RNA (tRNA) to a growing chain of amino acids (called a polypeptide chain because the amino acids are linked together by peptide bonds). A chain more than 100 amino acids long is called a protein.

to perpetuate a harmful mutant gene. People with the galactosemia trait who are enabled to function normally can reproduce and pass on one of the recessive genes to their children. Without cultural interference, natural selection would prevent such reproduction. Usually, natural selection acts to retain only those mutations that aid survival.

Even though most mutations may not be adaptive, those that are will multiply in a population relatively quickly, by natural selection. As Theodosius Dobzhansky has suggested:

> Consistently useful mutants are like needles in a haystack of harmful ones. A needle in a haystack is hard to find, even though one may be sure it is there. But if the needle is valuable, the task of finding it is facilitated by setting the haystack on fire and looking for the needle among the ashes. The role of the fire in this parable is played in biological evolution by natural selection.[31]

The black moth that was spotted in Manchester in 1850 probably resulted from a mutation. If the tree trunks had been light colored, that moth or its offspring probably would have died out. But as industrialization increased and the tree trunks became darker, a trait that was once maladaptive became adaptive.

Genetic recombination and mutation are the sources of new variations, but evolutionary biologists have identified two other processes that are important in distributing those variations through populations: genetic drift and gene flow.

GENETIC DRIFT

The term **genetic drift** refers to various random processes that affect gene frequencies in small, relatively isolated populations. Genetic drift is also known as the *Wright effect,* after the geneticist Sewall Wright, who first directed attention to this process. Over time in a small population, genetic drift may result in a neutral or nearly neutral gene becoming more or less frequent just by chance.[32]

One variety of genetic drift, called the *founder principle,* occurs when a small group recently derived from a larger population migrates to a relatively isolated location.[33] If a particular gene is absent just by chance in the migrant group, the descendants are also likely to lack that gene, assuming that the group remains isolated. Similarly, if all members of the original migrant group just by chance carried a particular gene, their descendants would also be likely to share that gene. Isolation can occur for physical reasons, such as when a group moves to a previously uninhabited place and does not return. The populations that traveled over the Bering land bridge from Asia to North America could not readily return when the sea level rose. This may explain why Native Americans have a higher proportion of individuals with type O blood than other populations—the first migrants may have had, by

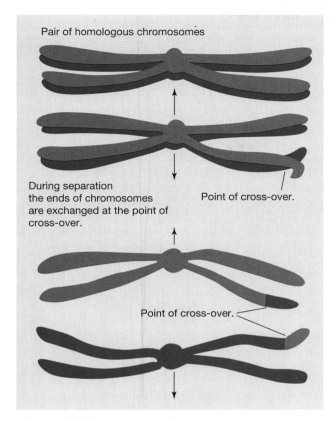

Pair of homologous chromosomes

During separation
the ends of chromosomes
are exchanged at the point of
cross-over.

Point of cross-over.

Point of cross-over.

Figure 3–6 *Crossing Over*

Source: Noel T. Boaz and Alan J. Almquist, *Biological Anthropology*. Copyright © 1997. Reprinted by permission of Pearson Education, Inc., Upper Saddle River, NJ 07458.

chance, a predominance of individuals with type O blood.

Or the isolation can occur for social reasons. A religious sect of Dunkers emigrated from Germany to the United States in the early 1700s. The fact that the 50 original families kept to themselves probably explains why some of their gene frequencies differ from what is found in both the German and general U.S. populations.[34]

GENE FLOW

Gene flow is the process whereby genes pass from one population to another through mating and reproduction. Unlike the other processes of natural selection and genetic drift, which generally increase the differences between populations in different environments, gene flow tends to work in the opposite direction—it *decreases* differences between populations. Two populations at opposite ends of a region may have different frequencies of a particular gene, but the populations located between them have an intermediate gene frequency because of gene flow between them. The variation in gene frequency from one end of the region to the other is called a **cline.** In Europe, for example, there is a cline in the distribution of blood type B, which gradually diminishes in frequency from east to west.[35]

Most genetically determined characteristics in humans have gradually or clinally varying frequencies as one moves from one area to another. Neighboring regions have more similar gene frequencies than regions widely separated. But these clines do not always coincide, which makes the concept of "race" as applied to humans not very useful for understanding human biological variation.[36] We discuss this in more detail in the chapter on human variation.

Gene flow may occur between distant as well as close populations. Long-range movements of people, to trade or raid or settle, may result in gene flow. But they do not always do so.

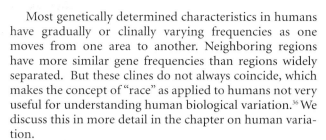

The Origin of Species

One of the most controversial aspects of Darwin's theory was the suggestion that one species could, over time, evolve into another. A **species** is a population that consists of organisms able to interbreed and produce fertile and viable offspring. In general, individuals from one species cannot successfully mate with members of a different species because of genetic and behavioral differences. If members of different species did mate, it is unlikely that the egg would be fertilized, or, if it were, that the embryo would survive. If the offspring were born, it would soon die or be infertile. But how could one species evolve into another? What is the explanation for this differentiation? How does one group of organisms become so unlike another group with the same ancestry that it forms a totally new species?

Speciation, or the development of a new species, may occur if one subgroup of a species finds itself in a radically different environment. In adapting to their separate environments, the two populations may undergo enough genetic changes to prevent them from interbreeding, should they renew contact. Numerous factors can prevent the exchange of genes. Two species living in the same area may breed at different times of the year, or their behavior during breeding—their courtship rituals—may be distinct. The difference in body structure of closely related forms may in itself bar interbreeding. Geographic barriers may be the most common barriers to interbreeding.

Once species differentiation does occur, the evolutionary process cannot be reversed; the new species can no longer mate with other species related to its parent population. Humans and gorillas, for example, have the same distant ancestors, but their evolutionary paths have diverged irreversibly.

Natural Selection of Behavioral Traits

Until now we have discussed how natural selection might operate to change a population's physical traits, such as the

CURRENT ISSUES
Do We Need to Fear Genetic Engineering?

So much is known about molecular genetics that it is now possible to alter individual genes and even whole organisms in very precise ways. The revolution occurred very quickly after the structure of DNA was first identified in 1953 by James Watson and Francis Crick. Particular genetic traits could then be linked to particular sequences of DNA messages. In the 1970s, the development of recombinant DNA techniques allowed researchers to splice pieces of DNA from one organism into the DNA of another, in precise locations. Researchers learned how to make copies by putting these "recombined" strands into host organisms such as bacteria, which reproduce by cloning. The applications of these techniques are potentially enormous. Biotechnology companies are already doing genetic engineering to manufacture medicines (such as insulin and a vaccine against hepatitis B) and to produce more desirable plant and animal products (for example, a strain of tomato that can be shipped when it's ripe without spoiling). They are also working on how to reintroduce altered cells into organisms to fix genetic defects. As of now, about 4,000 human disorders are known to be caused by defects in a few genes; theoretically, they should be fixable some day by genetic engineering. As more becomes known about the precise location of genes and the DNA sequences that convey particular information, much more engineering will be possible. Already some imagine that genetic therapy will eventually cure various cancers and heart disease.

Might there be risks associated with such interventions? Some fear that recombinant DNA engineering may have disastrous consequences. Could a dangerous runaway strain of bacteria or virus be produced in the lab? Might a kind of Frankenstein be produced? Could unscrupulous governments mandate certain kinds of alterations? Do we have reason to entertain such fears?

It is important to remind ourselves that although DNA alteration by recombinant techniques is new, genetic engineering is not new. Humans have genetically altered plants and animals for thousands of years. We usually do not call it genetic engineering—we call it domestication or breeding. To be sure, the mechanism of traditional genetic engineering, selective breeding, is different from DNA splicing, but the effect is genetic alteration nonetheless. By breeding for preferred traits, humans are able to produce breeds of horses, dogs, cattle, varieties of corn and beans, and all of the other animals and plants we depend on for food, fiber, and other materials and chemicals. All of them are different, often very different, from their wild progenitors. Humans have also domesticated micro-organisms. An example that goes back thousands of years is the yeast used for brewing beer and baking bread; a more recent example is a particular mold used to produce penicillin. And

---

color of moths or the neck length of giraffes. But natural selection can also operate on the behavioral characteristics of populations. Although this idea is not new, it is now receiving more attention. The approaches called **sociobiology**[37] and **behavioral ecology**[38] involve the application of evolutionary principles to the behavior of animals. Behavioral ecology is interested in how all kinds of behavior are related to the environment; sociobiology is particularly interested in social organization and social behavior. The typical behaviors of a species are assumed to be adaptive and to have evolved by natural selection. For example, why do related species exhibit different social behaviors even though they derive from a common ancestral species?

Consider the lion, as compared with other cats. Although members of the cat family are normally solitary creatures, lions live in social groups called *prides*. Why? George Schaller has suggested that lion social groups may have evolved primarily because group hunting is a more successful way to catch large mammals in open terrain. He has observed that not only are several lions more successful in catching prey than are solitary lions, but several lions are more likely to catch and kill large and dangerous prey such as giraffes. Then, too, cubs are generally safer from predators when in a social group than when alone with their mothers. Thus, the social behavior of lions may have evolved primarily because it provided selective advantages in the lions' open-country environment.[39]

It is important to remember that natural selection operates on expressed characteristics, or the *phenotype*, of an individual. In the moth example, the color of the moth is

live vaccines that are deliberately weakened viruses, as, for example, in the vaccine against polio, have already been widely used to prevent illness.

So what does our past engineering tell us about the risks of future engineering? In general, the past suggests that no serious harm is attributable to domestication. In fact, domesticated animals and plants are less likely to do well if reintroduced into the wild than their wild cousins. They usually need human help to eat, to get shelter from the elements, and to care for their offspring. So why should genetic engineering be any different? It has basically the same purpose as selective breeding—humans want organisms, large or small or microscopic, to be useful to humans. So far, the available evidence indicates that organisms altered genetically to satisfy human needs are no threat to humans because they are unlikely to survive without human assistance. Needless to say, that does not obviate the need to test for risks. It is reassuring that even though DNA in nature can cross over from one organism to another, such natural genetic alteration is not generally harmful to us.

People may mostly be afraid that a dangerous microbe could be accidentally released from a laboratory and multiply uncontrollably. But, as already noted, any microbe or new genetic form is unlikely to be as hardy as its wild cousins. If a bacterium is mistakenly released, it is not going into an artificially empty environment like a sterile petri dish. The natural environment is already filled with bacteria (most of them beneficial to humans), as well as organisms that attack bacteria. In short, it is not so easy to produce a harmful microbe.

The improbability of making destructive organisms does not mean that humans should not guard against the possibility. That is why we have government agencies to certify new products, along with guidelines for testing procedures and oversight panels. A new product of recombinant DNA research has to be approved before it can be widely used.

Can humans use such technology for eugenic purposes, such as creating superhumans or for biological warfare? Possibly. But recombinant DNA techniques are not the problem. After all, the lack of such technology has not prevented genocide, ethnic cleansing, sterilization, and rape. The absence of recombinant technology did not prevent the use of natural biological weapons (such as smallpox-infected blankets given to Native Americans in the nineteenth century) or the manufacture and use of poison gas in World War I and since. It is not technology or the absence of it that explains evil; it is other things. If we want to reduce the risk of human violence, we have to understand why it occurs. More research might help make us safer.

Sources: Allan M. Campbell, "Microbes: The Laboratory and the Field," Bernard D. Davis, "The Issues: Prospects versus Perceptions" and "Summary and Comments: The Scientific Chapters," and Henry I. Miller, "Regulation," all in Bernard D. Davis, ed., *The Genetic Revolution: Scientific Prospects and Public Perceptions* (Baltimore: Johns Hopkins University Press, 1991), pp. 28–44, 1–8, 239–65, 196–211; Paul Berg and Maxine Singer, *Dealing with Genes: The Language of Heredity* (Mill Valley, CA: University Science Books, 1992), pp. 221–44.

part of its phenotype, subject to natural selection. Behavior is also an expressed characteristic. If hunting in groups, a behavioral trait, gets you more food, then individuals who hunt in groups will do better. But we must also remember that natural selection requires traits to be heritable. Can the concept of heritability be applied to learned behavior, not just genetically transmitted behavior? And, even more controversially, if the concept of heritability can include learning, can it also include cultural learning?

Early theorizing in sociobiology and behavioral ecology appeared to emphasize the genetic component of behavior. For example, Edward O. Wilson, in his book *Sociobiology,* defined sociobiology as "the systematic study of the biological causes of behavior."[40] But Bobbi Low points out that, although the term *biology* may have been interpreted to mean "genetic," most biologists understand that expressed or observable characteristics are the results of genes and environment, and life history, all interacting. Behavior is a product of all three. If we say that some behavior is heritable, we mean that the child's behavior is more likely to resemble the parents' behavior than the behavior of others.[41] Learning from a parent could be an important part of why the offspring is like the parent. If the child is more like the parent than like others, then the likeness is heritable, even if it is entirely learned from the parent.

The sociobiological approach has aroused considerable controversy in anthropology, probably because of its apparent emphasis on genes, rather than experience and

Prides of lions that live in open country are more successful in catching large animals than are solitary lions. This social behavior may have evolved because it provided selective advantages in the lion's open-country environment.

learning, as determinants of human behavior. Anthropologists have argued that the customs of a society may be more or less adaptive because cultural behaviors also have reproductive consequences. It is not just an individual's behavior that may have reproductive consequences. So does natural selection also operate in the evolution of culture? Most biologists think not. They say there are substantial differences between biological and cultural evolution. How do cultural evolution and biological evolution compare? To answer this question, we must remember that the operation of natural selection requires three conditions, as we aleady noted: variation, heritability or mechanisms that duplicate traits in offspring, and differential reproduction because of heritable differences. Do these three requirements apply to cultural behavior?

In biological evolution, variability comes from genetic recombination and mutation. In cultural evolution, it comes from recombination of learned behaviors and from invention.[42] Cultures are not closed or reproductively isolated, as species are. A species cannot borrow genetic traits from another species, but a culture can borrow new things and behaviors from other cultures. The custom of growing corn, which has spread from the New World to many other areas, is an example of this phenomenon. As for the requirement of heritability, although learned traits obviously are not passed to offspring through purely genetic inheritance, parents who exhibit adaptive behavioral traits are more likely to "reproduce" those traits in their children, who may learn them by imitation or by parental instruction. Children and adults may also copy adaptive traits they see in people outside the family. Finally, as for the requirement of differential reproduction, it does not matter whether the trait in question is genetic or learned or both. As Henry Nissen emphasized, "behavioral incompetence leads to extinction as surely as does morphological disproportion or deficiency in any vital organ. Behavior is subject to selection as much as bodily size or resistance to disease."[43]

Many theorists are comfortable with the idea of applying the theory of natural selection to cultural evolution, but others prefer to use different terminology when dealing with traits that do not depend on purely genetic transmission from one generation to the next. For example, Robert Boyd and Peter Richerson discuss human behavior as involving "dual inheritance." They distinguish cultural transmission, by learning and imitation, from genetic transmission, but they emphasize the importance of understanding both and the interaction between them.[44] William Durham also deals separately with cultural transmission, using the term *meme* (analogous to the term

Mountain lions live in wooded environments and hunt individually. Here we see one that has killed a mule deer in western Montana.

gene) for the unit of cultural transmission. He directs our attention to the interaction between genes and culture, calling that interaction "coevolution," and provides examples of how genetic evolution and cultural evolution may lead to changes in each other, how they may enhance each other, and how they may even oppose each other.[45]

So biological and cultural evolution in humans may not be completely separate processes. As we will discuss, some of the most important biological features of humans—such as our relatively large brains—may have been favored by natural selection because our ancestors made tools, a cultural trait. Conversely, the cultural trait of informal and formal education may have been favored by natural selection because humans have a long period of immaturity, a biological trait.

As long as the human species continues to exist and the social and physical environment continues to change, there is reason to think that natural selection of biological and cultural traits will also continue. However, as humans learn more and more about genetic structure they will become more and more capable of curing genetically caused disorders and even altering the way evolution proceeds. Today, genetic researchers are capable of diagnosing genetic defects in developing fetuses, and parents can and do decide often whether to terminate a pregnancy. Soon genetic engineering will probably allow humans to fix defects and even try to "improve" the genetic code of a growing fetus. Whether and to what extent humans should alter genes will undoubtedly be the subject of continuing debate. Whatever the decisions we eventually make about genetic engineering, they will affect the course of human biological and cultural evolution.

Summary

1. If we think of the history of the universe in terms of 12 months, the history of human-like primates would take up only about one and a half hours. The universe is some 15 billion years old; modern-looking humans have existed for about 100,000 years.

2. Ideas about evolution took a long time to take hold because they contradicted the biblical view of events; species were viewed as fixed in their form by the creator. But in the eighteenth and early nineteenth centuries increasing evidence suggested that evolution was a viable theory. In geology, the concept of uniformitarianism suggested that the earth is constantly subject to shaping and reshaping by natural forces working over vast stretches of time. A number of thinkers during this period began to discuss evolution and how it might occur.

3. Charles Darwin and Alfred Wallace proposed the mechanism of natural selection to account for the evolution of species. Basic principles of the theory of natural selection are that (1) every species is composed of a great variety of individuals, some of which are better adapted to their environment than others; (2) offspring inherit traits from their parents at least to some degree and in some

way; and (3) since better adapted individuals generally produce more offspring over the generations than the poorer adapted, the frequency of adaptive traits increases in subsequent generations. In this way, natural selection results in increasing proportions of individuals with advantageous traits.

4. Mendel's and subsequent research in genetics and our understanding of the structure and function of DNA and mRNA help us to understand the biological mechanisms by which traits may be passed from one generation to the next.

5. Natural selection depends on variation within a population. The four sources of biological variation are genetic recombination, mutation, genetic drift, and gene flow.

6. Speciation, the development of a new species, may occur if one subgroup becomes separated from other subgroups. In adapting to different environments, these subpopulations may undergo enough genetic changes to prevent interbreeding, even if they reestablish contact. Once species differentiation occurs, it is believed that the evolutionary process cannot be reversed.

7. Natural selection can also operate on the behavioral characteristics of populations. The approaches called sociobiology and behavioral ecology involve the application of evolutionary principles to the behavior of animals. Much controversy surrounds the degree to which the theory of natural selection can be applied to human behavior, particularly cultural behavior. There is more agreement that biological and cultural evolution in humans may influence each other.

Glossary Terms

allele	homozygous
balancing selection	meiosis
behavioral ecology	messenger RNA (mRNA)
chromosome	mitosis
cline	mutation
crossing-over	natural selection
directional selection	normalizing selection
DNA	phenotype
dominant	recessive
gene	ribosome
gene flow	segregation
genetic drift	sociobiology
genotype	speciation
heterozygous	species

Critical Questions

1. Do you think the theory of natural selection is compatible with religious beliefs? Explain your reasoning.

2. How might the discovery of genetic cures and the use of genetic engineering affect the future of evolution?

3. Why do you think humans have remained one species?

 Internet Exercises

1. Explore the Evolution and the Nature of Science Institutes (ENSI) Web site at **http://www.indiana.edu/~ensiweb/**, and go through several of the evolution lessons.

2. Visit the home page of *Evolution* (*International Journal of Organic Evolution*) at **http://lsvl.la.asu.edu/evolution/**. By looking at the table of contents, provide a bibliography of at least 15 articles related to human evolution.

3. Visit the Museum of Paleontology's evolution exhibit halls at **http://www.ucmp.berkeley.edu/history/evolution.html**, and write a review of the exhibits presented there.

 Suggested Reading

BOYD, R., AND RICHERSON, P. J. *Culture and the Evolutionary Process*. Chicago: University of Chicago Press, 1985. The authors develop mathematical models to analyze how biology and culture interact under the influence of evolutionary processes.

BRANDON, R. N. *Adaptation and Environment*. Princeton, NJ: Princeton University Press, 1990. After defining basic concepts regarding adaptation and the theory of natural selection, the author emphasizes that the process of adaptation and its outcomes cannot be understood without analysis of the environment.

CHIRAS, D. D. *Human Biology: Health, Homeostasis, and the Environment*, 2nd ed. St. Paul, MN: West, 1995. An introductory textbook in human biology. See chapters 3–5 for a detailed discussion of chromosomes, DNA, RNA, principles of heredity, and genetic engineering.

DEVILLERS, C., AND CHALINE, J. *Evolution: An Evolving Theory*. New York: Springer-Verlag, 1993. Aimed at the general audience, this book addresses the questions: What is the place of humans in the living world? What is evolution? How can the observed data be explained? Appendixes give more detailed information.

DOBZHANSKY, T. *Mankind Evolving: The Evolution of the Human Species*. New Haven, CT: Yale University Press, 1962. A classic demonstration that the mechanisms of evolution, primarily natural selection, are still active.

DURHAM, W. H. *Coevolution: Genes, Culture, and Human Diversity*. Stanford, CA: Stanford University Press, 1991. A discussion of the evolution of culture that considers how theory and research point to the interaction of genes and culture in human populations.

EISELEY, L. *Darwin's Century: Evolution and the Men Who Discovered It*. New York: Anchor Books, 1958. A classic history of evolutionary thought and the growth of modern evolutionary theory.

MAYR, E. *The Growth of Biological Thought: Diversity, Evolution, and Inheritance*. Cambridge, MA: Belknap Press of Harvard University Press, 1982. A history of ideas that discusses the successful and unsuccessful attempts to understand problems in the study of evolution.

MAYR, E. *One Long Argument: Charles Darwin and the Genesis of Modern Evolutionary Thought*. Cambridge, MA: Harvard University Press, 1993. A concise look at evolutionary theory.

4

The Living Primates

The goal of *primatology*, the study of primates, is to understand how different primates have adapted anatomically and behaviorally to their environments. The results of such studies may help us to understand the behavior and evolution of the human primate.

But how can living primates such as chimpanzees tell us anything about humans or the primates that were our ancestors? After all, each living primate species has its own history of evolutionary divergence from the earliest primate forms. All living primates, including humans, evolved from earlier primates that are now extinct. Nonetheless, by observing how humans and other primates differ from and resemble each other, we may be able to infer how and why humans diverged from the other primates.

In conjunction with fossil evidence, anatomical and behavioral comparisons of living primates may help us reconstruct what early primates were like. For example, if we know that modern primates that swing through the trees have a particular kind of shoulder bone structure, we can infer that similar fossil bones probably belonged to an animal that also swung through the trees. Differing adaptations of living primates may also suggest why certain divergences occurred in primate evolution. If we know what traits belong to humans, and to humans alone, this knowledge may suggest why the line of primates that led to humans branched away from the line leading to chimpanzees and gorillas.

In this chapter we first examine the common features of the living primates. Next we introduce the different animals that belong to the order Primates, focusing on the distinctive characteristics of each major type. Then we discuss possible explanations of some of the varying adaptations exhibited by the different primate species. We close with a look at the traits that make humans different from all other primates. The purpose of this chapter is to help us understand more about humans. Therefore, we emphasize the features of primate anatomy and behavior that perhaps have the greatest bearing on human evolution.

Common Primate Traits

All primates belong to the class Mammalia, and they share all the common features of mammals. Except for humans, the bodies of primates are covered with dense hair or fur, which provides insulation. Even humans have hair in various places, though perhaps not always for insulation. Mammals are *warm-blooded;* that is, their body temperature is more or less constantly warm and usually higher than that of the air around them. Almost all mammals give birth to live young that develop to a considerable size within the mother and are nourished by suckling from the mother's mammary glands. The young have a relatively long period of dependence on adults after birth. This period is also a time of learning, for a great deal of adult mammal behavior is learned rather than instinctive. Play

is a learning technique common to mammal young and is especially important to primates, as we shall see later in this chapter.

The primates have a number of physical and social traits that set them apart from other mammals.

PHYSICAL FEATURES

No one of the primates' physical features is unique to primates; animals from other orders share one or more of the characteristics described below. But the complex of all these physical traits *is* unique to primates.[1]

Many skeletal features of the primates reflect an **arboreal** (tree-living) existence. All primate hind limbs are structured principally to provide support, but the "feet" in most primates can also grasp things (see Figure 4–1). Some primates—orangutans, for instance—can suspend themselves from their hind limbs. The forelimbs are especially flexible, built to withstand both pushing and pulling forces. Each of the hind limbs and forelimbs has one bone in the upper portion and two bones in the lower portion (with the exception of the tarsier). This feature has little changed since the time of the earliest primate ancestors. It has remained in modern primates (although many other mammals have lost it) because the double bones give great mobility for rotating arms and legs.

Another characteristic structure of primates is the clavicle, or collarbone. The clavicle also gives primates great freedom of movement, allowing them to move the shoulders both up and down and back and forth. Although humans obviously do not use this flexibility for arboreal activity, they do use it for other activities. Without a clavicle we could not throw a spear or a ball; no fine tools could be made and no doorknobs turned if we did not have rotatable forearms.

Primates generally are **omnivorous;** that is, they eat all kinds of food, including insects and small animals, as well as fruits, seeds, leaves, and roots. The teeth of primates reflect this omnivorous diet. The chewing teeth—the **molars** and **premolars**—are unspecialized, particularly in comparison with those of other groups of animals, such as the grazers. The front teeth—the **incisors** and **canines**—are often very specialized, principally in the lower primates. For example, in many prosimians the slender, tightly packed lower incisors and canines form a "dental comb" the animals use in grooming or for scraping hardened tree gum (which is a food for them) from tree trunks.[2]

Primate hands are extremely flexible. All primates have **prehensile**—grasping—hands, which can be wrapped around an object. Primates have five digits on both hands and feet (in some cases, one digit may be reduced to a stub), and their nails, with few exceptions, are broad and flat, not clawlike. This structure allows them to grip objects; the hairless, sensitive pads on their fingers, toes, heels, and palms also help them to grip. Most primates have **opposable thumbs,** a feature that allows an even more precise and powerful grip.

Vision is extremely important to primate life. Com-

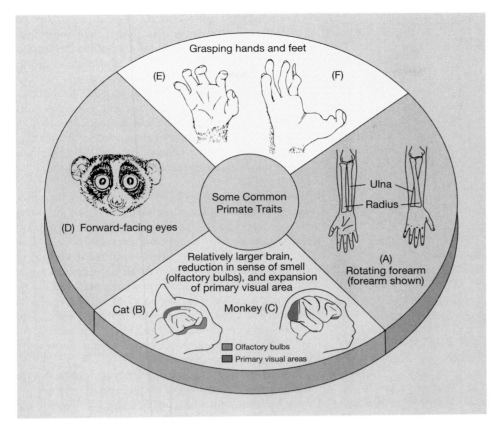

Figure 4–1 *Some Common Primate Traits*

Source: (A) From Ronald G. Wolff, *Functional Chordate Anatomy* (Lexington, MA: D. C. Heath and Company, 1991), p. 255. Reprinted with permission of D. C. Heath. (B, C) From Terrence Deacon, "Primate Brains and Senses," in Stephen Jones, Robert Martin, and David Pilbeam, eds., *The Cambridge Encyclopedia of Human Evolution* (New York: Cambridge University Press, 1992, p. 110. (D) From Matt Cartmill, "Non-Human Primates," in ibid., p. 25. (E, F) From ibid., p. 24. Copyright © by Cambridge University Press. Reprinted by permission of Cambridge University Press.

pared with other mammals, primates have a relatively larger portion of the brain devoted to vision rather than smell. Primates are characterized by *stereoscopic,* or depth, *vision*. Their eyes are directed forward rather than sideways, as in other animals—a trait that allows them to focus on an object (insects or other food or a distant branch) with both eyes at once. Most primates also have color vision, perhaps to recognize when plant foods are ready to eat.

Another important primate feature is a large brain relative to body size. That is, primates generally have larger brains than animals of similar size, perhaps because their survival depends on an enormous amount of learning, as we discuss later. In general, animals with large brains seem to mature more slowly and to live longer than animals with small brains.[3] The more slowly an animal matures and the longer it lives, the more it can learn.

Finally, the primate reproductive system sets this order of animals apart from other mammals. Males of most primate species have a pendulous penis that is not attached to the abdomen by skin, a trait shared by a few other animals, including bats and bears. Females of most primate species have two nipples on the chest (a few prosimians have more than two nipples). The uterus is usually constructed to hold a single fetus (only the marmosets and tamarins typically give birth to twins), not a litter, as with most other animals. This reproductive system can be seen as emphasizing quality over quantity—an adaptation possibly re-

lated to the dangers of life in the trees, particularly the risk of falls.[4] Primate infants tend to be relatively well developed at birth, although humans, apes, and some monkeys have helpless infants. Most infant primates, except humans, can cling to their mothers from birth. Primates typically take a long time to mature. For example, the rhesus monkey is not sexually mature until about 3 years of age, the chimpanzee not until about age 9.

SOCIAL FEATURES

For the most part, primates are social animals. And just as physical traits such as grasping hands and stereoscopic vision may have developed as adaptations to the environment, so may have many patterns of social behavior. For most primates, particularly those that are **diurnal**—that is, active during the day—group life may be crucial to survival, as we will see later in this chapter.

DEPENDENCY AND DEVELOPMENT IN A SOCIAL CONTEXT Social relationships begin with the mother and other adults during the fairly long dependency period of primates. (For the dependency period of primates, the infancy and juvenile phases, see Figure 4–2.) The prolonged dependency of infant monkeys and apes probably offers an evolutionary advantage in that it allows infants more time to observe and learn the complex behaviors essential to survival while enjoying the care and protection of mature adults.

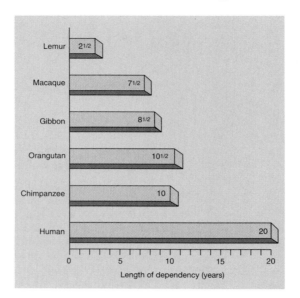

Figure 4–2 *A Comparison of the Dependency Periods of Primate Offspring*

Source: Data from Alison Jolly, *The Evolution of Primate Behavior,* 2nd ed. (New York: Macmillan, 1985), p. 292.

Primates without a warm, social relationship with a mother or another individual do not appear to develop appropriate patterns of social interaction. In a series of classic experiments with rhesus monkeys, Harry Harlow investigated the effects of maternal neglect and isolation on offspring.[5] He found that as a result of either inadequate mothering or isolation from other infants, some monkeys are unable to lead normal social lives. They develop aberrant sexual activities and may even become juvenile delinquents. Harlow mated socially deprived female monkeys with well-adjusted males. When these females gave birth, their behavior was not at all motherly, and they

Primates can learn from direct teaching, but they learn mostly by imitation and trial-and-error.

often rejected their babies entirely. Their abnormal behavior was offered as evidence that mothering is more than instinctive. Harlow's experiments underline the importance of maternal care and attention for monkeys and, as a corollary, for humans.

In many primate groups the mother is not the only individual providing care to the dependent young. Among gray langur monkeys, the birth and subsequent rearing of a baby absorb the attention of most female members of the troop.[6] And in some primate species, the father may spend as much time caring for infants as the mother.[7]

PRIMATES AT PLAY Harlow's investigations have provided other information about social learning in young primates. The experiments that showed the importance of maternal care to baby rhesus monkeys also revealed that play is another crucial ingredient of normal development during the dependency period. Just as monkeys raised without mothers showed abnormal behavior as adults, so did monkeys raised with mothers but with no peers to play with. In fact, when some of the monkeys raised without mothers were allowed a regular playtime with peers, many of them behaved more normally. Subsequent work has supported Harlow's findings.[8]

Play is important for learning.[9] It provides practice for the physical skills necessary or useful in adulthood. For example, young monkeys racing through the trees at top speed are gaining coordination that may save their lives if they are chased by predators later on. Play is also a way of learning social skills, particularly in interacting and communicating with other members of the group. Some dom-

APPLIED ANTHROPOLOGY
Endangered Primates

In contrast to many human populations that are too numerous for their resources, many populations of nonhuman primates face extinction because they are not numerous enough. The two trends—human overpopulation and nonhuman primate extinctions—are related. Were it not for human expansion in many parts of the world, the nonhuman primates living in those habitats would not be endangered. Various lemur and other prosimian species of Madagascar, the mountain gorilla and red colobus monkeys of Africa, and the lion tamarin monkeys of Brazil are among the species most at risk.

Many factors are responsible for the difficulties faced by nonhuman primates, but most of them are directly or indirectly the result of human activity. Perhaps the biggest problem is the destruction of tropical rain forest, the habitat of most nonhuman primates, because of encroaching agriculture and cattle ranching and the felling of trees for wood products. The people who live in these areas are partly responsible for the threats to nonhuman primates—population pressure in the human populations increases the likelihood that more forest will be cleared and burned for agriculture, and

A golden lion tamarin.

in some areas nonhuman primates are an important source of hunted food. But world market forces are probably more important. The increasing need for "American" hamburger in fast food restaurants has accelerated the search for places to raise beef inexpensively. There is also enormous demand for wood products from tropical forests; Japan imports half of all the timber from rain forests to use for plywood, cardboard, paper, and furniture.

Some would argue that it is important to preserve all species. Primatologists remind us that it is especially important to preserve primate diversity. One reason is the scientific one of needing those populations to study and understand how humans are similar and different and how they came to be that way. Another reason is the usefulness of nonhuman primates in biomedical research on human diseases; we share many of our diseases, and many of our genes, with our primate relatives. (As we noted in the first chapter, chimpanzees share 99 percent of their genes with humans.) The film *The Planet of the Apes,* in which the humans are subordinate to the apes, tells us that the primates in zoos could have been us.

So how can nonhuman primates be protected from us? There really are only two major ways: Either human population growth in many places has to be curtailed, or we have to preserve substantial populations of nonhuman primates in protected parks and zoos. Both are difficult but humanly possible.

Sources: Russell A. Mittermeier and Eleanor J. Sterling, "Conservation of Primates," in Steve Jones, Robert Martin, and David Pilbeam, eds., *The Cambridge Encyclopedia of Human Evolution* (Cambridge: Cambridge University Press, 1992), pp. 33–36; Toshisada Nishida, "Introduction to the Conservation Symposium," in Naosuke Itoigawa, Yukimaru Sugiyama, Gene P. Sackett, and Roger K. R. Thompson, *Topics in Primatology,* vol. 2 (Tokyo: University of Tokyo Press, 1992), pp. 303–304.

inance relationships seem to be established partly through the rough-and-tumble games that older juveniles play, where winning depends on such factors as size, strength, and agility. These qualities, or the lack of them, may influence the individual's status throughout adult life. (Other factors also help determine an individual's status. For instance, the mother's status has been shown to be very important in some primates.[10])

LEARNING FROM OTHERS   We know that primates, nonhuman and human alike, learn many things in social groups. Among humans, children often imitate others, and adults often deliberately teach the young. In English we say, "Isn't it cute how Tommy 'apes' his father." But do apes (and monkeys) imitate others, or do they just learn to do similar things whether or not a model is observed? There is controversy among researchers as to how much imitation versus independent learning occurs in nonhuman primates. Even more arguable is whether deliberate teaching occurs among nonhuman primates.[11]

Some fieldworkers have suggested that chimpanzees may learn by imitation to use tools. For example, Jane Goodall cited an occasion when a female with diarrhea picked up a handful of leaves to wipe her bottom. Her 2-year-old infant watched closely, and then twice picked up leaves to wipe its own, clean behind.[12] Termite "fishing," using a grass stalk to withdraw termites from a termite mound, is probably the best known example of chimpanzee tool use. Immature chimpanzees in the wild have been observed to watch attentively and pick up stalks while others are "fishing." And mothers let their infants hold on to the stalks while the mothers "fish." But some observers do not think these reports provide clear evidence of imitation or teaching. Even though the mother lets the infant hold on to the "fishing" stalk, the infant is doing the activity with her, not watching it and then independently repeating it soon after.[13]

Classification of Primates

Classification provides a useful way to refer to groups of species that are similar in biologically important ways.

Sometimes classification schemes vary because the classifiers emphasize somewhat different aspects of similarity and difference. For instance, one type of classification stresses the evolutionary branching that led to the primates of today; another the quantity of shared features. A third approach considers the evolutionary lines as well as similarity and difference of features, but not all features are equally weighted. More "advanced" and specialized features that develop in an evolutionary line are emphasized.[14] Figure 4–3 gives a classification scheme that follows this last approach.[15]

Despite the different ways to classify, there is generally little disagreement about how the various primates should be classified. Most of the disagreement, as we shall see when we discuss the various primates, revolves around the classification of tarsiers and humans.

The order Primates is often divided into two suborders: the **prosimians**—literally, premonkeys—and the **anthropoids.** The prosimians include lemurs, lorises, and tarsiers. The anthropoid suborder includes New World monkeys, Old World monkeys, the lesser apes (gibbons, siamangs), the great apes (orangutans, gorillas, chimpanzees), and humans.

The Various Primates

Now that we have discussed their common features, let us focus on some of the ways in which the primates living in the world today vary.

Figure 4–3 *A Simplified Classification of the Living Primates*

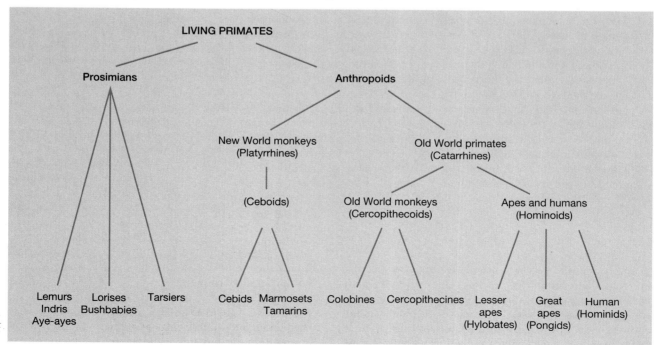

The bushbaby is a small arboreal prosimian that eats both fruit and insects. It is an energetic nocturnal animal that moves by vertical clinging and leaping.

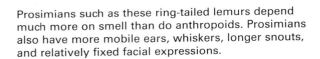

Prosimians such as these ring-tailed lemurs depend much more on smell than do anthropoids. Prosimians also have more mobile ears, whiskers, longer snouts, and relatively fixed facial expressions.

PROSIMIANS

The prosimians resemble other mammals more than the anthropoid primates do. For example, the prosimians depend much more on smell for information than do anthropoids. Also in contrast with the anthropoids, they typically have more mobile ears, whiskers, longer snouts, and relatively fixed facial expressions. The prosimians also exhibit many traits shared by all primates, including grasping hands, stereoscopic vision, and enlarged visual centers in the brain.

LEMURLIKE FORMS Lemurs and their relatives, the indris and the aye-ayes, are found only on two island areas off the southeastern coast of Africa, Madagascar and the Comoro Islands. These primates range in size from the mouse lemur to the 4-foot-long indri. Members of the lemur group usually produce single offspring, although twins and even triplets are common in some species. Many of the species in this group are **quadrupeds**—animals that move on all fours; they walk on all fours in the trees as well as on the ground. Some species, such as the indris, use their hind limbs alone to push off from one vertical position to another in a mode of locomotion called **vertical clinging and leaping.**

Lemurs are mostly vegetarians, eating fruit, leaves, bark, and flowers. Lemur species vary greatly in their group size. Many lemur species, particularly those that are **nocturnal** (active during the night), are solitary during their active hours. Others are much more social, living in groups ranging in size from a small family to as many as 60 members.[16] An unusual feature of the lemurlike primates is that females often dominate males, particularly over access to food. In most primates, and in most other mammals, female dominance is rarely observed.[17]

LORISLIKE FORMS Members of the loris group, found in both Southeast Asia and sub-Saharan Africa, are all nocturnal and arboreal. They eat fruit, tree gum, and insects, and usually give birth to single infants.[18] There are two major subfamilies, the lorises and the bushbabies (galagos), and they show wide behavioral differences. Bushbabies are quick, active animals that hop between branches and tree trunks in the vertical-clinging-and-leaping pattern. On the ground they often resort to a kangaroolike hop. Lorises are much slower, walking sedately along branches hand over hand in the quadrupedal fashion.

With the use of searchlights and technical aids such as radio tracking, field researchers have learned a good deal about these nocturnal primates. For example, we know that among bushbabies, females, particularly mothers and young adult daughters, stay together in small groups,

Nocturnal tree-living tarsiers, like this one in the Philippines, are the only primates that depend completely on animal foods. Their enormous eyes equip them to find insects and other prey in the night. Their elongated ankle bones (tarsals) make them very good at vertical clinging and leaping.

TARSIERS The nocturnal, tree-living tarsiers, found now only on the islands of the Philippines and Indonesia, are the only primates that depend completely on animal foods. They are usually insect-eaters, but they sometimes capture and eat other small animals. They are well equipped for night vision, possessing enormous eyes, extraordinary eyesight, and enlarged visual centers in the brain. The tarsiers get their name from their elongated tarsal bones (the bones of the ankle), which give them tremendous leverage for their long jumps. Tarsiers are very skilled at vertical clinging and leaping. They live in family groups composed of a mated pair and their offspring. Like some higher primates, male and female tarsiers sing together each evening to advertise their territories.[20]

The classification of tarsiers is somewhat controversial. Instead of placing them with the suborder prosimians, as we have done here, some classifiers group tarsiers with anthropoids. In this other classification scheme the suborders of primates are labeled *strepsirhines* (which includes lemurs and lorises) and *haplorhines* (which includes tarsiers and anthropoids). Tarsiers have chromosomes similar to those of other prosimians; they also have claws for grooming on some of their toes, more than two nipples, and a uterus shaped like that of other prosimians (two-horned). Like bushbabies, tarsiers move about through

whereas the males disperse. Newborns are born in nests or hollows of trees (which related females may share), and mothers return to nurse them regularly. A few days after birth, a mother may carry her infant in her mouth to nearby trees, "parking" it while she eats.[19]

Figure 4–4 *Features of Platyrrhines and Catarrhines*

Source: Based on Noel T. Boaz and Alan J. Almquist, *Biological Anthropology*. Copyright © 1997. Reprinted by permission of Pearson Education, Inc., Upper Saddle River, NJ 07458.

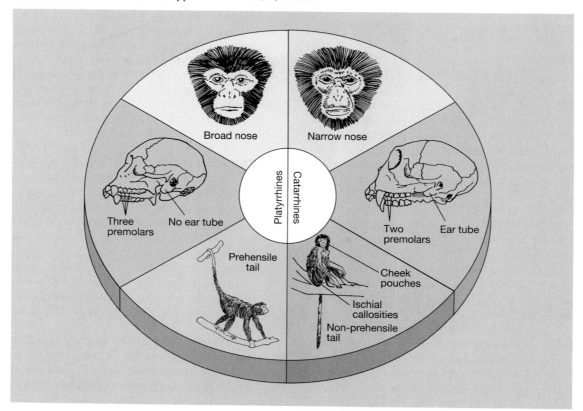

vertical clinging and leaping. In other respects tarsiers are more like the anthropoids. They have a reduced dependence on smell; not only are their noses smaller, but they lack the wet, doglike snout of lemurs. In common with the anthropoids, their eyes are closer together and are protected by bony orbits. Reproductively, the tarsier, like anthropoids, has a placenta that allows contact between the mother's blood and that of the fetus.[21]

ANTHROPOIDS

The anthropoid suborder includes humans, apes, and monkeys. Most anthropoids share several traits in varying degree. They have rounded braincases; reduced, nonmobile outer ears; and relatively small, flat faces instead of muzzles. They have highly efficient reproductive systems. They also have highly dextrous hands.[22] The anthropoid order is divided into two main groups: **platyrrhines** and **catarrhines** (see Figure 4–4). These groups take their names from the nose shape of the different anthropoids, but as we shall see they differ in other features as well. Platyrrhines have broad, flat-bridged noses, with nostrils facing outward; these monkeys are found only in the New World, in Central and South America. Catarrhines have narrow noses with nostrils facing downward. Catarrhines include monkeys of the Old World (Africa, Asia, and Europe), as well as apes and humans.

The squirrel monkey, like all platyrrhines, almost never leaves the trees. It is well suited to an arboreal lifestyle; note how it uses both hands and feet to grasp branches.

NEW WORLD MONKEYS Besides the shape of the nose and the position of the nostrils, other anatomical features distinguish the New World monkeys (platyrrhines) from the catarrhine anthropoids. The New World species have three premolars, whereas the Old World species have two. Some New World monkeys have a prehensile (grasping) tail; no Old World monkeys do. All the New World monkeys are completely arboreal; they vary a lot in the size of their groups; and their food ranges from insects to nectar and sap to fruits and leaves.[23]

Two main families of New World monkeys have traditionally been defined. One family, the *callitrichids,* contains marmosets and tamarins; the other family, the *cebids,* contains all the other New World monkeys. Although scholars recognize some problems with this division, it is a useful one for gaining a basic understanding of the New World monkeys. The callitrichids are very small, have claws instead of fingernails, and give birth to twins who mature in about two years. Perhaps because twinning is so common and the infants have to be carried, callitrichid mothers cannot take care of them alone. Fathers and older siblings have often been observed carrying infants. Indeed, males may do more carrying than females. Callitrichid groups may contain a mated pair (monogamy) or a female mated to more than one male (polyandry). The callitrichids eat a lot of fruit and tree sap, but like other very small primates, they obtain a large portion of their protein requirements from insects.[24]

Cebids are generally larger than callitrichids, take about twice as long to mature, and tend to bear only one offspring at a time.[25] The cebids vary widely in size, group composition, and diet. For example, squirrel monkeys weigh about 2 pounds, whereas woolly spider monkeys weigh more than 16 pounds. Some cebids have small groups with one male-female pair, others have groups of up to 50 individuals. Some of the smallest cebids have a diet of leaves, insects, flowers, and fruits, whereas others are mostly fruit-eaters with lesser dependence on seeds, leaves, or insects.[26]

OLD WORLD MONKEYS The Old World monkeys, or **cercopithecoids,** are related more closely to humans than to New World monkeys. They have the same number of teeth as apes and humans. The Old World monkey species are not as diverse as their New World cousins, but they live in a greater variety of habitats. Some live both in trees and on the ground; others, such as the gelada baboon, are completely **terrestrial,** or ground-living. Macaques are found both in tropical jungles and on snow-covered mountains, and they range from the Rock of Gibraltar to Africa to northern India, Pakistan, and Japan. There are two major subfamilies of Old World monkeys.

Colobine Monkeys The colobine group includes Asian langurs, the African colobus monkeys, and several other species. These monkeys live mostly in trees, and their diet consists principally of leaves and seeds. Their digestive tracts are equipped to obtain maximum nutrition from a

Grooming is an important part of social behavior for Old World monkeys. Here two Japanese macaques groom one another.

high-cellulose diet; they have pouched stomachs, which provide a large surface area for breaking down plant food, and very large intestinal tracts.

One of the most noticeable features of colobines is the flamboyant color typical of newborns. For example, in one species dusky gray mothers give birth to brilliant orange babies.[27] Observational studies suggest that the colobines

This langur, like all catarrhines, has a relatively narrow nose with nostrils that point downward. Langurs are Asian members of the colobine family and are primarily leaf-eaters.

are also unusual among the primates (except for humans) in that mothers let other group members take care of their infants shortly after birth. But males who are not members of the group are dangerous for infants; males trying to enter and take over a group have been observed to kill infants. Although this description may suggest that a one-male group is the typical group structure, there does not appear to be a typical pattern for a given species. When more than one site of a species has been studied, both one-male and multiple-male groups have been found.[28]

Cercopithecine Monkeys The cercopithecine subfamily of monkeys includes more terrestrial species than any other subfamily of Old World monkeys. Many of these species are characterized by a great deal of **sexual dimorphism** (the sexes look very different); the males are larger, have longer canines, and are more aggressive than the females. Cercopithecines depend more on fruit than do colobines. They are also more capable of surviving in arid and seasonal environments.[29] Pouches inside the cheeks allow cercopithecines to store food for later eating and digestion. An unusual physical feature of these monkeys is the *ischial callosities,* or callouses, on their bottoms—an adaptation that enables them to sit comfortably in trees or on the ground for long periods of time.[30]

Studies of baboons and macaques suggest that closely related females form the core of a local group, or *troop.* In large groups, which are common among rhesus monkeys,

A troop of baboons in Kenya spends most of its time on the ground.

many social behaviors seem to be determined by degree of biological relatedness. For example, an individual is most likely to sit next to, groom, or help an individual who is closely related maternally.[31] Moreover, a closely related subgroup is likely to stay together when a large troop divides.[32]

THE HOMINOIDS: APES AND HUMANS The **hominoid** group includes three separate families: the lesser apes, or **hylobates** (gibbons and siamangs); the great apes, or **pongids** (orangutans, gorillas, and chimpanzees); and humans, or **hominids.** Several characteristics distinguish the hominoids from the other primates. Their brains are relatively large, especially the areas of the cerebral cortex associated with the ability to integrate data. All hominoids have fairly long arms, short, broad trunks, and no tails. The wrist, elbow, and shoulder joints of hominoids allow a greater range of movement than in other primates. Hominoid hands are longer and stronger than those of other primates. These skeletal features probably evolved along with the hominoids' unique abilities in suspensory locomotion. Unlike other anthropoids, who move quadrupedally along the ground or along tops of tree branches, hominoids often suspend themselves from below the branches and swing or climb hand over hand from branch to branch.[33] This suspensory posture also translates to locomotion on the ground; all hominids, at least occasionally, move bipedally, as we discuss in more detail in the chapter on the first hominids.

The dentition of hominoids demonstrates some unique features as well (see Figure 4–5). Hominoid molars are flat and rounded compared to those of other anthropoids, and have what is called a **"Y-5" pattern** on the lower molars—that is, the lower molars have five cusps with a Y-shaped groove opening toward the cheek running

between them. Other anthropoids have what is called a **bilophodont** pattern—their molars have two long ridges or "loafs" running parallel to the cheeks. All hominoids except for humans also have long canine teeth that project beyond the tops of the other teeth, and a corresponding space on the opposite jaw, called a **diastema,** where the canine sits when the jaws are closed. The contact of the upper canine and the lower third premolar creates a sharp cutting edge, in part due to the premolar being elongated to accommodate the canine.[34] These dental features are related to the hominoids' diets, which often include both fibrous plant materials, which can be efficiently cut with sharp canines against elongated premolars, and soft fruits, which can be efficiently chewed with wide, flat molars.

The skeletal and dental features shared by the hominoids point toward their common ancestry. Their blood proteins show many similarities, too. This blood likeness is particularly strong among chimpanzees, gorillas, and humans. For this reason, primatologists think chimpanzees and gorillas are evolutionarily closer to humans than are the lesser apes and orangutans, which probably branched off at some earlier point. We discuss the fossil evidence that supports an early split for the orangutans in the next chapter.

Gibbons and Siamangs The agile gibbons and their close relatives the siamangs are found in the jungles of Southeast Asia. The gibbons are small, weighing only about 11 to 15 pounds. The siamangs are somewhat larger, but no more than 25 pounds. Both are mostly fruit-eaters, although they also eat leaves and insects. They are spectacular **brachiators;** their long arms and fingers let them swing hand over hand through the trees.[35] A gibbon can move more than 30 feet in a single forward swing.

Figure 4–5

Difference in dentition between an Old World monkey (left) and an ape (right). In Old World monkeys the cusps of the lower molars form two parallel ridges; in apes, the five cusps form a Y-shaped pattern. Source: Adapted from Noel T. Boaz and Alan J. Almquist, Essentials of Biological Anthropology (Upper Saddle River, NJ: Prentice Hall, 1999), p. 164.

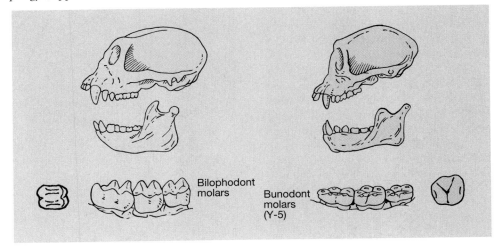

A white-handed gibbon demonstrates its ability as a brachiator.

Gibbons and siamangs live in small family groups consisting of an adult pair, who appear to mate for life, and one or two immature offspring. When the young reach adulthood, they are driven from home by the adults. There is little sexual dimorphism—males and females do not differ in size or appearance—nor is there any clear pattern of dominance by either sex. These lesser apes are also highly territorial; an adult pair advertises their territory by singing and defends it by chasing others away.[36]

Orangutans Orangutans survive only on the islands of Borneo and Sumatra. Unlike gibbons and siamangs, they are clearly recognizable as males or females. Males not only weigh almost twice as much as females (up to 200 pounds), but they also have large cheek pads, throat pouches, beards, and long hair.[37] Like gibbons and siamangs, orangutans are primarily fruit-eaters and arboreal. They are the heaviest of the arboreal primates, and perhaps for this reason they move slowly and laboriously through the trees. Orangutans are unusual among the higher primates in living basically solitary lives, except for mothers and their young; however, a recent field study of orangutans on Sumatra found that groups of as many as 10 adults fed together in the same tree.[38]

Different ideas have been proposed about the solitary habit of the orangutans that live in the mountainous areas of Borneo. One is that there may be insufficient food in any one tree or home range to support more than a single adult orangutan, a pretty large animal, as animals go. To obtain sufficient food each day without having to travel over a huge area, orangutans thus may live alone rather than in groups.[39] Another idea is that animals live in groups when they are subject to heavy predation; the large size of orangutans may make them immune to attacks from most animals, so living alone may be a viable option.[40] A third idea, which on the face of it seems opposite to the second, is that living alone may be an adaptation to heavy predation by humans. The orangutan's best defense against humans with guns may be to hide alone in the trees.[41]

Gorillas Gorillas are found in the lowland areas of western equatorial Africa and in the mountain areas of Congo, Uganda, and Rwanda.[42] Unlike the other apes, who are mostly fruit-eaters, gorillas mostly eat other parts of plants—stems, shoots (for example, bamboo), pith, leaves, roots, and flowers. The amount of fruit eaten varies greatly. In many populations fruit-eating is rare; in some, however, fruit is a common part of the diet.[43]

Gorillas are by far the largest of the surviving apes. In their natural habitats, adult males weigh up to 450 pounds and females up to 250 pounds. To support the weight of massive chests, gorillas travel mostly on the ground on all fours in a form of locomotion known as **knuckle walking:** They walk on the thickly padded middle joints of their fingers. Gorillas' arms and legs, especially those of the young, are well suited for climbing. As adults, their heavier bodies make climbing more precarious.[44] They sleep on the ground or in tub-shaped nests they make from non-food plants each time they bed down.[45]

Gorillas tend to live in groups consisting of a dominant male, called a *silverback,* other adult males, adult females, and immature offspring. Both males and females, when mature, seem to leave the groups into which they were

A young gorilla shows how it knuckle-walks. The back feet are flat on the ground, and only the knuckles of the "hands" touch the ground.

born to join other groups. The dominant male is very much the center of attention; he acts as the main protector of the group and the leader in deciding where the group will go next.[46]

Chimpanzees   Perhaps because they are more sociable and easier to find, chimpanzees have been studied far more than gorillas. Chimpanzees live in the forested areas of Africa, from Sierra Leone in the west to Tanzania in the east.

There are two distinct species of chimpanzee—the common chimpanzee (*Pan troglodytes*) and the *bonobo,* or pygmy, chimpanzee (*Pan paniscus*). While they share many features in common (indeed, they were not recognized as distinct species until 1929), bonobos tend to be more slender than common chimpanzees, with longer limbs and digits, smaller heads, darker faces, and a distinct part in their hair. Unlike common chimpanzees, bonobos show almost no sexual dimorphism in dentition or skeletal structure. More significant seem to be differences in social behavior. Bonobos are more gregarious than common chimpanzees, and groups tend to be more stable. Groups also tend to be centered around females rather than males.[47] Some of these behavioral differences have led some scholars to suggest that bonobos are likely to be more closely related to humans than common chimpanzees,[48] although this view remains controversial.[49]

Although they are primarily fruit-eaters, chimpanzees

A bonobo mother with infant. Her slender limbs, dark face, and the part in her hair are some of the traits that distinguish bonobos from common chimpanzees.

Chimpanzees, though they spend much time in the trees, can also move very quickly on the ground.

show many similarities to their close relatives, the gorillas. Both are arboreal and terrestrial. Like gorillas, chimpanzees are good climbers, especially when young, and they spend many hours in the trees. But they move best on the ground, and when they want to cover long distances they come down from the trees and move by knuckle walking. Occasionally, they stand and walk upright, usually when they are traveling through tall grass or are trying to see long distances. Chimpanzees sleep in tree nests that they carefully prepare anew, complete with a bunch of leaves as a pillow, each time they bed down.[50]

Chimpanzees (including bonobos) are less sexually dimorphic than the other great apes. Males weigh a little more than 100 pounds on the average, females somewhat less. But males have longer canines.

For some time it was thought that chimpanzees ate only plant food. Although most of their diet is vegetarian, among common chimpanzees a significant amount comes from meat. After three decades of studies at Gombe Park in Tanzania and elsewhere, researchers have found that common chimpanzees not only eat insects, small lizards, and birds, but they also actively hunt and kill larger animals.[51] They have been observed hunting and eating monkeys, young baboons, and bushbucks in addition to smaller prey. At Gombe, the red colobus monkey is by far the most often hunted animal. So it is not only humans who endanger other primates (recall the box "Endangered Primates"); the red colobus monkey population is very small in areas of intense chimpanzee hunting. Hunting appears to be undertaken more often during the dry season when food is scarce.[52] Prey is caught mostly by the males, which hunt either alone or in small groups. It is then shared with—or, perhaps more accurately, begged by—as many as 15 other chimpanzees in friendly social gatherings that may last up to nine hours.[53]

Despite considerable observation, the organization of chimpanzee social groups is still not clear. Groups of common chimpanzees usually are multimale and multifemale, but the size may range considerably from a few to 100 or so members. In Gombe, males typically remain in their natal group throughout life, and females often move to a neighboring group; but males in Guinea do not tend to stay in their natal groups.[54] It appears that chimpanzees come together and drift apart depending upon circumstances such as the availability of food and the risk of predation.[55]

Hominids   According to the classification we use here, the hominoids we call hominids include only one living species—modern humans. Humans have many distinctive characteristics that set them apart from other anthropoids and other hominoids, which lead many to place humans in a category separate from the pongids. (These traits are discussed later in this chapter and also throughout much of the rest of the book.) However, others believe that the differences are not so great as to justify a separate hominid category for humans. For example, humans, chimpanzees, and gorillas are very similar in their proteins and DNA. And it is widely agreed that the lines leading to humans, chimpanzees, and gorillas diverged from a common ancestor perhaps 5 million to 6 million years ago.[56] Whether we stress the similarities or differences between humans and apes does not matter that much; what does matter is that we try to understand the reasons for those similarities and differences.

Explanations of Variable Primate Adaptations

Thus far we have discussed the common features of primates and introduced the different primates that survive in the world today. Now let us examine possible explanations, suggested by research, of some of the ways in which the surviving primates vary.

BODY SIZE

Surviving primates vary enormously in body size, ranging from the 2 or so ounces of the average gray mouse lemur to the 350 pounds of the average male gorilla. What accounts for this sizable variation? Three factors seem to predict body size—the time of day the species is active, where it is active (in the trees or on the ground), and the kinds of food eaten.[57] All the nocturnal primates are small; and among the primates active during the day, the arboreal ones tend to be smaller than the terrestrial ones. Finally, species that eat mostly leaves tend to be larger than species that eat mostly fruits and seeds.

Why do these factors predict size? One important consideration is the general relationship in mammals between body weight and energy needs. Generally, larger animals require more absolute energy, but smaller animals require much more energy for their body weight. That being so, smaller animals (and small primates) need more energy-rich food. Insects, fruits, tree gum, and sap are full of calories and tend to be more important in the diet of small primates. Leaves are relatively low in energy, so leaf-eaters have to consume a lot of food to get enough energy. They

Figure 4–6

As this graph shows, larger animals generally have larger brains. Primates generally have even larger brains than we would expect from their body weight. Note that most of the primates (as indicated by the colored circles) fall above the line showing the relationship between brain weight and body weight. The brains in primates are about twice as heavy as the brains of non-primate mammals of the same body weight. Source: From Terrence W. Deacon, "Primate Brains and Senses," in Stephen Jones, Robert Martin, and David Pilbeam, eds., *The Cambridge Encyclopedia of Human Evolution* (New York: Cambridge University Press, 1992), p. 111. Copyright © by Cambridge University Press. Reprinted by permission of Cambridge University Press.

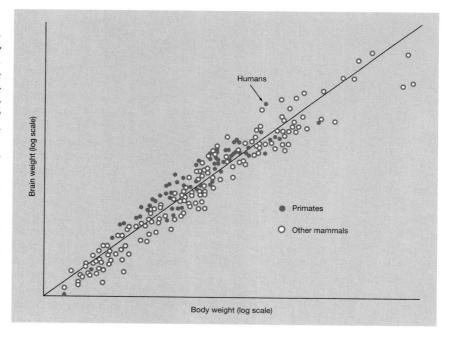

RESEARCH FRONTIERS

Researcher at Work: Katharine Milton

Katharine Milton is Professor of Anthropology at the University of California, Berkeley, with an avid interest in the scientific study of monkeys. But that is far from how she started out. Born in Alabama, Milton went to Sweet Briar College in Virginia. She was an English major in college and went on to receive her M.A. in that subject at the University of Iowa. It wasn't until later, while she was living in Argentina, that she discovered her great interest in animal behavior and primates in particular.

After receiving her Ph.D. from New York University, with a dissertation on the "economics" of the howler monkeys of Panama, she was fortunate to be able to study the woolly spider monkey—a little-known endangered monkey species living in southeastern Brazil. Because so little was known about them, she

started out doing a basic review of their diet and behavior. Woolly spider monkeys look like spider monkeys, so they were assumed also to be fruit-eaters as are the spider monkeys. But Milton discovered through systematic observation over a year's time that this "commonsense" view was wrong. As she put it: "Apparently no one ever connected the short lifespan of captive woolly spider monkeys with the fact that perhaps, just perhaps, they were being fed the wrong food. Zoos, listen up—if you are ever fortunate enough to obtain a woolly spider monkey or two, be sure to give them leafy matter as their major dietary component, not ripe sugary fruits!"

Much of Milton's research has been devoted to understanding the implications of diet for both nonhuman and human primates.

Compared with fruit-eaters, leaf-eating primates are generally larger, require relatively less area to feed in, and have relatively smaller brains. Why? Milton suggested that despite the energy costs of a larger brain, the greater intellectual difficulties of remembering locations of dispersed high-quality food (for example, fruit, which provides more nutrients by weight than leaves) favored greater mental development in such primates.

Sources: Katharine Milton, "The Evolution of a Physical Anthropologist," in Peter N. Peregrine, Carol R. Ember, and Melvin Ember, eds., *Physical Anthropology: Original Readings in Method and Practice* (Upper Saddle River, NJ: Prentice Hall, 2002); Katharine Milton, "Foraging Behaviour and the Evolution of Primate Intelligence," in Richard W. Bryne and Andrew Whiten, eds., *Machiavellian Intelligence: Social Expertise and the Evolution of Intellect in Monkeys, Apes, and Humans* (Oxford: Clarendon Press, 1988), pp. 285–305.

also need large stomachs and intestines to extract the nutrients they need, and a bigger gut in turn requires a bigger skeleton and body.[58] Small primates, which eat insects and other rich foods, probably would compete with birds for food. However, most very small primates are nocturnal, whereas most forest-living birds are diurnal.

Energy requirements may also explain why arboreal primates are usually smaller. Moving about in trees usually requires both vertical and horizontal motion. The energy required to climb vertically is proportional to weight, so larger animals require more energy to climb. But the energy for traveling horizontally, as on the ground, is not proportionate to weight, so larger animals use energy more efficiently on the ground than in the trees.[59] An additional consideration is the amount of weight that can be supported by small tree branches, where foods such as fruits are mostly located. Small animals can go out to small branches more safely than large animals. Also, ground dwellers might be bigger because large size is a protection against predation.[60]

RELATIVE BRAIN SIZE

Larger primates usually have larger brains, but larger animals of all types generally have larger brains (see Figure 4–6). Thus primatologists are interested in *relative brain size*, that is, the ratio of brain size to body size.

Perhaps because human primates have the largest brain relatively of any primate, we tend to think a larger brain is "better." However, a large brain does have "costs." From an energy perspective, the development of a large brain requires a great deal of metabolic energy; therefore it should not be favored by natural selection unless the benefits outweigh the costs.[61]

Fruit-eating primates tend to have relatively larger brains than leaf-eating primates do. This difference may be due to natural selection in favor of more capacity for memory, and therefore relatively larger brains, in fruit-eaters. Leaf-eaters may not need as much memory, because they depend on food that is more readily available in time and space, and therefore they may not have to remember where food might be found. In contrast, fruit-eaters may need greater memory and brain capacity because their foods ripen at different times and in separate places that have to be remembered to be found.[62] The brain requires large supplies of oxygen and glucose. Because leaf-eating primates do not have as much glucose in their diets as fruit-eating primates, they may also not have the energy reserves to support relatively large brains.[63]

GROUP SIZE

Primate groups vary in size from solitary males and females with young (orangutans) to a few individuals and young (for example, gibbons) to 100 or more individuals in some Old World monkey troops.[64] What factors might account for such variation?

Nocturnal activity is an important predictor not only of small body size but also of small group size. Nocturnal primates feed either alone or in pairs.[65] John Terborgh has noted that most nocturnal predators hunt by sound, so a nocturnal animal might best avoid attack by being silent.[66] Groups are noisy, and therefore nocturnal animals might be more likely to survive by living alone or in pairs.

On the other hand, a large group might provide advantages in the daytime. The more eyes, ears, and noses a group has, the more quickly a would-be predator might be detected—and perhaps avoided. Also, a larger group would have more teeth and strength to frighten or mob a predator that actually attacked.[67] But this line of reasoning would lead us to expect that all diurnal terrestrial species would have large groups. Yet not all do. Other factors must be operating. One seems to be the amount and density of food. If food resources occur in small amounts and in separate places, only small groups can get enough to eat; if food occurs in large patches, there will be enough to support large groups.[68] An additional factor may be competition over resources. One suggestion is that substantial but separated patches of resources are likely to be fought over, and therefore individuals living in larger groups might be more likely to obtain access to them.[69]

Distinctive Human Traits

We turn now to some of the features that distinguish us—humans—from the other primates. Although we like to think of ourselves as unique, many of the traits we discuss here are at the extreme of a continuum that can be traced from the prosimians through the apes.

PHYSICAL TRAITS

Of all the primates, only humans consistently walk erect on two feet. Gibbons, chimpanzees (particularly bonobos), and gorillas (and some monkeys too) may stand or walk on two feet some of the time, but only for very short periods. All other primates require thick, heavy musculature to hold their heads erect; this structure is missing in humans, for our heads are more or less balanced on top of our spinal columns. A dish-shaped pelvis (peculiar to humans), a lumbar curve in the spine, straight lower limbs, and arched, nonprehensile feet are all related to human **bipedalism.** Because we are fully bipedal, we can carry objects without impairing our locomotor efficiency. (In the chapter on the first hominids we consider the effects that bipedalism may have had on such diverse traits as tool-making, prolonged infant dependency, and the division of labor by gender.)

Although many primates have an opposable thumb, which enables them to grasp and examine objects, the greater length and flexibility of the human thumb allow us to handle objects with greater dexterity. We are capable of both a power grip, to hold large or heavy objects firmly, and a precision grip, to hold small or delicate objects without dropping or breaking them. We also have remarkable hand-eye coordination, as well as a remarkably sophisticated brain.

The human brain is large and complex, particularly the **cerebral cortex,** the center of speech and other higher mental activities. The brain of the average adult human measures more than 1,300 cubic centimeters, compared with 525 cubic centimeters for the gorilla, the primate with the next largest brain. The frontal areas of the human brain are also larger than those of other primates, so that humans have more prominent foreheads than monkeys or gorillas. Humans have special areas of the brain that are dedicated to speech and language. The large human brain requires an enormous amount of blood, and the way blood is carried to and from the brain is also unique.[70] We'll talk more about the human brain and its evolution in the chapter on the emergence of the genus *Homo.*

Human teeth reflect our completely omnivorous diet, and they are not very specialized, which may reflect the fact that we use tools and cooking to prepare our food. As discussed earlier, other hominoids have long canines and a diastema, whereas human canines do not usually project beyond the tops of the other teeth. This allows humans to move their jaws both vertically and horizontally when chewing; horizontal movement would be prevented by the long upper canines of the other hominoids. Human molars have thicker enamel than the molars of other hominoids, and both horizontal movement and thickened molars may be related to a dietary emphasis on coarse grains and seeds, something we'll discuss further in the chapter on the first hominids. The human jaw is shaped like a parabolic arch, rather than a U-shape, as in the apes, and is composed of relatively thin bones and light muscles. Humans have chins; other primates do not.

One other distinctive human trait is the sexuality of human females, who may engage in intercourse at any time throughout the year; most other primate females engage in sex only periodically, just around the time they can conceive.[71] Humans are also unusual among the primates in having female-male bonding.[72] Later, in the discussion of the origins of culture, we examine some theories suggesting why male-female bonding, which in humans we call "marriage," may have developed. It used to be thought

that more or less continuous female sexuality may be related to female-male bonding, but comparative research
on mammals and birds contradicts this idea. Those mammals and birds that have more frequent sex are not more
likely to have male-female bonding.[73]

Why, then, does human female sexuality differ from
that of most other primates? One suggestion is that more
or less continuous female sexuality became selectively advantageous in humans after female-male bonding developed in conjunction with local groups consisting of at
least several adult males and adult females.[74] More specifically, the combination of group living *and* male-female
bonding—a combination unique to humans among the
primates—may have favored a switch from the common
higher-primate pattern of periodic female sexuality to the
pattern of more or less continuous female sexuality. Such
a switch may have been favored in humans because periodic rather than continuous female sexuality would undermine female-male bonding in multimale-multifemale
groups.

Field research on nonhuman primates strongly suggests that males usually attempt to mate with any females
ready to mate. If the female (or females) a male was
bonded to was not interested in sex at certain times, but
other females in the group were, it seems likely that the
male would try to mate with those other females. Frequent
"extramarital affairs" might jeopardize the male-female
bond and thereby presumably reduce the reproductive
success of both males and females. Hence natural selection
may have favored more or less continuous sexuality in human females if humans already had the combination of
group living (and the possibility of "extramarital affairs")
and marriage. If bonded adults lived alone, as do gibbons,
noncontinuous female sexuality would not threaten
bonding, because "extramarital" sex would not be likely to
occur. Similarly, seasonal breeding would also pose little
threat to male-female bonds, because all females would be
sexually active at more or less the same time.[75] So the fact
that the combination of group living and male-female
bonding occurs only in humans may explain why continuous female sexuality developed in humans. The bonobo,
or pygmy chimpanzee, female does engage in intercourse
throughout the year, but bonobos do not have male-
female bonding and the females are not interested in sex
quite as often as human females.[76]

BEHAVIORAL ABILITIES

In comparison with other primates, a much greater proportion of human behavior is learned and culturally patterned. As with many physical traits, we can trace a continuum in the learning abilities of all primates. The great
apes, including orangutans, gorillas, and chimpanzees, are
probably about equal in learning ability.[77] Old and New
World monkeys do much less well in learning tests, and,
surprisingly, gibbons perform more poorly than most
monkeys.

TOOLMAKING The same kind of continuum is evident in inventiveness and toolmaking. There is no evidence that any nonhuman primates except great apes
use tools, although several species of monkeys use
"weapons"—branches, stones, or fruit dropped onto
predators below them on the ground. Chimpanzees both
fashion and use tools in the wild. As we have noted, they
strip leaves from sticks and then use the sticks to "fish" termites from their mound-shaped nests. They use leaves to
mop up termites, to sponge up water, or to wipe themselves clean.

One example of chimpanzee tool use suggests planning. In Guinea, West Africa, observers watched a number
of chimpanzees crack oil palm nuts with two stones. The
"platform" stone had a hollow depression; the other stone
was used for pounding. The observers assumed that the
stones had been brought by the chimpanzees to the palm
trees, because no stones like them were nearby and the
chimps were observed to leave the pounding stone on top
of or near the platform stone when they were finished.[78]
Observers in other areas of West Africa have also reported
that chimpanzees use stones to crack nuts. In one location
in Liberia, an innovative female appeared to have started
the practice; it seems to have been imitated within a few
months by 13 others who previously showed no interest in
the practice.[79]

In captivity, chimpanzees have also been observed to be
inventive toolmakers. One mother chimpanzee was seen
examining and cleaning her son's teeth, using tools she
had fashioned from twigs. She even extracted a baby tooth
he was about to lose.[80]

Humans have usually been considered the only toolmaking animal, but observations such as these call for
modification of the definition of toolmaking. If we define
toolmaking as adapting a natural object for a specific purpose, then at least some of the great apes are toolmakers
too. Perhaps it would be more accurate to say humans are
the only habitual toolmaking animal, just as we say

Chimps in the wild use tools—in this case, a stick to pry
insects out of a fallen tree trunk. As far as we know,
though, they don't use tools to make other tools, as
humans do.

humans are the only habitual bipedal hominoid, even though the other hominoids all can and do walk bipedally sometimes. As far as we know, though, humans are unique in their ability to use one tool to make another.

LANGUAGE   Only humans have spoken, symbolic language. But, as with toolmaking abilities, the line between human language and the communications of other primates is not as sharp as we once thought. In the wild, vervet monkeys make different alarm calls to warn of different predators. Observers playing tape recordings of these calls found that monkeys responded to them differently, depending on the call. If the monkeys heard an "eagle" call, they looked up; if they heard a "leopard" call, they ran high into the trees.[81]

Common chimpanzees are also communicative, using gestures and many vocalizations in the wild. Researchers have used this "natural talent" to teach chimpanzees symbolic language in experimental settings. In their pioneering work, Beatrice T. Gardner and R. Allen Gardner raised a female chimpanzee named Washoe and trained her to communicate with startling effectiveness by means of American Sign Language hand gestures.[82] After a year of training, she was able to associate gestures with specific activities. For example, if thirsty, Washoe would make the signal for "give me" followed by the one for "drink." As she learned, the instructions grew more detailed. If all she wanted was water, she would merely signal for "drink." But if she craved soda pop, as she did more and more, she prefaced the drink signal with the sweet signal—a quick touching of the tongue with her fingers. Later, the Gardners had even more success in training four other chimpanzees, who were taught by fluent deaf users of American Sign Language.[83]

Bonobos have provided strong evidence that they understand simple grammatical "rules," very much like 2-year-old humans. Pointing to graphic symbols for different particular meanings, a bonobo named Kanzi regularly communicated sequences of types of symbols; for example, he would point to a symbol for a verb ("bite") and then point to a symbol for an object ("ball," "cherry," "food").[84]

OTHER HUMAN TRAITS   Although many primates are omnivores, eating insects and small reptiles in addition to plants—some even hunt small mammals—only humans hunt very large animals. Also, humans are one of the few primates that are completely terrestrial. We do not even sleep in trees, as many other ground-living primates do. Perhaps our ancestors lost their perches when the forests receded, or cultural advances such as weapons or fire may have eliminated the need to seek nightly shelter in the trees. In addition, as we have noted, we have the longest dependency period of any of the primates, requiring extensive parental care and support for up to 20 years or so.

Finally, humans are unlike almost all other primates in having a division of labor by gender in food-getting and food sharing in adulthood. Among nonhuman primates, both females and males forage for themselves after infancy. Humans have more gender-role specialization, perhaps because men, unencumbered by infants and small children, were freer to hunt and chase large animals.

Having examined our distinctive traits and the traits we share with other primates, we need to ask what selective forces may have favored the emergence of primates, what forces may have favored the line of divergence leading to the first hominids, and what forces led to the emergence of the genus *Homo*. These questions are the subjects of the next three chapters.

Summary

1. Although no living primate can be a direct ancestor of humans, we do share a common evolutionary history with the other surviving primates. Studying the behavioral and anatomical features of our closest living relatives may help us make inferences about primate evolution. Studying distinctive human traits may help us understand why the line of primates that led to humans branched away from the line leading to chimpanzees and gorillas.

2. No one trait is unique to primates. However, primates do share the following features: two bones in the lower part of the leg and in the forearm, a collarbone, flexible prehensile (grasping) hands, stereoscopic vision, a relatively large brain, only one (or sometimes two) offspring at a time, long maturation of the young, and a high degree of dependence on social life and learning.

3. The order Primates is divided into two suborders: the prosimians and the anthropoids. Compared with the anthropoids, prosimians depend more on smell for information. They have mobile ears, whiskers, longer snouts typically, and relatively fixed facial expressions. Anthropoids have rounded braincases; reduced, nonmobile outer ears; and relatively small, flat faces instead of muzzles. They have highly dextrous hands.

4. The anthropoid order is divided into two main groups: platyrrhines (monkeys of the New World) and catarrhines. The catarrhines are subdivided into cercopithecoids (Old World monkeys) and hominoids (apes and humans). The anthropoid apes consist of the hylobates, or lesser apes (gibbons and siamangs), and the pongids, or great apes (orangutans, gorillas, and chimpanzees).

5. Along with the gorilla, the chimpanzee has proteins and DNA remarkably similar to those of humans, as well as anatomical and behavioral similarities to humans. Wild chimpanzees have been seen to create and use tools, modifying a natural object to fulfill a specific purpose. High conceptual ability is also demonstrated by both the chimpanzee's and the gorilla's facility in learning sign language.

6. Variable aspects of the environment, differences in activity patterns, and variation in diet may explain many of the traits that vary in the primates. Nocturnal primates tend to be small and to live alone or in very small groups. Among diurnal species, the arboreal primates tend to be

smaller and to live in smaller social groups than terrestrial primates. Fruit-eaters have relatively larger brains than leaf-eaters.

7. The differences between humans and the other anthropoids show us what makes humans distinctive as a species. Humans are totally bipedal; they walk on two legs and do not need the arms for locomotion. The human brain, particularly the cerebral cortex, is the largest and most complex. In contrast to females of almost all other primates, human females may engage in sexual intercourse at any time throughout the year. Human offspring have a proportionately longer dependency stage. And in comparison with other primates, more human behavior is learned and culturally patterned. Spoken, symbolic language and the use of tools to make other tools are uniquely human behavioral traits. Humans also generally have a division of labor in food-getting and food sharing in adulthood.

 ## Glossary Terms

anthropoids
arboreal
bilophodont
bipedalism
brachiators
canines
catarrhines
cercopithecoids
cerebral cortex
diastema
diurnal
hominids
hominoid
hylobates
incisors
knuckle walking

molars
nocturnal
omnivorous
opposable thumbs
platyrrhines
pongids
prehensile
premolars
prosimians
quadrupeds
sexual dimorphism
terrestrial
vertical clinging
 and leaping
"Y-5" pattern

 ## Critical Questions

1. How could you infer that a fossil primate lived in the trees?
2. Why are primates so smart?
3. Under what conditions would the ability to communicate be adaptive?
4. Why are humans immature for so long?

 ## Internet Exercises

1. The Duke University Primate Center (**http://www.duke.edu/web/primate/index.html**) is devoted to research on and conservation of prosimians. Click on the Animals button and read about how prosimians differ from anthropoidal primates and the differences among lemurs, lorises, galagos, pottos, and tarsiers. Also, use this site to find out which prosimians are most endangered.

2. Visit the Primate Gallery site at **http://www. selu.com/~bio/PrimateGallery/main.html** and read about the primate of the week. Look at the new images at **http://www.selu.com/~bio/PrimateGallery/new/images.html**.

3. Visit the Great Ape Project at **http://www.greatapeproject.org/** and click on the latest news reports. Read one of the reports of interest to you and summarize the article.

4. Want to hear some primate vocalizations? Go to the Web site at **http://www.indiana.edu/~primate/primates.html** and listen to vocalizations from a number of different primates.

 ## Suggested Reading

CHENEY, D., AND SEYFARTH, R. *How Monkeys See the World.* Chicago: University of Chicago Press, 1990. A thoughtful, balanced attempt to find out how monkeys think and the extent to which their view of the world is similar to ours.

FLEAGLE, J. G., JANSON, C. H., AND REED, K. E., EDS. *Primate Communities.* Cambridge: Cambridge University Press, 1999. An interesting collection of essays examining variation in primate communities.

GRAY, J. P. *Primate Sociobiology.* New Haven, CT: HRAF Press, 1985. A survey and discussion of empirical studies that tested 396 possible explanations, mostly derived from sociobiological theory, of many aspects of variation in primate behavior.

JONES, S., MARTIN, R., AND PILBEAM, D., EDS. *The Cambridge Encyclopedia of Human Evolution.* Cambridge: Cambridge University Press, 1992. About a third of this comprehensive book reviews information about primate classification, conservation, aspects of and variation in physique, physiology, behavior, and cognitive abilities of the living primates.

MCGREW, W. *Chimpanzee Material Culture: Implications for Human Evolution.* Cambridge: Cambridge University Press, 1992. A careful description and analysis of tool use among chimpanzees.

PARKER, S. T., AND GIBSON, K. R., EDS. *"Language" and Intelligence in Monkeys and Apes: Comparative Developmental Perspectives.* New York: Cambridge University Press, 1990. A volume of 20 papers that apply frameworks from human developmental psychology and evolutionary biology to comparative studies of primate abilities.

ROWE, N. *The Pictorial Guide to the Living Primates.* East Hampton, NY: Pogonias Press, 1996. A beautiful successor to J. R. Napier and P. H. Napier's *Handbook of Living Primates* (New York: Academic Press, 1967), with a photograph or illustration of each of the living primates. This is the most complete collection of images yet published in a single source.

SMUTS, B. B., CHENEY, D. L., SEYFARTH, R. M., WRANGHAM, R. W., AND STRUHSAKER, T. T., EDS. *Primate Societies.* Chicago: University of Chicago Press, 1987. An extensive review, by some 50 primatologists, of primate species that have been studied in the wild.

5

Primate Evolution: From Early Primates to Hominoids

CHAPTER OUTLINE

The Emergence of Primates

The Emergence of Anthropoids

The Miocene Anthropoids:
Monkeys, Apes, and Hominids(?)

The Divergence of Hominids
from the Other Hominoids

rimate paleontologists and paleoanthropologists focus on various questions about primate evolution. How far back in time did the primates emerge? What did they look like? What conditions favored them? How did the early primates diverge after that point? What kinds of niches did the different primates occupy? Although our concern as anthropologists is largely with the emergence of humans, and with the primates that are in the ancestral line leading to humans, we must remember that evolution does not proceed with a purpose or to give rise to any particular species; rather, organisms adapt, or fail to adapt, to the environments in which they find themselves. Thus, the primate fossil record is full of diversity; it is also full of apparent extinctions. Probably most of the primate lineages of the past never left any descendants at all.[1]

The reconstruction of primate evolution requires the finding of fossil remains. Although many fossils have been discovered and continue to be discovered, the fossil record is still very incomplete. If geological strata are not uplifted, exposed by erosion, or otherwise accessible in the areas where ancient primates lived, paleoanthropologists cannot recover their fossils. The fossils that are found are usually fragmented or damaged, and judgments about what the organism looked like may be based on one or just a few pieces. As we discussed in the chapter on how we discover the past, piecing together the evolutionary history of the primates requires much more than recovering fossil remains. The knowledge gained from anatomical studies of living species can allow us to make inferences about physical and behavioral traits that are likely to have been associated with the fossil features. Dating techniques developed in geology, chemistry, and physics are used to estimate the age of fossil remains (see Figure 5–1). And studies of ancient plants and animals, geography, and climate help us reconstruct the environments of ancient primates.

Although much of primate evolution is not yet known or is still controversial, there is a lot we do know. We know that as of the early Eocene epoch, which began about 55 million years ago, primates with some of the features of modern prosimians had already emerged. Primates with monkey- and apelike features appeared in the Oligocene epoch, beginning about 34 million years ago. The Miocene epoch, beginning about 24 million years ago, saw the appearance of many different kinds of apes. The ancient primates we know from fossils had some of the features of today's primates, but none of the ancient primates looked like the primates of today.

In this and the following chapters we describe the main features of current theory and evidence about primate evolution, from the origin of primates to the origin of modern humans. In this chapter we deal with that part of the story before the emergence of definite bipedal hominids. Our overview in this chapter covers the period from about 65 million years ago to the end of the Miocene, a little over 5 million years ago (see Figure 5–1).

The Emergence of Primates

When did the primates first emerge? This question turns out to be hard to answer from the currently known fossil record. Some paleoanthropologists have suggested that fossil finds from the **Paleocene** epoch, which began about 65 million years ago, are from archaic primates. These are the *plesiadapiforms*. They have been found in both Europe and North America, which in the Paleocene were one landmass. The most well known of the plesiadapiforms is ***Plesiadipis.*** This squirrel-like animal had a large snout and large incisors. It also had a large nasal cavity and eye orbits located on the sides of the skull, suggesting a well-developed sense of smell and little or no stereoscopic vision (depth perception). The fingers of *Plesiadipis* had claws, and its hands and feet did not appear to allow for grasping. These features suggest that *Plesiadipis* was not a primate. However, the elbow and ankle joints suggest great mobility, and despite the large incisors the teeth suggest a primatelike omnivorous diet. The structure of their inner ears also resembled that of modern primates. Because it had these primatelike features, some scholars believe that the plesiadipiforms were archaic primates.[2]

Other paleoanthropologists find so few similarities between the plesiadapiforms and later obvious primates that they do not include the plesiadapiforms in the order Primates.[3] There is no dispute, however, about fossils dating from the early **Eocene**, about 55 million years ago. These oldest definite primates appear in two major groups of prosimians—*adapids* and *omomyids*. Because these two kinds of primate are different from each other in major ways, and because they both appeared rather abruptly at the border of the Paleocene and Eocene, there presumably was an earlier common primate ancestor. But what it was is not yet known, or at least there is no consensus about it among paleoanthropologists. Even if we do not know exactly what the earliest primate looked like, the presence of the prosimians in the Eocene tells us that we need to look to an earlier time to explain the emergence of the primates. The circled P in Figure 5–2 represents the unknown common ancestor, which lived in the late Cretaceous, according to Robert D. Martin. Others think the common ancestor emerged in the Paleocene.

Now we turn to the conditions that may have favored the emergence of the primates.

THE ENVIRONMENT

It is generally agreed that the earliest primate may have emerged by the Paleocene, 65 million to 55 million years ago, and perhaps earlier, in the late **Cretaceous.** What was the environment like in those times? The beginning of the Paleocene marked a major geological transition, what geologists call the transition from the Mesozoic to the Cenozoic era. About 75 percent of all animal and plant life that lived in the last part of the Cenozoic (the late Cretaceous)

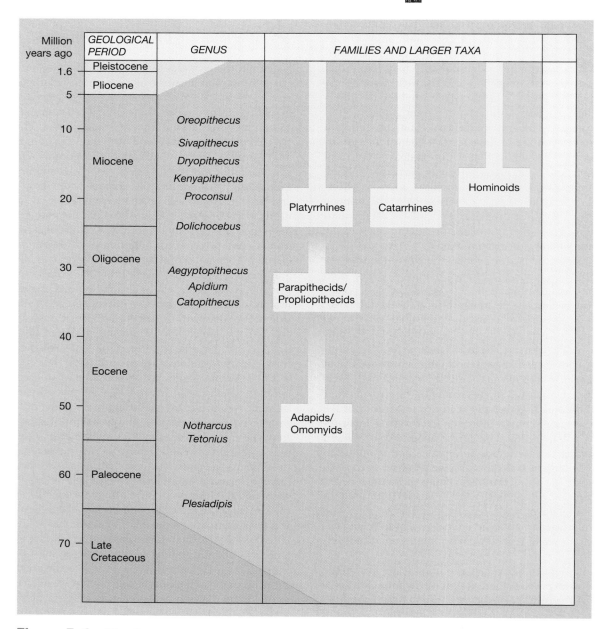

Figure 5–1 *The Evolution of the Primates*

vanished by the early Paleocene. The extinction of the dinosaurs is the most famous of these disappearances.[4]

The climate of the Cretaceous period was almost uniformly damp and mild, but temperatures began falling at the end of the Cretaceous. Around the beginning of the Paleocene epoch, both seasonal and geographic fluctuations in temperature began to develop. The climate became much drier in many areas, and vast swamplands disappeared. The climate of the Paleocene was generally somewhat cooler than in the late Cretaceous, but by no means cold. Forests and savannas thrived in fairly high latitudes. Subtropical climates existed as far north as latitude 62 in Alaska.[5]

One important reason for the very different climates of the past is **continental drift** (Figure 5–3). In the early Cretaceous (ca. 135 million years ago), the continents were actually clumped into two large landmasses or "supercontinents"—*Laurasia,* which included North America and Eurasia, and *Gondwanaland,* which included Africa, South America, India, Australia, and Antarctica. By the beginning of the Paleocene (ca. 65 million years ago) Gondwanaland had broken apart, with South America drifting west away from Africa, India drifting east, and Australia and Antarctica drifting south. As the continents changed position, they moved into locations with different climatic conditions. More importantly, however, the very move-

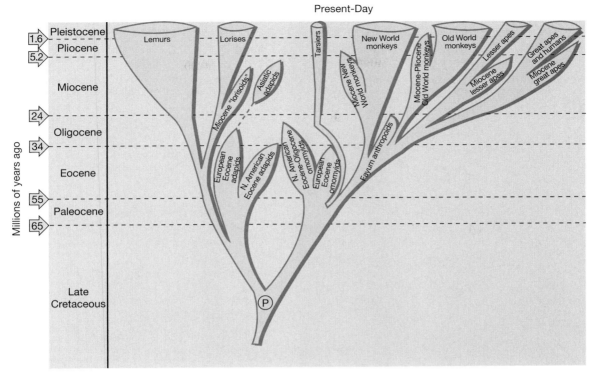

Figure 5–2

A view of the evolutionary relationships between early primates and living primates, adapted from one suggested by R. D. Martin. The primate lineages that do not extend to the present day indicate presumed extinctions. Branching from a common "stalk" suggests divergence from a common ancestor. ℗ represents the unknown common ancestor of all primates. Source: From Robert D. Martin, *Primate Origins and Evolution: A Phylogenetic Reconstruction* (Princeton, NJ: Princeton University Press, 1990). The dates for the Paleocene, Eocene, Oligocene, and the beginning of the Miocene are from William A. Berggren, Dennis V. Kent, John D. Obradovich, and Carl C. Swisher III, "Toward a Revised Paleogene Geochronology," in Donald R. Prothero and William A. Berggren, eds., *Eocene-Oliocene Climatic and Biotic Evolution* (Princeton, NJ: Princeton University Press, 1992), pp. 29–45. The dates for the end of the Miocene, Pliocene, and Pleistocene are from Steve Jones, Robert Martin, and David Pilbeam, eds., *The Cambridge Encyclopedia of Human Evolution.* Copyright © by Cambridge University Press. Reprinted by permission of Cambridge University Press.

ment of the continents affected the climate, sometimes on a global scale.[6]

   CD-ROM Simulation II-7

Large landmasses affect wind and weather patterns differently than smaller landmasses, so weather patterns across Laurasia would have been different from weather in the subsequently separated continents. When continents collide, mountain ranges are formed, and mountains can also have a profound effect on weather patterns. Clouds drop their moisture as they meet a mountain range, and therefore the side away from the prevailing movement of weather systems is often very dry (a condition called a *rain shadow*), whereas the other side (called the *windward side*) is often wet. When the location of continents prevents the movement of ocean currents from the tropics to the poles,

the earth's climate becomes colder. Continental drift and climate change had profound effects on the evolution of the primates.[7]

With changes in climate come changes in vegetation. Although the first deciduous trees (that lose their leaves in winter) and flowering plants (called *angiosperms*) arose during the Cretaceous, it was during the late Paleocene and early Eocene that large trees with large fruits and seeds became common.[8] New species of animals evolved as the climate and environment changed. Although some mammals date from the Cretaceous, the Paleocene saw the evolution and diversification of many different types of mammal, and the expansion and diversification of deciduous trees and flowering plants probably played a large role in mammalian expansion and diversification. Indeed, primate paleontologists think primates evolved from one of these mammalian *radiations,* or extensive diversifications, probably from the **insectivore** order of mammals, including modern shrews and moles, that is adapted to

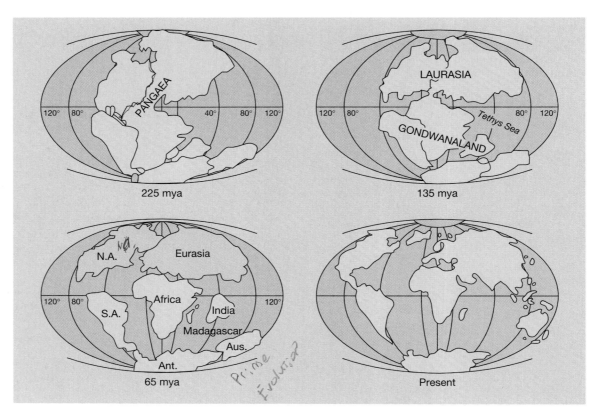

Figure 5–3 *Continental Drift*

The supercontinent Pangea split into Laurasia and Gondwanaland 135 million years ago (mya). These further divided into the continents as we know them today. Source: Noel T. Boaz and Alan J. Almquist, *Biological Anthropology.* Copyright © 1997. Reprinted by permission of Pearson Education, Inc., Upper Saddle River, NJ 07458.

eating insects—insects that would have lived off the new deciduous trees and flowering plants.

To put it simply, the new kinds of plant life opened up sources of food and protection for new animal forms. Of most interest to us is that the new plant life provided an abundant food supply for insects. The result was that insects proliferated in both number and variety, and in turn there was an increase in *insectivores*—the mammals that ate the insects. The insectivores were very adaptable and were able to take advantage of many different habitats—under the ground, in water, on the ground, and above the ground, including the woody habitat of bushes, shrubs, vines, and trees. It was the last kind of adaptation, above the ground, that may have been the most important for primate evolution. The woody habitat had been exploited only partially in earlier periods. But then several different kinds, or *taxa,* of small animals, one of which may have been the archaic primate, began to take advantage of the woody habitat.

WHAT IN PARTICULAR MAY HAVE FAVORED THE EMERGENCE OF PRIMATES?

The traditional explanation of primate origins is called the *arboreal theory.* According to this view, the primates

evolved from insectivores that took to the trees. Different paleoanthropologists emphasized different possible adaptations to life in the trees. In 1912, G. Elliot Smith suggested that taking to the trees favored vision over smell. Searching for food by sniffing and feeling with the snout might suit terrestrial insectivores, but vision would be more useful in an animal that searched for food in the maze of tree branches. With smaller snouts and the declining importance of the sense of smell, the eyes of the early primates would have come to face forward. In 1916, Frederic Wood Jones emphasized changes in the hand and foot. He thought that tree climbing would favor grasping hands and feet, with the hind limbs becoming more specialized for support and propulsion. In 1921, Treacher Collins suggested that the eyes of the early primates came to face forward not just because the snout got smaller. Rather, he thought that three-dimensional binocular vision would be favored because an animal jumping from branch to branch would be more likely to survive if it could accurately judge distances across open space.[9] In 1968, Frederick Szalay suggested that a shift in diet—from insects to seeds, fruits, and leaves—might have been important in the differentiation of primates from insectivores.[10]

Arboreal theory still has some proponents, but Matt

Cartmill highlighted some crucial weaknesses in the theory.[11] He argued that tree living is not a good explanation for many of the primate features because there are living mammals that dwell in trees but seem to do very well without primate-like characteristics. One of the best examples, Cartmill says, is the tree squirrel. Its eyes are not front-facing, its sense of smell is not reduced in comparison with other rodents, it has claws rather than nails, and it lacks an opposable thumb. Yet these squirrels are very successful in trees. They can leap accurately from tree to tree, they can walk over or under small branches, they can go up and down vertical surfaces, and they can even hang from their hind legs to get food below them. Furthermore, other animals have some primate traits but do not live in trees or do not move around in trees as primates do. For example, carnivores, such as cats, hawks, and owls, have forward-facing eyes, and the chameleon, a reptile, and some Australian marsupial mammals that prey on insects in bushes and shrubs have grasping hands and feet.

Cartmill thinks, then, that some factor other than moving about in trees may account for the emergence of the primates. He proposes that the early primates may have been basically insect-eaters, and that three-dimensional vision, grasping hands and feet, and reduced claws may have been selectively advantageous for hunting insects on the slender vines and branches that filled the undergrowth of tropical forests. Three-dimensional vision would allow the insect hunter to gauge the prey's distance accurately. Grasping feet would allow the predator to move quietly up narrow supports to reach the prey, which could then be grabbed with the hands. Claws, Cartmill argues, would make it difficult to grasp very slender branches. And the sense of smell would have become reduced, not so much because it was no longer useful, but because the location of the eyes at the front of the face would leave less room for a snout. (See the box "Matt Cartmill Reexamines His Own Theory" for a discussion of Cartmill's recent revision in response to criticisms.)

Robert Sussman's theory builds on Cartmill's *visual predation theory* and on Szalay's idea about a dietary shift.[12] Sussman accepts Cartmill's point that the early primates were likely to eat and move about mostly on small branches, not on large trunks and branches (as do squirrels). If they did, grasping hands and feet, and nails rather than claws (as squirrels have) would have been advantageous. Sussman also accepts Szalay's point that the early primates probably ate the new types of plant food (flowers, seeds, and fruits) that were beginning to become abundant, as flowering trees and plants spread throughout the world. But Sussman asks an important question: If the early primates ate mostly plant foods rather than quick-moving insects, why did they become more reliant on vision than on smell? Sussman suggests it was because the early primates were probably nocturnal (as many prosimians still are): If they were to locate and manipulate small food items at the ends of slender branches in dim light, they would need improved vision.

We still have very little fossil evidence of the earliest primates. When more fossils become available, we may be better able to evaluate the various explanations that have been suggested for the emergence of primates.

THE EARLY PRIMATES: WHAT THEY LOOKED LIKE

The earliest definite (undisputed) primates, dating back to the Eocene epoch, appear abruptly in what is now North America, Europe, and Asia about 55 million years ago. At that time Laurasia, the supercontinent made up of North America and Eurasia linked though Greenland was still a single landmass, though it would separate by the middle Eocene. Africa was not yet connected to Eurasia, nor was India, but both would make contact with the Eurasian landmass by the end of the Oligocene, initiating dramatic climatic changes that we will discuss later. The beginning of the Eocene was warmer and less seasonal than the Paleocene, and vast tropical forests abounded.[13]

The anatomy of the diverse Eocene primates suggests that they already had many of the features of modern primates—nails rather than claws, a grasping, opposable first toe, and a bony bar around the side of the eye socket.[14] Vertical clinging and leaping was probably a common method of locomotion. Eocene prosimians not only moved around the way modern prosimians do; some were similar skeletally to living prosimians.

EARLY EOCENE PRIMATES: OMOMYIDS AND ADAPIDS

Two groups of prosimians appear in the early Eocene. One group, called **omomyids,** had many tarsierlike features; the other group, **adapids,** had many lemurlike features. The omomyids were very small, no bigger than squirrels; the adapids were kitten- and cat-sized.

Omomyids are considered tarsierlike because of their large eyes, long tarsal bones, and very small size. The large eyes suggest that they were active at night; the smaller-sized omomyids may have been insect-eaters and the larger ones may have relied more on fruit.[15] Most of the omomyids had dental formulas characteristic of modern prosimians: two incisors and three premolars on each side of the lower jaw rather than the three incisors and four premolars of early mammals.[16] The importance of vision is apparent in a fossilized skull of the Eocene omomyid *Tetonius.* Imprints in the skull show that the brain had large occipital and temporal lobes, the regions associated with perception and the integration of visual memory.[17]

The lemurlike adapids were more active during the day and relied more on leaf and fruit vegetation. In contrast to the omomyids, adapid remains show considerable sexual dimorphism in the canines. And they retain the four premolars characteristic of earlier mammals (although with fewer incisors).[18] One adapid known from its abundant fossil finds is *Notharctus.* It had a small, broad face with full stereoscopic vision and a reduced muzzle. It appears to have lived in the forest and had long, powerful hind legs for leaping from tree to tree.[19]

RESEARCH FRONTIERS

Matt Cartmill Reexamines His Own Theory of Primate Origins

Matt Cartmill originally conceived his visual predation theory to explain primate origins because he thought that the arboreal theory did not explain enough. Why do other animals, such as tree squirrels, manage very well in the trees, even though they don't have primate traits? Cartmill's theory attracted some criticism. How did he respond?

One criticism, by J. Allman, is that if visual predation is such an important predictor of forward-facing eyes, then why don't some visual predators have such eyes? Cats and owls have forward-facing eyes, but mongooses and robins do not. A second criticism, by Paul Garber, is that if claws were disadvantageous for moving on slender branches, why does at least one small primate—the Panamanian tamarin—feed on insects among small twigs and vines but have claws on four of its five digits? And Robert Sussman pointed out that most small nocturnal prosimians eat more fruit than insects. Sussman suggests that the need for precise finger manipulation to grasp small fruits and flowers at the ends of small branches, while hanging on by the hind feet, might favor both clawless digits and grasping extremities.

Cartmill acknowledged these problems and responded to them by revising his theory. He also suggests how new research could test some of the implications of his revised theory.

In regard to the problem of forward-facing eyes, Cartmill says that Allman's own research suggests a solution: namely, that forward-facing eyes are advantageous for seeing something in front more clearly in dim light. Daytime predators have eye pupils that constrict to see ahead more clearly, so fully forward-facing eyes are not necessary for daytime predation. Nocturnal predators relying on sight are more likely to have forward-facing eyes because constricting pupils would be disadvantageous at night. So Cartmill now believes that the earliest primates were probably nocturnal. And he now thinks that they also probably ate fruit (in addition to insects), as Sussman suggests, just as many contemporary nocturnal prosimians do. If they ate fruit and insects at the ends of small branches and twigs, claws may have been disadvantageous. The Panamanian tamarin is not a case to the contrary; it has claws, to be sure, but it also eats tree gum on the tree trunks to which it clings, using its claws as a tree squirrel does.

Cartmill thinks that his modified theory explains the changes in primate vision better than Sussman's theory. For example, how can we explain stereoscopic, forward-facing eyes in the early primates? Sussman says that the early primates were fruit-eaters, but Cartmill points out that, although stereoscopic, forward-facing eyes are not necessary for getting nonmoving fruit. Rather, forward-facing eyes might be essential for catching insects.

Cartmill suggests how future research on other arboreal mammals may help us answer some of the remaining questions about the origins of primates. Arboreal marsupials, for instance, tend to have grasping hind feet with clawless divergent first toes, and many have reduced claws on some other toes and fingers. The eyes of arboreal marsupials are also somewhat convergent (not as much, of course, as the eyes of primates). One genus of marsupial, an opposum in South America (*Caluromys*), has many additional primatelike features, including a relatively large brain, more forward-facing eyes, a short snout, and a small number of offspring at one time. Studies by Tab Rasmussen suggest that *Caluromys* fits both Cartmill's and Sussman's theories because it eats fruit on terminal branches and catches insect prey with its hands. More field research on marsupials and other animals with some primatelike habits or features could tell us a lot more. So would new fossil finds.

Sources: Matt Cartmill, "Explaining Primate Origins," in Peter N. Peregrine, Carol R. Ember, and Melvin Ember, eds., *Physical Anthropology: Original Readings in Method and Practice* (Upper Saddle River, NJ: Prentice Hall, 2002); Matt Cartmill, "New Views on Primate Origins," *Evolutionary Anthropology,* 1 (1992): 105–11; Robert Sussman, "Primate Origins and the Evolution of Angiosperms," *American Journal of Primatology,* 23 (1991): 209–23; D. Tab Rasmussen, "Primate Origins: Lessons from a Neotropical Marsupial," *American Journal of Primatology,* 22 (1990): 263–77.

There was a great deal of diversity among all mammals during the Eocene epoch, and the primates were no exception. Evolution seems to have proceeded rapidly during those years. Both the omomyids and adapids had a few features that suggest links between them and the anthropoids that appear later, in the Oligocene, but there is no agreement that either group gave rise to the anthropoids.[20] Although the omomyids had some resemblances to modern tarsiers and the adapids had some resemblances to lemurs and lorises, paleoanthropologists are not sure that either group was ancestral to modern prosimians. But it is generally thought that the populations ancestral to lemurs and lorises as well as tarsiers did emerge in the Eocene or even earlier, in the late Paleocene.[21]

The Emergence of Anthropoids

The anthropoids of today—monkeys, apes, and humans—are the most successful living primates and include well over 150 species. Unfortunately, the fossil record documenting the emergence of the anthropoids is extremely spotty, and there is no clear fossil record of the Old World forms (the catarrhines) in the two areas where they are most abundant today—the rain forests of sub-Saharan Africa and Southeast Asia.[22] Some paleoanthropologists think that recent Eocene primate finds from China, Southeast Asia, and Algeria have anthropoid affinities, but there is no clear agreement on their evolutionary status.[23]

Although the Fayum depression is a desert today, it was a tropical forest in the Oligocene. The area is littered with the fossilized remains of tropical plants and the animals that fed on them, including primates.

Undisputed remains of early anthropoids date from a somewhat later period, the late Eocene and early Oligocene, about 34 million years ago, in the **Fayum** area, southwest of Cairo, Egypt. One of the earliest fossil primates at Fayum is *Catopithecus*, dating to around 35 million years ago. Several recent finds have made it one of the best known late Eocene primates. *Catopithecus* was about the size of a modern marmoset or squirrel monkey. Its dentition suggests a mixed diet of fruit and insects. Its eyes were small, suggesting it was active during the day (diurnal). The few skeletal remains of *Catopithecus* suggest it was an agile arboreal quadruped. It may be the best candidate for the earliest anthropoid, though how it was related to other primates is still debated.[24]

OLIGOCENE ANTHROPOIDS

The Fayum is an uninviting area of desert badlands, but it has yielded a remarkable array of early anthropoid fossils. During the **Oligocene** epoch, 34 million to 24 million years ago, the Fayum was a tropical rain forest very close to the shores of the Mediterranean Sea. The area had a warm climate, and it contained many rivers and lakes. The Fayum, in fact, was far more inviting than the northern continents then, for the climates of both North America and Eurasia were beginning to cool during the Oligocene. The general cooling seems to have resulted in the virtual disappearance of primates from the northern areas, at least for a time.

Oligocene anthropoids from the Fayum are grouped into two main types: the monkeylike **parapithecids** and the apelike **propliopithecids.** Dating from 35 million to 31 million years ago,[25] the parapithecids and the propliopithecids had enough features to be unquestionably classified as anthropoids.

PARAPITHECIDS The monkeylike parapithecids had three premolars (in each quarter), as do most prosimians and the New World monkeys. They were similar to modern anthropoids, with a bony partition behind the eye sockets, broad incisors, projecting canines, and low, rounded cusps on their molars. But they had prosimian-like premolars and relatively small brains. The parapithecids were small, generally weighing under 3 pounds, and resembled the squirrel monkeys living now in South and Central America.[26] Their relatively small eye sockets suggest that they were not nocturnal. Their teeth suggest that they ate mostly fruits and seeds. Locomotion is best known from one of the parapithecids, *Apidium*, an arboreal quadruped that also did a considerable amount of leaping.[27] The parapithecids are the earliest definite anthropoid group, and although there is still disagreement among paleoanthropologists, most believe that the emergence of the anthropoids preceded the split between the New World monkeys (platyrrhines) and the Old World monkeys (catarrhines).[28]

That parapithecids may be ancestral to New World monkeys (platyrrhines) raises an interesting puzzle in

A reconstruction of what two Oligocene primates might have looked like. In the foreground is a group of *Aegyptopithecus,* in the background are two individuals of *Apidium.* Some of the fauna that shared the Fayum region with these early primates are also shown.

primate evolution: the origin of the New World monkeys. Anthropoidal primates such as *Dolichocebus,* a small fruit-eating monkey similar to the modern squirrel monkey,[29] appear suddenly and without any apparent ancestors in South America around 25 million years ago. Since the parapithecids predate the appearance of anthropoids in South America, and resemble them in many ways, it seems reasonable to view them as part of the population ancestral to the New World monkeys.[30]

But how did anthropoidal primates get from Africa to South America? Although the continents were closer together in the late Oligocene, when primates first appear in South America, at least 3,000 kilometers separated South America and Africa. An extended continental shelf and islands created by lower sea levels in the late Oligocene may have made it possible to "island-hop" from Africa to South America over ocean stretches as short as 200 kilometers, but that is still a long distance for an arboreal primate.

Going from Africa to Europe and North America, which were still joined in the late Oligocene, is not a likely route either. North America and South America were not joined until some 5 million years ago, so even if the ancestors of the New World monkeys made it to North America, they would still have needed to make a long ocean crossing to reach South America. One suggestion is that the ancestors of the New World monkeys "rafted" across the Atlantic on large mats of vegetation. Such "rafts," of matted plants, roots, and soil, break away from the mouths of major rivers today, and they can be quite large. It seems an unlikely scenario, but many scholars believe such drifting vegetation must have been the means of bringing anthropoids to South America.[31]

PROPLIOPITHECIDS The other type of anthropoid found in the Fayum, the propliopithecids, had the dental formula of modern catarrhines. This trait clearly places the propliopithecids with the catarrhines.[32] In contrast with the parapithecids, which had three premolars, the propliopithecids had only two premolars, as do modern apes, humans, and Old World monkeys. Propliopithecids shared with the parapithecids the anthropoid dental characteristics of broad lower incisors, projecting canines, and lower molars with low, rounded cusps. And, like parapithecids, propliopithecids had a bony partition behind the eye socket.

Aegyptopithecus, the best-known propliopithecid, probably moved around quadrupedally in the trees, and weighed about 13 pounds. Its molars were low with large cusps, and it had relatively large incisors, suggesting that *Aegyptopithecus* ate mostly fruit. Its eyes were relatively small, and thus it was probably active during the day. It had a long muzzle and a relatively small brain. Endocasts of the brain cavity suggest *Aegyptopithecus* had a relatively large area of the brain dedicated to vision and a relatively small area dedicated to smell. The skulls of *Aegyptopithecus* show considerable sexual dimorphism, and individuals also changed dramatically as they aged, developing bony ridges along the top and across the back of the skull, much like modern great apes. Although its teeth, jaws, and some aspects of the skull were apelike, the rest of *Aegypto-*

The fossil skull of an *Aegyptopithecus* from the Fayum. Its dentition, its small, bony eye sockets, and its relatively large brain make it an unambiguous ancestor of Old World monkeys and apes.

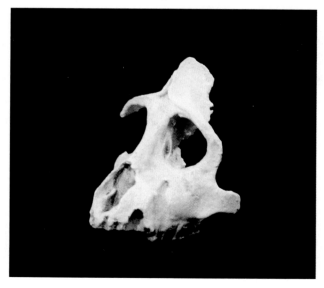

pithecus's skeleton was monkeylike,[33] and they are classified by most scholars as primitive catarrhines. Because the propliopithecids lack the specialized characteristics of living Old World monkeys and apes (catarrhines), but share the dental formula of the catarrhines, some paleoanthropologists think that the propliopithecids included the ancestor of both the Old World monkeys and the hominoids (apes and humans).[34]

The Miocene Anthropoids: Monkeys, Apes, and Hominids(?)

During the **Miocene** epoch, 24 million to 5.2 million years ago, monkeys and apes clearly diverged in appearance, and numerous kinds of apes appeared in Europe, Asia, and Africa. In the early Miocene, the temperatures were considerably warmer than in the Oligocene. From early to late Miocene, conditions became drier,[35] particularly in East Africa. The reasons for this relate again to continental drift. By about 18 million years ago, Africa came into contact with Eurasia, ending the moderating effect that the Tethys Sea, which separated Africa from Eurasia, had on the climates of both continents. The contact of Africa and, more significantly, India with the Eurasian continent also initiated mountain building, changing established weather patterns. The overall effect was that southern Eurasia and eastern Africa became considerably drier than they had been. Once again, these changes appear to have significantly influenced primate evolution.

We can infer that late in the Miocene, between about 8 million and 5 million years ago, the direct ancestor of humans—the first hominid—may have emerged in Africa.

The inference about *where* hominids emerged is based on the fact that undisputed hominids lived in East Africa after about 5 million years ago. The inference about *when* hominids emerged is based not on fossil evidence but on comparative molecular and biochemical analyses of modern apes and humans. As we will see in the next chapter, the effect of a drier climate and the creation of more open, grassland environments may have directly influenced the evolution of the hominids.

One of the Miocene apes (known or unknown) was ancestral to hominids, so our discussion here deals mostly with the *proto-apes*—anthropoids with some apelike characteristics—of the early Miocene and the definite apes of the middle and late Miocene. But before we get to the apes, we should say something about monkeys and prosimians in the Miocene. Unfortunately, monkey fossils from the early Miocene are rare. In the New World, the whole Miocene fossil record is quite empty. There are only a few primate fossils found in Colombia and Argentina; they show close affinities with present-day South American monkeys. In the Old World, early Miocene monkey fossils have been found only in northern Africa. The situation is different for the middle and late Miocene: Old World monkey fossils become much more abundant than ape fossils.[36] As for prosimians, fossils from the Miocene are scarce, but we know that at least some adapids survived into the middle Miocene in India and the late Miocene in China.[37] Some lorislike prosimians appear in East Africa, Pakistan, and India during the Miocene.[38]

EARLY MIOCENE PROTO-APES

Most of the fossils from the early Miocene are described as proto-apes. They have been found mostly in Africa. The

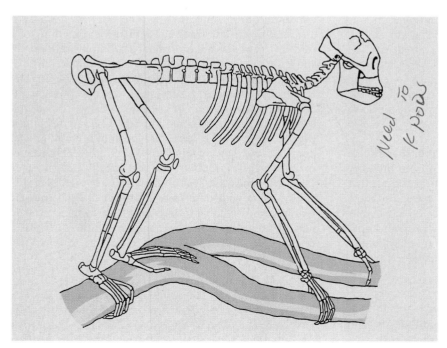

Figure 5–4

The forelimbs and hind limbs of Proconsul africanus *(dating from about 20 million years ago) are about the same length, suggesting that it moved on all fours on the tops of branches.* Proconsul africanus *was the smallest of the* Proconsul *species, weighing about 22 to 26 pounds. Source:* From *New Interpretation of Ape and Human Ancestry* by R. Ciochon and R. Corruccina, eds. Copyright © 1983 by Plenum Publishers. Reprinted by permission of Plenum Publishers.

A reconstruction of what *Heliopithecus,* a close relative of *Kenyapithecus,* may have looked like.

best-known genus is **Proconsul,** found in sites in Kenya and Uganda that are about 20 million years old.[39]

All of the various *Proconsul* species that have been found were much bigger than any of the anthropoids of the Oligocene, ranging from about the size of a gibbon to that of a female gorilla.[40] They lacked a tail. That lack is one of the most definitive features of hominoids, and most paleoanthropologists now agree that *Proconsul* was definitely hominoid, but quite unlike any ape living today. Modern hominoids have many anatomical features of the shoulder, elbow, wrists, and fingers that are adapted for locomotion by suspension (brachiation). Suspension was apparently not *Proconsul*'s method of getting around. Its elbows, wrists, and fingers may have permitted brachiation,[41] but, like the Oligocene anthropoids, *Proconsul* was primarily an arboreal quadruped (see Figure 5–4). Some of the larger forms may have sometimes moved on the ground. Judging by teeth, most *Proconsul* species appear to have been fruit-eaters, but larger species may have also consumed leaves.[42]

If *Proconsul* is the best-known group of the many kinds of primates with some hominoid features from the early Miocene, some recent finds from East Africa suggest that other types of proto-ape were also on the scene. But these other finds are fragmentary and not clearly classifiable. *Proconsul* may or may not have been ancestral to later apes and humans, but given its combination of monkeylike and apelike features, it may have looked a lot like the common ancestor of apes and humans.[43]

MIDDLE MIOCENE APES

The first definitely apelike finds come from East Africa in the middle Miocene, 16 million to 10 million years ago.

The fossils, on Maboko Island and nearby locations in Kenya, include several kinds of primate—a prosimian, several types of Old World monkeys, and a definite hominoid, **Kenyapithecus.**[44]

Kenyapithecus has many of *Proconsul*'s features, but its molars resemble those of more modern hominoids. And, in contrast to *Proconsul, Kenyapithecus* was probably more terrestrial. It also had very thickly enameled teeth and robust jaws, suggesting a diet of hard, tough foods, or possibly a great deal of grit in the food because *Kenyapithecus* lived mostly on the ground. Finds similar to *Kenyapithecus* appear in Europe and Turkey. Whether *Kenyapithecus* is ancestral to the later apes and humans is something of a puzzle.[45] Its molars are more modern, but its limbs do not show the capacity for brachiation that is characteristic of all the later apes.[46] Then again, perhaps Sue Savage-Rumbaugh is correct in suggesting that the common ancestor of apes and humans was essentially a biped. According to her argument, knuckle walking may have evolved as a mode of terrestrial locomotion only in later apes. Because they are knuckle walkers, living apes cannot make a snapping motion with the hand (which is called "abducting the wrist"), as humans uniquely can.[47] This last ability, along with other things hands can do if they are not involved in locomotion, may have been crucial in making complete bipedalism adaptive in the earliest humans, as we will discuss in the next chapter.

LATE MIOCENE APES

From the end of the middle Miocene into the late Miocene, the apes diversified and moved into many areas. Fossils are abundant in Europe and Asia, less so in Africa. This does not mean that apes were more numerous than monkeys. In fact, the fossil record suggests that monkeys in the Old World became more and more numerous than apes toward the end of the Miocene, and this trend continues to the present day. There are many more monkey than ape species now. The climate throughout the Miocene was turning cooler and drier, which probably favored more drought-resistant plants with thicker cell walls. Modern monkeys tend to be more adapted than apes for eating leaves, so monkeys may have had an advantage in the changing environment toward the end of the Miocene, and since.[48]

One well-known late Miocene ape from Europe is *Oreopithecus,* which dates from about 8 million years ago. It is particularly interesting because, despite being well represented by fossils, including nearly complete ones preserved in beds of hard coal, its classification is enigmatic. *Oreopithecus* was clearly adapted to life in thickly forested marshlands. It had extremely long arms and hands and mobile joints, and was likely an agile brachiator. Its dentition suggests it had a diet that consisted mostly of leaves. However, the dentition and skull of *Oreopithecus* also had a number of unique features that suggest affinity to some Old World monkeys. In short, *Oreopithecus* had an apelike body and a monkeylike head. Because of its suspensory locomotion and other apelike features, most scholars today consider it an early, albeit specialized, ape.[49]

Most paleoanthropologists divide the later Miocene apes into at least two main groups: the sivapithecids, represented primarily by the genus *Sivapithecus* and found primarily in western and southern Asia, and the dryopithecids, represented primarily by the genus *Dryopithecus* and found primarily in Europe.[50]

SIVAPITHECIDS At one time **Sivapithecus,** which dates from roughly 13 million to 8 million years ago, was thought to be ancestral to hominids. It had flat and thickly enameled molars, smaller canines, and less sexual dimorphism than other Miocene apes, and in some reconstructions (now considered faulty) had a parabolic dental arcade—all hominid features. It also lived in a mixed woodland-grassland environment, and the wear on its teeth suggested a diet of coarse grasses and seeds, much like the diet of the later early hominids (although some scholars argue that the *Sivapithecus* diet was focused on fruit with coarse pits rather than on grasses and seeds). However, as more fossil material was uncovered, scholars recognized that *Sivapithecus* was remarkably similar to the modern orangutan in the face, and it is now thought to be ancestral to the orangutan.[51]

The closely related *Gigantopithecus* was similar in its teeth to *Sivapithecus,* but, as its name suggests, it was huge, perhaps 10 feet tall erect.[52] Some paleoanthropologists suggest that *Gigantopithecus* weighed over 600 pounds and got even larger over the nearly 10 million years of its existence.[53] (See the box "What Happened to *Gigantopithecus*?") *Gigantopithecus* was restricted to the forests of Southeast Asia, and is thought to have had a diet focused on bamboo.

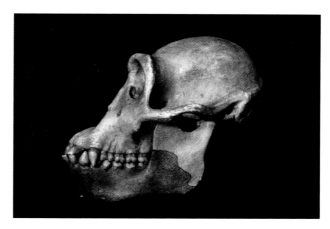

The reconstructed skull of a *Dryopithecus* strongly resembles that of modern African apes.

DRYOPITHECIDS *Dryopithecus,* which appears about 15 million years ago, was a chimpanzee-sized ape that lived in the forests of Eurasia. It was mainly arboreal and apparently omnivorous. *Dryopithecus* had thinner tooth enamel than *Sivapithecus,* lighter jaws, and pointed molar cusps. In the palate, jaw, and midface, *Dryopithecus* looked like the African apes and humans. In contrast to later hominoids, however, *Dryopithecus* had a very short face and a relatively small brow ridge.[54]

The fingers and elbows of *Dryopithecus* and *Sivapithecus* suggest that they were much more capable of suspending themselves than were earlier hominoids. *Sivapithecus* may have moved about more on the ground than *Dryopithecus,* but both were probably mostly arboreal.[55] Indeed, recent finds of *Dryopithecus* hand, arm, shoulder, and leg bones strongly suggest that *Dryopithecus* was highly efficient at suspensory locomotion and probably moved through the trees like modern orangutans do.

It is still very difficult to identify the particular evolutionary lines leading from the Miocene apes to modern apes and humans. Only the orangutans have been linked to a late Miocene ape genus, *Sivapithecus*, so presumably that lineage continued into modern times.[56] *Dryopithecus* disappears from the fossil record after about 10 million years ago, leaving no descendants, perhaps because less rainfall and more seasonality reduced the forests where they lived.[57]

The Divergence of Hominids from the Other Hominoids

The later Miocene apes are best known from Europe and Asia. There is almost a complete gap in the African fossil record between 13.5 million and 5 million years ago.[58] This gap is unfortunate for our understanding of human evolution because the earliest known bipedal primates (hominids) appear in Africa near the beginning of the Pliocene, after 5 million years ago. To understand the

RESEARCH FRONTIERS

What Happened to Gigantopithecus?

In studying human evolution we tend to focus on the primate lineages that presumably are ancestral to modern humans and our closest primate cousins. There were, however, other primate lineages that left no apparent descendants but were very successful in the sense that they persisted for millions of years. The first definite primates, the omomyids and the adapids, first appeared early in the Eocene and stayed for more than 20 million years, much longer than bipedal hominids have been around! Why some primates were successful for so long is an important question; so is why they became extinct. To understand evolution, we need to investigate not only why some form may have survived for a while; we need also to investigate why it died out. For example, what happened to the largest primate, *Gigantopithecus*, that ever lived?

A paleoanthropologist, Russell Ciochon, and an archaeologist, John Olsen, have searched for clues to understanding the extinction of "Giganto," as they call it, which apparently left no

descendants living in the world today. Ciochon and Olsen think that the largest form of *Gigantopithecus, G. blacki*, persisted for at least 5 million years and did not become extinct until about 250,000 years ago. And if you count earlier *Gigantopithecus* forms, the genus may have been around for nearly 10 million years. Ciochon and Olsen think it likely that Giganto and *Homo erectus*, a hominid that looked very much like modern humans from the head down, met up about a quarter of a million years ago in at least two Asian locations—now parts of China and Vietnam. The possible contact with *H. erectus* may have been partly responsible for the demise of Giganto.

What did Giganto look like? Reconstruction requires some guesswork, particularly with Giganto, because the only remains we have are teeth and jaw fragments. But we can reasonably infer some of Giganto's features and measurements from the body proportions of existing apes and the more complete fossil remains of extinct apes. Thus,

Gigantopithecus probably lived mostly on bamboo. It is the largest primate known to us. The genus survived for about 10 million years and only became extinct 250,000 years ago. Bill Munns is shown here with the model of "Giganto" that he and Russell Ciochon reconstructed.

it is estimated that Giganto was 10 feet tall and weighed over 600 pounds.

What did Giganto eat? Ciochon's guess is that Giganto ate

---

evolutionary links between the apes of the Miocene and the hominids of Africa, we need more fossil evidence from late Miocene times in Africa.

However, we do have some idea about the transition to hominids. The molecular biology of the various modern primates suggests when the last common ancestor of humans and our closest primate relatives, chimpanzees, probably lived.

THE MOLECULAR CLOCK

In 1966, on the basis of biochemical comparisons of blood proteins in the different surviving primates, Vincent

Sarich and Allan Wilson estimated that gibbons diverged from the other hominoids about 12 million years ago, orangutans 10 million years ago, and the other apes (gorillas and chimps) from hominids only 4.5 million years ago. These estimates depended on the assumption that the more similar in chemistry the blood proteins of different primates are—for instance, comparing chimpanzees and humans—the closer those primates are in evolutionary time. In other words, the more similar the blood proteins of related species, the more recently they diverged.[59]

But knowing that species are close molecularly does not translate into evolutionary time unless it is assumed that molecular changes occur at a constant rate. After all,

mostly bamboo from the then-plentiful bamboo forests. The large size of the jaw, the wear patterns on the teeth, and the fact that large primates eat mostly foods with a lot of cellulose all suggest a diet of bamboo or something like it. Another kind of evidence suggests the same conclusion. A student had suggested to Ciochon that he look for phytoliths on the fossil teeth of Giganto. Phytoliths are microscopic granules of silicon dioxide that enter a plant's cells and take their shape. When the plants decompose, the phytoliths remain. Different plants have phytoliths of different shapes.

So, on the chance that phytoliths were on the fossil teeth from Giganto, the researchers looked microscopically at the teeth. They found phytoliths that belong to a family of grasses as well as phytoliths from a kind of fruit. Bamboo is a kind of grass, so the phytoliths found on the Giganto teeth are consistent with both bamboo- and fruit-eating. The teeth revealed something else too. Many showed pitting of the tooth enamel (hypoplasias), which suggests that Giganto suffered periodically from malnutrition. (Hypoplasias are produced by dietary insufficiencies.)

Bamboo forests are found almost everywhere in China and Southeast Asia, but for reasons not yet understood they dwindle every 20 years or so. If Giganto ate bamboo, it would have had a serious problem every so often, which is consistent with the hypoplasias. Could the extinction of Giganto be linked to something that happened to the bamboo forests? Perhaps. Giant pandas, which are bamboo-eaters almost exclusively, are now at risk of extinction because of the spread of humans throughout China and Southeast Asia. Bamboo is used by humans for shelter, boats, tools, and food (bamboo shoots), and the bamboo forests are now drastically reduced. In their time, *H. erectus* may also have reduced the bamboo forests, thus contributing to the demise of Giganto. It is also possible that *H. erectus* hunted Giganto for food. This possibility is very speculative, but nonhuman primates have been hunted for food by many recent human societies. Like the giant panda, Giganto was probably very slow-moving and easy to hunt, as are most megaherbivores.

Humans in different places tell stories about huge, hairy, humanlike creatures—"Bigfoot" or

Sasquatch in northwestern North America, the "Abominable Snowman" or Yeti of the Himalayas. Is it possible that Giganto is still around? Ciochon and Olsen point out that no recent Giganto bones have been found, so it is very unlikely that Giganto is still out there. But perhaps humans continue to believe it because they encountered Giganto in the not-so-distant past. After all, Australian aborigines still tell stories referring to events that happened more than 30,000 years ago.

What we do know is that *Gigantopithecus* persisted for a very long time, until humans came on the scene. Researchers have learned a lot about Giganto from very fragmentary remains. If more fossils are found in the future, we can expect that more will come to be known about the gigantic ape.

a reliable "molecular clock" should not slow down or speed up from one period of time to another. To maximize the likelihood of molecular change at a constant rate, researchers try to examine molecular characteristics that are probably neutral in terms of adaptation. (Natural selection can speed up the rate of molecular change in the case of a characteristic that is very advantageous or very disadvantageous.) The rate of change in a neutral characteristic is calculated from the time of some divergence that is absolutely dated. For example, if we know that two lineages split 20 million years ago, and we know the degree of molecular difference between a contemporary representative of each, we can estimate the rate of change that produced

that degree of difference. Given such an estimated rate of change (in a particular characteristic), we can estimate the amount of time that has elapsed since other pairs of related species diverged from each other.[60]

Subsequent comparative studies of the living primates have employed a variety of techniques, including comparisons of amino acid sequences, chromosomal structures, and the degree of matching of DNA strands from different species. These studies have confirmed the probable recency of the hominid divergence from chimpanzees and gorillas. Although the different techniques yield slightly different estimates, the results are not that divergent. Most of the recent comparisons place the split somewhat earlier than the Sarich and Wilson estimates, but not by much. The common ancestor of chimpanzees and hominids is estimated to have lived 5 million to 6 million years ago, the common ancestor of gorillas and hominids a little farther back.[61]

So what does the fossil evidence tell us about where and when hominids first emerged? Unfortunately, the answer is nothing as yet: We still do not have any definitely hominid fossils in Africa from the end of the Miocene, 8 million to 5 million years ago, the presumed place and time hominids emerged. And definitely hominid fossils dating from the late Miocene have not been found anywhere else. All we know for sure now is that primates with undisputably hominid characteristics lived about 4 million years ago in East Africa. We turn to these undisputed hominids in the next chapter.

Summary

1. We cannot know with certainty how primates evolved. But fossils, a knowledge of ancient environments, and an understanding of comparative anatomy and behavior give us enough clues to have a tentative idea of when, where, and why primates emerged and diverged.

2. The surviving primates—prosimians, New World monkeys, Old World monkeys, apes, and humans—are thought to be descendants of small, originally terrestrial insectivores (the order, or major grouping, of mammals, including modern shrews and moles, that is adapted to feeding on insects). However, exactly who the common ancestor was and when it emerged are not yet known.

3. Fossils dating from the early Eocene, about 55 million years ago, are definitely primates. They appear to fall into two major groups of prosimians—adapids and omomyids. These two kinds of primate are different from each other in major ways, and they both appeared rather abruptly at the border of the Paleocene and Eocene, so their common ancestor would have had to emerge earlier, probably in the Paleocene.

4. What conditions may have favored the emergence of the primates? The proliferation of insects led to an increase in insectivores—the mammals that ate the insects, some of which lived above ground, in the woody habitat of bushes, shrubs, vines, and trees. Eventually, trees with large flowers and fruits evolved. The exploitation of resources in the woody habitat was probably the key adaptation in the emergence of the primates.

5. The traditional view of primate evolution was that arboreal (tree) life would have favored many of the common primate features, including distinctive dentition, greater reliance on vision over smell, three-dimensional binocular vision, and grasping hands and feet. A second theory proposes that some of the distinctive primate characteristics were selectively advantageous for hunting insects on the slender vines and branches that filled the undergrowth of forests. A third theory suggests that the distinctive features of primates (including reliance more

on vision than on smell) were favored because the early primates were nocturnal and ate flowers, fruits, and seeds, which they had to locate on slender branches in dim light.

6. Undisputed remains of early anthropoids unearthed in Egypt date from the early Oligocene (after 34 million years ago). They include the monkeylike parapithecids and the propliopithecids with apelike teeth.

7. During the Miocene epoch (24 million to 5.2 million years ago), monkeys and apes clearly diverged in appearance, and numerous kinds of apes appeared in Europe, Asia, and Africa. Most of the fossils from the early Miocene are described as proto-apes. From the end of the middle Miocene into the late Miocene, the apes diversified and spread geographically. Most paleoanthropologists divide the later Miocene apes into at least two main groups: dryopithecids, found primarily in Europe, and sivapithecids, found primarily in western and southern Asia.

8. The fossil record does not tell us who the first hominid was, but biochemical and genetic analyses of modern apes and humans suggest that the hominid-ape split occurred during the late Miocene (after about 6 million years ago). Because undisputed hominids lived in East Africa after about 4 million years ago, the first hominid probably emerged in Africa.

Glossary Terms

adapids	Miocene
Aegyptopithecus	Oligocene
continental drift	omomyid
Cretaceous	Paleocene
Dryopithecus	parapithecids
Eocene	*Plesiadipis*
Fayum	*Proconsul*
insectivore	propliopithecids
Kenyapithecus	*Sivapithecus*

Critical Questions

1. What an animal eats and how it gets its food are suggested by its skeletal anatomy. Discuss possible examples in the evolution of the primates.

2. Why do you suppose there are more monkey than ape species?

3. We like to think of the human lineage as biologically unique, which of course it is (like all evolutionary lineages). But some paleoanthropologists say that humans, chimpanzees, and gorillas are so similar that all three should be grouped as hominids. What do you think, and why do you think so?

Internet Exercises

1. Visit the primate evolution page at **http://www. primate.wisc.edu/pin/evolution.html** and follow some of

the links to other pages. Write an essay describing what you found on those pages and how they compared to what you read in this chapter.

2. Visit the University of Leeds Web site and read the lecture by Bill Sellars on primate evolution at **http://www.leeds.ac.uk/chb/lectures/anthl_09.html**.

3. Mary Leakey is best known for her work at Olduvai Gorge, where early hominids were found. But she also played a role in discoveries of anthropoids from the Miocene. Read the article about her at **http://www.sciam. com/explorations/121696explorations.html** and summarize what those discoveries were.

4. Go to **http://www.cruzio.com/~cscp/beard.htm** and read the article Searching for Our Primate Ancestors in China.

 ## Suggested Reading

ANDREWS, P., AND STRINGER, C. *Human Evolution: An Illustrated Guide.* London: British Museum, 1989. A brief introduction to primate and human evolution, illustrated by color reconstructions of many fossil finds.

BEGUN, D. "Miocene Apes." In P. N. Peregrine, C. R. Ember, and M. Ember, eds., *Physical Anthropology: Original Readings in Method and Practice* (Upper Saddle River, NJ: Prentice Hall, 2002). An up-to-date survey of the diversity among Miocene hominoids. Suggests that humans evolved from knuckle walkers.

CARTMILL, M. "Explaining Primate Origins." In P. N. Peregrine, C. R. Ember, and M. Ember, eds., *Physical Anthropology: Original Readings in Method and Practice* (Upper Saddle River, NJ: Prentice Hall, 2002). A review of the major theories of primate origins with a close look at criticisms of his own theory.

CONROY, G. C. *Primate Evolution.* New York: Norton, 1990. Conveys both the consensus and the points of disagreement in theories of primate evolution. Assumes some basic knowledge of physical anthropology and biology.

FLEAGLE, J. G. *Primate Adaptation and Evolution*, 2nd ed. San Diego: Academic Press, 1999. A textbook that examines the comparative anatomy, behavioral ecology, and paleontology of humans and their nearest relatives. Chapters 10–16 are particularly relevant to this chapter.

FLEAGLE, J. G., AND KAY, R. F., EDS. *Anthropoid Origins.* New York: Plenum, 1994. Based on a conference, this book brings together technical information about recent discoveries and current theories concerning the origin and early evolution of anthropoid primates—monkeys, apes, and humans.

MARTIN, R. D. *Primate Origins and Evolution: A Phylogenetic Reconstruction.* Princeton, NJ: Princeton University Press, 1990. The author draws together findings from comparisons of living primates, the fossil record, and molecular evidence to make a provisional synthesis of primate phylogeny.

6

The First Hominids

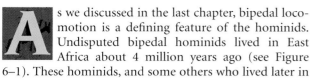s we discussed in the last chapter, bipedal loco-motion is a defining feature of the hominids. Undisputed bipedal hominids lived in East Africa about 4 million years ago (see Figure 6–1). These hominids, and some others who lived later in eastern and southern Africa, are generally classified in the genus ***Australopithecus.*** In this chapter we discuss what we know or suspect about the emergence of australo-pithecines and their relationship to later hominids, in-cluding ourselves.

 The Evolution of Bipedal Locomotion

Perhaps the most crucial change in early hominid evolu-tion was the development of *bipedal locomotion,* or walk-ing on two legs. We know from the fossil record that other important physical changes—including the expansion of the brain, modification of the female pelvis to allow bigger-brained babies to be born, and reduction of the

Figure 6–1
The Evolution of the Australopithecines

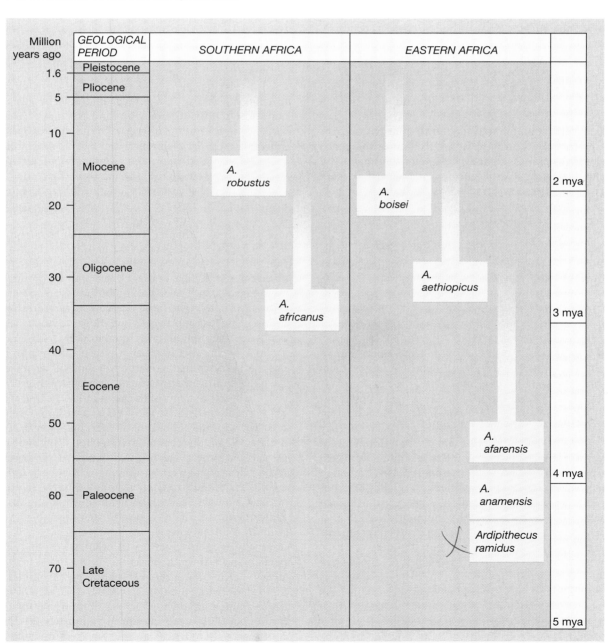

face, teeth, and jaws—did not occur until about 2 million years after the emergence of bipedalism. Other human characteristics, such as an extended period of infant and child dependency and increased meat-eating, may also have developed after that time.

We do not know whether bipedalism developed quickly or gradually, because the fossil record for the period between 8 million and 4 million years ago is very skimpy. We do know, on the basis of their skeletal anatomy, that many of the Miocene anthropoids were capable of assuming an upright posture. For example, *brachiation,* swinging by the arms through the trees, puts an animal in an upright position; so does climbing up and down trees with the use of grasping hands and feet. It is also likely that the protohominids were capable of occasional bipedalism, just as many modern monkeys and apes are.[1]

As we noted at the end of the last chapter, definitely bipedal hominids apparently emerged first in Africa. The physical environment in Africa was changing from extensive tropical forest cover to more discontinuous patches of forest and open country.[2] About 16 million to 11 million years ago, a drying trend set in that continued into the Pliocene. Gradually, the African rain forests, deprived of intense humidity and rainfall, dwindled in extent; areas of **savanna** (grasslands) and scattered deciduous woodlands became more common. The tree-dwelling primates did not completely lose their customary habitats, because some tropical forests remained in wetter regions, and natural selection continued to favor the better adapted tree dwellers in those forested areas. But the new, more open country probably favored characteristics adapted to ground living in some primates as well as other animals. In the evolutionary line leading to humans, these adaptations included bipedalism.

THEORIES FOR THE EVOLUTION OF BIPEDALISM

What in particular may have favored the emergence of bipedal hominids? There are several possible explanations for this development. One idea is that bipedalism was adaptive for life amid the tall grasses of the savannas because an erect posture may have made it easier to spot ground predators as well as potential prey.[3] This theory does not adequately account for the development of bipedalism, however. Baboons and some other Old World monkeys also live in savanna environments, yet, although they can stand erect, and occasionally do so, they have not evolved fully bipedal locomotion. And recent evidence suggests that the area where early hominids lived in East Africa was not predominantly savanna; rather, it seems to have been a mix of woodland and open country.[4]

Other theories stress the importance of freeing the hands. If some hand activity is critical while an animal is moving, selection may favor bipedalism because it frees the hands to perform other activities at the same time. What hand activities might have been so critical?

Gordon Hewes suggested that carrying food in the

hands was the critical activity; if it were necessary to carry food from one locale to another, moving about only on the hind limbs would have been adaptive.[5] Hewes emphasized the importance of carrying hunted or scavenged meat, but many paleoanthropologists now question whether early hominids hunted or even scavenged.[6] However, the ability to carry any food to a place safe from predators may have been one of the more important advantages of bipedalism. C. Owen Lovejoy has suggested that food carrying might have been important for another reason. If males provisioned females and their babies by carrying food back to a home base, the females would have been able to conserve energy by not traveling and therefore might have been able to produce and care for more babies.[7] Thus, whatever the advantages of carrying food, the more bipedal a protohominid was, the more it might reproduce.

But carrying food or provisioning families might not have been the only benefit of freeing the hands; feeding itself may have been more efficient. Clifford Jolly has argued that bipedalism would have allowed early hominids to efficiently harvest small seeds and nuts because both hands could be used to pick up food and move it directly to the mouth.[8] Natural selection would not have favored bipedalism just for locomotion, but also for more efficient foraging. In the changing environments of East Africa, where forests were giving way to more open woodlands and savannas, an advantage in foraging for small seeds and nuts might well have proven important for survival, and thus have been favored by natural selection.

Bipedalism might also have been favored by natural selection because the freeing of the hands would allow protohominids to use, and perhaps even make, tools that they could carry with them as they moved about. Consider how advantageous such tool use might have been. Sherwood Washburn noted that some contemporary ground-living primates dig for roots to eat, "and if they could use a stone or a stick they might easily double their food supply."[9] David Pilbeam also suggests why tool use by the more open-country primates may have appreciably increased the number and amount of plant foods they could eat: In order to be eaten, many of the plant foods in the grassy areas probably had to be chopped, crushed, or otherwise prepared with the aid of tools.[10] Tools may also have been used to kill and butcher animals for food. Without tools, primates in general are not well equipped physically for regular hunting or even scavenging. Their teeth and jaws are not sharp and strong enough, and their speed afoot is not fast enough. So the use of tools to kill and butcher game might have enlarged even further their ability to exploit the available food supply.

Finally, tools may have been used as weapons against predators, which would have been a great threat to the relatively defenseless ground-dwelling protohominids. In Milford Wolpoff's opinion, it was the advantage of carrying weapons *continuously* that was responsible for transforming occasional bipedalism to completely bipedal locomotion.[11] In particular, Sue Savage-Rumbaugh has suggested that the ability to abduct or snap the wrist would have permitted early humans "to perfect both throwing and rock-striking skills [for toolmaking] and consequently to develop throwing as a much more effective predator defense system than apes could ever manage."[12]

But some anthropologists question the idea that tool use and toolmaking favored bipedalism. They point out that the first clear evidence of stone tools appears more than 2 million years *after* the emergence of bipedalism. So how could toolmaking be responsible for bipedalism? Wolpoff suggests an answer. Even though bipedalism appears to be at least 2 million years older than stone tools, it is not unlikely that protohominids used tools made of wood and bone, neither of which would be as likely as stone to survive in the archaeological record. Moreover, unmodified stone tools present in the archaeological record might not be recognizable as tools.[13]

Some researchers have taken a closer look at the mechanics of bipedal locomotion to see if it might be a more efficient form of locomotion in the savanna-woodland environment, where resources are likely to be scattered. Compared with the quadrapedal locomotion of primates such as chimpanzees, bipedalism appears to be more efficient for long-distance travel (see Figure 6–2). But why travel long distances? If the ancestors of humans had the manipulative ability and tool-using capability of modern chimpanzees (for example, using stones to crack nuts), *and* those ancestors had to move around in a more open environment, then those individuals who could efficiently travel longer distances to exploit those resources might do better.[14]

Finally, bipedalism might have been favored by natural selection as a way of regulating body temperature, particularly in the increasingly hot and dry environments of East Africa at the end of the Miocene and the beginning of the Pliocene. Peter Wheeler has argued that a bipedal posture limits the area of the body directly exposed to the sun, especially when the sun is at its hottest, mid-day.[15] Bipedal posture would also facilitate convective heat loss by allowing heat to rise up and away from the body rather than being trapped underneath it. (We radiate a lot of body heat through the head.) Cooling through the evaporation of sweat would also be facilitated by a bipedal posture, as more skin area would be exposed to cooling winds. Thus, natural selection may have favored bipedalism because it reduced heat stress in the warming environments of East Africa.

All theories about the origin of bipedalism are speculative. We do not yet have direct evidence that any of the factors we have discussed were actually responsible for bipedalism. Any or all of the factors may explain the transformation of an occasionally bipedal protohominid to a completely bipedal hominid.

THE "COSTS" OF BIPEDALISM

We must remember that there are also "costs" to bipedal walking. Bipedalism makes it harder to overcome gravity to supply the brain with sufficient blood,[16] and the weight of the body above the pelvis and lower limbs puts greater stress on the hips, lower back, knees, and feet. As Adrienne Zihlman points out, the stresses on the lower body are even greater for females.[17] Females have to support extra weight during pregnancy, and as mothers they usually are responsible for carrying nursing infants. So whatever the advantages of bipedalism, they must be greater than the disadvantages—or our ancestors never would have become bipedal.

We must also remember that the evolution of bipedalism required some dramatic changes in the ancestral ape skeleton. While apes today can and do walk bipedally, they cannot do so efficiently or for long periods of time. To be habitually bipedal, the ancestral ape skeleton had to be modified, and the major changes that allowed the early hominids to become fully bipedal occurred primarily in the skull, pelvis, knees, and feet.[18] Let's take a look at each of these changes.

In both ancient and modern apes, the spinal column enters the skull toward the back, which makes sense because apes generally walk on all fours, with the spine roughly parallel to the ground. In bipedal hominids, the spinal column enters the skull at the bottom, through a hole called the **foramen magnum.** Thus, when hominids became bipedal, the skull ended up on top of the spinal column.

The shape of ancient and modern ape pelvises is considerably different from that of a bipedal hominid. Ape pelvises are long and flat, forming a bony plate in the lower back to which the leg muscles attach. In bipedal hominids the pelvis is bowl-shaped, which supports the internal organs and also lowers the body's center of gravity, allowing better balance on the legs. The hominid pelvis also provides a different set of muscle attachments and shifts the orientation of the femurs (the upper leg bones) from the side of the pelvis to the front. These changes allow hominids to move their legs forward in a bipedal stride (and do things like kick a soccer ball). Apes, in comparison, move their legs forward (when they walk bipedally) by shifting their pelvis from side to side, not by kicking each leg forward alternately as we do.[19]

Another change associated with the hominid ability to kick the leg forward is our "knock-kneed" posture. Ape legs hang straight down from the pelvis. Bipedal hominid legs, on the other hand, angle inward toward one another. This configuration not only helps us move our legs forward but also helps us maintain a center of gravity in the midline of our bodies, so that our center of gravity does not shift from side to side when we walk or run.

Finally, the feet of bipedal hominids have two major changes compared to those of apes. First, hominid feet have an enlarged group of ankle bones forming a robust heel that can withstand the substantial forces placed on them as a result of habitual bipedalism. Second, hominid feet have an arch, which also aids in absorbing the forces endured by the feet during bipedal locomotion. We know this arch is vital to our ability to be habitually bipedal because "flat-footed" people who lack it have chronic problems in their feet, ankles, knees, and back.[20]

When did these changes take place? We don't know for sure, but fossils from East Africa—Ethiopia, Tanzania, and Kenya—clearly show that bipedal hominids lived there between 4 million and 3 million years ago, perhaps even earlier. In fact, there is some evidence that *Ardipithecus ramidus*, perhaps a hominid ancestor, walked bipedally as early as 4.4 million years ago.

Ardipithecus: The First Bipedal Ape?

In 1992, a team of researchers led by anthropologist Tim White began surveying a 4.4-million-year-old fossil deposit at Aramis, in the Middle Awash region of Ethiopia.

Figure 6–2 *Skeletal Evidence of Bipedalism*

Because humans move about on their legs only, the human skeleton differs from the skeleton of the great ape. The human head is more or less balanced on the backbone (see the feature marked 3 in the figure). There is no need for powerful muscles at the back of the neck, as in the great ape. The human vertebral column (see 4 in the figure) has a forward curvature in the neck and lower back regions. These two extra curves, along with the curvature in the middle back region, allow the backbone to act more like a spring, which is advantageous given that the legs have to bear all the weight and given the need to balance on one leg with each stride. Bipedal locomotion has favored a human pelvis (see 1 in the figure) that is lower and broader than the ape pelvis. In contrast to the apes, the legs in humans are longer than the arms and represent a larger proportion of the body weight (see 2 in the figure); this change lowers the body's center of gravity and is advantageous with bipedalism. The most obvious adaptation to bipedalism is the human foot (see 5 in the figure). The big toe is not opposed to the other toes, as in the other primates, and the foot can no longer grasp. When we walk, the big toe is the last point of contact with the ground before the leg swings forward, which explains why the big toe has become aligned with the other toes. Source: From Stephen Jones, Robert Martin, and David Pilbeam, eds., The Cambridge Encyclopedia of Human Evolution (New York: Cambridge University Press, 1992), p. 8. Copyright © by Cambridge University Press. Reprinted by permission of Cambridge University Press.

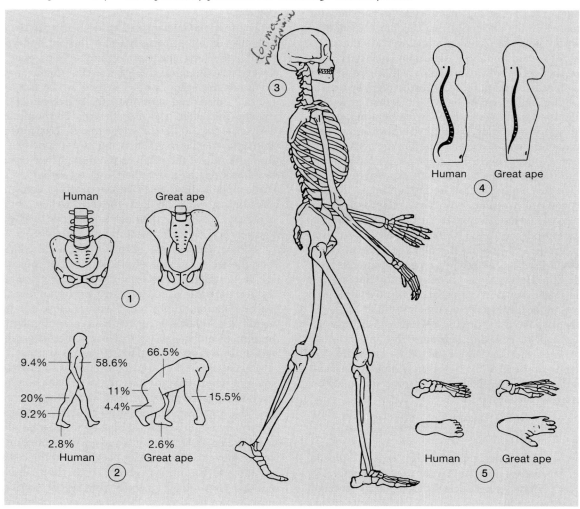

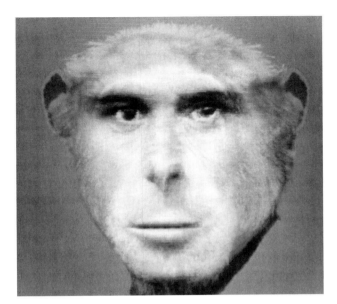

We do not know what the common ancestor of humans and chimpanzees looked like, but this computerized image of a hybrid between a modern human and a modern chimpanzee face hauntingly reminds us that we are not that far apart.

There they discovered a remarkable find—17 fossils of what may be the earliest hominid (some 90 more have been found since). Although initially published as a new australopithecine species, White and his colleagues decided that *ramidus,* the species name given to the new fossils, was distinct enough from the australopithecines to warrant a new genus: *Ardipithecus.*[21]

What makes **Ardipithecus ramidus** unique is the combination of apelike dentition along with evidence of bipedal locomotion and an overall hominidlike skeleton. Like apes, *A. ramidus* has relatively small cheek teeth with thin enamel and relatively large canines. However, its arm bones seem hominidlike, and the base of its skull shows the foramen magnum positioned underneath the skull, just as in definitely bipedal hominids.[22] While more evidence is needed to be sure, *Ardipithecus ramidus* appears to be the earliest hominid yet found.

Australopithecus: The First Definite Hominid

Although some doubt remains about the status of *Ardipithecus* as a hominid genus, there is no doubt that the australopithecines (members of the genus *Australopithecus*) were hominids (Figure 6–3 shows australopithecine sites). Their teeth share the basic hominid characteristics of small canines, flat and thickly enameled molars, and a parabolic dental arch, and there is unambiguous evidence that even the earliest australopithecines were fully bipedal. Not only do their skeletons reflect bipedal locomotion, but at Laetoli, Tanzania, more than 50 hardened humanlike

footprints about 3.6 million years old give striking confirmation that the hominids there were fully bipedal. The bipedalism of the australopithecines does not mean that these earliest definite hominids were terrestrial all of the time. All of the australopithecines, including the later ones, seem to have been capable of climbing and moving in trees, judging by arm versus leg length and other skeletal features.[23]

The australopithecines show considerable variability, and paleoanthropologists divide the genus *Australopithecus* into at least six species.[24] And there may have been others; recent finds are considered by some scholars to represent two new australopithecine species, *A. bahrelghazali* and *A. garhi* (see the box "Surprising New Australopithecines"). Most scholars divide the various australopithecine species into two groups, the "gracile" australopithecines and the "robust" australopithecines.

The **gracile australopithecines** include *A. anamensis, A. afarensis,* and *A. africanus.* All of them have smaller dentition and lighter facial and dental musculature than the robust australopithecines. **Australopithecus anamensis,** which may be 4.2 million years old, is the earliest australopithecine, and has been found only in northern Kenya. Other hominids found in East Africa from 4 million to 3 million years ago are classified by most paleoanthropologists as belonging to the species **Australopithecus afarensis.** A few paleoanthropologists do not think that these hominids should be placed in a separate species, because they resemble the later hominid species **Australopithecus africanus,** which lived between about 3 million and 2 million years ago, primarily in southern Africa. But the temporal and spatial separation of these forms leads many paleoanthropologists to argue that they were different species.

The **robust australopithecines** have larger dentition than the gracile species, and massive faces and jaws. Some individuals had a ridge of bone called a **sagittal crest** on the top of their heads; the ridge anchored the heavy musculature for their large teeth and jaws. The earliest robust species is **Australopithecus aethiopicus,** which lived in eastern Africa between 2.7 and 2.3 million years ago. Most paleoanthropologists think that the later robust australopithecines, who lived between 2.5 and 1 million years ago, consist of two species: the East African species **Australopithecus boisei** and the South African species **Australopithecus robustus.**

The picture that emerges from this brief overview of the australopithecines is one of diversity. There seem to have been many different species of australopithecine, and even within species there seems to be a relatively high level of variation.[25] All shared similar environments in eastern and southern Africa, but those environments were diverse and changing. Forests were giving way to open woodlands and grasslands. Large lakes were formed and then broken apart through uplifting and volcanic activity in the rift valley of eastern Africa. And the climate continued to warm until the end of the Pliocene, some 2 million years ago. The apparent diversity of the australopithecines may

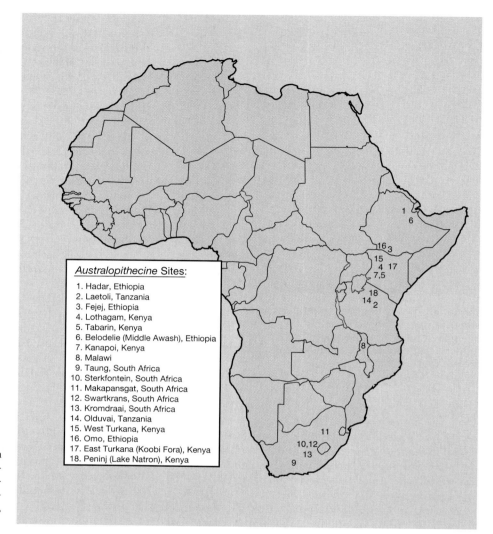

Figure 6–3
Australopithecine Sites

Source: From Russell L. Ciochon and John G. Fleagle, eds., *The Human Evolution Source Book.* Copyright © 1993. Reprinted by permission of Pearson Education, Inc., Upper Saddle River, NJ 07458.

Australopithecine Sites:

1. Hadar, Ethiopia
2. Laetoli, Tanzania
3. Fejej, Ethiopia
4. Lothagam, Kenya
5. Tabarin, Kenya
6. Belodelie (Middle Awash), Ethiopia
7. Kanapoi, Kenya
8. Malawi
9. Taung, South Africa
10. Sterkfontein, South Africa
11. Makapansgat, South Africa
12. Swartkrans, South Africa
13. Kromdraai, South Africa
14. Olduvai, Tanzania
15. West Turkana, Kenya
16. Omo, Ethiopia
17. East Turkana (Koobi Fora), Kenya
18. Peninj (Lake Natron), Kenya

reflect an *adaptive radiation* (a dispersal and divergence) of bipedal hominids to these dynamic environmental conditions.[26] Whatever the cause, diversity seems to be the key word when thinking about the australopithecines. Let's take a closer look at the diverse species of *Australopithecus*.

Gracile Australopithecines

Australopithecus anamensis The earliest australopithecine species is *A. anamensis,* which has been found in several locations in northern Kenya and is dated between 3.9 and 4.2 million years ago.[27] While there is controversy about some of the specimens included in *A. anamensis,* the general picture is that it was a small bipedal hominid with teeth similar to those of the later *A. afarensis.*[28] The more controversial specimens have long bones, suggesting well-developed bipedalism, but their elbow and knee joints look more like those of the later *Homo* genus than like those of any other species of *Australopithecus.* It has been said that *A. anamensis* is "*afarensis*-like from the neck up and *Homo*-like from the neck down."[29]

Australopithecus afarensis *A. afarensis* is perhaps the most well-represented australopithecine species. Remains from at least two dozen individuals were unearthed at Laetoli, Tanzania.[30] Although the remains there consisted largely of teeth and jaws, there is no question that the Laetoli hominids were bipedal, because it was at the Laetoli site that the now-famous trail of footprints was found. Two hominids walking erect and side by side left their tracks in the ground 3.6 million years ago. The remains of at least 35 individuals have been found at another site, Hadar, in Ethiopia. The Hadar finds are remarkable for their completeness. Whereas paleoanthropologists often find just parts of the cranium and jaws, many parts of the skeleton were also found at Hadar. For example, paleoanthropologist Donald Johanson found 40 percent of the skeleton of a female hominid he named Lucy, after the Beatles' song "Lucy in the Sky with Diamonds."[31]

Dating of the hominid remains at Laetoli suggests that the hominids there lived between 3.8 million and 3.6 million years ago.[32] Although Lucy and the other hominids at

CURRENT ISSUES
Surprising New Australopithecines

In his description of the new species *Australopithecus garhi*, Ethiopian paleoanthropologist Berhane Asfaw explained that the word *garhi* means "surprise" in the Ethiopian language. The name is a fitting one, for neither he nor his colleagues nor the rest of the paleoanthropological community was expecting to find a new australopithecine species when they began working in the Middle Awash in 1996. In 1992, the same team had discovered *Ardipithecus ramidus*. *Australopithecus anamensis* and *Australopithecus bahrelghazali* were discovered in the following years. Within five years, four new early hominoids had been discovered.

Surprising, too, were the skeletal and dental traits of *A. garhi*, which was found in rock dating to approximately 2.5 million years ago. Asfaw and his colleagues expected the new find to resemble one of the previously known australopithecine species, but it did not. While clearly not *Homo*, the teeth and jaws were also clearly not like *A. afarensis* or any of the robust australopithecines. *A. garhi* has larger molars than *A. afarensis*, yet does not have the huge face and jaws of the robust australopithecines. It also lacks the enlarged brain of early *Homo*. Several limb bones

were found in the same rock layers, and these do resemble *A. afarensis*. *A. garhi*, then, looks to be an *afarensis*-like creature but with greatly enlarged molars.

Most surprising of all, however, was the fact that the remains of butchered animals were found in the same rock layer as the *A. garhi* remains. Several bones found near the *A. garhi* fossils show unambiguous cut marks and signs of having been broken with a stone tool. Unfortunately, no stone tools have been found, but the evidence for butchery suggests they must have been used. And since no other species of hominid have been found in the area, it is reasonable to think that *A. garhi* was the toolmaker and butcher. Asfaw and his colleagues suggest that *A. garhi* is in the right place, at the right time, and has the right physical and behavioral traits to be the direct ancestor of early *Homo*.

Equally surprising is *Australopithecus bahrelghazali*, not so much because of its physical features, but because it was found further west, in what is now central Chad. *A. bahrelghazali* is the first early hominid to be found outside of the Rift Valley (in East Africa), and until *A. bahrelghazali* surfaced, few thought early hominids were present anywhere

else. *A. bahrelghazali* dates to about 3 million years ago, and is very similar to contemporary *A. afarensis* fossils from the Rift Valley. It differs from *A. afarensis* in some distinct ways (its premolars, for example, have thinner enamel and more well-defined roots), but the important difference is where *A. bahrelghazali* lived. Most scholars assume the early hominids represent a specific adaptation to the Rift Valley. The discovery of an early australopithecine some 2,500 kilometers west of the Rift Valley calls this assumption into question.

A. bahrelghazali is represented by a single, fragmentary jaw, and only a handful of skull and limb fragments represent *A. garhi*. While the finds are intriguing, we will not know how important either species is, or how they may change our understanding of early hominid evolution, until more fossils from them are found.

Sources: Berhane Asfaw, Tim White, Owen Lovejoy, Bruce Latimer, Scott Simpson, and Glen Suwa, "*Australopithecus garhi:* A New Species of Early Hominid from Ethiopia," *Science*, 284 (1999): 629–36; Michel Frunet, Alain Beauvilain, Yves Coppens, Elile Heintz, Aladji H. E. Moutaye, and David Pilbeam, "The First Australopithecine 2500 Kilometers West of the Rift Valley (Chad)," *Nature*, 378 (1995): 273–75.

Hadar were once thought to be about as old as those at Laetoli, recent dating suggests that they are somewhat younger—less than 3.2 million years old. Lucy probably lived 2.9 million years ago.[33] The environment Lucy lived in was semiarid, upland savanna with rainy and dry seasons.[34]

The existence of such extensive fossil collections has al-

lowed paleoanthropologists such as Donald Johanson and Tim White to develop a portrait of this ancient hominid species. *A. afarensis* was a small hominid, but, like most of the living great apes, was sexually dimorphic. Females weighed perhaps 65 pounds and stood a little more than 3 feet tall; males weighed more than 90 pounds and stood about 5 feet tall.[35]

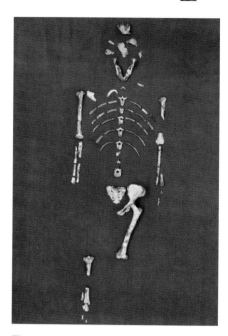

The 40-percent-complete skeleton of a female *Australopithecus afarensis* named "Lucy" by its discoverer, Donald Johanson.

A. *afarensis* teeth were large compared to their body size, and they had thick molar enamel. They also had large, apelike canines, which, on some specimens, projected beyond the adjacent teeth. However, even the longer canines did not rub against the lower teeth or fit into a diastema (a space between the teeth), and thus did not prevent side-to-side movement of the lower jaw.[36] This is important, because side-to-side movement of the lower jaw allowed A. *afarensis* to efficiently chew small seeds and nuts. The thick enamel on the molars and wear patterns on the molar crowns suggest that such small, hard materials made up a significant part of the diet of A. *afarensis*.[37] The cranium of A. *afarensis* reflects its dentition. The face juts forward because of the large teeth and jaws, and the base of the skull flares out to provide attachment areas for large neck muscles to support the heavy face. The brain is small, about 400 cubic centimeters (cc), but relatively large for an animal this size.[38]

The arms and legs of A. *afarensis* were about the same length, and the fingers and toe bones are curved, suggesting they were heavily muscled. Most scholars believe these limb proportions and strong hands and feet point to a partially arboreal life-style.[39] In other words, it appears that A. *afarensis* spent a lot of time in the trees, probably feeding, sleeping, and avoiding terrestrial predators. The pelvis and leg bones of A. *afarensis*, however, demonstrate that it moved bipedally when on the ground. The pelvis is wide and flaring, but has the bowl-like shape of all later hominids. The legs angle inward, and the feet have an arch and an ankle much like later hominids.[40] Detailed analyses

of the Laetoli footprints suggest that A. *afarensis* may have had a shorter and less efficient stride than modern humans.[41]

While A. *afarensis* is the most well-represented australopithecine species, it was not the first one discovered. That distinction rests with *Australopithecus africanus*.

Australopithecus africanus In 1925, Raymond Dart, professor of anatomy at the University of Witwatersrand in Johannesburg, South Africa, presented the first evidence that an erect bipedal hominid existed in the Pliocene epoch. As he separated bones from a matrix of material found in the Taung cave on the edge of the Kalahari Desert, Dart realized he was looking at more than the remains of an ape. He described the experience:

> On December 23, [1924,] the rock parted. I could view the face from the front, although the right side was still embedded. The creature that had contained this massive brain was no giant anthropoid such as a gorilla. What emerged was a baby's face, an infant with a full set of milk teeth and its permanent molars just in the process of erupting.[42]

By the teeth Dart identified the fossil as the remains of a 5- to 7-year-old child (although recent analysis by elec-

Mary Leakey's expedition discovered a trail about 70 yards long of 3.6-million-year-old fossilized footprints at Laetoli, Tanzania. Shown here is one of the footprints that were left by two adults who were clearly upright walkers. The footprint shows a well-developed arch and forward-facing big toe.

tron microscope suggests that the child was no more than three and a half[43]). He named the specimen *Australopithecus africanus,* which means "southern ape of Africa." Dart was certain the skull was that of a bipedal animal. He based his conclusion on the fact that the foramen magnum faced downward, indicating that the head was carried directly over the spine. Furthermore, the Taung child's incisors and canine teeth were short, and therefore definitely more human- than apelike.

Dart's conclusion met with widespread skepticism and opposition. Not the least of the problems was that scientists at the time believed hominids had originated in Asia. But there were probably other reasons: Dart had found only one fossil; it was an infant rather than an adult; and no other hominid fossils had yet been found in Africa. Other australopithecines were not discovered until the 1930s, when Robert Broom recovered some fossils from the Sterkfontein cave near Johannesburg. Dart's and Broom's conclusions did not begin to be accepted until after 1945, when Wilfred Le Gros Clark, a professor of anatomy at Oxford, supported the hominid status of their finds.[44]

Since the Taung child's discovery more than 75 years ago, the remains of hundreds of other similar australopithecines have been unearthed from caves at Sterkfontein and Makapansgat in South Africa. From this abundant evidence a fairly complete picture of *A. africanus* can be drawn: "The brain case is rounded with a relatively well-developed forehead. Moderate brow ridges surmount a rather projecting face."[45] The estimated cranial capacity for the various finds from Taung and Sterkfontein is between 428 and 485 cc.[46]

Like *A. afarensis, A. africanus* was very small; the adults were $3^1/_2$ to $4^1/_2$ feet tall, weighed 60 to 90 pounds, and were sexually dimorphic.[47] The large, chinless jaw of *A. africanus* resembles that of *A. afarensis,* but some of the

A reconstruction of an *Australopithecus africanus* mother and child picking berries in a tree. Like *A. afarensis, A. africanus* probably spent time in trees both feeding and avoiding predators.

dental features of *A. africanus* are similar to those of modern humans—broad incisors and small, short canines. And, although the premolars and molars were larger than in modern humans, their form was very similar. Presumably, function and use were also similar.

Dating of the australopithecine finds from the South African limestone caves is somewhat difficult because none of the absolute dating techniques can be applied. But relative dating is possible. Comparisons of the fauna found in the strata with fauna found elsewhere suggest that the South African *A. africanus* lived between 3 million and 2 million years ago. The climate was probably semi-arid, not too different from the climate of today.[48]

ROBUST AUSTRALOPITHECINES

The robust australopithecines lived in eastern Africa and in southern Africa from about 2.5 million to 1 million years ago, and are quite distinct from the gracile australopithecines. Indeed, some paleoanthropologists think these

Fossil skull of an *Australopithecus africanus* (STS 5) nicknamed "Mrs. Ples" found by Robert Broom at Sterkfontein cave in 1947.

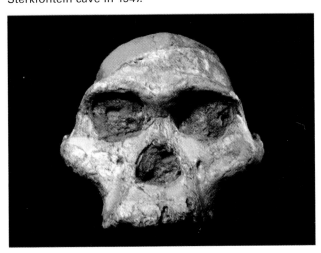

RESEARCH FRONTIERS

New Finds of Early "Robust" Australopithecines Are Puzzling

Where do the robust australopithecines, with their big jaws and bony skull ridges, fit into the evolution of humans? Paleoanthropologists agree that the robust australopithecines are a side branch of human evolution, but when did they diverge from the *Homo* line? The very early date of some robust australopithecine fossils in East Africa presents a puzzle, according to paleoanthropologist Henry McHenry. These fossils, classified as *Australopithecus aethiopicus,* date apparently from about 2.5 million years ago. If the late robust forms—*A. robustus* and *A. boisei*—descend from *A. aethiopicus,* and if the line leading to *Homo* had already split off from an earlier australopithecine (see Figure 6–4), then why do the late robust australopithecines resemble *Homo erectus* more than they resemble the australopithecines who were their presumed ancestors?

The late robust australopithecines are like *H. erectus* in hav-ing a relatively large brain (as compared with *A. africanus*), reduced prognathism (lower face projection), and a deep jaw joint. If they diverged recently from the *Homo* line, similarity to *Homo* would not present a puzzle. But if the robust line diverged earlier, as the 2.5-million-year-old *A. aethiopicus* suggests, the late robust forms should be much more divergent from *Homo.* After all, the further back in time the two lines diverge, the more you would expect the later examples in each to differ.

What could explain some of the similarities between the late robust australopithecines and the *Homo* line? McHenry suggests two possible explanations, both involving convergence. He points out that *convergence,* the independent appearance of similar structures in different lines of descent, can obscure the issue of how far back there was common ancestry. Bats, birds, and butterflies have wings, but they are not closely related—their common ancestor is way back in evolutionary time. One possible explanation for the similarities between the late robust australopithecines and the *Homo* line is that the late robust forms descend from the early robust forms but resemble *H. erectus* because of convergence. A second possibility is that the late robust forms and *Homo* share a recent, not yet found ancestor; if they do, then the early robust forms were not ancestral to the late robust forms. Convergence, not close common ancestry, might then explain the resemblance between the late and early robust forms.

McHenry prefers the second possibility. On the basis of his analysis of trait similarities, McHenry thinks that the two late robust australopithecine species (*A. robustus* and *A. boisei*) share a common ancestor but that ancestor was not the early robust form, *A. aethiopicus.* In many ways, the late robust forms are not that similar to *A. aethiopicus.*

fossils are so different that they deserve to be classified in a different genus, which they call *Paranthropus,* literally, "beside humans." Robust australopithecines were found first in South African caves, in Kromdraai and in Swartkrans, and later in East Africa, in the Omo Basin in Ethiopia, on the east and west sides of Lake Turkana in Kenya, and Olduvai Gorge in Tanzania.[49] Most paleoanthropologists classify the South African robust australopithecines from about 1.8 million to 1 million years ago as *A. robustus* and the East African robust forms from 2.2 million to 1.3 million years ago as *A. boisei.*[50] The third robust species, *A. aethiopicus,* is even earlier, dating back more than 2.5 million years ago, and may have been ancestral to *A. boisei* (see the box "New Finds of Early 'Robust' Australopithecines Are Puzzling").

In contrast to the gracile australopithecines, the robust australopithecines had thicker jaws, with larger molars and premolars but smaller incisors, more massive muscle attachments for chewing, and well-developed sagittal crests and ridges to support heavy chewing.[51] In addition, *A. robustus* and *A. boisei* have somewhat larger cranial capacities (about 490–530 cc) than any of the gracile species.

It used to be thought that the robust australopithecines were substantially bigger than the other australopithecines—hence the term *robust.* But recent calculations suggest that these australopithecines were not substantially different in body weight or height from the other australopithecines. The robustness is primarily in the skull and jaw, most strikingly in the teeth. If the robust forms

One of the best examples of *A. aethiopicus* is a nearly complete skull (the "Black Skull"). It is no doubt robust. It has huge premolars and molars and an enormous sagittal crest. But in other ways it resembles *A. afarensis:* protruding muzzle, shallow jaw joint, and small braincase. McHenry thinks that convergent evolution produced the resemblances between the early and late robust australopithecines and the convergence happened because of strong selective pressure for heavy chewing. Features good for heavy chewing have evolved in other primates as well, in evolutionary lines far removed from the human line. *Giganto-pithecus,* with its enormous premolars and molars, was one such primate. Thus, although McHenry still considers the late robust australopithecines to constitute a side branch to the *Homo* line, his analysis suggests that *A. robustus* and *A. boisei* were not as far from *Homo* as previously thought.

Timothy Bromage, who has studied fossil facial growth, and Randall Susman, who has studied the hominid thumb, have other suggestions about the robust australopithecines. Bromage has used the scanning electron microscope to study images of fossil faces (see the box on Bromage in Chapter 1), particularly to see how the face would have grown from infancy to adulthood. The maturing face changes in shape by a combination of deposition of bone in some locations and resorption of bone in other locations. So, for instance, a jaw becomes more protruding when bone deposits on the forward-facing surfaces and resorbs on the opposite surfaces. Scanning electron microscopy can reveal whether bone is deposited or resorbed. Bromage found differences between the growth patterns of the robust australopithecines and *A. africanus. Australopithecus africanus* and even early *Homo* finds are more apelike in their growth pattern than the later robust australopithecines.

Susman has studied thumb bones and attached musculature to see what traits would be needed to make tools. Modern humans have longer but stouter thumbs than apes, so they can perform the kind of precision grasping needed for toolmaking. Did any early hominids have such precision-grasping ability? Susman thinks that all the australopithecines after about 2.5 million years ago, including the robust ones, had toolmaking hand capabilities. This doesn't mean that they made tools, only that they could have.

The robust australopithecines, with their small foreheads, extremely flat cheeks, and enormous jaws, may have looked very different from the forms in the *Homo* line, but they could be closer to us evolutionarily than we once thought.

Sources: Henry M. McHenry, " 'Robust' Australopithecines, Our Family Tree, and Homoplasy," and Timothy G. Bromage, "Paleoanthropology and Life History, and Life History of a Paleoanthropologist," in Peter N. Peregrine, Carol R. Ember, and Melvin Ember, eds., *Physical Anthropology: Original Readings in Method and Practice* (Upper Saddle River, NJ: Prentice Hall, 2002); Randall L. Susman, "Fossil Evidence for Early Hominid Tool Use," *Science,* September 9, 1994, 1570–73.

were larger in body size, their slightly bigger brain capacity would not be surprising, since larger animals generally have larger brains. However, the body of the robust forms is similar to that of *A. africanus,* so the brain of the robust australopithecines was relatively larger than the brain of *A. africanus.*[52]

Australopithecus aethiopicus

A. aethiopicus is the earliest and also the least known of the robust australopithecines. *A. aethiopicus* is represented by a small group of fossils found in northern Kenya and southern Ethiopia dating between 2.3 million and 2.7 million years ago, including one spectacular find—a nearly complete skull (known as the "Black Skull" because of its dark color) found in 1985.[53] Even though we have only a few fossils, it seems clear that *A. aethiopicus* was quite different from other australopithecines. They differ from *A. afarensis* specimens from roughly the same region and perhaps even the same time period by having much larger dentition, particularly molars, huge cheek bones, projecting and dish-shaped (round and flat) faces, and large sagittal crests. But they are similar to *A. afarensis* in most other ways. Overall, *A. aethiopicus* resembles *A. afarensis* with a massively "scaled-up" dental apparatus.[54]

Australopithecus robustus

In 1936, Robert Broom, then curator of vertebrate paleontology at the Transvaal museum in South Africa, began visiting quarries seeking fossils for the museum, particularly hominids that might support Raymond Dart's earlier discovery of the Taung child. In 1938, a quarry manager gave Broom a hominid jaw that had been found in a nearby cave called Kromdraai. Broom immediately began excavating in the cave, and within days was able to piece together the skull of what would prove to be a new australopithecine species—*Australopithecus robustus.*[55]

While Broom had expected another example of *Australopithecus africanus* (he had found an *A. africanus* skull in 1936), this one was different. It had larger teeth, a massive jaw, and a flatter face than *A. africanus.*[56] Indeed, after further study, Broom decided that the fossil represented an entirely new hominid genus: *Paranthropus.* Broom's genus designation was not widely accepted at the time (scholars thought the specimen represented a species of *Australopithecus*), but as we noted earlier many scholars today believe the robust australopithecines are unique enough to warrant the separate *Paranthropus* genus.

During the 1940s Broom added many new fossils of *A. robustus* and *A. africanus* to the collections of the Transvaal Museum. But his discoveries also raised a problem. How did two strikingly different hominid species evolve in the same environment? In 1954, John T. Robinson proposed that *A. africanus* and *A. robustus* had different dietary adaptations—*A. africanus* being an omnivore (dependent on meat and plants) and *A. robustus* a vegetarian, with a need for heavy chewing. Robinson's view was hotly debated for many years. Evidence from electron microscopy supports Robinson's view that *A. robustus* ate mostly small hard objects such as seeds, nuts, and tubers. But how different was *A. africanus* in this respect? Recent analyses suggest that *A. africanus* also practiced fairly heavy chewing.[57]

The idea that *A. robustus* was just a vegetarian is also questioned by a relatively new chemical technique that analyzes strontium-calcium ratios in teeth and bones to estimate the proportion of plant versus animal food in the diet. This new kind of analysis suggests that *A. robustus* was an omnivore.[58] Thus *A. robustus* may have needed large teeth and jaws to chew seeds, nuts, and tubers, but that doesn't mean that it didn't eat other things too.

Was *A. robustus* adapted, then, to a drier, more open environment than *A. africanus*? This is a possibility, but the evidence is controversial. At any rate, most paleoanthropologists think that *A. robustus* died out shortly after 1 million years ago[59] and is not ancestral to our own genus, *Homo.*[60]

Australopithecus boisei Legendary paleoanthropologist Louis Leakey began his search for a human ancestor in 1931 at Olduvai Gorge in western Tanzania. It was not until 1959 that his efforts paid off with the discovery of *Australopithecus boisei* (named after a benefactor, Charles Boise). The nearly 30 years that Leakey, his wife, Mary Leakey, and their children (including paleoanthropologist Richard Leakey) worked at Olduvai before finding *A. boisei* were not wasted. The Leakeys assembled a rich collection of nonhominid fossils and established a detailed understanding of the ancient environment of the region.[61] As we discuss in the next chapter, they also amassed a remarkable collection of ancient stone tools. So, on a hot July morning, when Mary Leakey rushed to tell Louis, who was sick in bed, that she had discovered the hominid they

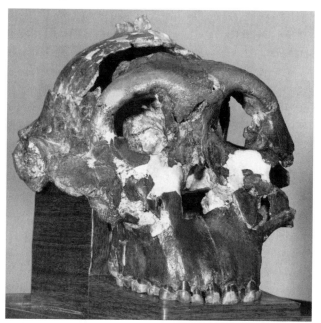

Fossil skull of *Australopithecus boisei* found by Louis and Mary Leakey in 1959. Note its huge face and teeth and its sagittal crest.

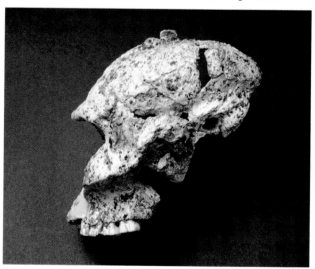

Fossil skull of an *Australopithecus robustus* (SK46) found by Robert Broom at Swartkrans cave in 1949. Note its sagittal crest, massive cheek bones, and huge molars.

had long been searching for, the Leakeys were able to immediately place their find into a rich environmental and perhaps cultural context.

The discovery of *A. boisei* was particularly important because it demonstrated that early hominids were present in East Africa. Until the Leakeys found *A. boisei,* it was thought that South Africa was the homeland of the hominids. Indeed, Leakey initially assigned *A. boisei* to a new genus—*Zinjanthropus*—to highlight its location (*Zinj* means "East Africa" in Arabic). Today we know that the most ancient fossil hominids are all found in East Africa, but in 1959 simply finding a fossil hominid in East Africa was remarkable.

What did *A. boisei* look like? Compared with *A. robustus, A. boisei* had even more extreme features that reflected a huge chewing apparatus—enormous molar teeth and

expanded premolars that look like molars, a massive, thick and deep jaw, thick cheek bones, and a more pronounced sagittal crest.[62] Indeed, *A. boisei* has been called a "hyper-robust" australopithecine—a name that definitely captures the species.

A. boisei lived between about 2.3 and 1.3 million years ago. Like *A. robustus,* it seems to have lived in a dry, open environment and ate a lot of coarse seeds, nuts, and roots. And, like *A. robustus,* most paleoanthropologists think *A. boisei* is not ancestral to our genus, *Homo.*[63] We don't know for sure whether *A. boisei* was the maker of the stone tools the Leakeys found at Olduvai for, as we will learn in the next chapter, it lived alongside at least two other hominid species—*Homo habilis* and *Homo erectus*—who are perhaps the more likely toolmakers.

One Model of Human Evolution

At this point you may well be wondering how all these species fit together. Figure 6–4 shows one model entertained by paleoanthropologists about how the known fossils may be related. The main disagreement among paleontologists concerns which species of *Australopithecus* were ancestral to the line leading to modern humans. For example, the model shown in Figure 6–4 suggests that *A. africanus* is not ancestral to *Homo,* only to one line of robust australopithecines. *Australopithecus afarensis* is viewed as ancestral to both lines of robust australopithecines and to the line leading to modern humans. Those who think that *A. afarensis* was the last common ancestor of all the hominid lines shown in Figure 6–4 think the split to *Homo* occurred over 3 million years ago.[64]

Despite the uncertainty and disagreements about what species was ancestral to the *Homo* line, there is widespread agreement among paleoanthropologists about other aspects of early hominid evolution: (1) There were at least two separate hominid lines between 3 million and 1 million years ago; (2) the robust australopithecines were not ancestral to modern humans but became extinct after 2 million years ago; and (3) *Homo habilis* (and successive *Homo* species) were in the direct ancestral line to modern humans. It is our direct ancestors, the first members of the *Homo* genus, to whom we turn in the next chapter.

Figure 6–4 *Phylogenetic Time Lines*

Source: Adapted from *New York Times,* September 5, 1995, p. C9. (Maeve Leakey, Ian Tattersall, *The Fossil Trail.*) Dates changed slightly to reflect recent redating.

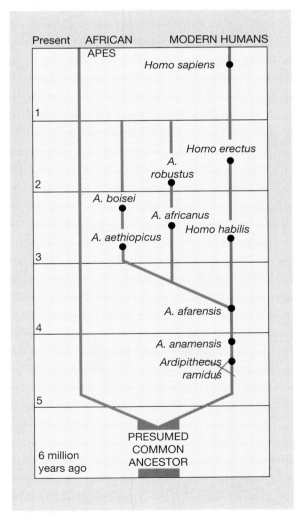

 CD-ROM Interactive Exercise II-8

 Summary

1. The drying trend in climate that began about 16 million to 11 million years ago diminished the extent of

CURRENT ISSUES
Cladistic Analysis

Traditional models of human evolution take the form of a phylogenetic tree like that shown in Figure 6–4. The models are usually based on several lines of evidence, including the age of the species, their locations, and, most importantly, the characteristics they seem to share with other species. In many ways phylogenetic trees are subjective, since they are often based on those items the designer of the tree thinks are the most important characteristics shared, or not shared, by a group of species. In recent years, many paleoanthropologists have found *cladistic analysis* to be a more useful way of looking at the relationships between species.

Cladistic analysis focuses exclusively on the *derived traits* (traits that have changed over time) in a group of species. One lists the changes in a given trait for each species in the analysis, and then orders the various species in terms of their ages. Finally, one diagrams the relationships between species by age and the direction of change in the trait being analyzed. The result is a *cladogram*, such as that shown first in this box, which illustrates the relationships between species based on changes in a single trait. In this case, the change is in en-

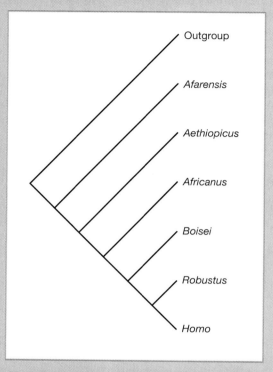

Cladogram Based on Endocranial Volume

Source: From Henry McHenry, " 'Robust' Australopithecines, Our Family Tree, and Homoplasy," in Peregrine, Ember, and Ember, *Physical Anthropology.*

docranial volume or, to put it more simply, brain size. The "outgroup" here defines the most primitive form. As one moves up the left-right sloping line, one reaches branching points where endocranial volume changes. Here *A. robustus* and early *Homo* are more like one another than any others in the cladogram;

African rain forests and gave rise to areas of savanna (grasslands) and scattered deciduous woodlands. The new, more open country probably favored characteristics adapted to ground living in some primates. In the evolutionary line leading to humans, these adaptations included bipedalism.

2. One of the crucial changes in early hominid evolu-

tion was the development of bipedalism. There are several theories for this development: It may have increased the emerging hominid's ability to see predators and potential prey while moving through the tall grasses of the savanna; by freeing the hands for carrying, it may have facilitated transferring food from one place to another; tool use, which requires free hands, may have favored two-legged

early *Homo*, *A. robustus*, and *A. boisei* are more like one another than the others; and so on.

One of the main benefits of this approach is that it is a formal procedure: Assumptions must be made clear, and traits used in the analysis must also be defined precisely. This allows the results of a cladistic analysis to be less affected by an unacknowledged bias or subjective preconception than traditional phylogenetic trees are prone to. Often cladistic analyses lead to quite different pictures of evolutionary relationships, compared with traditional phylogenetic trees.

The second figure in this box represents a cladogram of early hominid species based on 77 traits. It suggests that early *A. robustus* and *A. boisei* are more like one another on these traits than like other species, and thus are likely to share a common ancestor. Early *Homo* shares a common ancestor with *A. robustus* and *A. boisei*. All three share a common ancestor with *A. africanus*. *A. afarensis* is the least like the others, and shares a common ancestor with all the rest. Compare this with Figure 6–4. There are a number of similarities, and yet the close relationship between the robust australopithecines and early *Homo* is not apparent in the traditional phylogeny. Though we will probably never know the true phylogenetic relationships among our ancient ancestors, many scholars believe cladistic analyses provide the best approximations.

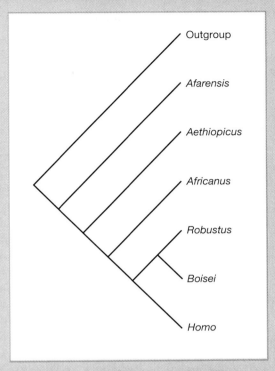

The Most Parsimonious Cladogram

Source: From Henry McHenry, " 'Robust' Australopithecines, Our Family Tree, and Homoplasy," in Peregrine, Ember, and Ember, *Physical Anthropology.*

Sources: Henry McHenry, " 'Robust' Australopithecines, Our Family Tree, and Homoplasy," in Peter N. Peregrine, Carol R. Ember, and Melvin Ember, eds., *Physi-* *cal Anthropology: Original Readings in Method and Practice* (Upper Saddle River, NJ: Prentice Hall, 2002); Willi Hennig, *Phylogenetic Systematics* (Urbana: University of Illinois Press, 1966).

walking; and bipedalism may have made long-distance traveling more efficient.

3. *Ardipithecus ramidus,* a species dating to 4.4 million years ago, may have walked bipedally and may be the earliest hominid. Undisputed hominids dating between 4 million and 3 million years ago have been found in East Africa. These definitely bipedal hominids are now generally classified in the genus *Australopithecus.*

4. At least six species of australopithecine have been identified, and these are generally divided into two types: gracile and robust. The gracile australopithecines have relatively smaller teeth and jaws, and include *A. anamensis,* *A. afarensis,* and *A. africanus.* The robust australopithecines have relatively larger teeth and jaws, and are

more muscular than the gracile australopithecines. They include *A. aethiopicus, A. robustus,* and *A. boisei.*

Glossary Terms

Ardipithecus ramidus
Australopithecus
Australopithecus aethiopicus
Australopithecus afarensis
Australopithecus africanus
Australopithecus anamensis
Australopithecus boisei

Australopithecus robustus
foramen magnum
gracile australopithecine
robust australopithecine
sagittal crest
savanna

Critical Questions

1. How could there have been more than one species of hominid living in East Africa at the same time?

2. What may have enabled australopithecines to survive in the face of many ground predators?

3. What evolutionary processes can you envision that may have led the genus *Australopithecus* to divide into two major types: gracile and robust?

Internet Exercises

1. Visit **http://www.talkorigins.org/faqs/homs/ specimen.html** to view some of the prominent hominid fossils. Based on the Web site, write a brief summary of your findings pertaining to *Australopithecus afarensis* and Donald Johanson.

2. Visit the hominid species time line at **http:// www.wsu.edu:8001/vwsu/gened/learn-modules/ top_longfor/timeline/timeline.html** and look through the pages relating to the australopithecines.

3. Examine the Hooper Virtual Natural History Museum exhibit on the "Aquatic Ape" hypothesis of hominid origins at **http://www.wf.carleton.ca/Museum/aquatic/ intro1.htm**. Write an essay critically evaluating this hypothesis.

4. Look at the early human phylogeny presented on the Smithsonian Institution Hall of Human Ancestors Web site (**http://www.mnh.si.edu/anthro/humanorigins/ ha/a_tree.html**). Examine how it compares to the phylogeny presented in this chapter.

Suggested Reading

CONROY, G. C. *Primate Evolution.* New York: Norton, 1990. Chapter 6 summarizes the fossil record for the australopithecines and early *Homo,* discusses the geography and climate of the early sites, and explains the biomechanical principles of bipedalism.

GRINE, F. E., ED. *Evolutionary History of the "Robust" Australopithecines.* New York: Aldine, 1988. A great deal of controversy has surrounded the "robust" australopithecines. In a 1987 workshop, participants from many different fields summarized recent knowledge of this group of australopithecines.

JOHANSON, D., AND EDEY, M. *Lucy: The Beginnings of Humankind.* New York: Simon & Schuster, 1981. An engaging description of the discovery, reconstruction, and significance of *Australopithecus afarensis.*

PEREGRINE, P. N., EMBER, C. R., AND EMBER M., EDS. *Physical Anthropology: Original Readings in Method and Practice.* Upper Saddle River, NJ: Prentice Hall, 2002. Several chapters in this book deal with the evolution of early hominids and their cultures: T. G. Bromage, "Paleoanthropology and Life History, and Life History of a Paleoanthropologist"; H. M. McHenry, " 'Robust' Australopithecines, Our Family Tree, and Homoplasy"; S. W. Simpson, "*Australopithecus afarensis* and Human Evolution"; and J. D. Speth, "Were Our Ancestors Hunters or Scavengers?"

PHILLIPSON, D. W. *African Archaeology,* 2nd ed. Cambridge: Cambridge University Press, 1993. A summary and interpretation of the archaeological evidence in Africa and what it tells us about human history from its beginnings to historic times. Chapters 2 and 3 are particularly relevant to this chapter.

TATTERSALL, I. *The Fossil Trail: How We Know What We Think We Know about Human Evolution.* New York: Oxford University Press, 1995. A readable introduction to paleoanthropology and research on the australopithecines.

7

The Origins of Culture
and the Emergence of *Homo*

n the last chapter we discussed the origins of bipedalism and how that fundamental hominid means of locomotion was established and refined in the australopithecines. In this chapter we will consider a number of trends in hominid evolution, including the use of patterned or nearly standardized stone tools, considered one sign of the emergence of culture. It is assumed, but not known for sure, that patterned stone tools were made by the first members of our own genus, *Homo*, for it is in the genus *Homo* that we see a number of trends that probably relate to patterned stone tool making—expansion of the brain, modification of the female pelvis to accommodate bigger-brained babies, and reduction in the teeth, face, and jaws.

Even though stone tools are found at various sites in East Africa before the time early *Homo* appeared, most anthropologists surmise that members of these early *Homo* species, rather than the australopithecines, made those tools (see Figure 7–1). After all, early *Homo* had a brain capacity almost one-third larger than the australopithecines'. But the fact is that none of the earliest stone tools is clearly associated with early *Homo*, so it is impossible as yet to know who made them. As we noted in the box in the previous chapter about the robust lines, all the hominids found after 2.5 million years had a thumb capable of toolmaking, so all of them may have been toolmakers.[1] We turn now to a discussion of those tools and what archaeologists infer about the life-styles of their makers, the

Figure 7–1 *The Evolution of Early* **Homo**

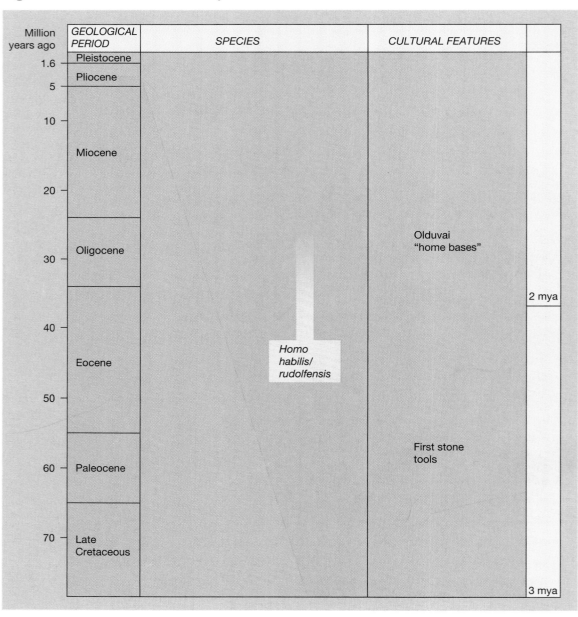

Olduvai Gorge, Tanzania. The stratigraphy of the fossil beds is clearly visible. Bed I, where evidence of early human culture was found, is at the very bottom of the Gorge.

hominids (whoever they were) who lived between about 2.5 million and 1.5 million years ago.

Early Hominid Tools

The earliest identifiable stone tools found so far come from various sites in East Africa and date from about 2.5 million years ago,[2] and maybe earlier. The oldest tools, some 3,000 in number, were discovered recently at Gona, Ethiopia. The tools range from very small flakes (thumb-size) to cobble or core tools that are fist-size.[3] These early tools were apparently made by striking a stone with another stone, a technique called **percussion flaking.** Both the sharp-edged flakes and the sharp-edged cores (the pieces of stone left after flakes are removed) were probably used as tools.

What were those earliest stone tools used for? What do they tell us about early hominid life-styles? Unfortunately, little can be inferred about life-styles from the earliest tool sites because little else was found with the tools. In contrast, finds of later tool assemblages at Olduvai Gorge in Tanzania have yielded a rich harvest of cultural information. The Olduvai site was uncovered accidentally in 1911, when a German entomologist followed a butterfly into the gorge and found fossil remains. As we discussed in the last chapter, Louis and Mary Leakey beginning in the 1930s searched the gorge for clues to the evolution of early humans. Of the Olduvai site, Louis Leakey wrote,

> [It] is a fossil hunter's dream, for it shears 300 feet through stratum after stratum of earth's history as through a gigantic layer cake. Here, within reach, lie countless fossils and artifacts which but for the faulting and erosion would have remained sealed under thick layers of consolidated rock.[4]

The oldest cultural materials from Olduvai (Bed I) date from Lower Pleistocene times. The stone *artifacts* (things made by humans) include core tools and sharp-edged flakes. Flake tools predominate. Among the core tools, so-called *choppers* are common. Choppers are cores that have been partially flaked and have a side that might have been used for chopping. Other core tools, with flaking along one side and a flat edge, are called *scrapers.* Whenever a stone has facets removed from only one side of the cutting edge, we call it a **unifacial tool.** If the stone has facets removed from both sides, we call it a **bifacial tool.** Although there are some bifacial tools in the early stone tool assemblages, they are not as plentiful or as elaborated as in later tool traditions. The kind of tool assemblage found in Bed I and to some extent in later (higher) layers is referred to as **Oldowan** (see Figure 7–2).[5]

Early Hominid Life-Styles

Archaeologists have speculated about the life-styles of early hominids from Olduvai and other sites. Some of these speculations come from analysis of what can be done with the tools, microscopic analysis of wear on the tools, and examination of the marks the tools make on bones; other speculations are based on what is found with the tools.

Archaeologists have experimented with what can be done with Oldowan tools. The flakes appear to be very versatile; they can be used for slitting the hides of animals, dismembering animals, and whittling wood into sharp-pointed sticks (wooden spears or digging sticks). The larger stone tools (choppers and scrapers) can be used to hack off branches or cut and chop tough animal joints.[6] Those who have made and tried to use stone tools for

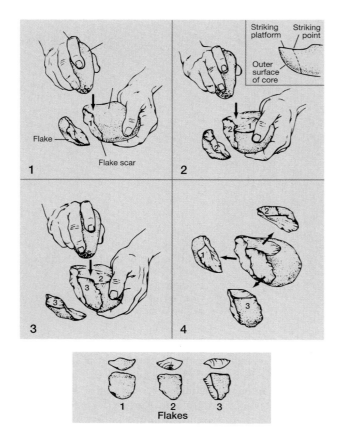

Figure 7–2 *The Production of a Simple Oldowan Chopper Core and the Resultant Flakes*

Source: From "The First Technology" by R. Freyman in *Scientific American.* Reprinted by permission of the artist, Ed Hanson.

various purposes are so impressed by the sharpness and versatility of flakes that they wonder whether most of the core tools were really used as tools. The cores could mainly be what remained after wanted flakes were struck off.[7]

Archaeologists surmise that many early tools were also made of wood and bone, but these do not survive in the archaeological record. For example, present-day populations use sharp-pointed digging sticks for extracting roots and tubers from the ground; stone flakes are very effective for sharpening wood to a very fine point.[8]

None of the early flaked stone tools can plausibly be thought of as a weapon. So, if the toolmaking hominids were hunting or defending themselves with weapons, they had to have used wooden spears, clubs, or unmodified stones as missiles. Later Oldowan tool assemblages also include stones that were flaked and battered into a rounded shape. The unmodified stones and the shaped stones might have been lethal projectiles.[9]

Experiments may indicate what can be done with tools, but they cannot tell us what was *actually* done with them. Other techniques, such as microscopic analysis of the wear on tools, are more informative. Early studies looked at the microscopic scratches formed when a tool was used in dif-

ferent ways. Scratches parallel to the edge of a tool often occur when a tool is used in a sawing motion; perpendicular scratches suggest whittling or scraping.[10] Lawrence Keeley used high-powered microscopes in his experimental investigations of tools and found that different kinds of "polish" develop on tools when they are used on different materials. The polish on tools used for cutting meat is different from the polish on tools used for woodworking. On the basis of microscopic investigation of the 1.5-million-year-old tools from the eastern side of Lake Turkana, Keeley and his colleagues concluded that at least some of the early tools were probably used for cutting meat, others for cutting or whittling wood, and still others for cutting plant stems.[11]

In the 1950s and 1960s, Olduvai Gorge revealed the presence of both Oldowan tools and the remains of broken bones and teeth from many different animal species. For many years it seemed plausible to assume that hominids were the hunters and the animals their prey. But, as we discussed in the chapter on how we discover the past, archaeologists had to reexamine this assumption with the emergence of the field of *taphonomy,* which studies the processes that can alter and distort an assemblage of bones. So, for example, flowing water can bring bones and artifacts together, which may have happened at Olduvai Gorge about 1.8 million years ago. (The area of what is now the gorge bordered the shores of a shallow lake at that time.) And other animals such as hyenas could have brought carcasses to some of the same places that hominids spent time. Taphonomy requires archaeologists to consider all the possible reasons things may be found together.[12]

But there is little doubt that shortly after 2 million years ago hominids were cutting up animal carcasses for meat. Microscopic analyses show that cut marks on animal bones were unambiguously created by stone flake tools, and microscopic analyses of polish on stone tools indicate

A replica of an Oldowan stone tool is used to chop into a large bone to extract the nutrient-rich marrow. Few animals have jaws powerful enough to break open the bones of large mammals, but stone tools would have allowed early humans to do so.

CURRENT ISSUES

How Do You Know Something Is a Tool?

When you look at photographs or drawings of early stone tools, do you ever wonder how paleoanthropologists can distinguish them from ordinary rocks? It is not always easy. Paleoanthropologists mainly look for flakes or rocks with flakes removed, but rocks can be flaked by knocking against other rocks in a riverbed or rolling down a craggy hill. To tell that a core tool is not a naturally flaked rock, paleoanthropologists typically look for three distinct features.

First, the tool has to be made of the right kind of rock. The rock must be both *flakable* and *durable*. You can flake shale, for example, but it is not durable. Many metamorphic rocks are durable, but you cannot flake them because there are too many flaws in the rock. Most stone tools are made from obsidian, quartz, flint, or chert.

Second, paleoanthropologists look for *bilateral flaking*. Bilateral flaking occurs when flakes are struck from two sides of a stone to form a cutting edge. Natural processes may knock a couple of flakes from one side of a stone but will rarely knock them off from opposite sides.

Third, paleoanthropologists look for *retouching*. Retouching occurs when additional flakes are removed from an existing tool in order to resharpen it. Again, natural processes may knock a series of flakes from one side of a rock but will rarely create something resembling a retouched cutting edge.

Paleoanthropologists may also look for a distinct *striking platform* on flakes. A striking platform is the place where the blow landed that knocked the flake from the core. When a flake is struck from a core, it leaves a clean scar that can be used as a striking platform to knock a flake from the opposite side of the core. On flakes made by humans, the striking platform is often the scar left by a previous flake. Just as bilateral flaking is rare in nature, so too is a flake scar with a clearly prepared striking platform.

With these features, paleoanthropologists can usually distinguish naturally flaked rocks from stone tools. But this is not always the case, and many paleoanthropologists have made mistakes. Indeed, one of the most famous mistakes was made by Louis Leakey, one of the first paleoanthropologists to identify early hominid tools. In the late 1960s, Leakey claimed that a site in California called Calico Hills contained early human tools. This claim was met by disbelief, as no evidence of early humans has ever been found in North America, and, as we discuss in the chapter on the Upper Paleolithic world, there is good evidence that modern-looking humans were the continent's first inhabitants. However, because it was Leakey who made the claim, it had to be taken seriously. A group of respected paleoanthropologists met at the site on Leakey's request to make a determination. Their finding? The alleged stone tools were natural objects, not made by humans.

Calico Hills is an important cautionary tale. How do you know something is a tool? In addition to the tool's physical features, paleoanthropologists must also consider the context in which it is found. When alleged tools are found in the absence of hominids or with no other clear evidence of stone tool use, as in the case of Calico Hills, and the context does not suggest the possibility of tools, paleoanthropologists should question their presence.

Sources: Vance Haynes, "The Calico Site: Artifacts or Geofacts?" *Science,* 181 (1973): 305–10; Leland Patterson, "Criteria for Determining the Attributes of Man-Made Lithics," *Journal of Field Archaeology,* 10 (1983): 297–307.

that the polish is consistent with butchering. We still do not know for sure whether the hominids around Olduvai Gorge were just scavenging meat (taking meat from the kills of other animals) or hunting the animals.

On the basis of her analysis of cut marks on bone from Bed I in Olduvai Gorge, Pat Shipman suggested that scavenging, not hunting, was the major meat-getting activity of the hominids living there between 2 million and 1.7 million years ago. For example, the cut marks made by the stone tools usually (but not always) overlie teeth marks made by carnivores. This suggests that the hominids were often scavenging the meat of animals killed and partially eaten by nonhominid predators. The fact that the cut marks were sometimes made first, however, suggested to Shipman that the hominids were also sometimes the hunters.[13] On the other hand, prior cut marks may indicate only that the hominids scavenged before carnivores had a chance to consume their prey.

The artifact and animal remains from Bed I and the lower part of Bed II at Olduvai suggest a few other things about the life-styles of the hominids there. First, it seems that the hominids moved around during the year; most of the sites in what is now the Olduvai Gorge appear to have been used only in the dry season, as indicated by an analysis of the kinds of animal bones found there.[14] Second, whether the early Olduvai hominids were hunters or scavengers, they apparently exploited a wide range of animals. Although most of the bones are from medium-sized antelopes and wild pigs, even large animals such as elephants and giraffes seem to have been eaten.[15] It is clear, then, that the Olduvai hominids scavenged or hunted for meat, but we cannot tell yet how important meat was in their diet.

There is also no consensus about how to characterize the Olduvai sites that contain concentrations of stone tools and animal bones. In the 1970s, there was a tendency to think of them as home bases to which hominids (presumably male) brought meat to share with others (presumably nursing mothers and young children). Indeed, Mary Leakey identified two locations where she thought early hominids had built simple structures (see Figure 7–3). One was a stone circle that she suggested formed the base of a small brush windbreak. The other was a circular area of dense debris surrounded by an area virtually without debris. Leakey suggested that the area lacking debris may represent the location of a ring of thorny brush with which early hominids surrounded their campsite in order to keep out predators—much like pastoralists living in the region do today.[16] But archaeologists today are not so sure these sites were home bases. For one thing, carnivores also frequented the sites. Places with meaty bones lying around

may not have been so safe for hominids to use as home bases. Second, the animal remains at the sites had not been completely dismembered and butchered. If the sites had been hominid home bases, we would expect more complete processing of carcasses.[17] Third, natural processes as simple as trees growing through a site can create circular areas of debris such as the ones Leakey identified as structures, and without better evidence that early hominids made them, one cannot be sure that the circles of debris were indeed structures.[18]

If these sites were not home bases, what were they? Some archaeologists are beginning to think that these early sites with many animal bones and tools may just have been places where hominids processed food but did not live. Why would the hominids return repeatedly to a particular site? Richard Potts suggests one possible reason—that hominids left caches of stone tools and stones for toolmaking at various locations to facilitate recurrent food-collecting and -processing activities.[19] Future research may tell us more about early hominid life. Did they have home bases, or did they just move from one processing site to another? How did they protect themselves from predators? They apparently did not have fire to keep the predators away. Did they climb trees to get away or to sleep?

STONE TOOLS AND CULTURE

Regardless of the answers to these questions, the presence of patterned stone tools means that these early hominids had probably developed culture. Archaeologists consider a pattern of behavior, such as a particular way to make a tool that is shared and learned by a group of individuals, to be a sign of cultural behavior. To be sure, toolmaking does not imply that early humans had anything like the com-

Figure 7–3 *Olduvai "Hut"*

A ring of stones and bones found in Bed I of Olduvai Gorge that Mary Leakey interpreted as the remains of an ancient hut.

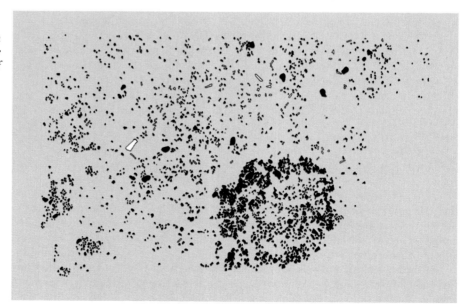

plex cultures of humans today. As we note later in this chapter, when we discuss the social behavior of living primates, chimpanzees have patterns of tool use and toolmaking that appear to be shared and learned, but they do not have that much in the way of cultural behavior.

What, exactly, makes human **culture** so different from other forms of animal behavior? Anthropologists have spent more than a century trying to answer this question, and there is still no widely accepted answer. One thing is clear, however: Culture must be understood as a set of interrelated processes, not as a thing.[20] What are the processes that make up culture? Let's consider some of the more important ones.

First, culture is *learned* and *shared*. This is the fundamental difference between culture and most other forms of animal behavior. Culture is not a set of innate behaviors but, rather, a set of learned ones. Culture is something individuals acquire during their lifetimes as they mature and interact with others. Interaction is key here, because not only are cultural behaviors learned, they are learned through interaction with others, through education, through shared experiences. Culture, then, is a social process, not an individual one.

Second, culture is generally *adaptive*. What this means is that most of the learned and shared behaviors that make up a culture are thought to have developed and spread through a group of people because they help that group of people survive in a given environment. Thus, cultural behaviors may be favored by natural selection just as genes are. The extent to which human culture is a product of natural selection is hotly debated, but few anthropologists would argue that culture is not a key aspect of human adaptation. What makes culture quite different from the behavioral systems of other animals is that, because culture is learned and shared rather than innate, humans can develop new behaviors quickly and adapt to diverse and changing conditions with relative ease. Adaptation, then, is perhaps the most significant process of culture.

Change is the third major process of culture, for culture is always *changing*. As we just discussed, culture change regularly occurs as new and beneficial means of adaptation are developed and shared. But anthropologists also assume that when new behaviors are developed they tend to become integrated with existing behaviors. That is, new behaviors that conflict with established ones may lead to one or the other changing. For example, a group of early humans could not have both scavenged meat and, at the same time, had a prohibition against eating meat that they did not themselves kill. Such a situation would create a contradiction, and something would have to change. Working out contradictions between new, highly beneficial behaviors and established but less beneficial ones may be one of the reasons that cultures are so dynamic.

So, culture is a dynamic system of learned and shared behavior that helps humans adapt to their environments. But how did this dynamic set of interrelated processes we call culture shape the behavior of early humans? To help answer that question paleoanthropologists often look to the living primates and their systems of social behavior. Most paleoanthropologists feel that primate societies, particularly those of the great apes, offer a model of early hominid behavior that can aid us in understanding not only the roots of human culture but also the ways in which culture or cultural behavior differs from other systems of primate behavior.

Primate Social Behavior

All primates are social beings—much more social than most other mammals. But primate social behavior differs from culture in a number of important ways.

First, primate social behavior is largely *innate*, not learned and shared.[21] While there are learned and shared behaviors among many primate groups (chimpanzees, for example, use sticks to "fish" for tools, a learned behavior that is taught to juveniles), most behaviors are not thought to be learned. Primate behaviors appear largely to be *stimulus-determined responses;* that is, they are responses to particular stimuli that are innate in the individual or developed over time through conditioning, through repeated exposure to the same stimuli and the rewards associated with those responses.

Second, primate social behavior does not change rapidly. When primates encounter new situations, they tend to respond out of their existing behavioral repertoire rather than develop new behaviors. And while primates do sometimes create new behaviors (for example, Japanese macaques on Koshima Island developed techniques for cleaning sweet potatoes and wheat), innovative behavior tends to be the rare exception among primate groups.[22]

Primate social behavior tends not to be dynamic or learned and shared, but it is thought to be adaptive, like human culture. How? What are the benefits of being social?

WHY BE SOCIAL?

One reason for being social is that it allows group learning to take place.[23] While most primate behaviors are stimulus-determined responses, those responses are typically conditioned over time in primate groups. Alarm calls among vervets, for example, may trigger an initial response in an individual to escape from threat, but the particular route of escape—to a tree or along the ground—is conditioned by observing and following the behaviors of other individuals in the group. Over time an individual vervet is conditioned to run up a tree in response to a "leopard" alarm, and to seek safety under a tree or bush in response to an "eagle" alarm.[24] Such conditioning may be easier in groups because there are more models.

Another reason for being social is for group protection. All primates lack claws, and most do not have long enough canines to be used as defensive weapons. Thus primates

Many primates, like these chimpanzees, group together when threatened.

must rely on their numbers to defend against predators. Large groups provide lots of eyes to watch for the approach of predators, and large groups can either confuse or frighten a predator and therefore prevent attack. Among savanna-dwelling baboons, for example, the approach of a predator (typically lions) evokes a call of warning. The group rapidly creates a defensive formation, with mothers and infants at the center, females and adolescent males around them, and adult males on the outside. The adult males will work together to distract and threaten the predator while the rest of the group moves to safety. Without this group defense, an individual baboon would be easy prey.[25]

Finally, social behavior provides some advantages in foraging.[26] A lone individual can forage only over a small area. A group, on the other hand, can cover a much larger area, creating a greater likelihood that highly nutritious or desirable foods will be found. When rich food sources are found, most primates will call to others in the group to let them know, and soon the group as a whole will benefit from the discovery. In some cases foraging may involve cooperation. For example, male chimpanzees will work together to hunt and kill baboons and small mammals. A single chimpanzee would likely be unable to track and kill other animals, but through cooperative hunting chimpanzees can be successful predators (see the box "Chimpanzee Hunting Behavior").

With all these benefits, why aren't all animals more social? The answer is that there are also many drawbacks to sociability.

DRAWBACKS TO SOCIABILITY

One of the major problems with being social is stress.[27] When animals live in social groups there is always conflict and stress. Individuals get in each other's way, tempers flare, fights erupt—it is a pattern we can easily understand. Most often, conflict stems from competition for resources, which is a second major problem associated with

being social. Whenever animals live together there will be some resources that are not adequate for all. Even if food resources are plentiful, most animals will compete for access to mates. This leads to competition and, ultimately, to conflict and further stress. A third drawback to sociability is disease.[28] Individuals living in groups create not only a situation ripe for competition and stress, but also one where disease can easily spread from one individual to another.

For primates, however, these drawbacks appear to be less significant than the benefits that sociability provides. One reason is that primates have developed some behavioral mechanisms to reduce the drawbacks. To ease stress, primates groom one another. Grooming is not only soothing in itself but also creates bonds between individuals, which can lessen conflict and stress.[29] Although it may seem paradoxical, dominance hierarchies seem to ease competition. Many primate societies have clear dominance hierarchies. While conflict certainly surrounds their establishment and maintenance, stable dominance hierar-

Grooming creates bonds between members of primate groups and helps to ease social tensions.

RESEARCH FRONTIERS
Chimpanzee Hunting Behavior

When Jane Goodall first began studying the chimpanzees at Gombe, it was thought that chimpanzees were pure vegetarians. When she first documented chimpanzees eating meat, the reports were greeted with skepticism. As more research was done on the Gombe chimpanzees, it became clear that not only do chimpanzees eat meat, but they eat it regularly during the dry season when other foods are relatively scarce. Thus meat is an important part of the chimpanzee diet. Researcher Craig Stanford spent several years watching the red colobus monkey troops that are the most common prey of the Gombe chimpanzees. He found that not only do chimpanzees stalk these monkeys, they actively hunt them, often in large groups of 35 or more. He also found that chimpanzees are the major predators of red colobus monkey in the Gombe Reserve.

Just how much meat do the Gombe chimpanzees eat? Stanford estimates that the 45 chimpanzees in one study group ate about 1,500 pounds of meat a year. During the dry season, when hunting is most common, chimpanzees eat about a pound of meat a week. This figure comes close to the amount of meat eaten by some contemporary human hunters during lean periods of the year.

How do the chimpanzees go about hunting and killing their prey? A typical hunt begins when a chimpanzee troop encounters a troop of red colobus monkeys. The adult chimpanzees (often males) will surround the colobus troop, which often takes refuge in a tree. The chimpanzees entice the male colobus monkeys to attack and chase them, and in the confusion the chimpanzees try to grab an immature colobus or an infant away from its mother. Adult monkeys venturing too close to the chimpanzees or unlucky enough to fall out of the tree may also be surrounded and killed. Kills are made either with a bite to the head or by flailing the animal against the ground. Once a kill is made, other chimpanzees will beg meat from the successful hunters. Sharing is likely after a successful hunt, particularly between males and females.

The fact that the Gombe chimpanzees actively hunt in large groups may have important implications for our understanding of early hominid behavior. For one thing, it makes it very likely that early hominids hunted small animals, such as monkeys.

However, we also know that early hominids were butchering large game. While many carcasses butchered by early hominids show evidence that they were scavenged rather than hunted, not all do. Could early hominids have hunted large game? The fact that chimpanzees hunt in large groups certainly makes the idea plausible. A single hunter would find it hard or impossible to kill an antelope-sized animal with the simple stone tools made by early hominids, but a group of hunters might be able to isolate, overwhelm, and dispatch even a very large animal. If contemporary chimpanzees are capable of similar behaviors, it seems reasonable to suggest that our ancient hominid ancestors were capable of those behaviors too.

Sources: Craig B. Stanford, "Chimpanzee Hunting Behavior and Human Evolution," in Peter N. Peregrine, Carol R. Ember, and Melvin Ember, eds., *Physical Anthropology: Original Readings in Method and Practice* (Upper Saddle River, NJ: Prentice Hall, 2002); Craig B. Stanford, Janette Wallis, Hilali Matama, and Jane Goodall, "Patterns of Predation by Chimpanzees on Red Colobus Monkeys in Gombe National Park, Tanzania, 1982–1991," *American Journal of Physical Anthropology,* 94 (1994): 213–29; Jane Goodall, *Through a Window* (Boston: Houghton Mifflin, 1990).

chies ease competition by clearly establishing the order of access to resources.[30] Finally, the relatively high mobility of most primate groups is a way of easing the possibility of disease spreading. Individuals too sick to keep up with the group are left behind, and therefore cannot infect others. In these and other ways primates have developed mechanisms to help alleviate the drawbacks of sociability.

 ## The Evolution of Culture

It seems clear that the early hominids, like other primates, were social beings. It also seems clear from the archaeological record that the early hominids were making and using stone tools on a regular basis. As we discussed earlier, tools are frequently found in discrete concentrations and often in association with animal bones and other debris from human activity. And, as we have already noted, a number of paleoanthropologists have argued that such concentrations of debris may represent campsites or even small shelters. Home bases of some sort may have been a part of early hominid culture.

Whether they reflect home bases or not, large numbers of animal bones and tools are found in discrete locations, and these accumulations suggest that the areas were being used by groups of individuals over periods of time. In such a situation sharing of food is very likely. It seems counterintuitive to think that individuals would have purposely brought food to a common location only to keep it to themselves. And although we must move into the realm of pure speculation, it does seem reasonable to think that closely related individuals, like parents, children, and siblings, would be more likely to associate and share food with one another than more distantly related individuals. This speculation is supported by the fact that when food sharing takes place among chimpanzees it is usually among closely related individuals.[31] Thus, the ancient locations of early hominid social activity may be evidence of family groups.

It is interesting that the archaeological record of early hominids may represent some of the essential features of modern human culture. These include home bases, sharing, and families. If we think of culture as a process, such a combination of features seems quite likely to form the foundation of human culture. Culture is learned and shared, so a common place where learning and sharing occur—a home base—is something we should expect in early hominid cultures. Culture is adaptive, and adaptation has two important facets—survival and reproduction. Thus, we would expect families and the sharing of food at the base of human culture. How would such a system of social behavior—the creation of a common meeting, resting, and living place for a group of related individuals to share food—have evolved? Let's consider one model.

ONE MODEL FOR THE EVOLUTION OF CULTURE

Early *Homo* had a brain almost one-third larger than that of the australopithecines. As we discuss later in the section on trends in hominid evolution, one of the possible consequences of brain expansion was the lessening of maturity at birth. That babies were born more immature may at least partly explain the lengthening of the period of infant and child dependency in hominids. Compared with other animals, we spend not only a longer proportion of our life span, but also the longest absolute period, in a dependent state. Prolonged infant dependency has probably been of great significance in human cultural evolution. According to Theodosius Dobzhansky,

> it is this helplessness and prolonged dependence on the ministrations of the parents and other persons that favors . . . the socialization and learning process on which the transmission of culture wholly depends. This may have been an overwhelming advantage of the human growth pattern in the process of evolution.[32]

It used to be thought that the australopithecines had a long period of infant dependency, just as modern humans do, but the way their teeth apparently developed suggests that the early australopithecines followed an apelike pattern of development. Thus, prolonged maturation may be relatively recent, but just how recent is not yet known.[33]

Although some use of tools for digging, defense, or scavenging may have influenced the development of bipedalism, full bipedalism may have made possible more

Figure 7–4

Comparison of the estimated cranial capacities of Australopithecus africanus, Homo erectus, *and* Homo sapiens, *demonstrating the expansion of the brain in hominid evolution. Source:* Estimated cranial capacities from Ian Tattersall, Eric Delson, and John van Couvering, eds., *Encyclopedia of Human Evolution and Prehistory.* Reproduced by permission of Routledge, Inc., part of The Taylor & Francis Group.

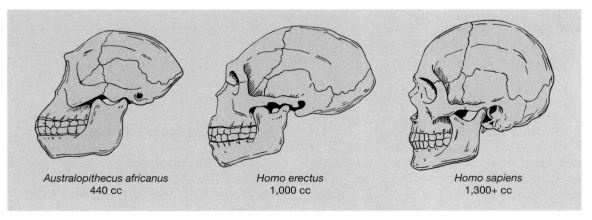

Australopithecus africanus
440 cc

Homo erectus
1,000 cc

Homo sapiens
1,300+ cc

efficient toolmaking and consequently more efficient foraging and scavenging. As we have seen, there are archaeological signs that early hominids may have been scavenging (and perhaps even hunting) animals at least as far back as the late Pliocene. Indeed, we have fairly good evidence that early hominids were butchering and presumably eating big game some 2 million years ago.

Whenever it was that hominids began to scavenge for game and perhaps hunt regularly, the development of scavenging would require individuals to travel long distances frequently in search of suitable carcasses. Among groups of early *Homo*, longer infant and child dependency may have fostered the creation of home bases. The demands of childbirth and caring for a newborn might have made it difficult for early *Homo* mothers to travel for some time after the birth. Certainly, it would have been awkward, if not impossible, for a mother carrying a nursing child to travel long distances on a regular basis. Because early *Homo* males (and perhaps females without young children) would have been freer to roam farther from home, they probably became the scavengers or hunters. While they were away seeking carcasses or small game, women with young children may have gathered wild plants within a small area that could be covered without traveling far from the home base.

The creation of home bases among early *Homo* groups may have increased the likelihood of food sharing. If mothers with young children were limited to gathered plant foods near a home base, the only way to ensure that they and their children could obtain a complete diet would have been to share the other foods obtained elsewhere. With whom would such sharing take place? Most likely with close relatives. Sharing with them would have made it more likely that their offspring would survive to have offspring. Thus early *Homo* groups located at a home base and connected by bonds of family and sharing could have encouraged the development of the learned and shared behaviors that we call *culture*.

Obviously this is a "just-so" story—a tale that we never may be able to prove really happened. However, it is a tale that is consistent with the archaeological record. Patterned stone tools do not appear until early *Homo* came on the scene. And with early *Homo* we see the start of several trends in hominid evolution that appear to be related to the manufacture and use of patterned stone tools—the expansion of the brain, the modification of the female pelvis to accommodate bigger-brained babies, and a general reduction in the size of teeth, face, and jaws.

Trends in Hominid Evolution

EXPANSION OF THE BRAIN

The australopithecines had relatively small cranial capacities, about 380 to 530 cubic centimeters (cc)—not much larger than that of chimpanzees. But around 2.3 million years ago, close to the time that patterned stone tools first appear, some hominids showed evidence of enlarged brain capacity. These hominids, early *Homo*, had cranial capacities averaging about 630–640 cc, which is about 50 percent of the brain capacity of modern humans (average slightly more than 1,300 cc). (See Figure 7–4.) A later member of our genus, *Homo erectus*, which may have first appeared about 1.8 million years ago, had a cranial capacity averaging about 895–1,040 cc, or about 70 percent of the brain capacity of modern humans.[34]

The australopithecines were small, and the earliest *Homo* finds were hardly bigger, so much of the increase in brain size over time might have been a result of later hominids' bigger bodies. When we correct for body size, however, it turns out that brain size increased not only absolutely but also relatively after 2 million years ago. Between about 4 million and 2 million years ago, relative brain size remained just about the same. Only in the last 2 million years has the hominid brain doubled in relative size and tripled in absolute size.[35]

What may have favored the increase in brain size? As we have noted earlier, many anthropologists think that the increase is linked to the emergence of stone tool making about 2.5 million years ago. The reasoning is that stone tool making was important for the survival of our ancestors, and therefore natural selection would have favored bigger-brained individuals because they had motor and conceptual skills that enabled them to be better toolmakers. According to this view, the expansion of the brain and more and more sophisticated toolmaking would have developed together. Other anthropologists think that the expansion of the brain may have been favored by other factors, such as warfare, hunting, longer life, and language.[36] Whatever the factors favoring bigger brains, they also provided humans with an expanded capacity for culture. Thus, along with bipedalism, the expansion of the brain marks a watershed in human evolution. (See the box "Brains and Blood" for a discussion of some of the physiological problems that had to be overcome in order for the brain to expand.)

As the hominid brain expanded, natural selection also favored the widening of the female pelvis to allow larger-brained babies to be born. But there was probably a limit to how far the pelvis could widen and still be adapted to bipedalism. Something had to give, and that something was the degree of physical development of the human infant at birth—for instance, the human infant is born with cranial bones so plastic that they can overlap. Because birth takes place before the cranial bones have hardened, the human infant with its relatively large brain can pass through the opening in the mother's pelvis. Human infants are born at a relatively early stage of development, and are wholly dependent on their parents for many years. As we have noted, this lengthy period of infant dependency may have been an important factor in the evolution of culture.

CURRENT ISSUES
Brains and Blood

The human brain is the most complex organ in the body—and the most demanding. The brain must have a constant supply of oxygen and sugar to function, and that means it requires a lot of blood. The brain also generates heat, yet the brain is very sensitive to heat changes—a few degrees too hot and the brain will be damaged. These two demands—blood supply and temperature control—are linked in the human brain, according to paleoanthropologist Dean Falk.

Falk has examined the evolution of the human brain using endocasts. She has particularly studied the vessels that carry blood to and from the brain (see the figure in this box). These vessels can be seen on endocasts in two ways. Like other brain features, they leave an impression on the inside of the cranium, but endocasts also reveal the small holes in the cranial bones, called *emissary foramena,* through which blood vessels run. Using these clues, Falk has been able to

reconstruct the way blood moved in and out of the brain in early hominids.

According to Falk, bipedalism raised a major obstacle in hominid brain evolution. With the brain perched on top of the head, the circulatory system had to keep blood flow constant. In quadrupedal apes, blood from the brain drains directly into the jugular vein. But the additional pull of gravity on the blood in a bipedal ape, Falk argues, would put too much stress on the jugular, potentially causing it to rupture. Australopithecines apparently overcame this problem by developing large sinuses in the back of the brain, which slowed the blood flow when the animal stood up. But as the brain and its demand for blood increased in early *Homo,* a more efficient system had to be developed to maintain blood flow to and from the enlarging brain.

Falk argues that early *Homo* developed two separate systems to drain blood from the brain.

One is the system of large vessels, similar to the one in australopithecines, that drains blood across the top and down the sides of the brain and into the jugular. Unlike the australopithecines, however, members of the *Homo* genus use this system as the primary blood drainage system only when lying down. Falk argues that in early *Homo* a secondary system of smaller blood vessels, called the *emissary system,* evolved to help drain blood from the brain when individuals were standing upright. Falk suggests that by developing the use of both blood drainage systems, early *Homo* was able to maintain a large brain supplied with blood whether lying down or standing up.

Falk's ideas about controlling brain temperature are more controversial. She argues that the emissary system of blood vessels not only helps drain blood from the brain but also serves as a "radiator" to help cool the brain. Falk suggests that these small

REDUCTION OF THE FACE, TEETH, AND JAWS

As in the case of the brain, substantial changes in the face, teeth, and jaws do not appear in hominid evolution until after about 2 million years ago. The australopithecines all have cheek teeth that are very large relative to their estimated body weight, perhaps because the diet of the australopithecines was especially high in plant foods,[37] including small, tough objects such as seeds, nuts, and tubers. The australopithecines have thick jawbones, probably also related to their chewing needs. The australopithecines have relatively large faces that project forward below the eyes. But when we get to the *Homo* forms, we see reduction in the size of the face, cheek teeth, and jaws (see Figure 7–5). It would seem that natural selection in favor

of a bigger and stronger chewing apparatus was relaxed. One reason might be that members of the *Homo* genus ate foods that were easier to chew. Such foods might have included roots, fruits, and meat. As we discuss later, it may have been the development of habitual tool use and the control of fire that allowed members of the *Homo* genus to change their diet to include easier to chew foods, including meat. If food is cooked and easy to chew, individual humans with smaller jaws and teeth would not be disadvantaged, and therefore the face, cheek teeth, and jaw would get smaller on average over time.

OTHER EVOLVED TRAITS

The fossil evidence, which we discuss below and in the next chapter, suggests when, and in which hominids,

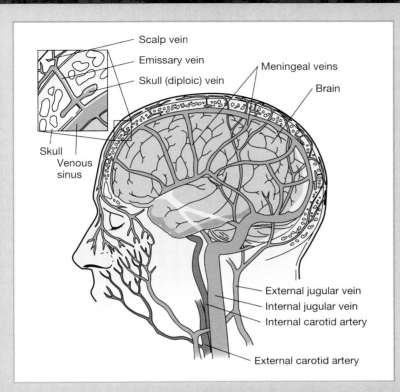

Scalp vein

Emissary vein

Skull (diploic) vein

Meningeal veins

Brain

Skull
Venous
sinus

External jugular vein

Internal jugular vein

Internal carotid artery

External carotid artery

Source: Illustration copyright © 1993 by Carol Donner. Reprinted by permission of Carol Donner.

search, they are valuable in illustrating an important point about the expansion of the brain. Growing the brain in a bipedal hominoid was not a simple process, but required the solving of at least two problems—maintaining blood flow and temperature. When we think about trends in hominid evolution such as the expansion of the brain, we must remember that the changes we discuss were often accompanied by other significant physiological changes. The expansion of the human brain was not simply a process of "scaling up" the ancient hominoid brain, but required new anatomy so that a larger brain could be supplied with blood and cooled.

Sources: Dean Falk, *Brain Dance* (New York: Henry Holt, 1992); Dean Falk, "A Good Brain Is Hard to Cool," *Natural History,* August 1993, 65–66.

vessels carry blood that has been cooled on the face and scalp into the center of the brain, where it is warmed and then carried out of the brain, taking some of the brain's heat with it. The emissary system, then, not only helps maintain blood flow in the brain but also helps to regulate the brain's internal temperature.

Whether or not Falk's ideas are supported through future re-

---

changes occurred in brain size and in the face, teeth, and jaws. Other changes in the evolution of hominids cannot yet be confidently dated with regard to time and particular hominid. For example, we know that modern humans are relatively hairless compared with the other surviving primates. But we do not know when hominids became relatively hairless, because fossilized bones do not tell us whether their owners were hairy. On the other hand, we suspect that most of the other characteristically human traits developed after the brain began to increase in size, during the evolution of the genus *Homo.*

What is the evidence that the physical and behavioral changes we have been discussing occurred during the evolution of the *Homo* genus? We shall now consider the earliest *Homo* fossils and how they are associated with brain expansion and the reduction of the face, jaws, and teeth.

　CD-ROM Interactive Exercise II-9

 Early Homo Fossils

Hominids with a brain absolutely and relatively larger than that of the australopithecines appear about 2.3 million years ago. These hominids, classified in our own genus, *Homo,* are generally divided into two species: **Homo habilis** and **Homo rudolfensis.** Both are known primarily from the western parts of Kenya and Tanzania, but remains have been found elsewhere in eastern and

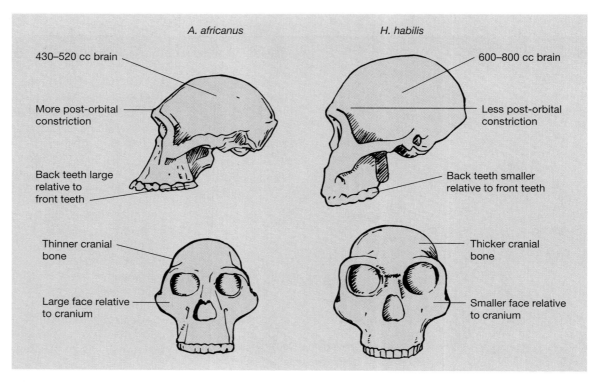

Figure 7–5 *Comparison of* A. africanus *and* H. habilis

The skull of a *Homo habilis/rudolfensis* (ER-1470) found by Richard Leakey in 1972. Note its high forehead and large braincase.

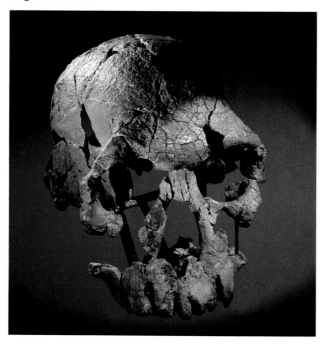

southern Africa, including the Omo Basin of Ethiopia and Sterkfontein cave in South Africa. Both lived in the same place and time as the robust australopithecine, *Australopithecus boisei*, and may later have lived at the same time as *Homo erectus*.

Homo habilis appears to be the earlier of these two species, appearing around 2.3 million years ago. Compared with the australopithecines, *H. habilis* had a significantly larger brain, averaging 630–640 cc,[38] and reduced molars and premolars.[39] The rest of the skeleton is reminiscent of the australopithecines, including the presence of powerful hands and relatively long arms, suggesting that *H. habilis* was at least partially arboreal. *H. habilis* may also have been sexually dimorphic like the australopithecines, as individuals seem to have greatly differed in size.

Homo rudolfensis is roughly contemporary with *Homo habilis*, and shares many of its features. Indeed, many paleoanthropologists make no distinction between the two species, putting *H. rudolfensis* into *H. habilis*. Those who do see them as distinct species point to the larger and more thickly enameled cheek teeth of *H. rudolfensis*, its flatter and broader face, and its more modernlike limb proportions. Even with its larger teeth and broader face, the dentition of *H. rudolfensis* is considerably reduced over the australopithecines and, like *H. habilis*, its brain is at least a third larger.

We have little postcranial skeletal material for either

early *Homo* species, so it is impossible to tell whether the female pelvis had changed. But, with brains averaging a third larger than the australopithecines', it seems likely that some modifications must have developed to allow these bigger-brained babies to be born. We do know that changes in the female pelvis to accommodate bigger-brained babies can be seen in *Homo erectus,* and it is to this species that we turn in the next chapter.

Summary

1. The earliest identifiable stone tools found so far come from various sites in East Africa and date from about 2.5 million years ago. Flake tools predominate, but choppers are also common. Choppers are cores that have been partially flaked and have a side that might have been used for chopping. These early stone tools are referred to as Oldowan.

2. Archaeologists have experimented with what can be done with Oldowan tools. The flakes appear to be very versatile; they can be used for slitting the hides of animals, dismembering animals, and whittling wood. The choppers can be used to hack off branches or cut and chop tough animal joints. Shortly after 2 million years ago, hominids were cutting up animal carcasses for meat, mostly obtained through scavenging rather than hunting.

3. There are archaeological sites dating as early as 2 million years ago that contain concentrations of stone tools and animal bones. Some scholars think these might have been early hominid home bases; others do not. If these sites were not home bases, what were they? Some archaeologists are beginning to think that these early sites with many animal bones and tools may just have been places where hominids processed food but did not live.

4. The presence of stone tools and perhaps home bases suggests that early hominids had culture. Culture is a dynamic, adaptive process of learned, shared, and integrated behaviors. Many primate social behaviors are adaptive, and some primates have a few learned and shared behaviors, but none comes close to the dynamic system of social behavior that is culture.

5. One of the reasons primates are social is that being social allows group learning to take place. Another reason for being social is for group protection. Finally, social behavior provides some advantages in foraging. While there are many benefits to being social, there is one major drawback—stress. Primates have developed several ways to minimize social stress, including dominance hierarchies and grooming.

6. Important physical changes in early hominids that led to the evolution of our genus, *Homo*, include the expansion of the brain, the modification of the female pelvis to allow bigger-brained babies to be born, and the reduction of the face, teeth, and jaws. These physical changes are seen in the species *Homo habilis* and *Homo rudolfensis,* both of which date to around 2.3 million years ago. Early

Homo appears to have used tools and scavenged or possibly hunted meat, so culture, or the evolution of cultural behavior, seems to have played a role in these physical changes as well.

Glossary Terms

bifacial tool	Oldowan
culture	percussion flaking
Homo habilis	unifacial tool
Homo rudolfensis	

Critical Questions

1. Why might early hominids have begun to make stone tools? How would stone tools have been more useful than wood or bone tools?

2. What might have been some of the advantages of home bases for early hominids? What might have been some of the disadvantages?

3. In what ways are human social behavior more complex than that of other primates?

4. How do the physical changes that occur in early hominids correlate with the apparent changes in their behavior?

Internet Exercises

1. Visit the Hooper Virtual Natural History Museum (**http://www.wf.carleton.ca/Museum/1.html**) and examine one or more of the exhibits on human evolution; then visit the exhibits on human evolution at the Mankato EMuseum (**http://emuseum.mankato.msus.edu/biology/humanevolution/index.shtml**). Compare and contrast the exhibits at the two virtual museums.

2. Go to the *Journal of Human Evolution*'s home page at **http://www.academicpress.com/jhevol** and examine the table of contents for several recent issues. Describe the types of research currently being done on hominid origins and early hominid culture.

3. Visit the Palomar college page on early hominid culture (**http://daphne.palomar.edu/homo/homo_3.htm**) and write a brief essay describing what new information or insights you gained.

4. Explore the University of Minnesota, Duluth's early *Homo* pages, located at **http://www.d.umn.edu/cla/faculty/troufs/anth1602/pchomo-e.html**.

Suggested Reading

DELSON, E., ED. *Ancestors: The Hard Evidence.* New York: Alan R. Liss, 1985. A collection of papers on human evolution and the fossil evidence for it. Some are quite technical, but all are informative. The papers in section IV (pp. 91–201) are most relevant to early hominids.

SCHICK, K., AND TOTH, N. *Making Silent Stones Speak.* New York: Simon & Schuster, 1993. A large part of understanding past tool traditions is making them and using them. The authors describe their experimental work and relate it to the archaeologically recovered tool traditions of the past.

RASMUSSEN, T., ED. *The Origin and Evolution of Humans and Humanness.* Boston: Jones and Bartlett, 1993. A collection of essays examining early hominids and the origins of culture.

TATTERSALL, I. *The Human Odyssey.* New York: Prentice Hall, 1993. A well-illustrated overview of human evolution written for a general audience.

TATTERSALL, I. AND SCHWARTZ, J. *Extinct Humans.* Boulder, CO: Westview, 2000. A beautifully illustrated guide to fossil humans. All of the early hominids are covered in detail, including *H. habilis* and *H. rudolfensis*.

8

Homo erectus and the Origins of Language

omo erectus evolved very shortly after *Homo habilis,* probably about 1.8 million years ago (see Figure 8–1). **Homo erectus** was the first hominid species to be widely distributed in the Old World. Examples of *H. erectus* were first found in Java, later in China, and still later in Africa. Most paleoanthropologists agree that some human ancestor moved from Africa to Asia at some point. Until recently, it was assumed that it was *H. erectus* who moved, because *H. erectus* lived in East Africa about 1.6 million years ago but not until after about 1 million years ago in Asia.[1] Recent redating, however, suggests that *H. erectus* in Java may be somewhat older, dating to perhaps 1.8 million years ago.[2]

And new *H. erectus* fossils from Dmanisi, Georgia, have recently been dated to 1.7 million years ago.[3] If this dating is accurate, early hominids may have moved out of Africa earlier, or *H. erectus* may have emerged elsewhere.

There is also a question of whether there is only one species of *H. erectus* or whether *H. erectus* contains several distinct species. Some scholars see enough differences between Asian and African populations of *H. erectus* to argue that they should be separated into two distinct species, *Homo erectus* for the Asian populations and *Homo ergaster* for the African ones. Furthermore, *Homo erectus* (or *Homo ergaster*) fossils are also found in Europe; but some paleoanthropologists think that the finds in Europe typically

Figure 8–1 *The Evolution of* Homo erectus

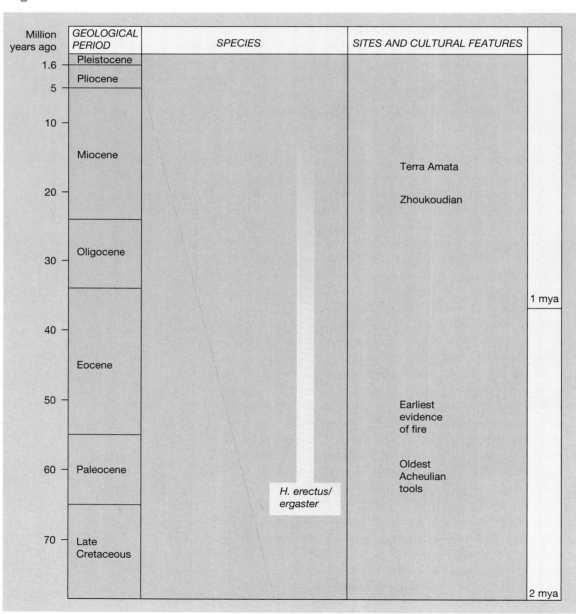

classified as *H. erectus* are actually early examples of *H. sapiens*.[4] Others think these European fossils, and similar ones in southern Africa and the Near East, should be grouped into a distinct species, *Homo heidelbergensis*. It is all a bit confusing. Later we will try to sort it all out.

The Discovery of *Homo erectus*

In 1891, Eugene Dubois, a Dutch anatomist digging in Java, found what he called *Pithecanthropus erectus,* meaning "erect ape man." (We now refer to this hominid as *Homo erectus*.) The discovery was not the first humanlike fossil found; Neandertals, which we discuss in the next chapter, were known many years earlier. But no one was certain, not even Dubois himself, whether the fossil he found in Java was an ape or a human.

The actual find consisted of a cranium and a thighbone. For many years it was thought that the fragments were not even from the same animal. The skull was too large to be that of a modern ape but was smaller than that of an average human, having a cranial capacity between the average ape's 500 cubic centimeters (cc) and the average modern human's 1,300 cc. The thighbone, however, matched that of a modern human. Did the two fragments in fact belong together? The question was resolved many years later by fluorine analysis. If fossils from the same deposit contain the same amount of fluorine, they are the same age. The skull fragment and thighbone found by Dubois were tested for fluorine content and found to be the same age.

A discovery by G. H. R. von Koenigswald in the mid-1930s, also in Java, not only confirmed Dubois' earlier speculations and extended our knowledge of the physical characteristics of *Homo erectus* but also gave us a better understanding of this early human's place in time. Since then, many more *H. erectus* fossils have been found in Java. These *H. erectus* in Java were thought not to be more than 1 million years old;[5] now argon-argon dating puts some of the Java specimens back to a time 1.8 million years ago.[6]

Between the times of Dubois' and von Koenigswald's discoveries, Davidson Black, a Canadian anatomy professor teaching in Peking (Beijing), China, set out to investigate a large cave at nearby Zhoukoudian where a fossilized tooth had been found. Confident that the tooth came from a hitherto unknown hominid genus, he obtained funds to excavate the area extensively. After two years of excavation, he and his colleagues found a skull in limestone whose owner was dubbed "Peking man." Black died in 1934, and his work was carried on by Franz Weidenreich.

It was not until the 1950s that *H. erectus* fossils were uncovered in northern Africa (see Figure 8–2). Many finds since then come from East Africa, particularly two sites— Olduvai Gorge in Tanzania and the Lake Turkana region of Kenya. An almost complete skeleton of a boy was found at Nariokotome, on the western side of Lake Turkana, dating from about 1.6 million years ago. The Olduvai finds are from about 1.2 million years ago.[7]

PHYSICAL CHARACTERISTICS OF HOMO ERECTUS

The *Homo erectus* skull generally was long, low, and thickly walled, with a flat frontal area and prominent brow

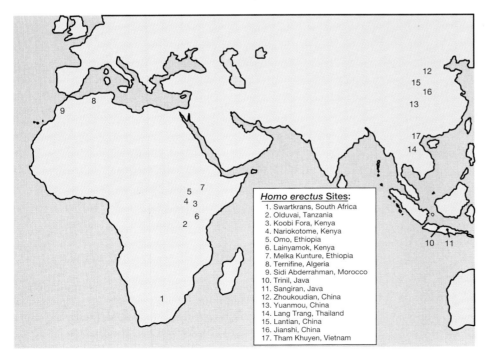

Figure 8–2
Homo erectus *Sites*

Source: From Russell L. Ciochon and John G. Fleagle, eds., *The Human Evolution Source Book.* Copyright © 1993. Reprinted by permission of Pearson Education, Inc., Upper Saddle River, NJ 07458.

Homo erectus Sites:
1. Swartkrans, South Africa
2. Olduvai, Tanzania
3. Koobi Fora, Kenya
4. Nariokotome, Kenya
5. Omo, Ethiopia
6. Lainyamok, Kenya
7. Melka Kunture, Ethiopia
8. Ternifine, Algeria
9. Sidi Abderrahman, Morocco
10. Trinil, Java
11. Sangiran, Java
12. Zhoukoudian, China
13. Yuanmou, China
14. Lang Trang, Thailand
15. Lantian, China
16. Jianshi, China
17. Tham Khuyen, Vietnam

ridges. It has a unique pentagonal shape when looked at from the back, formed in part by a rounded ridge, called a **sagittal keel,** running along the crest of the skull. There is also a ridge of bone running horizontally along the back of the skull, called an **occipital torus,** which adds to the skull's overall long shape (see Figure 8–3).[8]

Compared with early *Homo, H. erectus* had relatively small teeth. *H. erectus* was the first hominid to have third molars that were smaller than the second or first molars, as in modern humans. The molars also had an enlarged pulp cavity, called **taurodontism,** which may have allowed the teeth to withstand harder use and wear than the teeth of modern humans. But the jaw was lighter and thinner than in either early *Homo* or the australopithecines, and the face was less **prognathic,** or forward-thrusting, in the upper and lower jaw.

The brain, averaging 895–1,040 cc, was larger than that found in any of the australopithecines or early *Homo* species, but smaller than the average brain of a modern human.[9] Endocasts, which provide a picture of the surface of the brain, suggest that it was organized more like the brain of modern humans than like that of australopithecines.

Homo erectus had a prominent, projecting nose, in contrast to the australopithecines' flat, nonprojecting nose.[10] From the neck down, *H. erectus* was practically indistinguishable from *H. sapiens.* In contrast to the smaller australopithecines and early *Homo* species who lived in East Africa around the same time, *H. erectus* was comparable to modern humans in size. The almost complete skeleton of the boy at Nariokotome suggests that he was about 1.6 meters tall when he died, and about 11 years of age; researchers estimate that he would have been 1.9 meters tall had he lived to maturity. About 1.6 million years ago, the Nariokotome region was probably open grassland, with

The skull of a *Homo erectus/ergaster* (ER-3733) from East Africa.

trees mostly along rivers.[11] *Homo erectus* in East Africa was similar in size to Africans today who live in a similarly open, dry environment.[12] *H. erectus* was also less sexually dimorphic than either the australopithecines or early *Homo.* The degree of sexual dimorphism in *H. erectus* was comparable to that in modern humans.

Those scholars who distinguish African populations as a distinct species, *Homo ergaster,* point to several differences between them and other *Homo erectus* populations: The cranial proportions differ in *Homo ergaster;* the brow ridge is thinner and is arched above each of the eye sockets; the eye sockets are more rounded; and the face is oriented more vertically below the skull, among others. On the other hand, some scholars believe the differences between *Homo erectus* and modern humans are not large enough to call us different species, and argue that *Homo erectus* populations should be lumped into *Homo sapiens.*[13] These arguments will not be settled any time soon, and for the purposes of this book we will stick with the single taxon, *Homo erectus* (see the box "*Homo erectus*: One or More Species?").

The Evolution of *Homo erectus*

The evolution of *Homo erectus* reflects a continuation of the general evolutionary trends we discussed in the last chapter. The brain continued to expand, increasing more than a third over early *Homo* (just as early *Homo* had increased more than a third over the australopithecines).

Figure 8–3   **Homo erectus *Features***

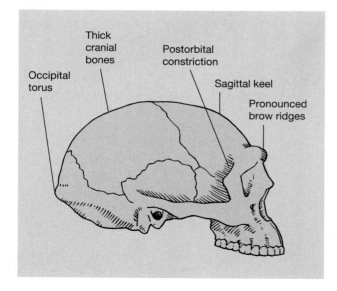

Occipital torus

Thick cranial bones

Postorbital constriction

Sagittal keel

Pronounced brow ridges

RESEARCH FRONTIERS
Homo erectus: *One or More Species?*

In living populations it is possible to tell whether two different primates belong to different species. Can they interbreed? And are the offspring fertile? If the answer to either question is no, we are dealing with different species. But how can we tell species apart in the fossil record? Paleoanthropologists must judge by degree of difference between them. Once two populations stop interbreeding, they will begin to develop divergent traits. But how different do they have to be for us to call them different species?

Because the fossil record does not reveal mating patterns, it is not surprising that paleoanthropologists have differences of opinion about whether two fossils represent the same species or not. And paleoanthropologists have different predispositions; some tend to be "splitters," identifying more different species, and others tend to be "lumpers," identifying fewer different species. In the 1920s and 1930s, splitting was common; almost every new find of what we now call *Homo erectus* was assigned to a different species or even a different genus. For example, *Pithecanthropus erectus* is now called *H. erectus* from Java, and *Sinanthropus pekinensis* is now *H. erectus* from near Peking (Beijing). Franz Weidenreich in the 1940s suggested this lumping, which dominated classification through the 1960s and 1970s. But, in the 1980s, Peter Andrews, Christopher Stringer, and Bernard Wood proposed that the Asian and African fossils previ-

ously grouped as *H. erectus* were different enough to be split into two separate species—one Asian (*H. erectus*) and one African (*H. ergaster*). So once again there were opposing hypotheses about those fossils. Was *H. erectus* one or two species?

To discover which hypothesis is more likely to be correct, Andrew Kramer analyzed various skull measurements for the Asian and African fossils and two other groups—modern humans, who we know belong to the same species, and a mixed set of early hominids, who are conventionally classified as belonging to two or three different species. Kramer reasoned that if the African and Asian fossils are not more variable than the modern humans, we can conclude that those fossils belong to one species, *H. erectus*. And the mixed set of ancient hominids should be more variable than the modern humans.

The 16 Asian and African skulls in Kramer's analysis (that might or might not be from a single species, *H. erectus*) were the ones available that could provide the required measurements. They ranged in dating from 1.8 million to 500,000 years ago; other things being equal, such a great range in dating should make for more variability and therefore more likelihood that the 16 supposed *H. erectus* skulls would show more variability than the sample of modern humans. Kramer wanted to compare the 16 with the same number of modern skulls. But how does one choose 16 modern

skulls from the many available? (He had measurements from 2,533 skulls.) One random sample would not be sufficient. One can never know for sure how representative a particular random sample of 16 is. So Kramer used 1,000 different random samples of 16 each from the 2,533 modern skulls available. For each trait compared, he computed a measure of variability for the sample of 16. What were the results of the comparisons? The 16 supposed *H. erectus* skulls were no more variable than most of the modern human samples, strongly suggesting that they did come from the same species. To test this conclusion further, Kramer compared the modern samples with the mixed sample of ancient hominids (the skulls used were again ones that allowed the required measurements). Because the mixed ancient sample presumably came from more than one species, it should look more variable than the modern human samples. And it did. Almost all of the modern human samples were less variable than the mixed ancient sample.

So Kramer's research strongly suggests that the hominids in Asia and Africa between 1.8 million years and 500,000 years ago were all *Homo erectus*.

Source: Andrew Kramer, "The Natural History and Evolutionary Fate of *Homo erectus*," in Peter N. Peregrine, Carol R. Ember, and Melvin Ember, eds., *Physical Anthropology: Original Readings in Method and Practice* (Upper Saddle River, NJ: Prentice Hall, 2002).

The face, teeth, and jaws continued to shrink, taking on an almost modern form. An increasing use and variety of tools may have led to a further development of the brain. *Homo erectus* was eating and probably cooking meat, and this may have led to further reduction in the teeth and jaws.

One additional change in *Homo erectus* is an apparent reduction in the extent of sexual dimorphism to almost modern levels. Recall that the australopithecines and early *Homo* were quite sexually dimorphic. *Homo erectus* does not appear to be as sexually dimorphic as these earlier hominids. What might have caused this change? In other primates, sexual dimorphism appears to be linked to social systems in which males are at the top of dominance hierarchies and dominant males control sexual access to multiple females. In contrast, lack of sexual dimorphism seems most pronounced in both primates and other animals where *pair bonding* exists—that is, where one male and one female form a breeding pair that lasts for a long period of time.[14] Could pair bonding have developed in *Homo erectus*? It seems likely.

Recall from the last chapter that early *Homo* seems to have established some of the basic elements of human culture, including home bases, family groups, and sharing. Another basic element of recent human culture, one that is present in all known cultures, is *marriage*. Marriage is a socially recognized sexual and economic bond between two individuals that is intended to continue throughout the lifetimes of the individuals and that can produce socially accepted children. It is essentially a pair bond that is formalized through human culture into a set of behaviors, expectations, and obligations that extend beyond the pair to those individuals' families. With marriage, then, the competition between males for access to females may have diminished, lessening the importance of sexual dimorphism. But why might marriage have developed in *Homo erectus*?

In animal species where females can feed themselves and their babies after birth, pair bonding is rare. But in species where females cannot feed both themselves and their babies, pair bonding is common. Why? We think it is because a pair bond provides the best solution to the problem of providing food to the mother—a male can obtain food and bring it back to his female partner and children.[15] Most primates lack pair bonding. This may be because primate infants are able to cling to their mother's fur soon after birth, so that the mother's hands are free to forage. (Interestingly, human infants demonstrate a residual form of this innate ability to cling during their first few weeks of life, called the *Moro reflex*. If a human infant feels it is falling backward, it will automatically stretch out its arms and clench its fists.[16])

We have no way of knowing if *Homo erectus* had fur like other primates, but we think probably not because, as we discuss below, we think they may have worn clothing. The brain in *Homo erectus* may also have already expanded enough that *Homo erectus* infants, like modern human infants, could not adequately support their heads

This De Brazza monkey has no problem traveling with her infant, as it can cling tightly to her fur. *Homo erectus* mothers probably had no fur to hold on to and had to carry their infants.

even if they could hold onto their mother's fur. In any case, when early hominids began to depend on scavenging and hunting for food (and skins for clothing), it would have been difficult and hazardous for mothers with infants to engage in these activities with their infants along. Marriage would have been an effective solution to this problem.

Another important aspect of the evolution of *Homo erectus* was the movement of populations out of eastern and southern Africa. As with the lessening of sexual dimorphism, it seems likely that cultural innovations were key to allowing *Homo erectus* to move into new environments. Why? Because upon entering new environments *Homo erectus* would have been faced with new (and generally colder) climatic conditions, new and different sources of raw material for tools, and new plants and animals to rely on for food. All animals adapt to such changes through natural selection, but natural selection typically takes a relatively long time and requires physical changes in the adapting organisms. *Homo erectus* was able to adapt to new environments very quickly and without apparent physical changes. This suggests that the primary mechanisms of adaptation for *Homo erectus* were cultural rather than biological.

What cultural adaptations might *Homo erectus* have made? Fire might have been one cultural adaptation to colder climates. As we discuss below, there is tantalizing evidence that *Homo erectus* used fire. But fire can only warm people when they are stationary; it doesn't help when people are out collecting food. To be mobile in colder climates, *Homo erectus* may have begun wearing animal furs for warmth. Some *Homo erectus* tools look like the hide-processing tools used by more recent human groups,[17] and it seems unlikely that *Homo erectus* could have survived in some of the colder locations where they have been found in eastern Europe and Asia without some form of clothing. And if *Homo erectus* was wearing furs for warmth, it seems likely they must have been hunting. *Homo erectus* could not have depended on scavenging to acquire skins—the skin is the first thing predators destroy when they dismember a carcass. *Homo erectus* would have had to kill fur-bearing animals themselves if they wanted intact skins for clothing.

It is interesting to consider that in eastern Africa *Homo erectus* co-existed with at least one other species of hominid (*A. boisei*), and possibly with as many as three (*A. boisei, A. africanus,* and *H. habilis/rudolfensis*). Why did *Homo erectus* survive and flourish while these other species went extinct? Again, culture may be the answer. *A. boisei* seems to have been a specialized grasslands species. Their large molars and powerful dental architecture allowed them to eat hard grass seeds and other coarse materials that other hominids could not chew. However, they had to compete with the many other grassland animals who also relied on these plants, but who also reproduced faster and had speed to help them escape from predators. Early *Homo* was apparently a tool user and relied at least in part on scavenging and hunting, but compared to *Homo erectus,* early *Homo* technology was crude and their social organization was not as complex. *Homo erectus* appears to have been better organized to scavenge and hunt and to defend themselves against predators. These differences in culture may have provided enough of an advantage to *Homo erectus* that they drove early *Homo* to extinction.

This scenario, just like the one we suggested for the evolution of early *Homo*, is a "just-so" story that may or may not be true. But it does fit the facts we know about *Homo erectus* and the area in which it evolved. And, regardless of this story's particular accuracy, there seems no doubt that the development of a more complex culture was vital to the evolution of *Homo erectus.*

Lower Paleolithic Cultures

The stone tool traditions of *Homo erectus* are traditionally called **Lower Paleolithic.** This refers specifically to "core" tool techniques, in which a core of stone, rather than a flake, is used as the basic raw material for finished tools

(we will talk more about Lower Paleolithic stone tool technology later). Since stone tools are the most common cultural material in the archaeological record of these ancient peoples, the entire culture of *Homo erectus* is often termed *Lower Paleolithic,* a practice we follow here.

The archaeological finds of tools and other cultural artifacts dating from 1.5 million years to about 200,000 years ago are assumed to have been produced by *Homo erectus.* But fossils are not usually associated with these materials. Therefore it is possible that some of the tools during this period were produced by hominids other than *H. erectus,* such as australopithecines earlier and *H. sapiens* later. The so-called *Acheulian* tool assemblages dating from 1.5 million years ago to more than a million years later are very similar to each other, and *H. erectus* is the only hominid that spans the entire period. Thus it is conventionally assumed that *H. erectus* was responsible for most if not all of the Acheulian tool assemblages we describe below.[18]

THE ACHEULIAN TOOL TRADITION

A stone tool-making tradition known as the **Acheulian** was named after the site at St. Acheul, France, where the first examples were found. But the oldest Acheulian tools recovered are from East Africa, on the Peninj River, Tanzania, dating back about 1.5 million years.[19] In contrast to Oldowan, Acheulian assemblages have more large tools created according to standardized designs or shapes. Oldowan tools have sharp edges made by a few blows. Acheulian toolmakers shaped the stone by knocking more flakes off most of the edges. Many of these tools were made from very large flakes that had been struck from very large cores or boulders.

One of the most characteristic and common tools in the Acheulian tool kit is the so-called **hand axe,** which is a teardrop-shaped, bifacially flaked tool with a thinned sharp tip. Other large tools resemble cleavers and picks. There were also many kinds of flake tools, such as scrapers with a wide edge.

Early Acheulian tools appeared to have been made by blows with a hard stone, but later tools are wider and flatter and may have been made with a soft "hammer" of bone or antler.[20] This **soft hammer** technique of making stone tools was an important innovation. Tools made by a **hard hammer** technique, rock against rock, have limits in terms of their sharpness and form, because only large and thick flakes can be made with a hard hammer technique (unless the flintknapper is very skillful and the stone being used has unique qualities). Flakes created by soft hammer flaking are much thinner and longer than hard hammer flakes, and the flintknapper generally has better control over their size and shape. This means that thinner and sharper tools can be made, as well as tools with complex shapes. Hand axes can be made with either technique, as their shape is simple, but those made using a soft hammer have much thinner and sharper edges.[21]

Were hand axes made for chopping trees, as their name suggests? We cannot be sure what they were used for, but

CURRENT ISSUES

Putting Faces on Fossils

Have you ever wondered how we know what early humans looked like? We have pictures of them throughout this book, but how did the artists determine what to sculpt or draw? The answer lies in the field of forensic anthropology and more particularly in the field of facial reconstruction.

Facial reconstruction is based on knowledge of skull musculature and the thickness of soft tissue, determined over many years (the first such analysis was done in 1895) from cadavers and, more recently, magnetic resonance images of living people. From these measurements, forensic anthropologists have established a standard set of 21 to 34 locations on the skull where the average soft tissue thicknesses are known. The first step in facial reconstruction is to mark these locations on a cast of the skull to be reconstructed, using pegs that

Homo erectus, *seen in this skull and facial reconstruction, had prominent brow ridges, a thickly walled skull, and a low forehead. Its brain capacity was about 70 percent of that of modern humans.* H. erectus *was hardly distinguishable from modern humans from the neck down.*

are the same length as the thickness of muscle and soft tissue at that location. Clay is then used to cover the skull cast to the

depth of these pegs (the musculature of the face is first modeled in more sophisticated reconstructions, then clay is used to

---

experiments with them suggest that they are not good for cutting trees; they seem more suited for butchering large animals.[22] Lawrence Keeley microscopically examined some Acheulian hand axes, and the wear on them is more consistent with animal butchery. They may have been used for woodworking, particularly hollowing and shaping wood, and they are also good for digging.[23] William Calvin has even suggested that hand axes could be used as projectiles thrown like a discus into herds of animals in the hope of injuring or killing an animal.[24]

Acheulian tools are found widely in Africa, Europe, and western Asia, but bifacial hand axes, cleavers, and picks are not found as commonly in eastern and southeastern Asia.[25] Because H. erectus has been found in all areas of the Old World, it is puzzling why the tool traditions seem to differ from west to east. Recently, some archaeologists have suggested that large bifacial tools may be lacking in eastern and southeastern Asia because H. erectus in Asia had a better material to make tools out of—bamboo.

Bamboo is used today in Southeast Asia for many purposes, including incredibly sharp arrows and sticks for digging and cutting. Geoffrey Pope has shown that bamboo is found in those areas of Asia where hand axes and other large bifacial tools are missing.[26]

BIG-GAME EATING

Some of the Acheulian sites have produced evidence of big-game eating. F. Clark Howell, who excavated sites at Torralba and Ambrona, Spain, found a substantial number of elephant remains and unmistakable evidence of human presence in the form of tools. Howell suggests that the humans at those sites used fire to frighten elephants into muddy bogs, from which they would be unable to escape.[27] To hunt elephants in this way, the humans would have had to plan and work cooperatively in fairly large groups.

But do these finds of bones of large and medium-sized

represent the soft tissues, up to the depth of the pegs).

The size and shape of the nose are reconstructed based on the size and shape of the nasal opening. The size and shape of lips and ears are more difficult to determine, and the skull itself can tell the forensic anthropologist almost nothing about hair or eye color, whether the person had facial hair, or how the person's hair was cut. Those aspects of facial reconstruction require some artistic intuition, and it is helpful to know something about the person, such as sex, age, and ethnicity.

But what about ancient humans? The standard measurements used to reconstruct faces from modern human skulls cannot be assumed to work for ancient skulls. For those, the forensic anthropologists have to go back to the basis of facial reconstruction—muscle and soft tissue. When reconstructing the faces of ancient humans, forensic anthropologists begin with a careful reconstruction of skull musculature, often aided by the comparative anatomy of modern great apes. Once the muscles are in place, glands, fatty tissue, and skin are added, and the face begins to take shape. The size and shape of the nose are determined much like that for modern humans, from the size and shape of the nasal opening. Lips, ears, eyes, and hair are, however, subject to almost pure guesswork—we really have no way of knowing how hairy our ancestors were, whether they had full lips like ours or thin lips like other great apes, or whether their ears were large or small.

Though based on study of the likely muscular anatomy in fossils and the comparative anatomy of modern humans and great apes, it is important to realize that the reconstruction of ancient faces is in part an artistic exercise. We can never know for sure what, for example, *Homo erectus* really looked like. We do not know how hairy they were or how they "styled" their hair. We do not know if their ears were like ours. We do not know the color of their eyes or skin. This is why reconstructions vary in the ways they depict ancient humans. We need to keep in mind when we look at reconstructions that they are educated, perhaps biased, guesses, and not true depictions of ancient people.

Sources: John Prag and Richard Neave, *Making Faces: Using Forensic and Archaeological Evidence* (College Station: Texas A&M University Press, 1997); Stephanie Moser, *Ancestral Images: The Iconography of Human Origins* (Ithaca, NY: Cornell University Press, 1998).

animals, in association with tools, tell us that the humans definitely were big-game hunters? Some archaeologists who have reanalyzed the evidence from Torralba think that the big game may have been scavenged. Because the Torralba and Ambrona sites are near ancient streams, many of the elephants could have died naturally, their bones accumulating in certain spots because of the flow of water.[28] What seems fairly clear is that the humans did deliberately butcher different kinds of game—different types of tools are found with different types of animal.[29] Thus, whether the humans hunted big game at Torralba and Ambrona is debatable; all we can be sure of, as of now, is that they consumed big game and probably hunted smaller game.

CONTROL OF FIRE

One way in which *H. erectus* is thought to have hunted is by using *fire drives*—a technique still used by hunting and gathering peoples in recent times. It is highly effective: Animals are driven out of their hiding places and homes by fire and dispatched by hunters positioned downwind of the oncoming flames. Most peoples who use this technique today set fires deliberately, but fires caused by lightning strikes may have also been utilized. Did *H. erectus* set these fires? Because *H. erectus* was the first hominid to be found throughout the Old World and in areas with freezing winters, most anthropologists presume that *H. erectus* had learned to control fire, at least for warmth. There is archaeological evidence of fire in some early sites, but fires can be natural events. Thus, whether fire was under deliberate control by *H. erectus* is difficult to establish.[30]

Suggestive but not conclusive evidence of the deliberate use of fire comes from Kenya in East Africa and is over 1.4 million years old.[31] More persuasive, but still not definite, evidence of human control of fire, dating from nearly 500,000 years ago, comes from the cave at Zhoukoudian in China where *H. erectus* fossils have been found.[32] In that

Homo erectus ate—and probably hunted—large game animals, and they probably also learned to control fire.

cave are thousands of splintered and charred animal bones, apparently the remains of meals. There are also layers of ash, suggesting human control of fire.

But recent analysis raises questions about these finds. The most serious problem is that human remains, tools, and ash rarely occur together in the same layers. In addition, there are no hearths at the Zhoukoudian site. Fires can spontaneously occur with heavy accumulation of organic matter, so clear evidence of human control of fire is still not definitely attested. Even the inference that humans brought the animals to the cave for butchering is only possibly a correct guess. Throughout the cave there is evidence of hyenas and wolves, and they, not the humans, may have brought many of the animal parts to the cave.[33]

Evidence of the deliberate use of fire comes from Europe somewhat later. Unfortunately, the evidence of control of fire at these European sites is not associated with *H. erectus* fossils either, so the link between deliberate use of fire and *H. erectus* cannot be definitely established yet. The lack of clear evidence does not, of course, mean that *H. erectus* did not use fire. After all, *H. erectus* did move into cold areas of the world, and it is hard to imagine how that could have happened without the deliberate use of fire. Such a move is also hard to imagine if *H. erectus* were relatively hairless and did not get warm skins from hunting.

Clothing, therefore, may have been necessary, but fire might have been more important, not only for warmth. Cooking would also be possible. The control of fire was a major step in increasing the energy under human control. Cooking made all kinds of possible food (not just meat) more safely digestible and therefore more usable. Fires would also have kept predators away, a not inconsiderable advantage given that there were many.

CAMPSITES

Acheulian sites were usually located close to water sources, lush vegetation, and large stocks of herbivorous animals. Some camps have been found in caves, but most were in open areas surrounded by rudimentary fortifications or windbreaks. Several African sites are marked by stony rubble brought there by *H. erectus*, possibly for the dual purpose of securing the windbreaks and providing ammunition in case of a sudden attack.[34]

The presumed base campsites display a wide variety of tools, indicating that the camp was the center of many group functions. More specialized sites away from camp have also been found. These are marked by the predominance of a particular type of tool. For example, a butchering site in Tanzania contained dismembered hippopotamus carcasses and rare heavy-duty smashing and cutting tools. Workshops are another kind of specialized site encountered with some regularity. They are characterized by tool debris and are located close to a source of natural stone suitable for toolmaking.[35]

A camp has been excavated at the Terra Amata site near Nice, on the French Riviera. The camp appears to have been occupied in the late spring or early summer, judging by the pollen found in fossilized human feces. The excavator describes stake holes driven into the sand, paralleled by lines of stones, presumably marking the spots where the people constructed huts of roughly 30 by 15 feet (Figure 8–4). A basic feature of each hut was a central hearth that seems to have been protected from drafts by a small wall built just outside the northeast corner of the hearth. The evidence suggests that the Terra Amata occupants gathered seafood such as oysters and mussels, did some fishing, and hunted in the surrounding area. The animal remains suggest that they obtained both small and large animals but mostly got the young of larger animals such as stags, elephants, boars, rhinoceroses, and wild oxen. Some of the huts contain recognizable toolmakers' areas, scattered with tool debris; occasionally, the impression of an animal skin shows where the toolmaker actually sat.[36]

RELIGION AND RITUAL

Thus far we have discussed the life-styles of Lower Paleolithic and, in the last chapter, of late Pliocene peoples, but we have not talked about the less material aspects of life, such as religion and ritual. What beliefs did *Homo erectus* hold about the world around them? Did they take part in rituals? Did *H. erectus* have religion? So far, the answer seems to be no. The data we have to answer these questions are limited, but there are, in fact, some hints that ritual and religion may have been a part of Lower Paleolithic culture.

Remains of *red ochre* (oxidized clay) have been found

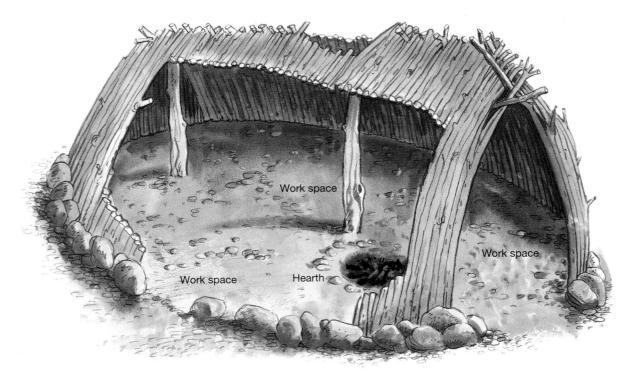

Figure 8–4 *A Reconstruction of the Oval Huts Built at Terra Amata*

These huts were approximately 30 feet by 15 feet. *Source:* Copyright © 1969 by Eric Mose. Reprinted by permission of Eric Mose, Jr.

on a number of Lower Paleolithic sites.[37] This may be significant because in many later cultures, even modern ones, red ochre has been used to represent blood or, more generally, life in rituals of various types. Ochre seems to be particularly important in burial rituals, and human remains sprinkled with red ochre have been found in many parts of the world and dating as far back as the Middle Paleolithic (about 200,000 years ago). However, there is no evidence that *Homo erectus* buried their dead, nor any evidence that ochre was used in rituals. It may have been used for body decoration, or simply for protection against insects or sunburn.

More significant, and even more controversial, is the suggestion made by the excavators of Zhoukoudian (in north China) that some of the *H. erectus* remains there showed evidence of ritual cannibalism.[38] The foramen magnum of some specimens had been deliberately enlarged and the facial bones had been deliberately broken away from the cranium on others. Apparently, the reason was to remove the brain for ritual consumption. Ritual cannibalism has been widely reported among living peoples, so its presence among ancient peoples is not impossible. But in the absence of formal burial rituals, cannibalism seems improbable. In addition, scholars point out that the parts of the skull that seem to have been purposely enlarged (to remove the brain) are those that are also the weakest points on the skull, and may have broken away because of decay or disturbance over the millennia.

At this point, we simply cannot say whether religion and ritual were parts of Lower Paleolithic culture.

Language

Another question we have few direct ways of answering is the question of language. Did *Homo erectus* have language? Dean Falk has examined the external structures of the brain by studying cranial endocasts—the impressions the brain leaves on the inside of the cranium. She argues that some of the areas of the brain known to be linked with speech are present on *Homo habilis* brains.[39] On the other hand, Philip Lieberman has argued that the vocal tract of *Homo erectus* was not capable of producing speech sounds, at least not those used in human languages today.[40] But does this mean *Homo erectus* could not have had language? The question requires us to have some understanding of what language is.

WHAT IS LANGUAGE?

Language is the primary system of human communication, but systems of communication are not unique to human beings. Other animal species communicate in a variety of ways. One way is by sound. A bird may communicate by a call that "this is my territory"; a squirrel may utter a cry that leads other squirrels to flee from danger.

This wolf is using vocal communication, but it is not like human language.

Another means of animal communication is odor. An ant releases a chemical when it dies, and its fellows then carry it away to the compost heap. Apparently the communication is highly effective; a healthy ant painted with the death chemical will be dragged to the funeral heap again and again. Another means of communication, body movement, is used by bees to convey the location of food sources. Karl von Frisch discovered that the black Austrian honeybee—by choosing a round dance, a wagging dance, or a short, straight run—can communicate not only the precise direction of the source of food but also its distance from the hive.[41]

Although primates use all three methods of communication—sound, odor, and body movement—it is sound that most concerns us here because spoken language is human beings' major means of communication. Nonhuman primates communicate vocally too, making various kinds of calls (but not very many of them). In the past, only human communication was thought to be symbolic. Recent research suggests that some monkey and ape calls in the wild are also symbolic.

When we say that a communication (call, word, sentence) is *symbolic,* we mean at least two things. First, the communication has meaning even when its *referent* (whatever is referred to) is not present. Second, the meaning is arbitrary; the receiver of the message could not guess its meaning just from the sound(s) and does not know the meaning instinctively. In other words, symbols

have to be learned. There is no compelling or "natural" reason that the word *dog* in English should refer to a smallish four-legged omnivore that is the bane of letter carriers.

As we discussed briefly in the last chapter, scientists who have observed vervet monkeys in their natural environment consider at least three of their alarm calls to be symbolic because each of them *means* (refers to) a different kind of predator—eagles, pythons, or leopards—and monkeys react differently to each call. Experimentally, in the absence of the referent, investigators have been able to evoke the normal reaction to a call by playing it back electronically.[42]

Another indication that the vervet alarm calls are symbolic is that infant vervets appear to need some time to learn the referent for each. When they are very young, infants apply a particular call to more animals than adult vervets apply the call to. So, for example, infant vervets will often make the eagle warning call when they see any flying bird. The infants learn the appropriate referent apparently through adult vervets' repetition of infants' "correct" calls; in any case, the infants gradually learn to restrict the call to eagles.[43] This process is probably not too different from the way a North American infant in an English-speaking family first applies the "word" *dada* to all adult males and gradually learns to restrict it to one person.

All of the nonhuman vocalizations we have described so far enable individual animals to convey messages. The sender gives a signal that is received and "decoded" by the receiver, who usually responds with a specific action or reply. How is human vocalization different? Since monkeys and apes appear to use symbols at least some of the time, it is not appropriate to emphasize symbolism as the distinctive feature of human language. However, there is a significant quantitative difference between human language and other primates' systems of vocal communication. All human languages employ a much larger set of symbols. Another and perhaps more important difference is that the other primates' vocal systems tend to be *closed*—that is, different calls are not often combined to produce new, meaningful utterances. In contrast, human languages are *open* systems, governed by complex rules about how sounds and sequences of sounds can be combined to produce an infinite variety of meanings.

The idea that humans can transmit many more complex messages than any other animal does not begin to convey how different human language is from other communication systems. No chimpanzee could say the equivalent of "I'm going to the ball game next Wednesday with my friend Jim if it's not raining." Humans not only can talk (and think) with language about things completely out of context; they also can be deliberately or unconsciously ambiguous in their messages. If a person asks you for help, you could say, "Sure, I'll do it when I have time," leaving the other person uncertain about whether your help is ever going to materialize.

Primates in the wild do not exhibit anything close to human language. But recent successful attempts to teach

Sue Savage-Rumbaugh gives the bonobo Kanzi a hug after his successful completion of a comprehension and syntax quiz on the symbol keyboard he uses to communicate.

apes to communicate with humans and with each other using human-created signs have led some scholars to question the traditional assumption that the gap between human and other animal communication is enormous. Even the bird brain of a parrot named Alex seems to be capable of some symbolic communication. When he is not willing to continue a training session, Alex says: "I'm sorry . . . Wanna go back."[44] Chimpanzees Washoe and Nim and the gorilla Koko were taught hand signs based on American Sign Language (ASL; used by the hearing impaired in the United States). The chimpanzee Sarah was trained with plastic symbols.

More recently, Lana, Sherman, Austin, and a bonobo, Kanzi, have been trained on symbol keyboards connected to computers. Sherman and Austin began to communicate with each other about actions they were intending to do, such as the types of tools they needed to solve a problem. And they were able to classify items into categories, such as "food" and "tools." In contrast to other apes, Kanzi learned symbols just by seeing humans point to them when they spoke to him. He did not need rewards or to have his hands put in the right position. And he understood a great deal of what was spoken to him. For example, when he was 5 years old, Kanzi heard someone talk about throwing a ball in the river, and he turned around and did so. Kanzi has come closest of all the "students" to having a primitive English grammar when he strings symbols together.[45] If chimpanzees and other primates have the capacity to use nonspoken language and even to understand spoken language, then the difference between humans and nonhumans may not be as great as people used to think.

Are these apes really using language? There is a lot of agreement among investigators that nonhuman primates have the ability to "symbol"—to refer to something (or a class of things) with an arbitrary "label" (gesture or sequence of sounds).[46] For example, the gorilla Koko (with a repertoire of about 375 signs) extended the sign for *drinking straw* to plastic tubing, hoses, cigarettes, and radio an-

tennae. Washoe originally learned the sign *dirty* to refer to feces and other soil and then began to use it insultingly, as in "dirty Roger," when her trainer Roger Fouts refused to give her things she wanted. Even the mistakes made by the apes suggest that they are using signs symbolically, just as words are used in spoken language. For example, the sign *cat* may be used for dog if the animal learned *cat* first (just as the Embers' daughter Kathy said "dog" to all pictures of four-footed animals, including elephants, when she was 18 months old).

In spite of the new evidence, Jane Hill believes that the answer about whether apes use language is still controversial because language is not one unitary thing. For instance, there does not appear to be anything comparable to linguistic rules in ape "language." Humans may make lists and speeches, tell stories, argue, and recite poetry. Apes do none of those things. But apes do have some of the capacities for some of the elements of human language. Therefore, understanding their capacities may help us better understand the evolution of human language.[47]

THE ORIGINS OF LANGUAGE

Most speculation about the origins of language has centered on the question of how natural selection may have favored the open quality of language. All known human languages are "open" in the sense that utterances can be combined in various ways to produce new meanings.[48] Somehow a call system of communication was eventually changed to a system based on small units of sound that can be put together in many different ways to form meaningful utterances. For example, an English speaker can combine *care* and *full* (*careful*) to mean one thing, then use each of the two elements in other combinations to mean different things. *Care* can be used to make *carefree*, *careless*, or *caretaker*; *full* can be used to make *powerful* or *wonderful*. And because language is a system of shared symbols, it can be re-formed into an infinite variety of expressions and be understood by all who share these symbols. In this way, for example, T. S. Eliot could form a sentence never before formed—"in the room the women come and go/talking of Michelangelo"[49]—and the sense of his sentence, though not necessarily his private meaning, could be understood by all speakers of English.

One group of theoreticians of grammar suggests that there may be a *language-acquisition device* in the brain, as innate to humans as call systems are to other animals.[50] As the forebrain evolved, this device may have become part of our biological inheritance. Whether such a mechanism exists is not clear. But we do know that the actual development of individual language is not completely biologically determined; if it were, all human beings would speak the same brain-generated language. Instead, about 4,000 to 5,000 mutually unintelligible languages have been identified. More than 2,000 of them were still spoken as of recently, most by peoples who did not traditionally have a system of writing. Indeed, the earliest writing systems are not that old; they appeared only about 5,000 years ago.[51]

Can we learn anything about the origins of language by studying the languages of modern nonliterate and technologically simpler societies? The answer is no, because such languages are not simpler or less developed than ours. The sound systems, vocabularies, and grammars of technologically simpler peoples are in no way inferior to those of peoples with more complex technology.[52] Of course, people in other societies, and even some people in our own society, will not be able to name the sophisticated machines used in our society. All languages, however, have the potential for doing so. All languages possess the amount of vocabulary their speakers need, and all languages expand in response to cultural changes. A language that lacks terminology for some of our conveniences may have a rich vocabulary for events or natural phenomena that are of particular importance to the people in that society.

If there are no primitive languages, and if the earliest languages have left no traces that would allow us to reconstruct them, does that mean we cannot investigate the origins of language? Some linguists think that understanding the way children acquire language, which we discuss shortly, can help us understand the origins of language (see the box "Mother-Infant Communication and the Origin of Language"). Recently, other linguists have suggested that an understanding of how creole languages develop will also tell us something about the origins of language.

CREOLE LANGUAGES Some languages developed in various areas where European colonial powers established commercial enterprises that relied on imported labor, generally slaves. The laborers in one place often came from several different societies and in the beginning would speak with their masters and with each other in some kind of *pidgin* (simplified) version of the masters' language. Pidgin languages lack many of the building blocks found in the languages of whole societies, building blocks such as prepositions (*to, on*, and so forth) and auxiliary verbs (designating future and other tenses). Many pidgin languages developed into and were replaced by so-called *cre-*

ole languages, which incorporate much of the vocabulary of the masters' language but also have a grammar that differs from it and from the grammars of the laborers' native languages.[53]

Derek Bickerton argues that there are striking grammatical similarities in creole languages throughout the world. This similarity, he thinks, is consistent with the idea that there is a universal grammar inherited by all humans. Creole languages, therefore, may resemble early human languages. All creoles use intonation instead of a change in word order to ask a question. The creole equivalent of the question "Can you fix this?" would be "You can fix this?" The creole version puts a rising inflection at the end; in contrast, the English version reverses the subject and verb without much inflection at the end. All creoles express the future and the past in the same grammatical way, by the use of particles (such as the English *shall*) between subject and verb, and they all employ double negatives, as in the Guyana English creole "Nobody no like me."[54]

It is possible that there are many things about language that are universal, that all languages are similar in many respects, because of the way humans are "wired" or because people in all societies have similar experiences. For example, names for frogs may usually contain *r* sounds because frogs make them.[55]

CHILDREN'S ACQUISITION OF LANGUAGE Apparently a child is equipped from birth with the capacity to reproduce all the sounds used by the world's languages and to learn any system of grammar. The language the child learns is the one spoken by the parents or caretakers.

Children's acquisition of the structure and meaning of language has been called the most difficult intellectual achievement in life. If that is so, it is pleasing to note that they accomplish it with relative ease and vast enjoyment. This "difficult intellectual achievement" may in reality be a natural response to the capacity for language that is one of humans' genetic characteristics. All over the world children begin to learn language at about the same age, and in no culture do children wait until they are 7 or 10 years old. By 12 or 13 months of age, children are able to name a few objects and actions, and by 18 to 20 months they can make one key word stand for a whole sentence: "Out!" for "Take me out for a walk right now"; "Juice!" for "I want some juice now." Evidence suggests that children acquire the concept of a word as a whole, learning sequences of sounds that are stressed or at the ends of words (for example, "raffe" for giraffe). Even hearing-impaired children learning signs in ASL tend to acquire and use signs in a similar fashion.[56]

Children the world over tend to progress to two-word sentences at about 18 to 24 months of age. In their sentences they express themselves in "telegraph" form—using nounlike words and verblike words but leaving out the seemingly less important words. So a two-word sentence such as "Shoes off" may stand for "Take my shoes off" or "More milk" may stand for "Give me more milk, please."[57] They do not utter their two words in random order, some-

NEW PERSPECTIVES ON GENDER
Mother-Infant Communication and the Origin of Language

Most models for the origin of human language identify tool use and hunting as major factors driving the development of language skills in early humans. In order to make complex tools like hand axes, one needs to be able to think abstractly about how to flake the stone into the desired shape. Most models of language origin suggest that language was fostered because one has to be able to convey these abstract ideas in order to teach others how to make complex tools. Similarly, most models of language origin suggest that language was needed for humans to stalk and kill large game animals. Individuals would have had to carefully plan and coordinate hunts, and this would have fostered language.

Problems with these models of language origin are well recognized. Flintknappers have suggested that observation and imitation are more important than vocal communication in learning to make stone tools. Most contemporary hunters communicate with hand signals rather than speech during hunts. In fact, greater dependence on hunting predicts the use of sign language. But despite these problems, the view that tool use and hunting promoted language is still widely accepted. Feminist scholars have raised another objection: gender bias. They suggest that toolmaking and hunting are typically male roles, so that these models

of language origin see males as the producers of human language. Several have suggested alternative models that give women a primary role in language origins.

Catherine Borchert and Adrienne Zihlman have argued that language may have developed through mother-infant communication. Borchert and Zihlman suggest that the problems faced by hominid mothers and infants that we have already discussed as important for the origin of culture—the long period of dependency and the difficulty hominid mothers with young infants would have had in feeding themselves—may also have played a key role in the origin of language. The extreme dependency of human infants on their mothers may have been one important factor. Infants would have had to convey both distress and desire to their mothers. Anyone who has ever been around infants knows that they are able to let you know when they are content, when they are in distress, and when they want something, even though they cannot talk. Borchert and Zihlman argue that many uniquely human traits like crying, smiling, laughing, and cooing may have evolved as a way for mothers and infants to communicate, and such communication may well have provided the beginnings of human language.

Borchert and Zihlman also

point out that child rearing in human groups is a social process with many caretakers, not just the mother, looking after children. Communication would have been essential in these interactions as well, both for the mother and the child. The mother would have needed to be able to convey known needs and preferences to caretakers of her child and more significantly, the child would have had to be able to communicate with caretakers who were not their mother. Sharing child care would have required a shared communication system that all members of the group, both adults and infants, could understand. Again, Borchert and Zihlman suggest it may have been these social interactions among mothers, infants, and caretakers that formed the foundation for human language, and not toolmaking and hunting.

Sources: Catherine Borchert and Adrienne Zihlman, "The Ontogeny and Phylogeny of Symbolizing," in M. LeC. Foster and L. J. Botsharow, *The Life of Symbols* (Boulder, CO: Westview, 1990), pp. 15–44; Adrienne Zihlman, "Women's Bodies, Women's Lives: An Evolutionary Perspective," in M. E. Morbeck, A. Galloway, and A. Zihlman, eds., *The Evolving Female: A Life-History Perspective* (Princeton, NJ: Princeton University Press, 1997), pp. 185–97; William Divale and Clifford Zipin, "Hunting and the Development of Sign Language: A Cross-Cultural Test," *Journal of Anthropological Research,* 33 (1977): 185–201.

times saying "off " first, other times saying "shoes" first. If a child says "Shoes off," then he or she will also say "Clothes off" and "Hat off." They seem to select an order that fits the conventions of adult language, so they are

likely to say "Daddy eat," not "Eat Daddy." In other words, they tend to put the subject first, as adults do. And they tend to say "Mommy coat" rather than "Coat Mommy" to indicate "Mommy's coat."[58] Adults do not utter sentences

Children learn language naturally and with apparent ease. Here English-speaking children are learning a second language in school—Chinese.

such as "Daddy eat," so children seem to know a lot about how to put words together with little or no direct teaching from their caretakers. Consider the 5-year-old who, confronted with the unfamiliar "Gloria in Excelsis," sings quite happily, "Gloria eats eggshells." To make the words fit the structure of English grammar is more important than to make the words fit the meaning of the Christmas pageant.

If there is a basic grammar imprinted in the human mind, we should not be surprised that children's early and later speech patterns seem to be similar in different languages. We might also expect children's later speech to be similar to the structure of creole languages. And it is, according to Derek Bickerton.[59] The "errors" children make in speaking are consistent with the grammar of creoles. For example, English-speaking children 3 to 4 years old tend to ask questions by intonation alone, and they tend to use double negatives, such as "I don't see no dog," even though the adults around them do not speak that way and consider the children's speech wrong.

Future research on children's acquisition of language and on the structure of creole languages may bring us closer to an understanding of the origins of human language.

Lower Paleolithic Language?

We know that language is a universal human capacity that is, at least in part, "hard-wired" into our brains. We also know that some of the structures of the brain that are important for language were present in the earliest members of our genus. We have seen that modern apes have the ability to acquire rudimentary forms of language in specific settings, and that all humans acquire language in an apparently universal manner. Does this mean that our Lower Paleolithic ancestors, and *Homo erectus* in particular, had language? Or were they only beginning to develop what would later become this distinctive human capacity?

One of the most striking things about language is its diversity. As noted earlier, there are some 2,000 languages currently spoken and perhaps an equal number that have recently gone extinct. Language and culture are intimately linked, and we know that the diversity of languages in the world is paralleled by a similar diversity of cultures. Lower Paleolithic culture lacks apparent diversity (or at least the diversity of modern culture). Hand axes from different parts of the world show some divergence, but the basic form and technique of manufacture are much the same. Similarly, language, like culture, is constantly changing and innovating, and we might expect peoples with language to have constant change in their material culture, as we find among modern humans. But Lower Paleolithic material culture remained remarkably unchanged for more than a million years.

Perhaps more significantly, language is a complex system of symbolic communication, and in modern cultures complex symbolic communication is not restricted to spoken language but is represented in the entire range of material culture. We find stylistic variation, artistic expression, and experimentation widely expressed in the material culture of modern peoples. People today use material culture to convey ideas and beliefs, along with status, wealth, and identity. Lower Paleolithic material culture lacks art, shows little in the way of stylistic variation or experimentation, and does not appear to have been used to convey meaning to others.[60]

Together, the material record of Lower Paleolithic peoples suggests that complex symbolic communication was not present, and it therefore seems likely that *Homo erectus* did not have language, at least not language as we know it today.[61] Their social behavior and ability to move into new and challenging environments suggest that they must have had a complex system of communication, but it also does not seem to have had the productive and highly symbolic elements of human language. Most scholars today believe that language is a more recent development—perhaps as recent as the last 50,000 years, a time when human culture began to display the kinds of complex symbolic communication (such as art) that Lower Paleolithic cultures seem to lack. We consider the evolution of modern humans and their cultures in the next chapter.

Summary

1. *Homo erectus* emerged about 1.8 million to 1.6 million years ago. It had a larger brain capacity than *Homo habilis* and an essentially modern postcranial skeleton. What differentiates *Homo erectus* most from modern humans is the shape of the skull, which is long, low, and has prominent brow ridges.

2. *Homo erectus* was the first hominid species to be widely distributed in the Old World. Some of the locations where *Homo erectus* lived in eastern Europe and Asia were quite cold, and *Homo erectus* was able to adapt to these new and often colder environments through culture.

3. Lower Paleolithic tools and other cultural artifacts from about 1.6 million to about 200,000 years ago were probably produced by *H. erectus*. Acheulian is the name given to the most well-known tool tradition of this period. Acheulian tools include both small flake tools and large tools, but hand axes and other large bifacial tools are characteristic.

4. Although it is presumed that *H. erectus* had learned to use fire to survive in areas with cold winters, there is no definite evidence of the control of fire by *H. erectus*. There is evidence in some sites of big-game eating, but whether *H. erectus* hunted those animals is debatable. There is little evidence of ritual behavior among *H. erectus*.

5. Language is an exceptionally complex symbolic communication system. Living apes have been able to acquire some rudimentary language skills, but language seems to be a unique human capacity. Studies of the brain, of creole languages, and of child language acquisition suggest that language is "hard-wired" into our brains. While cranial endocasts suggest *Homo erectus* had some of the brain structures for language, there is little additional evidence that *Homo erectus* had language.

Glossary Terms

Acheulian	occipital torus
hand axe	prognathic
hard hammer	sagittal keel
Homo erectus	soft hammer
Lower Paleolithic	taurodontism

Critical Questions

1. How did *Homo erectus* culture differ from the culture of earlier hominids?

2. When compared to earlier hominids, *Homo erectus* is larger, has a larger brain, and smaller teeth. How might these physical changes correlate with apparent behavioral changes in *Homo erectus*?

3. What evidence is there that *Homo erectus* had language? What evidence is there that *Homo erectus* did not have language?

4. *Homo erectus* lived in many places in the Old World. What enabled them to spread so widely?

Internet Exercises

1. Go to the Smithsonian Institution Hall of Human Ancestors site at **http://www.mnh.si.edu/anthro/humanorigins/ha/ances_start.html**. Examine the QTVR image of *Homo ergaster* (WT 15000). Compare it with the other QTVR images of hominid skulls you can view on the site.

2. Go to **http://www.cruzio.com/~cscp/maps.htm** to view sites where fossil hominids have been found in China.

3. Explore a site devoted to stone tool technology at **http://www.hf.uio.no/iakn/roger/lithic/sarc.html**. Look in particular for earlier stone tool technologies.

Suggested Reading

CHIA, L. *The Story of Peking Man: From Archaeology to Mystery.* Oxford: Oxford University Press, 1990. A history of research at the Zhoukoudian site, including an interesting examination of the mysterious loss of all the early fossil material during World War II.

KRAMER, A. "The Natural History and Evolutionary Fate of *Homo erectus.*" In P. N., Peregrine, C. R. Ember, and M. Ember, eds., *Physical Anthropology: Original Readings in Method and Practice.* Upper Saddle River, NJ: Prentice Hall, 2002. An overview of *Homo erectus* and the multiregional hypothesis of modern human origins.

RIGHTMIRE, G. P. *The Evolution of* Homo erectus: *Comparative Anatomical Studies of an Extinct Human Species.* Cambridge: Cambridge University Press, 1990. A review of the anatomical features of *Homo erectus* and how they changed over time.

SHIPMAN, P. *The Man Who Found the Missing Link: Eugene Dubois and His Lifelong Quest to Prove Darwin Right.* New York: Simon & Schuster, 2001. A new biography of Eugene Dubois and his discovery of *Homo erectus.*

WALKER, A., AND SHIPMAN, P. *The Wisdom of the Bones: In Search of Human Origins.* New York: Knopf, 1996. An informative account of the discovery and analysis of a *Homo erectus* skeleton, written for the nonprofessional.

9

The Emergence of *Homo sapiens*

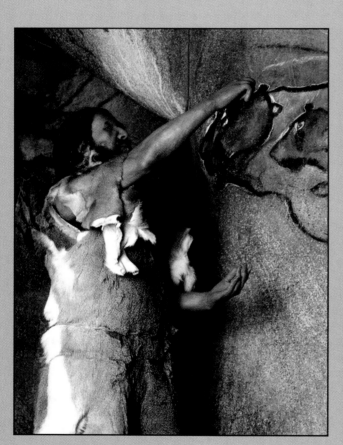

ntil about 20 years ago, paleoanthropologists thought that our species *Homo sapiens* evolved in the last 50,000 years. Now we know that our species appeared earlier (see Figure 9–1). The date of about 50,000 years ago is for Europe, but recent finds in southern Africa and elsewhere indicate the presence of *Homo sapiens* at least 100,000 years ago. Completely modern-looking humans, ***Homo sapiens sapiens,*** appeared about 50,000 years ago. One paleoanthropologist, Christopher Stringer, characterizes the modern human, *Homo sapiens sapiens,* as having "a domed skull, a chin, small eyebrows, brow ridges, and a rather puny

skeleton."[1] Some of us might not like to be called puny, but except for our larger brain, most modern humans definitely are puny compared with *Homo erectus* and even with earlier forms of our own species, *H. sapiens.* We are relatively puny in several respects, including our thinner and lighter bones, as well as our smaller teeth and jaws.

In this chapter we discuss the fossil evidence, as well as the controversies, about the transition from *H. erectus* to modern humans, which may have begun 500,000 years ago. We also discuss what we know archaeologically about the Middle Paleolithic cultures between about 300,000 and 40,000 years ago.

Figure 9–1 *Timeline for the Emergence of Modern Humans**

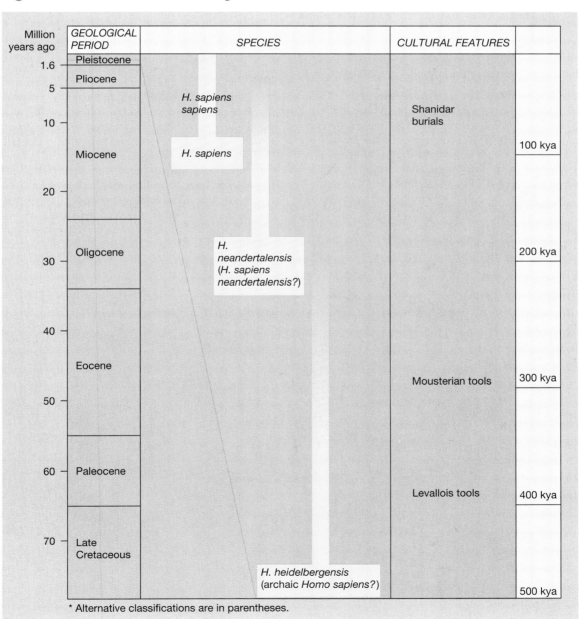

* Alternative classifications are in parentheses.

The Transition from *Homo erectus* to *Homo sapiens*

Most paleoanthropologists agree that *H. erectus* evolved into *H. sapiens*, but they disagree about how and where the transition occurred. There is also disagreement about how to classify some fossils from about 500,000 to 200,000 years ago that have a mix of *H. erectus* and *H. sapiens* traits.[2] A particular fossil might be called *H. erectus* by some anthropologists and "archaic" *Homo sapiens* by others. And, as we shall see, still other anthropologists see so much continuity between *H. erectus* and *H. sapiens* that they think it is completely arbitrary to call them different species. According to these anthropologists, *H. erectus* and *H. sapiens* may just be earlier and later varieties of the same species and therefore all should be called *H. sapiens*. (*H. erectus* would then be *H. sapiens erectus*.)

HOMO HEIDELBERGENSIS

In recent years scholars have suggested that the "transitional" fossils share common traits and may actually represent a separate species—***Homo heidelbergensis,*** named after a jaw found in 1907 in the village of Mauer near Heidelberg, Germany.[3] Other specimens that have been suggested as members of this species have been found in many parts of the world: Bodo, Hopefield, Ndutu, Elandsfontein, and Rabat in Africa; Bilzingsleben, Petralona, Arago, Steinheim, and Swanscombe in Europe; and Dali and Solo in Asia.

Homo heidelbergensis differs from *Homo erectus* in hav-

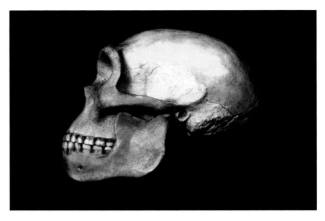

A reconstructed skull of *Homo heidelbergensis,* based on the mandible found at Mauer, Germany. While resembling *Homo erectus, Homo heidelbergensis* has smaller teeth and jaws and a larger brain.

ing smaller teeth and jaws, a much larger brain (on the order of 1,300 cc), a skull that lacks a sagittal keel and occipital torus, a brow ridge that divides into separate arches above each eye, and an overall robusticity in its skeleton (see Figure 9–2). *Homo heidelbergensis* differs from *Homo sapiens* in retaining a large and prognathic face with relatively large teeth and jaws, a brow ridge, a long, low cranial vault with a sloping forehead, and in its overall robusticity.[4] Many scholars question whether *Homo heidelbergensis* represents one or several species of Middle Pleistocene hominid, or whether it is indeed a separate species at all. Many would argue that *Homo heidelbergensis* should be considered an archaic *Homo sapiens*. As noted, some

Figure 9–2

Comparison of the crania of Homo heidelbergensis, Homo neandertalensis, *and* Homo sapiens, *showing important differences.*

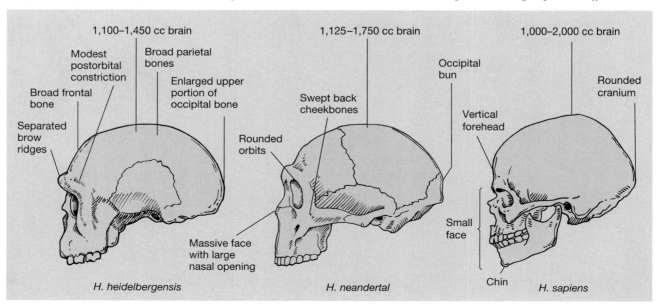

scholars also argue that *Homo erectus* should be included in the *Homo sapiens* species.

 CD-ROM Interactive Exercise II-10

NEANDERTALS: HOMO SAPIENS OR HOMO NEANDERTALENSIS?

There may be disagreement about how to classify the mixed-trait fossils from 500,000 to 200,000 years ago, but recently an outright battle has emerged about many of the fossils that are less than 200,000 years old. Some anthropologists argue that they were definitely *Homo sapiens* and classify them as *Homo sapiens neandertalensis*. Others, that they were part of a distinct species, **Homo neandertalensis,** more commonly referred to as the **Neandertals.** The Neandertals have been a confusing hominid fossil group since the first specimen was found in 1856. Somehow through the years, the Neandertals have become the victims of their cartoon image, which usually misrepresents them as burly and more ape than human. Actually, they might go unnoticed in a cross section of the world's population today. Were they part of our species? For a while the answer seemed to be yes. But recent archaeological and genetic evidence has led many to question the relationship between Neandertals and modern humans, and

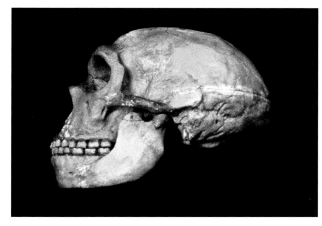

The reconstructed skull of a *Homo neandertalensis* man found at La Chapelle-aux-Saints, France.

today the tide seems to be turning against those who would group them together. Let's take a look at some of the history of research on the Neandertals.

In 1856, three years before Darwin's publication of *The Origin of Species,* a skullcap and other fossilized bones were discovered in a cave in the Neander Valley (*tal* is the German word for "valley"), near Düsseldorf, Germany. The fossils in the Neander Valley were the first that scholars could tentatively consider as an early hominid. (The fossils classified as *Homo erectus* were not found until later

Boule's reconstruction of Neandertal (left) as displayed at Chicago's Field Museum in 1929, and a more recent reconstruction (right). The recent reconstruction makes Neandertal seem more like modern humans.

in the nineteenth century, and the fossils belonging to the genus *Australopithecus* not until the twentieth century.) After Darwin's revolutionary work was published, the Neandertal find aroused considerable controversy. A few evolutionist scholars, such as Thomas Huxley, thought that the Neandertal was not that different from modern humans. Others dismissed the Neandertal as irrelevant to human evolution; they saw it as a pathological freak, a peculiar, disease-ridden individual. However, similar fossils turned up later in Belgium, Yugoslavia, France, and elsewhere in Europe, which meant that the original Neandertal find could not be dismissed as an oddity.[5]

The predominant reaction to the original and subsequent Neandertal-like finds was that the Neandertals were too "brutish" and "primitive" to have been ancestral to modern humans. This view prevailed in the scholarly community until well into the 1950s. A major proponent of this view was Marcellin Boule, who claimed between 1908 and 1913 that the Neandertals would not have been capable of complete bipedalism. Boule and others may have been misled by the bowed leg bones, due to the vitamin-deficiency disease called rickets, in some Neandertal specimens. Since the 1950s, however, a number of studies have disputed Boule's claim, and it is now generally

agreed that the skeletal traits of the Neandertals are completely consistent with bipedalism.

Perhaps more important, when the much more ancient australopithecine and *H. erectus* fossils were accepted as hominids in the 1940s and 1950s, anthropologists realized that the Neandertals did not look that different from modern humans—despite their sloping foreheads, large brow ridges, flattened braincases, large jaws, and nearly absent chins (see Figure 9–2).[6] After all, they did have larger brains (averaging more than 1,450 cc) than modern humans (slightly more than 1,300 cc).[7] Some scholars believe that the large brain capacity of Neandertals suggests that they were capable of the full range of behaviors characteristic of modern humans. Their skeletons did, however, attest to one behavioral trait markedly different from behaviors of most modern humans: Neandertals apparently made very strenuous use of their bodies.[8]

It took almost 100 years for scholars to accept the idea that Neandertals were not that different from modern humans and therefore should be classified as *Homo sapiens neandertalensis*. But in the last few years there has been a growing debate over whether the Neandertals in western Europe were ancestral to modern-looking people who lived later in western Europe, after about 40,000 years ago.

Figure 9–3 Homo sapiens *Sites*

Source: From Russell L. Ciochon and John G. Fleagle, eds., *The Human Evolution Source Book.* Copyright © 1993. Reprinted by permission of Pearson Education, Inc., Upper Saddle River, NJ 07458.

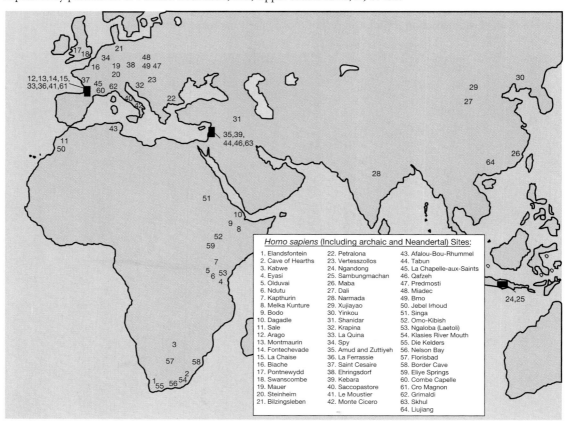

Neandertals lived in other places besides western Europe. A large number of fossils from central Europe strongly resemble those from western Europe, although some features, such as a projecting midface, are less pronounced.[9] Neandertals have also been found in southwestern Asia (Israel, Iraq) and Central Asia (Uzbekistan). One of the largest collections of Neandertal fossils comes from Shanidar cave in the mountains of northeastern Iraq, where Ralph Solecki unearthed the skeletons of nine individuals (see site 31 in Figure 9–3).[10]

What has changed scholars' opinions of the Neandertals so that they are now most commonly seen as not belonging to the *Homo sapiens* group?

In 1997, a group of researchers from the United States and Germany published findings that forced a reconsideration of the Neandertals and their relationship to modern humans. These scholars reported that they had been able to extract DNA from the original Neandertal specimen found in 1856.[11] The DNA they extracted was not nuclear DNA—the material that makes up the human genome. Rather, it came from a tiny structure found in all eukaryotic cells (that is, cells with a membrane-bound nucleus and DNA in the chromosomes) called *mitochondria*. Mitochondria produce enzymes needed for energy production, and they have their own DNA, which replicates when a cell replicates but is not thought to be under any pressure from natural selection.[12]

The only source of change in mitochondrial DNA (usually referred to as *mtDNA*) is random mutation. Mitochondrial DNA is inherited only from mothers in animals; it is not carried into an egg cell by sperm, but is left with the sperm's tail on the outside of the egg. These unique characteristics make it possible to use mtDNA to measure the degree of relatedness between two species, and even to say how long ago those species diverged.[13] The longer two species have been separated, the more differences there will be in their mtDNA, which is thought to mutate at a fairly constant rate of about 2 percent per million years. Thus, the number of differences between the mtDNA of two organisms can be converted into an estimated date in the past when those organisms stopped being part of the same breeding population. While controversy remains over many of the details of how and why mtDNA mutates and about its accuracy for determining absolute dates of divergence, most scholars agree that it is a powerful tool for examining relative degrees of relatedness between species.[14]

How similar is Neandertal mtDNA to modern human DNA? Not as similar as many scholars would have expected. Among individual modern humans, there are usually five to ten differences in the sequence of mtDNA examined by the U.S. and German researchers. Between modern humans and the Neandertal specimen, there tend to be about 25 differences—more than three times that among modern humans (see Figure 9–4). This suggested to the researchers that the ancestors of modern

Figure 9–4 *Differences in mtDNA Sequences among Humans, the Neandertal, and Chimpanzees*

The x-axis shows the number of sequence differences; the y-axis shows the percent of individuals that share that number of sequence differences. Source: Reprinted from *Cell*, 90 (1997): 25 with permission from Elsevier Science.

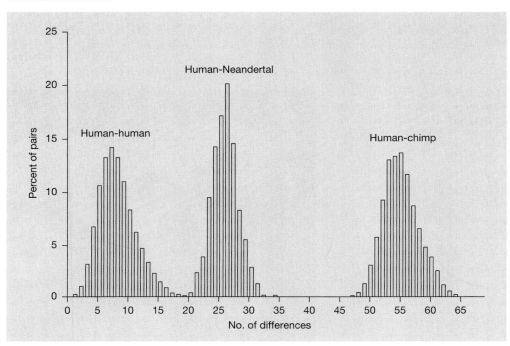

humans and the Neandertal must have diverged about 600,000 years ago.[15] If the last common ancestor of ours and the Neandertal lived that long ago in the past, the Neandertal would be a much more distant relative than previously thought. While many issues are still to be addressed in this study, as well as a need for it to be replicated on other Neandertal specimens, it does seem to reinforce some of the more recent archaeological findings from Europe and the Near East that are relevant to the issues.

It has been known for decades that both modern human and Neandertal fossils are found in the same locations in parts of the Levant, but recent improvements in dating technology and newly discovered fossils have even more clearly demonstrated that the two kinds of hominid coexisted. In fact, several caves in the Mount Carmel region of Israel contain both modern human and Neandertal occupations. The fact that these two groups of hominids co-inhabited the Near East for perhaps as much as 30,000 years strongly suggests that the two are different species.[16] And finds in Europe seem to corroborate that assessment. As early modern humans began moving into Europe they appear to have displaced populations of Neandertals already living there. Sites with tools thought to be associated with Neandertals disappear throughout Europe as sites with tools thought to be associated with modern humans expand their range (there are, unfortunately, very few fossils from this time period—roughly 40,000 years ago—to make certain who made the tools).[17] Significantly, the area of Europe (Iberia) last colonized by modern humans contains the very latest Neandertal fossils yet found, dating to some 30,000 years ago.[18]

With all this evidence pointing to Neandertals not being part of the modern human species, why is there an ongoing debate? In part this is because none of the evidence is conclusive, and much of it can be interpreted in alternate ways. There is also evidence suggesting that Neandertals were not all that different physically from modern

humans (see the box "Neandertal Growth and Development"). Perhaps more importantly, however, Neandertal culture, typically referred to as Middle Paleolithic after the predominant tool technology, has some features that make it seem similar to the culture of early modern humans.

Middle Paleolithic Cultures

The period of cultural history associated with the Neandertals is traditionally called the **Middle Paleolithic** in Europe and the Near East and dates from about 300,000 years to about 40,000 years ago.[19] For Africa, the term *Middle Stone Age* is used instead of Middle Paleolithic. The tool assemblages from this period are generally referred to as *Mousterian* in Europe and the Near East and as *post-Acheulian* in Africa.

CD-ROM Interactive Exercise II-11

TOOL ASSEMBLAGES

THE MOUSTERIAN The Mousterian type of tool complex is named after the tool assemblage found in a rock shelter at Le Moustier in the Dordogne region of southwestern France. Compared with an Acheulian assemblage, a **Mousterian tool assemblage** has a smaller proportion of large core tools such as hand axes and cleavers and a bigger proportion of small flake tools such as scrapers.[20] Although many flakes struck off from a core were used "as is," the Mousterian is also characterized by flakes that were often altered or "retouched" by striking

The Neandertal on the left has bigger brow ridges and a more sloping forehead than the Cro-Magnon on the right. The Neandertal brain was larger on average than the Cro-Magnon brain.

RESEARCH FRONTIERS
Neandertal Growth and Development

One of the reasons many scholars think the Neandertals did not belong to the *Homo sapiens* species is that their material culture was impoverished compared with that of early modern humans who lived at the same time. Since much of contemporary human behavior is dependent on learning that takes place during our long period of infant dependency, could it be that Neandertals matured more rapidly than modern humans and thus had a shorter period of time in which to learn cultural behaviors?

Paleoanthropologist Nancy Minugh-Purvis decided to test this idea by examining growth and development of the skull and face in Neandertals. Minugh-Purvis's study of Neandertal growth and development was feasible largely because Neandertals buried their dead. Juvenile and infant skeletons are rare in the archaeological record and often do not preserve well. In juveniles and infants, many of the bones are still growing and thus are relatively delicate. They are also smaller than adult bones, and a wider variety of scavengers can consume them. But because Neandertals buried their dead, a number of well-preserved juvenile and infant skeletons are available for study. Indeed, Minugh-Purvis was able to locate more than 100 Neandertal skeletons, ranging in age from newborns to young adults.

To chart the way the skull and face of Neandertals grew from infancy to adulthood, Minugh-Purvis measured the available fossils on a set of standard *anthro-pometric indices*—indices that are widely used in physical anthropology to compare the size and shape of bones. She found that newborn Neandertals and modern humans do not differ very much, but that Neandertal infants tend to have thicker cranial bones than modern humans and perhaps heavier musculature. Many of the more striking features of adult Neandertals—a large face with a protruding nose, brow ridges, and a long skull—are not present in infants. These typical Neandertal characteristics begin to appear in children. For example, a 4-year-old Neandertal from the site of Engis, Belgium, already has brow ridges. A 7-year-old from the site of La Quinta in France not only has brow ridges but also a large, protruding nose and face and a long skull. Finally, a 10-year-old from the site of Teshik-Tash in Uzbekistan has all of the typical Neandertal features, and is basically identical to an adult Neandertal except in size.

In short, Neandertals are born similar to modern humans, but by the age of about 10 have developed all of the striking physical features that differentiate Neandertals from modern humans. What does this tell us about Neandertal growth and development? Minugh-Purvis suggests that it was much like our own. Indeed, she argues that many of the physical differences between the Neandertal face and skull and those of modern humans might not be due to genetic differences but rather to behavioral ones. Neandertal teeth show wear patterns that suggest they were used as tools, particularly to hold objects while working on them with the hands. The teeth and jaws were apparently placed under tremendous stress from these uses. Minugh-Purvis suggests that the prognathic face and heavy musculature may be a result of the teeth and jaws being used as tools from a young age, rather than from developmental differences between modern humans and Neandertals.

However, there are other differences between Neandertals and modern humans that cannot be explained by behavior. The overall picture that appears from Minugh-Purvis's study is that Neandertals did indeed mature slightly faster than modern humans. But was their maturation fast enough to account for the lack of cultural elaboration among the Neandertals? Did Neandertals grow so fast they had no time to learn? Minugh-Purvis suggests the differences are not that significant, and that other factors must be sought to explain the differences in cultural elaboration between Neandertals and modern humans.

Sources: Nancy Minugh-Purvis, "Neandertal Growth: Examining Developmental Adaptations in Earlier *Homo sapiens*," in Peter N. Peregrine, Carol R. Ember, and Melvin Ember, eds., *Physical Anthropology: Original Readings in Method and Practice* (Upper Saddle River, NJ: Prentice Hall, 2002); Erik Trinkaus, "The Neandertal Face: Evolutionary and Functional Perspectives on a Recent Hominid Face," *Journal of Human Evolution*, 16 (1987): 429–43; Christopher Stringer and Clive Gamble, *In Search of the Neanderthals* (New York: Thames and Hudson, 1993).

small flakes or chips from one or more edges (see Figure 9–5).[21] Studies of the wear on scrapers suggest that many were used for scraping hides or working wood. The fact that some of the tools, particularly points, were thinned or shaped on one side suggests that they were hafted or attached to a shaft or handle.[22]

Toward the end of the Acheulian period, a technique developed that enabled the toolmaker to produce flake tools of a predetermined size instead of simply chipping flakes away from the core at random. In this **Levalloisian method,** the toolmaker first shaped the core and prepared a "striking platform" at one end. Flakes of predetermined and standard sizes could then be knocked off. Although some Levallois flakes date as far back as 400,000 years ago, they are found more frequently in Mousterian tool kits.[23]

The tool assemblages in particular sites may be characterized as Mousterian, but one site may have more or fewer scrapers, points, and so forth, than another site. A number of archaeologists have suggested possible reasons for this variation. For example, Sally Binford and Lewis Binford suggested that different activities may have occurred in different sites. Some sites may have been used for butchering and other sites may have been base camps; hence the kinds of tools found in different sites should vary.[24] And Paul Fish has suggested that some sites may have more tools produced by the Levalloisian technique because larger pieces of flint were available.[25]

THE POST-ACHEULIAN IN AFRICA Like Mousterian tools, many of the post-Acheulian tools in Africa during the Middle Stone Age were struck off prepared cores in the Levalloisian way. The assemblages consist mostly of various types of flake tools. A well-described sequence of such tools comes from the area around the mouth of the Klasies River on the southern coast of South Africa. This area contains rock shelters and small caves in which early and later *Homo sapiens* lived. The oldest cultural remains in one of the caves may date back 120,000 years.[26] These earliest tools include parallel-sided flake blades (probably used as knives), pointed flakes (possibly spearpoints), burins or gravers (chisel-like tools), and scrapers. Similar tools discovered at Border cave, South Africa, may have been used almost 200,000 years ago.[27]

HOMESITES

Most of the excavated Middle Paleolithic homesites in Europe and the Near East are located in caves and rock shel-

Figure 9–5 *A Typical Mousterian Tool Kit*

A Mousterian tool kit emphasized sidescrapers (1–4), notches (5), points (6), and saw-toothed denticulates (7). How these stone artifacts were actually used is not known, but the points may have been joined to wood shafts, and denticulates could have been used to work wood. The tools illustrated here are from Mousterian sites in western Europe. Source: From Richard G. Klein, "Ice-Age Hunters of the Ukraine." Reprinted with permission of Nelson H. Prentiss.

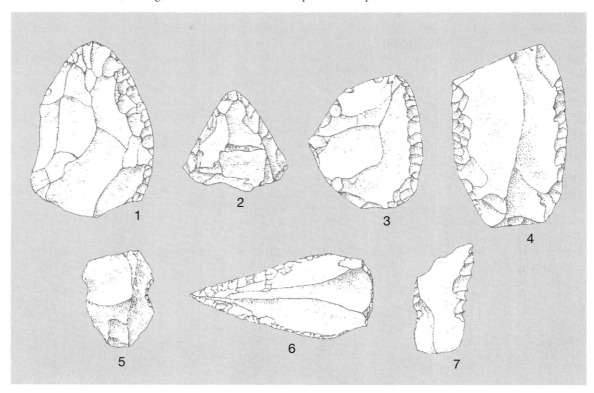

ters. The same is true for the excavated Middle Stone Age homesites in sub-Saharan Africa. We might conclude, therefore, that Neandertals (as well as many early modern humans) lived mostly in caves or rock shelters. But that conclusion could be incorrect. Caves and rock shelters may be overrepresented in the archaeological record because they are more likely to be found than are sites that originally were in the open but now are hidden by thousands of years, and many feet, of sediment. Sediment is the dust, debris, and decay that accumulate over time; when we dust the furniture and vacuum the floor, we are removing sediment.

Still, we know that many Neandertals lived at least part of the year in caves. This was true, for example, along the Dordogne River in France. The river gouged deep valleys in the limestone of that area. Below the cliffs are rock shelters with overhanging roofs and deep caves, many of which were occupied during the Middle Paleolithic. Even if the inhabitants did not stay all year, the sites do seem to have been occupied year after year.[28] Although there is evidence of some use of fire in earlier cultures, Middle Paleolithic humans seem to have relied more on fire. There are thick layers of ash in many rock shelters and caves and evidence that hearths were used to increase the efficiency of the fires.[29]

Quite a few Neandertal homesites were in the open. In Africa, open-air sites were located on floodplains, at the edges of lakes, and near springs.[30] Many open-air sites have been found in Europe, particularly eastern Europe. The occupants of the well-known site at Moldova in western Russia lived in river-valley houses framed with wood and covered with animal skins. Bones of mammoths, huge elephants now extinct, surround the remains of hearths and were apparently used to help hold the animal skins in place. Even though the winter climate near the edge of the glacier nearby was cold at that time, there still would have been animals to hunt because the plant food for the game was not buried under deep snow.

The hunters probably moved away in the summer to higher land between the river valleys. In all likelihood, the higher ground was grazing land for the large herds of animals the Moldova hunters depended on for meat. In the winter river-valley sites, archaeologists have found skeletons of wolf, arctic fox, and hare with their paws missing. These animals probably were skinned for pelts that were made into clothing.[31]

GETTING FOOD

How Neandertals and early modern humans got their food probably varied with their environment. In Africa, they lived in savanna and semiarid desert. In western and eastern Europe, they had to adapt to cold; during periods of increased glaciation, much of the environment was steppe grassland and tundra.

The European environment during this time was much richer in animal resources than the tundra of northern countries is today. Indeed, the European environment in-

habited by Neandertals abounded in game, both big and small. The tundra and alpine animals included reindeer, bison, wild oxen, horses, mammoths, rhinoceroses, and deer, as well as bears, wolves, and foxes.[32] Some European sites have also yielded bird and fish remains. For example, people in a summer camp in northern Germany apparently hunted swans and ducks and fished for perch and pike.[33] Little, however, is known about the particular plant foods the European Neandertals may have consumed; the remains of plants are unlikely to survive thousands of years in a nonarid environment.

In Africa, too, early *Homo sapiens* varied in how they got food. For example, we know that the people living at the mouth of the Klasies River in South Africa ate shellfish as well as meat from small grazers such as antelopes and large grazers such as eland and buffalo.[34] But archaeologists disagree about how the Klasies River people got their meat when they began to occupy the caves in the area.

Richard Klein thinks they hunted both large and small game. Klein speculates that because the remains of eland of all ages have been found in Cave 1 at the Klasies River site, the people there probably hunted the eland by driving them into corrals or other traps, where animals of all ages could be killed. Klein thinks that buffalo were hunted differently. Buffalo tend to charge attackers, which would make it difficult to drive them into traps. Klein believes

Neandertals (reconstructed) hunted a wide variety of game, including deer.

that, because bones from mostly very young and very old buffalo are found in the cave, the hunters were able to stalk and kill only the most vulnerable animals.[35]

Lewis Binford thinks the Klasies River people hunted only small grazers and scavenged the eland and buffalo meat from the kills of large carnivores. He argues that sites should contain all or almost all of the bones from animals that were hunted. According to Binford, since more or less complete skeletons are found only from small animals, the Klasies River people were not, at first, hunting all the animals they used for food.[36]

But new evidence suggests that people were hunting big game as much as 400,000 years ago. Wooden spears that old were recently found in Germany in association with stone tools and the butchered remains of more than ten wild horses. The heavy spears resemble modern aerodynamic javelins, which suggests they would have been thrown at large animals such as horses, not at small animals. This new evidence strongly suggests that hunting, not just scavenging, may be older than archaeologists once thought.[37]

FUNERAL RITUALS?

Some Neandertals were deliberately buried. At Le Moustier, the skeleton of a boy 15 or 16 years old was found with a beautifully fashioned stone axe near his hand. Near Le Moustier, graves of five other children and two adults, apparently interred together in a family plot, were discovered. These finds, along with one at Shanidar cave in Iraq, have aroused speculation about the possibility of funeral rituals.

The evidence at Shanidar consists of pollen around and on top of a man's body. Pollen analysis suggests that the flowers included ancestral forms of modern grape hyacinths, bachelor's buttons, hollyhocks, and yellow flowering groundsels. John Pfeiffer speculated about this find:

> A man with a badly crushed skull was buried deep in the cave with special ceremony. One spring day about 60,000 years ago members of his family went out into the hills, picked masses of wild flowers, and made a bed of them on the ground, a resting place for the deceased. Other flowers were probably laid on top of his grave; still others seem to have been woven together with the branches of a pinelike shrub to form a wreath.[38]

Can we be sure? Not really. All we really know is that there was pollen near and on top of the body. It could have gotten there because humans put flowers in the grave, or it could have gotten there for other, even accidental, reasons.

The Emergence of Modern Humans

Cro-Magnon humans, who appear in western Europe about 35,000 years ago, were once thought to be the

As this reconstruction illustrates, Neandertals were the first humans to purposely bury their dead.

earliest specimens of modern humans, or *Homo sapiens sapiens*. (The Cro-Magnons are named after the rock shelter in France where they were first found, in 1868.[39]) But we now know that modern-looking humans appeared earlier outside of Europe. As of now, the oldest unambiguous fossils classified as *H. sapiens* come from Africa. Some of these fossils, discovered in one of the Klasies River mouth caves, are possibly as old as 100,000 years.[40] Other *Homo sapiens* fossils of about the same age have been found in Border cave in South Africa, and a find at Omo in Ethiopia may be an early *H. sapiens*.[41] Remains of anatomically modern humans (*Homo sapiens sapiens*) found at two sites in Israel, at Skhul and Qafzeh, which used to be thought to date back 40,000 to 50,000 years, may be 90,000 years old.[42] There are also anatomically modern human finds in Borneo, at Niah, from about 40,000 years ago and in Australia, at Lake Mungo, from about 30,000 years ago.[43]

These modern-looking humans differed from the Neandertals and other early *H. sapiens* in that they had higher, more bulging foreheads, thinner and lighter bones, smaller faces and jaws, chins (the bony protuberances that remain after projecting faces recede), and only slight brow ridges (or no ridges at all; see Figure 9–2).

THEORIES ABOUT THE ORIGINS OF MODERN HUMANS

Two theories about the origins of modern humans continue to be debated among anthropologists. One, which can be called the *single-origin theory*, suggests that modern humans emerged in just one part of the Old World and then spread to other parts, replacing Neandertals. (Africa is generally thought to be the place of modern humans' origin.) The second theory, which has been called the *multiregional theory*, suggests that modern humans evolved in various parts of the Old World after *Homo erectus* spread out of Africa.[44]

SINGLE-ORIGIN THEORY According to the single-origin theory, the Neandertals did not evolve into modern humans. Rather, Neandertals became extinct after 35,000 years ago because they were replaced by modern humans. The presumed place of origin of the first modern humans has varied over the years as new fossils have been discovered. In the 1950s, the source population was presumed to be Neandertals in the Near East, who were referred to as "generalized" or "progressive" Neandertals. Later, when earlier *Homo sapiens* were found in Africa, paleoanthropologists postulated that modern humans emerged first in Africa and then moved to the Near East and from there to Europe and Asia. Single-origin theorists think that the originally small population of *H. sapiens sapiens* had some biological or cultural advantage, or both, that allowed them to spread and replace Neandertals.

The main evidence for the single-origin theory comes from the mtDNA of living peoples. In 1987, Rebecca Cann and her colleagues presented evidence that the mtDNA from a sample of people from the United States, New Guinea, Africa, and East Asia showed differences suggesting that their common ancestor lived only 200,000 years ago (see the box "DNA Evidence and the 'Out-of-Africa' Theory of Modern Human Origins"). They further claimed that, since the amount of variation among individuals was greatest in African populations, the common ancestor of all lived in Africa.[45] (It is generally the case that people living in a homeland exhibit more variation than any emigrant descendant population.) Thus was born what the media called the "mitochondrial Eve" and the "Eve hypothesis" for the origins of modern humans.

There were many problems with this initial study, but over the years those problems have been addressed and new and better mtDNA analyses have been performed. Most scholars now agree that the mtDNA of modern humans shows a remarkably small degree of variation (in fact less than half the variation found in most chimpanzee populations), which strongly suggests that we all share a very recent, common ancestry.[46]

The recent mtDNA analyses of Neandertals, and the archaeological evidence suggesting that Neandertals and modern humans lived separately in Europe and the Near East, tend to support the single-origin theory. However, the lack of unambiguous *Homo sapiens* skeletal material from Africa in the 150,000–200,000-year-ago time range makes it impossible as yet to support the single-origin theory through the fossil record. Even if we had such evidence, it would not necessarily question the validity of the multiregional theory of human origins.

MULTIREGIONAL THEORY According to the multiregional theory, *Homo erectus* populations in various parts of the Old World gradually evolved into anatomically modern-looking humans. The theorists espousing this view believe that the "transitional" or "archaic" *H. sapiens* and the Neandertals represent phases in the gradual development of more "modern" anatomical features. Indeed, as we have noted, some of these theorists see so much continuity between *Homo erectus* and modern humans that they classify *Homo erectus* as *Homo sapiens erectus*.

Continuity is the main evidence used by the multiregional theorists to support their position. In several parts of the world there seem to be clear continuities in distinct skeletal features between *Homo erectus* and *Homo sapiens*. For example, *Homo erectus* fossils from China tend to have

Figure 9–6 *Fossil Evidence for Regional Continuity*

Continuity in southeast Asian and Australian populations: Skulls of (a) Homo erectus, *(b) early* Homo sapiens, *and (d) modern* Homo sapiens, *all from southeast Asia and Australia, have similar foreheads, brow ridges, and occipital and facial shapes, while skulls from Africa, represented here by (c), an early* Homo sapiens, *have different forms. The similarity in southeast Asian and Australian populations over more than 500,000 years argues for regional continuity rather than replacement.*

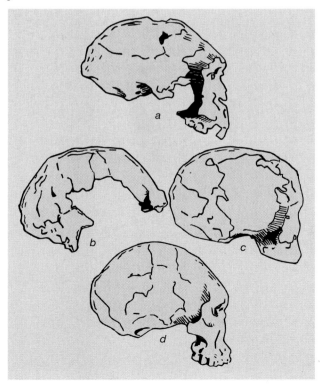

CURRENT ISSUES

DNA *Evidence and the "Out-of-Africa" Theory of Modern Human Origins*

Paleoanthropologists used to believe that the humans (hominids) diverged from apes (pongids) more than 10 million years ago. Then molecular biologists started comparing the blood proteins and DNA of living primate species. The results of the comparisons indicated that the probable time of divergence should be pushed up to 5 million to 6 million years ago. Molecular biology now has entered another paleoanthropological debate, this time about the origin of modern-looking humans. On the basis of comparisons of mitochondrial DNA (mtDNA) in various populations of living humans, molecular biologists generally support the "out-of-Africa" theory—the view that modern-looking humans emerged first in Africa and then spread throughout the world, replacing Neandertals.

Mitochondrial DNA is found in the mitochondrion, a part of the cell that converts food into energy for the cell. There are three advantages to using mtDNA over other kinds of DNA found in cell nuclei. The first is that mtDNA comprises only 37 genes; the fewer the genes, the easier the comparisons. Second, many neutral mutations accumulate rapidly and steadily in mtDNA, making it easier to find markers of similarity and difference in recent populations. (The more similar the mutations, the closer are two populations to a common ancestor.) The third advantage of mitochrondrial DNA is that it is inherited only from the mother, making it less complicated to trace evolutionary

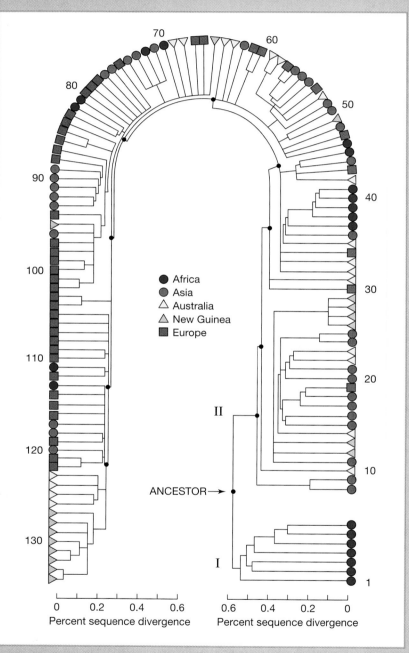

"Tree" diagram comparing mtDNA sequences of humans from different geographic regions. The total difference (percent sequence divergence) suggests that humans share a common ancestor who lived in Africa about 200,000 years ago. Source: With permission, from *Annual Review of Anthropology,* Volume 17 © 1988 by Annual Reviews www.AnnualReviews.org.

lines. Because mtDNA is passed on through the maternal line, molecular biologists refer to the ancestor of all modern humans as "Eve." Of course, there wasn't just one "Eve"; there must have been more than one of her generation with similar mtDNA.

Comparing the mtDNA of humans from different geographic regions and using computer software to create branching "tree" diagrams, the molecular researchers claim that the simplest or most parsimonious of the obtained solutions traces modern human mtDNA back to females who lived some 200,000 years ago. They also suggest that the mtDNA evidence is consistent with paleoanthropological evidence indicating that modern-looking humans appeared first in Africa, somewhat later in the Near East, and later still in Europe and Asia.

Critics of the out-of-Africa theory point out that the acceptability of the model depends on dubious assumptions. Perhaps the most telling criticism is that the solutions obtained so far are not the only ones possible. Actually, there are thousands of solutions possible in constructing tree diagrams from mtDNA data. The solutions obtained so far may point to an African origin of modern humans, but other possible solutions may suggest other scenarios. Why should we assume that the solutions obtained so far cover all the reasonable possibilities?

A second criticism of the out-of-Africa theory points to fossil evidence suggesting continuous evolution toward modern-looking traits in various regions of the world. In other words, the fossil record is not consistent

with the idea that modern-looking traits were introduced from outside those regions. The out-of-Africa theory must be wrong, critics argue, if physical traits persist in even just one region other than Africa, from the time of early humans to modern humans. For the out-of-Africa theory assumes that humans from southern Africa completely replaced Neandertals, with no gene flow between them. If this is what happened, the fossil record should show some discontinuity over time. But in Southeast Asia and Australia the fossils spanning 700,000 years (from *Homo erectus* to modern-looking humans) have similar features throughout that span of time. For instance, they have sloping rather than vertical frontal bones (foreheads), in contrast to early modern skulls in South Africa (such as at Border cave), which have more vertical foreheads. In China there are shovel-shaped incisors from ancient times to modern times; African populations, early and late, lack this trait. So the persistence of distinctive traits in different regions (shovel-shaped incisors in China and sloping foreheads in Southeast Asia and Australia) is not consistent with the idea that modern-looking humans completely replaced previous human populations in those regions.

There is also a lack of archaeological evidence to support the idea that an invading modern population came out of southern Africa. An invading population might have a very different tool kit, but in the Near East, where both Neandertal and modern human fossils are found with tools, the two have similar tool kits. In Asia, too, there is no discontinuity in technology, as we

might expect with an invading population.

We would expect an invading population that replaced all other human populations to have had some significant superiority. If not technological, then what? Some out-of-Africa theorists have suggested that the earliest modern humans had language, whereas previous human populations did not. But the evidence from anatomy regarding capacity for spoken language is still controversial.

As with most controversies, the out-of-Africa one may be resolved with additional fossil evidence and more deliberate hypothesis tests of alternative interpretations.

Sources: For support of the out-of-Africa theory, see Linda Vigilant, Mark Stoneking, Henry Harpending, Kristen Hawkes, and Allan C. Wilson, "African Populations and the Evolution of Human Mitochondrial DNA," *Science*, September 27, 1991, 1503; and Allan C. Wilson and Rebecca L. Cann, "The Recent African Genesis of Humans," *Scientific American*, April 1992, 68–73. For critiques of the out-of-Africa theory, see David W. Frayer, "Testing Theories and Hypotheses about Human Origins," and Susan Weller, "The Research Process," in Carol R. Ember, Melvin Ember, Peter N. Peregrine, eds., *Research Frontiers in Anthropology* (Upper Saddle River, NJ: Prentice Hall, 1998). Prentice Hall/Simon & Schuster Custom Publishing; and Alan G. Thorne and Milford H. Wolpoff, "The Multiregional Evolution of Humans," *Scientific American*, April 1992, 76–83.

broader faces with more horizontal cheekbones than specimens from elsewhere in the world, traits that also appear in modern Chinese populations.[47] Southeast Asia provides more compelling evidence, according to multiregional theorists. There, a number of traits—relatively thick cranial bones, a receding forehead, an unbroken brow ridge, facial prognathism, relatively large cheekbones, and relatively large molars—appear to persist from *Homo erectus* through modern populations.[48] But others suggest that these traits cannot be used to establish a unique continuation from *Homo erectus* in Southeast Asia because these traits are found in modern humans all over the world. And still others argue that the traits are not as similar as the multiregional theorists claim.[49]

In support of their position, multiregional theorists argue that the mtDNA evidence supports multiregional evolution rather than a single-origin of modern humans, that the mtDNA evidence may reflect the emigration of *Homo erectus* out of Africa rather than the emigration of *Homo sapiens sapiens*. This interpretation would mean that the accepted rate of mutation in mtDNA is wrong, that mtDNA actually mutates much more slowly than currently thought.[50] However, this interpretation is contradicted by established correlations between differences in mtDNA among human groups known to have colonized New Guinea and Australia at particular points in time, which seem to fit the accepted rate of mutation, and with the divergence between humans and apes, the date of which also seems to accord with the accepted faster rate of mtDNA mutation.

To explain why human evolution would proceed gradually and in the same direction in various parts of the Old World, multiregional theorists point to cultural improvements in cutting-tool and cooking technology that occurred all over the Old World. These cultural improvements may have relaxed the prior natural selection for heavy bones and musculature in the skull. The argument is that unless many plant and animal foods were cut into small pieces and thoroughly cooked in hearths or pits that were efficient thermally, they would be hard to chew and digest. Thus people would have needed robust jaws and thick skull bones to support the large muscles that enabled them to cut and chew their food. But robust bone and muscle would no longer be needed after people began to cut and cook more effectively.[51]

INTERMEDIATE THEORIES The single-origin and multiregional theories are not the only possible interpretations of the available fossil record. There is also the intermediate interpretation that there may have been some replacement of one population by another, some local continuous evolution, and some interbreeding between early modern humans, who spread out of Africa, and populations encountered in North Africa, Europe, and Asia.[52] As the biologist Alan Templeton has noted, the debates over a single-origin versus multiregional evolution "are based on the myth that replacement of one physical feature in a fossil series with another feature can only be cre-

ated by one population replacing another (by exterminating them, for example), but such fossil patterns could be a reflection of one genotype replacing another through gene flow and natural selection. Morphological replacement should not be equated with population replacement when one is dealing with populations that can interbreed."[53]

What Happened to the Neandertals?

Regardless of which theory (single-origin or multiregional) is correct, it seems clear that Neandertals and modern humans (*H. sapiens sapiens*) coexisted in Europe and the Near East for at least 20,000 years, and maybe as long as 60,000 years. What happened to the Neandertals? Three answers have generally been considered. First, they interbred with modern humans and the unique Neandertal characteristics slowly disappeared from the interbreeding population. Second, they were killed off by modern humans. Third, they were driven to extinction due to competition with modern humans. Let's take a look at each of these scenarios.

The interbreeding scenario seems the most probable, yet evidence supporting it is weak. If modern humans and Neandertals interbred, we should be able to find "hybrid" individuals in the fossil record. In fact, a group of scholars has recently argued that an Upper Paleolithic skeleton from Portugal demonstrates a combination of modern human and Neandertal features.[54] The finding remains controversial, however, because it is a child's skeleton (approximately 4 years old) and its Neandertal-like features have not been corroborated by other scholars. More significantly, if the interbreeding hypothesis is correct, then the mtDNA analysis we have discussed several times in this chapter must be wrong. On the other hand, recent research on Neandertal tools suggests they adopted new techniques of tool manufacture that are thought to be uniquely associated with modern humans[55] (we discuss these in more detail in the next chapter). If Neandertals were learning from modern humans, then the idea that they could have interbred and perhaps been absorbed within the modern human population gains credibility.

The genocide scenario, that modern humans killed off Neandertals, has appeal as a sensational story, but little evidence. Not a single "murdered" Neandertal has ever been found, and one might wonder, in a fight between the powerful Neandertals and the more gracile modern humans, who might get the better of whom.

Finally, the extinction scenario, that Neandertals simply could not compete with modern humans, seems to have the best archaeological support. As we discussed earlier, there appear to be "refugee" populations of Neandertals in Iberia as recently as perhaps 30,000 years ago. The "retreat" of Neandertals from the Near East, eastern Europe, and finally western Europe following the movement of modern humans into the region seems to support the "refugee" interpretation.[56] More importantly, physical anthropologist Erik Trinkaus has argued, based on both physical characteristics of the Neandertal skeleton and their apparent patterns of behavior, that Neandertals were less efficient hunters and gatherers than modern humans.[57] If this is true, a modern human group would have been able to live and reproduce more easily than a Neandertal group in the same territory, and this would likely drive the Neandertals away. When there were no new territories to run to, the Neandertals would go extinct—precisely what the archaeological record seems to suggest.

But were modern humans and their cultures really that much more efficient than Middle Paleolithic cultures? As we will see in the next chapter, the Upper Paleolithic does seem to mark a watershed in the evolution of human culture, allowing humans to expand their physical horizons throughout the world and their intellectual horizons into the realms of art and ritual.

 ## Summary

1. Most anthropologists agree that *Homo erectus* began to evolve into *Homo sapiens* after about 500,000 years ago. But there is disagreement about how and where the transition occurred. The mixed traits of the transitional fossils include large cranial capacities (well within the range of modern humans), together with low foreheads and large brow ridges, which are characteristic of *H. erectus* specimens. The earliest definite *H. sapiens,* who did not look completely like modern humans, appeared about 100,000 years ago.

2. *Homo sapiens* have been found in many parts of the Old World—in Africa and Asia as well as in Europe. Some of these *H. sapiens* may have lived earlier than the Neandertals of Europe. There is still debate over whether the Neandertals in western Europe became extinct or survived and were ancestral to the modern-looking people who lived in western Europe after about 40,000 years ago.

3. The period of cultural history associated with the Neandertals is traditionally called the *Middle Paleolithic* in Europe and the Near East and dates from about 300,000 to about 40,000 years ago. For Africa, the term *Middle Stone Age* is used. The assemblages of flake tools from this period are generally referred to as *Mousterian* in Europe and the Near East and as *post-Acheulian* in Africa. Compared with an Acheulian assemblage, a Mousterian tool assemblage has a smaller proportion of large hand axes and cleavers and a larger proportion of small flake tools such as scrapers. Some Mousterian sites show signs of intentional burial.

4. Fossil remains of fully modern-looking humans, *Homo sapiens sapiens,* have been found in Africa, the Near East, Asia, and Australia, as well as in Europe. The oldest of these fossils have been found in South Africa and may be 50,000 to 100,000 years old.

5. Two theories about the origins of modern humans continue to be debated among anthropologists. One, the *single-origin theory*, suggests that modern humans emerged in just one part of the Old World—the Near East and, more recently, Africa have been the postulated places of origin—and spread to other parts of the Old World, superseding Neandertals. The second theory, the *multiregional theory*, suggests that modern humans emerged in various parts of the Old World, becoming the varieties of humans we see today.

 ## Glossary Terms

Cro-Magnon
Homo heidelbergensis
Homo neandertalensis
Homo sapiens sapiens
Levalloisian method

Middle Paleolithic
Mousterian tool assemblage
Neandertal

 ## Critical Questions

1. If the single-origin or "out-of-Africa" theory were correct, by what mechanisms could *Homo sapiens* have been able to replace *Homo erectus* and *Homo neandertalensis* populations?

2. If modern human traits emerged in *Homo erectus* populations in different areas more or less at the same time, what mechanisms would account for similar traits emerging in different regions?

3. How do Middle Paleolithic cultures differ from Lower Paleolithic cultures?

 ## Internet Exercises

1. Learn about how the face of a Neandertal child was reconstructed by visiting the Computer-Assisted Paleoanthropology site at **http://www.ifi.unizh.ch/staff/zolli/ CAP/Main.htm**.

2. Visit the Smithsonian Institution page on *Homo heidelbergensis* at **http://www.mnh.si.edu/anthro/ humanorigins/ha/heid.htm**.

3. Visit the Neandertals and Modern Humans page at **http://www.neanderthal-modern.com**. Follow the regional links and compare and contrast several of the regions in terms of the archaeological and fossil material that has been recovered.

4. Visit the Neanderthal Museum (**http://www. neanderthal.de/e_thal/fs_2.htm**) and explore the presentation of Neandertals and their culture. Compare the interpretation of the Neandertals with the one presented in this chapter.

Suggested Reading

DIBBLE, H. L., AND MELLARS, P., EDS. *The Middle Paleolithic: Adaptation, Behavior, and Variability* (Philadelphia: University Museum, 1992). A collection of papers that presents data and rethinking about the variability in behavior during the Middle Paleolithic. The focus is on Europe and the Near East.

MELLARS, P. *The Neanderthal Legacy: An Archaeological Perspective from Western Europe.* Princeton, NJ: Princeton University Press, 1996. Focuses on the archaeological rather than the fossil record of Neandertals, and includes detailed discussions of Neandertal tool kits and archaeological sites.

PEREGRINE, P. N., EMBER, C. R., AND EMBER, M., EDS. *Physical Anthropology: Original Readings in Method and Practice.* Upper Saddle River, NJ: Prentice Hall, 2002. Especially relevant to this chapter are D. W. Frayer, "Testing Theories and Hypotheses about Modern Human Origins"; A. Kramer, "The Natural History and Evolutionary Fate of *Homo erectus*"; N. Minugh-Purvis, "Neandertal Growth: Examining Developmental Adaptations in Earlier *Homo sapiens*"; and I. Tattersall, "Paleoanthropology and Evolutionary Theory."

STRINGER, C. *In Search of the Neanderthals: Solving the Puzzle of Human Origins.* London: Thames and Hudson, 1993. A comprehensive and detailed account of research on the Neandertals.

TATTERSALL, I. *The Last Neanderthal: The Rise, Success, and Mysterious Extinction of Our Closest Human Relatives.* Boulder, CO: Westview, 1999. A well-written, up-to-date overview of the Neandertals, with wonderful illustrations.

TRINKAUS, E., ED. *The Emergence of Modern Humans: Biocultural Adaptations in the Later Pleistocene.* Cambridge: Cambridge University Press, 1989. Physical anthropologists and archaeologists review and debate what is known and not known about the Neandertals and the transition to modern humans.

TRINKAUS, E., AND SHIPMAN, P. *The Neandertals: Changing the Image of Mankind.* New York: Knopf, 1993. An interesting history of research on the Neandertals along with a clear discussion of current interpretations.

10

The Upper Paleolithic World

he period of cultural history in Europe, the Near East, and Asia known as the **Upper Paleolithic** (see Figure 10–1) dates from about 40,000 years ago to the period known as the *Neolithic* (beginning about 10,000 years ago, depending on the area). In Africa, the cultural period comparable to the Upper Paleolithic is known as the *Later Stone Age* and may have begun much earlier. In North and South America the period begins when humans first entered the New World, some time before 12,000 years ago (these colonizers are typically called *Paleo-Indians*) and continues until what are called *Archaic traditions* emerged some 10,000 years ago. To simplify terminology, we use the term *Upper Paleolithic* to refer to cultural developments in all areas of the Old World during this period.

In many respects, life-styles during the Upper Paleolithic were similar to life-styles before. People were still mainly hunters and gatherers and fishers who probably lived in small mobile bands. They made their camps out in the open in skin-covered huts and in caves and rock shelters. And they continued to produce smaller and smaller stone tools.

But the Upper Paleolithic is also characterized by a variety of new developments. One of the most striking is the emergence of art—painting on cave walls and stone slabs, and carving tools, decorative objects, and personal ornaments out of bone, antler, shell, and stone. (Perhaps for this as well as other purposes, people began to obtain materials from distant sources.) Because more archaeological sites date from the Upper Paleolithic than from any previous period and some Upper Paleolithic sites seem larger than any before, many archaeologists think that the human population increased considerably during the Upper Paleolithic.[1] And new inventions, such as the bow and arrow, the spear-thrower, and tiny replaceable blades that could be fitted into handles, appear for the first time.[2]

The Last Ice Age

The Upper Paleolithic world had an environment very different from today's. The earth was gripped by the last ice age, with glaciers covering Europe as far south as Berlin and Warsaw, and North America as far south as Chicago. To the south of these glacial fronts was a tundra zone extending in Europe to the Alps and in North America to the Ozarks, Appalachians, and well out onto the Great Plains (see Figure 10–2). Environmentally, both Europe and North America probably resembled contemporary Siberia and northern Canada. Elsewhere in the world conditions were not as extreme, but were still different from conditions today.[3]

For one thing, the climate was different. Annual temperatures were as much as 10 degrees Celsius below today's, and changes in ocean currents would have made temperature contrasts (that is, the differences between summer and winter months) more extreme as well. The changing ocean currents also changed weather patterns, and Europe experienced heavy annual snowfall. Not all the world was cold, however; still the presence of huge ice sheets in the north changed the climate throughout the world. North Africa, for example, appears to have been

Figure 10–1 *Places and Events in the Upper Paleolithic*

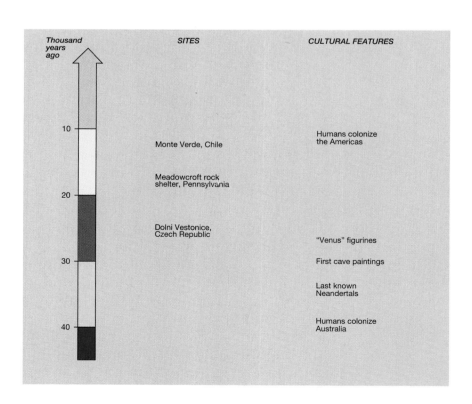

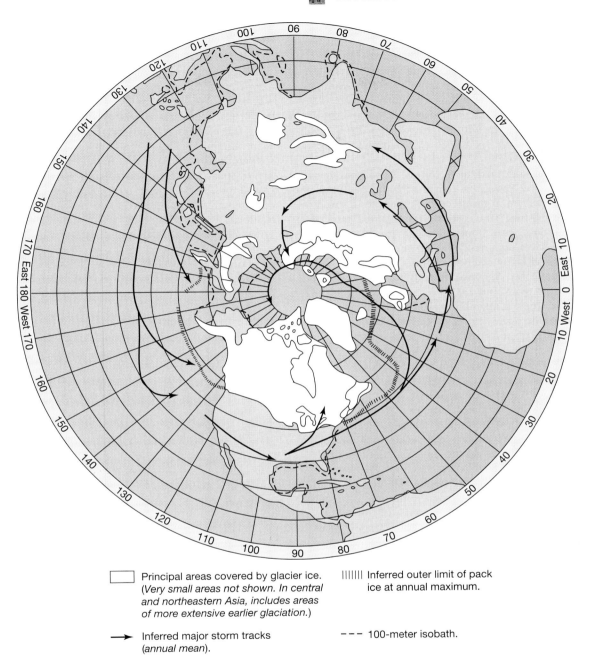

Principal areas covered by glacier ice.
(*Very small areas not shown. In central
and northeastern Asia, includes areas
of more extensive earlier glaciation.*)

||||||| Inferred outer limit of pack
ice at annual maximum.

→ Inferred major storm tracks
(*annual mean*).

– – – 100-meter isobath.

Figure 10–2   *The Extent of Glaciation during the Upper Paleolithic*

Source: From *Physical Anthropology*, 7e by P. Stein and B. Rowe. Used by permission of The McGraw Hill Companies, Inc.

much wetter than today, and South Asia was apparently drier. And everywhere the climate seems to have been highly variable.[4]

The plants and animals of the Upper Paleolithic world were adapted to these extreme conditions. Among the most important, and dramatic, were the large game animals collectively known as *Pleistocene megafauna*.[5] These animals, as their name suggests, were huge compared to their contemporary descendants. In North America, for example, giant ground sloths stood some 8–10 feet tall and

weighed several thousand pounds. Siberian mammoths were the largest elephants ever to live—some standing more than 14 feet tall. In East Asia, species such as the woolly rhinoceros and giant deer were present.

Upper Paleolithic Europe

With the vast supplies of meat available from megafauna, it is not surprising that many Upper Paleolithic cultures relied on hunting, and this was particularly true of the Upper Paleolithic peoples of Europe, on whom we focus here. Their way of life represents a common pattern throughout the Old World. But as people began to use more diverse resources in their environments, the use of local resources allowed Upper Paleolithic groups in much of the Old World to become more sedentary than their predecessors. They also began to trade with neighboring groups in order to obtain resources not available in their local territories.[6]

As was the case in the known Middle Paleolithic sites, most of the Upper Paleolithic remains that have been excavated were situated in caves and rock shelters. In southwestern France, some groups seem to have paved parts of the shelter floors with stones. Tentlike structures were built in some caves, apparently to keep out the cold.[7] Some open-air sites have also been excavated.

The site at Dolni Vestonice in what is now the Czech Republic, dated to around 25,000 years ago, is one of the first for which there is an entire settlement plan.[8] The settlement seems to have consisted of four tentlike huts, probably made from animal skins, with a great open hearth in the center. Around the outside were mammoth bones, some rammed into the ground, which suggests that the huts were surrounded by a wall. All told, there were bone heaps from about 100 mammoths. Each hut probably housed a group of related families—about 20 to 25 people. (One hut was approximately 27 by 45 feet and had five hearths distributed inside it, presumably one for each family.) With 20 to 25 people per hut, and assuming that all four huts were occupied at the same time, the population of the settlement would have been 100 to 125.

Up a hill from the settlement was a fifth and different kind of hut. It was dug into the ground and contained a bake oven and more than 2,300 small, fired fragments of animal figurines. There were also some hollow bones that may have been musical instruments. Another interesting feature of the settlement was a burial find, of a woman with a disfigured face. She may have been a particularly important personage; her face was found engraved on an ivory plaque near the central hearth of the settlement.

UPPER PALEOLITHIC TOOLS

Upper Paleolithic toolmaking appears to have had its roots in the Mousterian and post-Acheulian traditions, because flake tools are found in many Upper Paleolithic sites. But the Upper Paleolithic is characterized by a preponderance of *blades;* there were also burins, bone and antler tools, and microliths. In addition, two new techniques of toolmaking appeared—*indirect percussion* and *pressure flaking.* Blades were found in Middle Paleolithic assemblages, but they were not widely used until the Upper Paleolithic. Although blades can be made in a variety of ways, **indirect percussion** using a hammer-struck punch was common in the Upper Paleolithic. After shaping a core into a pyramidal or cylindrical form, the toolmaker put a punch of antler, wood, or other hard material into position and struck it with a hammer. Because the force is readily directed, the toolmaker was able to strike off consistently shaped **blades,** which are more than twice as long as they are wide[9] (see Figure 10–3).

The Upper Paleolithic is also noted for the production of large numbers of bone, antler, and ivory tools; needles, awls, and harpoons made of bone appear for the first time.[10] The manufacture of these implements may have been made easier by the development of many varieties of burins. **Burins** are chisel-like stone tools used for carving (see Figure 10–4); bone and antler needles, awls, and projectile points could be produced with them.[11] Burins have been found in Middle and Lower Paleolithic sites but are present in great number and variety only in the Upper Paleolithic.

Pressure flaking also appeared during the Upper Paleolithic. Rather than using percussion to strike off flakes as in previous technologies, pressure flaking works by employing pressure with a bone, wood, or antler tool at the edge of the tool to remove small flakes. Pressure flaking would usually be used in the final stages of retouching a tool.[12]

As time went on, all over the Old World smaller and smaller blade tools were produced. The very tiny ones, called **microliths,** were often hafted or fitted into handles, one blade at a time or several blades together, to serve as

Figure 10–3

One way to remove blades from a core is to hit them with a punch using indirect percussion. The object being struck is the punch, which is made of bone or horn. Source: From Brian M. Fagan, *In the Beginning* (Boston: Little, Brown, 1972), p. 195.

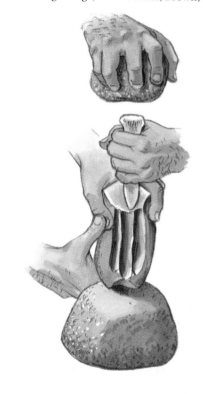

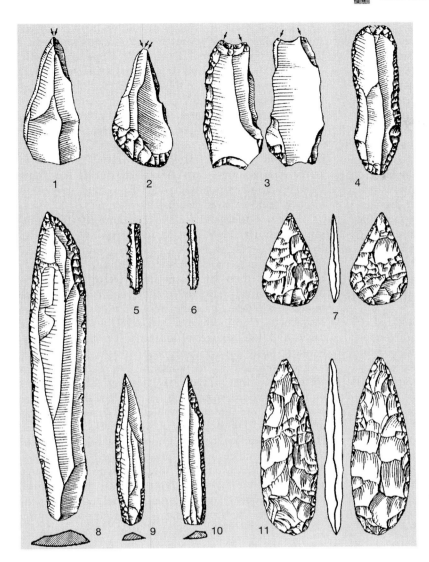

Figure 10–4

Upper Paleolithic tool kit from Hungary and Czechoslovakia. Burin (1), burin scraper (2), multiple burin (3), end-scraper on retouched blade (4), denticulated-backed bladelets (5, 6), pointed retouched blade (8), gravette points (9, 10), and bifacial points (7, 11). Source: From François Bordes, *The Old Stone Age,* trans. J. E. Anderson (New York: World University Library, 1968).

spears, adzes, knives, and sickles. The hafting required inventing a way to trim the blade's back edge so that it would be blunt rather than sharp. In this way the blades would not split the handles into which they might be inserted; the blunting would also prevent the users of an unhafted blade from cutting themselves.[13]

Some archaeologists think that the blade technique was adopted because it made for more economical use of flint. André Leroi-Gourhan of the Musée de l'Homme in Paris calculated that with the old Acheulian technique, a 2-pound lump of flint yielded 16 inches of working edge and produced only two hand axes. If the more advanced Mousterian technique were used, a lump of equal size would yield 2 yards of working edge. The indirect percussion method of the Upper Paleolithic would yield as much as 25 yards of working edge.[14] With the same amount of material, a significantly greater number of tools could be produced. Getting the most out of a valuable resource may have been particularly important in areas lacking large flint deposits. Then again, if the population was increas-

ing, that by itself would require more tools and more working edge to be produced.

Jacques Bordaz suggested that the evolution of toolmaking techniques, which continually increased the amount of usable edge that could be gotten out of a lump of flint, was significant because people could then spend more time in regions where flint was unavailable. Another reason for adopting the blade toolmaking technique may have been that it made for easy repair of tools. For example, the cutting edge of a tool might consist of a line of razorlike microliths set into a piece of wood. The tool would not be usable if just one of the cutting edge's microliths broke off or was chipped. But if the user carried a small prepared core of flint from which an identical-sized microlith could be struck off, the tool could be repaired easily by replacing the lost or broken microlith. A spear whose point was lost could be repaired similarly. Thus, the main purpose of the blade toolmaking technique may not have been to make more economical use of flint but rather to allow easy replacement of damaged blades.[15]

HOW WERE THE TOOLS USED? Ideally, the study of tools should reveal not only how the implements were made but also how they were used. One way of suggesting what a particular tool was used for in the past is to observe the manner in which similar tools are used by members of recent or contemporary societies, preferably societies with subsistence activities and environments similar to those of the ancient toolmakers. This method of study is called reasoning from **ethnographic analogy.** The problem with such reasoning, however, is obvious: We cannot be sure that the original use of a tool was the same as the present use. When selecting recent or contemporary cultures that may provide the most informative and accurate comparisons, we should try to choose those that derive from the ancient culture we are interested in. If the cultures being compared are historically related—prehistoric and recent Pueblo cultures in the southwestern United States, for example—there is a greater likelihood that the two groups used a particular kind of tool in similar ways and for similar purposes.[16]

Another way of suggesting what a particular kind of tool was used for is to compare the visible and microscopic wear marks on the prehistoric tools with the wear marks on similar tools made and experimentally used by contemporary researchers. The idea behind this approach is that different uses leave different wear marks. A pioneer in this research was S. A. Semenov, who re-created prehistoric stone tools and used them in a variety of ways to find out which uses left which kinds of wear marks. For example, by cutting into meat with his re-created stone knives, he produced a polish on the edges that was like the polish found on blades from a prehistoric site in Siberia. This finding led Semenov to infer that the Siberian blades were probably also used to cut meat.[17]

The tools made by Upper Paleolithic peoples suggest that they were much more effective hunters and fishers than their predecessors.[18] During the Upper Paleolithic, and probably for the first time, spears were shot from a spear-thrower rather than thrown with the arm. We know this because bone and antler **atlatls** (the Aztec word for "spear-thrower") have been found in some sites. A spear propelled off a grooved board could be sent through the air with increased force, causing it to travel farther and hit harder, and with less effort by the thrower. The bow and arrow was also used in various places during the Upper Paleolithic; and harpoons, used for fishing and perhaps for hunting reindeer, were invented at this time.

These new tools and weapons for more effective hunting and fishing do not rule out the possibility that Upper Paleolithic peoples were still scavenging animal remains. Olga Soffer suggests that Upper Paleolithic peoples may have located their settlements near places where many mammoths died naturally in order to make use of the bones for building (see Figure 10–5). For example, in Moravia the mammoths may have come to lick deposits of calcite and other sources of magnesium and calcium, particularly during the late spring and early summer when resources were short and mortality was high. Consistent with the idea that humans may not have killed so many of the enormous mammoths is the fact that in some places there are few human-made cut marks on mammoth bones. For example, at Dolni Vestonice, where bones of 100 mammoths were found, few bones show cut marks from butchering and few bones were found inside the huts. In contrast, the site is littered with bison, horse, and reindeer bones, suggesting that these other animals were deliberately killed and eaten by humans. If the people had been able to kill all the mammoths we find the

Figure 10–5

Here we see the type of mammoth-bone shelters constructed about 15,000 years ago on the East European Plain. Often mammoth skulls formed part of the foundation for the tusk, long bone, and wooden frame, covered with hide. As many as 95 mammoth mandibles were arranged around the outside in a herringbone pattern. Ten men and women could have constructed this elaborate shelter of 258 square feet in six days, using 46,000 pounds of bone.

remains of, why would they have hunted so many other animals?[19]

UPPER PALEOLITHIC ART

The earliest discovered traces of art are beads and carvings, and then paintings, from Upper Paleolithic sites. We might expect that early artistic efforts were crude, but the cave paintings of Spain and southern France show a marked degree of skill. So do the naturalistic paintings on slabs of stone excavated in southern Africa. Some of those slabs appear to have been painted as much as 28,000 years ago, which suggests that painting in Africa is as old as painting in Europe.[20] But painting may be even older than that. The early Australians may have painted on the walls of rock shelters and cliff faces at least 30,000 years ago and maybe as much as 60,000 years ago.[21]

Peter Ucko and Andrée Rosenfeld identified three principal locations of paintings in the caves of western Europe: (1) in obviously inhabited rock shelters and cave entrances—art as decoration or "art for art's sake"; (2) in "galleries" immediately off the inhabited areas of caves; and (3) in the inner reaches of caves, whose difficulty of access has been interpreted by some as a sign that magical-religious activities were performed there.[22]

The subjects of the paintings are mostly animals. The paintings are on bare walls, with no backdrops or environmental trappings. Perhaps, like many contemporary peoples, Upper Paleolithic men and women believed that the drawing of a human image could cause death or injury. If that were indeed their belief, it might explain why human figures are rarely depicted in cave art. Another explanation for the focus on animals might be that these

A piece of abstract, three-dimensional art from Dolni Vestonice, Czech Republic.

people sought to improve their luck at hunting. This theory is suggested by evidence of chips in the painted figures, perhaps made by spears thrown at the drawings. But if hunting magic was the chief motivation for the paintings, it is difficult to explain why only a few show signs of having been speared. Perhaps then the paintings were inspired by the need to increase the supply of animals. Cave art seems to have reached a peak toward the end of the Upper Paleolithic period, when the herds of game were decreasing.

The particular symbolic significance of the cave paintings in southwestern France is more explicitly revealed, perhaps, by the results of Patricia Rice and Ann Paterson's statistical study.[23] The data suggest that the animals portrayed in the cave paintings were mostly the ones that the painters preferred for meat and for materials such as hides. For example, wild cattle (bovines) and horses are portrayed more often than we would expect by chance, probably because they were larger and heavier (meatier) than the other animals in the environment. In addition, the paintings mostly portray animals that the painters may have feared the most because of their size, speed, natural weapons such as tusks and horns, and unpredictability of behavior. That is, mammoths, bovines, and horses are portrayed more often than deer and reindeer. Thus, the paintings are consistent with the idea that "the art is related to the importance of hunting in the economy of Upper Paleolithic people."[24] Consistent with this idea, according to the investigators, is the fact that the art of the cultural period that followed the Upper Paleolithic also seems to reflect how people got their food. But in that period, when getting food no longer depended on hunting large game (because they were becoming extinct), the art ceased to focus on portrayals of animals.

Upper Paleolithic art was not confined to cave paintings. Many spear shafts and similar objects were decorated with figures of animals. Alexander Marshack has an interesting interpretation of some of the engravings made during the Upper Paleolithic. He believes that as far back as 30,000 years ago, hunters may have used a system of notation, engraved on bone and stone, to mark the phases of the moon. If this is true, it would mean that Upper Paleolithic people were capable of complex thought and were consciously aware of their environment.[25] In addition, figurines representing the human female in exaggerated form have been found at Upper Paleolithic sites. Called *Venuses*, these figurines portray women with broad hips and large breasts and abdomens.

What the Venus figurines symbolized is still controversial. Most scholars believe these figurines represented a goddess or fertility symbol, but that belief is not universally held. For example, LeRoy McDermott has argued that Venus figurines are not symbolic representations at all but rather accurate self-portraits made by pregnant women. Their exaggerated breasts, hips, and stomachs are distortions that can be attributed to the perspective gained by a person looking down at herself, as is the lack of facial details on many of the figurines.[26] Others have argued that

NEW PERSPECTIVES ON GENDER

Women in Upper Paleolithic Art

It is a common misperception that depictions of the human form in Upper Paleolithic art are restricted to Venus figurines. On the contrary, there are many other depictions of humans, both female and male, running the whole range of ages from infants to old people. For women, figures of obese or pregnant women, like those sometimes depicted in Venus figurines, appear to be only one type in a wide range of images, many of which offer accurate rather than stylized representations.

In a survey of Upper Paleolithic art, Jean-Pierre Duhard found that all shapes and sizes of women as well as all age ranges were present. Indeed, he argued that a range of female body types can be seen. One engraved figure from Gönnersdorf cave on the Rhine River, for example, depicts four women. Three are the same size, but one is smaller and has small breasts—she may be an adolescent. Of the three larger figures, one appears to have a child tied to her back, and she also has large, rounded breasts, as opposed to the flat and pointed breasts of the other two. Duhard argued that this is an accurate depiction of four women, one with a child she is breast-feeding.

Duhard also argued that while depictions of women are common in Upper Paleolithic art, similar depictions of men and children are comparatively rare. He suggested this disparity may reflect women's status in Upper Paleolithic societies. Most depictions of women show them in some motherhood role—pregnant, in childbirth, or carrying

Image of Four Women from Gönnersdorf Cave

Source: From Jean-Pierre Duhard, "Upper Paleolithic Figures as a Reflection of Human Morphology and Social Organization," *Antiquity,* 67 (1993): 86.

an infant (and perhaps walking with older children). Duhard suggested that women's roles as mothers may have given them a privileged status in Upper Paleolithic life, which may be why that status is the most frequently depicted subject in Upper Paleolithic art.

In a similar way, Patricia Rice has argued that Venus figurines accurately reflect the social importance of women in Upper Paleolithic society. She demonstrated that a range of body types and ages are represented in Venus figurines, and argued that, since the Venuses depict real women of all ages, not just pregnant women, they should be seen as symbols of "womanhood" rather than "motherhood." The wide distribution of Venus figurines and their apparent importance to Upper Paleolithic peoples reflect, according to Rice, the recognized

importance of women in Upper Paleolithic society. Arguing along similar lines, Olga Soffer examined the clothing worn by some Venus figures. Soffer and her colleagues show that woven items are the most frequently depicted, and argue that, since these woven items would have been highly valued in Upper Paleolithic society, their presence on some Venus figurines suggests that some women held positions of high status in Upper Paleolithic society.

Sources: Jean-Pierre Duhard, "Upper Paleolithic Figures as a Reflection of Human Morphology and Social Organization," *Antiquity,* 67 (1993): 83–91; Patricia Rice, "Prehistoric Venuses: Symbols of Motherhood or Womanhood?" *Journal of Anthropological Research,* 37 (1981): 402–14; Olga Soffer, J. M. Adovasio, and D. C. Hyland, "The 'Venus' Figurines: Textiles, Basketry, Gender, and Status in the Upper Paleolithic," *Current Anthropology,* 41 (2000): 511–37.

The Venus of Willendorf, one of the most famous Venus figurines.

the figurines are examples of early erotica made by males for their sexual gratification or education. Still others suggest they were made by females to instruct young women in pregnancy and childbirth.[27]

The controversies surrounding Venus figurines provide insight into a basic problem in archaeology: There is often little or no evidence available that allows us to accept or reject a particular interpretation (see the box "Women in Upper Paleolithic Art"). Rather, in most cases we have to balance data and interpretation to come to an informed judgment, recognizing that our judgment today will likely change as new data are uncovered.

Upper Paleolithic Cultures in Africa and Asia

Europe was not the only region where Upper Paleolithic peoples thrived. In North Africa, for example, Upper Paleolithic peoples hunted large animals on the grasslands that covered the region during that period. They lived in small communities located within easy access to water and other resources, and moved regularly, probably to follow the animal herds. Trade took place between local groups, particularly for high-quality stone used in making tools.[28] In eastern and southern Africa, a way of life known as the *Later Stone Age* developed that persisted in some areas until very recently. People lived in small, mobile groups, hunting large animals and collecting a wide variety of plant foods. Interaction was common among these bands. Among their ethnographically known descendants, indi-

viduals would regularly switch their membership from one band to another.[29]

In South Asia the Upper Paleolithic saw an increasingly sedentary life-style developing along the banks of freshwater streams. The Upper Paleolithic peoples in South Asia combined hunting, fishing, and gathering with seasonal movements to exploit seasonally abundant resources.[30] In East and Southeast Asia ocean resources became vital to coastal-dwelling peoples, while those inland lived primarily in caves, hunting and collecting broadly in the local environment. Many of these sites appear to have been occupied for long periods of time, suggesting some degree of sedentism. During the Upper Paleolithic, peoples from Asia also populated Australia, New Guinea, and some of the islands of western Melanesia, clearly demonstrating the ability of these peoples to navigate on the sea and to use its resources.[31]

The Earliest Humans and Their Cultures in the New World

So far in this chapter we have dealt only with the Old World—Africa, Europe, and Asia. What about the New World—North and South America? How long have humans lived there, and what were their earliest cultures like?

Because only *Homo sapiens sapiens* fossils have been found in North and South America, migrations of humans to the New World had to have taken place some time after the emergence of *H. sapiens sapiens*. But exactly when these migrations occurred is subject to debate, particularly about when people got to areas south of Alaska. On the basis of similarities in biological traits such as tooth forms and blood types, and on possible linguistic relationships, anthropologists agree that Native Americans originally came from Asia. The traditional assumption is that they came to North America from Siberia, walking across a land bridge (Beringia) that is now under water (the Bering Strait) between Siberia and Alaska. The ice sheets or glaciers that periodically covered most of the high latitudes of the world contained so much of the world's water (the ice sheets were thousands of feet thick in some places) that Beringia was dry land in various periods (see Figure 10–6). For example, there was a land bridge for a while until the last 10,000 years or so. Since then, the glaciers have mostly melted, and the Bering "bridge" has been completely covered by a higher sea level.

CD-ROM Interactive Exercise II-12

Until recently, the prevailing view was that humans were not present south of Alaska until after 11,500 years ago. Now it appears from an archaeological site called Monte Verde in Chile that modern humans got to southern South America by at least 12,500 years ago, and maybe

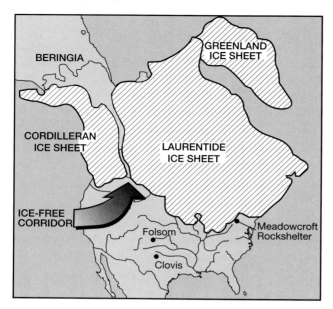

Figure 10–6 *Beringia and the Ice Sheets*

Source: David K. Meltzer, "Pleistocene Peopling of the Americas," *Evolutionary Anthropology*, Vol. 1, 1993. Copyright © 1993. Reprinted by permission of Wiley-Liss, Inc., a subsidiary of John Wiley & Sons, Inc.

initely not hunters of mammoths and other big game, as the contemporaneous Clovis people of North America were. In other words, it looks like the earliest inhabitants of the New World—in Chile, Brazil, North America—varied in culture. The people in the Amazon lived by collecting fruits and nuts, fishing, and hunting small game. They lived in caves with painted art on the walls and left 30,000 stone chips from making tips of spears, darts, or harpoons.[34]

There is no disagreement that humans were living south of Canada around 11,000 years ago. The *Clovis people,* as they are called (after an archaeological site near Clovis, New Mexico), left finely shaped spear points in many locations in North America. And we have human skeletal remains from after 11,000 years ago. Now that the Monte Verde site has been reliably dated, we know that there were people south of Canada before the Clovis people were in New Mexico. And there are other possible sites of pre-Clovis occupation, although many archaeologists do not agree that the presumed tools at these sites were made by humans (these objects could have been made by rockfalls or other natural forces) or that the sites are accu-

A jury of visiting archaeologists at the Monte Verde site in Chile confirmed that modern humans arrived in southern South America at least 12,500 years ago.

as much as 33,000 years ago. The Monte Verde site contains more than 700 stone tools, the remains of hide-covered huts, and a child's footprint next to a hearth.[32] The site suggests that there was at least one wave of human migration into the New World before 11,500 years ago, by walking and/or perhaps in boats. Even when the last glaciers were at their fullest extent, there was a small ice-free corridor through which people could have walked. And there were ice-free corridors earlier.

It was geologically possible then for humans to have walked into the New World at various times, and they could have traveled by boat, too (see box "Alternative Avenues of Entry into the New World"). Parts of the Beringia land bridge were exposed from about 60,000 to 25,000 years ago. It wasn't until between 20,000 and 18,000 years ago that the land bridge was at its maximum. When did the last land bridge disappear? It was widely believed that the land bridge was flooded around 14,000 years ago, but recent evidence suggests that walking across Beringia was still possible until about 10,000 years ago. An ice-free corridor between the Laurentide and Cordilleran ice sheets may have been present after 25,000 years ago, but that corridor is not likely to have supported big game, and permitted humans to hunt enough for sustenance, until after about 14,000 years ago. So some investigators suggest that moving through the ice-free corridor to what is now south of Canada was not likely until after that time.[33]

The people there may or may not have hunted big game, but just a little while later there were people living in the Amazon jungle of what is now Brazil who were def-

CURRENT ISSUES

Alternative Avenues of Entry into the New World

The most widely accepted model for how humans entered the New World is the one presented in the body of this textbook: by walking across Beringia, which joined Asia and North America at the end of the last ice age, when sea levels were lower than today. There is good evidence to support this model, both archaeological and geological. But there are also some problems.

One of the most persistent problems with the Beringia model is the presence of archaeological sites in both North and South America dated to time periods before glacial ice had retreated far enough to allow access to North America. In addition, several of the South American sites appear to be earlier than the earliest North American sites, which seems contradictory to a model based on humans moving into the New World from north to south.

Alternative models for human entry into the New World, which solve some of the problems with the Beringia model, have been proposed. The one with more support suggests that humans came to the New World from Asia by boat. These people would have moved along the sea edge of the glaciers, subsisting on fish and sea mammals. Once past the glaciers, they either would have moved farther down the coast, perhaps all the way to the tip of

South America, or proceeded inland into North America. Small groups of people may have made such voyages on many occasions, and it may be that none established communities that lasted more than a few generations.

Some scholars posit that the few very early archaeological sites may be the remnants of these early explorers. The small numbers would leave only a small archaeological record, so it is not surprising that more material has not been found. The fact that early occupations at a number of sites are separated from later occupations by soil showing no signs of human presence may also be evidence that these early explorers were present, but died out. Additional support for the coastal migration model has recently come from archaeological explorations of ancient coastlines now lying deep beneath the Bering Sea. Archaeologists have found stone tools in locations that would have been coastal during the last ice age.

A second, and more controversial, model is that humans may have come to the New World by boat from Europe. Like those who may have boated from Asia, these Europeans would have moved along the glacial ice front, not across the open sea. They would have fished and hunted sea mammals during their voyage, which may have

taken many generations. The primary evidence for this model are the Clovis stone tools made by the Paleo-Indians. Archaeologists and stone tool experts Bruce Bradley and Dennis Stanford have argued that the techniques used to manufacture Clovis tools bear little resemblance to techniques used by peoples in eastern Asia, but are identical to those used by the Solutrean peoples of Europe. One major problem with this model is that the Solutrean period ends about 17,000 years ago, and the earliest evidence of Solutrean-like tools in North America does not appear until at least 12,000 years ago.

Both of the alternative models for human entry into the New World have some archaeological support and provide explanations for the presence of very early sites. It still appears that a large migration of humans from Asia began about 12,500 years ago, probably across Beringia, and that it was those people who successfully colonized the New World.

Sources: Thomas Dillehay, *The Settlement of the Americas* (New York: Basic Books, 2000); Lawrence Guy Strauss, "Solutrean Settlement of North America? A View of Reality," *American Antiquity*, 65 (2000): 219–26; Michael Parfit, "Who Were the First Americans?" *National Geographic*, December 2000, 41–67; Eliot Marshall, "Pre-Clovis Sites Fight for Acceptance," *Science*, 291 (2001): 1730–32.

rately dated. One site that may be another pre-Clovis site is the Meadowcroft Rockshelter in western Pennsylvania.[35] In the bottom third of a stratum that seems to date from 19,600 to 8,000 years ago, the Meadowcroft site shows clear signs of human occupation—a small fragment

of human bone, a spearpoint, and chipped knives and scrapers. If the dating is accurate, the tools would be about 12,800 years old. William Parry suggests we need to date the human bone found in the site. If the bone turns out to date from before 12,000 years ago, few anthropologists would question the conclusion that humans occupied the Meadowcroft site before the time of the Clovis people.[36]

According to the comparative linguists Joseph Greenberg and Merritt Ruhlen, there were three waves of migration into the New World.[37] They compared hundreds of languages in North and South America, grouping them into three different language families. Because each of these language families has a closer relationship to an Asian language family than to the other New World language families, it would appear that three different migrations came out of Asia. The first arrivals spoke a language that diverged over time into most of the languages found in the New World, the Amerind family of languages; the speakers of these related languages came to occupy all of South and Central America as well as most of North America. Next came the ancestors of the people who speak languages belonging to the Na-Dené family, which today includes Navaho and Apache in the southwestern United States and the various Athapaskan languages of northern California, coastal Oregon, northwestern Canada, and Alaska. Finally, perhaps 4,000 years ago, came the ancestors of the Inuit (Eskimo) and Aleut (the latter came to occupy the islands southwest of Alaska and the adjacent mainland), who speak languages belonging to the Inuit-Aleut family.

Christy Turner's study of New World teeth supports the Greenberg and Ruhlen proposal of three separate migrations. Turner looked at the proportions of shovel-shaped incisors, a common Asian trait, in New World populations. The varying proportions fall into three distinct groupings, the same three suggested by the linguists[38] (see Figure 10–7). But a recent genetic analysis suggests that Inuit-Aleut may have split from Na-Dené in the New World.[39] The peopling of the New World may have even been more complicated. There could have been four separate migrations from the Old World, from different regions of Asia.[40]

THE PALEO-INDIANS

Archaeological remains of early New World hunters, called *Paleo-Indians,* have been found in the United States, Mexico, and Canada. Just south of the farthest reaches of the last glaciation, the area east of the Rockies known as the High Plains abounded with mammoths, bison, wild camels, and wild horses. The tools found with mammoth kills are known as the *Clovis complex,* which includes the

Figure 10–7

Inuit (Eskimos) and Aleuts, speakers of Na-Dené languages, and other Native American language groups differ in the frequency of shovel-shaped incisors. These genetic differences seem to reflect three waves of migration into the New World. Source: From Christy G. Turner II, "Telltale Teeth," *Natural History,* January 1987, p. 8. Courtesy of *Natural History* magazine.

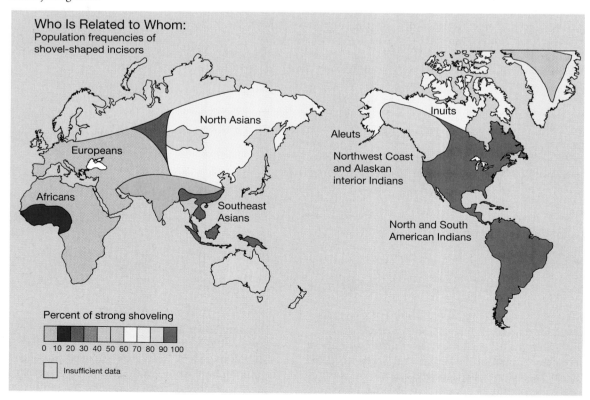

Clovis points.

Clovis projectile point as well as stone scrapers and knives and bone tools. The Clovis projectile point is large and leaf-shaped, flaked on both sides. It has a broad groove in the middle, presumably so that the point could be attached to a wooden spear shaft.[41] Because one mammoth was found with eight Clovis points in it, there is little dispute that Clovis people hunted large game.[42] Recent dating places most Clovis sites between 11,200 and 10,900 years ago.[43]

The mammoth disappeared about 10,000 years ago, and the largest game animal became the now-extinct large, straight-horned bison. The hunters of that bison used a projectile point called the *Folsom point,* which was much smaller than the Clovis point. Tools are also found with many other kinds of animal remains, including wolf, turtle, rabbit, horse, fox, deer, and camel, so the bison hunters obviously depended on other animals as well.[44] In the Rio Grande valley, the Folsom toolmakers characteristically established a base camp on low dune ridges overlooking both a large pond and broad, open grazing areas. If we assume that the pond provided water for the grazing herds, the people in the camp would have been in an excellent position to watch the herds.[45]

As the climate of what is now the American Southwest became drier, the animals and the cultural adaptations changed somewhat. About 9,000 years ago the smaller modern bison replaced the earlier straight-horned variety.[46] Base camps began to be located farther from ponds and grazing areas and closer to streams. If the ponds were no longer reliable sources of water during these drier times, the animals probably no longer frequented them, which would explain why the hunters had to change the sites of their base camps. Not much is known about the plant foods these Paleo-Indian people may have exploited, but on the desert fringes plant gathering may have been vital. In Nevada and Utah, archaeologists have found milling stones and other artifacts for processing plant food.[47]

The Olsen-Chubbuck site, a kill site excavated in Colorado, shows the organization that may have been involved in hunting bison.[48] In a dry gulch dated to 6500 B.C.

were the remains of 200 bison. At the bottom were complete skeletons and at the top, completely butchered animals. This find clearly suggests that Paleo-Indian hunters deliberately stampeded the animals into a natural trap—an arroyo, or steep-sided dry gully. The animals in front were probably pushed by the ones behind into the arroyo. Joe Ben Wheat estimated that the hunters may have obtained 55,000 pounds of meat from this one kill. If we judge from nineteenth-century Plains Indians, who could prepare bison meat to last a month, and estimate that each person would eat a pound a day, the kill at the Olsen-Chubbuck site could have fed more than 1,800 people for a month (they probably did not all live together throughout the year). The hunters must have been highly organized not only for the stampede itself but also for butchering. It seems that the enormous carcasses had to be carried to flat ground for that job. In addition, the 55,000 pounds of meat and hides had to be carried back to camp.[49]

Although big game may have been most important on the High Plains, other areas show different adaptations. For example, Paleo-Indian people in woodland regions of what is now the United States seem to have depended more heavily on plant food and smaller game. In some woodland areas, fish and shellfish may have been a vital

The "river of bones" at the Olsen-Chubbuck site. These are the remains of bison that Paleo-Indian hunters stampeded into an arroyo.

part of the diet.[50] On the Pacific coast, some Paleo-Indian people developed food-getting strategies more dependent on fish.[51] And in other areas, the lower Illinois River valley being one example, Paleo-Indian people who depended on game and wild vegetable foods managed to get enough food to live in permanent villages of perhaps 100 to 150 people.[52]

Once humans colonized the Americas, they established a way of life very similar to that of their Upper Paleolithic cousins in the Old World, a life generally based on big-game hunting. As time went on, life became more sedentary, with increasing interaction among local groups.

The End of the Upper Paleolithic

After about 10,000 years ago, the glaciers began to disappear; and with their disappearance came other environmental changes. The melting of the glacial ice caused the oceans to rise, and, as the seas moved inland, the waters inundated some of the richest fodder-producing coastal plains, creating islands, inlets, and bays. Other areas were opened up for human occupation as the glaciers retreated and the temperatures rose.[53] The cold, treeless plains, tundras, and grasslands eventually gave way to dense mixed forests, mostly birch, oak, and pine, and the Pleistocene megafauna became extinct. The warming waterways began to be filled with fish and other aquatic resources.[54]

Archaeologists believe that these environmental changes induced some populations to alter their food-getting strategies. When the tundras and grasslands disappeared, hunters could no longer obtain large quantities of meat simply by remaining close to large migratory herds of animals, as they probably did during Upper Paleolithic times. Even though deer and other game were available, the number of animals per square mile (density) had decreased, and it became difficult to stalk and kill animals sheltered in the thick woods. Thus, in many areas people seemed to have turned from a reliance on big-game hunting to the intensive collecting of wild plants, mollusks, fish, and small game to make up for the extinction of the large game animals they had once relied upon.

THE MAGLEMOSIAN CULTURE OF NORTHERN EUROPE

Some adaptations to the changing environment can be seen in the cultural remains of the settlers in northern Europe who are called *Maglemosians* by archaeologists. Their name derives from the peat bogs (*magle mose* in Danish means "great bog") where their remains have been found.

To deal with the new, more forested environment, the Maglemosians made stone axes and adzes to chop down trees and form them into various objects. Large timbers appear to have been split for houses; trees were hollowed

out for canoes; and smaller pieces of wood were made into paddles. The canoes presumably were built for travel and perhaps for fishing on the lakes and rivers that abounded in the postglacial environment.

We do not know to what extent the Maglemosians relied on wild plant foods, but there were a lot of different kinds available, such as hazelnuts. However, we do know many other things about the Maglemosians' way of life. Although fishing was fairly important, as suggested by the frequent occurrence of bones from pike and other fish, as well as fishhooks, these people apparently depended mainly on hunting for food. Game included elk, wild ox, deer, and wild pig. In addition to many fishing implements and the adzes and axes, the Maglemosians' tool kit included the bow and arrow. Some of their tools were ornamented with finely engraved designs. Ornamentation independent of tools also appears in amber and stone pendants and small figurines representing, for example, the head of an elk.[55]

Like the Maglemosian finds, many of the European post–Upper Paleolithic sites are along lakes, rivers, and oceanfronts. But these sites probably were not inhabited year round; there is evidence that at least some groups moved seasonally from one place of settlement to another, perhaps between the coast and inland areas.[56] Finds such as *kitchen middens* (piles of shells) that centuries of post–Upper Paleolithic seafood-eaters had discarded and the remains of fishing equipment, canoes, and boats indicate that these people depended much more heavily on fishing than had their ancestors in Upper Paleolithic times.

THE ARCHAIC CULTURES OF EASTERN NORTH AMERICA

A related set of adaptations to the changing environment can be seen among the peoples who inhabited eastern North America at the end of the ice age. As the climate became warmer and drier, the flora and fauna of North America changed. Megafauna, as elsewhere in the world, went extinct, and were replaced by smaller mammals, particularly deer. The availability of meat was greatly reduced—hunters could count on coming home with pounds, not tons, of meat. Warmer adapted plants replaced cold adapted plants, and were used for food to replace the meat that was no longer available. Warmer adapted plants had advantages as food resources for humans over cold adapted ones because edible seeds, fruits, and nuts were more common, and often more plentiful and accessible, on the warmer adapted plants. Thus a much greater diversity of plants and animals came to be used by the Archaic peoples.[57]

The Archaic peoples of North America, like the Maglemosian peoples in Europe, began to follow a more sedentary life-style. Two forms of Archaic settlement appear to have been typical. One was a residential base camp, which would have been inhabited seasonally by several, probably related, families. The other was a special-purpose camp,

Some examples of Archaic ground stone tools from eastern North America. They include axes (top left), an adze (bottom left), an atlatl weight (bottom right), a hammer, and a stone to crack nuts (top right).

which would have been a short-term habitation near a particular resource or perhaps used by a group of hunters for a short period of time.[58] On the Atlantic coast, for example, individual groups apparently moved seasonally along major river valleys, establishing summer base camps in the piedmont and winter camps near the coast. Special-purpose camps were created year round as groups went out from the base camp to hunt and collect particular resources, such as stone for making tools.[59]

One of the innovations of the Archaic peoples was the development of ground stone woodworking tools. Axes, adzes, and tools for grinding seeds and nuts become more and more common in the tool kit.[60] This probably reflects the emergence of greater areas of forest following the retreat of the glaciers from North America, but it also demonstrates a greater reliance on forest products and, most likely, a greater use of wood and wood products. Fish and shellfish also came to be relied upon in some areas, and this too reflects the adjustment made by the Archaic peoples to the changing conditions they faced at the end of the last ice age.

The innovation of most lasting importance in both the New and Old Worlds, however, was the development of domesticated plants and animals. In both parts of the world, peoples at the end of the ice age began to experiment with plants. By around 14,000 years ago in the Old World, and 10,000 years ago in the New World, some species had been domesticated. It is this fundamental change in food-getting—the invention of agriculture—to which we turn in the next chapter.

Summary

1. The period of cultural history known as the Upper Paleolithic in Europe, the Near East, and Asia or the Later Stone Age in Africa dates from about 40,000 years

ago to about 14,000 to 10,000 years ago. During this time the world was locked in an ice age, with glaciers covering much of northern Europe and North America, and annual temperatures as much as 10 degrees Celsius below today's.

2. The Upper Paleolithic tool kit is characterized by the preponderance of blades; there were also burins, bone and antler tools, and (later) microliths. In many respects, life-styles were similar to life-styles before. People were still mainly hunters and gatherers and fishers who probably lived in highly mobile bands. They made their camps out in the open and in caves and rock shelters.

3. The Upper Paleolithic is also characterized by a variety of new developments: new techniques of toolmaking, the emergence of art, population growth, and new inventions such as the bow and arrow, the spear-thrower (atlatl), and the harpoon.

4. Only *Homo sapiens sapiens* remains have been found in the New World. The prevailing opinion is that humans migrated to the New World over a land bridge between Siberia and Alaska in the area of what is now the Bering Strait. Until recently it was thought that humans were not present south of Alaska until after 11,500 years ago. Now it appears from an archaeological site called Monte Verde in Chile that modern humans got to southern South America by at least 12,500 years ago and perhaps as much as 33,000 years ago.

5. At the end of the ice age, around 14,000 years ago, the climate began to become more temperate. Many large animals relied upon by Upper Paleolithic peoples for food went extinct, and at the same time new, warmer-adapted plants provided a rich new food source. Around the world people began to use more plant foods and a broader range of resources overall. In many parts of the world people began experimenting with domesticating plants and animals.

Glossary Terms

atlatls	indirect percussion
blades	microliths
burins	pressure flaking
ethnographic analogy	Upper Paleolithic

Critical Questions

1. How do Upper Paleolithic tools differ from Middle Paleolithic tools? What is the significance of these differences in terms of human culture?

2. Upper Paleolithic cave paintings arouse our imaginations. We have described some research that tested ideas about what these paintings might mean. Can you think of other ways to understand the significance of cave art?

3. What factors might have led humans to colonize the New World?

Internet Exercises

1. Take a virtual tour through the cave of Lascaux at **http://www.culture.fr/culture/arcnat/lascaux/en/**. View the remarkable paintings made by Upper Paleolithic peoples, and learn how they were made. When you are done, test your knowledge with the site's questionnaire.

2. In 1997, a team of experts accepted the findings from a site in Chile named Monte Verde suggesting that humans were in the New World earlier than traditionally thought. Look at the press release at **http://www. nationalgeographic.com/society/ngo/events/97/ monteverde/ dallas.html**. But recently scholars have raised new questions about the site. These are summarized in *Discovering Archaeology* at **http://www. discoveringarchaeology.com/0699toc/6special-mv1. shtml**. Write a brief essay summarizing the debate and the main points raised on both sides.

3. Visit the Institute for Ice Age Studies' Web site at **http://www.insticeagestudies.com/** and read the news about current research into the European Upper Paleolithic. Summarize the most recent discoveries.

Suggested Reading

BAHN, P., AND VERTUT, J. *Images of the Ice Age.* New York: Facts on File, 1988. A well-illustrated introduction to Upper Paleolithic art.

DICKSON, D. BRUCE. *The Dawn of Belief: Religion in the Upper Paleolithic of Southwestern Europe.* Tucson: University of Arizona Press, 1990. An introduction to Upper Paleolithic life and art, focusing on the origins of religion.

MELTZER, D. J. *Search for the First Americans.* Washington, DC: Smithsonian Institution, 1993. An overview of research on Paleo-Indian cultures.

SOFFER, O. *The Upper Paleolithic of the Central Russian Plain.* Orlando, FL: Academic Press, 1985. An examination of Upper Paleolithic life in glacial Europe.

SOFFER, O., AND PRASLOV, N. D., EDS. *From Kostenki to Clovis: Upper Paleolithic Paleo-Indian Adaptations.* New York: Plenum, 1993. A collection of essays that examine Upper Paleolithic peoples in Asia and North America, seeking commonalities and connections.

Origins of Food Production and Settled Life

oward the end of the period known as the Upper Paleolithic, people seem to have gotten most of their food from hunting migratory herds of large animals, such as wild cattle, antelope, bison, and mammoths. These hunter-gatherers were probably highly mobile in order to follow the migrations of the animals. Beginning about 14,000 years ago, people in some regions began to depend less on big-game hunting and more on relatively stationary food resources, such as fish, shellfish, small game, and wild plants (see Figure 11–1). In some areas, particularly Europe and the Near East, the exploitation of local, relatively permanent resources may account for an increasingly settled way of life. The cultural period in which these developments took place is usually called the *Epipaleolithic* in the Near East and the *Mesolithic* in Europe. Other areas of the world show a similar switch to what is called *broad-spectrum* food-collecting, but they do not always show an increasingly settled life-style, as for example in Mesoamerica where this period is called the *Archaic*.

We see the first clear evidence of a changeover to **food production**—the cultivation and domestication of plants and animals—in the Near East, about 8000 B.C.[1] This shift, called the *Neolithic revolution* by archaeologist V. Gordon Childe, occurred, probably independently, in other areas of the Old and New Worlds within the next few thousand years. In the Old World there were independent centers of domestication in China, Southeast Asia (what is now Malaysia, Thailand, Cambodia, and Vietnam), and

Africa around 6000 B.C.[2] In the New World there were centers of cultivation and domestication in the highlands of Mesoamerica (about 7000 B.C.), the central Andes around Peru (about 7000 B.C.), and the Eastern Woodlands of North America (about 2000 B.C., but perhaps earlier).[3] Most of the world's major food plants and animals were domesticated well before 2000 B.C. Also developed by that time were techniques of plowing, fertilizing, fallowing, and irrigation.[4] Figure 11–2 shows the regions of the world that domesticated today's main food crops.

In this chapter we discuss what is believed about the origins of food production and settled life, called **sedentarism**—how and why people in different places may have come to cultivate and domesticate plants and animals and to live in permanent villages. **Agriculture** (which we use here to refer to all types of domestic plant cultivation) and a sedentary life did not necessarily develop together. In some regions of the world, people began to live in permanent villages before they cultivated and domesticated plants and animals, whereas in other places people planted crops without settling down permanently. Much of our discussion focuses on the Near East and Mesoamerica, the areas we know best archaeologically for the developments leading to food production and settled life. As much as we can, however, we try to indicate how data from other areas appear to suggest patterns different from, or similar to, those in the Near East and Mesoamerica.

Figure 11–1
The Evolution of Domestication

Source: Dates for animal domestication are from Juliet Clutton-Brock, "Domestication of Animals," in Stephen Jones, Robert Martin, and David Pilbeam, eds., *The Cambridge Encyclopedia of Human Evolution* (New York: Cambridge University Press, 1992), p. 384.

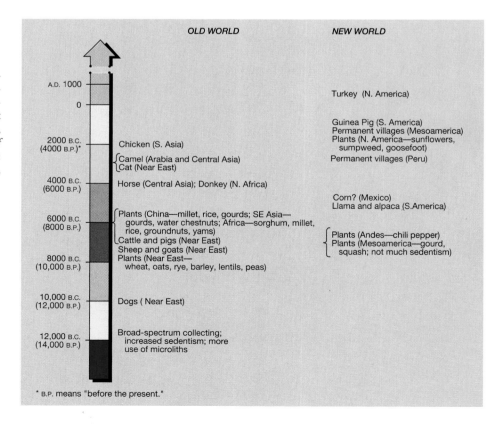

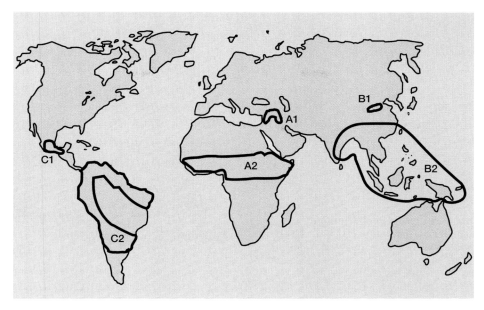

Figure 11–2 *Original Locations of the World's Main Food Crops*

The world's main food crops were originally domesticated in different regions: (A1) barley, wheat, peas, lentils, and chickpeas in the Near East; (A2) various millets, sorghum, groundnuts, yams, dates, coffee, and melons in Africa; (B1) various millets and rice in North China; (B2) rice, bananas, sugar cane, citrus fruits, coconuts, taro, and yams in Southeast Asia; (C1) maize or corn, squash, beans, and pumpkins in Mesoamerica; (C2) lima beans, potatoes, sweet potatoes, manioc, and peanuts in lowland and highland South America. There was also independent domestication in North America, but (except for sunflower) the plants domesticated there are not common crops today. Source: From Frank Hole, "Origins of Agriculture," in Stephen Jones, Robert Martin, and David Pilbeam, eds., *The Cambridge Encyclopedia of Human Evolution* (New York: Cambridge University Press, 1992), p. 376. Copyright © by Cambridge University Press. Reprinted by permission of Cambridge University Press.

 Preagricultural Developments

THE NEAR EAST

In the Near East there seems to have been a shift from mobile big-game hunting to the utilization of a broad spectrum of natural resources at the end of the Upper Paleolithic, similar to those changes that happened in Europe which we discussed at the end of the last chapter.[5] There is evidence that people subsisted on a variety of resources, including fish, mollusks, and other water life; wild deer, sheep, and goats; and wild grains, nuts, and legumes.[6] The increased utilization of stationary food sources such as wild grain may partly explain why some people in the Near East began to lead more sedentary lives during the Epipaleolithic.

Even today, a traveler passing through the Anatolian highlands of Turkey and other mountainous regions in the Near East may see thick stands of wild wheat and barley growing as densely as if they had been cultivated. Wielding flint sickles, Epipaleolithic people could easily have harvested a bountiful crop from such wild stands. Just how productive these resources can be was demonstrated in a field experiment duplicating prehistoric conditions. Using the kind of flint-blade sickle an Epipaleolithic worker would have used, researchers were able to harvest a little over two pounds of wild grain in an hour. A family of four, working only during the few weeks of the harvest season, probably could have reaped more wheat and barley than they needed for the entire year.[7]

The amount of wild wheat harvested in the experiment prompted Kent Flannery to conclude, "Such a harvest would almost necessitate some degree of sedentism—after all, where could they go with an estimated metric ton of clean wheat?"[8] Moreover, the stone equipment used for grinding would have been a clumsy burden to carry. Part of the harvest would probably have been set aside for immediate consumption, ground, and then cooked either by roasting or boiling. The rest of the harvest would have been stored to supply food for the remainder of the year. A grain diet, then, could have been the impetus for the construction of roasters, grinders, and storage pits by some preagricultural people, as well as for the construction of solid, fairly permanent housing. Once a village was built, people may have been reluctant to abandon it. We can visualize the earliest preagricultural settlements

Hayonim, one of the many caves in which the Natufians built relatively permanent settlements. Archaeologists are at work at the site.

clustered around such naturally rich regions, as archaeological evidence indeed suggests they were.

THE NATUFIANS OF THE NEAR EAST   Eleven thousand years ago the Natufians, a people living in the area that is now Israel and Jordan, inhabited caves and rock shelters and built villages on the slopes of Mount Carmel in Israel. At the front of their rock shelters they hollowed out basin-shaped depressions in the rock, possibly for storage pits. Examples of Natufian villages are also found at the Eynan site in Israel.

Eynan is a stratified site containing the remains of three villages in sequence, one atop another. Each village consisted of about 50 circular *pit houses*. The floor of each house was sunk a few feet into the ground, so that the walls of the house consisted partly of earth, below ground level, and partly of stone, above ground level. Pit houses had the advantage of retaining heat longer than houses built above the ground. The villages appear to have had stone-paved walks; circular stone pavements ringed what seem to be permanent hearths; and the dead were interred in village cemeteries.

The tools suggest that the Natufians harvested wild grain intensively. Sickles recovered from their villages have a specific sheen, which experiments have shown to be the effect of flint striking grass stems, as the sickles would have been used in the cutting of grain. The Natufians are the earliest Mesolithic people known to have stored surplus crops. Beneath the floors of their stone-walled houses they constructed plastered storage pits. In addition to wild grains, the Natufians exploited a wide range of other resources.[9] The remains of many wild animals are found in Natufian sites; Natufians appear to have concentrated on hunting gazelle, which they would take by surrounding whole herds.[10]

The Natufians, as well as food collectors in other areas at the time, show many differences as compared with food collectors in earlier periods.[11] Not only was Natufian food collection based on a more intensive use of stationary resources such as wild grain, but the archaeological evidence suggests increasing social complexity. Natufian sites on the average were five times larger than those of their predecessors. Communities were now occupied for most of the year, if not year round. Burial patterns suggest more social differences between people. Although the available wild cereal resources appear to have enabled the Natufians to live in relatively permanent villages, their diet seems to have suffered. Their tooth enamel shows signs of nutritional deficiency, and their stature declined over time.[12]

MESOAMERICA

A similar shift toward more broad-spectrum hunting and gathering occurred in the New World at the end of the Paleo-Indian period, about 10,000 years ago. Climate change seems to have been vital here too, as it was in the Old World. The retreat of glacial ice from North America and overall warmer and wetter climate brought dramatic changes to plant and animal communities throughout North America and Mesoamerica. Pleistocene megafauna, such as mammoths, mastodon, rhinoceros, giant ground sloth, and others, as well as a variety of smaller game animals, such as the horse, all went extinct in a relatively short period of time.[13] Hunting strategies shifted toward a broader range of game species, particularly deer, antelope, bison, and small mammals. At the same time, deciduous woodlands and grasslands expanded, providing a range of new plants to exploit. Ground stone woodworking tools such as axes and adzes first appeared, as did nut-processing tools such as mortars and pestles. Shellfish began to be exploited in some areas. Throughout North America and Mesoamerica people began to expand the range of plants and animals they relied upon.[14]

THE ARCHAIC PEOPLES OF HIGHLAND MESO-AMERICA   In Highland Mesoamerica, the mountainous regions of central and southern Mexico, we also see a shift from big-game hunting to a broader use of resources, in part due to a change in climate more like today's. Altitude became an important factor in the hunting and collecting regime, as different altitudes have different plant and animal resources. Valleys tend to have scrubby, grassland vegetation, whereas foothills and mountains have "thorn forests" of cactuses and succulents giving way to oak and pine forests at higher altitudes, where there is more moisture. This vertical zonation means that a wide range of plants and animals were available in relatively close proximity—different environments were close by—and the Archaic peoples took advantage of these varied conditions to hunt and collect a broad range of resources.[15]

About 8,000 years ago the Archaic peoples in Mesoamerica appear to have moved seasonally between communities of two different sizes: camps with 15 to 30 residents (*macrobands*) and camps with only 2 to 5 residents (*microbands*). Macroband camps were located near seasonally abundant resources, such as acorns or mesquite pods. Several families would have come together when these resources were in season, both to take advantage of them and to work together to harvest them while they were plentiful, to perform rituals, and simply to socialize. Microband camps were also inhabited seasonally, probably by a single family, when groups were not assembled into macroband camps. Remains of these microband camps are often found in caves or rock shelters from which a variety of environments could be exploited by moving either upslope or downslope from the campsite.[16]

Unlike the Natufians of the Near East, there is no evidence of social differences among the Archaic peoples of Highland Mesoamerica. The largest social unit, the macroband camp, was probably composed of related family groups, and leadership in these groups was probably informal. There is little evidence of ritual behavior beyond the presence of what may have been a ceremonial dance floor at Gheo-Shih, a macroband campsite in the Valley of Oaxaca. In short, life-styles remained much like the simple

and egalitarian ones of the Paleo-Indians, despite the transition to a much broader strategy of food collection.

OTHER AREAS

People in other areas of the world also shifted from hunting big game to collecting many types of food before they began to practice agriculture. The still-sparse archaeological record suggests that such a change occurred in Southeast Asia, which may have been one of the important centers of original plant and animal domestication. The faunal remains in inland sites there indicate that many different sources of food were being exploited from the same base camps. For example, at these base camps we find the remains of animals from high mountain ridges as well as lowland river valleys, birds and primates from nearby forests, bats from caves, and fish from streams. The few coastal sites indicate that many kinds of fish and shellfish were collected and that animals such as deer, wild cattle, and rhinoceros were hunted.[17] The preagricultural developments in Southeast Asia probably were responses to changes in the climate and environment, including a warming trend, more moisture, and a higher sea level.[18]

In Africa, too, the preagricultural period was marked by a warmer, wetter environment. The now-numerous lakes, rivers, and other bodies of water provided fish, shellfish, and other resources that apparently allowed people to settle more permanently than they had before. For example, there were lakes in what is now the southern and central Sahara Desert, where people fished and hunted hippopotamuses and crocodiles. This pattern of broad-spectrum food-collecting seems also to have been characteristic of the areas both south and north of the Sahara.[19] One area showing increased sedentism is the Dakhleh Oasis in the Western Desert of Egypt. Between 9,000 and 8,500 years ago, the inhabitants lived in circular stone huts on the shores of rivers and lakes. Bone harpoons and pottery are found there and in other areas from the Nile Valley through the central and southern Sahara westward to

This !Kung woman, like other broad-spectrum hunters and gatherers, gathers food from a wide range of plants.

what is now Mali. Fishing seems to have allowed people to remain along the rivers and lakes for much of the year.[20]

WHY DID BROAD-SPECTRUM COLLECTING DEVELOP?

It is apparent that the preagricultural switch to broad-spectrum collecting was fairly common throughout the world. Climate change was probably at least partly responsible for the exploitation of new sources of food. For example, the worldwide rise in sea level because of glacial melting may have increased the availability of fish and shellfish. Changes in climate may have also been partly responsible for the decline in the availability of big game, particularly the large herd animals. In addition, it has been suggested that another possible cause of that decline was human activity, specifically overkilling of some of these animals. The evidence suggesting overkill is that the extinction in the New World of many of the large Pleistocene animals, such as the mammoth, coincided with the movement of humans from the Bering Strait region to the southern tip of South America.[21]

The overkill hypothesis has been questioned on the basis of bird as well as mammal extinctions in the New World. An enormous number of bird species also became extinct during the last few thousand years of the North American Pleistocene, and it is difficult to argue that human hunters caused all of those extinctions. Because the bird and mammal extinctions occurred simultaneously, it is likely that most or nearly all the extinctions were due to climatic and other environmental changes.[22] Then again, the example of the New Zealand moas, which went extinct soon after humans colonized the islands, may be instructive. Moas had low reproductive rates; computer simulations suggest their population would have been very sensitive to increases in adult mortality. Because many large animals have low reproductive rates like moas, human overhunting may have been responsible for their extinction.[23]

The decreasing availability of big game may have stimulated people to exploit new food resources. But they may have turned to a broader spectrum of resources for another reason—population growth (see Figure 11–3). As Mark Cohen has noted, hunter-gatherers were "filling up" the world, and they may have had to seek new, possibly less desirable sources of food.[24] (We might think of shellfish as more desirable than mammoths, but only because we don't have to do the work to get such food. A lot of shellfish have to be collected, shelled, and cooked to produce the animal protein obtainable from one large animal.) Consistent with the idea that the world was filling up around this time is the fact that not until after 30,000 years ago did hunter-gatherers begin to move into previously uninhabited parts of the world, such as Australia and the New World.[25]

Broad-spectrum collecting may have involved exploitation of new sources of food, but that does not necessarily mean that people were eating better. A decline in stature

Figure 11–3 *Reconstructed Increases in World Population and Carrying Capacity for Humans during the Pleistocene*

Estimates of human population suggest that substantial increases preceded the movement of humans into more marginal areas. Further population increase preceded the emergence of broad-spectrum collecting. Source: Figure adapted from *Demographic Archaeology* by F. A. Hassan, copyright © 1981 by Academic Press, reproduced by permission of the publisher.

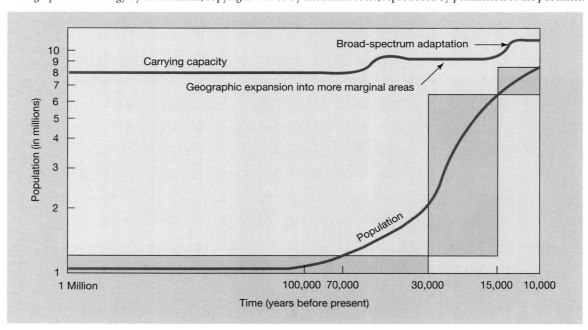

often indicates a poorer diet. During the preagricultural period, height apparently declined by as much as two inches in many parts of the Old World (Greece, Israel, India, and northern and western Europe).[26] This decline may have been a result of decreasing nutrition, but it could also be that natural selection for greater height was relaxed because leverage for throwing projectiles such as spears was not so favored after the decline of big-game hunting. (Greater limb-bone length, and therefore greater height, would enable a hunter to throw a spear with more force and farther.[27]) In other areas of the world, such as Australia and what is now the midwestern United States, skeletal evidence also suggests a decline in the general level of health with the rise of broad-spectrum collecting.[28]

BROAD-SPECTRUM COLLECTING AND SEDENTARISM

Does the switch to broad-spectrum collecting explain the increasingly sedentary way of life we see in various parts of the world in preagricultural times? The answer seems to be both yes and no. In some areas of the world—some sites in Europe, the Near East, Africa, and Peru—settlements became more permanent. In other areas, such as the semiarid highlands of Mesoamerica, the switch to broad-spectrum collecting was not associated with increasing sedentarism. Even after the Highland Mesoamericans began to cultivate plants, they still did not live in permanent villages.[29] Why?

It would seem that it is not simply the switch to broad-spectrum collecting that accounts for increasing sedentarism in many areas. Rather, a comparison of settlements on the Peruvian coast suggests that the more permanent settlements were located nearer, within three and a half miles, to most, if not all, of the diverse food resources exploited during the year than were temporary settlements. The community that did not have a year-round settlement seems to have depended on more widely distributed resources. What accounts for sedentarism may thus be the

nearness[30] or the high reliability and yield[31] of the broad-spectrum resources, rather than the broad spectrum itself.

SEDENTARISM AND POPULATION GROWTH

Although some population growth undoubtedly occurred throughout the hunting and gathering phase of world history, some anthropologists have suggested that populations would have increased dramatically when people began to settle down. The evidence for this suggestion comes largely from a comparison of recent nomadic and sedentary !Kung populations.

The settling down of a nomadic group may reduce the typical spacing between births.[32] Nomadic !Kung have children spaced four years apart on the average; in contrast, recently sedentarized !Kung have children about three years apart. Why might birth spacing change with settling down? There are several possibilities.

The spacing of children far apart can occur in a number of ways. One way, if effective contraceptives are not available, is prolonged sexual abstinence after the birth of a child—the postpartum sex taboo—which is common in recent human societies. Another way is abortion or infanticide.[33] Nomadic groups may be motivated to have children farther apart because of the problem of carrying small children. Carrying one small child is difficult enough; carrying two might be too burdensome. Thus, sedentary populations could have their children spaced more closely because carrying children would not always be necessary.

Although some nomadic groups may have deliberately spaced births by abstinence or infanticide, there is no evidence that such practices explain why four years separate births among nomadic !Kung. There may be another explanation, involving an unintended effect of how babies are fed. Nancy Howell and Richard Lee have suggested that the presence of baby foods other than mother's milk may be responsible for the decreased birth spacing in sedentary agricultural !Kung groups.[34] It is now well established that

A !Kung group moving camp. When hunters and gatherers move, they have to carry their children and all their possessions with them. Spacing births an average of four years apart helps to ensure that a woman will not have to carry more than two children at a time.

the longer a mother nurses her baby without supplementary foods, the longer it is likely to be before she starts ovulating again. Nomadic !Kung women have little to give their babies in the way of soft, digestible food, and the babies depend largely on mother's milk for two to three years. But sedentary !Kung mothers can give their babies soft foods such as cereal (made from cultivated grain) and milk from domesticated animals. Such changes in feeding practices may shorten birth spacing by shortening the interval between birth and the resumption of ovulation. In preagricultural sedentary communities, it is possible that baby foods made from wild grains might have had the same effect. For this reason alone, therefore, populations may have grown even before people started to farm or herd.

Another reason sedentary !Kung women may have more babies than nomadic !Kung women has to do with the ratio of body fat to body weight. Some investigators suspect that a critical minimum of fat in the body may be necessary for ovulation. A sedentary !Kung woman may have more fatty tissue than a nomadic !Kung woman, who walks many miles daily to gather wild plant foods, often carrying a child with her. Thus, sedentary !Kung women might resume ovulating sooner after the birth of a baby and so for that reason alone may be likely to have more closely spaced children. If some critical amount of fat is necessary for ovulation, that would explain why in our own society many women who have little body fat—long-distance runners, gymnasts, and ballet dancers are examples—do not ovulate regularly.[35]

MICROLITHIC TECHNOLOGY

Technologically, these preagricultural cultures did not differ radically from Upper Paleolithic cultures.[36] The trend

Figure 11–4 *Seed Heads of Wild and Domesticated Wheat*

Note the larger and more numerous seeds on domesticated wheat. Source: From Past in Perspective by K. Feder. Copyright © 2000 by Mayfield Publishing Company. Reprinted by permission of the publisher.

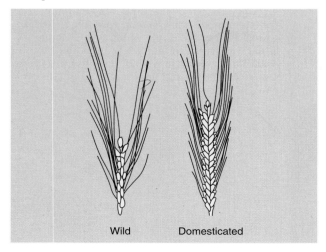

Wild   Domesticated

toward smaller and lighter tools continued. Microliths, small blades half an inch to two inches long, which were made in late Upper Paleolithic times, were now used in quantity. In place of the one-piece flint implement, the preagricultural peoples in Europe, Asia, and Africa equipped themselves with *composite tools*—that is, tools made of more than one material.

Microliths, too small to be used one at a time, could be fitted into grooves in bone or wood to form arrows, harpoons, daggers, and sickles. A sickle, for example, was made by inserting several microliths into a groove in a wooden or bone handle. The blades were held in place by resin. A broken microlith could be replaced like a blade in a modern razor. Besides being adaptable for many uses, microliths could be made from many varieties of available stone. Since they did not need the large nodules to make large core and flake tools, people using microliths could work with smaller nodules to make the small blades.[37]

The Domestication of Plants and Animals

Neolithic means "of the new stone age"; the term originally signified the cultural stage in which humans invented pottery and ground-stone tools. We now know, however, that both were present in earlier times, so we cannot define a Neolithic state of culture purely on the basis of the presence of pottery and ground-stone tools. At present, archaeologists generally define the **Neolithic** in terms of the presence of domesticated plants and animals. In this type of culture, people began to produce food rather than merely collect it.

The line between food-collecting and food-producing occurs when people begin to plant crops and to keep and breed animals. How do we know when this transition occurred? In fact, archaeologically we do not see the beginning of food production; we can see signs of it only after plants and animals show differences from their wild varieties. When people plant crops, we refer to the process as *cultivation*. It is only when the crops cultivated and the animals raised are *modified*—different from wild varieties—that we speak of plant and animal **domestication.**

We know, in a particular site, that domestication occurred if plant remains have characteristics different from those of wild plants of the same types (see Figure 11–4). For example, wild grains of barley and wheat have a fragile **rachis**—the seed-bearing part of the stem—which shatters easily, releasing the seeds. Domesticated grains have a tough rachis, which does not shatter easily. In addition, the grain of wild barley and wheat has a tough shell protecting the seed from premature exposure, whereas domesticated grain has a brittle shell that can be easily separated, which facilitates preparing the seed for grinding into flour.

How did the domesticated plants get to be different from the wild varieties? Artificial or human selection, deliberate or accidental, obviously was required. Consider how the rachis of wheat and barley may have changed. As we said, when wild grain ripens in the field, the rachis shatters easily, scattering the seed. This trait is selectively advantageous under wild conditions; it is nature's method of propagating the species. Plants with a tough rachis, therefore, have only a slight chance of reproducing themselves under natural conditions, but they are more desirable for planting. When humans arrived with sickles and flails to collect the wild stands of grain, the seeds harvested probably contained a high proportion of tough-rachis mutants, because these could best withstand the rough treatment of harvest processing. If planted, the harvested seeds would be likely to produce tough-rachis plants. If in each successive harvest seeds from tough-rachis plants were the least likely to be lost, tough-rachis plants would come to predominate.[38]

Domesticated species of animals also differ from the wild varieties. For example, the horns of wild goats in the Near East are shaped differently from those of domesticated goats.[39] But differences in physical characteristics may not be the only indicators of domestication. Some ar-

chaeologists believe that imbalances in the sex and age ratios of animal remains at particular sites also suggest that domestication had occurred. For example, at Zawi Chemi Shanidar in Iraq, the proportion of young to mature sheep remains was much higher than the ratio of young to mature sheep in wild herds. One possible inference to be drawn is that the animals were domesticated, the adult sheep being saved for breeding purposes while the young were eaten. (If mostly young animals were eaten, and only a few animals were allowed to grow old, most of the bones found in a site would be from the young animals that were killed regularly for food.[40])

DOMESTICATION IN THE NEAR EAST

For some time most archaeologists have thought that the Fertile Crescent (see Figure 11–5), the arc of land stretching up from Israel and the Jordan Valley through southern Turkey and then downward to the western slopes of the Zagros Mountains in Iran, was one of the earliest centers of plant and animal domestication. We know that several

Figure 11–5   *Early Agricultural Settlements in the Near East*

Modern cities are represented by a dot, early settlements by a square. The yellow color indicates the area known as the Fertile Crescent.

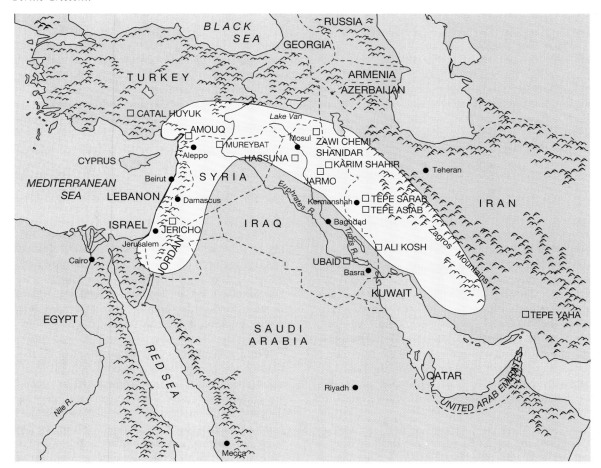

RESEARCH FRONTIERS
Did Dogs (and Cats) Domesticate Themselves?

Early evidence of a close relationship between dogs and people comes from an archaeological site in northern Israel dating to nearly 12,000 years ago. At that site, archaeologists found the grave of an elderly woman, lying on her right side with her legs folded up, with a dog under her left hand. The Embers' dog was always happy to greet them when they came home. She also was a retriever, an alarm system, could follow a scent, and ate everything that dropped on the floor. Do any of these attributes explain why humans all over the world have had domesticated descendants of wolves around the house for the last 10,000 to 15,000 years?

Dogs were probably the first animals domesticated by humans, some thousands of years before plants, sheep, and goats were domesticated in the Near East. Humans were starting to settle down in semipermanent camps and villages, as they began to depend less on big game

(which they would have had to follow over long distances) and more on relatively stationary food resources, such as fish, shellfish, small game, and wild plants rich in carbohydrates, proteins, and oils.

Why would humans have been interested in taming wolves at that time? One theory is that humans were shifting their prey from large animals to small, and they needed dogs for tracking wounded game or for retrieving killed game from bodies of water or underbrush. Dogs might also have been useful as alarm-givers in case predators came close. Finally, dogs might have helped to keep a camp clean, by scavenging garbage.

The Embers think that this last use of dogs suggests an alternative theory of dog domestication. Perhaps it wasn't so much that humans domesticated dogs, but that some wolves domesticated themselves by hanging around human camps. Why would wolves be interested in

those humans who were first settling down? It couldn't have been the possibility of a human dinner, because that would have been a possibility for millions of years before. So perhaps something else lured wolves to those early settled camps and villages. What was different about those early settlements? For the first time in human history, people were staying put for considerable periods of time—months at a time, *year after year*—because they could count on being able to "harvest" and live on the wild resources of the area. If they lived in a place for years, even if only seasonally, they would eventually have a problem with garbage.

The residues of meals, in particular, would have been a problem. They might not only come to stink; they might also attract rodents and bigger threats to health and children. What could the people do about this problem? Well, as any camper nowadays realizes, they could have buried the garbage so that its

varieties of domesticated wheat were being grown there after about 8000 B.C., as were oats, rye, barley, lentils, peas, and various fruits and nuts (apricots, pears, pomegranates, dates, figs, olives, almonds, and pistachios).[41] It appears that animals were first domesticated in the Near East. Dogs were first domesticated before the rise of agriculture, around 10,000 B.C. (see the box "Did Dogs (and Cats) Domesticate Themselves?"), goats and sheep around 7000 B.C., and cattle and pigs around 6000 B.C.[42]

Let us look at two early Neolithic sites in the Near East to see what life there may have been like after people began to depend on domesticated plants and animals for food.

ALI KOSH At the stratified site of Ali Kosh in what is now southwestern Iran (see Figure 11–5), we see the re-

mains of a community that started out about 7500 B.C. living mostly on wild plants and animals. Over the next 2,000 years, until about 5500 B.C., agriculture and herding became increasingly important. After 5500 B.C., we see the appearance of two innovations—irrigation and the use of domesticated cattle—that seem to have stimulated a minor population explosion during the following millennium.

From 7500 to 6750 B.C., the people at Ali Kosh cut little slabs of raw clay out of the ground to build small, multiroom structures. The rooms excavated by archaeologists are seldom more than 7 by 10 feet, and there is no evidence that the structures were definitely houses where people actually spent time or slept. Instead, they may have been storage rooms. On the other hand, house rooms of even smaller size are known in other areas of the world, so

scent would not attract unwelcome visitors. But eventually they would have run out of room for garbage pits in or close to the settlement. Of course, they could have moved the settlement. But maybe they didn't want to. After all, they had spent a lot of time and effort building a permanent house that was warm in the winter and dry in the rains. And they had a lot of things stored there. So what *could* they do?

Maybe people didn't have to do anything. Maybe those wolves hanging around the neighborhood solved the problem for our ancestors. How? By scavenging, which is something most dogs (particularly larger ones, like the first domesticated dogs) do quite naturally and efficiently. The Embers' dog ate anything (except maybe undressed lettuce). So even a few tame wolves or domesticated dogs could have kept a garbage pit or pile from stinking and growing. And the people "feeding" that pit or pile could stay put in one place for a long time, safe from smells, vermin, and disease. Dogs may have mostly domesticated themselves because it was good for some of

them as well as for those pre-agricultural humans.

A similar theory may explain the domestication of cats. Cats are especially good at catching and killing mice. Masses of mice skeletons (of the house mouse) begin to appear in basements of Near East dwellings after the emergence of agriculture. It is possible that humans purposely tried to domesticate cats to catch mice, but it is more likely that cats would have domesticated themselves by adapting to life near or in a granary or storage cellar. Of course, humans might have helped the process of domestication a little, by killing the more ferocious wild cats that were attracted to the settlement. The same was probably true for the wolves attracted to garbage. Even if you didn't at first want to "pet" the canids or felids who were hanging around, you wouldn't want them to attack humans. Wolves in the wild have a dominance-submission hierarchy, so they would be preadapted to heeding a "dominant" human; those that were not sufficiently submissive could be killed.

How could these theories of

dog and cat domestication be tested? If dogs domesticated themselves as scavengers, archaeologists should find evidence of dog domestication (for example, changes in anatomy) only in sites that were occupied for a good part of the year over a period of years. Only under those circumstances would garbage be a problem and dogs a solution. Similarly, evidence of cat domestication should be found only in sites that show signs of year-to-year storage of grain. Only then would rodents be a problem and cats a solution. We hope archaeologists will make these tests in the future.

Sources: Juliet Clutton-Brock, "Domestication of Animals," and Frank Hole, "Origins of Agriculture," in Steve Jones, Robert Martin, and David Pilbeam, eds., *The Cambridge Encyclopedia of Human Evolution* (New York: Cambridge University Press, 1992), pp. 380–85, 373–79; Juliet Clutton-Brock, "Dog," and Roy Robinson, "Cat," in Ian L. Mason, *Evolution of Domesticated Animals* (New York: Longman, 1984), pp. 198–210, 217–25; Stephen Budiansky, *The Covenant of the Wild: Why Animals Chose Domestication* (New York: Morrow, 1992).

it is possible that the people at Ali Kosh in its earliest phase were actually living in those tiny, unbaked, "brick" houses. There is a bit of evidence that the people at Ali Kosh may have moved for the summer (with their goats) to the grassier mountain valleys nearby, which were just a few days' walk away.

We have a lot of evidence about what the people at Ali Kosh ate. They got some of their food from cultivated emmer wheat and a kind of barley and a considerable amount from domesticated goats. We know the goats were domesticated because wild goats do not seem to have lived in the area. Also, the fact that virtually no bones from elderly goats were found in the site suggests that the goats were domesticated and herded rather than hunted. Moreover, it would seem from the horn cores found in the site that mostly young male goats were eaten, so the females

probably were kept for breeding and milking. But with all these signs of deliberate food production, there is an enormous amount of evidence—literally tens of thousands of seeds and bone fragments—that the people at the beginning of Ali Kosh depended mostly on wild plants (legumes and grasses) and wild animals (including gazelles, wild oxen, and wild pigs). They also collected fish, such as carp and catfish, and shellfish, such as mussels, as well as waterfowl that visited the area during part of the year.

The flint tools used during this earliest phase at Ali Kosh were varied and abundant. Finds from this period include tens of thousands of tiny flint blades, some only a few millimeters wide. About 1 percent of the chipped stone found by archaeologists was **obsidian,** or volcanic glass, which came from what is now eastern Turkey, several hundred miles away. Thus, the people at Ali Kosh

A sickle made with microliths.

during its earliest phase definitely had some kind of contact with people elsewhere. This contact is also suggested by the fact that the emmer wheat they cultivated did not have a wild relative in the area.

From 6750 to 6000 B.C., the people increased their consumption of cultivated food plants; 40 percent of the seed remains in the hearths and refuse areas were now from emmer wheat and barley. The proportion of the diet coming from wild plants was much reduced, probably because the cultivated plants have the same growing season and grow in the same kind of soil as the wild plants. Grazing by the goats and sheep that were kept may also have contributed to the reduction of wild plant foods in the area and in the diet. The village may or may not have gotten larger, but the multiroom houses definitely had. The rooms were now larger than 10 by 10 feet; the walls were much thicker; and the clay-slab bricks were now held together by a mud mortar. Also, the walls now often had a coat of smooth mud plaster on both sides. The stamped-mud house floors were apparently covered with rush or reed mats (you can see the imprints of them). There were courtyards with domed brick ovens and brick-lined roasting pits. Understandably, considering

the summer heat in the area, none of the ovens found was inside a house.

Even though the village probably contained no more than 100 individuals, it participated in an extensive trading network. Seashells were probably obtained from the Persian Gulf, which is some distance to the south; copper may have come from what is now central Iran; obsidian was still coming from eastern Turkey; and turquoise somehow made its way from what is now the border between Iran and Afghanistan. Some of these materials were used as ornaments worn by both sexes—or so it seems from the remains of bodies found buried under the floors of houses.

After about 5500 B.C., the area around Ali Kosh begins to show signs of a much larger population, apparently made possible by a more complex agriculture employing irrigation and plows drawn by domesticated cattle. In the next thousand years, by 4500 B.C., the population of the area probably tripled. This population growth was apparently part of the cultural developments that culminated in the rise of urban civilizations in the Near East,[43] as we will see in the next chapter.

Population growth may have occurred in and around Ali Kosh but did not continue in all areas of the Near East after domestication. For example, one of the largest early villages in the Near East, 'Ain Ghazal (on the outskirts of what is now Amman, Jordan), suffered a decline in population and standard of living over time, perhaps because the environment around 'Ain Ghazal could not permanently support a large village.[44]

CATAL HÜYÜK On a windswept plateau in the rugged, mountainous region of southern Turkey stand the remains of a mud-brick town known as Catal Hüyük (see Figure 11–5). *Hüyük* is the Turkish word for a mound formed by a succession of settlements, one built on top of another.

About 5600 B.C., Catal Hüyük was an adobe town. Some 200 houses have been excavated, and they are inter-

Remains of the pueblo-like structures of Neolithic Catal Hüyük.

connected in *pueblo fashion* (each flat-roofed structure housed a number of families). The inhabitants decorated the walls of the houses with imaginative murals, and their shrines with symbolic statuary. The murals depict what seem to be religious scenes and everyday events. Archaeologists peeling away frescoes found layer upon layer of murals, indicating that old murals were plastered over to make way for fresh paintings. Several rooms are believed to have been shrine rooms. They contain many large bull murals and clay bull figurines and have full-sized clay heads of cattle on the walls. Other "shrine-room" murals depict scenes of life and death, painted in red and black, respectively. Clay statuettes of a pregnant woman and of a bearded man seated on a bull have also been found in these rooms.

Figure 11–6

Neolithic implements from Switzerland, including axes (1–5, 24), chisels made of stone and bone (6, 9), awls made of bone (11, 12), fling knives (7, 8), weaving implements made of clay and bone (14–16), and ornaments (18–22).

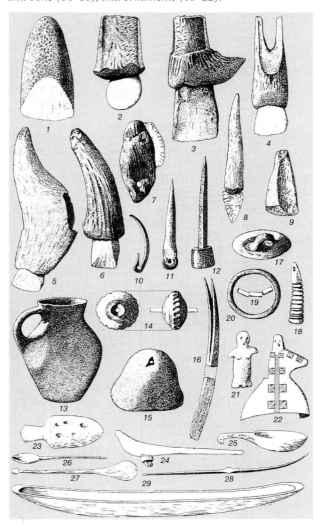

Farming was well advanced at Catal Hüyük. Lentils, wheat, barley, and peas were grown in quantities that produced a surplus. Archaeologists were astonished at the richly varied handicrafts, including beautifully carved wooden bowls and boxes, that the people of the town produced. These people also had obsidian and flint daggers, spearheads, lance heads, scrapers, awls, and sickle blades. Bowls, spatulas, knives, ladles, and spoons were made from bone. The houses contained belt hooks, toggles, and pins carved from bone. Evidence also suggests that men and women wore jewelry fashioned from bone, shell, and copper and that they used obsidian mirrors.[45] (See Figure 11–6 for similar tools and ornaments in Neolithic Switzerland.)

Because Catal Hüyük is located in a region with few raw materials, the town evidently depended on exchange with other areas to secure the rich variety of materials it used. Shells were procured from the Mediterranean, timber from the hills, obsidian from 50 miles away, and marble from western Turkey.

DOMESTICATION IN MESOAMERICA

A very different pattern of domestication is seen in Mesoamerica. Here the semi-nomadic Archaic hunting and gathering life-style persisted long after people first domesticated plants.[46] How can this be? Don't people have to settle near their crops to take care of them? Once they have domesticated plants, don't they stop collecting wild plants? The answer is no. In Mesoamerica, people sowed a variety of plants, but after doing so they went on with their seasonal rounds of hunting and gathering, and came back later to harvest what they had sown. Many of the early domesticates in Mesoamerica were not basic to subsistence, even if they were highly desirable. Domestication may have been a way for Archaic peoples to make desirable plants more common in their environment. For example, one of the first domesticates was the bottle gourd. These were not eaten but were used to carry water. Joyce Marcus and Kent Flannery hypothesize that the bottle gourd was domesticated by people deliberately planting them in areas where they did not grow naturally, so that as groups moved through those areas they always had access to gourds for carrying water.[47]

Bottle gourds are only one of many early domesticates from Highland Mesoamerica. Others include tomatoes, cotton, a variety of beans and squashes, and, perhaps most importantly, maize. Although the origins of *maize* (corn) are controversial, an early domesticated form dating from about 5000 B.C. has been found in Tehuacán, Mexico. Until 1970, the most widely accepted view was that maize was cultivated from a now-extinct "wild maize" that had tiny cobs topped by small tassels. Now most scholars believe that maize was domesticated from teosinte, a tall wild grass that still grows widely in Mexico, or that it resulted from a cross between a perennial variety of teosinte and a wild corn (see Figure 11–7).[48]

But teosinte is quite different from maize in several important ways. Teosinte stalks do look a lot like maize,

Teosinte

Maize

Figure 11–7 *Teosinte Plant, Spike, and Seeds and Maize Plant, Cob, and Kernels*

Note how much larger the domesticated maize spike and seeds are. Source: From *Past in Perspective* by K. Feder. Copyright © 2000 by Mayfield Publishing Company. Reprinted by permission of the publisher.

but teosinte has a "spike" to which 7 to 12 individual seeds are attached in a single row, unlike the maize cob, which has many seeds in many rows. Each teosinte seed has its own brittle shell, whereas the entire maize cob is covered with a tough husk. However, early maize was also considerably different from modern maize. The oldest maize cobs—dating to about 7,000 years ago—are tiny, only about an inch long. They have only a half-dozen rows of seeds, and each seed is tiny. One interesting fact about both ancient and modern maize is that it is almost completely dependent on humans to reproduce—the shift from seeds with brittle coats to cobs with a tough husk meant that someone had to open the husk without damaging the seeds in order for them to be dispersed and reproduce.[49]

Like maize and the bottle gourd, beans and squash were probably domesticated by simple manipulation of wild varieties. Runner beans, for example, grow naturally in the soils on the slopes outside of rock shelters and caves. It is not a stretch of the imagination to envision Archaic peoples harvesting these beans (for their roots to begin with—nondomestic runner bean seeds are tiny and probably were not eaten) and selectively planting those with desired qualities, like large seeds. Similarly, only the seeds of wild squashes were likely eaten by Archaic peoples, as the flesh of wild squashes often has an unattractive smell

and taste. But they may have selectively planted mutants with good-tasting flesh and larger seeds, eventually producing the domestic varieties over time.[50]

People who lived in Mesoamerica, Mexico and Central America, are often credited with the invention of planting maize, beans, and squash together in the same field. This planting strategy provides some important advantages. Maize takes nitrogen from the soil; beans, like all legumes, put nitrogen back into the soil. The maize stalk provides a natural pole for the bean plant to twine around, and the low-growing squash can grow around the base of the tall maize plant. Beans supply people with the amino acid lysine, which is missing in maize. Thus, maize and beans together provide all the essential amino acids that humans need to obtain from their food. Whether teosinte was or was not the ancestor of maize, it may have provided the model for this unique combination, as wild runner beans and wild squash occur naturally where teosinte grows.[51]

GUILA NAQUITZ The Guila Naquitz cave, excavated in the 1960s by Kent Flannery, provides a good picture of early domestication in Highland Mesoamerica. Here small groups of people, probably only a single family at a time, lived intermittently (and probably seasonally) over a period of 2,000 years (ca. 8900 B.C. to 6700 B.C.), the period during which plants were domesticated. The cave itself is

The thorn forest in the Valley of Oaxaca.

located in the thorn forest of the upper piedmont above the floor of the Valley of Oaxaca. The residents of Guila Naquitz hunted deer and peccary (a wild piglike animal) with spears and spear-throwers, and trapped small animals such as rabbits. They also collected plant foods from the surrounding area, particularly prickly pear fruits, cherries, acorns, and pinion nuts from the forests above the cave, along with agave hearts, onions, and various other nuts and fruits from a variety of thorn forest plants.[52]

Also found in Guila Naquitz cave are the remains of domesticated plants, including bottle gourd and several varieties of squashes. How did these come to be in the cave? Were the inhabitants planting fields of squashes? Probably not in the way one thinks of planting a field today. Squashes are common wild plants in Highland Mesoamerica, and thrive in disturbed soils such as those outside of caves. It may be that the inhabitants of the Guila Naquitz cave knew squashes would grow easily near their cave, and so actively planted some with better-tasting flesh or larger seeds than those that might naturally grow there.[53] Domestication and the use of domesticated plants would be rather informal—a supplement to a diet already rich in animal and plant species. This picture seems much different from that at Near Eastern sites such as Ali Kosh and Catal Hüyük. Domestication in Guila Naquitz appears to have been accomplished by hunters and gatherers who supplemented their basic diet with some desired plants (squashes with tasty flesh, for example); there was no "revolution" that enabled the people to rely on domesticated plants.

DOMESTICATION ELSEWHERE IN THE WORLD

SOUTH AMERICA AND THE EASTERN UNITED STATES   Outside of Mesoamerica, evidence of inde-
pendent domestication of plants comes from at least two areas in the New World: South America and the eastern United States. The first plants to be domesticated in the New World were members of the cucurbit family, including the bottle gourd and a variety of squashes, all domesticated some time after 7500 B.C. In addition to these and other plants domesticated in Mesoamerica, we can trace more than 200 domesticated plants to the Andes in South America, including potatoes, lima beans, peanuts, amaranth, and quinoa. The first clear domesticate was the chili pepper, dating back to about 7300 B.C., which makes domestication in the Andes about as old as in Mesoamerica.

Potatoes, one of the world's most important food plants, were domesticated in the Andes.

The origins of the root crops manioc and sweet potato are less certain, but those crops probably originated in lowland tropical forest regions of South America.[54]

Many of the plants grown in North America, such as corn, beans, and squash, were apparently introduced from Mesoamerica. However, at least three seed plants were probably domesticated independently in North America at an earlier time—sunflowers, sumpweed, and goosefoot. Sunflowers and sumpweed contain seeds that are highly nutritious in terms of protein and fat; goosefoot is high in starch and similar to corn in food value.[55] Sumpweed is an unusually good source of calcium, rivaled only by greens, mussels, and bones. It is also a very good source of iron (better than beef liver) and thiamine.[56] These plants may have been cultivated in the area of Kentucky, Tennessee, and southern Illinois beginning around 2000 B.C. (Corn was introduced about A.D. 200.)

All of the pre-corn domesticates are nutritionally superior to corn, so why did North American agriculturalists switch to a reliance on corn in the last 1,000 years?[57] In the archaeologist Bruce Smith's words, "With the exception of the sunflower, North American seed crops are not exactly household words."[58] Crop yields of corn would have had to be quite high to surpass the yields of those other crops, so perhaps the crucial factors were the time of harvest and the amount of effort required. Goosefoot, for example, was comparable to corn nutritionally. But harvesting and preparing it for storage took a lot of work and had to be done during the fall, the time of year when deer could be hunted intensively. So perhaps the incompatibility of goosefoot production and deer hunting, and the ease of harvesting corn and preparing it for storage, explain the switch to corn.[59]

On the whole, domestic animals were less important economically in the New World than they were in many parts of the Old World. In North America, dogs and turkeys were the main domesticated animals before the arrival of the Spanish. Dogs in North and South America probably descended from the North American wolf and were domesticated relatively early. Domesticated turkeys from about A.D. 500 have been found in pueblos in the American Southwest.[60] Their feathers were used for arrows, ornaments, and weaving, and their bones for tools; but they do not seem to have been used frequently for food. However, turkeys were an important food in Mexico, where they may have been independently domesticated, and in Central America. When Cortes came to Mexico in 1519, he found domesticated turkeys in great quantities.[61]

The central Andes was the only part of the New World where animals were a significant part of the economy. Used for meat, transportation, and wool, llamas and alpacas (members of the camel family) were domesticated as early as 5000 B.C. in the Andes.[62] Guinea pigs, misnamed because they are neither pigs nor from Guinea, are rodents that were domesticated in the Andes sometime later. They were an important source of food even before domestication.[63] Since they were domesticated, they have been raised in people's dwellings.

Animal domestication in the New World differed from that in the Old World because different wild species were found in the two hemispheres. The Old World plains and forests were the homes for the wild ancestors of the cattle, sheep, goats, pigs, and horses we know today. In the New World, the Pleistocene herds of horses, mastodons, mammoths, and other large animals were long extinct, allowing few opportunities for domestication of large animals.[64]

EAST ASIA The archaeological record for the domestication of seed crops is better known than for soft-flesh crops because the latter do not preserve well. The earliest clear evidence of cereal cultivation outside the Near East is from China. Late in the sixth millennium B.C. in North China there were sites where foxtail millet was cultivated. Storage pits, storage pots, and large numbers of grinding stones suggest that millet was an enormously important item in the diet. The wild-animal bones and the hunting and fishing tools that have been found suggest that people still depended on hunting and fishing somewhat, even though domesticated pigs (as well as dogs) were present. In South China, from about the same time, archaeologists have found a village by the edge of a small lake where people cultivated rice, bottle gourds, water chestnuts, and the datelike fruit called jujube. The people in South China also raised water buffalo, pigs, and dogs. And, as in the North China sites, some of their food came from hunting and fishing.[65]

Mainland Southeast Asia may have been a place of domestication as early as the Near East was. The dating of domestication in Southeast Asia is not yet clear; the dates of the oldest site with probable domesticates—Spirit cave in northwest Thailand—range from about 9500 B.C. to 5500 B.C. Some of the plants found at Spirit cave are not clearly distinguishable from wild varieties, but others, such as gourds, betel nut, betel leaf, and water chestnut, were probably domesticates.[66]

Most of the early cultivation in mainland Southeast Asia seems to have occurred in the plains and low terraces around rivers, although the main subsistence foods of early cultivators were probably the fish and shellfish in nearby waters. The first plants to be domesticated probably were not cereal grains, as they were in the Near East. Indeed, some early cultivated crops may not have been used for food at all. In particular, bamboo may have been used to make cutting tools and for a variety of building purposes, and gourds were probably used as containers or bowls. We do not know yet exactly when rice was first domesticated, but there is definite evidence of cultivated rice in Thailand after 4000 B.C. Other major food plants were domesticated first in Southeast Asia, including root crops, such as taro and yams, and tree crops, such as breadfruit, coconuts, and bananas.[67]

AFRICA Some plants and animals were domesticated first in Africa. Most of the early domestications probably occurred in the wide, broad belt of woodland-savanna country south of the Sahara and north of the equator.

A man harvesting sorghum in Burkina Faso. Sorghum is one of several plant species domesticated in Africa.

Among the cereal grains, sorghum was probably first domesticated in the central or eastern part of this belt, bulrush millet and a kind of rice (different from Asian rice) in the western part, and finger millet in the east. Groundnuts (peanuts) and yams were first domesticated in West Africa.[68] We do know that farming became widespread in the northern half of Africa after 6000 B.C.; investigators continue to debate whether the earliest crops grown there were indigenous or borrowed from the Near East. There is little doubt, however, that some of the plant foods were first domesticated in sub-Saharan Africa because the wild varieties occur there.[69] Many of the important domestic animals in Africa today—cattle, sheep, and goats—probably were domesticated first in the Near East, but most likely the donkey and guinea fowl were first domesticated in Africa.[70]

Why Did Food Production Develop?

We know that an economic transformation occurred in widely separate areas of the world beginning after about 10,000 years ago, as people began to domesticate plants and animals. But why did domestication occur? And why did it occur independently in many different places within a period of a few thousand years? Considering that people depended only on wild plants and animals for millions of

years, the differences in exactly when domestication first occurred in different parts of the world seem small. The spread of domesticated plants seems to have been more rapid in the Old World than in the New World, perhaps because the Old World spread was more along an east-west axis (except for the spread to sub-Saharan Africa), whereas the New World spread was more north-south. Spreading north and south may have required more time to adapt to variation in day lengths, climates, and diseases.[71]

There are many theories of why food production developed; most have tried to explain the origin of domestication in the area of the Fertile Crescent. Gordon Childe's theory, popular in the 1950s, was that a drastic change in climate caused domestication in the Near East.[72] According to Childe, the postglacial period was marked by a decline in summer rainfall in the Near East and northern Africa. As the rains decreased, people were forced to retreat into shrinking pockets, or *oases,* of food resources surrounded by desert. The lessened availability of wild resources provided an incentive for people to cultivate grains and to domesticate animals, according to Childe.

Robert Braidwood criticized Childe's theory for two reasons. First, Braidwood believed that the climate changes may not have been as dramatic as Childe had assumed, and therefore the "oasis incentive" may not have existed. Second, the climatic changes that occurred in the Near East after the retreat of the last glaciers had probably occurred at earlier interglacial periods too, but there had never been a similar food-producing revolution before. Hence, according to Braidwood, there must be more to the explanation of why people began to produce food than simply changes in climate.[73]

Braidwood and Gordon Willey claimed that people did not undertake domestication until they had learned a great deal about their environment and until their culture had evolved enough for them to handle such an undertaking: "Why did incipient food production not come earlier? Our only answer at the moment is that culture was not ready to achieve it."[74]

But most archaeologists now think we should try to explain why people were not "ready" earlier to achieve domestication. Both Lewis Binford and Kent Flannery suggest that *some change* in external circumstances must have induced or favored the changeover to food production.[75] As Flannery pointed out, there is no evidence of a great economic incentive for hunter-gatherers to become food producers. In fact, some contemporary hunter-gatherers obtain adequate nutrition with far *less* work than many agriculturalists. So what might push food collectors to become food producers?

Binford and Flannery thought that the incentive to domesticate animals and plants may have been a desire to reproduce what was wildly abundant in the most bountiful or optimum hunting and gathering areas. Because of population growth in the optimum areas, people might have moved to surrounding areas containing fewer wild resources. It would have been in those marginal areas that

RESEARCH FRONTIERS

You Are What You Eat: Chemical Analyses of Bones and Teeth

Archaeologists study ancient diets in several ways, most of them indirect. They can indirectly infer some of what ancient people ate from recovered food wastes. For example, if you find a lot of corncobs, chances are that the people ate a lot of corn. Plant and animal foods can be identified in the charred remains of cooking fires and (when preserved) in the ancient people's feces, or *coprolites*. Such inferences are usually biased in favor of hard food sources such as seeds, nuts, and grains (which are likely to be preserved); rarely are the remains of soft plants such as bananas or tubers found. Archaeologists can also indirectly infer diet from the artifacts they find, particularly, of course, ones we can be pretty sure were used in

obtaining or processing food. So, for example, if you find a stone with a flat or concave surface that looks like what people use in some places to grind corn, it is very likely that the ancient people also ground grain (or other hard things such as seeds) for food. But plant remains or implements do not tell us *how much* people relied on particular sources of food.

There is a more direct way to study ancient diets. Anthropologists have discovered that in many ways "you are what you eat." In particular, chemical analyses of bones and teeth, the most common remains found in excavations, can reveal distinctive traces of the foods that metabolically went into the bones and teeth.

One kind of informative chemical analysis involves the ratio of strontium to calcium in bone. This analysis can indicate the relative amounts of plant and animal food in the diet. So, for example, we know from strontium analysis of bones that just before the beginnings of cereal agriculture in the Near East, people were eating a lot of plant food, probably wild cereals that were intensively collected. Then there was a temporary decline in such collecting, suggesting overexploitation of the wild resources or at least their decreasing availability. This problem was presumably solved by the cultivation and domestication (modification) of cereals.

Carbon isotope ratios also can tell us what types of plants peo-

people might have first turned to food production in order to reproduce what they used to have.

The Binford-Flannery model seems to fit the archaeological record in the Levant, the southwestern part of the Fertile Crescent, where population increase did precede the first signs of domestication.[76] But, as Flannery admitted, in some regions, such as southwestern Iran, the optimum hunting-gathering areas do not show population increase before the emergence of domestication.[77]

The Binford-Flannery model focuses on population pressure in a small area as the incentive to turn to food production. Mark Cohen theorizes it was population pressure on a global scale that explains why so many of the world's peoples adopted agriculture within the span of a few thousand years.[78] He argues that hunter-gatherers all over the world gradually increased in population so that by about 10,000 years ago the world was more or less filled with food collectors. Thus people could no longer relieve population pressure by moving to uninhabited areas. To support their increasing populations, they would have had to exploit a broader range of less desirable wild foods; that is, they would have had to switch to broad-spectrum collecting, or they would have had to increase the yields of

the most desirable wild plants by weeding, protecting them from animal pests, and perhaps deliberately planting the most productive among them. Cohen thinks that people might have tried a variety of these strategies but would generally have ended up depending on cultivation because that would have been the most efficient way to allow more people to live in one place.

Recently, some archaeologists have returned to the idea that climatic change (not the extreme variety that Childe envisaged) might have played a role in the emergence of agriculture. It seems clear from the evidence now available that the climate of the Near East about 13,000 to 12,000 years ago became more seasonal: The summers got hotter and drier than before and the winters became colder. These climatic changes may have favored the emergence of annual species of wild grain, which archaeologically we see proliferating in many areas of the Near East.[79] People such as the Natufians intensively exploited the seasonal grains, developing an elaborate technology for storing and processing the grains and giving up their previous nomadic existence to do so. The transition to agriculture may have occurred when sedentary foraging no longer provided sufficient resources for the population. This could have hap-

ple were eating. Trees, shrubs, and temperate-zone grasses (for example, rice) have carbon isotope ratios that are different from those of tropical and subtropical grasses (such as millet and corn). People in China were relying heavily on cereals about 7,000 to 8,000 years ago, but the cereals were not the same in the north and south. Contrary to what we might expect, the carbon isotope ratios tell us that an originally temperate-zone cereal (rice) was the staple in subtropical southern China; in the more temperate north, an originally tropical or subtropical grass (millet) was most important. The dependence on millet in the north was enormous. It is estimated that 50 to 80 percent of the diet between 5000 and 500 B.C. came from millet.

In the New World, seed crops such as sunflower, sumpweed, and goosefoot were domesticated in eastern North America long before corn, introduced from Mexico, became the staple. We know this partly from the archaeology; the remains of the early seed crops are older than the remains of corn. Corn, an originally subtropical plant, has a carbon isotope ratio that is different from the ratio for the earlier, temperate-zone seed crops. Thus, the shift in carbon isotope ratios after A.D. 800–900 tells us that corn had become the staple.

Nonchemical analyses of human bones and teeth were traditionally used by physical anthropologists and archaeologists to study similarities and differences between peoples in different geographic regions, between living humans and possible fossil ancestors, and between living humans and other surviving primates. Much of the research involved surface measurements, particularly of the skull (outside and inside). In recent years, physical anthropologists and archaeologists have begun to study the "insides" of bones and teeth. The new kinds of chemical analysis mentioned here are part of that trend. In N. J. van der Merwe's pithy words: "The emphasis in studies of human evolution has . . . shifted from a preoccupation with the brain to an equal interest in the stomach."

Sources: N. J. van der Merwe, "Reconstructing Prehistoric Diet," in Stephen Jones, Robert Martin, and David Pilbeam, eds., *The Cambridge Encyclopedia of Human Evolution* (New York: Cambridge University Press, 1992), pp. 369–72; Clark Spenser Larsen, "Bare Bones Anthropology: The Bioarchaeology of Human Remains," in Peter N. Peregrine, Carol R. Ember, and Melvin Ember, eds., *Archaeology: Original Readings in Method and Practice* (Upper Saddle River, NJ: Prentice Hall, 2002).

pened because sedentarization led to population increase and therefore resource scarcity,[80] or because local wild resources became depleted after people settled down in permanent villages.[81] In the area of Israel and Jordan where the Natufians lived, some of the people apparently turned to agriculture, probably to increase the supply of grain, whereas other people returned to nomadic food collection because of the decreasing availability of wild grain.[82]

Change to a more seasonal climate might also have led to a shortage of certain nutrients for food collectors. In the dry seasons certain nutrients would have been less available. For example, grazing animals get lean when grasses are not plentiful, so meat from hunting would have been in short supply in the dry seasons. Although it may seem surprising, some recent hunter-gatherers have starved when they had to rely on lean meat. If somehow they could have increased their carbohydrate or fat intake, they might have been more likely to get through the periods of lean game.[83] So it is possible that some wild-food collectors in the past thought of planting crops to get them through the dry seasons when hunting, fishing, and gathering did not provide enough carbohydrates and fat for them to avoid starvation.

Mesoamerica presents a very different picture, because the early domesticates were not important to subsistence. Theories about population pressure and nutrient shortage don't seem to fit Mesoamerica well. However, there were apparently shortages of desired plants, such as bottle gourds, and domestication may well have occurred as humans actively sowed these desired plants. The difference between this model and the ones described above is that humans in Mesoamerica were apparently not forced into domestication by climate change or population pressure, but actively turned to domestication to obtain more of the most desired or useful plant species. The most interesting case is maize, which only became a staple food some 2,500 or more years after it was first domesticated. Why did it become a staple? Probably both because it was a suitable staple crop (especially when intercropped with beans and squash, as discussed earlier) and because people liked it, so they grew it in large quantities. Over time, and perhaps because of conflict, population pressure, and other forces similar to those that apparently led to domestication in the Near East, people in Mesoamerica and later North and South America came to rely upon maize as their dietary mainstay.

Consequences of the Rise of Food Production

We know that intensive agriculture (permanent rather than shifting cultivation) probably developed in response to population pressure, but we do not know for sure that population pressure was even partly responsible for plant and animal domestication in the first place. Still, population growth certainly accelerated after the rise of food production (see Figure 11–8). There were other consequences too. Paradoxically, perhaps, health seems to have declined. Material possessions, though, became more elaborate.

ACCELERATED POPULATION GROWTH

As we have seen, settling down (even before the rise of food production) may have increased the rate of human population growth. But population growth definitely accelerated after the emergence of farming and herding, possibly because the spacing between births was reduced further and therefore fertility (the number of births per mother) increased. Increased fertility may have been advantageous because of the greater value of children in farming and herding economies; there is evidence from recent population studies that fertility rates are higher where children contribute more to the economy.[84]

Not only may parents desire more children to help with chores; the increased workload of mothers may also (but inadvertently) decrease birth spacing. The busier a mother is, the less frequently she may nurse and the more likely her baby will be given supplementary food by other caretakers such as older siblings.[85] Less frequent nursing[86] and greater reliance on food other than mother's milk may result in an earlier resumption of ovulation after the birth of a baby. (Farmers and herders are likely to have animal milk to feed to babies, and also cereals that have been

transformed by cooking into soft, mushy porridges.) Therefore the spacing between births may have decreased (and the number of births per mother, in turn, increased) when mothers got busier after the rise of food production.

DECLINING HEALTH

Although the rise of food production may have led to increased fertility, this does not mean that health generally improved. In fact, it appears that health declined at least sometimes with the transition to food production. The two trends may seem paradoxical, but rapid population growth can occur if each mother gives birth to a large number of babies, even if many of them die early because of disease or poor nutrition.

The evidence that health may have declined sometimes after the rise of food production comes from studies of the bones and teeth of some prehistoric populations, before and after the emergence of food production. Nutritional and disease problems are indicated by such features as incomplete formation of tooth enamel, nonaccidental bone lesions (incompletely filled-in bone), reduction in stature, and decreased life expectancy. Many of the studied prehistoric populations that relied heavily on agriculture seem to show less adequate nutrition and higher infection rates than populations living in the same areas before agriculture. Some of the agricultural populations are shorter and had lower life expectancies.[87]

The reasons for a decline in health in those populations are not yet clear. Greater malnutrition can result from an overdependence on a few dietary staples that lack some necessary nutrients. Overdependence on a few sources of food may also increase the risk of famine because the fewer the staple crops, the greater the danger to the food supply posed by a weather-caused crop failure. But some or most nutritional problems may be the result of social and political factors, particularly the rise of different socioeconomic classes of people and unequal access, be-

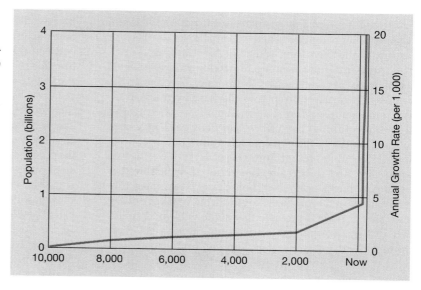

Figure 11–8 *Population Growth since 10,000 Years Ago*

The rate of population growth accelerated after the emergence of farming and herding 10,000 years ago. The rate of growth accelerated even more dramatically in recent times. Source: Adapted from Ansley J. Coale, The History of the Human Population. *Copyright © 1974 by Scientific American, Inc. All rights reserved.*

As this reconstruction shows, transforming grain into flour was a "daily grind," putting a great deal of stress on the lower back and knees. Studies of Neolithic skeletons of women show marks of stress on bone and arthritis, probably reflecting their long hours of work at the grinding stone. (*Source:* "The Eloquent Bones of Abu Hureyras," Roberto Osti. Courtesy of Scientific American, Aug. 1994, p. 73 top.)

tween and within communities, to food and other resources.[88]

As we will see in the next chapter, social stratification or considerable socioeconomic inequality seems likely to develop after the rise of food production. The effects of stratification and political dominance from afar on the general level of health may be reflected in the skeletal remains of prehistoric Native Americans who died in what is now Illinois between A.D. 950 and 1300, the period spanning the changeover in that region from hunting and gathering to agriculture. The agricultural people living in the area of Dickson's Mounds—burial sites named after the doctor who first excavated them—were apparently in much worse health than their hunter-gatherer ancestors. But curiously, archaeological evidence suggests that they were still also hunting and fishing. A balanced diet was apparently available, but who was getting it? Possibly it was the elite at Cahokia, 110 miles away, where perhaps 15,000 to 30,000 people lived, who were getting most of the meat and fish. The individuals near Dickson's Mounds who collected the meat and fish may have gotten luxury items such as shell necklaces from the Cahokia elite, but many of the people buried at Dickson's Mounds were clearly not benefiting nutritionally from the relationship with Cahokia.[89]

THE ELABORATION OF MATERIAL POSSESSIONS

In the more permanent villages that were established after the rise of food production about 10,000 years ago, houses became more elaborate and comfortable, and construction methods improved. The materials used in construction depended on whether timber or stone was locally available or whether a strong sun could dry mud bricks. Modern architects might find to their surprise that bubble-shaped houses were known long ago in Neolithic

Cyprus. Families in the island's town of Khirokitia made their homes in large, domed, circular dwellings shaped like beehives and featuring stone foundations and mud-brick walls. Often, more space was created by dividing the interior horizontally and firmly propping a second floor on limestone pillars.

Sizable villages of solidly constructed, gabled wooden houses were built in Europe on the banks of the Danube and along the rims of Alpine lakes.[90] Many of the gabled wooden houses in the Danube region were long, rectangular structures that apparently sheltered several family units. In Neolithic times these longhouses had doors, beds, tables, and other furniture that closely resembled those in modern-day societies. We know the people had furniture because miniature clay models have been found at their sites. Several of the chairs and couches seem to be models of padded and upholstered furniture with wooden frames, indicating that Neolithic European artisans were creating fairly sophisticated furnishings.[91] Such furnishings were the result of an advanced tool technology put to use by a people who, because they were staying in one area, could take time to make and use furniture.

For the first time, apparel made of woven textiles appeared. This development was not simply the result of the domestication of flax (for linen), cotton, and wool-growing sheep. These sources of fiber alone could not produce cloth. It was the development by Neolithic society of the spindle and loom for spinning and weaving that made textiles possible. True, textiles can be woven by hand without a loom, but to do so is a slow, laborious process, impractical for producing garments.

The pottery of the early Neolithic was similar to the plain earthenware made by some preagricultural groups and included large urns for grain storage, mugs, cooking pots, and dishes. To improve the retention of liquid, potters in the Near East may have been the first to glaze the earthenware's porous surface. Later, Neolithic ceramics

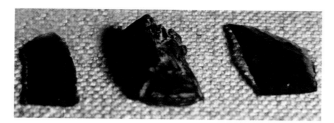

Obsidian blades from the Neolithic occupation at Jericho. The closest source of obsidian was in Anatolia, some 500 miles away from Jericho, so these must have been obtained through long-distance trade.

became more artistic. Designers shaped the clay into graceful forms and painted colorful patterns on the vessels.

It is probable that virtually none of these architectural and technological innovations could have occurred until humans became fully sedentary. Nomadic hunting and gathering peoples would have found it difficult to carry many material goods, especially fragile items such as pottery. It was only when humans settled in one place that these goods would have provided advantages, enabling villagers to cook and store food more effectively and to house themselves more comfortably.

There is also evidence of long-distance trade in the Neolithic, as we have noted. Obsidian from southern Turkey was being exported to sites in the Zagros Mountains of Iran and to what are now Israel, Jordan, and Syria in the Levant. Great amounts of obsidian were exported to sites about 190 miles from the source of supply; more than 80 percent of the tools used by residents of those areas were made of this material.[92] Marble was being sent from western to eastern Turkey, and seashells from the coast were traded to distant inland regions. Such trade suggests a considerable amount of contact among various Neolithic communities.

About 3500 B.C., cities first appeared in the Near East. These cities had political assemblies, kings, scribes, and specialized workshops. The specialized production of goods and services was supported by surrounding farming villages, which sent their produce to the urban centers. A dazzling transformation had taken place in a relatively short time. People had not only settled down, but they had also become "civilized," or urbanized. (The word *civilized* literally means to make "citified."[93]) Urban societies seem to have developed first in the Near East and somewhat later around the eastern Mediterranean, in the Indus Valley of northwestern India, in northern China, and in Mexico and Peru. In the next chapter we turn to the rise of these earliest civilizations.

Summary

1. In the period immediately before plants and animals were domesticated, there seems to have been a shift in many areas of the world to less dependence on big-game hunting and greater dependence on what is called broad-spectrum collecting. The broad spectrum of available resources frequently included aquatic resources such as fish and shellfish and a variety of wild plants and deer and other game. Climatic changes may have been partly responsible for the change to broad-spectrum collecting.

2. In some sites in Europe, the Near East, Africa, and Peru, the switch to broad-spectrum collecting seems to be associated with the development of more permanent communities. In other areas, such as the semiarid highlands of Mesoamerica, permanent settlements may have emerged only after the domestication of plants and animals.

3. The shift to the cultivation and domestication of plants and animals has been referred to as the Neolithic revolution, and it occurred, probably independently, in a number of areas. To date, the earliest evidence of domestication comes from the Near East about 8000 B.C. Dating for the earliest domestication in other areas of the Old World is not so clear, but the presence of different domesticated crops in different regions suggests that there were independent centers of domestication in China, Southeast Asia (what is now Malaysia, Thailand, Cambodia, and Vietnam), and Africa some time around or after 6000 B.C. In the New World, there appear to have been several early areas of cultivation and domestication: the highlands of Mesoamerica (about 7000 B.C.), the central Andes around Peru (about the same time), and the Eastern Woodlands of North America (about 2000 B.C.).

4. Theories about why food production originated remain controversial, but most archaeologists think that certain conditions must have pushed people to switch from collecting to producing food. Some possible causal factors include (1) population growth in regions of bountiful wild resources (which may have pushed people to move to marginal areas where they tried to reproduce their former abundance); (2) global population growth (which filled most of the world's habitable regions and may have forced people to utilize a broader spectrum of wild resources and to domesticate plants and animals); and (3) the emergence of hotter and drier summers and colder winters (which may have favored sedentarism near seasonal stands of wild grain; population growth in such areas may have forced people to plant crops and raise animals to support themselves).

5. Regardless of why food production originated, it seems to have had important consequences for human life. Populations generally increased substantially *after* plant and animal domestication. Even though not all early cultivators were sedentary, sedentarism did increase with greater reliance on agriculture. Somewhat surprisingly, some prehistoric populations that relied heavily on agriculture seem to have been less healthy than earlier populations that relied on food collection. In the more permanent villages that were established after the rise of food production, houses and furnishings became more elaborate, and people began to make textiles and to paint pot-

tery. These villages have also yielded evidence of increased long-distance trade.

Glossary Terms

agriculture
domestication
food production
Neolithic

obsidian
rachis
sedentarism

Critical Questions

1. What might cause people to work harder to get food?

2. How might people have domesticated sheep, goats, and cattle?

3. Do the various theories of the rise of food production explain why domestication occurred in many areas of the world within a few thousand years?

Internet Exercises

1. Visit the Catal Hüyük Web site (**http://catal.arch. cam.ac.uk/catal/catal.html**) and learn about the ongoing excavations. Write a brief summary of the most current discoveries.

2. Domestication of wild plants is not without its difficulties. Look at the description of attempts to cultivate wild rice at **http://www.hort.purdue.edu/newcrop/ proceedings1993/v2-235.html**. Explore the problems of shattering seed casings and increased disease with cultivation.

3. Explore animal domestication at **http://www.ag. usask.ca/exhibits/walkway/what/animdom.html**. Pick a domestic animal you are interested in and find out when and where it was domesticated.

4. Visit the Origins of Maize Web site at **http://farma. qfb.umich.mx/orimaize.htm** to learn about current research into how maize was domesticated.

Suggested Reading

COHEN, M. N. "Were Early Agriculturalists Less Healthy than Food Collectors?" In P. N. Peregrine, C. R. Ember, and M. Ember, eds., *Archaeology: Original Readings in Method and Practice.* Upper Saddle River, NJ: Prentice Hall, 2002. A specially written chapter for an undergraduate audience, reviewing the evidence for a decline in health with the advent of agriculture.

COWAN, C. W., AND WATSON, P. J., EDS. *The Origins of Agriculture: An International Perspective.* Washington, DC: Smithsonian Institution Press, 1992. Summarizes the geography, climate, botany, and archaeology of the events associated with the emergence of plant cultivation in different parts of the Old and New Worlds.

HENRY, D. O. *From Foraging to Agriculture: The Levant at the End of the Ice Age.* Philadelphia: University of Pennsylvania Press, 1989. An examination and discussion of theories about the origins of agriculture, with particular reference to the areas bordering the eastern Mediterranean.

HODDER, I. *The Domestication of Europe: Structure and Contingency in Neolithic Societies.* Oxford: Blackwell, 1990. Discusses the social changes experienced by northern European societies after the the adoption of agriculture.

MACNEISH, R. S. *The Origins of Agriculture and Settled Life.* Norman: University of Oklahoma Press, 1991. After reviewing previous theories about the origins of agriculture, the author puts forward his own model and reviews the archaeological sequences in each of the early regions of domestication in order to evaluate his theory.

PRICE, T. D., AND BROWN, J. A., EDS. *Prehistoric Hunter-Gatherers: The Emergence of Cultural Complexity.* Orlando, FL: Academic Press, 1985. A volume of papers by archaeologists on the beginnings of social complexity among hunter-gatherers. The scope is global; most of the chapters deal comparatively or cross-archaeologically with the various adaptations of hunter-gatherers in the past.

PRICE, T. D. AND GEBAUER, A. B., EDS. *Last Hunters, First Farmers: New Perspectives on the Prehistoric Transition to Agriculture.* Santa Fe, NM: School of American Research Press, 1995. A wide-ranging collection of papers from a 1992 conference on the transition to agriculture held at the School of American Research. Some of the papers are technical and difficult, but all are insightful.

SMITH, B. D. *The Emergence of Agriculture.* New York: Scientific American Library, 1995. A thorough and readable overview of agricultural origins.

12

Origins of Cities and States

rom the time agriculture first developed until about 6000 B.C., people in the Near East lived in fairly small villages. There were few differences in wealth and status from household to household, and apparently there was no governmental authority beyond the village. There is no evidence that these villages had any public buildings or craft specialists or that one community was very different in size from its neighbors. In short, these settlements had none of the characteristics we commonly associate with "civilization."

But some time around 6000 B.C., in parts of the Near East—and at later times in other places—a great transformation in the quality and scale of human life seems to have begun. For the first time we can see evidence of differences in status among households. For example, some are much bigger than others. Communities begin to differ in size and to specialize in certain crafts. And there are signs that some political officials had acquired authority over several communities, that what anthropologists call "chiefdoms" had emerged.

Somewhat later, by about 3500 B.C., we can see many, if not all, of the conventional characteristics of **civilization**: the first inscriptions, or writing; cities; many kinds of full-time craft specialists; monumental architecture; great differences in wealth and status; and the kind of strong, hierarchical, centralized political system we call the **state** (see Figure 12–1).

This type of transformation has occurred many times and in many places in human history. The most ancient civilizations arose in the Near East around 3500 B.C., in northwestern India after 2500 B.C., in northern China

around 1750 B.C., in the New World (Mexico and Peru) a few hundred years before the time of Christ, and in tropical Africa somewhat later.[1] At least some of these civilizations evolved independently of the others—for example, those in the New World and those in the Old World. Why did they do so? What conditions favored the emergence of centralized, statelike political systems? What conditions favored the establishment of cities? We ask this last question separately, because archaeologists are not yet certain that all the ancient state societies had cities when they first developed centralized government. In this chapter we discuss some of the things archaeologists have learned or suspect about the growth of ancient civilizations. Our discussion focuses primarily on the Near East and Mexico because archaeologists know the most about the sequences of cultural development in those two areas.

Archaeological Inferences about Civilization

The most ancient civilizations have been studied by archaeologists rather than historians because those civilizations evolved before the advent of writing. How do archaeologists infer that a particular people in the preliterate past had social classes, cities, or a centralized government?

As we have noted, it appears that the earliest Neolithic societies were *egalitarian;* that is, people did not differ much in wealth, prestige, or power. Some later societies

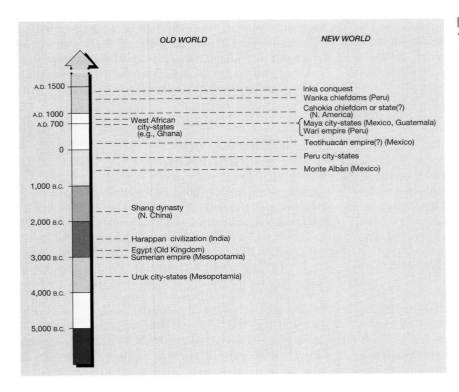

Figure 12–1
The Emergence of Civilization

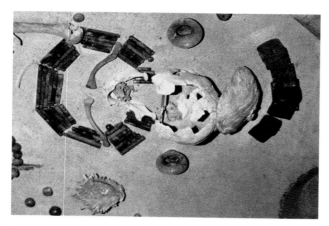

Replica of a burial from the Mayan site of Tikal. This individual was buried in a special funeral vault lined with jaguar and ocelot skins, and his body was adorned with more than 16 pounds of jade ornaments, including the massive necklace, headdress, and ear spools shown here. Archaeologists assume that such special treatment indicates elite status.

show signs of social inequality, indicated by burial finds. Archaeologists generally assume that inequality in death reflects inequality in life, at least in status and perhaps also in wealth and power. Thus, we can be fairly sure that a society had differences in status if only some people were buried with special objects, such as jewelry or pots filled with food. And we can be fairly sure that high status was assigned at birth rather than achieved in later life if we find noticeable differences in children's tombs. For example, some (but not all) child burials from as early as 5500 to 5000 B.C. at Tell es-Sawwan in Iraq, and from about 800 B.C. at La Venta in Mexico, are filled with statues and ornaments, suggesting that some children had high status from birth.[2] But burials indicating differences in status do not necessarily mean a society had significant differences in wealth. It is only when archaeologists find other substantial differences, as in house size and furnishings, that we can be sure the society had different socioeconomic classes of people.

Some archaeologists think that states first evolved around 3500 B.C. in greater Mesopotamia, the area now shared by southern Iraq and southwestern Iran. Archaeologists do not always agree on how a state should be defined, but most think that hierarchical and centralized decision making affecting a substantial population is the key criterion. Other characteristics are usually, but not always, found in these first states. They usually have cities with a substantial part of the population not involved directly in the collection or production of food (which means that people in cities are heavily dependent on people elsewhere); full-time religious and craft specialists; public buildings; and often an official art style. There is a hierarchical social structure topped by an elite class from which the leaders are drawn. The government tries to claim a monopoly on the use of force. (Our own state society says

that citizens do not have the right "to take the law into their own hands.") The state uses its force or threat of force to tax its population and to draft people for work or war.[3]

How can archaeologists tell, from the information provided by material remains, whether a society was a state or not? This depends in part on what is used as the criterion for a state. For example, Henry Wright and Gregory Johnson defined a state as a centralized political hierarchy with at least three levels of administration.[4] But how might archaeologists infer that such a hierarchy existed in some area? Wright and Johnson suggested that the way settlement sites differ in size is one indication of how many levels of administration there were in an area.

During the early Uruk period (just before 3500 B.C.), in what is now southwestern Iran, there were some 50 settlements that seem to fall into three groups in terms of size.[5] There were about 45 small villages, three or four "towns," and one large center, Susa. These three types of settlements seem to have been part of a three-level administration hierarchy, since many small villages could not trade with Susa without passing through a settlement intermediate in size. Because a three-level hierarchy is Wright and Johnson's criterion of a state, they think a state had emerged in the area by early Uruk times.

Evidence from the next period, middle Uruk, suggests more definitely that a state had emerged. This evidence takes the form of clay seals that were apparently used in trading.[6] *Commodity sealings* were used to keep a shipment of goods tightly closed until it reached its destination, and *message sealings* were used to keep track of goods sent and received. The clay seals found in Susa include many message seals and *bullae*, clay containers that served as bills of lading for goods received. The villages, in contrast, had few message seals and bullae. Again, this finding suggests that Susa administered the regional movement of goods and that Susa was the "capital" of the state.

Let us turn now to the major features of the cultural sequences leading to the first states in southern Iraq.

Cities and States in Southern Iraq

Farming communities older than the first states have not been found in the arid lowland plains of southern Iraq—the area known as Sumer, where some of the earliest cities and states developed (see Figure 12–2). Perhaps silt from the Tigris and Euphrates rivers has covered them. Or, as has been suggested, Sumer may not have been settled by agriculturalists until people learned how to drain and irrigate river-valley soils otherwise too wet or too dry for cultivation. At any rate, small communities depending partly on agriculture had emerged in the hilly areas north and east of Sumer early in the Neolithic. Later, by about 6000 B.C., a mixed herding-farming economy developed in those areas.

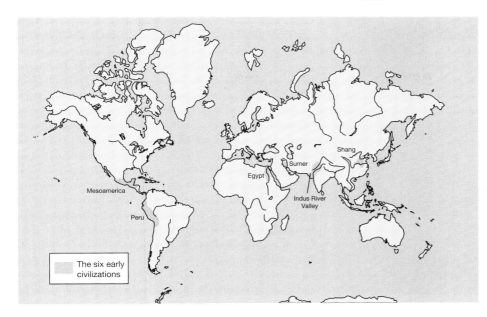

Figure 12–2
Six Early Civilizations

Source: Adapted from *The Origins of the State and Civilization: The Process of Cultural Evolution* by Elman R. Service. Copyright © 1975 by W. W. Norton & Company, Inc. Used by permission of W. W. Norton & Company, Inc.

THE FORMATIVE ERA

Elman Service called the period from about 5000 to 3500 B.C. the *formative era,* for it saw the coming together of many changes that seem to have played a part in the development of cities and states. Service suggested that with the development of small-scale irrigation, lowland river areas began to attract settlers. The rivers provided not only water for irrigation but also mollusks, fish, and waterbirds for food. And they provided routes by which to import needed raw materials, such as hardwood and stone, that were lacking in Sumer.

Changes during this period suggest an increasingly complex social and political life. Differences in status are reflected in the burial of statues and ornaments with children. Different villages specialized in the production of different goods—pottery in some, copper and stone tools in others.[7] Temples were built in certain places that may have been centers of political as well as religious authority for several communities.[8] Furthermore, some anthropologists think that chiefdoms, each having authority over several villages, had developed by this time.[9]

SUMERIAN CIVILIZATION

By about 3500 B.C., there were quite a few cities in the area of Sumer. Most were enclosed in a fortress wall and surrounded by an agricultural area. About 3000 B.C. all of Sumer was unified under a single government. After that time, Sumer became an empire. It had great urban centers. Imposing temples, commonly set on artificial mounds, dominated the cities. In the city of Warka the temple mound was about 150 feet high. The empire was very complex and included an elaborate system for the administration of justice, codified laws, specialized government officials, a professional standing army, and even sewer systems in the cities. Among the many specialized crafts were

brickmaking, pottery, carpentry, jewelry making, leatherworking, metallurgy, basketmaking, stonecutting, and sculpture. Sumerians learned to construct and use wheeled wagons, sailboats, horse-drawn chariots, and spears, swords, and armor of bronze.[10]

As economic specialization developed, social stratification became more elaborate. Sumerian documents describe a system of social classes: nobles, priests, merchants, craftworkers, metallurgists, bureaucrats, soldiers, farmers, free citizens, and slaves. Slaves were common in Sumer; they often were captives, brought back as the spoils of war.

We see the first evidence of writing around 3000 B.C. The earliest Sumerian writings were in the form of ledgers containing inventories of items stored in the temples and records of livestock or other items owned or managed by the temples. Sumerian writing was wedge-shaped, or **cuneiform,** formed by pressing a stylus against a damp clay tablet. For contracts and other important documents, the tablet was fired to create a virtually permanent record. Egyptian writing, or hieroglyphics, appeared about the same time. **Hieroglyphics** were written on rolls woven from papyrus reeds, from which our word *paper* derives.

CD-ROM Interactive Exercise II-13

Cities and States in Mesoamerica

Cities and states emerged in Mesoamerica—Mexico and Central America—later than they did in the Near East. The later appearance of civilization in Mesoamerica may be linked to the later emergence of agriculture in the New World, as we saw in the last chapter, and possibly to the near-absence of large animals such as cattle and horses

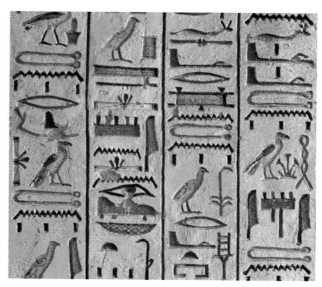

Examples of two of the earliest writing systems on earth. On the left is a cuneiform tablet and on the right is a section of a hieroglyphic panel.

that could be domesticated.[11] We focus primarily on the developments that led to the rise of the city-state of Teotihuacán, which reached its height shortly after the time of Christ. Teotihuacán is located in a valley of the same name, which is the northeastern part of the larger Valley of Mexico.

THE FORMATIVE PERIOD

The formative period in the area around Teotihuacán (1000–300 B.C.) was characterized initially by small, scattered farming villages on the hilly slopes just south of the Teotihuacán Valley. There were probably a few hundred people in each hamlet, and each of these scattered groups was probably politically autonomous. After about 500 B.C., there seems to have been a population shift to settlements on the valley floor, probably in association with the use of irrigation. Between about 300 and 200 B.C., small "elite" centers emerged in the valley; each had an earthen or stone raised platform. Residences or small temples of poles and thatch originally stood on these platforms. That some individuals, particularly those in the elite centers, were buried in special tombs supplied with ornaments, headdresses, carved bowls, and a good deal of food indicates some social inequality.[12] The various elite centers may indicate the presence of chiefdoms.

 CD-ROM Interactive Exercise II-14

THE CITY AND STATE OF TEOTIHUACÁN

About 150 years before the time of Christ, no more than a few thousand people lived in scattered villages in the

Teotihuacán Valley. In A.D. 100, there was a city of 80,000. By A.D. 500, well over 100,000 people, or approximately 90 percent of the entire valley population, seem to have been drawn or coerced into Teotihuacán.[13]

The layout of the city of Teotihuacán, which shows a tremendous amount of planning, suggests that from its beginning the valley was politically unified under a centralized state. Mapping has revealed that the streets and most of the buildings are laid out in a grid pattern following a basic modular unit of 57 square meters. Residential structures are often squares of this size, and many streets are spaced according to multiples of the basic unit. Even the river that ran through the center of the city was channeled to conform to the grid pattern. Perhaps the most outstanding feature of the city is the colossal scale of its architecture. Two pyramids dominate the metropolis, the so-called Pyramid of the Moon and the Pyramid of the Sun. At its base the latter is as big as the great Pyramid of Cheops in Egypt.

The thousands of residential structures built after A.D. 300 follow a standard pattern. Narrow streets separate the one-story buildings, each of which has high, windowless walls. Patios and shafts provide interior light. The layout of rooms suggests that each building consisted of several apartments; more than 100 people may have lived in one of these apartment compounds. There is variation from compound to compound in the size of rooms and the elaborateness of interior decoration, suggesting considerable variation in wealth.[14]

At the height of its power (A.D. 200–500), the metropolis of Teotihuacán encompassed an area larger than imperial Rome.[15] Much of Mesoamerica seems to have been influenced by Teotihuacán. Archaeologically, its influence is suggested by the extensive spread of Teotihuacán-style pottery and architectural elements. Undoubtedly, large

The city of Teotihuacán, which had its peak in 500 A.D., was a planned city built on a grid pattern. At the center was the Pyramid of the Sun shown here.

numbers of people in Teotihuacán were engaged in production for, and the conduct of, long-distance trade. Perhaps 25 percent of the city's population worked at various specialized crafts, including the manufacture of projectile points and cutting and scraping tools from volcanic obsidian. Teotihuacán was close to major deposits of obsidian, which was apparently in some demand over much of Mesoamerica. Materials found in graves indicate that there was an enormous flow of foreign goods into the city, including precious stones, feathers from colorful birds in the tropical lowlands, and cotton.[16]

THE CITY OF MONTE ALBÁN

Teotihuacán probably was not the earliest city-state in Mesoamerica. There is evidence of political unification somewhat earlier, about 500 B.C., in the Valley of Oaxaca, in southern Mexico, with the city of Monte Albán at its center. Monte Albán presents an interesting contrast to

Teotihuacán. Whereas Teotihuacán seems to have completely dominated its valley, containing almost all its inhabitants and craftspeople, Monte Albán did not. The various villages in the Valley of Oaxaca seem to have specialized in different crafts, and Monte Albán did not monopolize craft production. After the political unification of the valley, cities and towns other than Monte Albán remained important; the population of Monte Albán grew only to 30,000 or so. Unlike Teotihuacán, Monte Albán was not an important commercial or market center, it was not laid out in a grid pattern, and its architecture was not much different from that of other settlements in the valley.[17]

Monte Albán did not have the kinds of resources that Teotihuacán had. It was located on top of a mountain in the center of the valley, far from either good soil or permanent water supplies that could have been used for irrigation. Even finding drinking water must have been difficult. No natural resources for trade were nearby, nor is

The city of Monte Albán served primarily as an administrative center. The main plaza of the temple complex, shown here, may have been the center of government.

there much evidence that Monte Albán was used as a ceremonial center. Because the city was at the top of a steep mountain, it is unlikely that it could have been a central marketplace for valleywide trade.

Why, then, did Monte Albán rise to become one of the early centers of Mesoamerican civilization? Richard Blanton suggested it may have originally been founded in the late formative period (500–400 B.C.) as a neutral place where representatives of the different political units in the valley could reside to coordinate activities affecting the whole valley. Thus Monte Albán may have been like the cities of Brasília, Washington, D.C., and Athens, all of which were originally founded in "neutral," nonproductive areas. Such a center, lacking obvious resources, would not, at least initially, threaten the various political units around it. Later it might become a metropolis dominating a more politically unified region, as Monte Albán came to do in the Valley of Oaxaca.[18]

OTHER CENTERS OF MESOAMERICAN CIVILIZATION

In addition to Teotihuacán and Oaxaca, there were other Mesoamerican state societies, which developed somewhat later. For example, there are a number of centers with monumental architecture, presumably built by speakers of Mayan languages, in the highlands and lowlands of modern-day Guatemala and the Yucatán Peninsula of modern-day Mexico. On the basis of surface appearances, the Mayan centers do not appear to have been as densely populated as Teotihuacán or Monte Albán. But it is now evident that the Mayan centers were more densely populated and more dependent on intensive agriculture than was once thought,[19] and recent translations of Mayan picture writing indicate a much more developed form of writing than previously thought.[20] It is apparent now that Mayan urbanization and cultural complexity were underestimated because of the dense tropical forest that now covers much of the area of Mayan civilization.

 CD-ROM Interactive Exercise II-15

 ## The First Cities and States in Other Areas

So far we have discussed the emergence of cities and states in southern Iraq and Mesoamerica whose development is best, if only imperfectly, known archaeologically. But other state societies probably arose more or less independently in many other areas of the world as well (see Figure 12–2). We say "independently," because such states seem to have emerged without colonization or conquest by other states.

Almost at the same time as the Sumerian empire, the

great dynastic age was beginning in the Nile Valley in Egypt. The Old Kingdom, or early dynastic period, began about 3100 B.C., with a capital at Memphis. The archaeological evidence from the early centuries is limited, but most of the population appears to have lived in largely self-sufficient villages. Many of the great pyramids and palaces were built around 2500 B.C.[21]

Elsewhere in Africa states also arose. In what is present-day Ethiopia the Axum (or Aksum) state evolved beginning sometime early in the first millennium A.D., and ultimately became a center of trade and commerce between Africa and the Arabian Peninsula. Among the unique accomplishments of the Axum state were multistory stone residences built in a singular architectural style. Axum is also notable as being perhaps the first officially Christian state in the world.[22]

In sub-Saharan Africa, by A.D. 800, the savanna and forest zones of western Africa had a succession of city-states. One of them was called Ghana, and it became a major source of gold for the Mediterranean world (as did other states in what came to be known as the "Gold Coast").[23] In the Congo River basin a powerful kingdom had evolved by A.D. 1200, with cities described as having tens of thousands of residences and a king that was recognized as an equal by the Portuguese king in the early 1500s.[24] Farther south, states apparently arose in several areas early in the second millennium A.D. One of these was responsible for the large, circular stone structures known today as the Great Zimbabwe.[25]

Memphis, the capital of Egypt's Old Kingdom.

In the Indus Valley of northwestern India, a large state society had developed by 2300 B.C. This Harappan civilization did not have much in the way of monumental architecture, such as pyramids and palaces, and it was also unusual in other respects. The state apparently controlled an enormous territory—over a million square kilometers. There was not just one major city but many, each built according to a similar pattern and with a municipal water and sewage system.[26]

The Shang dynasty in northern China (1750 B.C.) has long been cited as the earliest state society in the Far East. But recent research suggests that an even earlier one, the Xia dynasty, may have emerged in the same general area by 2200 B.C.[27] In any case, the Shang dynasty had all the earmarks of statehood: a stratified, specialized society; religious, economic, and administrative unification; and a distinctive art style.[28]

In South America, a group of distinct state societies may have emerged after 200 B.C. in the area of modern-day Peru.[29] Each of the major river valleys leading from the Andes to the sea witnessed the development of a complex agricultural system dependent on irrigation. The separate, but similar, states participated in a widespread system of religious symbols and beliefs called Chavín. The various states included the well-known Moche state, creators of some of the most remarkable effigy ceramics ever known, and the Nazca state, the people of which constructed a huge landscape of intaglios (inscribed images and lines) on the hard ground of highland deserts. By A.D. 700, these regional states were integrated into a large, militaristic empire called Wari (or Huari).[30]

And in North America a huge settlement, with over 100 earthen mounds (one of them, Monk's Mound, is the largest pre-Columbian structure north of Mexico), and covering an area of more than 13 square kilometers, developed near present-day St. Louis late in the first millennium A.D. The site is called Cahokia, and it was certainly the center of a large and powerful chiefdom. Whether it had achieved a state level of organization is controversial. There is evidence for religious and craft specialists and there is clear social stratification, but whether or not the leaders of Cahokian society were able to govern by force is still unclear.[31]

 CD-ROM Interactive Exercise II-16

 # Theories about the Origin of the State

We have seen that states developed in many parts of the world. Why did they evolve when and where they did? A number of theories have been proposed. We consider those that have been discussed frequently by archaeologists.[32]

IRRIGATION

Irrigation seems to have been important in many of the areas in which early state societies developed. Irrigation made the land habitable or productive in parts of Mesoamerica, southern Iraq, the Nile Valley, China, and South America. It has been suggested that the labor and management needed for the upkeep of an irrigation system led to the formation of a political elite, the overseers of the system, who eventually became the governors of the society.[33] Proponents of this view believe that both the city and civilization were outgrowths of the administrative requirements of an irrigation system.

Critics note that this theory does not seem to apply to all areas where cities and states may have emerged independently. For example, in southern Iraq, the irrigation systems serving the early cities were generally small and probably did not require extensive labor and management.

One of the cities of the Harappan civilization in the Indus Valley was Mohenjodaro. Seen here is an excavated large "bath" with surrounding rooms. Columns originally surrounded the pool. (Modern buildings appear in the background.) In contrast to other early civilizations, there was little display of grandeur. All Harappan cities were laid out according to the same plan.

NEW PERSPECTIVES ON GENDER

Effects of Imperialism on Women's Status

Archaeologists, and particularly women archaeologists, have begun to pay attention to the gender implications of archaeological materials. Do the findings from excavated houses imply anything about what women and men did where they lived? What do the findings in houses and other places suggest about the division of labor by gender? Can archaeology tell us about women's status in the culture and how it may have changed over time? Recent research suggests that if you look for gender-related results, you often can find some. As the title of a recent book indicated, new kinds of archaeology can be "engendered." For example, the archaeologist Cathy Costin has studied the effects of Inka (Inca) imperialism on women's status in a conquered area.

Costin participated in a research project that studied culture change in the Yanamarca Valley of highland Peru. The project focused on the development of chiefdoms among the indigenous Wanka ethnic group

between A.D. 1300 and 1470 and on the effects of the Inka conquest at the end of that period. According to the archaeology, most people before the Inka conquest were farmers, but some households specialized part time in the production of pottery, stone tools, and perhaps textiles. Documents written after the arrival of the Spanish suggest that the Wanka had developed chiefdoms about A.D. 1300, possibly as a result of intensified warfare among the various communities. A high level of conflict is inferred from the locations and configurations of the settlements: Most people lived in fortified (walled) communities located on hills above the valley floor. According to the documentary sources, the Wanka chiefs had achieved their positions because of success as war leaders.

We know from documents that the Wanka were conquered by the Inka during the reign of the emperor Pachakuti (about A.D. 1470). The Wanka region became a province within the Inka

empire, and bureaucrats from the capital at Cuzco came to govern the Wanka. The Inka conquerors, including military personnel, formed the highest class in the valley. The Wanka chiefs became vassals of the Inka state and imitators of Inka ways, using Inka-like pottery and building Inka-style additions to their homes. The economy of the valley became more specialized, apparently to meet the needs of the Inka. People in some villages still mostly farmed, but in other villages most households specialized in the production of pottery, stone tools, and other crafts. Skeletal remains indicate that the commoners became healthier and lived longer after the Inka conquest.

How did the Inka conquest affect the status of women? One key to an answer was suggested by the presence in the excavations of several thousand perforated round ceramic objects. They were spindle whorls, weights used in spinning to keep the thread tight and even. The

---

Large-scale irrigation works were not constructed until after cities had been fully established.[34] Thus, irrigation could not have been the main stimulus for the development of cities and states in Sumer. Even in China, for which the irrigation theory was first formulated, there is no evidence of large-scale irrigation as early as Shang times.[35]

Although large-scale irrigation may not always have preceded the emergence of the first cities and states, even small-scale irrigation systems could have resulted in unequal access to productive land and so may have contributed to the development of a stratified society.[36] In addition, irrigation systems may have given rise to border and other disputes between adjacent groups, thereby

prompting people to concentrate in cities for defense and stimulating the development of military and political controls.[37] Finally, as Robert Adams and Elman Service both suggested, the main significance of irrigation, either large or small scale, may have been its intensification of production, a development that in turn may have indirectly stimulated craft specialization, trade, and administrative bureaucracy.[38]

POPULATION GROWTH, CIRCUMSCRIPTION, AND WAR

Robert Carneiro has suggested that states may emerge because of population growth in an area that is physically or

thread (from llama and alpaca wool) was made into cloth, which became the major form of tax payment after the Inka took over. Each village had to produce a certain amount of cloth for the state tax collectors. The cloth collected was used to clothe men serving in the army and to "pay" other government personnel. The burden of producing the cloth fell on the traditional spinners and weavers, who we know from the post-Spanish documents were females of all ages.

Just before the Inka conquest, all households excavated had spindle whorls, indicating that the female occupants in all households spun and made cloth. More whorls were found the farther up the mountain the house was located, indicating that women who lived closer to the high grasslands, where the flocks of llamas and alpacas were kept, spun more thread than did women who lived farther down from the pastures. We might expect that elite women would do less work. But, to the contrary, the women in elite households seem to have produced more cloth than the women in commoner households, judging by the number of whorls in the households.

After the Inka conquest, households appear to have produced twice the amount of thread they did before, because there are twice the number of recovered spindle whorls. There is no indication, archaeological or documentary, that the women were freed from other tasks to make more time for spinning, so it would appear that women had to work harder under Inka domination to produce thread and cloth. But the producers do not appear to have benefited from the increased cloth production. Much if not most of the cloth produced was removed from the villages and taken to Inka storage facilities in the capital and redistributed from there.

In addition to working harder for the Inka, women seem to have fared worse than the men when it came to nutrition. Christine Hastorf's chemical analysis of bones from Inka-period graves suggests that women ate less maize (corn) than did men. It seems that the men were "eating out" more than women. Maize was often consumed as *chicha* beer, a key component of state-sponsored feasts, which were probably attended more by men than women. Men also worked more in state-organized agricultural and production projects, where they probably were rewarded with meat, maize, and *chicha* for their service to the state.

So, under Inka domination, Wanka women had to produce more and received less. Is this a general effect of imperialism? And, if so, why?

Sources: Elizabeth M. Brumfiel, "Distinguished Lecture in Archeology: Breaking and Entering the Ecosystem—Gender, Class, and Faction Steal the Show," *American Anthropologist,* 94 (1992): 551–67; Joan M. Gero and Margaret W. Conkey, eds., *Engendering Archaeology: An Introduction to Women and Prehistory* (Oxford: Blackwell, 1991); Cathy Lynne Costin, "Cloth Production and Gender Relations in the Inka Empire," in Peter N. Peregrine, Carol R. Ember, and Melvin Ember, eds., *Archaeology: Original Readings in Method and Practice* (Upper Saddle River, NJ: Prentice Hall, 2002); Christine Hastorf, "Gender, Space, and Food in Prehistory," in Gero and Conkey, eds., *Engendering Archaeology.*

socially limited. Competition and warfare in such a situation may lead to the subordination of defeated groups, who are obliged to pay tribute and to submit to the control of a more powerful group.[39] Carneiro illustrated his theory by describing how states may have emerged on the northern coast of Peru.

After the people of that area first settled into an agricultural village life, population grew at a slow, steady rate. Initially, new villages were formed as population grew. But in the narrow coastal valleys—blocked by high mountains, fronted by the sea, and surrounded by desert—this splintering-off process could not continue indefinitely. The result, according to Carneiro, was increasing land shortage and warfare between villages as they competed for land. Since the high mountains, the sea, and the desert blocked any escape for losers, the defeated villagers had no choice but to submit to political domination. In this way, chiefdoms may have become kingdoms as the most powerful villages grew to control entire valleys. As chiefs' power expanded over several valleys, states and empires may have been born.

Carneiro noted that physical or environmental circumscription may not be the only kind of barrier that gives rise to a state. Social circumscription may be just as important. People living at the center of a high-density area may find that their migration is blocked by surrounding settlements just as effectively as it could be by mountains, sea, and desert.

Ruins of the ancient city of Pisac in the Cuzco region of Peru.

Marvin Harris suggested a somewhat different form of circumscription. He argued that the first states with their coercive authority could emerge only in areas that supported intensive grain agriculture (and the possibility of high food production) and were surrounded by areas that could not support intensive grain agriculture. So people in such areas might put up with the coercive authority of a state because they would suffer a sharp drop in living standards if they moved away.[40]

Carneiro suggested that his theory applies to many areas besides the northern coast of Peru, including southern Iraq and the Indus and Nile valleys. Although there were no geographic barriers in areas such as northern China or the Mayan lowlands on the Yucatán Peninsula, the development of states in those areas may have been the result of social circumscription. Carneiro's theory seems to be supported for southern Iraq, where there is archaeological evidence of population growth, circumscription, and warfare.[41] And there is evidence of population growth before the emergence of the state in the Teotihuacán Valley.[42]

But population growth does not necessarily mean population pressure. For example, the populations in the Teotihuacán and Oaxaca valleys apparently did increase prior to state development, but there is no evidence that they had even begun to approach the limits of their resources. More people could have lived in both places.[43] Nor is population growth definitely associated with state formation in all areas where early states arose. For example, according to Wright and Johnson, there was population growth long before states emerged in southwestern Iran, but the population apparently declined just before the states emerged.[44]

In addition, Carneiro's circumscription theory leaves an important logical question unanswered: Why would the victors in war let the defeated populations remain and pay tribute? If the victors wanted the land so much in the first place, why wouldn't they try to exterminate the de-

feated and occupy the land themselves, which has happened many times in history?

LOCAL AND LONG-DISTANCE TRADE

It has been suggested that trade was a factor in the emergence of the earliest states.[45] Wright and Johnson theorized that the organizational requirements of producing items for export, redistributing the items imported, and defending trading parties would foster state formation.[46] Does the archaeological evidence support such a theory?

In southern Iraq and the Mayan lowlands, long-distance trade routes may indeed have stimulated bureaucratic growth. In the lowlands of southern Iraq, as we have seen, people needed wood and stone for building, and they traded with highland people for those items. In the Mayan lowlands, the development of civilization seems to have been preceded by long-distance trade. Farmers in the lowland regions traded with faraway places in order to obtain salt, obsidian for cutting blades, and hard stone for grinding tools.[47] In southwestern Iran, long-distance trade did not become very important until after Susa became the center of a state society, but short-distance trade may have played the same kind of role in the formation of states.

Kwang-chih Chang put forward a similar theory for the origin of states in China. He suggested that Neolithic societies in the Yellow River valley developed a long-distance trade network, which he called an *interaction sphere*, by about 4000 B.C. Trade spread cultural elements among the societies in the interaction sphere, so that they came to share some common elements (see Figure 12–3). Over time, these societies came to depend on each other both as trade partners and as cultural partners, and around 2000 B.C. they unified into a single political unit under the Shang dynasty.[48] Thus Chang sees political unification in China as an outgrowth of a preexisting system of trade and cultural interaction.

Figure 12–3 *Expansion of Regional Neolithic Cultures in China, 4000–3000 B.C.*

Source: From *Archaeology of Ancient China*, 4E by K-C. Chang. Reprinted by permission of Yale University Press.

THE VARIOUS THEORIES: AN EVALUATION

Why do states form? As of now, no one theory seems to fit all the known situations. The reason may be that different conditions in different places may have favored the emergence of centralized government. After all, the state, by definition, implies an ability to organize large populations for a collective purpose. In some areas, this purpose may have been the need to organize trade with local or far-off regions. In other cases, the state may have emerged as a way to control defeated populations in circumscribed ar-

eas. In still other instances, a combination of factors may have fostered the development of the state type of political system.[49]

The Consequences of State Formation

We have considered several areas where states arose, as well as a number of theories to explain the origin of states. But what were the consequences for the people living in those societies? The consequences seem to have been dramatic.

One of the ways states change the life-styles of people is by allowing for larger and denser populations.[50] As we have already seen, agriculture itself gives populations the potential to grow, and the development of a state only furthers that potential. Why? Because a state is able to build infrastructure—irrigation systems, roadways, markets—that allows both the production and distribution of agricultural products to become more efficient. States are able to coordinate information as well, and can use that information to manage agricultural production cycles and to anticipate or manage droughts, blights, or other natural disasters. States are also able to control access to land (through laws and a military) and thus can both maintain farmers on the land and prevent others (from either within or outside of the state) from removing the farmers or interfering with their ability to produce food.

With increased efficiency of agricultural production and distribution, states also allow many (if not most) people in the society to be relieved of food production. These people are freed to become craftspeople, merchants, and artists, as well as bureaucrats, soldiers, and political leaders. People may also live apart from agricultural fields, and thus cities with dense populations can arise. Cities can also arise in locations that are not suited to agriculture but that

The rise of states allows cities with dense populations to develop and, along with them, the many potentials and problems that cities and their populations create.

RESEARCH FRONTIERS
Imperialism, Colonialism, and the State

The first city-states seem to have emerged during the Uruk period, roughly the fourth millennium B.C., in the river valleys of southern Mesopotamia, now southern Iraq. From their very beginnings, these first city-states had "foreign trade." This trade may have been indispensable; the riverine environment, though fertile when drained and irrigated, lacked necessary raw materials such as hardwood and stone. The trade with other areas could have been peaceful and balanced, as between equals. After all, it is possible that when one area has something that another wants, and vice versa, the people on both sides could voluntarily arrange to satisfy each other's needs by bargaining and negotiating. But the archaeological evidence from the preliterate Uruk period, as well as the documentary evidence for shortly afterward, suggests that the first city-states in Mesopotamia were engaged in imperialism and colonialism from their very beginnings.

Just like the British and French, who first came to North America to explore and trade and often used force to protect their settlements and access to trade items, the Uruk city-states seem also to have dominated their peripheral, less developed trading "partners." For example, before 3000 B.C. there were fortified towns with Uruk-style pottery and administrative artifacts at river junctions in the north of Mesopotamia. Why did the Uruk people go there? One possibility is that they deliberately built outposts to secure their access to needed trade goods, including hides and dried meat.

There was no single state involved in this imperialism and colonialism. Southern Mesopotamia (Sumer) was not politically unified until after 3000 B.C. Rather, the various Uruk-period polities of the Tigris and Euphrates river valleys seem to have been intensely competitive. The walls around the cities indicate that they were probably subject to attack by their rivals at any time. The picture is reminiscent of the Greek city-states described by Thucydides. It is also like the

picture we get from the hieroglyphic writings of the Maya city-states in and around southern Mexico (A.D. 300–800), which, in a mixture of history and propaganda, extol the triumphs of the various rivalrous rulers. And, of course, we all are familiar with how Britain and Spain and Holland and France were rivalrous before and after the New World was discovered.

We know that the Greek city-states were imperialistic colonizers because we have historical evidence of the fact. Greek-speakers, from Athens and other polities, established colonies all over the Mediterranean—Syracuse in Sicily and Marseilles in France, for example. But what about the Uruk city-states? Why should we think they too were imperialistic colonizers? The archaeologist Guillermo Algaze recently reviewed the evidence. First there was the colonization of the plains of southwestern Iran, which people could get to from southern Mesopotamia in seven to ten days by foot or donkey caravan. Then, and maybe

perhaps are suited to trade (such as the cities on rivers in southern Mesopotamia) or defense (such as on top of a mountain, as in the case of Monte Albán). Art, music, and literature often flourish in such contexts, and these too are often consequences of the rise of states. Organized religion also often develops after states appear. Thus all the hallmarks we associate with civilization can be seen as resulting from the evolution of states.[51]

The development of states can have many negative impacts as well. When states develop people become governed by force, and are no longer able to say no to their leaders. Police and military forces can become instruments of oppression and terror.[52] On a less obvious level, the class stratification of states creates differences in access

to resources and an underclass of poor, uneducated, and frequently unhealthy people. Health issues are exacerbated by the concentration of people in cities, an environment in which epidemic diseases can flourish.[53] Without direct access to food supplies, people in cities also face the threat of malnutrition or outright starvation if food production and distribution systems fail.[54]

All states appear to be expansionistic, and the emergence of state warfare and conquest seems one of the most striking negative impacts of the evolution of states. In fact, more human suffering can probably be linked to state expansion than to any other single factor. Why do states expand? One basic reason may be that they are able to (see the box "Imperialism, Colonialism, and the State"). States

overlapping with the expansion into southwestern Iran, the Uruk polities established outposts or took over already existing settlements to the north and northwest, on the plains of what are now northern Iraq and Syria; these latter settlements were apparently all located at intersections of the important waterways and overland routes.

According to Algaze, the Uruk enclaves and outposts outside southern Mesopotamia fit what the comparative historian Philip Curtin calls *trade diaspora*. Curtin thinks that such movements develop after the emergence of cities, with their vulnerable populations. (An urban population is vulnerable because a city, by definition, is inhabited mostly by people who are dependent for their food on people who live outside the city.) Diaspora have taken various forms, but they all represent ways to organize exchange between areas with different but complementary resources. At one end of the range of possibilities—involving little or no political organization—commercial specialists remove themselves from their own society and settle as aliens somewhere else. At the other end of

the range of variation—the most politically organized—the expanding polity is involved from the beginning in the founding of outposts that secure the required trade.

Algaze thinks that the Uruk expansion was motivated by a lack of resources in southern Mesopotamia. But is that a complete explanation? Other areas of the world, at the time and since, have lacked resources, but they did not all become imperialistic colonizers. So what else, in addition to the need for external resources, might explain the Uruk expansion? And how can we explain why it eventually stopped? Algaze notes that when the Uruk settlers moved into southwestern Iran, they were entering an area that was not so densely settled, so they may have encountered only minimal resistance. Indeed, the various Uruk-period enclaves and outposts outside southern Mesopotamia were apparently larger and more complex than any previous communities in the peripheral areas. Perhaps, then, imperialism and colonialism are possible only in a world of unequals.

Years ago, the anthropologist Stanley Diamond argued that

"imperialism and colonialism are as old as the State." Does this mean that states are likely to practice imperialism and colonialism if they can get away with it? Or are only some conditions likely to predispose states to imperialism and colonialism? How strongly are imperialism and colonialism linked to state organization anyway? What makes a humane state possible? Perhaps future research, particularly cross-cultural and cross-historical research, will tell us.

Sources: Guillermo Algaze, *The Uruk World System: The Dynamics of Expansion of Early Mesopotamian Civilization* (Chicago: University of Chicago Press, 1993); Melinda A. Zeder, "After the Revolution: Post-Neolithic Subsistence in Northern Mesopotamia," *American Anthropologist,* 96 (1994): 97–126; Philip D. Curtin, *Cross-Cultural Trade in World History* (Cambridge: Cambridge University Press, 1984); Stanley Diamond, *In Search of the Primitive: A Critique of Civilization* (New Brunswick, NJ: Transaction Books, 1974); Joyce Marcus, "Maya Hieroglyphs: History or Propaganda?" in Peter N. Peregrine, Carol R. Ember, and Melvin Ember, eds., *Archaeology: Original Readings in Method and Practice* (Upper Saddle River, NJ: Prentice Hall, 2002).

have standing armies ready to fight or be sent to conquer enemies. Another reason for state expansion might be related to the threat of famine and disease, which is more likely with intensive agriculture.[55] Two of the authors of this text have found that in recent societies resource unpredictability is strongly associated with a higher frequency of warfare, and states fearful of shortfalls in resources may resort to war ahead of time as a means of gaining access to more resources (or of limiting the unpredictability of resources).[56] A third answer to the question of why states tend to expand might be that belligerence is simply part of the nature of states. States often arise through military means, and it may be vital to the continuation of some states that military power be continually

demonstrated.[57] Regardless of the causes, war and conquest are the consequences of state formation. Often, too, defeat in war is the fate of states.

 ## The Decline and Collapse of States

When you look over the list of ancient states we have discussed in this chapter—Monte Albán, Teotihuacán, Sumer, pharonic Egypt—you will notice one element common to them all: Each eventually collapsed; none maintained its power and influence into historic times. Why? It is an important question because, if collapse is the ultimate fate of many if not all states, then we can anticipate that our own state is likely to collapse eventually. Perhaps knowing something about how and why other states have fallen can prevent (or at least hold off) the fall of our own.

One suggested explanation for the decline and collapse of states is environmental degradation. If states originally arose where the environment was conducive to intensive agriculture and harvests big enough to support social stratification, political officials, and a state type of political system, then perhaps environmental degradation—declining soil productivity, persistent drought, and the like—contributed to the collapse of ancient states. The archaeologist Harvey Weiss has suggested that persistent drought helped to bring about the fall of the ancient Akkadian empire, in the Near East. By 2300 B.C., the Akkadians had established an empire stretching 1,300 kilometers from the Persian Gulf in what is now Iraq to the headwaters of the Euphrates River in what is now Turkey. But a century later the empire collapsed. Weiss thinks that a long-term drought brought the empire down, as well as other civilizations around at that time too. Many archaeologists doubted there was such a widespread drought, but new evidence indicates that the worst dry spell of the past 10,000 years began just as the Akkadians' northern stronghold was being abandoned.[58] The evidence of the drought, windblown dust in sediment retrieved from the bottom of the Persian Gulf, indicates that the dry spell lasted 300 years. Other geophysical evidence suggests that the drought was worldwide.[59]

Environmental degradation may occur for reasons other than natural events. The behavior of humans may sometimes be responsible. Consider the collapse of Cahokia, a city of at least 15,000 people that thrived for a while in the area where the Missouri and Mississippi rivers converge. In the twelfth century A.D., Cahokia had large public plazas, a city wall constructed from some 20,000 logs, and massive mounds. But within 300 years only the

mounds were left. Silt from flooding covered former croplands and settled areas. The geographer Bill Woods thinks that overuse of woodlands for fuel, construction, and defense led to deforestation, flooding, and persistent crop failure. The result was the abandonment of Cahokia. Timber depletion is also indicated by studies of charcoal from excavations in the area. Apparently the quality of wood used in construction declined over time, suggesting that choice trees got scarcer.[60]

Cahokia is just one example of degradation that may have been caused by human behavior. Another example is the increasing saltiness of soils caused by evaporation of water from fields that have been irrigated over long periods of time, as in what is now southern Iraq.

Civilizations may sometimes decline because human behavior has increased the incidence of disease. For example, many lowland Mayan cities were abandoned between A.D. 800 and 1000. Explanations of this collapse have ranged from overpopulation to resource depletion. But another factor may have been the increasing incidence of yellow fever. The clearing of forests and the consequent increase of breeding sites for mosquitoes may have favored the spread of the disease from areas farther south in Central America. Or the planting of particular trees by the Mayans in their urban areas may have increased the populations of co-resident monkeys who carried the disease (which mosquitoes transmitted to people).[61]

Another reason that some states have collapsed appears to be overextension. This is often one of the reasons given for the decline of the Roman Empire. By the time of its fall, beginning in the second century A.D., the empire had expanded throughout the Mediterranean region and into northwestern Europe. That huge area may simply have been too large to administer. "Barbarian" incursions on the peripheries of the empire went unchecked because it was too difficult, and too costly, to reinforce these far-flung frontiers. Sometimes these incursions became wholesale invasions that were exacerbated by famines,

Monk's Mound at Cahokia is the largest pre-Columbian structure north of Mexico.

The history of Ephesus, a former city lying in ruins in what is now western Turkey, illustrates the waxing and waning of states and empires. From about 1000 B.C. to 100 B.C., it was controlled by the Greeks, Lydians, Persians, Macedonians, and Romans, among others.

plagues, and poor leadership. By the time the last Roman emperor of the West was deposed in A.D. 476, the empire had withered to virtually nothing.[62]

Finally, internal conflict because of leaders' mismanagement or exploitation has been put forward to explain the collapse of states. For example, Peter Charnais has argued that the Byzantine Empire (the eastern half of the Roman Empire) collapsed because large, powerful landholders had been allowed to take over the land of too many small holders, creating a group of overtaxed, exploited peasants with no interest in maintaining the empire. When the landholders began vying with the emperor for power, civil wars erupted, leading to disunity that left the empire vulnerable to conquest.[63]

Many other ideas have been put forward to explain collapse, ranging from catastrophes to almost mystical factors such as "social decadence," but, as with theories for the origin of states, no single explanation seems to fit all or even most of the situations. While it is still not clear what specific conditions led to the emergence, or collapse, of the state in each of the early centers of civilization, the question of why states form and decline is a lively focus of research today. More satisfactory answers may come out of ongoing and future investigations.

Summary

1. Archaeologists do not always agree on how a state should be defined, but most seem to agree that hierarchi-

cal and centralized decision making affecting a substantial population is the key criterion. Most states have cities with public buildings, full-time craft and religious specialists, an official art style, and a hierarchical social structure topped by an elite class from which the leaders are drawn. Most states maintain power with a monopoly on the use of force. Force or the threat of force is used by the state to tax its population and to draft people for work or war.

2. Early state societies arose within the Near East in what is now southern Iraq and southwestern Iran. Southern Iraq, or Sumer, was unified under a single government just after 3000 B.C. It had writing, large urban centers, imposing temples, codified laws, a standing army, wide trade networks, a complex irrigation system, and a high degree of craft specialization.

3. Probably the earliest city-state in Mesoamerica developed around 500 B.C. in the Valley of Oaxaca, with a capital at Monte Albán. Somewhat later, in the northeastern section of the Valley of Mexico, Teotihuacán developed. At the height of its power, A.D. 200–500, the city-state of Teotihuacán appears to have influenced much of Mesoamerica.

4. City-states arose early in other parts of the New World: in Guatemala, the Yucatán Peninsula of Mexico, Peru, and possibly near St. Louis. In the Old World, early states developed in Africa, the Indus Valley of India, and northern China.

5. There are several theories of why states arose. The irrigation theory suggests that the administrative needs of maintaining extensive irrigation systems may have been

the impetus for state formation. The circumscription theory suggests that states emerge when competition and warfare in circumscribed areas lead to the subordination of defeated groups, which are obliged to submit to the control of the most powerful group. Theories involving trade suggest that the organizational requirements of producing exportable items, redistributing imported items, and defending trading parties would foster state formation. Which is correct? At this point, no one theory is able to explain the formation of every state. Perhaps different organizational requirements in different areas all favored centralized government.

6. When states arise they have a dramatic impact. Populations grow and become concentrated in cities. Agriculture becomes more efficient, allowing many people to be removed from food production. States provide a context in which what we commonly call civilization—art, music, literature, and organized religion—can develop and flourish. But states also provide a context in which warfare and political terror can flourish. The social differentiation found in states produces an underclass of poor and often unhealthy people. States are prone to epidemic disease and periodic famine.

7. All ancient states collapsed eventually. While we have no good answers to the question of why states collapse, research into this question may have implications for prolonging the lives of our modern state systems.

Glossary Terms

civilization
cuneiform
hieroglyphics
state

Critical Questions

1. Cities and states did not appear until after the emergence of food production. Why might food production be necessary, but not sufficient, for cities and states to develop?

2. Like the emergence of food production, the earliest cities and states developed within a few thousand years of each other. What might be the reasons?

3. Can you imagine a future world without states? What conditions might lead to that "state" of the world?

Internet Exercises

1. The Egyptian pyramids are often thought of as monuments associated with early cities and states. Visit the pyramids at the Web site **http://www.pbs.org/wgbh/nova/pyramid/** and summarize your findings.

2. Teotihuacán was one of the earliest city-states in Mesoamerica. Explore **http://archaeology.la.asu.edu/ARI_Web_2000/vm/mesoamerica/teo/index.htm** and write a brief essay about some aspect of this early city.

3. The Perseus Project at Tufts University offers an amazing array of information on classical civilizations. Visit its Web site at **http://www.perseus.tufts.edu/** and explore several links within the classics collection or one of their on-line exhibitions on ancient Greece or Rome.

4. Explore ongoing research projects on the ancient Near East at the Oriental Institute of the University of Chicago (**http://www-oi.uchicago.edu/OI/default.html**) and the University of Pennsylvania Museum (**http://www.museum.upenn.edu/**) Web sites. Describe one of the research projects you read about.

Suggested Reading

BLANTON, R. E., KOWALEWSKI, S. A., FEINMAN, G., AND APPEL, J. *Ancient Mesoamerica: A Comparison of Change in Three Regions,* 2nd ed. Cambridge: Cambridge University Press, 1993. A comparison and analysis of cultural development, and particularly the development of states, in three regions of Mesoamerica—the Valley of Oaxaca, the Valley of Mexico, and the eastern (Mayan) lowlands.

BURENHULT, G., ED. *Old World Civilizations: The Rise of Cities and States.* St. Lucia, Queensland, Australia: University of Queensland Press, 1994. A gorgeous book of color photographs surveying many of the ancient civilizations in Asia, Africa, and Europe.

BRUMFIEL, E. M., ED. *The Economic Anthropology of the State.* Lanham, MD: University Press of America, 1994. A collection of papers discussing states, both ancient and modern, and how they function, with a focus on the economy.

COHEN, R., AND SERVICE, E. R., EDS. *Origins of the State: The Anthropology of Political Evolution.* Philadelphia: Institute for the Study of Human Issues, 1978. A collection of theoretical and empirical papers on the possible origins of states.

FEINMAN, G. M., AND MARCUS, J., EDS. *Archaic States.* Santa Fe, NM: School of American Research Press, 1998. This collection of papers discusses the rise and fall of the ancient states in the Near East, India and Pakistan, Egypt, Mesoamerica, and the Andes, and presents some key questions for future research.

SANDERS, W. T., PARSONS, J. R., AND SANTLEY, R. S. *The Basin of Mexico: Ecological Processes in the Evolution of a Civilization.* New York: Academic Press, 1979. A description of a long-term archaeological project that investigated the evolution of civilization in the Valley of Mexico from 1500 B.C. to A.D. 1500, particularly as reflected in the history of its settlement.

SERVICE, E. R. *Origins of the State and Civilization: The Process of Cultural Evolution.* New York: Norton, 1975. An older but still highly informative discussion of state origins. Compares both historic and prehistoric cases of state origins to find similarities and trends.

13

Human Variation
and Adaptation

n the preceding chapters we discussed the emergence of people like ourselves, *Homo sapiens sapiens*. Just as the cultures of those human beings differed in some respects, so do the cultures of peoples in recent times. But anthropologists are also concerned with how recent human populations physically resemble or differ from each other, and why.

In any given human population, individuals vary in external features such as skin color or height and in internal features such as blood type or susceptibility to a disease. If you measure the frequencies of such features in different populations, you will typically find differences on average from one population to another. So, for example, some populations are typically darker in skin color than other populations.

Why do these physical differences exist? They may be largely the product of differences in genes. Or they may be largely due to growing up in a particular environment, physical and cultural. Or perhaps they are the result of an interaction between environmental factors and genes.

We turn first to the processes that may singly or jointly produce the varying frequencies of physical traits in different human populations. Then we discuss specific differences in external and internal characteristics and how they might be explained. Finally, we close with a critical examination of racial classification and whether it helps or hinders the study of human variation.

 Processes in Human Variation

ADAPTATION

Mutations—changes in the structure of a gene—are the ultimate source of all genetic variation. Because different genes make for greater or lesser chances of survival and reproduction, natural selection results in more favorable genes becoming more frequent in a population over time. We call this process **adaptation**. Adaptations are genetic changes that give their carriers a better chance to survive and reproduce than individuals without the genetic change who live in the same environment. It is the environment, of course, that favors the reproductive success of some traits rather than others.

How adaptive a gene or trait is depends on the environment; what is adaptive in one environment may not be adaptive in another. For example, in the chapter on genetics and evolution, we discussed the advantage that dark moths had over light moths when certain areas of England became industrialized. Predators could not easily see the darker moths against the newly darkened trees, and these moths soon outnumbered the lighter variety. Similarly, human populations live in a great variety of environments, so we would expect natural selection to favor different genes and traits in those different environments. As we shall see, variations in skin color and body build are among the many features that may be at least partly ex-

plainable by how natural selection works in different environments.

Adaptation through natural selection does not account for variation in frequencies of neutral traits—that is, traits that do not confer any advantages or disadvantages on their carriers. The sometimes different and sometimes similar frequencies of neutral traits in human populations may result, then, from genetic drift or gene flow. As we discussed in the chapter on genetics and evolution, genetic drift refers to variations in a population that appear because of random processes such as isolation (the "founder effect"), mating patterns, and the random segregation of chromosomes during meiosis. Gene flow involves the exchange of genes between populations. Neither genetic drift nor gene flow are adaptive processes, but they do result in differences between populations. Genetic drift may increase the differences between populations. Gene flow tends to work in the opposite direction—it tends to decrease differences between populations.

ACCLIMATIZATION

Natural selection may favor certain genes because of certain physical environmental conditions, as in the case of the moths in England. But the physical environment can sometimes produce variation even in the absence of genetic change. As we shall see, climate may influence the way the human body grows and develops, and therefore some kinds of human variation may be explainable largely as a function of environmental variation. We call this process *acclimatization*. **Acclimatization** involves physiological adjustments in individuals to environmental conditions. Acclimatizations may have underlying genetic factors, but they are not themselves genetic. Individuals develop them during their lifetimes, rather than being born with them.

Many acclimatizations are simple physiological changes in the body that appear and disappear as the environment changes. For example, when we are chilled, our bodies attempt to create heat by making our muscles work, a physiological response to the environment that we experience as shivering. Longer exposure to cold weather leads our bodies to increase our metabolic rates so that we generate more internal heat. Both these physiological changes are acclimatizations, one short term (shivering), one longer term (increased metabolic rate).

As we discuss later in this chapter, some long-term acclimatizations are difficult to distinguish from adaptations because they become established as normal operating processes, and they may persist even after the individual moves into an environment that is different from the one that originally fostered the acclimatization. It also appears that some acclimatizations are closely related to genetic adaptations. For example, tanning, an acclimatization among light-skinned people when exposed to high levels of solar radiation, is related to the adaptation of light skin color to environments with low solar radiation.

INFLUENCE OF THE CULTURAL ENVIRONMENT

Humans are not only influenced by their environments through adaptations and acclimatizations, but, as we have seen in the chapters on food production and on the state, humans can also dramatically affect their environments. Culture allows humans to modify their environments, and such modifications may lessen the likelihood of genetic adaptations and physiological acclimitizations. For example, the effects of cold may be modified by the culture traits of living in houses, harnessing energy to create heat, and clothing the body to insulate it. In these cultural ways, we alter our "microenvironments." Iron deficiency may be overcome by the culture trait of cooking in iron pots. If a physical environment lacks certain nutrients, people may get them by the culture trait of trading for them; trading for salt has been common in world history. Culture can also influence the direction of natural selection. As we shall see, the culture of dairying seems to have increased the frequency of genes that allow adults to digest milk.[1]

In addition, individual cultures sometimes practice behaviors that lead to physical variations between their members and between members of one culture and another. For example, elites in many highland Andean societies (the Inca, for example) practiced head binding. The heads of elite children were tightly bound with cloth. As the child grew, the binding forced the skull to take on an elongated, almost conical shape. This cultural practice, then, created physical variations among individuals that were intended to identify members of elite groups.[2] Many cultures have practices that are intended to create physical variations that distinguish members of their culture from members of other cultures. The Hebrew Bible, for example, tells the story of how Abraham was instructed by God to circumcise himself and all his male descendants as a sign of the covenant between them.[3] Thus all the descendants of Abraham share a culturally induced physical variation (lack of a foreskin) to identify themselves as a unique group.

In the next section we discuss some aspects of human (physical) variation for which we have explanations that involve one or more of the processes just described.

Physical Variation in Human Populations

The most noticeable physical variations among populations are those that are external, on the surface—body build, facial features, skin color, and height. No less important are those variations that are internal, such as variation in susceptibility to different diseases and differences in the ability to produce certain enzymes.

We begin our survey with some physical features that appear to be strongly linked to variation in climate, particularly variation in temperature, sunlight, and altitude.

BODY BUILD AND FACIAL CONSTRUCTION

Scientists have suggested that the body build of many birds and mammals may vary according to the temperature of the environment in which they live. Bergmann and Allen, two nineteenth-century naturalists, suggested some general rules for animals, but it was not until the 1950s that researchers began to examine whether these rules applied to human populations.[4] **Bergmann's rule** describes

Masai herdsmen illustrate Bergmann's rule. They have the long-limbed, lean body type that is often found in equatorial regions. Such a body type provides more surface area in relation to body mass and thus may facilitate the dissipation of body heat.

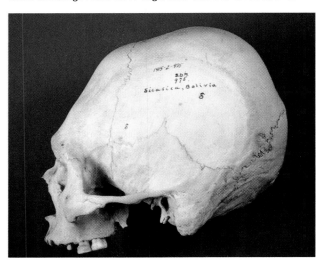

A cranium from Sicasica, Bolivia, showing the effects of head binding. Note how high and flat the forehead is.

what seems to be a general relationship between body size and temperature: The slenderer populations of a species inhabit the warmer parts of its geographic range, and the more robust populations inhabit the cooler areas.

D. F. Roberts's studies of variation in mean body weight of human populations in regions with widely differing temperatures have provided support for Bergmann's rule.[5] Roberts discovered that the lowest body weights were found among residents of areas with the highest mean annual temperatures, and vice versa. Figure 13–1 shows the relationship between body weight of males and average annual temperature for four different geographic populations. Although the slope of the relationship is slightly different for each group, the trend is the same—with colder temperatures, weight is greater. Looking at the general trend across populations (see the "Total" line), we see that where the mean annual temperatures are about freezing (0°C; 32°F), the average weight for males is about 65 kilograms (143 pounds); where the mean annual temperatures are about 25°C (77°F), men weigh, on the average, about 50 kilograms (110 pounds).

Allen's rule refers to another kind of variation in body build among birds and mammals: Protruding body parts (e.g., limbs) are relatively shorter in the cooler areas of a species' range than in the warmer areas. Research comparing human populations tends to support Allen's rule.[6]

The rationale behind these theories is that the long-limbed, lean body type often found in equatorial regions provides more surface area in relation to body mass and thus facilitates the dissipation of body heat. In contrast, the chunkier, shorter-limbed body type found among residents of cold regions promotes retention of body heat because the amount of surface area relative to body mass is lessened. The build of the Inuit (Eskimo) appears to exemplify Bergmann's and Allen's rules. The relatively large bodies and short legs of the Inuit may be adapted to the cold temperatures in which they live.

It is not clear whether differences in body build between populations are due solely to natural selection of different genes under different conditions of cold or heat. Some of the variations may be acclimatizations induced during the life span of individuals.[7] Alphonse Riesenfeld provided experimental evidence that extreme cold can affect body proportions during growth and development. Rats raised under conditions of extreme cold generally showed changes that resemble characteristics of humans in cold environments. These cold-related changes included shortening of the long bones, consistent with Allen's rule.[8]

Like body build, facial structure may also be affected by environment. Riesenfeld found experimentally that the facial width of rats increased in cold temperatures and their nasal openings grew smaller.[9] Because the rats raised in cold environments were genetically similar to those raised in warmer environments, we can confidently conclude that the environment, not genes, brought about these changes in the rats. How much the environment directly affects variation in the human face is not clear. We do

Figure 13–1 *Relationship between Body Weight of Males and Average Annual Temperature for Four Major Population Groups*

Source: From D. F. Roberts, "Body Weight, Race, and Climate," *American Journal of Physical Anthropology,* 11 (1953): Fig. 2, reproduced in Stephen Jones, Robert Martin, and David Pilbeam, eds., *The Cambridge Encyclopedia of Human Evolution.* Copyright © by Cambridge University Press. Reprinted by permission of Cambridge University Press.

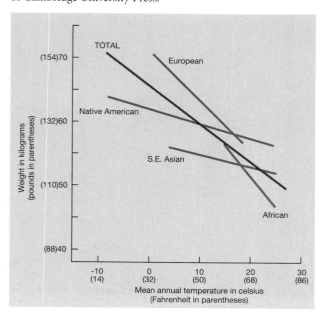

An Inuit hunter illustrates Allen's rule. He has a relatively large body and short limbs, which help him maintain body heat in the cold climate he inhabits.

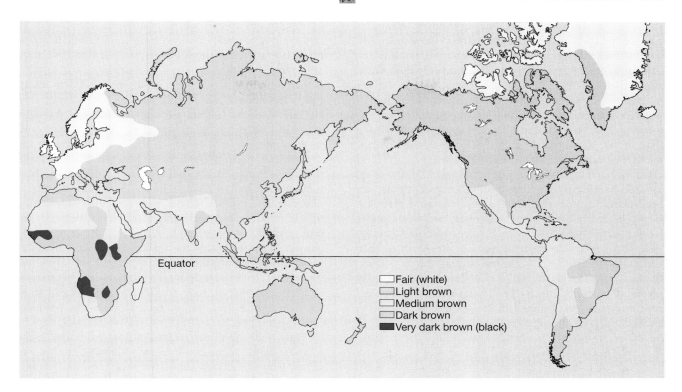

Figure 13–2 *Variation in Skin Color*

Source: From Biological Perspectives on Human Pigmentation by Ashley H. Robins. Copyright © by Cambridge University Press. Reprinted by permission of Cambridge University Press.

know that variation in climate is associated with facial variation. For example, people living in the humid tropics tend to have broad, short, flat noses, whereas people living in climates with low humidity (with cold or hot temperatures) tend to have long, thin noses. A narrow nose may be a more efficient humidifier of drier air than a broad nose.[10]

SKIN COLOR

Human populations obviously differ in average skin color. Many people consider skin color the most important indicator of "race," and they sometimes treat others differently solely on this basis. But anthropologists, in addition to being critical of prejudice, also note that skin color is not a good indicator of ancestry. For example, extremely dark skin is found most commonly in Africa. However, there are natives of southern India whose skin is as dark as or darker than that of many Africans. Yet these people are not closely related to Africans, either genetically or historically.

How can we explain the wide range of skin colors among the peoples of the world? The color of a person's skin depends on both the amount of dark pigment, or *melanin,* in the skin and the amount of blood in the small blood vessels of the skin.[11] Despite the fact that there is still much to understand about the genetics of skin color, we do have some theories that may partly account for variation in skin color.

The amount of melanin in the skin seems to be related to the climate in which a person lives. **Gloger's rule** states

that populations of birds and mammals living in warmer climates have more melanin and, therefore, darker skin, fur, or feathers, than do populations of the same species living in cooler areas. On the whole, this association with climate holds true for people as well as for other mammals and birds.

The populations of darker-skinned humans do live mostly in warm climates, particularly sunny climates (see Figure 13–2). Dark pigmentation seems to have at least one specific advantage in sunny climates. Melanin protects the sensitive inner layers of the skin from the sun's damaging ultraviolet rays; therefore, dark-skinned people living in sunny areas are safer from sunburn and skin cancers than are light-skinned people. Dark skin may also confer other important biological advantages in tropical environments, such as greater resistance to tropical diseases.[12]

What, then, might be the advantages of light-colored skin? Presumably, there must be some benefits in some environments; otherwise, all human populations would tend to have relatively dark skin. Although light-skinned people are more susceptible to sunburn and skin cancers, the ultraviolet radiation that light skin absorbs also facilitates the body's production of vitamin D. Vitamin D helps the body incorporate calcium and thus is necessary for the proper growth and maintenance of bones. Too much vitamin D, however, can cause illness. Thus, the light-colored skin of people in temperate latitudes maximizes ultraviolet penetration, perhaps ensuring production of sufficient amounts of vitamin D for good health, whereas the darker skin of people in tropical latitudes minimizes ultraviolet penetration, perhaps thereby preventing illness from too much vitamin D.[13] Light skin may also confer another advantage in colder environments: It is less likely to be damaged by frostbite.[14]

We now have direct evidence that confirms the connection between solar radiation and skin pigmentation. Anthropologists Nina Jablonski and George Chaplin used data from NASA satellites to determine the average amount of ultraviolet radiation people were exposed to in different parts of the world. They compared these average radiation amounts to data on skin reflectance (the lighter one's skin, the more light it reflects) and found that dark skin is more prevalent where ultraviolet radiation is more intense. Interestingly, there seems to be one notable exception—Native Americans tend to be lighter-skinned than expected. Jablonski and Chaplin suggest this is because they are recent migrants to the New World, and their skin colors have not adapted to the varying levels of ultraviolet radiation they encountered in the Americas, just as the skin colors of European colonizers have not.[15]

ADAPTATION TO HIGH ALTITUDE

Oxygen constitutes 21 percent of the air we breathe at sea level. At high altitudes, the percentage of oxygen in the air is the same, but because the barometric pressure is lower, we take in less oxygen with each breath.[16] We breathe more rapidly, our hearts beat faster, and all activity is more difficult. The net effects are discomfort and a condition known as **hypoxia,** or oxygen deficiency.

If high altitude presents such difficulties for many human beings, how is it that populations numbering in the millions can live out their lives, healthy and productive, at altitudes of 6,000, 12,000, or even 17,000 feet? Populations in the Himalayas and the Andes have adapted to their environments and do not display the symptoms suffered by low-altitude dwellers when they are exposed to high alti-

tudes. Moreover, high-altitude dwellers have come to terms physiologically with extreme cold, deficient nutrition, strong winds, rough countryside, and intense solar radiation.[17]

Early studies of Andean high-altitude dwellers found that they differed in certain physical ways from low-altitude dwellers. Compared with low-altitude dwellers, high-altitude Andean Indians had larger chests and greater lung capacity, as well as more surface area in the capillaries of the lungs (which was believed to facilitate the transfer of oxygen to the blood).[18] Early researchers thought that genetic changes had allowed the Andeans to maximize their ability to take in oxygen at the lower barometric pressure of their high-altitude environment. Recent research, however, has cast some doubt on this conclusion. It appears now that other populations living at high altitudes do not show the Andean pattern of physical differences. In the Himalayas, for example, low-altitude dwellers and high-altitude dwellers do not differ in chest size or lung size, even though both groups show adequate lung functioning.[19]

Thus, current research does not suggest that high-altitude living requires biological adaptations that are purely genetic. In fact, some evidence suggests that humans who grow up in a high-altitude environment may adapt to hypoxia during their lifetimes, as they mature. For example, Peruvians who were born at sea level but who grew up at high altitudes developed the same amount of lung capacity as people who spent their entire lives at high altitudes.[20] Consistent with a presumed environmental effect, the children of high-altitude Peruvians who grow up in the lowlands do not develop larger chests. What appeared to earlier researchers to be a genetic adaptation among highland Andean populations appears in fact to be an acclimatization that develops early in childhood and persists for the lifetime of an individual. As with other traits that have been studied, it appears that life experiences can have profound effects on how the body grows.

Highland Andean peoples have larger chests and greater lung capacity than people living at low altitude. These differences are thought to be acclimatizations to life at high altitude and the problem of hypoxia, or oxygen deficiency.

HEIGHT

Studies of identical twins and comparisons of the height of parents and children suggest that heredity plays a considerable role in determining height,[21] so genetic differences must at least partly explain differences between populations in average height. But if average height can increase dramatically in a few decades, as in Japan between 1950 and 1980 and in many other countries in recent times,[22] then environmental influences are also likely to be important.

The considerable variation in average height among human populations may be partly explained by temperature differences. The Dutch, in Europe, are among the tallest populations in the world on average, and the Mbuti of Zaire, in central Africa, are among the shortest.[23] We already know that weight is related to mean annual temperature (Bergmann's rule). Weight is also related to height (taller people are likely to be heavier). So, since the taller (heavier) Dutch live in a cooler climate, some of the population variation in height would appear to involve adaptation to heat and cold.[24] Other factors must also be operating, however, because tall and short peoples can be found in most areas of the world.

Many researchers think that poor nutrition and disease lead to reduced height and weight. In many parts of the world, children in higher social classes are taller on the average than children in lower social classes,[25] and this difference is more marked in economically poorer countries,[26] where the wealth and health differences between the classes are particularly large. During times of war and poor nutrition, children's stature often decreases. For example, in Germany during World War II, the stature of children 7 to 17 years of age declined as compared with previous time periods, despite the fact that stature had generally increased over time.[27]

More persuasive evidence for the effects of poor nutrition and disease comes out of longitudinal studies of the same individuals over time. For example, Reynaldo Martorell found that children in Guatemala who had frequent bouts of diarrhea were on the average over an inch shorter at age 7 than children without frequent diarrhea.[28] Although malnourished or diseased children can catch up in their growth, follow-up research on Guatemalan children suggests that if stunting occurs before 3 years of age, stature at age 18 will still be reduced.[29]

A controversial set of studies links a very different environmental factor to variation in height in human populations. The factor at issue is stress, physical and emotional, in infancy.[30] Contrary to the view that any kind of stress is harmful, it appears that some presumably stressful experiences in infancy are associated with greater height and weight. Experimental studies with rats provided the original stimulus for the studies investigating the possible effect of stress on height. The experiments showed that rats that were physically handled ("petted") by the experimenters grew to be longer and heavier than rats not petted. Researchers originally thought that this was because the petted rats had received "tender loving care." But someone noticed that the petted rats seemed terrified (they urinated and defecated) when petted by humans, which suggested that the petting might have been stressful. It turned out in subsequent studies that even more obviously stressful experiences such as electric shock, vibration, and temperature extremes also produced rats with longer skeletons as compared with unstressed rats.

Thomas Landauer and John Whiting thought that stress in human infants might similarly produce greater adult height. Many cultures have customs for treating infants that could be physically stressful, including circumcision, branding of the skin with sharp objects, piercing the nose, ears, or lips for the insertion of ornaments, molding and stretching the head and limbs for cosmetic purposes, and vaccination. In addition, Shulamith Gunders and John Whiting suggested that separating the baby from its mother right after birth is another kind of stress. In cross-cultural comparisons by Whiting and his colleagues,[31] it seems that *both* physical stress and mother-infant separation, *if practiced before 2 years of age,* predict greater adult height; males are on the average 2 inches taller in such societies. (It is important to note that the stresses being discussed are short in duration, often a one-time occurrence, and do not constitute

In recent times there has been a dramatic increase in average height, which may be due to one or more environmental factors. Here we see a Chinese American girl who is taller than her mother and almost as tall as her father.

RESEARCH FRONTIERS
Factors Affecting Fecundity

Fertility—that is, how many children women have—ranges widely from one human population to another. There are places where it is not uncommon for women to have ten or more children; there are others where the norm is less than two. Until relatively recently, it was assumed that the variation was due entirely to social and cultural factors—the later people marry, the less sex couples have, and the more they practice contraception, the fewer babies should be born. It was also assumed that if people did not exert restraint, fertility would naturally be very high. But now researchers are considering it likely that variation in human fertility may also be due to physiological factors. In other words, human *fecundity*—the physiological capacity to have offspring—may also vary in different populations.

In the chapter on the origins of food production we discussed how breast-feeding can affect fecundity. The physiological mechanisms are not yet fully understood, but we know that nursing somehow impedes the resumption of ovulation and hence increases the interval between births. We are also now beginning to understand the effects of nutrition and activity on fecundity, of individuals as well as populations. It appears that insufficient caloric intake—when activity increases dramatically but the diet remains the same, or when the amount of food consumed drops considerably—reduces the capacity to conceive and carry a baby to successful birth. But why should this be? Reproduction requires a substantial amount of extra energy. Since a mother may not survive a pregnancy or birth if she loses too many calories or nutrients to the fetus, natural selection should favor mechanisms that turn off reproductive capacity if a mother, fetus, or both have a reduced chance to survive. Insufficient caloric intake should activate such mechanisms.

To investigate the possible effects of nutrition and activity on fecundity, researchers need to measure reproductive potential (the likelihood of successful pregnancy). Lack of menstruation for months in the absence of pregnancy is a clear sign that a woman is not ovulating, but the presence of menstrual periods by itself does not indicate a high likelihood of successful pregnancy. A better indicator of the likelihood of successful pregnancy is a measure of the rise in levels of progesterone in the second half of the menstrual cycle: The more progesterone levels rise after ovulation, the more likely a fertilized egg will be viable. In the past, researchers had to rely on expensive and intrusive blood tests to measure progesterone levels, but now researchers have

---

prolonged stress or abuse, which can have opposite effects.)

Because the cross-cultural evidence is associational, not experimental, it is possible that the results are due to some factor confounded with infant stress. Perhaps societies with infant stress have better nutrition or have climates that favor tallness. Recently, using new cross-cultural comparisons, J. Patrick Gray and Linda Wolfe attempted to assess possible predictors of height differences between populations. The predictors compared were nutrition, climate, geography, physical stress, and mother-infant separation. Gray and Wolfe's analysis indicated which of those factors predicted adult height independently of the others. It turned out that geographic region, climatic zone, and customs of infant stress were all significant independent predictors of height.[32] So the results now available clearly show that the effect of infant stress cannot be discounted.

Persuasive evidence for the stress hypothesis also comes from an experimental study conducted in Kenya.[33] Landauer and Whiting arranged for a randomly selected sample of children to be vaccinated before they were 2 years old. Other children were vaccinated soon after they were 2. A few years later the two groups were compared with respect to height. Consistent with the cross-cultural evidence on the possible effect of stress on height, the children vaccinated before the age of 2 were significantly taller than the children vaccinated later. The children vaccinated before the age of 2 were selected randomly for early vaccination, so it is unlikely that nutritional or other differences between the two groups account for their differences in height.

As we noted earlier, in several areas of the world, people have been getting taller. What accounts for this recent trend toward greater height? Several factors may be involved. Some researchers think that it may be the result of

tests that can evaluate progesterone levels from saliva samples.

Research on women in industrial societies who engage in strenuous exercise (athletes and ballet dancers) has shown that such women are less likely to menstruate and therefore are less likely to ovulate than are less active women. With saliva tests, researchers can assess the effects of moderate levels of exercise and diet on reproductive potential, even in women who are menstruating. So, for example, researchers have discovered that women of normal weight who jog for recreation or go on moderate diets have lower levels of progesterone than do women who don't exercise or diet. Therefore the chances to give birth successfully are reduced for joggers and dieters.

We also have studies of ovarian function in nonindustrial societies. One study, among the Tamang of Nepal by Catherine Panter-Brick, Deborah Lotstein, and Peter Ellison, has documented that during the monsoon season when women work hard

at agriculture, many women lose weight and show evidence of reduced reproductive function. Nadine Peacock and Robert Bailey found that Lese women of Zaire tended to lose weight particularly during the later part of the "hungry" season (April, May, and June) before the new crops come in. The Lese had significantly fewer births nine months after the later part of the "hungry" season (January, February, March), suggesting that malnutrition reduces reproductive function. It is possible that the decline in reproduction was due to changes in behavior, such as avoidance of sex during the "hungry" months, but Peter Ellison's study of progesterone levels confirmed that it was nutrition that affected reproductive function—80 percent of the Lese women ovulated in April (a less "hungry" month), but only 65 percent ovulated in June (a more "hungry" month).

Much still needs to be studied, but the available research suggests that reproduction is finely tuned to the needs of the nursing

baby and to the caloric surpluses available to the mother. Voluntary behavior such as avoidance, abstinence, or contraception can reduce fertility. But fecundity can be reduced by physiological changes that occur in response to breast-feeding, exercise, and nutritional deficiency. These conditions can vary considerably from individual to individual and from one population to another, and hence reproductive function and fecundity also vary.

Sources: Peter T. Ellison, "Natural Variation in Human Fecundity," in Peter N. Peregrine, Carol R. Ember, and Melvin Ember, eds., *Physical Anthropology: Original Readings in Method and Practice* (Upper Saddle River, NJ: Prentice Hall, 2002); Catherine Panter-Brick, Deborah S. Lotstein, and Peter T. Ellison, "Seasonality of Reproductive Function and Weight Loss in Rural Nepali Women," *Human Reproduction,* 8 (1993): 684–90; Nadine Peacock and Robert Bailey, "Efe: Investigating Food and Fertility in the Ituri Forest," in Melvin Ember, Carol R. Ember, and David Levinson, eds., *Portraits of Culture: Ethnographic Originals* (Upper Saddle River, NJ: Prentice Hall, 1998). Prentice Hall/Simon & Schuster Custom Publishing.

improved nutrition and lower incidence of infectious diseases.[34] But it might also be that infant stress has increased as a result of giving birth in hospitals, which usually separate babies from mothers and also subject the newborns to medical tests, including the taking of blood. And various kinds of vaccinations have also become more common in infancy.[35]

In short, differences in human size seem to be the result of both adaptations and acclimatizations, with both of these, in turn, affected by cultural factors such as nutrition and stress. Human variation seems usually to be the result of several factors, not always genetic.

SUSCEPTIBILITY TO INFECTIOUS DISEASES

Certain populations seem to have developed inherited resistances to particular infectious diseases. That is, populations repeatedly decimated by certain diseases in the past

now have a high frequency of genetic characteristics that ameliorate the effects of these diseases. As Arno Motulsky pointed out, if there are genes that protect people from dying when they are infected by one of the diseases prevalent in their area, these genes will tend to become more common in succeeding generations.[36]

A field study of the infectious disease myxomatosis in rabbits supports this theory. When the virus responsible for the disease was first introduced into the Australian rabbit population, more than 95 percent of the infected animals died. But among the offspring of animals exposed to successive epidemics of myxomatosis, the percentage of animals that died from the disease decreased from year to year. The more epidemics the animals' ancestors had lived through, the smaller the percentage of current animals that died of the disease. Thus, the data suggested that the rabbits had developed a genetic resistance to myxomatosis.[37]

Infectious diseases seem to follow a similar pattern among human populations. When tuberculosis first strikes a population that has had no previous contact with it, the disease is usually fatal. But some populations seem to have inherited a resistance to death from tuberculosis. For example, the Ashkenazi Jews in America (those whose ancestors came from central and eastern Europe) are one of several populations whose ancestors survived many years of exposure to tuberculosis in the crowded European ghettos where they had previously lived. Although the rate of tuberculosis infection is identical among American Jews and non-Jews, the rate of tuberculosis mortality is significantly lower among Jews than among non-Jews in the United States.[38] After reviewing other data on this subject, Motulsky thought it likely "that the present relatively high resistance of Western populations to tuberculosis is genetically conditioned through natural selection during long contact with the disease."[39]

We tend to think of measles as a childhood disease that kills virtually no one, and we now have a vaccine against it. But when first introduced into populations, the measles virus can kill large numbers of people. In 1949, the Tupari Indians of Brazil numbered about 200 people. By 1955, two-thirds of the Tupari had died of measles, introduced into the tribe by rubber gatherers in the area.[40] Large numbers of people died of measles in epidemics in the Faeroe Islands in 1846, in Hawaii in 1848, in the Fiji Islands in 1874, and among the Canadian Inuit very recently. It is possible that where mortality rates from measles are low, populations have acquired a genetic resistance to death from this disease.[41]

But why is a population susceptible to a disease in the first place? The epidemiologist Francis Black suggests that lack of genes for resistance is not the whole answer. A high degree of genetic homogeneity in the population may also increase susceptibility.[42] A virus grown in one host is preadapted to a genetically similar new host and is therefore likely to be more virulent in the new host. For exam-

ple, the measles virus adapts to a host individual; when it replicates, the forms that the host cannot kill are those most likely to survive and continue replicating. When the virus passes to a new host with similar genes, the preadapted virus is likely to kill the new host. If, on the other hand, the next host is very different genetically, the adaptation process starts over again; the virus is not so virulent at first because the host can kill it.

Populations that recently came to an area, and that had a small group of founders (as was probably true for the first Native Americans and the Polynesian seafarers who first settled many islands in the Pacific), tended to have a high degree of genetic homogeneity. Therefore, epidemic diseases introduced by Europeans (such as measles) would be likely to kill many of the natives within the first few years after contact. It is estimated that 56 million people died in the New World after contact with Europeans, mostly because of introduced diseases such as smallpox and measles. Similarly caused depopulation occurred widely in the Pacific.[43]

Some researchers suggest that nongenetic factors may also partly explain differential resistance to infectious disease. For example, cultural practices may partly explain the epidemics of measles among the Yanomamö Indians of Venezuela and Brazil. The Yanomamö frequently visit other villages, and that, together with the nonisolation of sick individuals, promoted a very rapid spread of the disease. Because many individuals were sick at the same time, there were not enough healthy people to feed and care for the sick; mothers down with measles could not even nurse their babies. Thus, cultural factors may increase exposure to a disease and worsen its effect on a population.[44]

Epidemics of infectious disease may occur only if many people live near each other. Food collectors, who usually live in small dispersed bands, do not have enough people in and near the community to keep an epidemic going. Without enough people to infect, short-lived microorganisms that cause or carry diseases die out. In contrast,

Permanent settlements and high population densities allow diseases to spread rapidly and produce epidemics.

among agriculturalists, there are larger numbers of people in and around the community to whom a disease can spread. Permanent settlements, particularly urban settlements, also are likely to have poor sanitation and contaminated water.[45] Tuberculosis is an example of an infectious disease that, although very old, began to kill large numbers of people only after the emergence of sedentary, larger communities.[46]

SICKLE-CELL ANEMIA

Another biological variation is an abnormality of the red blood cells known as **sickle-cell anemia,** or **sicklemia.** This is a condition in which normal, disk-shaped red blood cells assume a crescent (sickle) shape when deprived of oxygen. The sickle-shaped red blood cells do not move through the body as readily as normal cells, and thus cause more oxygen deficiency and damage to the heart, lungs, brain, and other vital organs. In addition, the red blood cells tend to "die" more rapidly, and the anemia worsens still more.[47]

Sickle-cell anemia is caused by a variant form of the genetic instructions for hemoglobin, the protein that carries oxygen in the red blood cells.[48] Individuals who have sickle-cell anemia have inherited the same allele (Hb^S) from both parents and are therefore homozygous for that gene. Individuals who receive this allele from only one parent are heterozygous; they have one Hb^S allele and one allele for normal hemoglobin (Hb^A). Heterozygotes generally will not show the full-blown symptoms of sickle-cell disease, although in some cases a heterozygous individual may have a mild case of anemia. A heterozygous person has a 50 percent chance of passing on the sickle-cell allele to a child. And if the child later mates with another person who is also a carrier of the sickle-cell allele, the statistical probability is that 25 percent of their children will develop sickle-cell anemia. Without advanced medical care, most individuals with two Hb^S alleles are unlikely to live more than a few years.[49]

Why has the allele for sickle-cell persisted in various populations? If people with sickle-cell anemia do not usually live to reproduce, we would expect a reduction in the frequency of Hb^S to near zero through the process of *normalizing selection.* But the sickle-cell allele occurs fairly often in some parts of the world, particularly in the wet tropical belt of Africa, where frequencies may be between 20 and 30 percent, and in Greece, Sicily, and southern India.[50]

Because the sickle-cell gene occurs in these places much more often than expected, researchers in the 1940s and the 1950s began to suspect that heterozygous individuals (who carry one Hb^S allele) might have a reproductive advantage in a malarial environment.[51] If the heterozygotes were more resistant to attacks of malaria than the homozygotes for normal hemoglobin (who get the Hb^A allele from both parents), the heterozygotes would be more likely to survive and reproduce, and therefore the recessive Hb^S allele would persist at a higher than expected frequency in the population. This kind of outcome is an example of *balancing selection.*[52]

A number of pieces of evidence support the "malaria theory." First, geographic comparisons show that the sickle-cell allele tends to be found where the incidence of malaria is high (see Figure 13–3). Second, as land in the tropics is opened to yam and rice agriculture, the incidence of the sickle-cell allele also increases. The reason seems to be that malaria, carried principally by the *Anopheles gambiae* mosquito, becomes more prevalent as tropical forest gives way to more open land where mosquitoes can thrive in warm, sunlit ponds. Indeed, even among peoples of similar cultural backgrounds, the incidence of the sickle-cell allele increases with greater rainfall and surpluses of water. Third, children who are heterozygous for the sickle-cell trait tend to have fewer malarial parasites in their bodies than do homozygous normal individuals, and they are more likely to survive.[53] The sickling trait does not necessarily keep people from contracting malaria, but it greatly decreases the rate of mortality from malaria—and in evolutionary terms, the overall effect is the same.[54] Fourth, if there is no balancing selection because malaria is no longer present, we should find a rapid decline in the incidence of the sickle-cell allele. Indeed, we find such a decline in populations with African ancestry. Those who live in malaria-free zones of the New World have a much lower incidence of sicklemia than do those who live in malarial regions of the New World.[55]

Hb^S is not the only abnormal hemoglobin to have a distribution related to malaria. It seems that a number of abnormal hemoglobins may be widespread because of the advantage heterozygotes have against the disease. For example, another abnormal hemoglobin, Hb^E, occurs in populations from India through Southeast Asia and New Guinea where malaria occurs, but Hb^S is not that common. Why should Hb^E heterozygotes have resistance to malaria? One possibility is that malarial parasites are less able to survive in an individual's blood with some normal and some abnormal hemoglobin. Abnormal hemoglobin cells are more delicate and live less long, so they may not readily support malarial parasites.[56]

LACTASE DEFICIENCY

When American educators discovered that African American schoolchildren very often did not drink milk, they assumed that lack of money or education was the reason. These assumptions provided the impetus for establishing the school milk programs prevalent around the country. However, it now appears that after infancy many people lack an enzyme, lactase I, that is necessary for breaking down the sugar in milk, lactose, into simpler sugars that can be absorbed into the bloodstream.[57] Thus, a person without lactase cannot digest milk properly, and drinking it may cause bloating, cramps, stomach gas, and diarrhea. A study conducted in Baltimore among 312 "black" and

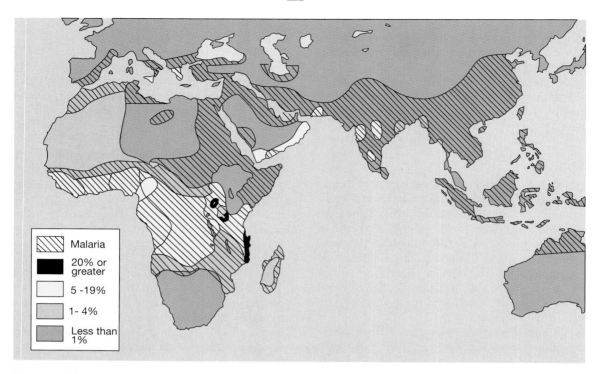

Figure 13–3 *Geographic Distribution of Sicklemia and Its Relationship to the Distribution of Malaria*

Source: From John Buettner-Janusch, *Physical Anthropology: A Perspective.* © 1973 by John Wiley & Sons, Inc. Reprinted by permission of John Wiley & Sons, Inc.

221 "white" children in grades 1 through 6 in two elementary schools indicated that 85 percent of the "black" children and 17 percent of the "white" children were milk-intolerant.[58]

More recent studies indicate that lactose intolerance occurs frequently in adults in many parts of the world.[59] The condition is common in Southeast and East Asia, India, the Mediterranean and the Near East, sub-Saharan Africa, and among Native North and South Americans. The widespread incidence of lactose intolerance should not be surprising. After infancy, mammals normally stop producing lactase.[60]

If lactose intolerance in adulthood in mammals is normal, we need to understand why only some human populations have the ability to make lactase I in adulthood and digest lactose. Why would selection favor this genetic ability in some populations but not in others? In the late 1960s, F. J. Simoons and Robert McCracken noted a relationship between lactose absorption and dairying (raising cows for milk). They suggested that with the advent of dairying, individuals with the genetic ability to produce lactase in adulthood would have greater reproductive success, and hence dairying populations would come to have a high proportion of individuals with the ability to break down lactose.[61]

But people in some dairying societies do not produce lactase in adulthood. Rather, they seem to have developed a cultural solution to the problem of lactase deficiency; they transform their milk into cheese, yogurt, sour cream, and other milk products that are low in lactose. To make these low-lactose products, people separate the lactose-rich whey from the curds or treat the milk with a bacterium (*Lactobacillus*) that breaks down the lactose, thus making the milk product digestible by a lactase-deficient person.[62]

So why in some dairying societies did natural selection favor a biological solution (the production in adulthood of the enzyme lactase) rather than the cultural solution? William Durham has collected evidence that natural selection may favor the biological solution in dairying societies farther from the equator. The theory is that lactose behaves biochemically like vitamin D, facilitating the absorption of calcium—but only in people who produce lactase so that they can absorb the lactose. Because people in more temperate latitudes are not exposed to that much sunlight, particularly in the winter, and therefore make less vitamin D in their skin, natural selection may have favored the lactase way of absorbing dietary calcium.[63] In other words, natural selection may favor lactase production in adulthood, as well as lighter skin, at higher latitudes (where there is less sunlight).

This is an example of how culture may influence the

(Top) Milking a cow in Barnstable, Massachusetts. Natural selection may favor production of the enzyme lactase, a genetic way of making milk digestible in dairying populations far from the equator. (Bottom) A Masai woman milking a cow in Kenya. Natural selection may favor the souring of milk, a cultural way of making it digestible in dairying populations close to the equator.

way natural selection favors some genes over others. Without dairying, natural selection may not have favored the genetic propensity to produce lactase. This propensity is yet another example of the complex ways in which genes, environment, and culture interact to create human variation.

 Race and Racism

Fortunately, internal variations such as lactase deficiency have never been associated with intergroup tensions—perhaps because such differences are not immediately obvious. Unfortunately, the same cannot be said for some of the more obvious external human differences such as skin color.

For as long as any of us can remember, countless aggressive actions—from fistfights to large-scale riots and civil wars—have stemmed from tensions and misunderstandings between various groups commonly referred to by many as races. *Race* has become such a common term that most of us take the concept for granted, not bothering to consider what it does, and does not, mean. We may talk about the "human race," which means that all humans belong to the same breeding population. Yet we are often asked to check a box to identify our particular "race." We discuss first how biologists sometimes use the term *race;* then we turn to why many biological anthropologists and others now conclude that the concept of race does not usefully apply to humans. We discuss how racial classifications are largely social constructions that have been used to justify discrimination, exploitation and even the extermination of certain categories of people.

RACE AS A CONSTRUCT IN BIOLOGY

Biological variation is not uniformly distributed in any species. While all members of a species can potentially interbreed with others, most matings take place within smaller groups or breeding populations. Through the processes of natural selection and genetic drift, populations inhabiting different geographic regions will exhibit some differences in biological traits. When differences within a species become sufficiently noticeable, biologists may classify different populations into different *varieties,* or **races.** If the term *race* is understood to be just a shorthand or classificatory way that biologists describe slight population variants within a species, the concept of race would probably not be controversial. Unfortunately, as applied to humans, racial classifications have often been confounded with **racism,** the belief that some races are innately inferior to others. The misuse and misunderstanding of the term *race* and its association with racist thinking is one reason why many biological anthropologists and others have suggested that the term should not be applied to human biological differences.

A second reason for not applying racial classification to humans is that humans have exhibited so much interbreeding that different populations are not clearly classifiable into discrete groups that can be defined in terms of the presence or absence of particular biological traits.[64] Therefore, many argue that race is not scientifically useful for describing human biological variation. The difficulty

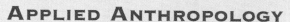

APPLIED ANTHROPOLOGY

Disparities in Death: African Americans Compared with European Americans

Everyone dies of something. Yet, if you consider cardiovascular disease, the leading cause of death in the United States, it turns out that after controlling for the effects of age and gender, African Americans die more often from that disease than European Americans. The same kind of disparity occurs also with almost every other major cause of death—cancer, cirrhosis of the liver, diabetes, injuries, infant mortality, and homicide. Medical anthropologists and health policy researchers want to know why. Without such understanding, it is hard to know how to reduce the disparity.

One reason may be subtle discrimination by the medical profession itself. For example, a European American with chest pain in the United States is more likely than an African American to be

given an angiogram, a medical procedure that injects radioactive dye into the heart to look for deficits in blood flow through the coronary arteries that supply blood to the heart. And even if coronary heart disease is detected by an angiogram, an African American is less likely to receive bypass surgery. Thus, the death rate from cardiovascular disease may be higher for African Americans than for European Americans because of unequal medical care.

Yet, while some difference in mortality may be due to disparity in medical treatment, this could only be part of the picture. African Americans may be more prone to cardiovascular disease because they are about twice as likely as European Americans to have high rates of hypertension (high blood pressure). But why

the disparity in hypertension? Three possible explanations, not mutually exclusive, are discussed in the research literature. The first is a possible difference in genetics. The second is a difference in life-style. The third is class difference.

Most of the Africans that came to the Americas were forcibly taken as slaves between the sixteenth and nineteenth centuries, largely from West Africa. In one comparative study of hypertension, African Americans had much higher blood pressure than Africans in Nigeria and the Cameroon, even in urban areas. People with African ancestry in the Caribbean were in the middle of the range. Life-style differences were also vast— the West Africans had plenty of exercise, were lean, and had low-fat and low-salt diets. Any possi-

---

in employing racial classification is evident by comparing the number of races that classifiers come up with. The number of racial categories has varied from as few as 3 to more than 37.[65]

How can groups be clearly divided into races if most adaptive biological traits show clinal or gradual differences from one region to another?[66] Skin color is a good example of clinal variation. In the area around Egypt, there is a gradient of skin color as one moves from north to south in the Nile Valley. Skin generally becomes darker closer to the equator (south) and lighter closer to the Mediterranean. But other adaptive traits may not have north-south clines, because the environmental predictors may be distributed differently. Nose shape varies with humidity, but clines in humidity do not particularly correspond to variation in latitude. So the gradient for skin color would not be the same as the gradient for nose shape. Because adaptive traits tend to be clinally distributed, there is no line you could draw on a world map that would separate "white" from "black" people or "whites" from "Asians."[67] Only traits that are neutral in terms of

natural selection will tend (because of genetic drift) to cluster in regions.[68]

Racial classification is problematic also because there is sometimes more physical, physiological, and genetic diversity *within* a single geographic group that might be called a race (e.g., Africans) than there is *between* supposed racial groups. Africans vary more among themselves than they do in comparison with people elsewhere.[69]

RACE AS A SOCIAL CATEGORY

If race, in the opinion of many biological anthropologists, is not a useful device for classifying humans, why is it so widely used? Racial classifications should be recognized for what they mostly are—social categories to which individuals are assigned, by themselves and others, on the basis of supposedly shared biological traits.[70]

If racial categories are mostly just social categories, we need to ask why they were invented. Part of the answer may be a desire to separate "my" group from others. Peo-

ble difference in genes would seem to be insignificant. Jared Diamond has suggested that individuals who could retain salt would have been most likely to survive the terrible conditions of the sailing ships that brought slaves to the New World. Many died on those voyages from diarrhea and dehydration (salt-depleting conditions). Retention of salt would have been a genetic advantage then, but disadvantageous in places such as the United States with high-salt, high-fat diets. Critics of this theory suggest that salt-depleting diseases were not the leading causes of death in the slave voyages; tuberculosis and violence were more frequent causes of death. Furthermore, critics say that the slave-ship theory would predict little genetic diversity in African American populations with respect to hypertension, but in fact there is great diversity.

Hypertension could be related also to differences in life-style and wealth. African Americans in the United States are disproportionately poorer. Study after study has noted that healthier life-style habits are generally correlated with higher positions on the socioeconomic ladder. Moreover, individuals from higher social positions are more likely to have health insurance and access to care in superior hospitals. But even after correcting for factors such as obesity, physical activity, and social class, the health differential persists—African Americans still have a much higher incidence of hypertension than European Americans.

William Dressler suggests that stress is another possible cause of higher rates of hypertension. Despite increased economic mobility in recent years, African Americans are still subject to prejudice and may consequently have more stress even if they have higher income. Stress is related to higher blood pressure. In a color-conscious society, a very dark-skinned individual walking in a wealthy neighborhood at night may be thought not to live there and may be stopped by the police. If Dressler is correct, darker-skinned African Americans who have objective indicators of higher status should have much higher blood pressure than would be expected from their relative education, age, body mass, or social class alone. And that seems to be true. Racism may affect health.

Sources: William W. Dressler, "Health in the African American Community: Accounting for Health Inequalities," *Medical Anthropological Quarterly*, 7 (1993): 325–45; Richard S. Cooper, Charles N. Rotimi, and Ryk Ward, "The Puzzle of Hypertension in African-Americans," *Scientific American*, February 1999, 56–63; Jared Diamond, "The Saltshakers' Curse—Physiological Adaptations That Helped American Blacks Survive Slavery May Now Be Predisposing Their Descendants to Hypertension," *Natural History* (10), October 1991.

ple tend to be ethnocentric, to view their culture as better than other cultures. We suggested that ethnocentrism has deep roots in our primate heritage, particularly the importance of family relations and social interactions in primate societies. Racial classifications may reflect the same tendency to divide "us" from "them," except that the divisions are supposedly based on biological differences.[71]

It is interesting to note that the features commonly used to classify races—skin color, hair form, nose and eye shape—are all surface facial features. No one has ever based a racial classification on the color or shape of the liver, or on the number of alveolar sacs in the lungs. Why not? Because those variations cannot be seen. People employ the concept of race to classify others quickly on the basis of readily visible features.[72] Race is a shorthand we use to categorize individuals as "us" or "them." Again, this seems to have strong links to our primate heritage. Primates are much more reliant on facial communication than most other mammals. Primates tend to have more muscles controlling the face than other mammals, and use them mainly for communicative gestures. A concern with race may be an extension of this basic primate focus on the face and facial features in communication.

We do know that racial classifications have often been, and still are, used by certain groups to justify discrimination, exploitation, or genocide. The "Aryan race" was supposed to be the group of blond-haired, blue-eyed, white-skinned people whom Adolf Hitler wanted to dominate the world, to which end he and others attempted to destroy as many members of the Jewish "race" as they could. (It is estimated that 6 million Jews and others were murdered in what is now called the Holocaust.[73]) But who are the Aryans? Technically, Aryans are any people, including the German-speaking Jews in Hitler's Germany, who speak one of the Indo-European languages. The Indo-European languages include such disparate modern tongues as Greek, Spanish, Hindi, Polish, French, Icelandic, German, Gaelic, and English. And many Aryans speaking these languages have neither blond hair nor blue eyes. Similarly, all kinds of people may be Jews, whether or not they descend from the ancient Near Eastern population that spoke the Hebrew language. There are light-skinned Danish Jews and darker Jewish Arabs. One of the most orthodox Jewish groups in the United States is based in New York City and is composed entirely of African Americans.

The arbitrary and social basis of most racial classifications becomes apparent when you compare how they differ from one place to another. Consider, for example, what used to be thought about the races in South Africa. Under apartheid, the system of racial segregation and discrimination, someone with mixed "white" and "black" ancestry was considered "colored." However, when important people of African ancestry from other countries would visit South Africa, they were often considered "white." Chinese were considered "Asian"; but the Japanese, who were important economically to South Africa, were considered "white."[74] In some parts of the United States, laws against interracial marriage continued in force through the 1960s. You would be considered a "negro" if you had an eighth or more "negro" ancestry (if one or more of your eight grandparents were "negro"). So only a small amount of "negro" ancestry made a person "negro," but a small amount of "white" ancestry did not make a person "white." Biologically speaking, this makes no sense, but socially it was another story.[75]

THE MYTHS OF RACISM

RACE AND CIVILIZATION Many persons hold the racist viewpoint that the biological inferiority of certain groups, which they call "races," is reflected in the supposedly "primitive" quality of their cultures. They will argue that the "developed" nations are "white" and the "underdeveloped" nations are not. (We put terms like "white," which are used as racial categories, in quotes to indicate the problematic nature of the categories.) But to make such an argument ignores much of history. Many of today's so-called underdeveloped nations—primarily in Asia, Africa, and South America—had developed complex

and sophisticated civilizations long before European nations expanded and acquired considerable power. The advanced societies of the Shang dynasty in China, the Mayans in Mesoamerica, and the African empire of Ghana were all founded and developed by "nonwhites."

Between 1523 and 1028 B.C., China had a complex form of government, armies, metal tools and weapons, and production and storage facilities for large quantities of grain. The early Chinese civilization also had writing and elaborate religious rituals.[76] From A.D. 300 to 900, the Mayans were a large population with a thriving economy. They built many large and beautiful cities in which were centered great pyramids and luxurious palaces.[77] According to legend, the West African civilization of Ghana was founded during the second century A.D. By A.D. 770, the time of the Sonniki rulers, Ghana had developed two capital cities—one Muslim and the other non-Muslim—each with its own ruler and both supported largely by Ghana's lucrative gold market.[78]

Considering how recently northern Europeans developed cities and central governments, it seems odd that some "whites" should label Africans, Native Americans, and others backward in terms of historical achievement, or biologically inferior in terms of capacity for civilization. But racists, both "white" and "nonwhite," choose to ignore the fact that many populations have achieved remarkable advances in civilization. Most significant, racists refuse to believe that they can acknowledge the achievements of another group without in any way downgrading the achievements of their own.

RACE, CONQUEST, AND THE ROLE OF INFECTIOUS DISEASE There are those who would argue that Europeans' superiority accounted for their ability to colonize much of the world during the last few hundred years. But it now appears that Europeans were able to dominate at least partly because many native peoples were susceptible to diseases brought by the Europeans.[79] Earlier, we discussed how continued exposure to epidemics of in-

The massive stone walls of Great Zimbabwe in southeast Africa, which date from the twelfth century to the fifteenth century, are evidence of a complex culture at a time when Europe was still in the Dark Ages.

fectious diseases, such as tuberculosis and measles, can cause succeeding generations to acquire a genetic resistance to death from such diseases. Smallpox had a long history in Europe and Africa; genetic resistance eventually made it mostly a survivable childhood disease. But in the New World it was quite another story. Cortez and the conquistadores were inadvertently aided by smallpox in their attempt to defeat the Aztecs of Mexico. In 1520, a member of Cortez's army unwittingly transmitted smallpox to the natives. The disease spread rapidly, killing at least 50 percent of the population, and so the Aztecs were at a considerable disadvantage in their battling with the Spanish.[80]

Outbreaks of smallpox repeatedly decimated many Native American populations in North America a century or two later. In the early nineteenth century, the Massachusett and Narragansett Indians, with populations of 30,000 and 9,000, respectively, were reduced by smallpox to a few hundred members. Extremely high mortality rates were also noted among the Crow, the Blackfoot, and other Native American groups during the nineteenth century. The germ theory alone may not completely explain these epidemics; Europeans may have deliberately encouraged the spread of one new disease, smallpox, by purposely distributing infected blankets to the natives. Motulsky calls the spread of smallpox "one of the first examples of biological warfare."[81]

RACE AND BEHAVIOR As an outgrowth of earlier attempts to show that inferior "races" have "primitive" cultures, some scholars have attempted to demonstrate behavioral differences between "races." One of the most active has been psychologist J. Philippe Rushton, whose 1995 book *Race, Evolution, and Behavior* purports to demonstrate behavioral differences between the "Negroid," "Caucasoid," and "Mongoloid" races in terms of sexual practices, parenting, social deviance, and family structure, among others.

Rushton argues that these behaviors have a genetic basis rooted in adaptations to particular environments. He suggests that "Negroids" are adapted to the warm environments of East Africa, where humans first evolved, through a reproductive strategy in which individuals have many offspring but put little energy into their children's upbringing and care. This strategy is known within evolutionary theory as *r-selected*, and is well documented among creatures such as fish, reptiles, and even some mammals (rabbits, for example).[82] Rushton further suggests that as humans left Africa they adapted to the "colder" climates of Asia by adopting a more *K-selected* reproductive strategy, which involves having few offspring but putting lots of energy into their upbringing and care. K-selected strategies are also well documented in the animal world, and it is interesting to note that apes are often presented as examples of highly K-selected species.[83]

The data Rushton uses to support his argument come almost entirely from modern nations, many with a history of racial discrimination (such as South Africa, Japan, and the United States). But if genetic differences in behavior

do exist among these three "races," differences that have their origins in the exodus of modern humans from Africa more than 100,000 years ago, then those differences should be apparent both between and among all the cultures of the world. That is, "Negroid" cultures should all share behaviors that are clearly different from "Caucasoid" cultures, "Caucasoid" cultures should all share behaviors that are different from "Mongoloid" cultures, and so on. Do such differences exist?

The authors of this text used information about the 186 cultures composing the Standard Cross-Cultural Sample to test whether Rushton's ideas hold up.[84] We examined 26 separate behaviors that Rushton predicted would differ among the races. Contrary to Rushton's predictions, most of them showed no differences between supposed "racial" groups. Only one of them showed the differences that Rushton predicted (frequency of homicide, which Rushton predicted would be higher among "Negroids" and lower among "Mongoloids" does indeed show this pattern), and five of them (sexual restraint, acceptance of rape, degree of political integration, level of social stratification, and level of technological specialization) demonstrated a pattern that was the *opposite* of what Rushton predicted. So Rushton's gross division of humans into these "races" does not generally predict variation in human behavior. His ideas appear plainly wrong and do not support the concept that it is scientifically useful to distinguish human "races."[85]

RACE AND INTELLIGENCE Attempts to document differences in intelligence among the so-called races have a fairly long history. One of the latest was a 1994 book, titled *The Bell Curve*, by Charles Murray and Richard Herrnstein (see the box "Differences in Average IQ Scores").

In the nineteenth century, European white supremacists tried to find scientific justification for what they felt was the genetically inherited mental inferiority of "blacks." They did this by measuring skulls. It was believed that the larger the skull, the greater the cranial capacity and the bigger (hence, also better) the brain. Although the skull-measuring mania quickly disappeared and is no longer considered seriously as a way to measure intelligence, other "facts" may be used to demonstrate the presumed intellectual superiority of "white" people—namely, statistics from intelligence tests.

The first large-scale intelligence testing in the United States began with our entry into World War I. Thousands of draftees were given the so-called Alpha and Beta IQ tests to determine military assignments. Later, psychologists arranged the test results according to the racial categories of "white" and "black" and found what they had expected—"blacks" scored consistently lower than "whites." This result was viewed as scientific proof of the innate intellectual inferiority of "blacks" and was used to justify further discrimination against them, both in and out of the army.[86]

Otto Klineberg's subsequent statistical analyses of IQ-test results demonstrated that "blacks" from northern

CURRENT ISSUES
Differences in Average IQ Scores—What Do They Mean?

In late 1994, a new book reignited controversy about the relationship between "race" and intelligence. Once again people thought they had evidence of African American "inferiority." But once again there were problems with the evidence. The book was *The Bell Curve*, by Richard Herrnstein and Charles Murray. It purported to show that the intelligence of an individual was largely inherited and unchangeable throughout the life span, that an individual's success was largely based on intelligence, and that African Americans were likely to remain at the bottom of society because they had less intelligence than European Americans. Herrnstein and Murray appealed to a lot of studies to buttress their argument. But their argument was still faulty.

If you look at the average scores on many standard intelligence tests, you might conclude, as racists have, that African Americans are less intelligent

than European Americans. The averages are different between the two groups; African Americans typically have lower scores. But what does this average difference mean? Herrnstein and Murray, like many before them, fail to distinguish between a measure, such as a particular IQ test, and what is supposedly being measured, intelligence. If a test only imperfectly measures what it purports to measure, lower average IQ scores merely mean lower scores on that particular IQ test; they do not necessarily reflect lower intelligence. There are many reasons why some smart people might not do well on particular kinds of IQ tests. For example, the way the tests are administered may affect performance, as may lack of familiarity with the format or the experiences and objects referred to. The test might also not measure particular kinds of intelligence such as social "smarts" and creativity.

If African Americans were re-

ally less intelligent, more than their average IQ scores would be lower. The whole frequency distribution of their individual scores should also be lower—they should have fewer geniuses and more retarded individuals. That is, the bell-shaped curve showing how their scores are distributed should range lower than the curve for other Americans, and African Americans should also have proportionately fewer scores at the very high end of the scale. But neither expectation is confirmed. According to research by Henry Grubb, the proportion of African Americans at the low end of the scale is not significantly different from the proportion of European Americans. And Grubb and Andrea Barthwell report that, on the basis of IQ tests administered by Mensa (a high-IQ society), the proportion of African Americans at the high end of the scale is not different from the proportion of European Americans. So the available

states scored higher than "blacks" from the South. Although dedicated racists explained that this difference was due to the northward migration of innately intelligent "blacks," most academics attributed the result to the influence of superior education and more stimulating environments in the North. When further studies showed that northern "blacks" scored higher than southern "whites," the better-education-in-the-North theory gained support, but again racists insisted such results were due to northward migration by all innately intelligent "whites."

As a further test of his conclusions, Klineberg gave IQ tests to "black" schoolgirls born and partly raised in the South who had spent varying lengths of time in New York City. He found that the longer the girls had been in the North, the higher their average IQ. In addition to providing support for the belief that "blacks" are not inherently

inferior to "whites," these findings suggested that cultural factors can and do influence IQ scores, and that IQ is not a fixed quantity.

The controversy about race and intelligence was fueled again in 1969 by Arthur Jensen.[87] He suggested that although the IQ scores of American "blacks" overlapped considerably with the IQ scores of "whites," the average score for "blacks" was 15 points lower than the average for "whites." IQ scores presumably have a large genetic component, so the lower average score for "blacks" implied to Jensen that "blacks" were genetically inferior to "whites." But others contend that the evidence presented by Jensen and more recently by Murray and Herrnstein implies no such thing.

The critics of the genetic interpretation point to at least two problems. First, there is widespread recognition now that IQ tests are probably not accurate measures of "intel-

evidence suggests that African Americans have lower average test scores, but not fewer very high scores or more very low scores (proportionately). Why, then, might their average scores be lower?

Grubb and Barthwell point out that the average scores are not lower on all IQ tests. One test that shows no significant difference is an untimed version of an intelligence test using pictures (the pictorial reasoning test). You can administer the pictorial reasoning test in one of two ways—timed or untimed. A person must finish the test by the end of a prescribed, relatively short time period; or the test-taker can respond to the questions without any time limit. African Americans have lower average scores than European Americans on the timed version of the pictorial reasoning test (although not as much lower as on other tests) but not on the untimed version. This finding suggests that a timed test measures or reflects more than just intelligence. What else besides intelligence might affect performance on a timed IQ test?

Familiarity with a particular format or the content could increase performance on a timed test. So could familiarity or comfort with speed. Although they do not have evidence for how African Americans feel about speed, Grubb and Barthwell cite a study that shows that discomfort with speed can affect performance on an IQ test. The study, conducted by A. Lieblich and S. Kugelmass, compared Jewish and Arab children in Israel. The Arab children scored lower than the Jewish children on the parts of a standard Wechsler intelligence test that were timed, but the Arab children scored the same or even higher on the parts that were untimed. Lieblich and Kugelmass concluded that the Arabs' poorer performance on the timed tests may reflect a cultural abhorrence of speed; "Time is of the Devil" is an Arab saying. Speed is not highly valued in some cultures. If unfamiliarity or discomfort with speed can affect performance on an IQ test, then clearly the test is not measuring intelligence only.

Critics have pointed to many other problems with the evidence presented in *The Bell Curve*. But the fundamental problem is the same as with all attempts to use differences in average IQ scores to make judgments about the capability of different groups. IQ tests may not adequately measure what they purport to measure. If they do not—and there are good reasons to think they do not—it is scientifically and morally incorrect to conclude that differences in average scores are caused by genetic differences in intelligence.

Sources: Richard J. Herrnstein and Charles Murray, *The Bell Curve: Intelligence and Class Structure in American Life* (New York: Free Press, 1994); Henry J. Grubb and Andrea G. Barthwell, "Superior Intelligence and Racial Equivalence: A Look at Mensa," paper presented at the 1996 annual meeting of the Society for Cross-Cultural Research; Henry J. Grubb, "Intelligence at the Low End of the Curve: Where Are the Racial Differences?" *Journal of Black Psychology*, 14 (1987): 25–34; Leon J. Kamin, "Behind the Curve," *Scientific American*, February 1995, 99–103.

ligence" because they are probably biased in favor of the subculture of those who construct the tests. That is, many of the questions on the test refer to things that "white," middle-class children are familiar with, thus giving such children an advantage.[88] So far, no one has come up with a "culture-fair," or bias-free, test. There is more agreement that, although the IQ test may not measure "intelligence" well, it may predict scholastic success or how well a child will do in the primarily "white"-oriented school system.[89]

A second major problem with a purely genetic interpretation of the IQ difference is that many studies also show that IQ scores can be influenced by the social environment. Economically deprived children, whether "black" or "white," will generally score lower than affluent "white" or "black" children. And training of children with low IQ scores clearly improves their test scores.[90] More dramatic evidence is provided by Sandra Scarr and her colleagues. "Black" children adopted by well-off "white" families have IQ scores above the average for "whites." And those "blacks" with more European ancestry do not have higher IQ scores.[91] So the average difference between "blacks" and "whites" in IQ cannot be attributed to a presumed genetic difference. For all we know, the 15-point average difference may be due completely to differences in environment or to test bias.

The geneticist Theodosius Dobzhansky reminded us that conclusions about the causes of different levels of achievement on IQ tests cannot be drawn until all people have equal opportunities to develop their potentials. He stressed the need for an open society operating under the democratic ideal, where all persons are given an equal opportunity to develop whatever gifts or aptitudes they possess and choose to develop.[92]

The Future of Human Variation

Laboratory fertilization, subsequent transplantation of the embryo, and successful birth have been accomplished with humans and nonhumans. *Cloning*—the exact reproduction of an individual from cellular tissue—has been achieved with frogs and sheep. And *genetic engineering*—the substitution of some genes for others—is increasingly practiced in nonhuman organisms. Indeed, as we discussed in the chapter on genetics and evolution, genetic engineering is now used in humans to eliminate certain disorders that are produced by defective genes. What are the implications of such practices for the genetic future of humans? Will it really be possible someday to control the genetic makeup of our species? If so, will the effects be positive or negative?

It is interesting to speculate on the development of a "perfect human." Aside from the serious ethical question of who would decide what the perfect human should be like, there is the serious biological question of whether such a development might in the long run be detrimental to the human species, for what is perfectly suited to one physical or social environment may be totally unsuited to another. The collection of physical, emotional, and intellectual attributes that might be "perfect" in the early twenty-first century might be inappropriate in the twenty-second.[93] Even defects such as the sickle-cell trait may confer advantages under certain conditions, as we have seen.

In the long run, the perpetuation of genetic variability is probably more advantageous than the creation of a "perfect" and invariable human being. In the event of dramatic changes in the world environment, absolute unifor-

Until all people have an equal education and opportunities to achieve, there is no way we can be sure that some people are smarter than others.

mity in the human species might be an evolutionary dead end. Such uniformity might lead to the extinction of the human species if new conditions favored genetic or cultural variations that were no longer present in the species. Perhaps our best hope for maximizing our chances of survival is to tolerate, and even encourage, the persistence of many aspects of human variation, both biological and cultural.[94]

 ## Summary

1. Physical variation—variation in the frequencies of physical traits—from one human population to another is the result of one or more of the following factors: adaptation, acclimatization, and the influence of the social or cultural environment.

2. Some physical variations in human populations involve genetic variation; other variations, including body build, facial construction, and skin color, may be adapted to variation in climate. Still other variations, such as the ability to make lactase, may be adapted partially to variation in cultural environment.

3. Most biological anthropologists today agree that race is *not* a useful way of referring to human biological variation because human populations do not unambiguously fall into discrete groups defined by a particular set of biological traits. Physical traits that are adaptive vary clinally, which makes it meaningless to divide humans into discrete racial entities. Rather it is suggested that racial classifications are mostly social categories that *are presumed* to have a biological basis.

4. Perhaps the most controversial aspect of racial discrimination is the relationship supposed between racial categories and intelligence. Attempts have been made to show, by IQ tests and other means, the innate intellectual superiority of one racial category over another. But there is doubt that IQ tests measure intelligence fairly. Because evidence indicates that IQ scores are influenced by both genes and environment, conclusions about the causes of differences in IQ scores cannot be drawn until all the people being compared have equal opportunities to develop their potentials.

 ## Glossary Terms

acclimatization	hypoxia
adaptation	race
Allen's rule	racism
Bergmann's rule	sickle-cell anemia
Gloger's rule	(sicklemia)

 ## Critical Questions

1. Why is skin color used more often than hair or eye color or body proportions in "racial" classifications?

2. If Europeans had been more susceptible to New World and Pacific diseases, would the world be different today?

3. How might studies of natural selection help increase tolerance of other populations?

Internet Exercises

1. Go look at **http://www.emory.edu/PEDS/SICKLE/ sicklept.htm** to find out what groups are most likely to have sickle-cell anemia (a group of inherited red blood cell disorders). Briefly discuss the cause and symptoms of this inherited disorder.

2. The site GeneLetter (**http://www.geneletter.org/**) contains information on current issues. If humans were cloned, how similar do you think the clones would be to each other? Using the search words "nature" and "nurture," find an article that explores this question and summarize its position.

3. Use the Human Genome Project Information site at **http://www.ornl.gov/hgmis/elsi/elsi.html** either to review your knowledge of molecular genetics or explore some of the ethical issues that may arise.

4. Read the American Anthropological Association's statements on race (**http://www.aaanet.org/stmts/ racepp.htm**) and race and intelligence (**http://www. aaanet.org/stmts/race.htm**) and use them to summarize the current position held by professional anthropologists concerning the concept of race.

Suggested Reading

DOBZHANSKY, T. *Mankind Evolving: The Evolution of the Human Species.* New Haven, CT: Yale University Press, 1962. A now-classic introduction to the interaction between cultural and biological components of human evolution. Keeping the technical details and vocabulary of genetics to a minimum, Dobzhansky discusses natural selection and biological fitness in human populations.

DURHAM, W. H. *Coevolution: Genes, Culture, and Human Diversity.* Stanford, CA: Stanford University Press, 1991. Intended as an update of Dobzhansky's *Mankind Evolving,* this book discusses recent theory and research on how the interaction of genes and culture helps determine human diversity.

MACKINTOSH, N. J. *IQ and Human Intelligence.* Oxford: Oxford University Press, 1998. Provides a detailed but readable overview of the many problems involved in measuring human intelligence.

MASCIE-TAYLOR, C. G. N., AND LASKER, G. W. *Applications of Biological Anthropology to Human Affairs.* New York: Cambridge University Press, 1991. This book discusses how biological anthropologists study fertility, childhood development, adult health, degenerative diseases, and aging.

MOLNAR, S. *Human Variation: Races, Types, and Ethnic Groups,* 4th ed. Upper Saddle River, NJ: Prentice Hall, 1998. A basic text on human biological diversity. Considers the biological principles underlying human variation and various aspects of that variation.

MONTAGU, A. *Man's Most Dangerous Myth: The Fallacy of Race,* 6th ed. Walnut Creek, CA: Alta Mira, 1997. A classic examination of racist thought, especially its social roots and history. Montagu offers insightful reasons to explain why the concept of race is so tenacious even in the face of strong scientific evidence against it.

MORAN, E. F. *Human Adaptability: An Introduction to Ecological Anthropology,* 2nd ed. Boulder, CO: Westview, 2000. An excellent overview of human acclimatization and adaptation, organized by environmental zone.

PEREGRINE, P. N., EMBER, C. R., AND EMBER, M. *Physical Anthropology: Original Readings in Method and Practice.* Upper Saddle River, NJ: Prentice Hall, 2002. Prentice Hall/ Simon & Schuster Custom Publishing. Several chapters in this book deal with the physical aspects of human variation and racism. They include P. T. Ellison, "Natural Variation in Human Fecunditiy"; J. P. Gray and L. Wolfe, "What Accounts for Population Variation in Height?"; and M. A. Little, "Growth and Development of Turkana Pastoralists."

SHANKLIN, E. *Anthropology and Race.* Belmont, CA: Wadsworth, 1994. This book is about the scientific uselessness of the concept of "race" and its abuses. The author thinks that anthropologists have a moral responsibility to combat racism.

SHIPMAN, P. *The Evolution of Racism: Human Differences and the Use and Abuse of Science.* New York: Simon & Schuster, 1994. Examines how evolutionary theory has impacted scientific views about race and racism.

14

Applied and Practicing Anthropology

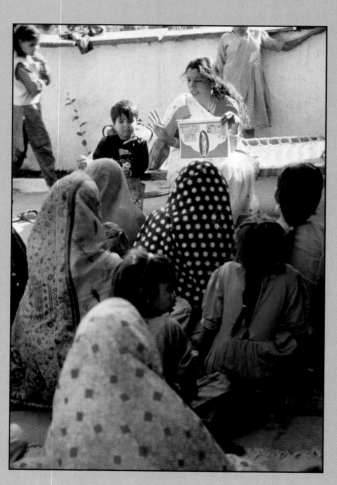

CHAPTER OUTLINE

Motives for Applying
and Practicing Anthropology

History and Types of Application

Ethics of Applied Anthropology

Evaluating the Effects
of Planned Change

Difficulties in Instituting
Planned Change

Cultural Resource Management

Forensic Anthropology

nthropology is no longer a merely academic subject. One out of two anthropologists in the United States is employed outside of colleges and universities. This situation reflects an increasing realization that anthropology, what it has discovered and can discover about humans, is useful. Anthropologists who call themselves applied or practicing anthropologists are usually employed in nonacademic settings, working for government agencies, international development agencies, private consulting firms, public health organizations, medical schools, public interest law firms, community development agencies, charitable foundations, and even profit-seeking corporations (see the box "Anthropology and Business"). Why are so many anthropologists hired to help solve practical problems? In this chapter and the next, we describe how anthropology has been, or could be, used to solve practical problems.

In discussing the work of those who call themselves applied and practicing anthropologists, this chapter first considers the motivations that led to the development of applied anthropology. We then discuss the history and types of application in the United States, the ethical issues involved in trying to improve people's lives, the difficulties in evaluating whether a program is beneficial, and the problems in instituting planned change. The final two sections in this chapter deal with cultural resource management (mainly work by archaeologists) and forensic anthropology—how anthropology (mainly physical anthropology) is being used in legal matters and in the investigation of crime. The next chapter deals with the growing specialty of medical anthropology, that is, the anthropology of health and illness.

Applied and practicing anthropologists are not the only ones interested in solving problems. Many researchers in anthropology and the other social sciences do *basic research* on social problems. Such research may involve fieldwork to get a broad understanding of cultural ideas and practices about health, illness, or violence. Or basic research may involve testing theories about the possible causes of specific problems. The results of such tests could suggest solutions to the problems if the causes, once discovered, can be reduced or eliminated. It is often the case that basic research has unintended payoffs. Even if a study is not directed to a practical problem, it may end up suggesting a solution.

Applied or **practicing anthropology** as a profession is explicitly concerned with making anthropological knowledge useful. Many applied anthropologists participate in or evaluate programs intended to improve people's lives. Applied or practicing anthropologists may be involved in one or more phases of a program: assembling relevant knowledge, developing plans, assessing the likely social and environmental impact of particular plans, implementing the program, and monitoring the program and its effects.[1] And there are still other ways to use anthropology. One of them, increasingly known to the public and discussed at the end of this chapter, is **forensic anthropology**—the use of anthropology to help solve crimes. Another frequent type of applied work is the "social impact" study required in connection with many programs funded by government or private agencies. For example, archaeologists are hired to study, record, and preserve "cultural resources" that will be disturbed or destroyed by construction projects.

Clearly, both basic and applied research may be motivated by a desire to improve the quality of human life. But it is often difficult to decide if a particular project is basic or applied. For example, consider a study of the possible causes of war; its results may suggest how the risk of war might be reduced. Is such a study basic or applied research? We would say it is both. The same could be said for archaeological research on a building site, which may be required by law to conserve or at least record the features of the site. The data found (and recorded or conserved) in the site might or might not be relevant to causal or other theoretical issues in archaeology or anthropology in general.

Argentine forensic anthropologist Patricia Bernardi, on the left, with a Bolivian assistant, unearths skeletons believed to belong to resistance soldiers who were killed by the Bolivian army.

APPLIED ANTHROPOLOGY

Anthropology and Business

Only relatively recently have businesspeople come to realize that anthropologists have useful knowledge to contribute, particularly with regard to the globalization of trade, the increase in international investments and joint ventures, and the spread of multinational corporations. What can anthropology offer? One of the most important contributions of anthropology is understanding how much culture can influence relationships between people of different cultures. For example, anthropologists know that communication is much more than the formal understanding of another language. People in some countries, such as the United States, expect explicit, straightforward verbal messages, but people in other countries are more indirect in their verbal messages. In Japan and China, for example, negative messages are less likely than messages expressing politeness and harmony. Many Eastern cultures have ways of saying no without saying the word.

It is also important to understand that different cultures may have different values. People in the United States place a high value on the individual, but the

Applied anthropologist Jill Kleinberg and clients.

importance of relationships with others may take precedence over individual needs in other places. People in the United States emphasize the future, youth, informality, and competitiveness, but in other societies the emphases are often the opposite. In any business arrangement, perhaps no difference is as salient as the value a culture places on time. As we say, "Time is money." If a meeting is arranged and the other person is late, say, 45 minutes, people from the United States consider it rude; but such a delay is well within the range of

acceptable behavior in many South American countries.

Anthropologists have helped businesses become aware of their own "cultures" (sometimes referred to as *organizational cultures*). The organizational culture of a business may interfere with the acceptance of new kinds of workers, or it may interfere with changing business needs. If parts of that culture need to be changed, it is necessary first to identify what the culture involves and to understand how and why it developed the way it did. Anthropologists know how to iden-

 ## Motives for Applying and Practicing Anthropology

Anthropologists have always cared and worried about the people they study, just as they care and worry about family and friends back home. It is upsetting if most of the families in your place of fieldwork have lost many of their babies to diseases that could be eliminated by medical care. It is upsetting when outside political

and economic interests threaten to deprive your fieldwork friends of their resources and pride. Anthropologists have usually studied people who are disadvantaged—by imperialism, colonialism, and other forms of exploitation—and so it is no wonder that we feel protective about these people, with whom we have lived and shared in the field.

But caring is not enough to improve others' lives. We may need basic research that allows us to understand how a condition might be successfully treated. A particular

tify cultural patterns on the basis of systematic observation and interviewing of individuals.

The anthropologist Jill Kleinberg studied six Japanese-owned firms in the United States to understand the impact of both the larger culture and the organizational culture of the workplace. All six firms employed both Japanese and Americans, although the Japanese dominated the managerial positions. The main goal of the study was to discover why there was considerable tension in the six firms. Kleinberg's first order of business was to interview people about their views of work and their jobs. She found clear differences between the Japanese and the American employees that seemed to reflect broader cultural differences. Americans wanted a clear definition of the job and its attached responsibilities, and they also wanted their job titles, authority, rights, and pay to match closely. The Japanese, on the other hand, emphasized the need to be flexible in their responsibilities as well as their tasks. They also felt that part of their responsibility was to help their co-workers. Americans were uncomfortable because the Japanese managers did not indicate exactly what the workers were supposed to do; even if there was a job description, the manager did not appear

to pay attention to it. Americans were given little information, were left out of decision making, and were frustrated by the lack of opportunity to advance. The Japanese thought that the Americans were too hard to manage, too concerned with money and authority, and too concerned with their own interests.

Dissatisfaction is a problem in any business. Absenteeism, high turnover, and lack of incentive on the job all detract from job performance and business capability. Kleinberg recommended giving all employees more information about the company as well as conducting training sessions about cross-cultural differences in business cultures. She also recommended making the Japanese philosophy of management more explicit during the hiring process so that the company would be able to find Americans who were comfortable with that philosophy. But she also suggested that the managerial structure be somewhat "Americanized" so that American employees could feel at ease. Finally, she recommended that Americans be given more managerial positions and contact with their Japanese counterparts overseas. These suggestions might not eliminate all problems, but they would increase mutual understanding and trust.

In a way, then, as Andrew Miracle notes, the work of the practicing anthropologist is similar to the shaman's in traditional societies. The people who call on shamans for help believe in their abilities to help, and the shaman tries to find ways to empower the client to think positively. To be sure, there are profound differences between a shaman and an applied anthropologist. Perhaps the most important is that the applied anthropologist uses research, not trance or magic, to effect an organizational cure. Like a shaman, however, the applied anthropologist must make an understandable diagnosis and help the client see the way to health and restored power.

Sources: Gary P. Ferraro, *The Cultural Dimension of International Business,* 4th ed. (Upper Saddle River, NJ: Prentice Hall, 2002); Jill Kleinberg, "Practical Implications of Organizational Culture Where Americans and Japanese Work Together," in Ann T. Jordan, ed., *Practicing Anthropology in Corporate America: Consulting on Organizational Culture, NAPA Bulletin No. 14* (Arlington, VA: American Anthropological Association, 1994); Andrew W. Miracle, "A Shaman to Organizations," in Carol R. Ember, Melvin Ember, and Peter N. Peregrine, eds., *Research Frontiers in Anthropology* (Upper Saddle River, NJ: Prentice Hall, 1998). Prentice Hall/Simon & Schuster Custom Publishing.

proposed "improvement" might actually not be an improvement; well-meaning efforts have sometimes produced harmful consequences. And even if we know that a change would be an improvement, there is still the problem of how to make that change happen. The people to be affected may not want to change. Is it ethical to try to persuade them? And, conversely, is it ethical *not* to try? Applied anthropologists must take all of these matters into consideration in determining whether and how to act in response to a perceived need.

Applied anthropology in the United States developed out of anthropologists' personal experiences with disadvantaged people in other cultures.[2] Today anthropologists are also interested in studying and solving problems in our own society. Indeed, as noted earlier, there are as many anthropologists now working in nonacademic settings as in academic settings.[3] These practicing anthropologists often work on specific projects that aim to improve people's lives, usually by trying to change behavior or the environment; or the anthropologists monitor or evaluate efforts by others to bring about change.[4] Usually the problems and projects are defined by the employers or clients (the client is sometimes the "target" population), not by the anthropologists.[5] But anthropologists are increasingly called upon to participate in deciding exactly what improvements might be possible, as well as how to achieve them.

History and Types of Application

In 1934, John Collier, the head of the federal Bureau of Indian Affairs, got legislation passed that provided protections for Native Americans: Land could no longer be taken away, lost land was supposed to be restored, tribal governments would be formed, and loans would be made available to reservations. This opened the way toward recognition of the useful roles that anthropologists could play outside academic settings. Collier employed some anthropologists to aid in carrying out the new policies. At about the same time, the Soil Conservation Service also hired anthropologists to help with projects related to Native American land use.[6] But until World War II, almost all of the few hundred anthropologists in the United States were still employed in colleges, universities, and museums, and applied anthropology was practically nonexistent.

Events in the 1940s encouraged more applied anthropology. In 1941, anthropologists founded the Society for Applied Anthropology and a new journal devoted to applied anthropology, now called *Human Organization*.[7] During World War II, anthropologists were hired in unprecedented numbers by the U.S. government to help in the war effort. Margaret Mead estimated that something like 295 of the 303 anthropologists in the United States at the time were in one way or another direct participants in the war effort.[8]

The government hired anthropologists to help improve morale, increase our understanding of enemies and allies, and prepare for military campaigns and occupation of the islands of Micronesia and other areas in and around the Pacific.[9] For example, applied anthropologists were called on for advice when perplexed U.S. military officials wanted to understand why their Japanese enemies refused to behave like "normal" people. One of the practices that most distressed military leaders was the tendency of Japanese soldiers to try and kill themselves rather than be taken prisoner. Certainly, U.S. prisoners of war did not behave in this manner. Eventually, in order to understand the Japanese code of honor, the military hired anthropologists as consultants to the Foreign Morale Analysis Division of the War Office's Information Department.

After working with the anthropologists, the U.S. military learned that a major reason for the "strange" behavior of the Japanese prisoners was their belief that to surrender in a wartime situation, even in the face of greatly superior odds, or to be taken prisoner, even when injured and unconscious and therefore unable to avoid capture, was a disgrace. The Japanese believed further that the U.S. sol-diers killed all prisoners. Thus, it is hardly surprising that so many captured Japanese soldiers preferred honorable death by their own hand. Once the U.S. military learned what the Japanese thought, they made efforts to explain to them that they would not be executed if captured, with the result that far more Japanese surrendered. Some prisoners even gave military information to the Americans—not to act against their own country but to try and establish new lives for themselves, since the disgrace of being captured prevented them from resuming their former lives.[10]

Anthropologists were enthusiastic about helping the government during World War II because they were overwhelmingly committed to winning the war. The government, in its turn, seemed eager for anthropological advice. But in the postwar period there was an enormous increase in higher education as returning veterans and, later, baby boomers went to college, and U.S. anthropologists increasingly found employment in universities and colleges. Anthropology became less concerned with applied problems and more concerned with theory and basic research.

The situation changed from the late 1970s on when interest in applied anthropology began to flourish. Some have attributed the increased interest to a shift in priorities in the aftermath of the Vietnam War; others cite declining employment opportunities in colleges and universities. Anthropologists who work in applied fields come out of all subfields of anthropology, although most are from ethnology. They may work on public and private programs at home and abroad to provide improvements in agriculture, nutrition, mental and physical health, housing, job opportunities, transportation, education, and the lives of women or minorities. They may work in business. Archaeologists may be hired to work in museums, or are employed to study, record, and preserve "cultural resources" that will be disturbed or destroyed by construction projects. Applied anthropologists who were trained in physical anthropology may work in the area of medicine, public health, and forensic investigations. And applied work in education and communication often utilizes the skills of linguists.[11]

Ethics of Applied Anthropology

Ethical issues always arise in the course of fieldwork, and anthropology as a profession has adopted certain principles of responsibility. Above all, an anthropologist's first responsibility is to those who are being studied; everything should be done to ensure that their welfare and dignity will be protected. Anthropologists also have a responsibility to those who will read about their research; research findings should be reported openly and truthfully.[12] But because applied anthropology often deals with planning and implementing changes in some target population, ethical responsibilities can become complicated. Perhaps the most important ethical question is: Will the change truly benefit the target population?

In May 1946, the Society for Applied Anthropology established a committee to draw up a specific code of ethics for professional applied anthropologists. After many meetings and revisions, a statement on ethical responsibilities was finally adopted in 1948, and in 1983, the statement was revised.[13] According to the code, the target community should be included as much as possible in the formulation of policy, so that people in the community may know in advance how the program will affect them. Perhaps the most important aspect of the code is the pledge not to recommend or take any action that is harmful to the interests of the community. The National Association of Practicing Anthropologists goes further: If the work the employer expects of the employee violates the ethical principles of the profession, the practicing anthropologist has the obligation to try to change those practices or, if change cannot be brought about, to withdraw from the work.[14]

Ethical issues are often complicated. Thayer Scudder described the situation of Gwembe Tonga villagers who were relocated after a large dam was built in the Zambezi Valley of central Africa. Economic conditions improved during the 1960s and early 1970s, as the people increasingly produced goods and services for sale. But then conditions deteriorated. By 1980, the villagers were in a miserable state; rates of mortality, alcohol drinking, theft, assault, and murder were up. Why? One reason was that they had cut back on producing their own food in favor of producing for the world market. Such a strategy works well when world market prices are high; however, when prices fall, so does the standard of living.[15] The situation described by Scudder illustrates the ethical dilemma for many applied anthropologists. As he said: "So how is it that I can still justify working for the agencies that fund such projects?" He points out that large-scale projects are almost impossible to stop. The anthropologist can choose to stand on the sidelines and complain or try to influence the project to benefit the target population as much as possible.[16]

The problem described by Scudder comes about in part because the anthropologist is not often involved until *after* a decision is made to go ahead with a change program. This situation has begun to change as applied anthropologists are increasingly asked to participate in earlier stages of the planning process. Anthropologists are also increasingly asked to help in projects initiated by the affected party. Such requests may range from help in solving problems in corporate organizations to helping Native Americans with land claims. Since the project is consistent with the wishes of the affected population, the results are not likely to put the anthropologist into an ethical dilemma.

Evaluating the Effects of Planned Change

The decision as to whether a proposed change would benefit the target population is not always easy to make. In certain cases, as when improved medical care is involved, the benefits offered to the target group would seem to be unquestionable—we all feel sure that health is better than illness. However, this may not always be true. Consider a public health innovation such as inoculation against disease. Although it would undoubtedly have a beneficial effect on the survival rate of a population, a reduction in the mortality rate might have unforeseen consequences that would in turn produce new problems. Once the inoculation program was begun, the number of children surviving would probably increase. But it might not be possible to increase the rate of food production, given the level of technology, capital, and land resources possessed by the target population. Thus, the death rate, because of starvation, might rise to its previous level and perhaps even exceed it. The inoculation program would not affect the death rate; it might merely change the causes of death. This example shows that even if a program of planned change has beneficial consequences in the short run, a great deal of thought and investigation have to be given to its long-term effects.

Debra Picchi raised questions about the long-term effects on the Bakairi Indians of a program by the National Brazilian Indian Foundation (FUNAI) to produce rice with machine technology.[17] The Bakairi of the Mato Grosso region largely practice slash-and-burn horticulture in gallery forests along rivers, with supplementary cattle raising, fishing, and hunting. In the early part of the twentieth century their population had declined to 150 people and they were given a relatively small reserve. Some of it was gallery forest, but a larger part was parched and infertile (*cerrado*). When the Bakairi population began to increase, FUNAI introduced a scheme to plant rice on formerly unused *cerrado* land, using machinery, insecticides, and fertilizer. FUNAI paid the costs for the first year and expected that by the third year the scheme would be self-supporting. The project did not go so well because FUNAI did not deliver all the equipment needed and did not provide adequate advice. So only half the expected rice was produced. Still, it was more food than the Bakairi had previously, so the program should have been beneficial to them.

But there were negative side effects, not anticipated. Nutritionally, to be sure, the Bakairi are growing an additional starchy food. But use of the *cerrado* for agriculture reduces the area on which cattle can be grazed; cattle are an important source of high-quality protein. So the now-mechanized agriculture has reduced the availability of animal protein. The mechanization also makes the Bakairi more dependent on cash for fuel, insecticides, fertilizer, and repairs. But cash is hard to come by. Only some individuals can be hired—usually men with outside experience who have the required knowledge of machinery. So the cash earned in the now-mechanized agriculture goes mainly to a relatively small number of people. It is debatable whether the new inequalities of income provide long-term effects that are beneficial to the Bakairi.

These failures were not the fault of anthropologists—

indeed, most instances of planned change by governments and other agencies usually have begun without the input of anthropologists at all. Applied anthropologists have played an important role in pointing out the problems with programs like these that fail to evaluate long-term consequences. Such evaluations are an important part of convincing governments and other agencies to ask for anthropological help in the first place. Ironically, failure experiences are learning experiences: Applied anthropologists who study previous examples of planned change can often learn a great deal about what is likely or not likely to be beneficial in the long run.

The benefits of programs or applied efforts are sometimes obvious. For example, Haiti has experienced serious deforestation. The process began in colonial times when the Spanish exported wood and the French cleared forests to grow sugarcane, coffee, and indigo. After Haiti's independence, foreign lumber companies continued to cut and sell hardwood. Wood is needed by the local population for fuel and for construction, but rapid population increases have increased the demand for fuel and wood and the trees were rapidly diminishing. The loss of tree cover also speeds up erosion of topsoil. Forestry experts, environmentalists, and anthropologists all agree about the need to stop this trend. How to bring about the appropriate change is not so easy. The poorer people become, the more likely they are to cut down trees to sell.[18] After numerous reforestation projects failed, an anthropologist was asked to help design a program that would work. And it did (see the box "Bringing the Trees Back to Haiti").

Difficulties in Instituting Planned Change

Whether a program of planned change can be successfully implemented depends largely on whether the targeted population wants the proposed change and likes the proposed program. Before an attempt can be made at cultural innovation, the innovators must determine whether the target population is aware of the benefits of the proposed change. Lack of awareness can be a temporary barrier to solving the problem at hand. For example, health workers have often had difficulty convincing people that they were becoming ill because something was wrong with their water supply. Many people do not believe that disease can be transmitted by water. At other times, the target population is perfectly aware of the problem. A case in point involved Taiwanese women who were introduced to family-planning methods beginning in the 1960s. The women knew they were having more children than they wanted or could easily afford, and they wanted to control their birth rate. They offered no resistance—they merely had to be given the proper devices and instructions, and the birth rate quickly fell to a more desirable, and more manageable, level.[19]

RESISTANCE BY THE TARGET POPULATION

Not all proposed change programs are beneficial to the target population. Sometimes resistance is rational. Applied anthropologists have pointed to cases where the judgment of the affected population has been better than that of the agents of change. One such example occurred during a Venezuelan government–sponsored program to give infants powdered milk. The mothers rejected the milk, even though it was free, on the grounds that it implied that the mothers' milk was no good.[20] But who is to say that the resistance was not in fact intuitively smart, reflecting an awareness that such a milk program would not benefit the children? Medical research now indicates quite clearly that mother's milk is far superior to powdered milk or formula. First, human milk best supplies the nutrients needed for human development. Second, it is now known that the mother, through her milk, is able to transmit antibodies (disease resistances) to the baby. And third, nursing delays ovulation and usually increases the spacing between births.[21]

The switchover to powdered milk and formula in many underdeveloped areas has been nothing short of a disaster, resulting in increased malnutrition and misery. For one thing, powdered milk must be mixed with water, but if the water and the bottles are not sterilized, more sickness is introduced. Then, too, if powdered milk has to be purchased, mothers without cash are forced to dilute the milk to stretch it. And if a mother feeds her baby formula or powder for even a short time, the process is tragically irreversible, for her own milk dries up and she cannot return to breast-feeding even if she wants to.

As the Venezuelan example suggests, individuals may be able to resist proposed medical or health projects because acceptance is ultimately a personal matter. Large development projects planned by powerful governments or agencies rarely are stoppable, but even they can be resisted successfully. The Kayapo of the Xingu River region of Brazil were able to cancel a plan by the Brazilian government to build dams along the river for hydroelectric power. The Kayapo gained international attention when some of their leaders appeared on North American and European television and then successfully organized a protest in 1989 by members of several tribal groups. Their success seemed to come in part from their ability to present themselves to the international community as guardians of the rain forest—an image that resonated with international environmental organizations that supported their cause. Although to outsiders it might seem that the Kayapo want their way of life to remain as it was, the Kayapo are not opposed to all change. In fact, they want greater access to medical care, other government services, and manufactured goods from outside.[22]

But even if a project *is* beneficial to a population, it may still meet with resistance. Factors that may hinder acceptance can be divided roughly into three, sometimes overlapping, categories: *cultural*, *social*, and *psychological* barriers.

APPLIED ANTHROPOLOGY
Bringing the Trees Back to Haiti

No one disagrees that Haiti needs to replace its rapidly disappearing trees. Not only are trees important for preventing soil erosion, but wood is needed for fuel and construction. Overpopulation has resulted in less and less land for poor farmers. As increasing numbers crowd into the cities, demand for charcoal increases. So poor people chop down the few remaining trees to sell for charcoal in the cities. Planners know that reforestation is needed, but traditional reforestation programs have failed miserably. Why?

Understanding why previous projects failed was the first step in helping Gerald Murray design an effective project. One problem seems to have been that previous projects were run through the government's Ministry of Agriculture. The seedling trees that were given away were referred to as "the state's trees." So, when project workers told farmers not to cut the new trees down so as to protect the environment, farmers took this statement to mean that the land on which the trees were planted might be considered government land, which the farmers could not care less about. In contrast, in the project proposed by Murray, private voluntary organizations rather than the Haitian government were used to distribute trees. The farmers were told that they were the owners of the trees. That ownership included the right to cut the trees and sell the wood, just as they sell crops. In previous projects farmers were given heavy, hard-to-transport seedlings that took a long time to

Reforestation in Haiti.

mature. They were told to plant in a large communal woodlot, an idea inconsistent with the more individualistic Haitian land tenure arrangements. In the new plan, the tree seedlings given away were fast-growing species that matured in as little as four years. In addition, the new seedlings were very small and could be planted quickly. Perhaps most important of all, the new trees could be planted in borders or interspersed with other crops, interfering little with traditional crop patterns.

To Murray's great surprise, by the end of two years, 2,500 Haitian households had planted 3 million seedlings. By the end of four years, 75,000 households had planted 20 million trees. Also, farmers were not rushing to cut down trees. Because growing trees do not spoil, farmers were postponing their cutting and

sales until they needed cash. So even though farmers were told that it was all right to cut trees down, a statement contrary to the message of previous reforestation projects, the landscape was filling up with trees.

Murray's lengthy participant observation and interviewing had helped him predict what might fit in with the Haitian farmers' needs. The idea that wood could be an important marketable cash crop was much more consistent with farmers' existing behavior—they already sold crops for cash when they needed it. The difference now was that instead of cutting down naturally grown wood, they were raising wood just as they raised other crops.

The more it becomes known that anthropologists can be helpful in implementing programs, the more often development and government agencies will turn to them for advice.

Sources: From "The Domestication of Wood in Haiti: A Case Study in Applied Evolution," from *Anthropological Praxis* by Robert Wulff and Shirley Fiske. Copyright © 1987 by Westview Press. Reprinted by permission of Perseus Books, L.L.C.

People from the affected area protesting a dam project in India.

Cultural barriers are shared behaviors, attitudes, and beliefs that tend to impede the acceptance of an innovation. For example, members of different societies may view gift giving in different ways. Particularly in commercialized societies, things received for nothing are often believed to be worthless. When the government of Colombia instituted a program of giving seedling orchard trees to farmers in order to increase fruit production, the farmers showed virtually no interest in the seedlings, many of which proceeded to die of neglect. When the government realized that the experiment had apparently failed, it began to charge each farmer a nominal fee for the seedlings. Soon the seedlings became immensely popular and fruit production increased.[23] The farmers' demand for the seedlings may have increased because they were charged a fee and therefore came to value the trees. The market demand for fruit may also have increased. Other examples of cultural resistance to change, which we discuss more in the next chapter, are beliefs about sex that make it difficult for people to follow medical guidelines for safer sex.

It is very important for agents of change to understand what the shared beliefs and attitudes are. First, indigenous cultural concepts or knowledge can sometimes be used effectively to enhance educational programs. For instance, in a program in Haiti to prevent child mortality from diarrhea, change agents used the terminology for traditional native herbal tea remedies (*rafrechi*, or cool refreshment) to identify the new oral rehydration therapy, which is a very successful medical treatment. In native belief, diarrhea is a "hot" illness and appropriate remedies have to have cooling properties.[24] Second, even if indigenous beliefs are not helpful to the campaign, not paying attention to contrary beliefs can undermine the campaign. But uncovering contrary beliefs is not easy, particularly when they do not emerge in ordinary conversation. In the next chapter, on medical anthropology, we discuss cultural theories about illness more extensively. The acceptance of planned change may also depend on social factors. Research suggests that acceptance is more likely if the change agent and the target or potential adopter are similar socially. But change agents may have higher social status and more education than the people they are trying to influence. So change agents may work more with higher-status individuals because they are more likely to accept new ideas. If lower-status individuals also have to be reached, change agents of lower status may have to be employed.[25]

Finally, acceptance may depend on psychological factors—that is, how the individuals perceive both the innovation and the agents of change. In the course of trying to encourage women in the southeastern United States to breast-feed rather than bottle-feed their infants, researchers discovered a number of reasons why women were reluctant to breast-feed their infants, even though they heard it was healthier. Many women did not have confidence that they would produce enough milk for their babies; they were embarrassed about breast-feeding in public; and their family and friends had negative attitudes.[26] In designing an educational program, change agents may have to address such psychological concerns directly.

DISCOVERING AND UTILIZING LOCAL CHANNELS OF INFLUENCE

In planning a project involving cultural change, the administrator of the project should find out what the normal channels of influence are in the population. In most communities, there are preestablished networks for communication, as well as persons of high prestige or influence who are looked to for guidance and direction. An understanding of such channels of influence is extremely valuable when deciding how to introduce a program of change. In addition, it is useful to know at what times, and in what sorts of situations, one channel is likely to be more effective in spreading information and approval than another.

An example of the effective use of local channels of influence occurred when an epidemic of smallpox broke out in the Kalahandi district of the state of Orissa in India. The efforts of health workers to vaccinate villagers against the disease were consistently resisted. The villagers, naturally suspicious and fearful of these strange men with their equally strange medical equipment, were unwilling to offer themselves, and particularly their babies, to the peculiar experiments the strangers wished to perform. Afraid of the epidemic, the villagers appealed for help to their local priest, whose opinions on such matters they trusted. The priest went into a trance, explaining that the illness was the result of the goddess Thalerani's anger with the people. She could be appeased, he continued, only by massive feasts, offerings, and other demonstrations of the villagers' worship of her. Realizing that the priest was the village's major opinion leader, at least in medical matters, the frustrated health workers tried to get the priest to convince his people to undergo vaccination. At first, the priest refused to cooperate with the strange men, but when his favorite nephew fell ill, he decided to try any means available to cure the boy. He thereupon went into another trance, telling the villagers that the goddess wished all her worshipers to be vaccinated. Fortunately, the people agreed, and the epidemic was largely controlled.[27]

If channels of influence are not stable, using influential persons in a campaign can sometimes backfire. In the educational campaign in Haiti to promote the use of oral rehydration therapy to treat diarrhea in children, Mme. Duvalier, the first lady of Haiti at the time, lent her name to the project. Because there were no serious social or cultural barriers to the treatment and mothers reported that children took to the solutions well, success was expected. But in the middle of the campaign, Haiti became embroiled in political turmoil and the first lady's husband was overthrown. Some of the public thought that the oral rehydration project was a plot by the Duvaliers to sterilize children, and this suspicion fueled resistance.[28] As the box on "Bringing the Trees Back to Haiti" shows, even after the Duvalier regime, people in Haiti were suspicious of any government-sponsored program.

Applied anthropologists often advocate integrating indigenous healers into medical change programs. This idea may encounter considerable resistance by the medical profession and by government officials who view such healers negatively. But this strategy may be quite effective in more isolated areas where indigenous healers are the only sources of health care. If they are involved in medical change programs, indigenous healers are likely to refer patients to hospitals when they feel unable to cope with an illness, and the hospitals choose sometimes to refer patients to the healers.[29]

Other social groups and their attitudes can play important roles in shaping the outcome of the change program. Most often the people who are being helped have few privileges, little political and economic power, and low prestige.[30] Change or development is often regarded as a threat to those with more privilege. If those who do have power object to the new program, they may effectively sabotage it. The development agent, then, not only has to reckon with the local community but may also have to persuade more powerful groups in the society that the new program should be introduced.

NEED FOR MORE COLLABORATIVE APPLIED ANTHROPOLOGY

Most large-scale programs of planned change originate with governments, international aid organizations, or other agencies. Even if the programs are well intentioned and even if the appropriate evaluations are made to ensure that the population will not be harmed, the population targeted for the change is usually not involved in the decision making. Some anthropologists, like Wayne Warry, think that applied anthropology should be more collaborative. Warry explains that he was asked by a Native Canadian elder whether he (Warry) would tolerate his own methods and interpretations if he were the native.[31] This question prompted him to involve himself in a project with Native Canadian collaborators, directed by the Mamaweswen Tribal Council. The project assesses healthcare needs and develops plans to improve local community health care. Funding is provided by the Canadian government as part of a program to transfer health care to the First Nations. Native researchers are conducting the surveys and workshops to keep the community informed about the project. The tribal council also reviews any publications and shares in any profits resulting from those publications.

Applied anthropologists may be increasingly asked to work on behalf of indigenous grass-roots organizations. The developing world has seen a proliferation of such groups. In some cases these small groups and networks of such groups are starting to hire their own technical assistance.[32] When such organizations do the hiring, they control the decision making. There is increasing evidence that grass-roots organizations are the key to effective development. For example, Kenyan farmers who belong to grass-roots organizations produce higher farm yields than those farmers who do not belong, even though the latter group is exposed to more agricultural extension agents.[33] Grass-roots organizations can succeed where government or outside projects fail. We have plenty of instances of people effectively resisting projects. Their willingness to change, and their participation in the crucial decision making, may be mostly responsible for the success of a change project.

Cultural Resource Management

Large-scale programs of planned change like those discussed earlier in this chapter have an impact not only on living people. They can also have an impact on the archaeological record left by the ancestors of living people. Recovering and preserving the archaeological record before programs of planned change disturb or destroy it is called **cultural resource management (CRM)**. CRM work is carried out by archaeologists who are often called "contract archaeologists" because they typically work under contract to a government agency.

Construction projects sometimes uncover archaeological sites as here in Beirut, Lebanon, which then may be studied by professional archaeologists.

What kinds of impact can programs of planned change have on the archaeological record? In the 1960s a large number of hydroelectric dam projects were initiated to provide flood control and to bring a stable source of electrical power to developing nations. In Egypt a dam was built on the Nile River at a site called Aswan. Archaeologists realized that once the dam was in place a huge lake would form behind it, submerging thousands of archaeological sites, including the massive temple of Rameses II. Something needed to be done; the archaeological record had to be salvaged or protected. In the language of CRM, there needed to be a *mitigation plan* put into action. And there was. As the Aswan dam was being built, archaeologists went to work excavating sites that would be flooded. Archaeologists and engineers designed a way to take apart the temple of Rameses II and rebuild it, piece by piece, on higher ground where it would not be flooded. By the time the dam was completed in 1965, hundreds of sites had been investigated and two entire temple complexes moved.

Large-scale development projects are not the only projects that involve CRM archaeologists. In many nations, including the United States and Canada, historic preservation laws require any project receiving federal funds to ensure that archaeological resources are protected or their damage mitigated. Highway construction projects in the United States are common places to find CRM archaeologists at work. Virtually all highway projects rely on federal funding, and before a highway can be built a complete archaeological survey of the proposed right-of-way has to be made. If archaeological sites are found, potential damage to them must be mitigated. A CRM archaeologist will work with the construction company, the state archaeologist, and perhaps a federal archaeologist to decide on the best course of action. In some cases the archaeological site will be excavated. In others the right-of-way may be moved. In still others, the decision is to allow the archaeological site to be destroyed, because it would be too costly

to excavate or the site may not be significant enough to warrant excavation. Regardless of the decision, the CRM archaeologist plays a crucial role in assessing and protecting the archaeological record.

CRM archaeologists do not work only for state or federal agencies. In many nations today CRM archaeologists are also working with native peoples to protect, preserve, and manage archaeological materials for them. Indeed, archaeologist John Ravesloot recently stated that "the future of American archaeology is with Indian communities functioning as active, not passive, participants in the interpretation, management, and preservation of their rich cultural heritage."[34] One example of such a working relationship is the Zuni Heritage and Historic Preservation Office. During the 1970s the Pueblo of Zuni decided it needed to train tribal members in archaeology in order to ensure that Zuni cultural resources and properties were managed properly. It hired three professional archaeologists and, with additional assistance from the National Park Service and the Arizona State Museum, initiated a program to train and employ tribal members in cultural resource management. Working with these non-Zuni archaeologists, the Pueblo of Zuni was able to establish its own historic preservation office that today manages and coordinates all historic preservation on the Zuni reservation, a task that was managed by the federal government until 1992. The Pueblo also established the Zuni Cultural Resource Enterprise, a Zuni-owned CRM business that employs both Zuni and non-Zuni archaeologists, and carries out contract archaeology projects both on and off the Zuni reservation.[35]

Cultural resource management is a growing field. Indeed, a 1994 survey conducted by the Society for American Archaeology showed that more than 25 percent of archaeologists in the United States are now employed in private CRM firms working on federally funded contracts, and another 25 percent work directly for state and federal agencies. Thus 50 percent of all employed archaeologists in the United States have jobs directly related to CRM.[36] As development and construction projects continue to affect the archaeological record, the need for well-trained CRM archaeologists is not likely to decline.

Forensic Anthropology

Many of us are fascinated by detective stories. We are interested in crimes and why they occur, and we like to read about them, fictional or not. Forensic anthropology is the specialty in anthropology that is devoted to solving crimes. It is attracting increasing attention by the public, and an increasing number of practitioners. One forensic anthropologist says she is called "the bone lady" by law enforcement people.[37] Like others in her line of work, she is asked to dig up or examine human bones to help solve crimes. Often the task is simple: Are these the bones of a man or woman? How old was the person? Forensic anthropologists can answer such questions fairly easily, particularly if the remains include most bones of the skeleton. Other times the question may be more difficult to answer. For example, can the forensic anthropologist say that a skull is probably from an Asian male? (The police suspect that the skeletal remains they found are from an Asian man who disappeared under mysterious circumstances five years before.) But it is difficult enough to assign an unambiguous "racial" classification to living persons. Bones alone are even more ambiguous because different features in the skeleton do not all vary in correlated ways. Still, the forensic anthropologist can suggest whether the skeletal remains show a constellation of features typically associated with a particular region of the world.

Sometimes the forensic anthropologist can suggest the cause of death when the law enforcement people are stumped. Stanley Rhine provides an example. He was asked to consult on a skeleton that turned out to be from a female in her late twenties and about five feet six inches tall. He examined x-rays of the skeleton. Halfway around the upper edge of the left second rib he saw a ding, a chip of bone missing. What could have caused such a tiny fragment to be broken off? Then he looked at the x-ray of the first left rib. Another chip had been broken off the lower border of that rib too. Then he looked at the x-ray of the adjacent clavicle (collarbone). That bone acts as a strut to hold the shoulder, curving over the first couple of ribs. Something amiss in both the first and second ribs suggested that there might be something unnatural on the clavicle. And that turned out to be the case. There were three shallow, roughly parallel scratches cut into the back side of the clavicle. The most likely cause would have been a sharp-edged object, like a knife, that had been thrust into the upper rib cage of the woman, perhaps penetrating her heart. The forensic anthropologist concluded that the woman had likely been killed by a stab wound (or wounds) down into the left shoulder next to the head. The chief medical investigator thought this forensic anthro-

pology was pretty "nifty," and from that time on Rhine was asked to consult more often on police cases.[38]

In recent years, Clyde Snow and other forensic anthropologists have been called on to confirm horrendous abuses of human rights. Governments have been responsible for the systematic killing of their citizens, and forensic anthropologists have helped to bring the perpetrators to justice. For example, Snow and other forensic anthropologists helped to confirm that the military dictatorship in Argentina in the 1980s was responsible for the deaths of many Argentine civilians who had "disappeared." The forensic anthropologists were also able to determine the location of mass graves and the identity of victims of state-organized brutality in Guatemala. In addition to bringing the perpetrators to justice, confirming the massacres and identifying the victims help the families of the "disappeared" put their anguish behind them. A special session (called "Uncovering the 'Disappeared': Clyde Snow and Forensic Anthropologists Work for Justice"[39]) at the annual meeting of the American Anthropological Association in November 2000 honored Snow and other forensic anthropologists.

Summary

1. Applied anthropology in the United States developed out of anthropologists' personal experiences with disadvantaged peoples. Applied, or practicing, anthropologists may be involved in one or more phases of programs that are designed to change peoples' lives: assembling relevant knowledge, constructing alternative plans, assessing the likely social and environmental impact of particular plans, implementing the programs, and monitoring the programs and their effects.

2. Today many anthropologists are finding employment outside of anthropology departments—in medical schools, health centers, development agencies, urban-planning agencies, and other public and private organizations.

3. The code of ethics for those who work professionally as applied anthropologists specifies that the target population should be included as much as possible in the formulation of policy, so that people in the community may know in advance how the program may affect them. But perhaps the most important aspect of the code is the pledge not to be involved in any plan whose effect will not be beneficial. It is often difficult to evaluate the effects of planned changes. Long-term consequences may be detrimental even if the changes are beneficial in the short run.

4. Even if a planned change will prove beneficial to its target population, the people may not accept it. And if the proposed innovation is not utilized by the intended target, the project cannot be considered a success. Target populations may reject or resist a proposed innovation for various reasons: because they are unaware of the need for the change; because they misinterpret the symbols used to explain the change or fail to understand its real purpose;

because their customs and institutions conflict with the change; or because they are afraid of it. The target population may also resist the proposed change because they unconsciously or consciously know it is not good for them.

5. To be effective, change agents may have to discover and use the traditional channels of influence in introducing their projects to the target population.

6. Cultural resource management usually takes the form of "contract archaeology" to record and/or conserve the archaeology of a building site.

7. Forensic anthropology is the use of anthropology to help solve crimes.

 Glossary Terms

applied anthropology or practicing anthropology
cultural resource management (CRM)
forensic anthropology

 Critical Questions

1. What particular advantages do anthropologists have in trying to solve practical problems?

2. Is it ethical to try to influence people's lives when they have not asked for help?

3 If you were interested in solving a practical problem, would you do basic or applied research on the problem? Why?

 Internet Exercises

1. The Applied Anthropology Computer Network (**http://www.oakland.edu/~dow/anthap.htm**) has frequently asked questions about applied anthropology. Find one question you are curious about and summarize the answer.

2. Check out the table of contents for *Human Organization,* the journal for the Society for Applied Anthropology: **http://www.sfaa.net/ho/**.

3. For an example of careers in nonacademic settings in one locality, go to the Web site **http://www.nku.edu/~anthro/careers.html**.

4. Go to the National Park Service's Cultural Resource Management Web site at **http://www.cr.nps.gov/crm/**. Click on the index; choose one issue and browse through the contents to get a feel for what is done in cultural resource management.

 Suggested Reading

FLUEHR-LOBBAN, C., ED. *Ethics and the Profession of Anthropology: Dialogue for a New Era.* Philadelphia: University of Pennsylvania Press, 1991. This edited volume contains historical and contemporary reviews of ethical issues regarding the profession of anthropology.

HIGGINS, P., AND PAREDES, A., EDS. *Classics of Practicing Anthropology: 1978–1998.* A collection of articles from the first 20 years of *Practicing Anthropology* that provides a snapshot of the variety of work undertaken in the last 25 years.

PODOLEFSKY, A., AND BROWN, P. J. *Applying Cultural Anthropology: An Introductory Reader.* Mountain View, CA: Mayfield, 1997. A selection of readings across a broad range of topics in cultural anthropology that are designed to show how anthropology is important in today's world. The selections show both the basic and applied elements in anthropological research.

POGGIE, J. J., JR., DEWALT, B. R., AND DRESSLER, W. W., EDS. *Anthropological Research: Process and Application.* Albany: State University of New York Press, 1992. The articles in this volume demonstrate how rigorous theory-testing research and innovative research methods can be brought to bear on practical and applied problems.

VAN WILLIGEN, J. *Applied Anthropology: An Introduction,* rev. ed. Westport, CT: Bergin & Garvey Paperback, 1993. With numerous examples of applied projects, this survey of applied anthropology deals with ethics in the subdiscipline, applied research methods, social impact assessment, evaluation research, action anthropology, community development, and the role of cultural broker.

15

Medical Anthropology

llness and death are significant events for people everywhere. No one is spared. So it should not be surprising that how people understand the causes of illness and death, how they behave, and what resources they marshal to cope with these events are extremely important parts of culture. Some argue that we will never completely understand how to treat illness effectively until we understand the cultural behaviors, attitudes, values, and the larger social and political milieux in which people live. Others argue that society and culture have little to do with the outcome of illness—the reason that people die needlessly is that they do not get the appropriate medical treatment.

But anthropologists, particularly medical anthropologists, who are actively engaged in studying health and illness, are increasingly realizing that biological *and* social factors need to be considered if we are to reduce human suffering. For instance, some populations have an appalling incidence of infant deaths due to diarrhea. The origin of this situation is mostly biological, in the sense that the deaths are caused by bacterial infection. But why are so many infants exposed to those bacteria? Usually, the main reason is social. The affected infants are likely to be poor. Because they are poor, they are likely to live with infected drinking water. Similarly, malnutrition may be the biological result of a diet poor in protein, but such a diet is usually also a cultural phenomenon, reflecting a society with classes of people with very unequal access to the necessities of life. In many ways, therefore, medical anthropology, and anthropology in general, are developing in the direction of a "biocultural synthesis."[1]

Medical anthropology is part of this developing synthesis. Indeed, the growth of jobs in medical anthropology is one of the more striking developments in contemporary anthropology. Medical anthropology has developed into a very popular specialty, and the Society for Medical Anthropology is now the second largest unit in the American Anthropological Association.[2]

The medical profession's ways of treating illness may be able to treat some conditions well, but by itself the medical profession cannot tell us why some groups are more affected than others, or why the effectiveness of treatment varies from group to group. This chapter discusses cultural variation in conceptions of health and illness, cultural universals and variables in how illness is treated, the political and social forces that affect health, and some contributions of medical anthropology to the study and treatment of particular diseases and health conditions.

Cultural Understandings of Health and Illness

Medical researchers and medical practitioners in the United States and other Western societies do not exist in a social vacuum. Many of their ideas and practices are influenced by the culture in which they live. We may think of medicine as purely based on "fact," but on reflection it is clear that many ideas stem from the culture in which the researchers reside. Consider the recent shift in attitudes toward birth. It was not so long ago in the United States that fathers were excluded from the birth, hospitals whisked the baby away from the mother and only brought the baby to her infrequently, and visitors (but not attending nurses and doctors) had to wear masks when holding the baby. Rationalizations were given for those practices, but looking back at them, they do not appear to be based on scientific evidence. Many medical anthropologists now argue that the *biomedical paradigm* (the system in which physicians are trained) itself needs to be understood as part of the culture.

Discovering the health-related beliefs, knowledge, and practices of a cultural group—its **ethnomedicine**—is one of the goals of medical anthropology. How do cultures view health and illness? What are their theories about the causes of illness? Do those theories impact on how illnesses are treated? What is the therapeutic process? Are there specialized medical practitioners, and how do they heal? Are there special medicines, and how are they administered? These are just some of the questions asked by the anthropological study of ethnomedicine.

CONCEPTS OF BALANCE OR EQUILIBRIUM

Many cultures have the view that the body should be kept in equilibrium or balance. The balance may be between hot and cold, or wet and dry, as in many cultures of Latin America and the Caribbean.[3] The notion of balance is not limited to opposites. For example, the ancient Greek system of medicine, stemming from Hippocrates, assumed that there were four "humors"—blood, phlegm, yellow bile, and black bile—that must be kept in balance. These humors have hot and cold and wet and dry properties. The Greek medical system was widely diffused in Europe and spread to parts of the Islamic world. In Europe, the humoral medical system was dominant until it was replaced by the germ theory in the 1900s.[4] In the Ayurvedic system, whose practice dates back 4,000 years in North India, Pakistan, Bangladesh, Sri Lanka, and in the Arab world, there are three humors (phlegm, bile, and flatulence), and a balance between hot and cold is also important.[5] The Chinese medical system, which dates back about 3,500 years, initially stressed the balance between the contrasting forces of *yin* and *yang* and later added the concept of humors, which were six in number in Chinese medicine.[6]

The concepts of hot and cold and *yin* and *yang* are illustrated in Emily Ahern's ethnographic description of the medical system of the Taiwanese Hokkien.[7] Both hot and cold substances are required by the body; when the body is out of balance, a lack of one substance can be restored by eating or drinking the missing substance. So, for example, when Ahern was faint with heat, she was told to drink some bamboo-shoot soup because it was "cold." In the winter, you need more hot substances; in the summer, you want fewer. Some people can tolerate more imbalance than others; the old, for instance, can tolerate less imbal-

In China and elsewhere, tai chi exercises are believed to bring harmony and balance.

ance than the young. A loss of blood means a loss of heat. So, for a month after childbirth, women eat mostly a soup made of chicken, wine, and sesame oil—all "hot" ingredients. Hot things to eat are generally oily, sticky, or come from animals; cold things tend to be soupy, watery, or made from plants.

The body also has *yin* and *yang* parts. The *yang* part is visible to the living. The *yin* part exists in the underworld in the shape of a house and tree. The roof of the house corresponds to a person's head, the walls to the skin, a woman's reproductive organs correspond to the flowers on the woman's tree, the roots of the tree to the legs, and so on. A shaman can enable villagers to go into a trance to look around in the underworld where the dead live. If a person has a health problem, a traveler may be sent to the underworld to see what is wrong with the person's *yin* house or tree. Fixing the *yin* house or tree should restore health to the *yang* part of the body. The *yin* world is also where ghosts reside; they sometimes may cause illness. In that case, people may ask for help from powerful gods who reside in the *yang* world.

SUPERNATURAL FORCES

The Taiwanese Hokkien believe that most illnesses have natural or physiological causes, but as is the case with many peoples, the belief that supernatural beings can cause illness is also very common. In fact, in a cross-cultural study of 139 societies, George P. Murdock found that only two societies did not have the belief that gods or spirits could cause illness, making such a belief a near-universal. And 56 percent of those sample societies thought that gods or spirits were the major causes of illness.[8] Sorcery and witchcraft are common in the world's societies. Although both sorcery and witchcraft are practiced by humans and may be used for good or evil, making people ill is one of their major uses. Illness can also be thought of as caused by the loss of one's soul, fate, retribu-

tion for violation of a taboo, or contact with a polluting or tabooed substance or object. Sorcery is believed to be a cause of illness by most societies on all continents; retribution because of violation of a taboo is also very frequent in all but one region of the world. The belief that soul loss can cause illness is absent in the area around the Mediterranean, uncommon in Africa, infrequent in the New World and the Pacific, and has its highest frequency in Eurasia.[9]

On Chuuk (Truk), an atoll in the central Pacific, serious illnesses and death are mainly believed to be the work of spirits. Occasionally, the spirits of relatives are to blame, although they usually do not cause serious damage. More often, illness is caused by the spirit of a particular locality or a ghost on a path at night.[10] Nowadays, one of two therapeutic options or their combination is often chosen—hospital medicine or Chuuk medicine. Chuuk medical treatment requires a careful evaluation of symptoms by the patient and his or her relatives, because different spirits inflict different symptoms. If the symptom match is clear, the patient may choose an appropriate Chuuk medical formula to cure the illness. The patient may also ask whether he or she has done something wrong, and if so, what might point to the appropriate spirit and countervailing formula. For example, there is a taboo on having sexual relations before going to sea. If a person who violated this prohibition becomes ill, the reef spirits will be suspected. The Chuuk medical formula is supposed to cure illness quickly and dramatically. It is for this reason that Chuuk patients ask for a discharge from a hospital if their condition does not improve quickly. If treatment fails, the Chuukese believe that they need to reevaluate the diagnosis, sometimes with the aid of a diviner.[11] In contrasting their theories of illness to the American germ theory, the people of Chuuk point out that while they have seen ghosts, they have never seen the germs that Americans talk about. Using both methods, some people recover and some do not, so the ultimate cause is a matter of faith.[12]

Among the Ojibwa, the most serious illnesses, the ones resistant to ordinary treatment, are thought to be due to retribution for doing wrong to another person, an animal, or a spirit. To cure such an illness, to yourself or to your children, you must reflect on your own conduct to see what you did wrong. Bad conduct cannot be withheld from the doctor or from the other people in the wigwam. On the contrary, only after confessing can medicine help.[13] The Hopi similarly believed that a patient was responsible for his or her own illness, but the cause might be not just improper actions but also bad thoughts and anxiety. Witches could also cause illness, but the action of witches was most effective against people who were depressed or worried; so good thoughts ward off illness.[14]

THE BIOMEDICAL PARADIGM

In most societies, people simply think that their ideas about health and illness are true. Often it is not until they confront another medical system that people develop any awareness that there may be another way of viewing things. Western medical practice has spread widely. People with other medical systems have had to recognize that their ideas about health and illness may be considered deficient by Western practitioners, so it is often necessary to decide which course (Western or non-Western) to follow in dealing with illness. Change, however, is not entirely one-way. For example, for a long time the Chinese practice of acupuncture was disparaged by the Western medical profession, but now more medical practitioners are recognizing that acupuncture may provide effective treatment of certain conditions.

Most medical anthropologists use the term **biomedicine** to refer to the dominant medical paradigm in Western cultures today, with the *bio* part of the word emphasizing the biological emphasis of this medical system. As Robert Hahn points out, biomedicine appears to focus on specific diseases and cures for those diseases. Health is not the focus, as it is thought to be the *absence* of disease. Diseases are considered to be purely natural, and there is relatively little interest in the person or the larger social and cultural systems. Doctors generally do not treat the whole body but tend to specialize, with the human body partitioned into zones that belong to different specialties. Death is seen as a failure, and biomedical practitioners do everything they can to prolong life, regardless of the circumstances under which the patient would live his or her life.[15]

One of the most important discoveries that profoundly changed the course of Western medicine was Louis Pasteur's isolation of the organisms responsible for some major infectious diseases. Pasteur's discoveries stimulated the search for other disease-causing germs using scientific methods. But the *germ theory* of disease, although powerful, may have led researchers to pay less attention to the patient and the patient's social and cultural milieux.[16] For an example of how anthropologists try to redress the balance, see the box "Exploring Why an Applied Project Didn't Work."

Treatment of Illness

Anthropologists who study diseases in this and other cultures can be roughly classified into two camps. First, there are those (the more relativistic) who think that the culture so influences disease symptoms, incidence, and treatment that there are few if any cultural universals about any illness. If each culture is unique, we should expect its conception and treatment of an illness to be unique too, not like beliefs and practices in other cultures. Second, there are those (the more universalistic) who see cross-cultural similarities in the conception and treatment of illness, despite the unique qualities (particularly in the belief system) of each culture. For example, native remedies may contain chemicals that are the same as, or similar in effect to, chemicals used in remedies by Western biomedicine.[17] The reader should note that our classification here of medical anthropologists is a crude one; many medical anthropologists do not fall unambiguously into one or the other group. And the reality might be that a given culture is very much like other cultures in some respects but unique in other respects.

In their extensive research on Maya ethnomedicine, Elois Ann Berlin and Brent Berlin make a strong case that although studies of the Maya have emphasized beliefs about illness that are based on supernatural causes, a good deal of Maya ethnomedicine is about natural conditions, their signs and symptoms, and the remedies used to deal with those conditions. In regard to gastrointestinal diseases, the Berlins found that the Maya have a wide-ranging and accurate understanding of anatomy, physiology, and symptoms. Furthermore, the remedies they use, including recommendations for food, drink, and herbal medicines, have properties that are not that different from those of the biomedical profession.[18]

Carole Browner also suggests that the emphasis on

Acupuncture, originally developed in China, is now used in Western countries.

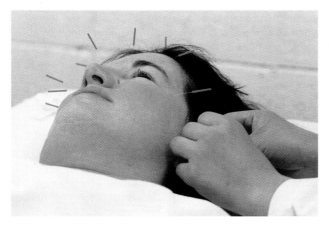

"hot-cold" theories of illness in Latin America has been overemphasized, to the neglect of other factors that influence choices about reproductive health and female health problems. In a study of the medical system in a highland Oaxacan community, Browner finds that certain plants are used to expel substances from the uterus—to facilitate labor at full-term, to produce an abortion, or to induce menstrual flow. Other plants are used to retain things in the uterus—to prevent excess blood loss during menstruation, to help healing after delivery, and to prevent miscarriage. Most of these plant remedies appear to work.[19]

The biomedical establishment has become increasingly aware of the value of studying the "traditional" medicinal remedies discovered or invented by people around the world. In studying the indigenous medicines of the Hausa of Nigeria, Nina Etkin and Paul Ross asked individuals to describe the physical attributes of more than 600 plants and their possible medicinal uses, more than 800 diseases and symptoms, and more than 5,000 prepared medicines. While many medicines were used for treating sorcery, spirit aggression, or witchcraft, most medicines were used for illnesses regarded by the Hausa as having natural causes. Malaria is a serious endemic medical problem in the Hausa region, as in many areas of Africa. The Hausa use approximately 72 plant remedies for conditions connected with malaria—among them anemia, intermittent fever, and jaundice. Experimental treatment of malaria in laboratory animals supports the efficacy of many of the Hausa remedies. But perhaps the most important part of the Etkin and Ross findings is the role of diet. While most medical research does not consider the possible medical efficacy of the *foods* that people eat in combating illness, food is, of course, consumed in much larger quantities and more often than medicine. It is noteworthy, therefore, that the Hausa eat many plants with antimalarial properties; in fact, dietary consumption of these plants appears to be greatest during the time of year when the risk of malarial infection is at its highest. Recent research has also discovered that foods and spices like garlic, onions, cinnamon, ginger, and pepper have antiviral or antibacterial properties.[20]

MEDICAL PRACTITIONERS

In our society we may be so used to consulting a full-time medical specialist (if we do not feel better quickly) that we tend to assume that biomedical treatment is the only effective medical treatment. If we are given a medicine, we expect it to have the appropriate medical effect and make us feel better. So, many in the biomedical system, practitioners and patients alike, are perplexed by the seeming effectiveness of other medical systems that are based in part on symbolic or ritual healing. As we noted earlier, many native plants have been shown to be medically effective, but their use is often accompanied by singing, dancing, noise-making, or rituals. Our difficulty in understanding the healing in such practices probably stems from the assumption in biomedicine that the mind is fundamentally different from the body. Yet, there is increasing evidence that the *form* of treatment may be just as important as the *content* of treatment.[21]

The practitioners who deal with more than the body are sometimes referred to as *personalistic* practitioners. In a personalistic view, illness may be viewed as being due to something in one's social life being out of order. The cause could be retribution for one's own bad behavior or thoughts, or the work of an angry individual practicing sorcery or witchcraft. Or a bad social situation or a bad relationship may be thought of as provoking physical symptoms because of anxiety or stress. In societies with occupational specialization, priests, who are formally trained full-time religious practitioners, may be asked to convey messages or requests for healing to higher powers.[22] Societies with beliefs in sorcery and witchcraft as causes of illness typically have practitioners who are believed to be able to use magic in reverse—that is, to undo the harm invoked by sorcerers and witches. Sometimes sorcerers or

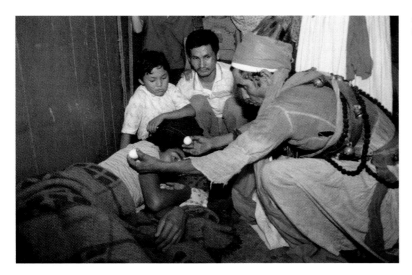

A shaman in Nepal holds up eggs to catch evil spirits affecting a sick person.

APPLIED ANTHROPOLOGY
Exploring Why an Applied Project Didn't Work

When applied projects do not succeed, it is important for researchers to try to figure why. Part of the problem may be that the intended recipients' ideas about how things work may be very different from the researchers' ideas. Consider the following example.

In Guatemala, village health-care workers were not only testing people for malaria but they were also offering free antimalarial drugs. Yet, surprisingly, a community survey found that only 20 percent of people with malaria symptoms took advantage of the free treatment. More surprisingly, most people with symptoms spent the equivalent of a day's wages to buy an injection that was not strong enough to be effective! Why? What was going on?

Finding the answer was not easy. First, researchers designed interviews to elicit folk concepts about illness. What kinds of illnesses are there? What are their causes? What are their symptoms, and how are different illnesses to be treated? They conducted interviews with a random sample of households to find out what illnesses people had and what they did about them. Then they asked people to consider different hypothetical scenarios (vignettes), with different types of people and different degrees of severity of illness, to find out what treatment they would choose. All of these methods were well thought out, but the answers still did not predict what people actually did when they thought they had malaria. Finally, the researchers devised precise comparisons of the kinds of pills passed out by health-care

workers and the pills and ampules for injections sold by the drugstore. They compared them two at a time, varying dosages and brands. People did think that more pills were more effective, as indeed they were. But they thought that the colorfully wrapped store-bought pill was more effective than the equivalent white unwrapped free pill, even though it was not. They also thought that one store-bought ampule used for injections, for which they would pay a day's wages, was more effective than four pills of any kind! In fact, one ampule was equivalent to only one pill.

Applied researchers often use such trial-and-error methods to find out how to get the information they need. Methods that work in one field setting don't always work in others. To get the

---

witches themselves may be asked to reverse illnesses caused by others. However, they may not be sought out because they are often feared and have relatively low status.[23] Shamans are perhaps the most important medical practitioners in societies lacking full-time occupational specialization.

THE SHAMAN   The *shaman*, usually a male part-time specialist, is often involved in healing.[24] Westerners often call shamans "witch doctors" because they don't believe that shamans can effectively cure people. Do shamans effectively cure? Actually, Westerners are not the only skeptics. A Native American named Quesalid from the Kwakiutl of the Pacific Northwest didn't believe that shamanism was effective either. So he began to associate with the shamans in order to spy on them and was taken into their group. In his first lessons, he learned

> a curious mixture of pantomime, prestidigitation, and empirical knowledge, including the art of simulating fainting and nervous fits, . . . sacred song, the technique for inducing

vomiting, rather precise notions of auscultation or listening to sounds within the body to detect disorders and obstetrics, and the use of "dreamers," that is, spies who listen to private conversations and secretly convey to the shaman bits of information concerning the origins and symptoms of the ills suffered by different people. Above all, he learned the ars magna. . . . The shaman hides a little tuft of down in the corner of his mouth, and he throws it up, covered with blood at the proper moment—after having bitten his tongue or made his gums bleed—and solemnly presents it to his patient and the onlookers as the pathological foreign body extracted as a result of his sucking and manipulations.[25]

His suspicions were confirmed, but his first curing was a success. The patient had heard that Quesalid had joined the shamans and believed that only he could heal him. Quesalid remained with the shamans for the four-year apprenticeship, during which he could take no fee, and he became increasingly aware that his methods worked. He visited other villages, competed with other shamans in curing hopeless cases and won, and finally seemed con-

information needed, researchers must sometimes let the subjects structure their own answers. At other times, as in this case, they may have to make very specific comparisons to get predictive answers. The people in the Guatemala study didn't believe that the free pills were strong enough to work, so they didn't use them. More research would be needed to uncover why they did not believe the free pills were effective. Was it because they were free? Was it because the store-bought drugs were attractively packaged? Or was there a belief that injections work better than pills? That's what the research process is like; it always leads to new questions, particularly more general questions requiring more extensive or more comparative research.

For example, the Guatemala project revealed why a particular program was not successful in a particular area. But how widespread are the interfering beliefs?

Are they found throughout Guatemala? Do they interfere with the introduction of other medicines? Are we dealing with problems that exist in other areas of Central and South America? Although we don't yet have answers to these more extensive questions, anthropologists have developed efficient methods for assessing variation in beliefs within and between cultures.

We now know that if we ask one or two informants, we cannot assume that the answer is cultural. But that doesn't mean that we need to ask hundreds of people. If a belief is cultural and therefore commonly held, asking 10 to 20 individuals the same question is sufficient to provide the researcher with a high probability that an answer is correct. (The agreement among respondents is called *cultural consensus*.) So, for example, Guatemalan respondents mostly agreed about which illnesses were contagious. But they dis-

agreed a lot about whether a particular disease should be treated with a "hot" or a "cold" remedy. Using cultural-consensus methods, researchers can compare rural and urban residents, and they can also compare informants in different cultures. When we have more of these systematic comparisons, medical anthropologists and health practitioners may have a better understanding of how to implement medical care.

Sources: Susan C. Weller, "The Research Process," in Carol R. Ember, Melvin Ember, and Peter N. Peregrine, eds., *Research Frontiers in Anthropology* (Upper Saddle River, NJ: Prentice Hall, 1998). Prentice Hall/Simon & Schuster Custom Publishing, and the research referred to therein; A. Kimball Romney, Susan C. Weller, and William H. Batchelder, "Culture as Consensus: A Theory of Culture and Informant Accuracy," *American Anthropologist,* 88 (1986): 313–38.

vinced that his curing system was more valid than those of other shamans. Instead of denouncing the trickery of shamans, he continued to practice as a renowned shaman.[26]

After working with shamans in Africa, E. Fuller Torrey, a psychiatrist and anthropologist, concluded that they use the same mechanisms and techniques to cure patients as psychiatrists and achieve about the same results. He isolated four categories used by healers the world over:

1. **The naming process.** If a disease has a name—"neurasthenia" or "phobia" or "possession by an ancestral spirit" will do—then it is curable; the patient realizes that the doctor understands his case.
2. **The personality of the doctor.** Those who demonstrate some empathy, nonpossessive warmth, and genuine interest in the patient get results.
3. **The patient's expectations.** One way of raising the patient's expectations of being cured is the trip to the doctor; the longer the trip—to the Mayo Clinic,

Menninger Clinic, Delphi, or Lourdes—the easier the cure. An impressive setting (the medical center) and impressive paraphernalia (the stethoscope, the couch, attendants in uniform, the rattle, the whistle, the drum, the mask) also raise the patient's expectations. The healer's training is important: The Ute has dreams analyzed; the Blackfoot has a seven-year training course; the American psychiatrist spends four years in medical school and three in hospital training and has diplomas on the wall. High fees also help to raise a patient's expectations. (The Paiute doctors always collect their fees before starting a cure; if they don't, it is believed that they will fall ill.)
4. **Curing techniques.** Drugs, shock treatment, conditioning techniques, and so on have long been used in many different parts of the world.[27]

Biomedical research is not unaware of the effect of the mind on healing. In fact, considerable evidence has accumulated that psychological factors can be very important in illness. Patients who believe that medicine will help them often recover quickly even if the medicine is only a sugar pill or a medicine not particularly relevant to their condition. Such effects are called *placebo* effects.[28] Placebos do not just have psychological effects. Although the mechanisms are not well understood, they may also alter body chemistry and bolster the immune system.[29]

Shamans may coexist with medical doctors. Don Antonio, a respected Otomi Indian shaman in central Mexico, has many patients, perhaps not as many as before modern medicine, but still plenty. In his view, when he was born God gave him his powers to cure, but his powers are reserved for removing "evil" illnesses (those caused by sorcerers). "Good" illnesses can be cured by herbs and medicine, and he refers patients with those illnesses to medical doctors; he believes that doctors are more effective than he could be in those cases. The doctors, however, do not seem to refer any patients to Don Antonio or other shamans![30]

PHYSICIANS   The most important full-time medical practitioner in the biomedical system is the physician, and the patient-physican relationship is central. In the ideal scheme of things, the physician is viewed as having the ability, with some limits, of being able to treat illness, alleviate suffering, and prolong the life of the patient, as well as offering promises of patient confidentiality and privacy. The patient relies on the physician's knowledge, skill, and ethics. Consistent with the biomedical paradigm, doctors tend to treat patients as having "conditions" rather than as complete persons. Physicians presumably rely on science for authoritative knowledge, but they place a good deal of importance on the value of their own clinical experience. Often physicians consider their own observations of the patient to be more valuable than the reports by the patient. Since patients commonly go to physicians to solve a particular condition or sickness, physicians tend to try to do something about it even in the face of uncertainty. Physicians tend to rely on technology for diagnoses and

treatment and place relatively low value on talking with patients. In fact, physicians tend to give patients relatively little information, and they may not listen very well.[31]

Despite the importance of physicians in biomedicine, patients do not always seek physician care. In fact, one-third of the population of the United States regularly consults with alternative practitioners, such as acupuncturists or chiropractors, often unbeknown to the physician. Somewhat surprisingly, individuals with more education are more likely to seek alternative care.[32]

Political and Economic Influences on Health

People with more social, economic, and political power in a society are generally healthier.[33] Inequality in health in socially stratified societies is not surprising. The poor usually have more exposure to disease because they live in more crowded conditions. And the poor are more likely to lack the resources to get quality care. For many diseases, health problems, and death rates, incidence or relative frequency varies directly with social class. In the United Kingdom, for example, people in the higher social classes are less likely to have headaches, bronchitis, pneumonia, heart disease, arthritis, injuries, and mental disorders, to name just a few of the differences.[34] Ethnic differences also predict health inequities. In South Africa under apartheid, the 14 percent minority population, referred to as "white," controlled most of the income of the country and most of the high-quality land. "Blacks" were restricted to areas with shortages of housing, inadequate housing, and little employment. To get a job, families often had to be disrupted; usually the husband would have to migrate to find work. "Blacks" lived, on average, about nine years less than "whites" in 1985 and "black" infants died at about seven times the rate of "white" infants. In the United States recently, the differences between African Americans and European Americans in health are not as stark as in South

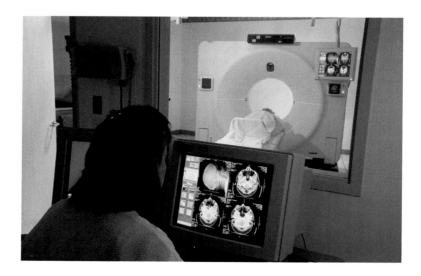

Biomedicine often uses high-tech equipment such as CAT scans to make diagnoses.

Africa, but those favoring European Americans are still substantial. As of 1987, the difference in life expectancy was seven years, and African American infant mortality was about twice the rate for European American infants. Robert Hahn has estimated that poverty accounts for about 19 percent of the overall mortality in the United States.[35]

Inequities because of class and ethnicity are not limited to within-society differences. Power and economic differentials *between* societies also have profound health consequences. Over the course of European exploration and expansion, indigenous peoples died in enormous numbers from introduced diseases, wars, and conquests; they had their lands expropriated and diminished in size and quality. When incorporated into colonial territories or into countries, indigenous people usually become minorities and they are almost always very poor. These conditions of life not only affect the incidence of disease, they also tend to lead to greater substance abuse, violence, depression, and other mental pathologies.[36]

 ## Health Conditions and Diseases

Medical anthropologists have studied an enormous variety of conditions. What follows is only a small sampling.

AIDS

Epidemics of infectious disease have killed millions of people within short periods of time throughout recorded history. The Black Death—bubonic plague—killed between 25 and 50 percent of the population of Europe, perhaps 75 million people, during the fourteenth century; an epidemic during the sixth century killed an estimated 100 million people in the Middle East, Asia, and Europe. Less noted in our history books, but also devastating, was the enormous depopulation that accompanied the expansion of Europeans into the New World and the Pacific from the 1500s on. Not only were people killed directly by European conquerors; millions also died from introduced diseases to which the natives had little or no resistance, diseases such as smallpox and measles that the Europeans brought with them but were no longer dying from.

The current state of medical science and technology may lull us into thinking that epidemics are a thing of the past. But the recent and sudden emergence of the disease we call **AIDS (acquired immune deficiency syndrome)** reminds us that new diseases, or new varieties of old diseases, can appear at any time. Like all other organisms, disease-causing organisms also evolve. The human immunodeficiency virus (HIV) that causes AIDS emerged only recently. Viruses and bacteria are always mutating, and new strains emerge that are initially a plague on our genetic resistance and on medical efforts to contain them.

Millions of people around the world already have the symptoms of AIDS, and millions more are infected with HIV but do not know they are infected. The World Health Organization estimated a few years ago that about 40 million adults and children would be infected and 15 million people would have AIDS by the year 2000.[37] The death toll is enormous and growing. AIDS is now the leading cause of death of people between the ages of 25 and 44 in the United States and Western Europe. It is the leading cause of adult death in many other countries as well.[38] AIDS is a frightening epidemic not only because of its death toll. It is also frightening because it takes a long time (on average, four years) after exposure for symptoms to appear. This means that many people who have been infected by HIV but do not know they are infected may continue, unknowingly, to transmit the virus to others.[39]

Transmission occurs mostly via sexual encounters, through semen and blood. Drug users may also transmit HIV by way of contaminated needles. Transmission by blood transfusion has been virtually eliminated in this and other societies by medical screening of blood supplies. In many countries, however, there is still no routine screening of blood prior to transfusions. HIV may be passed from a pregnant woman to her offspring through the placenta and after birth through her breast milk. The rate of transmission between a mother and her baby is 20 to 40 percent. Children are also at great risk because they are likely to be orphaned by a parent's death from AIDS. In 1995, one of ten children in Uganda was parentless.[40]

Many people think of AIDS as only a medical problem that requires only a medical solution, without realizing that there are behavioral, cultural, and political issues that need to be addressed as well. It is true that developing a vaccine or a drug to prevent people from getting AIDS and finding a permanent cure for those who have it will finally solve the problem. But, for a variety of reasons, we can expect that the medical solution alone will not be sufficient, at least not for a while. First, to be effective worldwide, or even within a country, a vaccine has to be inexpensive and relatively easy to produce in large quantities; the same is true of any medical treatment. Second, governments around the world have to be willing and able to spend the money and hire the personnel necessary to manage an effective program.[41] Third, future vaccination and treatment will require the people at risk to be willing to get vaccinated and treated, which is not always the case. Witness the fact that the incidence of measles is on the rise in the United States because many people are not having their children vaccinated.

There are now expensive drug treatments that significantly reduce the degree of HIV infection, but we do not know if an effective and inexpensive vaccine or treatment will be developed soon. In the meantime, the risk of HIV infection can be reduced only by changes in social, particularly sexual, behavior. But to persuade people to change their sexual behavior, it is necessary to find out exactly what they do sexually, and why they do what they do.

Research so far suggests that different sexual patterns are responsible for HIV transmission in different parts of the world. In the United States, England, northern Europe, Australia, and Latin America, the recipients of anal intercourse, particularly men, are the most likely individuals to acquire HIV infection; vaginal intercourse can also transmit the infection, usually from the man to the woman. Needle sharing can transmit the infection, too. In Africa, the most common mode of transmission is vaginal intercourse, and so women get infected more commonly in Africa than elsewhere.[42] In fact, in Africa there are slightly more cases of HIV in women as compared with men.[43]

Some researchers are arguing that while the immediate cause of HIV infection may be mostly related to sexual practice, larger political and social issues, such as poverty and gender inequality, increase the likelihood of such infection. For example, sexually transmitted diseases increase the risk of HIV infection three to five times, but the poor are less likely to get adequate treatment. And, in the developing world, rural and poorer areas are also more likely to get tainted blood transfusions. Gender inequality is likely to increase the likelihood that women have to submit to unsafe sex and women are even less likely than men to have access to adequate medical care.[44]

As of now, there are only two known ways to reduce the likelihood of sexual HIV transmission. One way is to abstain from sexual intercourse; the other is to use condoms. Educational programs that teach how AIDS spreads and what one can do about it may reduce the spread somewhat, but such programs may fail where people have incompatible beliefs and attitudes about sexuality. For example, people in some central African societies believe that deposits of semen after conception are necessary for a successful pregnancy and generally enhance a woman's health and ability to reproduce. It might be expected then that people who have these beliefs about semen would choose not to use condoms; after all, condoms in their view are a threat to public health.[45] Educational programs may also emphasize the wrong message. Promiscuity may increase the risk of HIV transmission, so hardly anyone would question the wisdom of advertising to reduce the number of sexual partners. And, at least in the homosexual community in the United States, individuals report fewer sexual partners than in the past. What was not anticipated, however, was that individuals in monogamous relationships, who may feel safe, are less likely to use condoms or to avoid the riskiest sexual practices. Needless to say, sex with a regular partner who is infected is not safe![46] In what may seem like something of a paradox, the United Nations observed that for most women in the world today, the major risk factor for being infected with HIV is being married.[47] It is not marriage, per se, that causes the risk of HIV infection; rather, the proximate cause may be the lower likelihood of condom use or abstinence between a husband and wife.

The stigmas associated with AIDS also hinder efforts to reduce its spread. In some societies, there is the widespread belief that homosexual men are particularly likely to get infected.[48] In other societies, AIDS may be thought to be due to promiscuity. If a woman asks a man to use a condom, she may be assumed to be a prostitute. In addition, many people mistakenly fear even proximity to AIDS victims, as if any kind of contact could result in infection.

To solve the problem of AIDS, we may hope that medical science will develop an effective and inexpensive vaccination or treatment that can be afforded by all. There is a vaccine that seems to reduce HIV infection in monkeys to hardly detectable levels.[49] Perhaps soon there will be a similar vaccine for humans. In the meantime, we can try to understand why people engage in certain risky sexual practices. Such understanding may allow us to design educational and other programs that would help inhibit the spread of AIDS.

MENTAL AND EMOTIONAL DISORDERS

When Western anthropologists first started describing mental illness in non-Western societies, there seemed to be unique illnesses in different cultures. These are referred to as *culture-bound syndromes*. For example, a mental disorder called *pibloktoq* occurred among some Eskimo adults of Greenland, usually women, who became oblivious to their surroundings and acted in agitated, eccentric ways. They might strip themselves naked and wander across the ice and over hills until they collapsed of exhaustion. Another disorder, *amok,* occurred in Malaya, Indonesia, and New Guinea, usually among males. It was characterized by John Honigmann as a "destructive maddened excitement . . . beginning with depression and followed by a period of brooding and withdrawal [culminating in] the final mobilization of tremendous energy during which the 'wild man' runs destructively berserk."[50] *Anorexia nervosa,* the disorder involving aversion to food, may be unique to the relatively few societies that idealize slimness.[51] (See the box "Eating Disorders, Biology, and the Cultural Construction of Beauty.")

Some scholars think that each society's views of personality and concepts of mental illness have to be understood in its own terms. Western understandings and concepts cannot be applied to other cultures. For example, Catherine Lutz suggested that the Western concept of depression cannot be applied to the Pacific island of Ifaluk. The people there have many words for thinking or feeling about "loss and helplessness," but all their words are related to a specific need for someone, such as when someone dies or leaves the island. Such thoughts and feelings of loss are considered perfectly normal, and there is no word in their language for general hopelessness or "depression."[52] Therefore Lutz questioned the applicability of the Western concept of depression as well as other Western psychiatric categories.

Other researchers are not so quick to dismiss the possible universality of psychiatric categories. Some think they have found a considerable degree of cross-cultural uniformity in conceptions of mental illness. Jane Murphy studied descriptions by the Inuit and the Yoruba, in Nigeria, of severely disturbed persons. She found that their descriptions not only were similar to each other but also corre-

APPLIED ANTHROPOLOGY
Eating Disorders, Biology, and the Cultural Construction of Beauty

Cultures differ about what they consider beautiful, including people. In many cultures, fat people are considered more beautiful than thin people. The second author of this book did fieldwork years ago on the islands of American Samoa. When he returned to the main island after three months on a distant island, he ran into a Samoan acquaintance, a prominent chief. The chief said: "You look good. You gained weight." In reality, the anthropologist had lost 30 pounds! The chief may not have remembered how heavy the anthropologist had been, but he clearly thought that fat was better than thin.

Why did he think so? One possible idea is that fat is considered beautiful in societies where hurricanes or other disasters frequently cause food shortages. The cultural preference for fat may reflect biological adaptability—people who are fat can better survive starvation. Being fat

may show that you have superior access to resources, mainly food. In such societies the wealthier may be those who are fatter. In other words, fat is beautiful where only the better-off are fat. Compare that situation with the situation in our culture. Clearly, we value thin more than fat. Thinness, for those who can afford it, may symbolize that you don't have to worry about your next meal, that you don't have to store up fat for a rainy day. In fact, in societies where food is bought and sold in the marketplace, those people with more wealth can always buy food. So it is not surprising that in such societies wealthier adults strive to be thin and thinness is considered beautiful. Only richer people look for personal trainers or the newest diet, and of course only they can afford to do so. For the poor, or the insecurely employed, fat may be the best protection against future deprivation.

Our cultural beliefs about what is considered a beautiful body impose enormous pressures on females to be thin. The effort to be thin can be carried to an extreme, resulting in anorexia and bulimia. If you suffer from these often fatal illnesses, you may regularly eat little and you may regularly force yourself to throw up, thus depriving your body of nutrients in the quest to be thinner and thinner. These conditions do not occur commonly among the very poor or in cultures that have frequent food scarcity. Anorexia is a malady found only in affluent cultures.

Sources: Peter J. Brown, "Culture and the Evolution of Obesity," in Aaron Podolefsky and Peter J. Brown, eds., *Applying Cultural Anthropology: An Introductory Reader,* 4th ed. (Mountain View, CA: Mayfield, 1999), p. 100; Martha O. Loustaunau and Elisa J. Sobo, *The Cultural Context of Health, Illness, and Medicine* (Westport, CT: Bergin and Garvey, 1997), p. 85; Naomi Wolf, *The Beauty Myth: How Images of Beauty Are Used against Women* (New York: Morrow, 1991).

sponded to North American descriptions of schizophrenia. The Inuit word for "crazy" is *nuthkavihak.* They use this word when something inside a person seems to be out of order. *Nuthkavihak* people are described as talking to themselves, believing themselves to be animals, making strange faces, becoming violent, and so on. The Yoruba have a word, *were,* for people who are "insane." People described as *were* sometimes hear voices, laugh when there is nothing to laugh at, and take up weapons and suddenly hit people.[53] Robert Edgerton found similarities in conceptions of mental illness in four East African societies. He noted not only that the four groups essentially agreed on the symptoms of psychosis but also that the symptoms they described were the same ones that are considered psychotic here.[54] Edgerton believed that the lack of exact translation in different cultures, such as the one pointed out by Lutz

regarding Ifaluk, does not make comparison impossible. If researchers can come to understand another culture's views of personality and if the researchers can manage to communicate these views to people of other cultures, we can compare the described cases and try to discover what may be universal and what may be found only in some cultures.[55]

Some mental illnesses, such as schizophrenia and depression, seem so widespread that many researchers think they are probably universal. Consistent with this idea is the fact that schizophrenic individuals in different cultures seem to share the same patterns of distinctive eye movements.[56] Still, cultural factors may influence the risk of developing such diseases, the specific symptoms that are expressed, and the effectiveness of different kinds of treatment.[57] There may be some truly culture-bound (nearly unique) syndromes, but others thought at one time to be unique may be culturally varying expressions of conditions that occur widely. *Pibloktoq,* for example, may be a kind of hysteria.[58]

Biological but not necessarily genetic factors may be very important in the etiology of some of the widespread disorders such as schizophrenia.[59] With regard to hysteria, Anthony Wallace theorized that nutritional factors such as calcium deficiency may cause hysteria and that dietary improvement may account for the decline of this illness in the Western world since the nineteenth century.[60] By the early twentieth century, the discovery of the value of good nutrition, coupled with changes in social conditions, had led many people to drink milk, eat vitamin-rich foods, and spend time in the sun (although spending a lot of time in the sun is no longer recommended because of the risk of skin cancers). These changes in diet and activity increased the intake of vitamin D and helped people to maintain a proper calcium level. Consequently, the number of cases of hysteria declined.

Regarding *pibloktoq,* Wallace suggested that a complex set of related variables may cause the disease. The Inuit live in an environment that supplies only a minimum amount of calcium. A diet low in calcium could result in two different conditions. One condition, rickets, would produce physical deformities potentially fatal in the Inuit hunting economy. Persons whose genetic makeup made them prone to rickets would be eliminated from the population through natural selection. A low level of calcium in the blood could also cause muscular spasms known as tetany. Tetany, in turn, may cause emotional and mental disorientation similar to the symptoms of *pibloktoq.* Such attacks last for only a relatively short time and are not fatal, so people who developed *pibloktoq* would have a far greater chance of surviving in the Arctic environment with a calcium-deficient diet than would people who had rickets.

Although researchers disagree about the comparability of mental illnesses among cultures, most agree that effective treatment requires understanding a culture's ideas about a mental illness—why people think it occurs, what treatments are believed to be effective, and how families and others respond to those afflicted.[61]

SUSTO *Susto* is often described as a "folk illness" or a culture-bound syndrome because there doesn't seem to be any direct counterpart in biomedical terms. In many areas of Latin America, it is believed that a person suffers *susto,* or becomes *astudado,* when a nonmaterial essence from the body becomes detached during sleep, or after suffering a fright. This essence is either held captive by supernatural forces or wanders freely outside the body.[62] Susto patients are described as restless during sleep, and listless, depressed, debilitated, and indifferent to food and hygiene during the day. Some researchers have suggested that people labeled as suffering from susto may in fact be suffering from mental illness. Believing that such conclusions were incomplete or premature, Arthur Rubel, Carl O'Nell, and Rolando Collado-Ardón designed a three-culture com-

parative study to evaluate whether susto victims were suffering from social, psychological, or organic problems. They compared individuals suffering with susto to other individuals matched by culture, age, and sex who defined themselves as "sick" when they came to health clinics (but who did not claim susto as their illness). The three cultures were Chichimec, Zapotec, and a Spanish-speaking mestizo community.[63]

From previous study of susto victims, Rubel and his colleagues hypothesized that susto was likely to strike people in socially stressful situations where they may think they are inadequate in required roles. For example, two cases of susto occurred among women who desperately wanted more children, but each had had a number of miscarriages (one had seven, the other two). In addition to measuring social stress, the researchers also had physicans evaluate organic problems with reference to the World Health Organization's International Classification of Diseases. Degree of psychiatric impairment was judged in an interview based on questions previously developed by other researchers. And seven years after the study, the researchers found out which, if any, of the studied individuals had died.

The research results supported the social stress hypothesis: Susto victims were significantly more likely to feel inadequate about social roles. The researchers did not expect to find evidence that susto victims had more psychiatric impairment or more organic disease. However, to their surprise, susto victims were also more likely to have had serious physical health problems. In fact, susto victims were more likely to have died in the seven years after the study. It is hard to say whether the susto victims had more disease because they were debilitated by susto or they were more prone to susto because they were physically sicker. The researchers guess that since many of the conditions that created social role impairment were of long duration (such as many miscarriages), it seemed likely that susto itself put its victims at risk for biological diseases.[64]

DEPRESSION Just as one kind of stress seems to be involved in the folk illness susto, researchers have considered the role of other kinds of stress in producing various other forms of mental illness. One of the most important stressors may be economic deprivation. Many studies have found that the lower classes in socially stratified societies have much higher proportions of all kinds of mental illness. Acute stressors like death of a loved one, divorce, loss of a job, or a natural disaster predict higher rates of mental illness for all social classes; however, these events take more of a toll in lower-class families.[65]

In a study designed to evaluate the effect of these and other stressors on the prevalence of depression in an African American community in a southern city, William Dressler combined fieldwork methods and hypothesis testing to try to better understand depression.[66] While many studies rely on treatment or hospitalization rates, Dressler decided that such rates drastically underestimate the incidence of depression, inasmuch as many people do not seek treatment. He decided to rely on a symptom checklist, which asked such questions as how often in the last week a person felt like crying, felt lonely, or felt hopeless about the future. While such checklists do not provide clear divisions for characterizing someone as mildly depressed or seriously depressed, they do allow researchers to compare people along a continuum.

Dressler measured a variety of different possible stressors, including life crises, economic worries, perceived racial inequality, and problems in social roles, and found that some of the objective stressors, like life crises and unemployment, predict depression in the expected direction *only* in the lower classes. That is, for lower-class African Americans, unemployment and other life crises predicted more depression, but that result was not found among middle- and upper-class individuals. These results are consistent with previous findings that many stressors take more of a toll among poorer individuals. On the other hand, more subjective economic stressors, such as feeling you are not making enough money, predict depression across all class lines. So does "social role" stress, such as thinking you are missing promotions because you are African American or thinking that your spouse expects too much.[67]

UNDERNUTRITION

What people eat is intrinsically connected to their survival and the ability of a population to reproduce itself, so we would expect that the ways people obtain, distribute, and consume food have been generally adaptive.[68] For example, the human body cannot synthesize eight amino acids. Meat can provide all of these amino acids, and combinations of particular plants can also provide them for a complete complement of protein. The combination of maize and beans in many traditional native American diets, or *tortillas* and *frijoles* in Mexico, can provide all the needed amino acids. In places where wheat (often made into bread) is the staple, dairy products combined with wheat also provide complete protein.[69] Even the way that people have prepared for scarcity, such as breaking up into mobile bands, cultivating crops that can better withstand drought, and preserving food in case of famine, are probably adaptive practices in unpredictable environments. As we see in the box on obesity, hypertension, and diabetes, geneticists have proposed that populations in famine-prone areas may have had genetic selection for "thrifty genes"—genes that allow individuals to need a minimum of food and store the extra in fatty tissue to get them past serious scarcity. Customary diets and genetic changes may have been selected over a long stretch of time, but many serious nutritional problems observed today are due to rapid culture change.

Often the switch to commercial or cash crops has harmful effects on nutrition. When the farmer-herders of the arid region in northeastern Brazil started growing sisal, a drought-resistant plant used for making twine and rope, many of them abandoned subsistence agriculture.

The small landholders turned most of their land into sisal growing and when the price of sisal fell they had to work as laborers for others to try to make ends meet. Food then had to be mostly bought, but if a laborer or sisal grower didn't earn enough, there was not enough food for the whole family.

Analysis of allocation of food in some households by Daniel Gross and Barbara Underwood suggests that the laborer and his wife received adequate nutrition, but the children often received much less than required. Lack of adequate nutrition usually results in retarded weight and height in children. As is commonly the case when there is substantial social inequality, the children from lower income groups weigh substantially less than those from higher income groups. But even though there were some economic differences before sisal production, the effects on nutrition appeared negligible before, judging from the fact that there was little or no difference in weight among adults from higher and lower socioeconomic positions who grew up prior to sisal production. But more recently, forty-five percent of the children from lower economic groups were undernourished as compared with 23 percent of the children from the higher economic groups.[70]

This is not to say that commercialization is always deleterious to adequate nutrition. For example, in the Highlands of New Guinea there is evidence that the nutrition of children improved when families started growing coffee for sale. However, in this case the families still had land to

A sisal plant in Bahia, Brazil. The switch to sisal production led to undernutrition in children.

APPLIED ANTHROPOLOGY

Obesity, Hypertension, and Diabetes: Health Consequences of Modernization?

Contact with the West first brought medical devastation to many populations previously unexposed to European illnesses. However, with the acceptance of modern medical care throughout much of the developing world, infant mortality has declined and life expectancies have gone up. These achievements have largely come about through the control of major epidemic diseases, such as smallpox (now eradicated), cholera, yellow fever, syphilis, and tuberculosis, as well as the inoculation of children against childhood diseases. Improvements in medical health are by no means uniform, however. The AIDS epidemic has spread throughout much of the world. Overall deaths from infectious diseases may have declined, but other health problems have increased. As more people survive into older ages, problems of hypertension, heart disease, cancer, and diabetes increase. Some of the increase in these chronic diseases is due to the aging of populations, but much of it appears to be due to changes in life-style that accompany modernization.

A good deal of research has focused on the Samoans of the South Pacific. The Samoans traditionally depended on root and tree crop horticulture. As did many other people in the modern world, Samoans increasingly moved to urban areas, worked for wages, and started buying most of their food. Researchers reported substantial increases, within a relatively short time, in rates of hypertension, diabetes,

and obesity across a wide range of age groups. For example, in 1990 about two-thirds of American Samoans were severely overweight, up substantially from the situation in the 1970s. And Samoans from more rural areas showed less hypertension and physiological signs of stress. Among the life-style changes thought to be responsible are less physical activity and changes in diet to low-fiber, high-calorie foods. Stress may also increase as more individuals buy material things and status goods without having the economic resources to support them.

What about genetic factors? Could some genetic predisposition be interacting with modernization to create obesity in the Samoan population? One possibility is referred to as the "thrifty gene." The geneticist James Neel suggested that individuals who have very efficient metabolisms and who can store calories in fatty tissue are most apt to survive and reproduce in environments with frequent famines or chronic food shortages. In time, populations in such environments would have a high prevalence of individuals with thrifty genes. What happens, though, when such individuals no longer need to exercise much or have access to high-calorie foods? Neel suggested that adult-onset diabetes might result, a scenario that is consistent with the increase in diabetes in Samoa and other parts of Polynesia. It is also consistent with the increase in obesity and hypertension.

The thrifty gene theory does not just pertain to the Samoans and other Polynesian populations. Probably most human populations had to cope with food uncertainty in the past. If the food supply increases with modernization, but it is accompanied by a reduction in physical activity and a switch to high-calorie diets, then increases in obesity, diabetes, and hypertension may frequently accompany modernization. Understanding both biological and cultural factors is essential in helping populations adapt to conditions of urban life.

Sources: John S. Allen and Susan M. Cheer, "The Non-Thrifty Genotype," *Current Anthropology,* 37 (1996): 831–42; James R. Bindon and Douglas E. Crews, "Changes in Some Health Status Characteristics of American Samoan Men: Preliminary Observations from a 12-Year Follow-up Study," *American Journal of Human Biology,* 5 (1993): 31–37; James R. Bindon, Amy Knight, William W. Dressler, and Douglas E. Crews, "Social Context and Psychosocial Influences on Blood Pressure among American Samoans," *American Journal of Physical Anthropology,* 103 (1997): 7–18; Stephen T. McGarvey, "The Thrifty Gene Concept and Adiposity Studies in Biological Anthropology," *Journal of the Polynesian Society,* 103 (1994): 29–42; J. D. Pearson, Gary D. James, and Daniel E. Brown, "Stress and Changing Lifestyles in the Pacific: Physiological Stress Responses of Samoans in Rural and Urban Settings," *American Journal of Human Biology,* 5 (1993): 49–60; World Bank, *World Development Report 1995. Workers in an Integrating World* (Oxford: Oxford University Press, 1995).

grow some crops for consumption. The extra money earned from coffee enabled them to buy canned fish and rice, which provided children with higher amounts of protein than the usual staple of sweet potatoes.[71]

Nutritional imbalances for females have a far-reaching impact on reproduction and the health of the infants they bear. In some cultures, the lower status of women has a direct bearing on their access to food. While the custom of feeding males first is well known, it is less often realized that females end up with less nutrient-dense food such as meat. Deprivation of food sometimes starts in infancy where girl babies, as in India, are weaned earlier than boy babies.[72] Parents may be unaware that their differential weaning practice has the effect of reducing the amount of high-quality protein that girl infants receive. Indeed, in Ecuador, Lauris McKee found that parents thought that earlier weaning of girls was helpful to them. They believed that mother's milk transmitted sexuality and aggression, both ideal male traits, to their infants and so it was important that girl babies be weaned early. Mothers weaned their girls at about 11 months and their boys about 20 months, a 9-month difference. McKee found that girl infants had a significantly higher mortality than boy infants in their second year of life, suggesting that the earlier weaning time for girls and their probable undernutrition may have been responsible.[73]

Making the World Better

Anthropology is now an applied as well as basic science. As this and the preceding chapter indicate, more and more people outside of anthropology find anthropological experiences and achievements useful. What anthropology has discovered, and what it can discover, about humans can help solve problems in the real world. No longer is what we do purely academic. Most of the problems anthropology can help with are of human making; therefore they are susceptible to human unmaking. The main thing limiting our efforts to make a better world may be the pessimists' assumption that problems are too hard to solve. Since we have already solved many problems, why not try to solve them all?

Summary

1. Medical anthropologists suggest that biological *and* social factors need to be considered if we are to understand how to treat illness effectively and reduce the suffering in human life.

2. Many of the ideas and practices of medical practitioners are influenced by the culture in which they reside. Understanding *ethnomedicine*—the medical beliefs and practices of a society or cultural group—is one of the goals of medical anthropology.

3. Many cultures have the view that the body should be kept in equilibrium or balance. The balance may be between hot and cold, or wet and dry, or there may be other properties that need to be balanced.

4. The belief that gods or spirits can cause illness is a near-universal. The belief in sorcery or witchcraft as a cause of illness is also very common.

5. Some anthropologists think that there are few cultural universals about conceptions of illness, or its treatment, but some researchers are finding evidence that many of the plant remedies used by indigenous peoples contain chemicals that are the same as, or similar in effect to, chemicals used in remedies by Western biomedicine.

6. In the biomedical system, medical practitioners emphasize disease and cures, focusing on the body of the patient, not the mind or the social circumstances of the patient. In some societies, healers are more "personalistic," and illness may be viewed as something out of order in one's social life. Shamans are perhaps the most important medical practitioners in societies lacking full-time specialization. Biomedical practitioners are becoming more aware of the psychological factors involved in healing.

7. People with more social, economic, and political power in a society are generally healthier. In socially stratified societies, the poor usually have increased exposure to disease because they are more likely to live in crowded and unsafe conditions and they are less likely to get access to quality care. Power and economic differentials between societies also have had profound health consequences.

8. The enormous death toll of AIDS, the leading cause of adult death in many countries today, will be reduced when medical science develops effective and inexpensive medicines to treat victims of HIV or AIDS and a vaccine to prevent individuals from getting HIV. In the meantime, if the death toll from AIDS is to be reduced, changes in attitudes, beliefs, and practices regarding sexual activity are needed.

9. Anthropologists debate the extent to which mental and emotional disorders are comparable across cultures. Some illnesses such as schizophrenia and depression seem so widespread as to be probably universal. Others, such as susto or anorexia nervosa, appear to be culture-bound syndromes.

10. The ways that people obtain, distribute, and consume food have been generally adaptive. Geneticists have proposed that populations in famine-prone areas may have had genetic selection for "thrifty genes." Many of the serious nutritional problems of today are due to rapid culture change, particularly those changes making for an increasing degree of social inequality.

 Glossary Terms

AIDS (acquired immune
  deficiency syndrome)

biomedicine
ethnomedicine

Critical Questions

1. Do people get sick just because they are exposed to germs?

2. Why do native remedies often contain chemicals that are the same as, or similar in effect to, chemicals used in remedies by Western biomedicine?

3. Why might people engage in sexual practices that increase their likelihood of contracting AIDS?

 Internet Exercises

1. Look over the contents of *Medical Anthropology Quarterly: International Journal for the Analysis of Health* to get an idea of what medical anthropologists publish. The Web site is at **http://www.cudenver.edu/sma/index.html**.

2. Look over the objectives of the Society for Ethnomedicine at **http://www.med.uni-muenchen.de/medpsy/ethno/agem-engl.html**.

3. UNICEF has a quiz on AIDS/HIV on the Web site **http://www.unicef.org/voy/learning/aids_disclaim.html**. Answer at least 20 questions on the quiz to test your knowledge. Summarize what you didn't know. Also, look at the UN site **http://www.unaids.org/** and check out the latest statistics on the prevalence of HIV/AIDS ("Epidemic Update").

Suggested Reading

FELDMAN, D. A., AND MILLER, J. W. *The AIDS Crisis: A Documentary History.* Westport, CT: Greenwood Press, 1998. A very readable history, including many relevant documents, of the AIDS epidemic that is affecting populations the world over.

GOODMAN, A. H., AND LEATHERMAN, T. L., EDS. *Building a New Biocultural Synthesis: Political-Economic Perspectives on Human Biology.* Ann Arbor: University of Michigan Press, 1998. This book represents efforts to develop a biocultural synthesis in human biology, mainly by discussing how disease incidence and treatment can be affected by the interaction of political-economic processes and local conditions.

HAHN, R. A. *Sickness and Healing: An Anthropological Perspective.* New Haven, CT: Yale University Press, 1995. An argument for a more anthropological medicine, one that considers the many culturally varying views of sickness and healing.

INHORN, M. C., AND BROWN, P. J., EDS. *The Anthropology of Infectious Disease.* Amsterdam: Gordon and Breach, 1997. This book reviews anthropological research on the many infectious diseases that attack humans, diseases that still remain the major causes of death worldwide.

LOUSTAUNAU, M. O., AND SOBO, E. J. *The Cultural Context of Health, Illness, and Medicine.* Westport, CT: Bergin and Garvey, 1997. Presents the achievements of medical anthropology and medical sociology and how they contribute to the delivery of effective health care in multicultural settings.

McELROY, A., AND TOWNSEND, P. K. *Medical Anthropology in Ecological Perspective,* 3rd ed. Boulder, CO: Westview, 1996. A survey of the field that emphasizes the health effects of interactions between human groups and their physical and biological environments.

Absolute Dating a method of dating fossils in which the actual age of a deposit or specimen is measured. Also known as chronometric dating.

Acclimatization impermanent physiological changes that people experience when they encounter a new environment.

Acculturation the process of extensive borrowing of aspects of culture in the context of superordinate-subordinate relations between societies; usually occurs as the result of external pressure.

Acheulian a stone toolmaking tradition dating from 1.5 million years ago. Compared with the Oldowan tradition, Acheulian assemblages have more large tools created according to standardized designs or shapes. One of the most characteristic and prevalent tools in the Acheulian tool kit is the so-called hand axe, which is a teardrop-shaped bifacially flaked tool with a thinned sharp tip. Other large tools might have been cleavers and picks.

Adapid a type of prosimian with many lemurlike features; appeared in the early Eocene.

Adaptation genetic changes that allow an organism to survive and reproduce in a specific environment.

Adaptive traits that enhance survival and reproductive success in a particular environment. Usually applied to biological evolution, the term is also often used by cultural anthropologists to refer to cultural traits that enhance reproductive success.

Aegyptopithecus an Oligocene anthropoid and probably the best-known propliopithecid.

Agriculture the practice of raising domesticated crops.

AIDS (Acquired Immune Deficiency Syndrome) a recent disease, almost always lethal, caused by the HIV virus.

Allele one member of a pair of genes.

Allen's Rule the rule that protruding body parts (particularly arms and legs) are relatively shorter in the cooler areas of a species' range than in the warmer areas.

Anthropoids one of the two suborders of primates; includes monkeys, apes, and humans.

Anthropological Linguistics the anthropological study of languages.

Anthropology a discipline that studies humans, focusing on the study of differences and similarities, both biological and cultural, in human populations. Anthropology is concerned with typical biological and cultural characteristics of human populations in all periods and in all parts of the world.

Applied (Practicing) Anthropology the branch of anthropology that concerns itself with applying anthropological knowledge to achieve practical goals, usually in the service of an agency outside the traditional academic setting.

^{40}Ar-^{39}Ar Dating used in conjunction with potassium-argon dating, this method gets around the problem of needing different rock samples to estimate potassium and argon. A nuclear reactor is used to convert the ^{39}Ar to ^{39}K, on the basis of which the amount of ^{40}K can be estimated. In this way, both argon and potassium can be estimated from the same rock sample.

Arboreal adapted to living in trees.

Archaeology the branch of anthropology that seeks to reconstruct the daily life and customs of peoples who lived in the past and to trace and explain cultural changes. Often lacking written records for study, archaeologists must try to reconstruct history from the material remains of human cultures. See also **Historical Archaeology.**

Ardipithecus ramidus perhaps the first hominid, dating to some 4.5 million years ago. Its dentition combines apelike and australopithecine-like features, and its skeleton suggests it was bipedal.

Artifact any object made by a human.

Atlatl Aztec word for "spear-thrower."

Australopithecus genus of Pliocene and Pleistocene hominids.

Australopithecus aethiopicus an early robust australopithecine.

Australopithecus afarensis a species of *Australopithecus* that lived 4 million to 3 million years ago in East Africa and was definitely bipedal.

Australopithecus africanus a species of *Australopithecus* that lived between about 3 million and 2 million years ago.

Australopithecus anamensis a species of *Australopithecus* that lived perhaps 4.2 million years ago.

Australopithecus boisei an East African robust australopithecine species dating from 2.2 million to 1.3 million years ago with somewhat larger cranial capacity than *A. africanus*. No longer thought to be larger than other australopithecines, it is robust primarily in the skull and jaw, most strikingly in the teeth. Compared with *A. robustus*, *A. boisei* has even more features that reflect a huge chewing apparatus.

Australopithecus robustus a robust australopithecine species found in South African caves dating from about 1.8 million to 1 million years ago. Not as large in the teeth and jaws as *A. boisei*.

Balancing Selection a type of selection that occurs when a heterozygous combination of alleles is positively favored even though a homozygous combination is disfavored.

Behavioral Ecology the study of how all kinds of behavior may be related to the environment. The theoretical orientation involves the application of biological evolutionary principles to the behavior (including social behavior) of animals, including humans. Also called sociobiology, particularly when applied to social organization and social behavior.

Bergmann's rule the rule that smaller-sized subpopulations of a species inhabit the warmer parts of its geographic range and larger-sized subpopulations the cooler areas.

Bifacial Tool a tool worked or flaked on two sides.

Bilophodont having four cusps on the molars that form two parallel ridges. This is the common molar pattern of Old World monkeys.

Biological Anthropology See **Physical Anthropology.**

Biomedicine the dominant medical paradigm in Western societies today.

Bipedalism locomotion in which an animal walks on its two hind legs.

Blade a thin flake whose length is usually more than twice its width. In the blade technique of toolmaking, a core is prepared by shaping a piece of flint with hammerstones into a pyramidal or cylindrical form. Blades are then struck off until the core is used up.

Brachiators animals that move through the trees by swinging hand over hand from branch to branch. They usually have long arms and fingers.

Burin a chisel-like stone tool used for carving and for making such artifacts as bone and antler needles, awls, and projectile points.

Canines the cone-shaped teeth immediately behind the incisors; used by most primates to seize food and in fighting and display.

Catarrhines the group of anthropoids with narrow noses and nostrils that face downward. Catarrhines include monkeys of the Old World (Africa, Asia, and Europe), as well as apes and humans.

Ceramics objects shaped from clay and baked at high temperature (fired) to make them hard. Containers such as pots and jars are typical ceramics, though they can take on many forms and uses.

Cercopithecoids Old World monkeys.

Cerebral Cortex the "gray matter" of the brain; the center of speech and other higher mental activities.

Chromosomes paired rod-shaped structures within a cell nucleus containing the genes that transmit traits from one generation to the next.

Chronometric Dating see **Absolute Dating.**

Civilization urban society, from the Latin word for "city-state."

Cline the gradually increasing (or decreasing) frequency of a gene from one end of a region to another.

Conservation techniques used on archaeological materials to stop or reverse the process of decay.

Continental Drift the movement of the continents over the past 135 million years. In the early Cretaceous (ca. 135 million years ago) there were two "supercontinents": *Laurasia,* which included North America and Eurasia, and *Gondwanaland,* which included Africa, South America, India, Australia, and Antarctica. By the beginning of the Paleocene (ca. 65 million years ago), Gondwanaland had broken apart, with South America drifting west away from Africa, India drifting east, and Australia and Antarctica drifting south.

Cretaceous geological epoch 135 million to 65 million years ago, during which dinosaurs and other reptiles ceased to be the dominant land vertebrates and mammals and birds began to become important.

Cro-Magnons humans who lived in western Europe about 35,000 years ago. Once thought to be the earliest specimens of modern-looking humans, or *Homo sapiens sapiens.* But it is now known that modern-looking humans appeared earlier outside of Europe; the earliest so far found lived in Africa.

Cross-Cultural Researcher an ethnologist who uses ethnographic data about many societies to test possible explanations of cultural variation.

Crossing-Over exchanges of sections of chromosomes from one chromosome to another.

Cultural Anthropology the study of cultural variation and universals.

Cultural Resource Management (CRM) the branch of applied anthropology that seeks to recover and preserve the archaeological record before programs of planned change disturb or destroy it.

Culture the set of learned behaviors, beliefs, attitudes, values, and ideals that are characteristic of a particular society or population.

Culture History a history of the cultures that lived in a given area over time. Until the 1950s building such culture histories was a primary goal of archaeological research.

Cuneiform wedge-shaped writing invented by the Sumerians around 3000 B.C.

Descriptive or Structural Linguistics the study of how languages are constructed.

Diastema a gap between the canine and first premolar found in apes.

Directional Selection a type of natural selection that increases the frequency of a trait (the trait is said to be positively favored, or adaptive).

Diurnal active during the day.

DNA deoxyribonucleic acid; a long, two-stranded molecule in the genes that directs the makeup of an organism according to the instructions in its genetic code.

Domestication modification or adaptation of plants and animals for use by humans. When people plant crops, we refer to the process as cultivation. It is only when the crops cultivated and the animals raised have been modified—are different from wild varieties—that we speak of plant and animal domestication.

Dominant the allele of a gene pair that is always phenotypically expressed in the heterozygous form.

Dryopithecus genus of ape from the later Miocene found primarily in Europe. It had thin tooth enamel and pointed molar cusps very similar to those of the fruit-eating chimpanzees of today.

Ecofacts natural items that have been used by humans. Things such as the remains of animals eaten by humans or plant pollens found on archaeological sites are examples of ecofacts.

Electron Spin Resonance Dating like thermoluminescence dating, this technique measures trapped electrons from surrounding radioactive material. The material to be dated is exposed to varying magnetic fields in order to obtain a spectrum of the microwaves absorbed by the tested material. Because heat is not required for this technique, electron spin resonance is especially useful for dating organic materials, such as bone and shell, that decompose if heated.

Eocene a geological epoch 55 million to 34 million years ago during which the first definite primates appeared.

Ethnographer a person who spends some time living with, interviewing, and observing a group of people so that he or she can describe their customs.

Ethnographic Analogy method of comparative cultural study that extrapolates to the past from recent or current societies.

Ethnography a description of a society's customary behaviors, beliefs, and attitudes.

Ethnohistorian an ethnologist who uses historical documents to study how a particular culture has changed over time.

Ethnology the study of how and why recent cultures differ and are similar.

Ethnomedicine the health-related beliefs, knowledge, and practices of a cultural group

Fayum a location southwest of Cairo, Egypt, where the world's best record of Oligocene primate fossils has been found.

Features artifacts of human manufacture that cannot be removed from an archaeological site. Hearths, storage pits, and buildings are examples of features.

Fission-Track Dating a chronometric dating method used to date crystal, glass, and many uranium-rich materials contemporaneous with fossils or deposits that are from 20 billion to 5 billion years old. This dating method entails counting the tracks or paths of decaying uranium-isotope atoms in the sample and then comparing the number of tracks with the uranium content of the sample.

Food Production the form of subsistence technology in which food-getting is dependent on the cultivation and domestication of plants and animals.

Foramen Magnum opening in the base of the skull through which the spinal cord passes en route to the brain.

Forensic Anthropology the use of anthropology to help solve crimes.

Fossils the hardened remains or impressions of plants and animals that lived in the past.

F-U-N Trio fluorine (F), uranium (U), and nitrogen (N) tests for relative dating. All three minerals are present in groundwater.

The older a fossil is, the higher its fluorine or uranium content will be and the lower its nitrogen content.

Gene chemical unit of heredity.

Gene Flow the process by which genes pass from the gene pool of one population to that of another through mating and reproduction.

Genetic Drift the various random processes that affect gene frequencies in small, relatively isolated populations.

Genotype the total complement of inherited traits or genes of an organism.

Genus a group of related species; pl., genera.

Gloger's Rule the rule that populations of birds and mammals living in warm, humid climates have more melanin (and therefore darker skin, fur, or feathers) than populations of the same species living in cooler, drier areas.

Gracile Australopithecines the earliest group of australopithecines, usually differentiated from the robust australopithecines (see below) by their lighter dentition and smaller faces.

Half-Life The time it takes for half of the atoms of a radioactive substance to decay into atoms of a different substance.

Hand Axe a teardrop-shaped stone tool characteristic of Acheulian assemblages.

Hard Hammer a technique of stone tool manufacture where one stone is used to knock flakes from another stone. Flakes produced through hard hammer percussion are usually large and crude.

Heterozygous possessing differing genes or alleles in corresponding locations on a pair of chromosomes.

Hieroglyphics "picture writing," as in ancient Egypt and in Mayan sites in Mesoamerica (Mexico and Central America).

Historical Archaeology a specialty within archaeology that studies the material remains of recent peoples who left written records.

Historical Linguistics the study of how languages change over time.

Holistic refers to an approach that studies many aspects of a multifaceted system.

Hominids the group of hominoids consisting of humans and their direct ancestors. It contains at least two genera: *Homo* and *Australopithecus*.

Hominoids the group of catarrhines that includes both apes and humans.

Homo genus to which modern humans and their ancestors belong.

Homo erectus the first hominid species to be widely distributed in the Old World. The earliest finds are possibly 1.8 million years old. The brain (averaging 895–1,040 cc) was larger than that found in any of the australopithecines or *H. habilis* but smaller than the average brain of a modern human.

Homo habilis early species belonging to our genus, *Homo*, with cranial capacities averaging about 630–640 cc, about 50 percent of the brain capacity of modern humans. Dating from about 2 million years ago.

Homo heidelbergensis a transitional species between *Homo erectus* and *Homo sapiens*.

Homo neandertalensis the technical name for the Neandertals, a group of robust and otherwise anatomically distinct hominids that are close relatives of modern humans—so close that some believe they should be classified as *Homo sapiens neandertalensis*.

Homo rudolfensis early species belonging to our genus, *Homo*. Similar enough to *Homo habilis* that some paleoanthropologists make no distinction between the two.

Homo sapiens all living people belong to one biological species, *Homo sapiens*, which means that all human populations on earth can successfully interbreed. The first *Homo sapiens* may have emerged by 200,000 years ago.

Homo sapiens sapiens modern-looking humans, undisputed examples of which appeared about 50,000 years ago; may have appeared earlier.

Homozygous possessing two identical genes or alleles in corresponding locations on a pair of chromosomes.

Human Paleontology the study of the emergence of humans and their later physical evolution. Also called paleoanthropology.

Human Variation the study of how and why contemporary human populations vary biologically.

Hylobates the family of hominoids that includes gibbons and siamangs; often referred to as the lesser apes (as compared with the great apes such as gorillas and chimpanzees).

Hypoxia a condition of oxygen deficiency that often occurs at high altitudes. The percentage of oxygen in the air is the same as at lower altitudes, but because the barometric pressure is lower, less oxygen is taken in with each breath. Often, breathing becomes more rapid, the heart beats faster, and activity is more difficult.

Incisors the front teeth; used for holding or seizing food and preparing it for chewing by the other teeth.

Indirect Percussion a toolmaking technique common in the Upper Paleolithic. After shaping a core into a pyramidal or cylindrical form, the toolmaker can put a punch of antler or wood or another hard material into position and strike it with a hammer. Using a hammer-struck punch enabled the toolmaker to strike off consistently shaped blades.

Insectivore the order or major grouping of mammals, including modern shrews and moles, that is adapted to feeding on insects.

Kenyapithecus an apelike primate from the Middle Miocene found in East Africa. It had very thickly enameled teeth and robust jaws, suggesting a diet of hard, tough foods. Probably somewhat terrestrial.

Knuckle Walking a locomotor pattern of primates such as the chimpanzee and gorilla in which the weight of the upper part of the body is supported on the thickly padded knuckles of the hands.

Levalloisian Method a method that allowed flake tools of a predetermined size to be produced from a shaped core. The toolmaker first shaped the core and prepared a "striking platform" at one end. Flakes of predetermined and standard sizes could then be knocked off. Although some Levallois flakes date from as far back as 400,000 years ago, they are found more frequently in Mousterian tool kits.

Lithics the technical name for tools made from stone.

Lower Paleolithic the period of the Oldowan and Acheulian stone tool traditions.

Maladaptive traits that diminish the chances of survival and reproduction in a particular environment. Usually applied to biological evolution, the term is often used by cultural anthropologists to refer to behavioral or cultural traits that are likely to disappear because they diminish reproductive success.

Marriage a socially approved sexual and economic union, usually between a man and a woman, that is presumed, both by the couple and by others, to be more or less permanent, and that subsumes reciprocal rights and obligations between the two spouses and between spouses and their future children.

Meiosis the process by which reproductive cells are formed. In this process of division, the number of chromosomes in the newly formed cells is reduced by half, so that when fertilization occurs the resulting organism has the normal number of chromosomes appropriate to its species, rather than double that number.

Mesolithic   the archaeological period in the Old World beginning about 12,000 B.C. Humans were starting to settle down in semipermanent camps and villages, as people began to depend less on big game (which they used to have to follow over long distances) and more on relatively stationary food resources such as fish, shellfish, small game, and wild plants rich in carbohydrates, proteins, and oils.

Messenger RNA   a type of ribonucleic acid that is used in the cell to copy the DNA code for use in protein synthesis.

Microlith   a small, razorlike blade fragment that was usually attached in a series to a wooden or bone handle to form a cutting edge.

Middle Paleolithic   the time period of the Mousterian stone tool tradition.

Miocene   the geological epoch from 24 million to 5.2 million years ago.

Mitosis   cellular reproduction or growth involving the duplication of chromosome pairs.

Molars   the large teeth behind the premolars at the back of the jaw; used for chewing and grinding food.

Mousterian Tool Assemblage   named after the tool assemblage found in a rock shelter at Le Moustier in the Dordogne region of southwestern France. Compared with an Acheulian assemblage, the Middle Paleolithic (40,000–300,000 years ago) Mousterian has a smaller proportion of large core tools such as hand axes and cleavers and a bigger proportion of small flake tools such as scrapers. Flakes were often altered or "retouched" by striking small flakes or chips from one or more edges.

Mutation   a change in the DNA sequence, producing an altered gene.

Natural Selection   the outcome of processes that affect the frequencies of traits in a particular environment. Traits that enhance survival and reproductive success increase in frequency over time.

Neandertal   the common name for the species *Homo neandertalensis*.

Neolithic   originally meaning "the new stone age," now meaning the presence of domesticated plants and animals. The earliest evidence of domestication comes from the Near East about 8000 B.C.

Nocturnal   active during the night.

Normalizing Selection   the type of natural selection that removes harmful genes that arose by mutation.

Obsidian   a volcanic glass that can be used to make mirrors or sharp-edged tools.

Occipital Torus   a ridge of bone running horizontally across the back of the skull in apes and some hominids.

Oldowan   the earliest stone tool making tradition, named after the tools found in Bed I at Olduvai Gorge, Tanzania, from about 2.5 million years ago. The stone artifacts include core tools and sharp-edged flakes made by striking one stone against another. Flake tools predominate. Among the core tools, so-called choppers are common.

Oligocene   the geological epoch 34 million to 24 million years ago during which definite anthropoids emerged.

Omnivorous   eating both meat and vegetation.

Omomyid   a type of prosimian with many tarsierlike features that appeared in the early Eocene.

Opposable Thumb   a thumb that can touch the tips of all the other fingers.

Paleoanthropologists   anthropologists who work in the field of paleoanthropology or human paleontology.

Paleoanthropology   see **Human Paleontology.**

Paleocene   the geological epoch 65 million to 55 million years ago.

Paleolithic   period of the early Stone Age, when flint, stone, and bone tools were developed and hunting and gathering were the means of acquiring food.

Parapithecids   small monkeylike Oligocene primates found in the Fayum area of Egypt.

Percussion Flaking   a toolmaking technique in which one stone is struck with another to remove a flake.

Phenotype   the observable physical appearance of an organism, which may or may not reflect its genotype or total genetic constitution.

Physical (Biological) Anthropology   the study of humans as biological organisms, dealing with the emergence and evolution of humans and with contemporary biological variations among human populations.

Platyrrhines   the group of anthropoids that have broad, flat-bridged noses, with nostrils facing outward; these monkeys are currently found only in the New World (Central and South America).

Pleistocene   a geological epoch that started 1.6 million years ago and, according to some, continues into the present. During this period, glaciers have often covered much of the earth's surface and humans became the dominant life form.

Plesiadipis   the most well known of the first primates, called the plesiadipiforms.

Pliocene   the geological epoch 5.2 million to 1.6 million years ago during which the earliest definite hominids appeared.

Pongids   hominoids whose members include both the living and extinct apes.

Potassium-Argon (K-Ar) Dating   a chronometric dating method that uses the rate of decay of a radioactive form of potassium (^{40}K) into argon (^{40}Ar) to date samples from 5,000 to 3 billion years old. The K-Ar method dates the minerals and rocks in a deposit, not the fossils themselves.

Practicing Anthropology   see **Applied Anthropology.**

Prehensile   adapted for grasping objects.

Prehistory   the time before written records.

Premolars   the teeth immediately behind the canines; used in chewing, grinding, and shearing food.

Pressure Flaking   toolmaking technique whereby small flakes are struck off by pressing against the core with a bone, antler, or wooden tool.

Primate   a member of the mammalian order Primates, divided into the two suborders of prosimians and anthropoids.

Primatologists   people who study primates.

Proconsul   the best-known genus of proto-apes from the Early Miocene.

Prognathic   a physical feature that is sticking out or pushed forward, such as the faces in apes and some hominid species.

Propliopithecids   apelike anthropoids dating from the early Oligocene, found in the Fayum area of Egypt.

Prosimians   literally "premonkeys," one of the two suborders of primates; includes lemurs, lorises, and tarsiers.

Quadrupeds   animals that walk on all fours.

Race   in biology, race refers to a subpopulation or variety of a species that differs somewhat in gene frequencies from other varieties of the species. All members of a species can interbreed and produce viable offspring. Many anthropologists do not think that the concept of race is usefully applied to humans because humans do not fall into geographic populations that can be easily distinguished in terms of different sets of biological or physical traits. Thus, race in humans is largely a culturally assigned category.

Rachis the seed-bearing part of a plant. In the wild variety the rachis shatters easily, releasing the seeds. Domesticated grains have a tough rachis, which does not shatter easily.

Racism the belief, without scientific basis, that one "race" is superior to others.

Radiocarbon (or Carbon-14, ^{14}C) Dating a dating method that uses the decay of carbon-14 to date organic remains. It is reliable for dating once-living matter up to 50,000 years old.

Recessive an allele phenotypically suppressed in the heterozygous form and expressed only in the homozygous form.

Relative Dating a method of dating fossils that determines the age of a specimen or deposit relative to a known specimen or deposit.

Ribosome a structure in the cell used in making proteins.

Robust Australopithecines a later group of australopithecines usually differentiated from the gracile australopithecines (see above) by their heavier dentition and larger faces.

Sagittal Crest a ridge of bone running along the top of the skull in apes and early hominids.

Sagittal Keel an inverted **V**-shaped ridge running along the top of the skull in *Homo erectus.*

Savanna tropical grassland.

Sedentarism settled life.

Segregation the random sorting of chromosomes in meiosis.

Sexual Dimorphism a marked difference in size and appearance between males and females of a species.

Sickle-Cell Anemia (Sicklemia) a condition in which red blood cells assume a crescent (sickle) shape when deprived of oxygen, instead of the normal (disk) shape. The sickle-shaped red blood cells do not move through the body as readily as normal cells, and thus cause damage to the heart, lungs, brain, and other vital organs.

Sites locations where the material remains of human activity have been preserved in a way that archaeologists or paleoanthropologists can recover them.

Sivapithecus a genus of ape from the later Miocene known for its thickly enameled teeth, suggesting a diet of hard, tough, or gritty items. Found primarily in western and southern Asia and now thought to be ancestral to orangutans.

Sociobiology see **Behavioral Ecology.**

Sociolinguistics the study of cultural and subcultural patterns of speaking in different social contexts.

Soft Hammer a technique of stone tool manufacure in which a bone or wood hammer is used to strike flakes from a stone.

Speciation the development of a new species.

Species a population that consists of organisms able to interbreed and produce viable and fertile offspring.

State a form of political organization that includes class stratification, three or more levels of hierarchy, and leaders with the power to govern by force.

Stratified an archaeological deposit that contains successive layers or strata.

Stratigraphy the study of how different rock formations and fossils are laid down in successive layers or strata. Older layers are generally deeper or lower than more recent layers.

Taphonomy the study of how natural processes form and disturb archaeological sites.

Taurodontism having teeth with an enlarged pulp cavity.

Taxonomy the classification of extinct and living organisms.

Terrestrial adapted to living on the ground.

Thermoluminescence Dating a dating technique that is well suited to samples of ancient pottery, brick, tile, or terracotta, which (when they were made) were heated to a high temperature that released trapped electrons. Such an object continues over time to trap electrons from radioactive elements around it, and the electrons trapped after manufacture emit light when heated. Thus, the age of the object can be estimated by measuring how much light is emitted when the object is heated.

Typology a way of organizing artifacts in categories based on their particular characteristics.

Unifacial Tool a tool worked or flaked on one side only.

Upper Paleolithic the time period associated with the emergence of modern humans and their spread around the world.

Uranium-Series Dating a technique for dating fossil sites that uses the decay of two kinds of uranium (^{235}U and ^{238}U) into other isotopes (such as ^{230}Th, thorium). Particularly useful in cave sites. Different types of uranium-series dating use different isotope ratios.

Vertical Clinging and Leaping a locomotor pattern characteristic of several primates, including tarsiers and galagos. The animal normally rests by clinging to a branch in a vertical position and uses its hind limbs alone to push off from one vertical position to another.

"Y-5" Pattern refers to the pattern of cusps on human molars. When looked at from the top, the cusps of the molars form a **Y** opening toward the cheek.

Notes

Chapter 1

1. Gail G. Harrison, "Primary Adult Lactase Deficiency: A Problem in Anthropological Genetics," *American Anthropologist,* 77 (1975): 812–35; William H. Durham, *Coevolution: Genes, Culture and Human Diversity* (Stanford, CA: Stanford University Press, 1991), pp. 228–37.
2. F. C. Chen and W. H. Li, "Genomic Divergence between Humans and Other Hominoids and the Effective Population Size of the Common Ancestor of Humans and Chimpanzees," *American Journal of Human Genetics,* 68 (2001): 444–56.
3. E. Chambers, *Applied Anthropology: A Practical Guide,* rev. ed. (Prospect Heights, IL: Waveland, 1989), as referred to in Gilbert Kushner, "Applied Anthropology," in William G. Emener and Margaret Darrow, eds., *Career Explorations in Human Services* (Springfield, IL: Charles C. Thomas, 1991).
4. Andrew W. Miracle, "A Shaman to Organizations," in Carol R. Ember, Melvin Ember, and Peter N. Peregrine, eds., *Research Frontiers in Anthropology* (Upper Saddle River, NJ: Prentice Hall/Simon & Schuster Custom Publishing, 1998). Prentice Hall/Simon & Schuster Custom Publishing; Kushner, "Applied Anthropology."
5. Leslie A. White, "The Expansion of the Scope of Science," in Morton H. Fried, ed., *Readings in Anthropology,* 2nd ed., vol. 1 (New York: Thomas Y. Crowell, 1968), pp. 15–24.
6. The exclamation point in the word !Kung signifies one of the clicking sounds made with the tongue by speakers of the !Kung language.
7. Edward T. Hall, *The Hidden Dimension* (Garden City, NY: Doubleday, 1966), pp. 144–53.

Chapter 2

1. Robert Martin, *Primate Origins and Evolution: A Phylogenetic Reconstruction* (Princeton, NJ: Princeton University Press, 1990), p. 42.
2. Robert Etienne, *Pompeii: The Day a City Died* (New York: Abrams, 1992).
3. Harold Dibble, P. Chase, S. McPherron, and A. Tuffreau, "Testing the Reality of a 'Living Floor' with Archaeological Data," *American Antiquity,* 62 (1997): 629–51.
4. Michael B. Schiffer, *Formation Processes of the Archaeological Record* (Albuquerque: University of New Mexico Press, 1987).
5. Glynn Isaac, ed., *Plio-Pleistocene Archaeology* (Oxford: Clarendon Press, 1997).
6. Brenda Fowler, *Iceman: Uncovering the Life and Times of a Prehistoric Man Found in an Alpine Glacier* (New York: Random House, 2000).
7. Anne Underhill, "Investigating Craft Specialization during the Longshan Period of China," in P. N. Peregrine, C. R. Ember, and M. Ember, eds., *Archaeology: Original Readings in Method and Practice.* (Upper Saddle River, NJ: Prentice Hall, 2002).
8. R. H. Michel, P. E. McGovern, and V. R. Badler, "The First Wine and Beer: Chemical Detection of Ancient Fermented Beverages," *Analytical Chemistry,* 65 (1993): 408A–13A.
9. Carla Sinopoli, "Learning about the Past through Archaeological Ceramics: An Example from Yijayanagara, India," in P. N. Peregrine, C. R. Ember, and M. Ember, eds., *Archaeology: Original Readings in Method and Practice* (Upper Saddle River, NJ: Prentice Hall, 2002).
10. Thomas Wynn, "The Intelligence of Later Acheulean Hominids," *Man,* 14 (1979): 371–91.
11. Lawrence Keeley, "The Functions of Paleolithic Flint Tools," *Scientific American,* 237 (1977): 108–26.
12. Martin, *Primate Origins and Evolution,* p. 42.
13. Richard F. Kay, "Teeth," in Ian Tattersall, Eric Delson, and John van Couvering, eds., *Encyclopedia of Human Evolution and Prehistory* (New York: Garland, 1988), pp. 578, 571–78.
14. Bernard Wood, "Hominid Paleobiology: Recent Achievements and Challenges," in Corruccini and Ciochon, eds., *Integrative Paths to the Past* (Englewood Cliffs, NJ: Prentice Hall, 1984), pp. 153, 147–65.
15. Glenn C. Conroy, *Primate Evolution* (New York: Norton, 1990), pp. 76–77.
16. Peter N. Peregrine, "Social Change in the Woodland-Mississippian Transition: A Study of Household and Community Patterns in the American Bottom," *North American Archaeologist,* 13 (1992): 131–47.
17. Alan Bilsborough, *Human Evolution* (New York: Blackie Academic & Professional, 1992), pp. 21–22.
18. Richard G. Klein, *The Human Career: Human Biological and Cultural Origins* (Chicago: University of Chicago, 1989), pp. 1–12.
19. Kenneth P. Oakley, "Analytical Methods of Dating Bones," in Don Brothwell and Eric Higgs, eds., *Science in Archaeology* (New York: Basic Books, 1963), p. 26.
20. Frank Hole and Robert F. Heizer, *An Introduction to Prehistoric Archeology,* 3rd ed. (New York: Holt, Rinehart & Winston, 1973), pp. 252–54.
21. F. H. Brown, "Methods of Dating," in Steve Jones, Robert Martin, and David Pilbeam, eds., *The Cambridge Encyclopedia of Human Evolution* (New York: Cambridge University Press, 1992), pp. 180, 470.
22. M. J. Aitken, *Thermoluminescence Dating* (London: Academic Press, 1985), pp. 1–4.
23. Ibid., pp. 191–202.
24. Ibid., pp. 4, 211–13.
25. John Kappelman, "The Attraction of Paleomagnetism," *Evolutionary Anthropology,* 2, no. 3 (1993): 89–99.
26. W. Gentner and H. J. Lippolt, "The Potassium-Argon Dating of Upper Tertiary and Pleistocene Deposits," in Don Brothwell and Eric Higgs, eds., *Science in Archaeology* (New York: Basic Books, 1963), pp. 72–84.
27. Klein, *The Human Career,* pp. 15–17.
28. Bilsborough, *Human Evolution,* pp. 23–24; Frank H. Brown, "Geochronometry," in Tattersall, Delson, and van Couvering, eds., *Encyclopedia of Human Evolution and Prehistory,* p. 225.
29. Brown, "Methods of Dating," pp. 182–83; Henry P. Schwarcz, "Uranium-Series Dating and the Origin of Modern Man," in Henry P. Schwarcz, *The Origin of Modern Humans and the Impact of Chronometric Dating* (Princeton, NJ: Princeton University Press, 1993), pp. 12–26.
30. Robert L. Fleischer, P. B. Price, R. M. Walker, and L. S. B. Leakey, "Fission-Track Dating of Bed I, Olduvai Gorge," *Science,* April 2, 1965, 72–74.
31. Robert L. Fleischer and Howard R. Hart, Jr., "Fission-Track Dating: Techniques and Problems," in W. A. Bishop and J. A.

Miller, eds., *Calibration of Hominid Evolution* (Toronto: University of Toronto Press, 1972), p. 474.

32. Fleischer et al., "Fission-Track Dating of Bed I, Olduvai Gorge."

33. Bruce G. Trigger, *A History of Archaeological Thought* (Cambridge: Cambridge University Press, 1989).

CHAPTER 3

1. Carl Sagan, "A Cosmic Calendar," *Natural History,* December 1975, 70–73.

2. Arthur O. Lovejoy, *The Great Chain of Being: A Study of the History of an Idea* (Cambridge, MA: Harvard University Press, 1964), pp. 58–63.

3. Quoted in ibid., p. 63.

4. Ibid., p. 183.

5. See Loren C. Eiseley, *Darwin's Century: Evolution and the Men Who Discovered It* (Garden City, NY: Doubleday, 1958), pp. 17–26; and Ernst Mayr, *The Growth of Biological Thought: Diversity, Evolution, and Inheritance* (Cambridge, MA: Belknap Press of Harvard University Press, 1982), pp. 171–75, 340–41.

6. Mayr, *The Growth of Biological Thought,* pp. 339–60.

7. Ernst Mayr, "The Nature of the Darwinian Revolution," *Science,* June 2, 1972, 981–89.

8. Alfred Russel Wallace, "On the Tendency of Varieties to Depart Indefinitely from the Original Type," *Journal of the Proceedings of the Linnaean Society,* August 1858, reprinted in Louise B. Young, ed., *Evolution of Man* (New York: Oxford University Press, 1970), p. 75.

9. Mayr, *The Growth of Biological Thought,* p. 423.

10. Darwin had a still longer title. It continued, *Or the Preservation of the Favoured Races in the Struggle for Life.* Darwin's notion of "struggle for life" is often misinterpreted to refer to a war of all against all. Although animals may fight with each other at times over access to resources, Darwin was referring mainly to their metaphorical "struggle" with the environment, particularly to obtain food.

11. Charles Darwin, *The Origin of Species,* excerpted in Young, ed., *Evolution of Man,* p. 78.

12. See Douglas Futuyma's *Science on Trial* (New York: Pantheon, 1982) for an overview of this long controversy.

13. Quoted in Ashley Montagu's introduction to Thomas H. Huxley, "Man's Place in Nature," in Young, ed., *Evolution of Man,* pp. 183–84.

14. Robert N. Brandon, *Adaptation and Environment* (Princeton, NJ: Princeton University Press, 1990), pp. 6–7.

15. George C. Williams, *Natural Selection: Domains, Levels, and Challenges* (New York: Oxford University Press, 1992), p. 7.

16. John Maynard Smith, *Evolutionary Genetics* (New York: Oxford University Press, 1989), pp. 42–45.

17. Charles Devillers and Jean Chaline, *Evolution: An Evolving Theory* (New York: Springer-Verlag, 1993), pp. 22–23.

18. G. A. Harrison, James M. Tanner, David R. Pilbeam, and P. T. Baker, *Human Biology: An Introduction to Human Evolution, Variation, Growth, and Adaptability,* 3rd ed. (Oxford: Oxford University Press, 1988), pp. 209–12.

19. William H. Durham, *Coevolution: Genes, Culture, and Human Diversity* (Stanford, CA: Stanford University Press, 1991), pp. 122–23.

20. Bruce Alberts, Dennis Bray, Julian Lewis, Martin Raff, Keith Roberts, and James D. Watson, *Molecular Biology of the Cell* (New York: Garland, 1983), p. 185.

21. Ibid., pp. 99–103.

22. George Beadle and Muriel Beadle, *The Language of Life* (Garden City, NY: Doubleday, 1966), p. 216.

23. Frederic Golden, Michael Lemonick, and Dick Thompson, "The Race Is Over," *Time,* July 3, 2000, 18–23; Thomas Hayden, "A Genome Milestone," *Newsweek,* July 3, 2000, 51–52; John Travis, "Human Genome Work Reaches Milestone," *Science News,* July 1, 2000, 4–5; Eliot Marshall, "Rival Genome Sequencers Celebrate a Milestone Together," *Science,* June 30, 2000, 2294–295; Elizabeth Pennisi, "Finally, the Book of Life and Instructions for Navigating It," *Science,* June 30, 2000, 2304–307.

24. Alberts et al., *Molecular Biology of the Cell,* pp. 107–11.

25. Paul Berg and Maxine Singer, *Dealing with Genes: The Language of Heredity* (Mill Valley, CA: University Science Books, 1992), p. 53.

26. Alberts et al., *Molecular Biology of the Cell,* pp. 107–11.

27. Ibid., p. 842.

28. Beadle and Beadle, *The Language of Life,* p. 123.

29. Alberts et al., *Molecular Biology of the Cell.*

30. Theodosius Dobzhansky, *Mankind Evolving: The Evolution of the Human Species* (New Haven, CT: Yale University Press, 1962), pp. 138–40.

31. Ibid., p. 139.

32. Harrison et al., *Human Biology,* pp. 205–206.

33. Ibid., pp. 205–208.

34. John Relethford, *The Human Species: An Introduction to Biological Anthropology* (Mountain View, CA: Mayfield, 1990), p. 94.

35. Harrison et al., *Human Biology,* pp. 198–200.

36. C. Loring Brace, "A Four-Letter Word Called Race," in Larry T. Reynolds and Leonard Leiberman, eds, *Race and Other Misadventures: Essays in Honor of Ashley Montagu in His Ninetieth Year* (New York: General Hall, 1996).

37. David P. Barash, *Sociobiology and Behavior* (New York: Elsevier, 1977).

38. J. R. Krebs and N. B. Davies, eds., *Behavioural Ecology: An Evolutionary Approach,* 2nd ed. (Sunderland, MA: Sinauer, 1984); J. R. Krebs and N. B. Davies, *An Introduction to Behavioural Ecology,* 2nd ed. (Sunderland, MA: Sinauer, 1987).

39. George B. Schaller, *The Serengeti Lion: A Study of Predator-Prey Relations* (Chicago: University of Chicago Press, 1972), cited in Edward O. Wilson, *Sociobiology: The New Synthesis* (Cambridge, MA: Belknap Press of Harvard University Press, 1975), p. 504.

40. Wilson, *Sociobiology,* quoted in Bobbi Low, "Behavioral Ecology, 'Sociobiology' and Human Behavior," in Carol R. Ember, Melvin Ember, and Peter N. Peregrine, eds., *Research Frontiers in Anthropology* (Upper Saddle River, NJ: Prentice Hall, 1998). Prentice Hall/Simon & Schuster Custom Publishing.

41. Low, "Behavioral Ecology, 'Sociobiology' and Human Behavior."

42. Donald T. Campbell, "Variation and Selective Retention in Socio-Cultural Evolution," in Herbert Barringer, George Blankstein, and Raymond Mack, eds., *Social Change in Developing Areas: A Re-Interpretation of Evolutionary Theory* (Cambridge, MA: Schenkman, 1965), pp. 19–49.

43. Henry W. Nissen, "Axes of Behavioral Comparison," in Anne Roe and George Gaylord Simpson, eds., *Behavior and Evolution* (New Haven, CT: Yale University Press, 1958), pp. 183–205.

44. Robert Boyd and Peter J. Richerson, *Culture and the Evolutionary Process* (Chicago: University of Chicago Press, 1985).

45. William H. Durham, *Coevolution: Genes, Culture, and Human Diversity* (Stanford, CA: Stanford University Press, 1991).

CHAPTER 4

1. The classic description of common primate traits is J. R. Napier and P. H. Napier, *A Handbook of Living Primates* (New York: Academic Press, 1967). See also Barbara B. Smuts, Dorothy L. Cheney, Robert M. Seyfarth, Richard W. Wrangham, and Thomas T. Struhsaker, eds., *Primate Societies* (Chicago: University of Chicago Press, 1987).

2. Simon K. Bearder, "Lorises, Bushbabies, and Tarsiers: Diverse Societies in Solitary Foragers," in Smuts et al., eds., *Primate Societies*, p. 14.

3. Alison F. Richard, *Primates in Nature* (New York: Freeman, 1985), p. 22ff.

4. Robert D. Martin, "Strategies of Reproduction," *Natural History*, November 1975, 50. The opossum, which is not a primate but lives in trees and has many babies at one time, is a marsupial and has a pouch in which to keep the babies when they are very young.

5. H. F. Harlow et al., "Maternal Behavior of Rhesus Monkeys Deprived of Mothering and Peer Association in Infancy," *Proceedings of the American Philosophical Society*, 110 (1966): 58–66.

6. Nancy A. Nicolson, "Infants, Mothers, and Other Females," in Smuts et al., eds., *Primate Societies*, p. 339.

7. See J. Patrick Gray, *Primate Sociobiology* (New Haven, CT: HRAF Press, 1985), pp. 144–63, for a discussion of research that attempts to explain the variation among primates in the degree of male parental care.

8. Anne E. Russon, "The Development of Peer Social Interaction in Infant Chimpanzees: Comparative Social, Piagetian, and Brain Perspectives," in Sue Taylor Parker and Kathleen Rita Gibson, eds., *"Language" and Intelligence in Monkeys and Apes: Comparative Developmental Perspectives* (New York: Cambridge University Press, 1990), p. 379.

9. Phyllis Jay Dohlinow and Naomi Bishop, "The Development of Motor Skills and Social Relationships among Primates through Play," in Phyllis Jay Dohlinow, ed., *Primate Patterns* (New York: Holt, Rinehart & Winston, 1972), pp. 321–25.

10. D. S. Sade, "Some Aspects of Parent-Offspring and Sibling Relationships in a Group of Rhesus Monkeys, with a Discussion of Grooming," *American Journal of Physical Anthropology*, 23 (1965): 1–17; and Glenn Hausfater, Jeanne Altmann, and Stuart Altmann, "Long-Term Consistency of Dominance Relations among Female Baboons," *Science*, August 20, 1982, 752–54.

11. Elisabetta Visaberghi and Dorothy Munkenbeck Fragaszy, "Do Monkeys Ape?" in Parker and Gibson, eds., *"Language" and Intelligence in Monkeys and Apes*, p. 265; Michael Tomasello, "Cultural Transmission in the Tool Use and Communicatory Signaling of Chimpanzees," in Parker and Gibson, eds., *"Language" and Intelligence in Monkeys and Apes*, pp. 304–305.

12. Jane van Lawick-Goodall, *In the Shadow of Man* (Boston: Houghton Mifflin, 1971), p. 242.

13. Visaberghi and Fragaszy, "Do Monkeys Ape?" pp. 264–65.

14. Robert Martin, "Classification and Evolutionary Relationships," in Steve Jones, Robert Martin, and David Pilbeam, eds., *The Cambridge Encyclopedia of Human Evolution* (Cambridge: Cambridge University Press, 1992), pp. 17–19; Glenn C. Conroy, *Primate Evolution* (New York: Norton, 1990), pp. 8–15.

15. This simplified chart of primate classification adapts information provided in Martin, "Classification and Evolutionary Relationships," p. 21.

16. G. A. Doyle and R. D. Martin, eds., *The Study of Prosimian Behavior* (New York: Academic Press, 1979); and Ian Tattersall, *The Primates of Madagascar* (New York: Columbia University Press, 1982).

17. Alison F. Richard, "Malagasy Prosimians: Female Dominance," in Smuts et al., eds., *Primate Societies*, p. 32.

18. Bearder, "Lorises, Bushbabies, and Tarsiers," p. 13.

19. Pierre Charles-Dominique, *Ecology and Behaviour of Nocturnal Primates*, trans. Robert D. Martin (New York: Columbia University Press, 1977), p. 258. See also Robert D. Martin and Simon K. Bearder, "Radio Bush Baby," *Natural History*, October 1979, 77–81; and Bearder, "Lorises, Bushbabies, and Tarsiers," pp. 18–22.

20. John MacKinnon and Kathy MacKinnon, "The Behavior of Wild Spectral Tarsiers," *International Journal of Primatology*, 1 (1980): 361–79.

21. Matt Cartmill, "Non-Human Primates," in Jones, Martin, and Pilbeam, eds., *The Cambridge Encyclopedia of Human Evolution*, p. 28; John G. Fleagle, *Primate Adaptation and Evolution*, 2nd ed. (San Diego: Academic Press, 1999), pp. 118–22.

22. Napier and Napier, *A Handbook of Living Primates*, pp. 32–33.

23. Richard, *Primates in Nature*, pp. 164–65.

24. Cartmill, "Non-Human Primates," p. 29; Anne Wilson Goldizen, "Tamarins and Marmosets: Communal Care of Offspring," in Smuts et al., eds., *Primate Societies*, p. 34. See also John F. Eisenberg, "Comparative Ecology and Reproduction of New World Monkeys," in Devra Kleinman, ed., *The Biology and Conservation of the Callitrichidae* (Washington, DC: Smithsonian Institution, 1977), pp. 13–22; and Robert W. Sussman and Warren G. Kinzey, "The Ecological Role of the Callitrichidae: A Review," *American Journal of Physical Anthropology*, 64 (1984): 419–49; Fleagle, *Primate Adaptation and Evolution*, pp. 168–74.

25. Eisenberg, "Comparative Ecology and Reproduction of New World Monkeys," pp. 15–17.

26. John G. Robinson, Patricia C. Wright, and Warren G. Kinzey, "Monogamous Cebids and Their Relatives: Intergroup Calls and Spacing," in Smuts et al., eds., *Primate Societies*, pp. 44–53; Carolyn Crockett and John F. Eisenberg, "Howlers: Variations in Group Size and Demography," in Smuts et al., eds., *Primate Societies*, pp. 54–68; John G. Robinson and Charles H. Janson, "Capuchins, Squirrel Monkeys, and Atelines: Socioecological Convergence with Old World Primates," in Smuts et al., eds., *Primate Societies*, pp. 69–82.

27. Sarah Blaffer Hrdy, *The Langurs of Abu: Female and Male Strategies of Reproduction* (Cambridge, MA: Harvard University Press, 1977), p. 18.

28. Ibid., pp. 18–19.

29. J. R. Napier, "Paleoecology and Catarrhine Evolution," in J. R. Napier and P. H. Napier, eds., *Old World Monkeys: Evolution, Systematics, and Behavior* (New York: Academic Press, 1970), pp. 80–82.

30. Linda Marie Fedigan, *Primate Paradigms: Sex Roles and Social Bonds* (Montreal: Eden Press, 1982), p. 11.

31. Ibid., pp. 123–24.

32. Phyllis C. Lee, "Home Range, Territory and Intergroup Encounters," in Robert A. Hinde, ed., *Primate Social Relationships: An Integrated Approach* (Sunderland, MA: Sinauer, 1983), p. 231.

33. Fleagle, *Primate Adaptation and Evolution*, p. 302.

34. W. E. LeGros Clark, *The Fossil Evidence for Human Evolution* (Chicago: University of Chicago Press, 1964), p. 184.

35. Holger Preuschoft, David J. Chivers, Warren Y. Brockelman, and Norman Creel, eds., *The Lesser Apes: Evolutionary and*

Behavioural Biology (Edinburgh: Edinburgh University Press, 1984).

36. C. R. Carpenter, "A Field Study in Siam of the Behavior and Social Relations of the Gibbon (*Hylobates lar*)," *Comparative Psychology Monographs*, 16, no. 5 (1940): 1–212; David John Chivers, *The Siamang in Malaya* (Basel: Karger, 1974); and David J. Chivers, ed., *Malayan Forest Primates: Ten Years' Study in Tropical Rain Forest* (New York: Plenum, 1980).

37. H. D. Rijksen, *A Fieldstudy on Sumatran Orang Utans* (Pongo Pygmaeus Abelii Lesson 1827): Ecology, Behaviour and Conservation (Wageningen, Netherlands: H. Veenman and Zonen B.V., 1978), p. 22.

38. Dennis Normile, "Habitat Seen Playing Larger Role in Shaping Behavior," *Science,* March 6, 1998, 1454–455.

39. Biruté M. F. Galdikas, "Orangutan Adaptation at Tanjung Puting Reserve: Mating and Ecology," in David A. Hamburg and Elizabeth R. McCown, eds., *The Great Apes* (Menlo Park, CA: Benjamin/Cummings, 1979), pp. 220–23.

40. Dorothy L. Cheney and Richard W. Wrangham, "Predation," in Smuts et al., eds., *Primate Societies*, p. 236.

41. Rijksen, *A Fieldstudy on Sumatran Orang Utans,* p. 321.

42. Dian Fossey, *Gorillas in the Mist* (Boston: Houghton Mifflin, 1983), p. xvi.

43. Russell H. Tuttle, *Apes of the World: Their Social Behavior, Communication, Mentality, and Ecology* (Park Ridge, NJ: Noyes, 1986), pp. 99–114.

44. George Schaller, *The Mountain Gorilla: Ecology and Behavior* (Chicago: University of Chicago Press, 1963). See also Schaller's *The Year of the Gorilla* (Chicago: University of Chicago Press, 1964).

45. Fossey, *Gorillas in the Mist,* p. 47.

46. A. H. Harcourt, "The Social Relations and Group Structure of Wild Mountain Gorillas," in Hamburg and McCown, eds., *The Great Apes*, pp. 187–92.

47. R. L. Sussman, ed., *The Pygmy Chimpanzee: Evolutionary Biology and Behavior* (New York: Plenum, 1984); F. J. White, "*Pan paniscus* 1973 to 1996: Twenty-three Years of Field Research," *Evolutionary Anthropology*, 5 (1996): 11–17.

48. Frans de Waal and Frans Lanting, *Bonobo: The Forgotten Ape* (Berkeley: University of California Press, 1997).

49. Craig B. Stanford, "The Social Behavior of Chimpanzees and Bonobos: Empirical Evidence and Shifting Assumptions," *Current Anthropology*, 39 (1998): 399–420.

50. Jane Goodall, "My Life among Wild Chimpanzees," *National Geographic*, August 1963, 272–308; and van Lawick-Goodall, *In the Shadow of Man*.

51. Geza Teleki, "The Omnivorous Chimpanzee," *Scientific American*, January 1973, 32–42.

52. Craig Stanford, "Chimpanzee Hunting Behavior and Human Evolution," in Peter N. Peregrine, Carol R. Ember, and Melvin Ember, eds, *Physical Anthropology: Original Readings in Method and Practice* (Upper Saddle River, NJ: Prentice Hall, 2002).

53. Ibid., pp. 35–41.

54. Normile, "Habitat Seen Playing Larger Role."

55. Tuttle, *Apes of the World,* pp. 266–69.

56. Morris Goodman, "Reconstructing Human Evolution from Proteins," in Jones, Martin, and Pilbeam, eds., *The Cambridge Encyclopedia of Human Evolution*, pp. 307–12.

57. T. H. Clutton-Brock and Paul H. Harvey, "Primate Ecology and Social Organization," *Journal of Zoology*, London, 183 (1977): 8–9.

58. L. C. Aiello, "Body Size and Energy Requirements," in Jones, Martin, and Pilbeam, eds., *The Cambridge Encyclopedia of Human Evolution*, pp. 41–44; Alison Jolly, *The Evolution of*

59. Aiello, "Body Size and Energy Requirements."

60. Jolly, The *Evolution of Primate Behavior,* pp. 53–54.

61. Sue Taylor Parker, "Why Big Brains Are So Rare," in Parker and Gibson, eds., *"Language" and Intelligence in Monkeys and Apes*, p. 130.

62. Katharine Milton, "Distribution Patterns of Tropical Plant Foods as an Evolutionary Stimulus to Primate Mental Development," *American Anthropologist,* 83 (1981): 534–48; T. H. Clutton-Brock and Paul H. Harvey, "Primates, Brains and Ecology," *Journal of Zoology*, London, 190 (1980): 309–23.

63. Katharine Milton, "Foraging Behaviour and the Evolution of Primate Intelligence," in Richard W. Bryne and Andrew Whiten, eds., *Machiavellian Intelligence: Social Expertise and the Evolution of Intellect in Monkeys, Apes, and Humans* (Oxford: Clarendon Press, 1988), pp. 285–305.

64. Jolly, The *Evolution of Primate Behavior*, p. 119.

65. Clutton-Brock and Harvey, "Primate Ecology and Social Organization," p. 9.

66. John Terborgh, *Five New World Primates: A Study in Comparative Ecology* (Princeton, NJ: Princeton University Press, 1983), pp. 224–25.

67. Jolly, *The Evolution of Primate Behavior,* p. 120.

68. Ibid., p. 122.

69. Richard W. Wrangham, "An Ecological Model of Female-Bonded Primate Groups," *Behaviour*, 75 (1980): 262–300.

70. Dean Falk, "Hominid Paleoneurology," *Annual Review of Anthropology*, 16 (1987): 13–30.

71. Female bonobo, or pygmy chimpanzees, engage in sexual intercourse nearly as often as human females. See Nancy Thompson-Handler, Richard K. Malenky, and Noel Badrian, "Sexual Behavior of *Pan paniscus* under Natural Conditions in the Lomako Forest, Equateur, Zaire," in Randall L. Susman, ed., *The Pygmy Chimpanzee: Evolutionary Biology and Behavior* (New York: Plenum, 1984), pp. 347–66. For a review of field research on pygmy chimpanzees, see White, "*Pan paniscus* 1973 to 1996."

72. By male-female bonding, we mean that at least one of the sexes is "faithful," that is, typically has intercourse with just one opposite-sex partner throughout at least one estrus or menstrual cycle or breeding season. Note that the bonding may not be monogamous; an individual may be bonded to more than one individual of the opposite sex. See Melvin Ember and Carol R. Ember, "Male-Female Bonding: A Cross-Species Study of Mammals and Birds," *Behavior Science Research*, 14 (1979): 37–41.

73. Ember and Ember, "Male-Female Bonding," p. 43; see also Carol R. Ember and Melvin Ember, "The Evolution of Human Female Sexuality: A Cross-Species Perspective," *Journal of Anthropological Research*, 40 (1984): 203–204.

74. Ember and Ember, "The Evolution of Human Female Sexuality," p. 207.

75. Ibid., pp. 208–209.

76. de Waal and Lanting, *Bonobo.*

77. Duane M. Rumbaugh, "Learning Skills of Anthropoids," in L. A. Rosenblum, ed., *Primate Behavior*, vol. 1 (New York: Academic Press, 1970), pp. 52–58.

78. Observation by others cited by Jolly, *The Evolution of Primate Behavior*, p. 53.

79. Alison C. Hannah and W. C. McGrew, "Chimpanzees Using Stones to Crack Open Oil Palm Nuts in Liberia," *Primates,* 28 (1987): 31–46.

80. "The First Dentist," *Newsweek,* March 5, 1973, 73.

81. Robert M. Seyfarth, Dorothy L. Cheney, and Peter Marler,

"Monkey Response to Three Different Alarm Calls: Evidence of Predator Classification and Semantic Communication," *Science,* November 14, 1980, 801–803.

82. R. Allen Gardner and Beatrice T. Gardner, "Teaching Sign Language to a Chimpanzee," *Science,* August 15, 1969, 664–72.

83. Beatrice T. Gardner and R. Allen Gardner, "Two Comparative Psychologists Look at Language Acquisition," in K. E. Nelson, ed., *Children's Language,* vol. 2 (New York: Halsted Press, 1980), pp. 331–69.

84. Patricia Marks Greenfield and E. Sue Savage-Rumbaugh, "Grammatical Combination in *Pan paniscus:* Processes of Learning and Invention in the Evolution and Development of Language," in Parker and Gibson, eds., *"Language" and Intelligence in Monkeys and Apes,* pp. 540–78.

CHAPTER 5

1. Russell L. Ciochon and Dennis A. Etler, "Reinterpreting Past Primate Diversity," in Robert S. Corruccini and Russell L. Ciochon, eds., *Integrative Paths to the Past: Paleoanthropological Advances in Honor of F. Clark Howell* (Englewood Cliffs, NJ: Prentice Hall, 1994), pp. 33, 37–67.

2. P. D. Gingerich, "*Plesiadipis* and the Delineation of the Order Primates," in B. Wood, L. Martin, and P. Andrews, eds., *Major Topics in Primate Evolution* (Cambridge: Cambridge University Press, 1986), pp. 32–46; F. S. Szalay, "Paleobiology of the Earliest Primates," in R. Tuttle, ed., *The Functional and Evolutionary Biology of the Primates* (Chicago: University of Chicago Press, 1972), pp. 3–35; F. S. Szalay, I. Tattersall, and R. Decker, "Phylogenetic Relationships of *Plesiadipis*—Postcranial Evidence," *Contributions to Primatology,* 5 (1975): 136–66.

3. John G. Fleagle, "Anthropoid Origins," in Corruccini and Ciochon, eds., *Integrative Paths to the Past,* pp. 20, 17–35; Ciochon and Etler, "Reinterpreting Past Primate Diversity," p. 41; Matt Cartmill, "Explaining Primate Origins," in Peter N. Peregrine, Carol R. Ember, and Melvin Ember, eds., *Physical Anthropology: Original Readings in Method and Practice* (Upper Saddle River, NJ: Prentice Hall, 2002).

4. Glenn C. Conroy, *Primate Evolution* (New York: Norton, 1990), pp. 49–53.

5. Ibid., p. 53.

6. J. K. A. Habicht, *Paleoclimate, Paleomagnetism, and Continental Drift* (Tulsa, OK: American Association of Petroleum Geologists, 1979).

7. Elizabeth S. Vrba, "On the Connection between Paleoclimate and Evolution," E. S. Vrba, G. H. Denton, T. C. Partridge, and L. H. Burckle, eds., in *Paleoclimate and Evolution* (New Haven, CT: Yale University Press, 1995), pp. 24–45.

8. Robert Sussman, "Primate Origins and the Evolution of Angiosperms," *American Journal of Primatology,* 23 (1991): 209–23.

9. Alison F. Richard, *Primates in Nature* (New York: Freeman, 1985), p. 31; and Matt Cartmill, "Rethinking Primate Origins," *Science,* April 26, 1974, 436–37.

10. Frederick S. Szalay, "The Beginnings of Primates," *Evolution,* 22 (1968): 32–33.

11. Cartmill, "Rethinking Primate Origins," pp. 436–43; for more recent statements by Cartmill, see his "New Views on Primate Origins," *Evolutionary Anthropology,* 1 (1992): 105–11, and his "Explaining Primate Origins."

12. Robert W. Sussman and Peter H. Raven, "Pollination by Lemurs and Marsupials: An Archaic Coevolutionary System," *Science,* May 19, 1978, 734–35.

13. Conroy, *Primate Evolution,* pp. 94–95.

14. Ibid., p. 99.

15. Fleagle, "Anthropoid Origins," pp. 22–23.

16. Conroy, *Primate Evolution,* p. 119.

17. Leonard Radinsky, "The Oldest Primate Endocast," *American Journal of Physical Anthropology,* 27 (1967): 358–88.

18. Ibid., p. 105; and Fleagle, "Anthropoid Origins," p. 21.

19. John P. Alexander, "Alas, Poor *Notharctus,*" *Natural History,* August 1992, 55–59; Conroy, *Primate Evolution,* p. 111.

20. Richard F. Kay, C. Ross, and B. A. Williams, "Anthropoid Origins," *Science,* 275 (1997): 797–804.

21. Robert D. Martin, *Primate Origins and Evolution: A Phyletic Reconstruction* (Princeton, NJ: Princeton University Press, 1990), p. 46; Conroy, *Primate Evolution,* p. 46.

22. Kay, Ross, and Williams, "Anthropoid Origins"; John G. Fleagle and Richard F. Kay, "The Paleobiology of Catarrhines," in Eric Delson, ed., *Ancestors: The Hard Evidence* (New York: Alan R. Liss, 1985), p. 25.

23. Fleagle, "Anthropoid Origins," pp. 44–45; J. Jaeger, T. Thein, M. Benammi, Y. Chaimanee, A. N. Soe, T. Lwin, T. Tun, S. Wai, and S. Ducrocq, "A New Primate from the Middle Eocene of Myanmar and the Asian Early Origins of Anthropoids," *Science,* 286 (1999): 528–30.

24. Elwyn L. Simons, "Skulls and Anterior Teeth of *Catopithecus* (Primates: Anthropoidea) from the Eocene Shed Light on Anthropoidean Origins," *Science,* 268 (1995): 1885–888; Elwyn L. Simons and D. T. Rassmussen, "Skull of *Catopithecus browni,* an Early Tertiary Catarrhine," *American Journal of Physical Anthropology,* 100 (1996): 261–92.

25. Fleagle, "Anthropoid Origins," p. 24.

26. Richard F. Kay, "Parapithecidae," in I. Tattersall, E. Delson, and J. van Couvering, eds., *Encyclopedia of Human Evolution and Prehistory* (New York: Garland, 2000), p. 441.

27. Ibid., pp. 441–42; Conroy, *Primate Evolution,* p. 156.

28. John G. Fleagle, *Primate Adaptation and Evolution* (San Diego: Academic Press, 1999), pp. 404–409.

29. A. L. Rosenberger, "Cranial Anatomy and Implications of *Dolichocebus,* a Late Oligocene Ceboid Primate," *Nature,* 279 (1979): 416–18.

30. John G. Fleagle and R. F. Kay, "The Phyletic Position of the Parapithecidae," *Journal of Human Evolution,* 16 (1987): 483–531.

31. L. C. Aiello, "The Origin of the New World Monkeys," in W. George and R. Lavocat, eds., *The Africa-South America Connection* (Oxford: Clarendon Press, 1993), pp. 100–18; W. C. Hartwig, "Pattern, Puzzles and Perspectives on Platyrrhine Origins," in R. S. Corruccini and R. L. Ciochon, eds., *Integrative Paths to the Past,* pp. 69–93.

32. Peter Andrews, "Propliopithecidae," in Tattersall, Delson, and van Couvering, eds., *Encyclopedia of Human Evolution and Prehistory,* pp. 486, 485–87.

33. Fleagle and Kay, "The Paleobiology of Catarrhines," pp. 25, 30; Conroy, *Primate Evolution,* pp. 160–61.

34. Fleagle, *Primate Adaptation and Evolution,* pp. 413–15. See also John G. Fleagle and Richard F. Kay, "New Interpretations of the Phyletic Position of Oligocene Hominoids," in Russell L. Ciochon and Robert S. Corruccini, eds., *New Interpretations of Ape and Human Ancestry* (New York: Plenum, 1983), p. 205.

35. Fleagle, *Primate Adaptation and Evolution,* p. 453.

36. Conroy, *Primate Evolution,* pp. 248–49.

37. Ibid., p. 56.

38. Martin, *Primate Origins and Evolution,* p. 56.

39. David Begun, "Miocene Apes," in Peregrine, Ember, and Ember, eds., *Physical Anthropology.*

40. Conroy, *Primate Evolution,* pp. 206–11.

41. Begun, "Miocene Apes."

42. Peter Andrews, "Proconsul," in Tattersall, Delson, and van Couvering, eds., *Encyclopedia of Human Evolution and Prehistory,* p. 485.

43. Begun, "Miocene Apes."

44. Ibid.

45. Carl Zimmer, "Kenyan Skeleton Shakes Ape Family Tree," *Science,* 285 (1999): 1335–337; Steve Ward, B. Brown, A. Hill, J. Kelley, and W. Downs, "*Equatorius:* A New Hominoid Genus from the Middle Miocene of Kenya," *Science,* 285 (1999): 1382–386.

46. Begun, "Miocene Apes"; and Jay Kelley, "The Evolution of Apes," in Steve Jones, Robert Martin, and David Pilbeam, eds., *The Cambridge Encyclopedia of Human Evolution* (New York: Cambridge University Press, 1992), pp. 225, 223–30.

47. E. Sue Savage-Rumbaugh, "Hominid Evolution: Looking to Modern Apes for Clues," in Duane Quiatt and Junichiro Itani, eds., *Hominid Culture in Primate Perspective* (Niwot: University Press of Colorado, 1994), pp. 7–49.

48. Conroy, *Primate Evolution,* pp. 185, 255.

49. T. Harrison, "A Reassessment of the Phylogenetic Relationships of *Oreopithecus bamboli,*" *Journal of Human Evolution,* 15 (1986): 541–84; T. Harrison and L. Rook, "Enigmatic Anthropoid or Misunderstood Ape? The Phylogenetic Status of *Oreopithecus bamboli* Reconsidered," in D. R. Begun, C. V. Ward, and M. D. Rose, eds., *Function, Phylogeny and Fossils: Miocene Hominoid Evolution and Adaptation* (New York: Plenum, 1997), pp. 327–362.

50. Fleagle, *Primate Adaptation and Evolution,* pp. 472–74.

51. S. Ward, "The Taxonomy and Phylogenetic Relationships of *Sivapithecus* Revisited," in Begun, Ward, and Rose, eds., *Function, Phylogeny and Fossils,* pp. 269–90.

52. Begun, "Miocene Apes."

53. Russell Ciochon, John Olsen, and Jamie James, *Other Origins: The Search for the Giant Ape in Human Prehistory* (New York: Bantam, 1990), pp. 99–102.

54. Begun, "Miocene Apes."

55. Ibid.

56. Fleagle, *Primate Adaptation and Evolution,* pp. 480–83.

57. Alan Bilsborough, *Human Evolution* (New York: Blackie Academic & Professional, 1992), p. 65.

58. Elwyn Simons, "The Primate Fossil Record," in Jones, Martin, and Pilbeam, eds., *The Cambridge Encyclopedia of Human Evolution,* p. 207.

59. Vincent M. Sarich and Allan C. Wilson, "Quantitative Immunochemistry and the Evolution of the Primate Albumins: Micro-Component Fixations," *Science,* December 23, 1966, 1563–566; Vincent M. Sarich, "The Origin of Hominids: An Immunological Approach," in S. L. Washburn and Phyllis C. Jay, eds., *Perspectives on Human Evolution,* vol. 1 (New York: Holt, Rinehart & Winston, 1968), pp. 99–121; and Roger Lewin, "Is the Orangutan a Living Fossil?" *Science,* December 16, 1983, 1222–223.

60. Jones, Martin, and Pilbeam, eds., *The Cambridge Encyclopedia of Human Evolution,* p. 293; Martin, *Primate Origins and Evolution,* pp. 693–709.

61. The material referred to in this paragraph is drawn from Jones, Martin, and Pilbeam, eds., *The Cambridge Encyclopedia of Human Evolution,* pp. 8, 293–321.

CHAPTER 6

1. M. D. Rose, "Food Acquisition and the Evolution of Positional Behaviour: The Case of Bipedalism," in David J. Chivers, Bernard A. Wood, and Alan Bilsborough, eds., *Food Acquisition and Processing in Primates* (New York: Plenum, 1984), pp. 509–24.

2. Alan Bilsborough, *Human Evolution* (New York: Blackie Academic & Professional, 1992), pp. 64–65.

3. Kenneth Oakley, "On Man's Use of Fire, with Comments on Tool-Making and Hunting," in S. L. Washburn, ed., *Social Life of Early Man* (Chicago: Aldine, 1964), p. 186.

4. John D. Kingston, Bruno D. Marino, and Andrew Hill, "Isotopic Evidence for Neogene Hominid Paleoenvironments in the Kenya Rift Valley," *Science,* May 13, 1994, 955–59.

5. Gordon W. Hewes, "Food Transport and the Origin of Hominid Bipedalism," *American Anthropologist,* 63 (1961): 687–710.

6. Pat Shipman, "Scavenging or Hunting in Early Hominids: Theoretical Framework and Tests," *American Anthropologist,* 88 (1986): 27–43; Erik Trinkaus, "Bodies, Brawn, Brains and Noses: Human Ancestors and Human Predation," in Matthew H. Nitecki and Doris V. Nitecki, eds., *The Evolution of Human Hunting* (New York: Plenum, 1987), p. 115.

7. C. Owen Lovejoy, "The Origin of Man," *Science,* January 23, 1981, 341–50.

8. Clifford Jolly, "The Seed-Eaters: A New Model of Hominid Differentiation Based on a Baboon Analogy," *Man,* 5 (1970): 5–28.

9. Sherwood Washburn, "Tools and Human Evolution," *Scientific American,* September 1960, 63.

10. David Pilbeam, *The Ascent of Man* (New York: Macmillan, 1972), p. 153.

11. Milford H. Wolpoff, "Competitive Exclusion among Lower Pleistocene Hominids: The Single Species Hypothesis," *Man,* 6 (1971): 602.

12. E. Sue Savage-Rumbaugh, "Hominid Evolution: Looking to Modern Apes for Clues," in Duane Quiatt and Junichiro Itani, eds., *Hominid Culture in Primate Perspective* (Niwot: University Press of Colorado, 1994), pp. 7–49.

13. M. H. Wolpoff, "*Ramapithecus* and Human Origins: An Anthropologist's Perspective of Changing Interpretations," in Russell L. Ciochon and Robert S. Corruccini, eds., *New Interpretations of Ape and Human Ancestry* (New York: Plenum, 1983), p. 666.

14. Adrienne L. Zihlman, "The Emergence of Human Locomotion: The Evolutionary Background and Environmental Context," in Toshisada Nishida, William C. McGrew, Peter Marler, Martin Pickford, and Frans B. M. de Waal, eds., *Topics in Primatology,* vol. 1, *Human Origins* (Tokyo: University of Tokyo Press, 1992), pp. 409–22.

15. Peter Wheeler, "The Evolution of Bipedality and Loss of Functional Body Hair in Hominids," *Journal of Human Evolution,* 13 (1984): 91–98; Peter Wheeler, "The Influence of Bipedalism in the Energy and Water Budgets of Early Hominids," *Journal of Human Evolution,* 23 (1991): 379–88.

16. D. Falk, "Enlarged Occipital/Marginal Sinuses and Emissary Foramina: Their Significance in Hominid Evolution," in Frederick E. Grine, ed., *Evolutionary History of the "Robust" Australopithecines* (New York: Aldine, 1988), pp. 85–96.

17. Zihlman, "The Emergence of Human Locomotion," p. 414.

18. C. Owen Lovejoy, "Evolution of Human Walking," *Scientific American,* 259 (1988): 82–89.

19. Leslie Aiello and Christopher Dean, *An Introduction to Human Evolutionary Anatomy* (London: Academic Press, 1990), pp. 268–74.

20. Ibid., pp. 507–508.

21. Timothy D. White, G. Suwa, and B. Asfaw, "Corrigendum: *Australopithecus ramidus,* a New Species of Early Hominid from Aramis, Ethiopia," *Nature,* 375 (1995): 88.

22. Timothy D. White, G. Suwa, and B. Asfaw, "*Australopithecus ramidus*, a New Species of Early Hominid from Aramis, Ethiopia," *Nature,* 371 (1994): 306–33.

23. Randall L. Susman, Jack T. Stern, Jr., and William L. Jungers, "Locomotor Adaptations in the Hadar Hominids," in Eric Delson, ed., *Ancestors: The Hard Evidence* (New York: Alan R. Liss, 1985), pp. 184–92. See also Rose, "Food Acquisition and the Evolution of Positional Behaviour."

24. Glenn C. Conroy, *Primate Evolution* (New York: Norton, 1990), p. 274. See also Elizabeth Culotta, "New Hominid Crowds the Field," *Science,* August 18, 1995, 918; and John Noble Wilford, "The Transforming Leap, from 4 Legs to 2," *New York Times,* September 5, 1995, p. C1ff.

25. John G. Fleagle, *Primate Adaptation and Evolution,* 2nd ed. (San Diego: Academic Press, 1999), pp. 511–15.

26. Ibid., p. 528.

27. Elizabeth Culotta, "New Hominid Crowds the Field," *Science,* August 18, 1995, 918.

28. Meave Leakey, C. S. Feibel, I. McDougall, and A. Walker, "New Four-Million-Year-Old Hominid Species from Kanapoi and Allia Bay, Kenya," *Nature,* 376 (1995): 565–71.

29. Ian Tattersall and Jeffrey Schwartz, *Extinct Humans* (Boulder, CO: Westview, 2000), p. 93.

30. Scott W. Simpson, "*Australopithecus afarensis* and Human Evolution," in Peter N. Peregrine, Carol R. Ember, and Melvin Ember, eds., *Physical Anthropology: Original Readings in Method and Practice* (Upper Saddle River, NJ: Prentice Hall, 2002); Tim D. White, Donald C. Johanson, and William H. Kimbel, "*Australopithecus africanus:* Its Phyletic Position Reconsidered," *South African Journal of Science,* 77 (1981): 445–70; and Donald C. Johanson and Tim D. White, "A Systematic Assessment of Early African Hominids," *Science,* January 26, 1979, 321.

31. Donald C. Johanson and Maitland Edey, *Lucy: The Beginnings of Humankind* (New York: Simon & Schuster, 1981), pp. 17–18.

32. Johanson and White, "A Systematic Assessment of Early African Hominids."

33. Roger Lewin, "Fossil Lucy Grows Younger, Again," *Science,* January 7, 1983, 43–44.

34. Conroy, *Primate Evolution,* pp. 291–92; Simpson, "*Australopithecus afarensis* and Human Evolution."

35. Fleagle, *Primate Adaptation and Evolution,* pp. 515–18.

36. Ibid., pp. 515, 520.

37. F. E. Grine, "Dental Evidence for Dietary Differences in *Australopithecus* and *Paranthropus:* A Quantitative Analysis of Permanent Molar Microwear," *Journal of Human Evolution,* 15 (1986): 783–822.

38. William H. Kimbel, T. D. White, and D. C. Johansen, "Cranial Morphology of *Australopithecus afarensis:* A Comparative Study Based on Composite Reconstruction of the Adult Skull," *American Journal of Physical Anthropology,* 64 (1984): 337–88.

39. William L. Jungers, "Relative Joint Size and Hominoid Locomotor Adaptations with Implications for the Evolution of Hominid Bipedalism," *Journal of Human Evolution,* 17 (1988): 247–65; Ronald J. Clarke and P. V. Tobias, "Sterkfontein Member 2 Foot Bones of the Oldest South African Hominid," *Science,* 269 (1995): 521–24.

40. Lovejoy, "Evolution of Human Walking."

41. Tattersall and Schwartz, *Extinct Humans,* pp. 88–89; Clarke and Tobias, "Sterkfontein Member 2 Foot Bones of the Oldest South African Hominid."

42. Raymond Dart, "*Australopithecus africanus:* The Man-Ape of South Africa," *Nature,* 115 (1925): 195.

43. Timothy G. Bromage and M. Christopher Dean, "Reevaluation of the Age at Death of Immature Fossil Hominids," *Nature,* October 10, 1985, pp. 525–27; B. Holly Smith, "Dental Development in *Australopithecus* and Early *Homo,*" *Nature,* September 25, 1986, pp. 327–30.

44. Niles Eldredge and Ian Tattersall, *The Myths of Human Evolution* (New York: Columbia University Press, 1982), pp. 80–90.

45. Pilbeam, *The Ascent of Man,* p. 107.

46. Ralph L. Holloway, "The Casts of Fossil Hominid Brains," *Scientific American,* July 1974, 106–15.

47. Frederick S. Szalay and Eric Delson, *Evolutionary History of the Primates* (New York: Academic Press, 1979), p. 504.

48. Conroy, *Primate Evolution,* pp. 280–82.

49. Ibid., pp. 294–303.

50. Henry M. McHenry, "'Robust' Australopithecines, Our Family Tree, and Homoplasy," in Peter N. Peregrine, Carol R. Ember, and Melvin Ember, eds., *Physical Anthropology: Original Readings in Method and Practice* (Upper Saddle River, NJ: Prentice Hall, 2002).

51. Szalay and Delson, *Evolutionary History of the Primates,* p. 504; Bernard A. Wood, "Evolution of Australopithecines," in Steve Jones, Robert Martin, and David Pilbeam, eds., *The Cambridge Encyclopedia of Human Evolution* (New York: Cambridge University Press, 1992), p. 236.

52. Henry M. McHenry, "New Estimates of Body Weight in Early Hominids and Their Significance to Encephalization and Megadontia in 'Robust' Australopithecines," in Grine, ed., *Evolutionary History of the "Robust" Australopithecines,* pp. 133–48; William L. Jungers, "New Estimates of Body Size in Australopithecines," in ibid., pp. 115–25.

53. Fleagle, "Primate Adaptation and Evolution," p. 522.

54. Frederick E. Grine, "Australopithecine Taxonomy and Phylogeny: Historical Background and Recent Interpretation," in R. L. Ciochon and J. G. Fleagle, eds., *The Human Evolution Source Book* (Englewood Cliffs, NJ: Prentice Hall, 1993), p. 204; Alan Walker and R. Leakey, "The Evolution of *Australopithecus boisei,*" in Grine, ed., *Evolutionary History of the "Robust" Australopithecines,* pp. 247–58.

55. Robert Broom, *Finding the Missing Link* (London: Watts, 1950).

56. Fleagle, *Primate Adaptation and Evolution,* p. 522.

57. McHenry, "'Robust' Australopithecines, Our Family Tree, and Homoplasy."

58. Ibid.

59. Frederick E. Grine, "Evolutionary History of the 'Robust' Australopithecines: A Summary and Historical Perspective," in Grine, ed., *Evolutionary History of the "Robust" Australopithecines,* pp. 515–16.

60. Christopher Stringer, "Evolution of a Species," *Geographical Magazine,* 57 (1985): 601–607.

61. Mary Leakey, *Olduvai Gorge: My Search for Early Man* (London: Collins, 1979); Louis Leakey, *Olduvai Gorge,* vol. 1: *A Preliminary Report on the Geology and Fauna* (Cambridge: Cambridge University Press, 1961).

62. McHenry, "'Robust' Australopithecines, Our Family Tree, and Homoplasy."

63. Fleagle, *Primate Adaptation and Evolution,* p. 529.

64. Wood, "Evolution of Australopithecines," p. 239.

CHAPTER 7

1. Randall Susman, "Fossil Evidence for Early Hominid Tool Use," *Science,* September 9, 1994, 1570.

2. Ibid.

3. "The First Tool Kit," *Science,* January 31, 1997, 623.

4. Louis S. B. Leakey, "Finding the World's Earliest Man," *National Geographic,* September 1960, 424.

5. J. Desmond Clark, *The Prehistory of Africa* (New York: Praeger, 1970), p. 68; Kathy Schick and Nicholas Toth, *Making Silent Stones Speak* (New York: Simon & Schuster, 1993), pp. 97–99.

6. Schick and Toth, *Making Silent Stones Speak,* pp. 153–70.

7. Ibid., p. 129.

8. Ibid., pp. 157–59.

9. Glynn Isaac, "The Archaeology of Human Origins: Studies of the Pleistocene in East Africa, 1971–1981," in Fred Wendorf and Angela E. Close, eds., *Advances in World Archaeology,* vol. 3 (Orlando, FL: Academic Press, 1984), p. 13.

10. John C. Whittaker, *Flintknapping: Making and Understanding Stone Tools* (Austin: University of Texas Press, 1994), pp. 283–85.

11. Reported in Schick and Toth, *Making Silent Stones Speak,* pp. 175–76.

12. John D. Speth, "Were Our Ancestors Hunters or Scavengers?" in Peter N. Peregrine, Carol R. Ember, and Melvin Ember, eds., *Physical Anthropology: Original Readings in Method and Practice* (Upper Saddle River, NJ: Prentice Hall, 2002).

13. Pat Shipman, "Scavenging or Hunting in Early Hominids: Theoretical Framework and Tests," *American Anthropologist,* 88 (1986): 27–43. For the idea that scavenging may have been an important food-getting strategy even for protohominids, see Frederick S. Szalay, "Hunting-Scavenging Protohominids: A Model for Hominid Origins," *Man,* 10 (1975): 420–29.

14. John D. Speth and Dave D. Davis, "Seasonal Variability in Early Hominid Predation," *Science,* April 30, 1976, 441–45.

15. Glynn Isaac, "The Diet of Early Man: Aspects of Archaeological Evidence from Lower and Middle Pleistocene Sites in Africa," *World Archaeology,* 2 (1971): 289.

16. Mary Leakey, *Olduvai Gorge: Excavations in Beds I and II* (Cambridge: Cambridge University Press, 1971).

17. Richard Potts, *Early Hominid Activities at Olduvai* (New York: Aldine, 1988), pp. 253–58.

18. Richard Potts, "Home Bases and Early Hominids," *American Scientist,* 72 (1984): 338–47.

19. Potts, *Early Hominid Activities at Olduvai,* pp. 278–81.

20. Eric Wolf, "Culture: Panacea or Problem," *American Antiquity,* 49 (1984): 393–400.

21. This statement is not as clear-cut as it may seem. Primate social behavior is very complex, and social learning is important. A well-balanced and insightful discussion of primate social behavior can be found in Dorothy Cheney and Robert Seyfarth, *How Monkeys See the World* (Chicago: University of Chicago Press, 1990); see also Gretchen Vogel, "Chimps in the Wild Show Stirrings of Culture," *Science,* 284 (1999): 2070–73.

22. John Frisch, "Individual Behavior and Intergroup Variability in Japanese Macaques," in P. C. Jay, ed., *Primates: Studies in Adaptation and Variability* (New York: Holt, Rinehart & Winston, 1968), pp. 243–52.

23. K. L. R. Hall, "Social Learning in Monkeys," in Jay, ed., *Primates,* pp. 383–97.

24. Cheney and Seyfarth, *How Monkeys See the World,* pp. 133–36.

25. John Fleagle, *Primate Adaptation and Evolution,* 2nd ed. (San Diego: Academic Press, 1999), p. 64; Robin Dunbar, *Primate Social Systems* (Ithaca, NY: Comstock, 1988), pp. 107–10.

26. Fleagle, *Primate Adaptation and Evolution,* pp. 64–65; Dunbar, *Primate Social Systems,* pp. 111–12.

27. Dunbar, *Primate Social Systems,* pp. 113–16.

28. Caroline Tutin and L. White, "The Recent Evolutionary Past of Primate Communities: Likely Environmental Impacts during the Past Three Millennia," in J. G. Fleagle, C. Janson, and K. E. Reed, eds., *Primate Communities* (Cambridge: Cambridge University Press, 1999), pp. 230–31.

29. Dunbar, *Primate Social Systems,* pp. 251–54.

30. Ibid., pp. 206–208.

31. Robert Boyd and Joan Silk, *How Humans Evolved,* 2nd ed. (New York: Norton, 2000), pp. 249–50.

32. Theodosius Dobzhansky, *Mankind Evolving: The Evolution of the Human Species* (New Haven, CT: Yale University Press, 1962), p. 196.

33. Timothy G. Bromage and M. Christopher Dean, "Re-Evaluation of the Age at Death of Immature Fossil Hominids," *Nature,* October 10, 1985, 525–27; B. Holly Smith, "Dental Development in *Australopithecus* and Early *Homo,*" *Nature,* September 25, 1986, 327–30.

34. Henry M. McHenry, "'Robust' Australopithecines, Our Family Tree, and Homoplasy," in Peregrine, Ember, and Ember, eds., *Physical Anthropology;* Philip V. Tobias, "The Craniocerebral Interface in Early Hominids: Cerebral Impressions, Cranial Thickening, Paleoneurobiology, and a New Hypothesis on Encephalization," in Robert S. Corruccini and Russell L. Ciochon, eds., *Integrative Paths to the Past: Paleoanthropological Advances in Honor of F. Clark Howell* (Englewood Cliffs, NJ: Prentice Hall, 1994), pp. 194–97.

35. Henry M. McHenry, "The Pattern of Human Evolution: Studies on Bipedalism, Mastication, and Encephalization," *Annual Review of Anthropology,* 11 (1982): 160–61.

36. Ibid., p. 162.

37. David Pilbeam and Stephen Jay Gould, "Size and Scaling in Human Evolution," *Science,* December 6, 1974, 899.

38. McHenry, "'Robust' Australopithecines, Our Family Tree, and Homoplasy"; Tobias, "The Craniocerebral Interface in Early Hominids."

39. Scott W. Simpson, "*Australopithecus afarensis* and Human Evolution," in Carol R. Ember, Melvin Ember, and Peter N. Peregrine, eds., *Research Frontiers in Anthropology* (Upper Saddle River, NJ: Prentice Hall, 1998). Prentice Hall/Simon & Schuster Custom Publishing.

CHAPTER 8

1. G. Philip Rightmire, "*Homo erectus,*" in Ian Tattersall, Eric Delson, and John van Couvering, eds., *Encyclopedia of Human Evolution and Prehistory* (New York: Garland, 1988), pp. 259–65.

2. C. C. Swisher III, G. H. Curtis, T. Jacob, A. G. Getty, A. Suprijo, and N. Widiasmoro, "Age of the Earliest Known Hominids in Java, Indonesia." *Science,* February 25, 1994, 1118–21.

3. Michael Balter and Ann Gibbons, "A Glimpse of Humans' First Journey out of Africa," *Science,* 288 (2000): 948–50; Leo Gabunia, A. Vekua, D. Lordkipanidze, et al., "Earliest Pleistocene Hominid Cranial Remains from Dmanisi, Republic of Georgia: Taxonomy, Geological Setting, and Age," *Science,* 288 (2000): 1019–25.

4. Milford H. Wolpoff and Abel Nkini, "Early and Early Middle Pleistocene Hominids from Asia and Africa," in Eric Delson, ed., *Ancestors: The Hard Evidence* (New York: A. R. Liss, 1985), pp. 202–205. See also G. Philip Rightmire, "The Tempo of Change in the Evolution of Mid-Pleistocene *Homo,*" in ibid., pp. 255–64; Michael Balter, "In Search of the First Europeans," *Science,* 291 (2001): 1722–25.

5. G. Philip Rightmire, *The Evolution of* Homo erectus: *Comparative Anatomical Studies of an Extinct Human Species* (Cambridge: Cambridge University Press, 1990), pp. 12–14.

6. Swisher et al., "Age of the Earliest Known Hominids in Java, Indonesia."

7. Rightmire, "*Homo erectus.*"

8. John Fleagle, *Primate Adaptation and Evolution,* 2nd ed. (San Diego: Academic Press), pp. 534–35; Michael Day, *Guide to Fossil Man,* 4th ed. (Chicago: University of Chicago Press, 1986), pp. 409–12; Andrew Kramer, "Natural History and Evolutionary Fate of *Homo erectus*," in P. N. Peregrine, C. R. Ember, and M. Ember, eds., *Physical Anthropology: Original Readings in Method and Practice* (Upper Saddle River, NJ: Prentice Hall, 2002).

9. Rightmire, "*Homo erectus*"; and Philip V. Tobias, "The Craniocerebral Interface in Early Hominids: Cerebral Impressions, Cranial Thickening, Paleoneurobiology, and a New Hypothesis on Encephalization," in Robert S. Corruccini and Russell L. Ciochon, eds., *Integrative Paths to the Past: Paleoanthropological Advances in Honor of F. Clark Howell* (Englewood Cliffs, NJ: Prentice Hall, 1994), pp. 194–97.

10. Robert G. Franciscus and Erik Trinkaus, "Nasal Morphology and the Emergence of *Homo erectus*," *American Journal of Physical Anthropology,* 75 (1988): 517–27.

11. Craig S. Feibel and Francis H. Brown, "Microstratigraphy and Paleoenvironments," in Alan Walker and Richard Leakey, eds., *The Nariokotome* Homo erectus *Skeleton* (Cambridge, MA: Harvard University Press, 1993), p. 39.

12. Christopher B. Ruff and Alan Walker, "Body Size and Body Shape," in Walker and Leakey, eds., *The Nariokotome* Homo erectus *Skeleton,* pp. 235, 254.

13. Milford Wolpoff, A. G. Thorne, J. Jelinek, and Zhang Yinyun, "The Case for Sinking *Homo erectus:* 100 years of *Pithecanthropus* Is Enough!" in J. L. Franzen, ed., *100 Years of Pithecanthropus: The* Homo Erectus *Problem. Courier Forshungsinstitut Senckenberg,* 171 (1993): 341–61.

14. Fleagle, *Primate Adaptation and Evolution,* p. 306.

15. Melvin Ember and Carol R. Ember, "Male-Female Bonding: A Cross-Species Study of Mammals and Birds," *Behavior Science Research* 14 (1979): 37–56; cf.; Owen Lovejoy, "The Origin of Man," *Science,* 211 (1981): 341–50.

16. Charles B. Clayman, ed., *American Medical Association Encyclopedia of Medicine* (New York: Random House, 1989), pp. 857–58.

17. Francois Bordes, *The Old Stone Age* (New York: McGraw-Hill, 1968), pp. 51–97.

18. David W. Phillipson, *African Archaeology,* 2nd ed. (Cambridge: Cambridge University Press, 1993), p. 57.

19. Kathy Schick and Nicholas Toth, *Making Silent Stones Speak* (New York: Simon & Schuster, 1993), pp. 227, 233.

20. Ibid., pp. 231–33; John C. Whittaker, *Flintknapping: Making and Understanding Stone Tools* (Austin: University of Texas Press, 1994), p. 27.

21. Bordes, *Old Stone Age,* pp. 24–25; Whittaker, *Flintknapping,* p. 27.

22. Schick and Toth, *Making Silent Stones Speak,* pp. 258–60; Whittaker, *Flintknapping,* p. 27.

23. Lawrence Keeley's analysis reported in Schick and Toth, *Making Silent Stones Speak,* p. 260; see that page for their analysis of tool use.

24. William H. Calvin, *The Throwing Madonna: Essays on the Brain* (New York: McGraw-Hill, 1983).

25. Hou Yamei, R. Potts, Y. Baoyin, et al., "Mid-Pleistocene Acheulean-like Stone Technology of the Bose Basin, South China," *Science,* 287 (2000): 1622–26.

26. Russell Ciochon, John Olsen, and Jamie James, *Other Origins: The Search for the Giant Ape in Human Prehistory* (New York: Bantam, 1990), pp. 178–83; Geoffrey G. Pope, "Bamboo and Human Evolution," *Natural History,* October 1989, 49–57.

27. F. Clark Howell, "Observations on the Earlier Phases of the European Lower Paleolithic," in *Recent Studies in Paleoanthropology, American Anthropologist,* special publication, April 1966, 111–40.

28. Richard G. Klein, "Reconstructing How Early People Exploited Animals: Problems and Prospects," in M. H. Nitecki and D. V. Nitecki, eds., *The Evolution of Human Hunting* (New York: Plenum, 1987), pp. 11–45; and Lewis R. Binford, "Were There Elephant Hunters at Torralba?" in ibid., pp. 47–105.

29. Leslie G. Freeman, "Torralba and Ambrona: A Review of Discoveries," in Corruccini and Ciochon, eds., *Integrative Paths to the Past,* pp. 597–637.

30. A good example of this problem is the ongoing debate about fire use at Zhoukoudian cave, as reported by Steve Wiener, Q. Xi, P. Goldberg, J. Liu, and O. Bar-Yousef, "Evidence for the Use of Fire at Zhoukoudian, China," *Science,* 281 (1998): 251–53.

31. Glynn Isaac, "The Archaeology of Human Origins: Studies of the Pleistocene in East Africa, 1971–1981," in Fred Wendorf and Angela E. Close, eds., *Advances in World Archaeology,* vol. 3 (Orlando, FL: Academic Press, 1984), pp. 35–36. Other evidence for deliberate use of fire comes from the Swartkrans cave in South Africa and is dated 1 million to 1.5 million years ago; see C. K. Brain and A. Sillen, "Evidence from the Swartkrans Cave for the Earliest Use of Fire," *Nature,* December 1, 1988, 464–66.

32. Richard G. Klein, *The Human Career: Human Biological and Cultural Origins* (Chicago: University of Chicago Press, 1989), p. 171.

33. Lewis R. Binford and Chuan Kun Ho, "Taphonomy at a Distance: Zhoukoudian, 'The Cave Home of Beijing Man'?" *Current Anthropology,* 26 (1985): 413–42.

34. J. Desmond Clark, *The Prehistory of Africa* (New York: Praeger, 1970), pp. 94–95.

35. Ibid., pp. 96–97.

36. Henry de Lumley, "A Paleolithic Camp at Nice," *Scientific American,* May 1969, pp. 42–50.

37. D. Bruce Dickson, *The Dawn of Belief* (Tucson: University of Arizona Press, 1990), pp. 42–44.

38. Ibid., p. 45; Ian Tattersall and Jeffrey Schwartz, *Extinct Humans* (Boulder, CO: Westview, 2000), p. 155.

39. Dean Falk, "Cerebral Cortices of East African Early Hominids," *Science,* 221 (1983): 1072–74; see also Philip Tobias, "The Brain of *Homo habilis:* A New Level of Organization in Cerebral Evolution," *Journal of Human Evolution,* 16 (1987): 741–61.

40. Philip Lieberman, *Uniquely Human: The Evolution of Speech, Thought, and Selfless Behavior* (Cambridge, MA: Harvard University Press, 1991), pp. 53–77.

41. Karl von Frisch, "Dialects in the Language of the Bees," *Scientific American,* August 1962, 78–87.

42. Dorothy Cheney and Robert Seyfarth, *How Monkeys See the World* (Chicago: University of Chicago Press, 1990), pp. 106–107.

43. Ibid., pp. 129–33.

44. Madhusree Mukerjee, "Field Notes: Interview with a Parrot," *Scientific American,* April 1996, 28.

45. E. S. Savage-Rumbaugh, "Language Training of Apes," in Steve Jones, Robert Martin, and David Pilbeam, eds., *The Cambridge Encyclopedia of Human Evolution* (Cambridge: Cambridge University Press, 1992), pp. 138–41.

46. Jane H. Hill, "Apes and Language," *Annual Review of Anthropology,* 7 (1978): 94.

47. Jane H. Hill, "Do Apes Have Language?" in Carol R. Ember, Melvin Ember, and Peter N. Peregrine, eds., *Research Frontiers in Anthropology* (Upper Saddle River, NJ: Prentice Hall, 1998). Prentice Hall/Simon and Schuster Custom Publishing.

48. C. F. Hockett and R. Ascher, "The Human Revolution," *Current Anthropology,* 5 (1964): 135–68.

49. T. S. Eliot, "The Love Song of J. Alfred Prufrock," in *Collected Poems, 1909–1962* (New York: Harcourt, Brace & World, 1963).

50. See Noam Chomsky, *Reflections on Language* (New York: Pantheon, 1975).

51. Wayne M. Senner, "Theories and Myths on the Origins of Writing: A Historical Overview," in Wayne M. Senner, ed., *The Origins of Writing* (Lincoln: University of Nebraska Press, 1989), pp. 1–26.

52. Franklin C. Southworth and Chandler J. Daswani, *Foundations of Linguistics* (New York: Free Press, 1974), p. 312. See also Franz Boas, "On Grammatical Categories," in Dell Hymes, ed., *Language in Culture and Society: A Reader in Linguistics and Anthropology* (New York: Harper & Row, 1964 [originally published 1911]), pp. 121–23.

53. Derek Bickerton, "Creole Languages," *Scientific American,* July 1983, 116–22.

54. Ibid., p. 122.

55. Brent Berlin, *Ethnobiological Classification: Principles of Categorization of Plants and Animals in Traditional Societies* (Princeton, NJ: Princeton University Press, 1992); Terence E. Hays, "Sound Symbolism, Onomatopoeia, and New Guinea Frog Names," *Journal of Linguistic Anthropology,* 4 (1994): 153–74.

56. Lila R. Gleitman and Eric Wanner, "Language Acquisition: The State of the State of the Art," in Eric Wanner and Lila R. Gleitman, eds., *Language Acquisition: The State of the Art* (Cambridge: Cambridge University Press, 1982), pp. 3–48; Ben G. Blount, "The Development of Language in Children," in Ruth H. Munroe, Robert L. Munroe, and Beatrice B. Whiting, eds., *Handbook of Cross-Cultural Human Development* (New York: Garland, 1981), pp. 379–402.

57. Roger Brown, "The First Sentence of Child and Chimpanzee," in Thomas A Sebeok and Jean Umiker-Sebeok, eds., *Speaking of Apes* (New York: Plenum, 1980), pp. 93–94.

58. Peter A. de Villiers and Jill G. de Villiers, *Early Language* (Cambridge, MA: Harvard University Press, 1979), p. 48; see also Wanner and Gleitman, eds., *Language Acquisition.*

59. Bickerton, "Creole Languages," p. 122.

60. William Noble and Ian Davidson, *Human Evolution, Language, and Mind* (Cambridge: Cambridge University Press, 1996), pp. 162–214.

61. Terrence Deacon, *The Symbolic Species: The Co-Evolution of Language and the Brain* (New York: Norton, 1997), pp. 365–75.

CHAPTER 9

1. Christopher Stringer, "Evolution of a Species," *Geographical Magazine,* 57 (1985): 601–607.

2. Ibid.

3. Philip Rightmire, "Human Evolution in the Middle Pleistocene: The Role of *Homo heidelbergensis.*" *Evolutionary Anthropology,* 6 (1997): 281–27.

4. Ibid.; John G. Fleagle, *Primate Adaptation and Evolution,* 2nd ed. (San Diego: Academic Press, 1999), pp. 535–37.

5. Frank Spencer, "The Neandertals and Their Evolutionary Significance: A Brief Historical Survey," in Fred H. Smith and Frank Spencer, eds., *The Origins of Modern Humans* (New York: A. R. Liss, 1984), pp. 1–50.

6. Erik Trinkaus, "Pathology and the Posture of the La Chapelle-aux-Saints Neandertal," *American Journal of Physical Anthropology,* 67 (1985): 19–41.

7. Christopher B. Stringer, "Neandertals," in Ian Tattersall, Eric Delson, and John van Couvering, eds., *Encyclopedia of Human Evolution and Prehistory* (New York: Garland, 1988), p. 370.

8. Erik Trinkaus and Pat Shipman, "Neandertals: Images of Ourselves," *Evolutionary Anthropology,* 1, no. 6 (1993): 198, 194–201.

9. Fred H. Smith, "Fossil Hominids from the Upper Pleistocene of Central Europe and the Origin of Modern Humans," in Smith and Spencer, eds., *The Origins of Modern Humans,* p. 187.

10. Erik Trinkaus, "Western Asia," in Smith and Spencer, eds., *The Origins of Modern Humans,* pp. 251–53.

11. Matthias Krings, A. Stone, R. W. Schmitz, H. Krainitzki, M. Stoneking, and S. Paabo, "Neandertal DNA Sequences and the Origin of Modern Humans," *Cell,* 90 (1997): 19–30.

12. Rebecca Cann, "DNA and Human Origins," *Annual Review of Anthropology,* 17 (1988): 127–43.

13. Ibid.

14. Linda Vigilant, M. Stoneking, H. Harpending, K. Hawkes, and A. Wilson, "African Populations and the Evolution of Human Mitochondrial DNA," *Science,* 253 (1991): 1503–1507.

15. Krings et al., "Neandertal DNA Sequences and the Origin of Modern Humans."

16. Ian Tattersall, *The Last Neanderthal* (Boulder, CO: Westview, 1999), pp. 115–16; Ann Gibbons, "The Riddle of Co-Existence," *Science,* 291 (2001): 1725–29.

17. Paul Mellars, *The Neanderthal Legacy* (Princeton, NJ: Princeton University Press, 1996), pp. 405–19.

18. Paul Mellars, "The Fate of the Neanderthals," *Nature,* 395 (1998): 539–40.

19. Lawrence Guy Strauss, "On Early Hominid Use of Fire," *Current Anthropology,* 30 (1989): 488–91.

20. Kathy D. Schick and Nicholas Toth, *Making Silent Stones Speak* (New York: Simon & Schuster, 1993), pp. 288–92.

21. Richard G. Klein, *The Human Career: Human Biological and Cultural Origins* (Chicago: University of Chicago Press, 1989), pp. 291–96.

22. Schick and Toth, *Making Silent Stones Speak,* pp. 288–92; John C. Whittaker, *Flintknapping: Making and Understanding Stone Tools* (Austin: University of Texas Press, 1994), pp. 30–31.

23. Klein, *The Human Career,* pp. 421–22.

24. Sally R. Binford and Lewis R. Binford, "Stone Tools and Human Behavior," *Scientific American,* April 1969, 70–84.

25. Paul R. Fish, "Beyond Tools: Middle Paleolithic Debitage Analysis and Cultural Inference," *Journal of Anthropological Research,* 37 (1981): 377.

26. Karl W. Butzer, "Geomorphology and Sediment Stratigraphy," in Ronald Singer and John Wymer, *The Middle Stone Age at Klasies River Mouth in South Africa* (Chicago: University of Chicago Press, 1982), p. 42.

27. David W. Phillipson, *African Archaeology,* 2nd ed. (Cambridge: Cambridge University Press, 1993), p. 63.

28. For the controversy about whether the inhabitants of the Dordogne Valley lived in their homesites year-round, see Lewis R. Binford, "Interassemblage Variability: The Mousterian and the 'Functional' Argument," in Colin Renfrew,

ed., *The Explanation of Culture Change: Models in Prehistory* (Pittsburgh: University of Pittsburgh Press, 1973).

29. Schick and Toth, *Making Silent Stones Speak*, p. 292.
30. Richard G. Klein, "The Ecology of Early Man in Southern Africa," *Science*, July 8, 1977, 120.
31. Richard G. Klein, "Ice-Age Hunters of the Ukraine," *Scientific American*, June 1974, 96–105.
32. François Bordes, "Mousterian Cultures in France," *Science*, September 22, 1961, 803–10.
33. Thomas C. Patterson, *The Evolution of Ancient Societies: A World Archaeology* (Englewood Cliffs, NJ: Prentice Hall, 1981).
34. Phillipson, *African Archaeology*, p. 64.
35. Richard G. Klein, "The Stone Age Prehistory of Southern Africa," *Annual Review of Anthropology*, 12 (1983): 38–39.
36. Lewis R. Binford, *Faunal Remains from Klasies River Mouth* (Orlando, FL: Academic Press, 1984), pp. 195–97. To explain the lack of complete skeletons of large animals, Klein (see note 35) suggests that the hunters may have butchered the large animals elsewhere because they could carry home only small cuts.
37. John Noble Wilford, "Ancient German Spears Tell of Mighty Hunters of Stone Age," *New York Times*, March 4, 1997, p. C6.
38. John E. Pfeiffer, *The Emergence of Man*, 3rd ed. (New York: Harper & Row, 1978), p. 155.
39. C. B. Stringer, J. J. Hublin, and B. Vandermeersch, "The Origin of Anatomically Modern Humans in Western Europe," in Smith and Spencer, eds., *The Origins of Modern Humans*, p. 107.
40. Singer and Wymer, *The Middle Stone Age at Klasies River Mouth in South Africa*, p. 149.
41. Günter Bräuer, "A Craniological Approach to the Origin of Anatomically Modern *Homo sapiens* in Africa and Implications for the Appearance of Modern Europeans," in Smith and Spencer, eds., *The Origins of Modern Humans*, pp. 387–89, 394; and Philip Rightmire, "*Homo sapiens* in Sub-Saharan Africa," in ibid., p. 320.
42. H. Valladas, J. L. Joron, G. Valladas, O. Bar-Yosef, and B. Vandermeersch, "Thermoluminescence Dating of Mousterian 'Proto-Cro-Magnon' Remains from Israel and the Origin of Modern Man," *Nature*, February 18, 1988, 614–16.
43. Stringer, Hublin, and Vandermeersch, "The Origin of Anatomically Modern Humans in Western Europe," p. 121.
44. For arguments supporting the single-origin theory, see the chapters by Günter Bräuer, F. Clark Howell, and C. B. Stringer et al. in Smith and Spencer, eds., *The Origins of Modern Humans*. For arguments supporting the multiregional theory, see the chapters by C. L. Brace et al., David W. Frayer, Fred H. Smith, and Milford H. Wolpoff et al. in the same volume.
45. Rebecca Cann, M. Stoneking, and A. C. Wilson, "Mitochondrial DNA and Human Evolution," *Nature*, 325 (1987): 31–36.
46. Vigilant et al., "African Populations and the Evolution of Human Mitochondrial DNA."
47. Milford Wolpoff, *Paleoanthropology*, 2nd ed. (Boston: McGraw-Hill, 1999), pp. 501–504, 727–31; David Frayer, M. Wolpoff, A. Thorne, F. Smith, and G. Pope, "Theories of Modern Human Origins: The Paleontological Test," *American Anthropologist*, 95 (1993): 24–27.
48. Wolpoff, *Paleoanthropology*, pp. 735–43; Frayer et al., "Theories of Modern Human Origins," pp. 21–24.
49. Daniel E. Lieberman, "Testing Hypotheses about Recent Human Evolution from Skulls: Integrating Morphology, Function, Development, and Phylogeny," *Current Anthropology*, 36 (1995): 159–97.
50. Alan Templeton, "The 'Eve' Hypotheses: A Genetic Critique and Reanalysis," *American Anthropologist*, 95 (1993): 51–72.
51. Erik Trinkaus, "The Neandertals and Modern Human Origins," *Annual Review of Anthropology*, 15 (1986): 193–218.
52. Ibid., p. 210.
53. Alan R. Templeton, "Gene Lineages and Human Evolution," *Science*, May 31, 1996, 1363. See also Francisco J. Ayala, "The Myth of Eve: Molecular Biology and Human Origins," *Science*, December 22, 1995, 1930–36; and his subsequent communication in *Science*, November 29, 1996, 1354.
54. Cidalia Duarte, J. Mauricio, P. B. Pettitt, P. Souto, E. Trinkaus, H. van der Plicht, and J. Zilhao, "The Early Upper Paleolithic Human Skeleton from the Abrigo do Lagar Velho (Portugal) and Modern Human Emergence in Iberia," *Proceedings of the National Academy of Sciences of the United States* 96 (1999): 7604–7609.
55. Paul Bahn, "Neanderthals Emancipated," *Nature*, 394 (1998): 719–20.
56. Tattersall, *The Last Neanderthal*, pp. 198–203.
57. Erik Trinkaus, "The Neandertals and Modern Human Origins," *Annual Review of Anthropology*, 15 (1986): 193–218; see also Erik Trinkaus and W. W. Howells, "The Neanderthals," *Scientific American*, December 1979, 118–33.

CHAPTER 10

1. Randall White, "Rethinking the Middle/Upper Paleolithic Transition," *Current Anthropology*, 23 (1982): 169–75.
2. Lawrence Guy Strauss, "Comment on White" [ibid.], *Current Anthropology*, 23 (1982): 185–86.
3. Alistar Dawson, *Ice Age Earth* (London: Routledge, 1992), pp. 24–71.
4. COHMAP Personnel, "Climatic Changes of the Last 18,000 Years," *Science*, 241 (1988): 1043–1052.
5. Paul S. Martin and H. E. Wright, eds., *Pleistocene Extinctions: The Search for a Cause* (New Haven, CT: Yale University Press, 1967).
6. Paul Mellars, "The Upper Paleolithic Revolution," in B. Cunliffe, ed., *The Oxford Illustrated Prehistory of Europe* (Oxford: Oxford University Press, 1994), pp. 42–78.
7. Thomas C. Patterson, *The Evolution of Ancient Societies: A World Archaeology* (Englewood Cliffs, NJ: Prentice Hall, 1981).
8. Bohuslav Klima, "The First Ground-Plan of an Upper Paleolithic Loess Settlement in Middle Europe and Its Meaning," in Robert J. Braidwood and Gordon R. Willey, eds., *Courses toward Urban Life: Archaeological Consideration of Some Cultural Alternatives*, Viking Fund Publications in Anthropology No. 32 (Chicago: Aldine, 1962), pp. 193–210.
9. John C. Whittaker, *Flintknapping: Making and Understanding Stone Tools* (Austin: University of Texas Press, 1994), p. 33; Kathy D. Schick and Nicholas Toth, *Making Silent Stones Speak* (New York: Simon & Schuster, 1993), pp. 293–99.
10. Whittaker, *Flintknapping*, p. 31.
11. Jacques Bordaz, *Tools of the Old and New Stone Age* (Garden City, NY: Natural History Press, 1970), p. 68.
12. Whittaker, *Flintknapping*, p. 33.
13. David W. Phillipson, *African Archaeology*, 2nd ed. (Cambridge: Cambridge University Press, 1993), p. 60.
14. Bordaz, *Tools of the Old and New Stone Age*, p. 68.
15. We thank Robert L. Kelly (personal communication) for bringing this possibility to our attention. See also

J. Desmond Clark, "Interpretations of Prehistoric Technology from Ancient Egyptian and Other Sources. Part II: Prehistoric Arrow Forms in Africa as Shown by Surviving Examples of the Traditional Arrows of the San Bushmen," *Paleorient*, 3 (1977): 136.

16. Robert Ascher, "Analogy in Archaeological Interpretation," *Southwestern Journal of Anthropology*, 17 (1961): 317–25.

17. S. A. Semenov, *Prehistoric Technology*, trans. M. W. Thompson (Bath, England: Adams & Dart, 1970), p. 103. For a more recent discussion of research following this strategy, see Lawrence H. Keeley, *Experimental Determination of Stone Tool Uses: A Microwear Analysis* (Chicago: University of Chicago Press, 1980).

18. Richard G. Klein, "Southern Africa before the Ice Age," in Robert S. Corruccini and Russell L. Ciochon, eds., *Integrative Paths to the Past: Paleoanthropological Advances in Honor of F. Clark Howell* (Englewood Cliffs, NJ: Prentice Hall, 1994), p. 508.

19. Olga Soffer, "Upper Paleolithic Adaptations in Central and Eastern Europe and Man-Mammoth Interactions," in Olga Soffer and N. D. Praslov, eds., *From Kostenki to Clovis: Upper Paleolithic–Paleo-Indian Adaptations* (New York: Plenum, 1993), pp. 38–40.

20. Phillipson, *African Archaeology*, p. 74.

21. Virginia Morell, "The Earliest Art Becomes Older—And More Common," *Science*, March 31, 1995, 1908–1909.

22. Peter J. Ucko and Andrée Rosenfeld, *Paleolithic Cave Art* (New York: McGraw-Hill, 1967).

23. Patricia C. Rice and Ann L. Paterson, "Cave Art and Bones: Exploring the Interrelationships," *American Anthropologist*, 87 (1985): 94–100. For similar results of a study of cave art in Spain, see Patricia C. Rice and Ann L. Paterson, "Validating the Cave Art–Archeofaunal Relationship in Cantabrian Spain," *American Anthropologist*, 88 (1986): 658–67.

24. Rice and Paterson, "Cave Art and Bones," p. 98.

25. Alexander Marshack, *The Roots of Civilization* (New York: McGraw-Hill, 1972).

26. LeRoy McDermott, "Self-Representation in Female Figurines," *Current Anthropology*, 37 (1996): 227–75.

27. For a review, see Marcia-Anne Dobres, "Venus Figurines," in B. Fagan, ed., *Oxford Companion to Archaeology* (Oxford: Oxford University Press, 1998), pp. 740–41.

28. Alicia Hawkins and M. Kleindienst, "Aterian," in P. N. Peregrine and M. Ember, eds., *Encyclopedia of Prehistory*, Vol. 1: *Africa* (New York: Kluwer Academic/Plenum, 2001), pp. 23–45.

29. Peter N. Peregrine, "Southern and Eastern Africa Later Stone Age," in Peregrine and Ember, eds., *Encyclopedia of Prehistory*, Vol. 1, pp. 272–73.

30. Vidula Jayaswal, "South Asian Upper Paleolithic," in P. N. Peregrine and M. Ember, eds., *Encyclopedia of Prehistory*, Vol. 8: *South and Southwest Asia* (New York: Kluwer Academic/Plenum, 2002).

31. Peter N. Peregrine and Peter Bellwood, "Southeast Asia Upper Paleolithic," in P. N. Peregrine and M. Ember, eds., *Encyclopedia of Prehistory*, Vol. 3: *East Asia and Oceania* (New York: Kluwer Academic/Plenum, 2001), pp. 307–309.

32. Kim A. McDonald, "New Evidence Challenges Traditional Model of How the New World Was Settled," *Chronicle of Higher Education*, March 13, 1998, A22.

33. John F. Hoffecker, W. Roger Powers, and Ted Goebel, "The Colonization of Beringia and the Peopling of the New World," *Science*, January 1, 1993, 46–53.

34. Ann Gibbons, "First Americans: Not Mammoth Hunters, but Forest Dwellers?" *Science*, April 19, 1995, 346–47; and A. C. Roosevelt et al., "Paleoindian Cave Dwellers in the Amazon: The Peopling of the Americas," *Science*, April 19, 1996, 373–84.

35. Thomas Dillehay, *The Settlement of the Americas* (New York: Basic Books, 2000).

36. William J. Parry, "When and How Did Humans Populate the New World?" in Peter N. Peregrine, Carol R. Ember, and Melvin Ember, eds., *Archaeology: Original Readings in Method and Practice* (Upper Saddle River, NJ: Prentice Hall, 2002).

37. Joseph H. Greenberg and Merritt Ruhlen, "Linguistic Origins of Native Americans," *Scientific American*, November 1992, 94–99.

38. Christy G. Turner II, "Teeth and Prehistory in Asia," *Scientific American*, February 1989, as reported in ibid.

39. Emöke J. E. Szathmary, "Genetics of Aboriginal North Americans," *Evolutionary Anthropology*, 1 (1993): 202–20.

40. McDonald, "New Evidence Challenges Traditional Model of How the New World Was Settled."

41. Joe Ben Wheat, "A Paleo-Indian Bison Kill," *Scientific American*, January 1967, 44–47.

42. Brian M. Fagan, *Ancient North America: The Archaeology of a Continent* (London: Thames and Hudson, 1991), p. 79.

43. John F. Hoffecker, W. Rogers Powers, and Ted Goebel, "The Colonization of Beringia and the Peopling of the New World," *Science*, January 1, 1993, 51.

44. J. D. Jennings, *Prehistory of North America* (New York: McGraw-Hill, 1968), pp. 72–88.

45. W. James Judge and Jerry Dawson, "Paleo-Indian Settlement Technology in New Mexico," *Science*, June 16, 1972, 1210–216.

46. Wheat, "A Paleo-Indian Bison Kill."

47. Brian M. Fagan, *People of the Earth: An Introduction to World Prehistory*, 6th ed. (Glenview, IL: Scott, Foresman, 1989), p. 221.

48. Wheat, "A Paleo-Indian Bison Kill."

49. Ibid.

50. Fagan, *People of the Earth*, p. 227.

51. Fagan, *Ancient North America*, p. 192.

52. Fagan, *People of the Earth*, p. 227.

53. Desmond Collins, "Later Hunters in Europe," in Desmond Collins, ed., *The Origins of Europe* (New York: Thomas Y. Crowell, 1976), pp. 88–125.

54. Chester S. Chard, *Man in Prehistory* (New York: McGraw-Hill, 1969), p. 171.

55. Grahame Clark, *The Earlier Stone Age Settlement of Scandinavia* (Cambridge: Cambridge University Press, 1975), pp. 101–61.

56. Erik B. Petersen, "A Survey of the Late Paleolithic and the Mesolithic of Denmark," in S. K. Kozlowski, ed., *The Mesolithic in Europe* (Warsaw: Warsaw University Press, 1973), pp. 94–96.

57. I. Randolph Daniel, "Early Eastern Archaic," in P. N. Peregrine and M. Ember, eds., *Encyclopedia of Prehistory*, Vol. 6: *North America* (Kluwer Academic/Plenum, 2001).

58. Kenneth Sassaman, "Early Archaic Settlement in the South Carolina Coastal Plain," in D. G. Anderson and K. E. Sassaman, eds., *The Paleoindian and Early Archaic Southeast* (Tuscaloosa: University of Alabama Press, 1996), pp. 58–83.

59. Ibid.

60. James A. Brown, "Summary," in J. L. Phillips and J. A. Brown, eds., *Archaic Hunters and Gatherers in the American Midwest* (New York: Academic Press, 1983), pp. 5–10.

CHAPTER 11

1. Naomi F. Miller, "The Origins of Plant Cultivation in the Near East," in C. Wesley Cowan and Patty Jo Watson, eds.,

The Origins of Agriculture (Washington, DC: Smithsonian Institution Press, 1992), pp. 41–42.

2. Gary W. Crawford, "Prehistoric Plant Domestication in East Asia," in Cowan and Watson, eds., *The Origins of Agriculture*, pp. 29–30; David W. Phillipson, *African Archaeology*, 2nd ed. (New York: Cambridge University Press, 1993), p. 118; Richard S. MacNeish, *The Origins of Agriculture and Settled Life* (Norman: University of Oklahoma Press, 1991), pp. 256, 268.

3. Kent V. Flannery, "The Research Problem," in Kent V. Flannery, ed., *Guila Naquitz: Archaic Foraging and Early Agriculture in Oaxaca, Mexico* (Orlando, FL: Academic Press, 1986), pp. 6–8; Deborah Pearsall, "The Origins of Plant Cultivation in South America," in Cowan and Watson, eds., *The Origins of Agriculture*, p. 197; Bruce D. Smith, "Prehistoric Plant Husbandry in Eastern North America," in Cowan and Watson, eds., *The Origins of Agriculture*, p. 101.

4. Frank Hole, "Origins of Agriculture," in Steve Jones, Robert Martin, and David Pilbeam, eds., *The Cambridge Encyclopedia of Human Evolution* (New York: Cambridge University Press, 1992), p. 375.

5. Lewis R. Binford, "Post-Pleistocene Adaptations," in Stuart Struever, ed., *Prehistoric Agriculture* (Garden City, NY: Natural History Press, 1971), pp. 45–49.

6. Kent V. Flannery, "The Origins of Agriculture," *Annual Review of Anthropology*, 2 (1973): 274.

7. Jack R. Harlan, "A Wild Wheat Harvest in Turkey," *Archaeology*, 20, no. 3 (June 1967): 197–201.

8. Kent V. Flannery, "The Origins and Ecological Effects of Early Domestication in Iran and the Near East," in Struever, ed., *Prehistoric Agriculture*, p. 59. Originally published in Peter J. Ucko and G. W. Dimbleby, eds., *The Domestication and Exploitation of Plants and Animals* (Chicago: Aldine, 1969).

9. James Mellaart, "Roots in the Soil," in Stuart Piggott, ed., *The Dawn of Civilization* (London: Thames & Hudson, 1961), pp. 41–64.

10. Donald O. Henry, *From Foraging to Agriculture: The Levant at the End of the Ice Age* (Philadelphia: University of Pennsylvania Press, 1989), pp. 214–15.

11. James A. Brown and T. Douglas Price, "Complex Hunter-Gatherers: Retrospect and Prospect," in T. Douglas Price and James A. Brown, *Prehistoric Hunter-Gatherers: The Emergence of Cultural Complexity* (Orlando, FL: Academic Press, 1985), pp. 435–41.

12. Henry, *From Foraging to Agriculture*, pp. 38–39, 209–10; Donald O. Henry, "Foraging, Sedentism, and Adaptive Vigor in the Natufian: Rethinking the Linkages," in Geoffrey A. Clark, ed., *Perspectives on the Past: Theoretical Biases in Mediterranean Hunter-Gatherer Research* (Philadelphia: University of Pennsylvania Press, 1991), pp. 365–68. See Deborah I. Olszewski, "Social Complexity in the Natufian? Assessing the Relationship of Ideas and Data," in Clark, ed., *Perspectives on the Past*, pp. 322–40, for some questions about the degree of social complexity in Natufian sites.

13. Paul S. Martin and H. E. Wright, eds., *Pleistocene Extinctions: The Search for a Cause* (New Haven, CT: Yale University Press, 1967).

14. A recent analysis of these changes is Steven Kuehn, "New Evidence for Late Paleoindian–Early Archaic Subsistence Behavior in the Western Great Lakes," *American Antiquity*, 63 (1998): 457–76; see also James Brown, "Long-Term Trends to Sedentism and the Emergence of Complexity in the American Midwest," in Price and Brown, eds., *Prehistoric Hunter-Gatherers*, pp. 201–31.

15. Joyce Marcus and Kent V. Flannery, *Zapotec Civilization* (London: Thames & Hudson, 1996), pp. 49–50.

16. Ibid., pp. 50–53.

17. Chester Gorman, "The Hoabinhian and After: Subsistence Patterns in Southeast Asia during the Late Pleistocene and Early Recent Periods," *World Archaeology*, 2 (1970): 315–16.

18. Kwang-Chih Chang, "The Beginnings of Agriculture in the Far East," *Antiquity*, 44, no. 175 (September 1970): 176. See also Gorman, "The Hoabinhian and After," pp. 300–19.

19. J. Desmond Clark, *The Prehistory of Africa* (New York: Praeger, 1970), pp. 171–72.

20. Phillipson, *African Archaeology*, pp. 111–12.

21. Paul S. Martin, "The Discovery of America," *Science*, March 9, 1973, 969–74.

22. Donald K. Grayson, "Pleistocene Avifaunas and the Overkill Hypothesis," *Science*, February 18, 1977, 691–92. See also Larry G. Marshall, "Who Killed Cock Robin? An Investigation of the Extinction Controversy," Donald K. Grayson, "Explaining Pleistocene Extinctions: Thoughts on the Structure of a Debate," and R. Dale Guthrie, "Mosaics, Allelochemics and Nutrients: An Ecological Theory of Late Pleistocene Megafaunal Extinctions," in Paul S. Martin and Richard G. Klein, eds., *Quaternary Extinctions: A Prehistoric Revolution* (Tucson: University of Arizona Press, 1984), pp. 785–806, 807–23, 259–98.

23. R. N. Holdaway and C. Jacomb, "Rapid Extinction of the Moas (Aves: Dinornithiformes): Model, Test, and Implications," *Science*, 287 (2000): 2250–257.

24. Mark Nathan Cohen, *The Food Crisis in Prehistory: Overpopulation and the Origins of Agriculture* (New Haven, CT: Yale University Press, 1977), pp. 12, 85.

25. Ibid., p. 85; and Fekri A. Hassan, *Demographic Archaeology* (New York: Academic Press, 1981), p. 207. For the view that hunter-gatherers were very unlikely to have lived in tropical forests before agriculture, see Robert C. Bailey, Genevieve Head, Mark Jenike, Bruce Owen, Robert Rechtman, and Elzbieta Zechenter, "Hunting and Gathering in Tropical Rain Forest: Is It Possible?" *American Anthropologist*, 91 (1989): 59–82.

26. Mark Nathan Cohen, *Health and the Rise of Civilization* (New Haven, CT: Yale University Press, 1989), pp. 112–13.

27. David W. Frayer, "Body Size, Weapon Use, and Natural Selection in the European Upper Paleolithic and Mesolithic," *American Anthropologist*, 83 (1981): 57–73.

28. Cohen, *Health and the Rise of Civilization*, pp. 113–15.

29. Kent V. Flannery, "The Origins of the Village as a Settlement Type in Mesoamerica and the Near East: A Comparative Study," in Ruth Tringham, ed., *Territoriality and Proxemics R1* (Andover, MA: Warner Modular, 1973), pp. 1–31.

30. Thomas C. Patterson, "Central Peru: Its Population and Economy," *Archaeology*, 24 (1971): 318–19.

31. Gregory A. Johnson, "Aspects of Regional Analysis in Archaeology," *Annual Review of Anthropology*, 6 (1977): 488–89. See also David R. Harris, "Settling Down: An Evolutionary Model for the Transformation of Mobile Bands into Sedentary Communities," in J. Friedman and M. J. Rowlands, eds., *The Evolution of Social Systems* (London: Duckworth, 1977), pp. 401–17.

32. Robert Sussman, "Child Transport, Family Size, and the Increase in Human Population Size during the Neolithic," *Current Anthropology*, 13 (April 1972): 258–67; and Richard B. Lee, "Population Growth and the Beginnings of Sedentary Life among the !Kung Bushmen," in Brian Spooner, ed., *Population Growth: Anthropological Implications* (Cambridge, MA: MIT Press, 1972), pp. 329–42.

33. For some examples of societies that have practiced infanticide, see Harris, "Settling Down," p. 407.

34. Nancy Howell, *Demography of the Dobe !Kung* (New York:

Academic Press, 1979); and Richard B. Lee, *The !Kung San: Men, Women, and Work in a Foraging Society* (Cambridge: Cambridge University Press, 1979).

35. Rose E. Frisch, "Fatness, Puberty, and Fertility," *Natural History,* October 1980, 16–27; and Howell, *Demography of the Dobe !Kung.*

36. Phillipson, *African Archaeology,* pp. 60–61.

37. S. A. Semenov, *Prehistoric Technology,* trans. M. W. Thompson (Bath, England: Adams & Dart, 1970), pp. 63, 203–204; John C. Whittaker, *Flintknapping: Making and Understanding Stone Tools* (Austin: University of Texas Press, 1994), pp. 36–37.

38. Daniel Zohary, "The Progenitors of Wheat and Barley in Relation to Domestication and Agricultural Dispersal in the Old World," in Ucko and Dimbleby, eds., *The Domestication and Exploitation of Plants and Animals,* pp. 47–66.

39. Kent V. Flannery, "The Ecology of Early Food Production in Mesopotamia," *Science,* March 12, 1965, 1252.

40. Ibid., p. 1253. For the view that a high proportion of immature animals does not necessarily indicate domestication, see Stephen Collier and J. Peter White, "Get Them Young? Age and Sex Inferences on Animal Domestication in Archaeology," *American Antiquity,* 41 (1976): 96–102.

41. Hole, "Origins of Agriculture," p. 376; MacNeish, *The Origins of Agriculture and Settled Life,* pp. 127–28.

42. Juliet Clutton-Brock, "Domestication of Animals," in Jones, Martin, and Pilbeam, eds., *The Cambridge Encyclopedia of Human Evolution,* p. 384.

43. Frank Hole, Kent V. Flannery, and James A. Neely, *Prehistory and Human Ecology of the Deh Luran Plain. Memoirs of the Museum of Anthropology No. 1* (Ann Arbor: University of Michigan, 1969).

44. See Alan H. Simmons, Ilse Köhler-Rollefson, Gary O. Rollefson, Rolfe Mandel, and Zeidan Kafafi, " 'Ain Ghazal: A Major Neolithic Settlement in Central Jordan," *Science,* April 1, 1988, 35–39.

45. James Mellaart, "A Neolithic City in Turkey," *Scientific American,* April 1964, 94–104.

46. Flannery, "The Research Problem," pp. 3–5; Heather Pringle, "The Slow Birth of Agriculture," *Science,* 282 (1998): 1446–450.

47. Marcus and Flannery, *Zapotec Civilization,* pp. 64–66.

48. Flannery, "The Research Problem," pp. 6–8.

49. Ibid., pp. 8–9; Marcus and Flannery, *Zapotec Civilization,* pp. 66–67.

50. Marcus and Flannery, *Zapotec Civilization,* pp. 65–66.

51. Ibid., pp. 66–68.

52. Kent V. Flannery, "Guila Naquitz in Spatial, Temporal, and Cultural Context," in K. V. Flannery, ed., *Guila Naquitz: Archaic Foraging and Early Agriculture in Oaxaca, Mexico* (Orlando, FL: Academic Press, 1986), pp. 31–42.

53. Kent V. Flannery, "Adaptation, Evolution, and Archaeological Phases: Some Implications of Reynolds' Simulation," in Flannery, ed., *Guila Naquitz,* p. 502.

54. MacNeish, *The Origins of Agriculture and Settled Life,* pp. 37, 47; Hole, "Origins of Agriculture," p. 376.

55. Bruce D. Smith, *Rivers of Change* (Washington, DC: Smithsonian Institution Press, 1992), pp. 163, 287.

56. Nancy B. Asch and David L. Asch, "The Economic Potential of *Iva annua* and Its Prehistoric Importance in the Lower Illinois Valley," in Richard I. Ford, ed., *The Nature and Status of Ethnobotany.* Anthropological Papers, Museum of Anthropology No. 67 (Ann Arbor: University of Michigan, 1978), pp. 301–42.

57. Smith, *Rivers of Change,* pp. 39, 274–75, 292; Smith, "Prehistoric Plant Husbandry in Eastern North America."

58. Smith, *Rivers of Change,* p. 6.

59. Ibid., p. 180.

60. Clutton-Brock, "Domestication of Animals," p. 385.

61. R. D. Crawford, "Turkey," in Ian L. Mason, *Evolution of Domesticated Animals* (New York: Longman, 1984), pp. 329–31.

62. Clutton-Brock, "Domestication of Animals," p. 385.

63. B. Müller-Haye, "Guinea Pig or Cuy," in Mason, *Evolution of Domesticated Animals,* p. 255.

64. Robert J. Wenke, *Patterns in Prehistory: Humankind's First Three Million Years,* 2nd ed. (New York: Oxford University Press, 1984), pp. 350, 397–98.

65. K. C. Chang, "In Search of China's Beginnings: New Light on an Old Civilization," *American Scientist,* 69 (1981): 148–60; MacNeish, *The Origins of Agriculture and Settled Life,* pp. 159–63.

66. MacNeish, *The Origins of Agriculture and Settled Life,* pp. 267–68.

67. Ibid.; Hole, "Origins of Agriculture," p. 376.

68. Phillipson, *African Archaeology,* p. 118.

69. Ibid.; MacNeish, *The Origins of Agriculture and Settled Life,* p. 314.

70. Clutton-Brock, "Domestication of Animals," p. 384.

71. Jared Diamond, "Location, Location, Location: The First Farmers," *Science,* November 14, 1997, 1243–244.

72. Cited in MacNeish, *The Origins of Agriculture and Settled Life,* p. 6.

73. Robert J. Braidwood, "The Agricultural Revolution," *Scientific American,* September 1960, 130.

74. Robert J. Braidwood and Gordon R. Willey, "Conclusions and Afterthoughts," in Robert J. Braidwood and Gordon R. Willey, eds., *Courses toward Urban Life: Archeological Considerations of Some Cultural Alternatives.* Viking Fund Publications in Anthropology No. 32 (Chicago: Aldine, 1962), p. 342.

75. Binford, "Post-Pleistocene Adaptations," pp. 22–49; and Flannery, "The Origins and Ecological Effects of Early Domestication in Iran and the Near East," pp. 50–70.

76. Gary A. Wright, "Origins of Food Production in Southwestern Asia: A Survey of Ideas," *Current Anthropology,* 12 (1971): 470.

77. Flannery, "The Research Problem," pp. 10–11.

78. Mark N. Cohen, "Population Pressure and the Origins of Agriculture," in Charles A. Reed, ed., *Origins of Agriculture* (The Hague: Mouton, 1977), pp. 138–41. See also Cohen, *The Food Crisis in Prehistory,* p. 279.

79. Roger Byrne, "Climatic Change and the Origins of Agriculture," in Linda Manzanilla, ed., *Studies in the Neolithic and Urban Revolutions.* British Archaeological Reports International Series 349 (Oxford, 1987), pp. 21–34, referred to in Mark A. Blumler and Roger Byrne, "The Ecological Genetics of Domestication and the Origins of Agriculture," *Current Anthropology,* 32 (1991): 23–35. See also Henry, *From Foraging to Agriculture,* pp. 30–38; and Joy McCorriston and Frank Hole, "The Ecology of Seasonal Stress and the Origins of Agriculture in the Near East," *American Anthropologist,* 93 (1991): 46–69.

80. Henry, *From Foraging to Agriculture,* p. 41.

81. McCorriston and Hole, "The Ecology of Seasonal Stress."

82. Henry, *From Foraging to Agriculture,* p. 54.

83. John D. Speth and Katherine A. Spielmann, "Energy Source, Protein Metabolism, and Hunter-Gatherer Subsistence Strategies," *Journal of Anthropological Archaeology,* 2 (1983): 1–31.

84. Benjamin White, "Demand for Labor and Population Growth in Colonial Java," *Human Ecology,* 1, no. 3 (March

1973): 217–36. See also John D. Kasarda, "Economic Structure and Fertility: A Comparative Analysis," *Demography,* 8, no. 3 (August 1971): 307–18.

85. Carol R. Ember, "The Relative Decline in Women's Contribution to Agriculture with Intensification," *American Anthropologist,* 85 (1983): 285–304.

86. Melvin Konner and Carol Worthman, "Nursing Frequency, Gonadal Function, and Birth Spacing among !Kung Hunter-Gatherers," *Science,* February 15, 1980, 788–91.

87. Anna Curtenius Roosevelt, "Population, Health, and the Evolution of Subsistence: Conclusions from the Conference," in Mark Nathan Cohen and George J. Armelagos, eds., *Paleopathology at the Origins of Agriculture* (Orlando, FL: Academic Press, 1984), pp. 559–84. See also Mark Nathan Cohen and George J. Armelagos, "Paleopathology at the Origins of Agriculture: Editors' Summation," in the same volume, pp. 585–602; Mark N. Cohen, "The Significance of Long-Term Changes in Human Diet and Food Economy," in Marvin Harris and Eric B. Ross, eds., *Food and Evolution: Toward a Theory of Human Food Habits* (Philadelphia: Temple University Press, 1987), pp. 269–73; Mark N. Cohen, "Were Early Agriculturalists Less Healthy Than Food Collectors?" in P. N. Peregrine, C. R. Ember, and M. Ember, eds, *Archaeology: Original Readings in Method and Practice* (Upper Saddle River, NJ: Prentice Hall, 2002). For evidence suggesting that the transition to food production was not generally associated with declining health, see James W. Wood, George R. Milner, Henry C. Harpending, and Kenneth M. Weiss, "The Osteological Paradox: Problems of Inferring Prehistoric Health from Skeletal Samples," *Current Anthropology,* 33 (1992): 343–70.

88. Roosevelt, "Population, Health, and the Evolution of Subsistence"; and Cohen and Armelagos, "Paleopathology at the Origins of Agriculture."

89. Alan H. Goodman and George J. Armelagos, "Disease and Death at Dr. Dickson's Mounds," *Natural History,* September 1985, 18. See also Alan H. Goodman, John Lallo, George J. Armelagos, and Jerome C. Rose, "Health Changes at Dickson Mounds, Illinois (A.D. 950–1300)," in Cohen and Armelagos, *Paleopathology at the Origins of Agriculture,* p. 300; Cohen, "Were Early Agriculturalists Less Healthy Than Food Collectors?"

90. Grahame Clark and Stuart Piggott, *Prehistoric Societies* (New York: Knopf, 1965), pp. 240–42.

91. Ibid., p. 235.

92. Colin Renfrew, "Trade and Culture Process in European Prehistory," *Current Anthropology,* 10 (April–June 1969): 156–57, 161–69.

93. *Webster's New World Dictionary,* Third College Edition (New York: Webster's New World, 1988).

CHAPTER 12

1. Robert J. Wenke, *Patterns in Prehistory: Humankind's First Three Million Years,* 3rd ed. (New York: Oxford University Press, 1990). See also Graham Connah, *African Civilizations: Precolonial Cities and States in Tropical Africa, an Archaeological Perspective* (Cambridge: Cambridge University Press, 1987); and Elman R. Service, *Origins of the State and Civilization: The Process of Cultural Evolution* (New York: Norton, 1975).

2. Kent V. Flannery, "The Cultural Evolution of Civilizations," *Annual Review of Ecology and Systematics,* 3 (1972): 399–426.

3. Ibid. See also Charles L. Redman, *The Rise of Civilization:*

From Early Farmers to Urban Society in the Ancient Near East (San Francisco: Freeman, 1978), pp. 215–16.

4. Henry T. Wright and Gregory A. Johnson, "Population, Exchange, and Early State Formation in Southwestern Iran," *American Anthropologist,* 77 (1975): 267.

5. The discussion in the remainder of this section draws from ibid., pp. 269–74. See also Gregory A. Johnson, "The Changing Organization of Uruk Administration on the Susiana Plain," in Frank Hole, ed., *Archaeology of Western Iran* (Washington, DC: Smithsonian Institution Press, 1987), pp. 107–39.

6. Ibid., pp. 271–72.

7. Flannery, "The Cultural Evolution of Civilizations."

8. Service, *Origins of the State and Civilization,* p. 207.

9. Ibid.; and Flannery, "The Cultural Evolution of Civilizations."

10. This description of Sumerian civilization is based on Samuel Noel Kramer, *The Sumerians: Their History, Culture, and Character* (Chicago: University of Chicago Press, 1963).

11. Jared Diamond, "The Accidental Conqueror," *Discover,* December 1989, 71–76.

12. Mary W. Helms, *Middle America* (Englewood Cliffs, NJ: Prentice Hall, 1975), pp. 34–36, 54–55. See also William T. Sanders, Jeffrey R. Parsons, and Robert S. Santley, *The Basin of Mexico: Ecological Processes in the Evolution of a Civilization* (New York: Academic Press, 1979).

13. Wenke, *Patterns in Prehistory*; and René Millon, "Teotihuacán," *Scientific American,* June 1967, 38–48.

14. René Millon, "Social Relations in Ancient Teotihuacán," in Eric R. Wolf, ed., *The Valley of Mexico: Studies in Pre-Hispanic Ecology and Society* (Albuquerque: University of New Mexico Press, 1976), pp. 215–20.

15. Millon, "Teotihuacán," pp. 38–44.

16. Helms, *Middle America,* pp. 61–63; see also Muriel Porter Weaver, *The Aztecs, Maya, and Their Predecessors,* 3rd ed. (San Diego: Academic Press, 1993).

17. Richard E. Blanton, "The Rise of Cities," in Jeremy A. Sabloff, ed., *Supplement to the Handbook of Middle American Indians,* vol. 1 (Austin: University of Texas Press, 1981), p. 397. See also Joyce Marcus, "On the Nature of the Mesoamerican City," in Evon Z. Vogt and Richard M. Leventhal, eds., *Prehistoric Settlement Patterns: Essays in Honor of Gordon R. Willey* (Albuquerque: University of New Mexico Press, 1983), pp. 195–242.

18. Richard Blanton, "The Origins of Monte Albán," in C. Cleland, ed., *Cultural Continuity and Change* (New York: Academic Press, 1976), pp. 223–32; and Richard Blanton, *Monte Albán: Settlement Patterns at the Ancient Zapotec Capital* (New York: Academic Press, 1978).

19. B. L. Turner, "Population Density in the Classic Maya Lowlands: New Evidence for Old Approaches," *Geographical Review,* 66, no. 1 (January 1970): 72–82. See also Peter D. Harrison and B. L. Turner II, eds., *Pre-Hispanic Maya Agriculture* (Albuquerque: University of New Mexico Press, 1978).

20. Stephen D. Houston, "The Phonetic Decipherment of Mayan Glyphs," *Antiquity,* 62 (1988): 126–35.

21. Robert J. Wenke, *Patterns in Prehistory: Humankind's First Three Million Years,* 2nd ed. (New York: Oxford University Press, 1984), p. 289.

22. Graham Connah, *African Civilizations* (Cambridge: Cambridge University Press, 1987), p. 67.

23. Brian M. Fagan, *People of the Earth: An Introduction to World Prehistory,* 6th ed. (Glenview, IL: Scott, Foresman, 1989), pp. 428–30.

24. Connah, *African Civilizations,* pp. 216–17.

25. Joseph Vogel, "De-Mystifying the Past: Great Zimbabwe, King Solomon's Mines, and Other Tales of Old Africa," in P. N. Peregrine, C. R. Ember, and M. Ember, eds., *Archaeology: Original Readings in Method and Practice* (Upper Saddle River, NJ: Prentice Hall, 2002).

26. Wenke, *Patterns in Prehistory,* pp. 305–20.

27. K. C. Chang, "In Search of China's Beginnings: New Light on an Old Civilization," *American Scientist,* 69 (1981): 148–60.

28. Kwang-Chih Chang, *The Archaeology of Ancient China* (New Haven, CT: Yale University Press, 1968), pp. 235–55.

29. Wenke, *Patterns in Prehistory,* p. 404.

30. For an overview, see Luis Lumbreras, *The Peoples and Cultures of Ancient Peru* (Washington, DC: Smithsonian Institution Press, 1974).

31. Melvin L. Fowler, "A Pre-Columbian Urban Center on the Mississippi," *Scientific American,* August 1975, 92–101.

32. For a more complete review of the available theories, see various chapters in Ronald Cohen and Elman R. Service, eds., *Origins of the State: The Anthropology of Political Evolution* (Philadelphia: Institute for the Study of Human Issues, 1978); see also chapter 1 in Melinda A. Zeder, *Feeding Cities: Specialized Animal Economy in the Ancient Near East* (Washington, DC: Smithsonian Institution Press, 1991).

33. Karl Wittfogel, *Oriental Despotism: A Comparative Study of Total Power* (New Haven, CT: Yale University Press, 1957).

34. Robert M. Adams, "The Origin of Cities," *Scientific American,* September 1960, 153. See also Henry T. Wright, "The Evolution of Civilizations," in David J. Meltzer, Don D. Fowler, and Jeremy A. Sabloff, eds., *American Archaeology Past and Future* (Washington, DC: Smithsonian Institution Press, 1986), pp. 323–65.

35. Paul Wheatley, *The Pivot of the Four Quarters* (Chicago: Aldine, 1971), p. 291.

36. Adams, "The Origin of Cities," p. 153.

37. Robert McC. Adams, *Heartland of Cities: Surveys of Ancient Settlement and Land Use on the Central Floodplain of the Euphrates* (Chicago: University of Chicago Press, 1981), p. 244.

38. Ibid., p. 243; and Service, *Origins of the State and Civilization,* pp. 274–75.

39. Robert L. Carneiro, "A Theory of the Origin of the State," *Science,* August 21, 1970, 733–38. See also William T. Sanders and Barbara J. Price, *Mesoamerica* (New York: Random House, 1968), pp. 230–32.

40. Marvin Harris, *Cultural Materialism: The Struggle for a Science of Culture* (New York: Random House, 1979), pp. 101–102. See also Wenke, *Patterns in Prehistory.*

41. T. Cuyler Young, Jr., "Population Densities and Early Mesopotamian Urbanism," in Peter J. Ucko, Ruth Tringham, and G. W. Dimbleby, eds., *Man, Settlement and Urbanism* (Cambridge, MA: Schenkman, 1972), pp. 827–42.

42. Sanders and Price, *Mesoamerica,* p. 141.

43. Richard E. Blanton, Stephen A. Kowalewski, Gary Feinman, and Jill Appel, *Ancient Mesoamerica: A Comparison of Change in Three Regions* (New York: Cambridge University Press, 1981), p. 224. For the apparent absence of population pressure in the Teotihuacán Valley, see Elizabeth Brumfiel, "Regional Growth in the Eastern Valley of Mexico: A Test of the 'Population Pressure' Hypothesis," in Kent V. Flannery, ed., *The Early Mesoamerican Village* (New York: Academic Press, 1976), pp. 234–50. For the Oaxaca Valley, see Gary M. Feinman, Stephen A. Kowalewski, Laura Finsten, Richard E. Blanton, and Linda Nicholas, "Long-Term Demographic Change: A Perspective from the Valley of Oaxaca, Mexico," *Journal of Field Archaeology,* 12 (1985): 333–62.

44. Wright and Johnson, "Population, Exchange, and Early

State Formation in Southwestern Iran," p. 276. Carneiro, however, argued the opposite: that the population grew just before the states emerged in southwestern Iran; see Robert L. Carneiro, "The Circumscription Theory: Challenge and Response," *American Behavioral Scientist,* 31 (1988): 506–508. Whether or not population declined, Frank Hole has suggested that climate change around that time may have forced local populations to relocate, some to centers that became cities; see his "Environmental Shock and Urban Origins," in Gil Stein and Mitchell S. Rothman, eds., *Chiefdoms and Early States in the Near East: The Organizational Dynamics of Complexity* (Madison, WI: Prehistory Press, 1994).

45. Karl Polanyi, Conrad M. Arensberg, and Harry W. Pearson, eds., *Trade and Market in the Early Empires* (New York: Free Press, 1957), pp. 257–62; and William T. Sanders, "Hydraulic Agriculture, Economic Symbiosis, and the Evolution of States in Central Mexico," in Betty J. Meggers, ed., *Anthropological Archaeology in the Americas* (Washington, DC: Anthropological Society of Washington, 1968), p. 105.

46. Wright and Johnson, "Population, Exchange, and Early State Formation in Southwestern Iran," p. 277.

47. William L. Rathje, "The Origin and Development of Lowland Classic Maya Civilization," *American Antiquity,* 36 (1971): 275–85.

48. Kwang-chih Chang, *Archaeology of Ancient China,* 4th ed. (New Haven, CT: Yale University Press, 1986), pp. 234–94.

49. For a discussion of how political dynamics may play an important role in state formation, see Elizabeth M. Brumfiel, "Aztec State Making: Ecology, Structure, and the Origin of the State," *American Anthropologist,* 85 (1983): 261–84.

50. Allen Johnson and Timothy Earle, *The Evolution of Human Societies* (Stanford: Stanford University Press, 1987), pp. 324–26.

51. V. Gordon Childe, "The Urban Revolution," *Town Planning Review,* 21 (1950): 3–17.

52. Service, *Origins of the State and Civilization,* pp. 12–15, 89–90.

53. Jared Diamond, *Guns, Germs, and Steel* (New York: Norton, 1997), pp. 205–207.

54. Robert Dirks, "Starvation and Famine," *Cross-Cultural Research,* 27 (1993): 28–69.

55. Johnson and Earle, *Evolution of Human Societies,* pp. 243–48; 304–306.

56. Carol R. Ember and Melvin Ember, "Resource Unpredictability, Mistrust, and War: A Cross-Cultural Study," *Journal of Conflict Resolution,* 36 (1992): 246–62.

57. R. Brian Ferguson and Neil L. Whitehead, "The Violent Edge of Empire," in R. B. Ferguson and N. Whitehead, eds, *War in the Tribal Zone* (Santa Fe, NM: School of American Research Press, 1992), pp. 1–30.

58. Harvey Weiss, M. A. Courty, W. Wetterstrom, F. Guichard, L. Senior, R. Meadow, and A. Curnow, "The Genesis and Collapse of Third Millennium North Mesopotamian Civilization," *Science,* 261 (1993): 995–1004.

59. Richard A. Kerr, "Sea-Floor Dust Shows Drought Felled Akkadian Empire," *Science,* January 16, 1998, 325–26.

60. "The Last of the Cahokians," *Science,* April 19, 1996, 351.

61. Robert L. Wilkinson, "Yellow Fever: Ecology, Epidemiology, and Role in the Collapse of the Classic Lowland Maya Civilization," *Medical Anthropology,* 16 (1995): 269–94.

62. Joseph Tainter, *The Collapse of Complex Societies* (Cambridge: Cambridge University Press, 1988), pp. 128–52.

63. Peter Charnais, "Economic Factors in the Decline of the Roman Empire," *Journal of Economic History,* 13 (1953): 412–24.

CHAPTER 13

1. See William H. Durham, *Coevolution: Genes, Culture, and Human Diversity* (Stanford, CA: Stanford University Press, 1991), pp. 154–225, for an extensive discussion of the relationship between genes and culture.

2. T. D. Steward, "Deformity, trephanating, and mutilation in South American Indian skeletal remains," in J. A. Steward, ed., *Handbook of South American Indians,* vol. 6: *Physical Anthropology, Linguistics, and Cultural Geography.* Bureau of American Ethnology Bulletin 143 (Washington, DC: Smithsonian Institution Press, 1950).

3. Genesis 17:9–15.

4. Joel M. Hanna, Michael A. Little, and Donald M. Austin, "Climatic Physiology," in Michael A. Little and Jere D. Haas, eds., *Human Population Biology: A Transdisciplinary Science* (New York: Oxford University Press, 1989), pp. 133–36; G. A. Harrison, James M. Tanner, David R. Pilbeam, and P. T. Baker, *Human Biology: An Introduction to Human Evolution, Variation, Growth, and Adaptability,* 3rd ed. (Oxford: Oxford University Press, 1988), pp. 504–507.

5. D. F. Roberts, "Body Weight, Race, and Climate," *American Journal of Physical Anthropology,* 2 (1953): 553–58. Cited in Stanley M. Garn, *Human Races,* 3rd ed. (Springfield, IL: Charles C. Thomas, 1971), p. 73. See also D. F. Roberts, *Climate and Human Variability,* 2nd ed. (Menlo Park, CA: Cummings, 1978).

6. Roberts, "Body Weight, Race, and Climate."

7. Harrison et al., *Human Biology,* p. 505.

8. Alphonse Riesenfeld, "The Effect of Extreme Temperatures and Starvation on the Body Proportions of the Rat," *American Journal of Physical Anthropology,* 39 (1973): 427–59.

9. Ibid., pp. 452–53.

10. J. S. Weiner, "Nose Shape and Climate," *Journal of Physical Anthropology,* 4 (1954): 615–18; A. T. Steegman, Jr., "Human Adaptation to Cold," in Albert Damon, ed., *Physiological Anthropology* (New York: Oxford University Press, 1975), pp. 130–66. See also Clark Spenser Larsen, "Bare Bones Anthropology: The Bioarchaeology of Human Remains," in P. N. Peregrine, C. R. Ember, and M. Ember, eds., *Archaeology: Original Readings in Method and Practice* (Upper Saddle River, NJ: Prentice Hall, 2002).

11. Harrison et al., *Human Biology,* pp. 308–10.

12. Anthony P. Polednak, "Connective Tissue Responses in Negroes in Relation to Disease," *American Journal of Physical Anthropology,* 41 (1974): 49–57. See also Richard F. Branda and John W. Eaton, "Skin Color and Nutrient Photolysis: An Evolutionary Hypothesis," *Science,* August 18, 1978, 625–26.

13. W. Farnsworth Loomis, "Skin-Pigment Regulation of Vitamin-D Biosynthesis in Man," *Science,* August 4, 1967, 501–506.

14. Peter W. Post, Farrington Daniels, Jr., and Robert T. Binford, Jr., "Cold Injury and the Evolution of 'White' Skin," *Human Biology,* 47 (1975): 65–80.

15. Constance Holden, "Selective Power of UV," *Science,* 289 (2000): 1461; Nina Jablonski and George Chaplin, "The Evolution of Human Skin Color," *Journal of Human Evolution,* 39 (2000): 57–106.

16. William A. Stini, *Ecology and Human Adaptation* (Dubuque, IA: Wm. C. Brown, 1975), p. 53.

17. Richard B. Mazess, "Human Adaptation to High Altitude," in Damon, ed., *Physiological Anthropology,* p. 168.

18. Lawrence P. Greksa and Cynthia M. Beall, "Development of Chest Size and Lung Function at High Altitude," in Little and Haas, eds., *Human Population Biology,* p. 223.

19. Ibid., p. 226.

20. A. Roberto Frisancho and Lawrence P. Greksa, "Development Responses in the Acquisition of Functional Adaptation to High Altitude," in Little and Haas, eds., *Human Population Biology,* p. 204.

21. Phyllis B. Eveleth and James M. Tanner, *Worldwide Variation in Human Growth,* 2nd ed. (Cambridge: Cambridge University Press, 1990), pp. 176–79.

22. Ibid., pp. 205–206.

23. Barry Bogin, *Patterns of Human Growth* (Cambridge: Cambridge University Press, 1988), pp. 105–106.

24. Harrison et al., *Human Biology,* p. 300.

25. Ibid., p. 198.

26. Rebecca Huss-Ashmore and Francis E. Johnston, "Bioanthropological Research in Developing Countries," *Annual Review of Anthropology,* 14 (1985): 482–83.

27. Harrison et al., *Human Biology,* pp. 385–86.

28. Reynaldo Martorell, "Interrelationships between Diet, Infectious Disease and Nutritional Status," in L. Greene and F. E. Johnston, eds., *Social and Biological Predictors of Nutritional Status, Physical Growth and Neurological Development* (New York: Academic Press, 1980), pp. 81–106.

29. Reynaldo Martorell, Juan Rivera, Haley Kaplowitz, and Ernesto Pollitt, "Long-Term Consequences of Growth Retardation during Early Childhood," paper presented at the Sixth International Congress of Auxology, September 15–19, 1991, Madrid.

30. Thomas K. Landauer and John W. M. Whiting, "Infantile Stimulation and Adult Stature of Human Males," *American Anthropologist,* 66 (1964): 1007–1028; S. Gunders and J. W. M. Whiting, "Mother-Infant Separation and Physical Growth," *Ethnology,* 7 (1968): 196–206; J. Patrick Gray and Linda D. Wolfe, "Height and Sexual Dimorphism of Stature among Human Societies," *American Journal of Physical Anthropology,* 53 (1980): 446–52; Thomas K. Landauer and John W. M. Whiting, "Correlates and Consequences of Stress in Infancy," in Ruth H. Munroe, Robert L. Munroe, and Beatrice B. Whiting, eds., *Handbook of Cross-Cultural Human Development* (New York: Garland, 1981), pp. 361–65.

31. Landauer and Whiting, "Infantile Stimulation and Adult Stature of Human Males"; Gunders and Whiting, "Mother-Infant Separation and Physical Growth"; Landauer and Whiting, "Correlates and Consequences of Stress in Infancy."

32. J. Patrick Gray and Linda Wolfe, "What Accounts for Population Variation in Height?" in Peter N. Peregrine, Carol R. Ember, and Melvin Ember, eds., *Physical Anthropology: Original Readings in Method and Practice* (Upper Saddle River, NJ: Prentice Hall, 2002).

33. Landauer and Whiting, "Correlates and Consequences of Stress in Infancy," p. 369.

34. Eveleth and Tanner, *Worldwide Variation in Human Growth,* p. 205.

35. Thomas K. Landauer, "Infantile Vaccination and the Secular Trend in Stature," *Ethos,* 1 (1973): 499–503.

36. Arno Motulsky, "Metabolic Polymorphisms and the Role of Infectious Diseases in Human Evolution," in Morris, ed., *Human Populations, Genetic Variation, and Evolution,* p. 223.

37. Ibid., p. 226.

38. Ibid., p. 229.

39. Ibid., p. 230.

40. Ibid., p. 233.

41. Ibid.

42. Francis L. Black, "Why Did They Die?" *Science,* December 11, 1992, 1739–40.
43. An examination of the epidemic diseases spread by Europeans can be found in chapter 11 of Jared Diamond's *Guns, Germs, and Steel* (New York: Norton, 1997).
44. James V. Neel, Willard R. Centerwall, Napoleon A. Chagnon, and Helen L. Casey, "Notes on the Effect of Measles and Measles Vaccine in a Virgin-Soil Population of South American Indians," *American Journal of Epidemiology,* 91 (1970): 418–29; Patrick Tierney in his *Darkness in El Dorado* (New York: Norton, 2000) has accused the Neel research team of fueling a measles outbreak among the Yanomamö by administering a harmful measles vaccine. But the scientific evidence indicates that Tierney is wrong. The vaccine used by Neel and associates was widely pretested and there was no way that the vaccine could have caused the epidemic. Measles was already spreading in the Amazon, which was why the vaccination program was initiated. See the statement by Bruce Alberts, president of the National Academy of Sciences, November 9, 2000, "Setting the Record Straight Regarding Darkness in El Dorado," which can be found at the Web address: http://www4.nationalacademies.org/nas/nashome.nsf.
45. Relethford, *The Human Species,* pp. 425–27, referring to A. McElroy and P. R. Townsend, *Medical Anthropology* (North Scituate, MA: Duxbury Press, 1979).
46. Charles F. Merbs, "A New World of Infectious Disease," *Yearbook of Physical Anthropology,* 35 (1992): 16.
47. Durham, *Coevolution,* pp. 105–107.
48. Ibid.
49. Ibid., p. 107.
50. Harrison et al., *Human Biology,* p. 231.
51. For a review of the early research, see Durham, *Coevolution,* pp. 123–27. The particular form of malaria that is discussed is caused by the species *Plasmodium falciparum.*
52. See Lorena Madigral, "Hemoglobin Genotype, Fertility, and the Malaria Hypothesis," *Human Biology,* 61 (1989): 311–25, for a report of her own research and a review of earlier studies.
53. Ibid., pp. 124–45.
54. Motulsky, "Metabolic Polymorphisms and the Role of Infectious Diseases in Human Evolution," p. 238.
55. Jared Diamond, "Who Are the Jews?" *Natural History,* November 1993, 16.
56. Stephen Molnar, *Human Variation: Races, Types and Ethnic Groups,* 4th ed. (Upper Saddle River, NJ: Prentice Hall, 1998), p. 158.
57. Durham, *Coevolution,* p. 230.
58. Jane E. Brody, "Effects of Milk on Blacks Noted," *New York Times,* October 15, 1971, p. 15.
59. Durham, *Coevolution,* pp. 233–35.
60. Relethford, *The Human Species,* p. 127.
61. Robert D. McCracken, "Lactase Deficiency: An Example of Dietary Evolution," *Current Anthropology,* 12 (1971): 479–500; see also references to the work of F. J. Simoons as referred to in Durham, *Coevolution,* pp. 240–41.
62. McCracken, "Lactase Deficiency," p. 480.
63. Durham, *Coevolution,* pp. 263–69.
64. Jonathan Marks, "Black, White, Other: Racial Categories Are Cultural Constructs Masquerading as Biology," *Natural History,* December 1994, 33; Eugenia Shanklin, *Anthropology and Race* (Belmont, CA: Wadsworth, 1994), pp. 15–17.
65. Molnar, *Human Variation,* p. 19.
66. C. Loring Brace, David P. Tracer, Lucia Allen Yaroch, John Robb, Kari Brandt, and A. Russell Nelson, "Clines and Clusters versus 'Race': A Test in Ancient Egypt and the Case of a Death on the Nile." *Yearbook of Physical Anthropology,* 36 (1993): 17–19.
67. Alison S. Brooks, Fatimah Linda Collier Jackson, R. Richard Grinker, "Race and Ethnicity in America," *Anthro Notes (National Museum of Natural History Bulletin for Teachers),* 15, no. 3 (Fall 1993): 11.
68. Brace et al., "Clines and Clusters versus 'Race,' " p. 19.
69. Brooks, Jackson, and Grinker, "Race and Ethnicity in America," pp. 12–13.
70. A review of the history and social roots of racial classification is given by Ashley Montagu in his book *Man's Most Dangerous Myth: The Fallacy of Race,* 6th ed. (Walnut Creek, CA: Alta Mira, 1997).
71. Melvin D. Williams, "Racism: The Production, Reproduction, and Obsolescence of Social Inferiority," in Ember, Ember, and Peregrine, eds., *Research Frontiers in Anthropology.*
72. John Fleagle, *Primate Adaptation and Evolution* (San Diego: Academic Press, 1999) p. 18.
73. Saul S. Friedman, "Holocaust," in *Academic American* [now *Grolier*] *Encyclopedia,* vol. 10 (Princeton, NJ: Arete, 1980), p. 206.
74. Marc Howard Ross, "Ethnocentrism and Ethnic Conflict," in Ember, Ember, and Peregrine, eds., *Research Frontiers in Anthropology.*
75. Marks, "Black, White, Other," p. 32.
76. L. Carrington Goodrich, *A Short History of the Chinese People,* 3rd ed. (New York: Harper & Row, 1959), pp. 7–15.
77. Michael D. Coe, *The Maya* (New York: Praeger, 1966), pp. 74–76.
78. Elizabeth Bartlett Thompson, *Africa, Past and Present* (Boston: Houghton Mifflin, 1966), p. 89.
79. William H. McNeill, *Plagues and Peoples* (Garden City, NY: Doubleday/Anchor, 1976).
80. Motulsky, "Metabolic Polymorphisms and the Role of Infectious Diseases in Human Evolution," p. 232.
81. Ibid.
82. R. H. MacArthur and E. O. Wilson, *Theory of Island Biogeography* (Princeton, NJ: Princeton University Press, 1967).
83. Donald C. Johansen and M. Edey, *Lucy: The Beginnings of Humankind* (New York: Simon and Schuster, 1981).
84. Peter N. Peregrine, Carol R. Ember, and Melvin Ember, "Teaching Critical Evaluation of Rushton," *Anthropology Newsletter,* 41, no. 2 (2000): 29–30.
85. Leonard Lieberman, "Scientific Insignificance," *Anthropology Newsletter,* 40, no. 8 (1999): 11–12.
86. Otto Klineberg, *Negro Intelligence and Selective Migration* (New York: Columbia University Press, 1935); and Otto Klineberg, ed., *Characteristics of the American Negro* (New York: Harper & Brothers, 1944).
87. Arthur Jensen, "How Much Can We Boost IQ and Scholastic Achievement?" *Harvard Educational Review,* 29 (1969): 1–123.
88. M. W. Smith, "Alfred Binet's Remarkable Questions: A Cross-National and Cross-Temporal Analysis of the Cultural Biases Built into the Stanford-Binet Intelligence Scale and Other Binet Tests," *Genetic Psychology Monographs,* 89 (1974): 307–34.
89. Theodosius Dobzhansky, *Genetic Diversity and Human Equality* (New York: Basic Books, 1973), p. 11.
90. Ibid., pp. 14–15.
91. Research by Sandra Scarr and others, reported in Robert Boyd and Peter J. Richerson, *Culture and the Evolutionary Process* (Chicago: University of Chicago Press, 1985), p. 56.
92. Theodosius Dobzhansky, *Mankind Evolving: The Evolution of the Human Species* (New Haven, CT: Yale University Press, 1962), p. 243.

93. J. B. S. Haldane, "Human Evolution: Past and Future," in Glenn L. Jepsen, Ernst Mayr, and George Gaylord Simpson, eds., *Genetics, Paleontology, and Evolution* (New York: Atheneum, 1963), pp. 405–18.

94. George Gaylord Simpson, *The Meaning of Evolution* (New York: Bantam, 1971), pp. 297–308.

CHAPTER 14

1. Gilbert Kushner, "Applied Anthropology," in William G. Emener and Margaret Darrow, eds., *Career Explorations in Human Services* (Springfield, IL: Charles C. Thomas, 1991), pp. 46–61.

2. Margaret Mead, "The Evolving Ethics of Applied Anthropology," in Elizabeth M. Eddy and William L. Partridge, eds., *Applied Anthropology in America* (New York: Columbia University Press, 1978), pp. 426–29.

3. Barbara Frankel and M. G. Trend, "Principles, Pressures and Paychecks: The Anthropologist as Employee," in Carolyn Fluehr-Lobban, ed., *Ethics and the Profession of Anthropology: Dialogue for a New Era* (Philadelphia: University of Pennsylvania Press, 1991), p. 177.

4. Robert A. Hackenberg, "Scientists or Survivors? The Future of Applied Anthropology under Maximum Uncertainty," in Robert T. Trotter II, ed., *Anthropology for Tomorrow: Creating Practitioner-Oriented Applied Anthropology Programs* (Washington, DC: American Anthropological Association, 1988), p. 172.

5. Kushner, "Applied Anthropology."

6. William L. Partridge and Elizabeth M. Eddy, "The Development of Applied Anthropology in America," in Elizabeth M. Eddy and William L. Partridge, eds., *Applied Anthropology in America*, 2nd ed. (New York: Columbia University Press, 1987), pp. 25–26.

7. Ibid., pp. 31–40.

8. Margaret Mead, "Applied Anthropology: The State of the Art," in Anthony F. C. Wallace, J. Lawrence Angel, Richard Fox, Sally McLendon, Rachel Sady, and Robert Sharer, eds., *Perspectives on Anthropology 1976, American Anthropological Association Special Publication No. 10* (Washington, DC: American Anthropological Association, 1977), p. 149.

9. Partridge and Eddy, "The Development of Applied Anthropology," pp. 31–40.

10. George M. Foster, *Applied Anthropology* (Boston: Little, Brown, 1969), p. 200.

11. Partridge and Eddy, "The Development of Applied Anthropology," p. 52.

12. "Appendix C: Statements on Ethics: Principles of Professional Responsibility, Adopted by the Council of the American Anthropological Association, May 1971" (as amended through May 1976), and "Appendix I: Revised Principles of Professional Responsibility, 1990," in Fluehr-Lobban, ed., *Ethics and the Profession of Anthropology*, pp. 239–42, 274–79.

13. "Appendix A: Report of the Committee on Ethics, Society for Applied Anthropology," and "Appendix F: Professional and Ethical Responsibilities, SfAA," in ibid., pp. 239–42, 262–64.

14. "Appendix H: National Association of Practicing Anthropologists' Ethical Guidelines for Practitioners, 1988," in ibid., pp. 270–73.

15. Thayer Scudder, "Opportunities, Issues, and Achievements in Development Anthropology since the Mid-1960s: A Personal View," in Eddy and Partridge, eds., *Applied Anthropology in America*, 2nd ed., pp. 184–210.

16. Ibid., p. 204ff.

17. Debra Picchi, "The Impact of an Industrial Agricultural Project on the Bakairi Indians of Central Brazil," *Human Organization*, 50 (1991): 26–38; for a more general description of the Bakairi, see Debra Picchi, "Bakairi: The Death of an Indian," in Melvin Ember, Carol R. Ember, and David Levinson, eds., *Portraits of Culture: Ethnographic Originals* (Upper Saddle River, NJ: Prentice Hall, 1998). Prentice Hall/Simon & Schuster Custom Publishing.

18. Gerald F. Murray, "The Domestication of Wood in Haiti: A Case Study in Applied Anthropology," in Aaron Podolefsky and Peter J. Brown, *Applying Cultural Anthropology: An Introductory Reader*, 3rd ed. (Mountain View, CA: Mayfield, 1997), p. 131.

19. Arthur H. Niehoff, *A Casebook of Social Change* (Chicago: Aldine, 1966), pp. 255–67.

20. Foster, *Applied Anthropology*, pp. 8–9.

21. Derrick B. Jelliffe and E. F. Patrice Jelliffe, "Human Milk, Nutrition, and the World Resource Crisis," *Science*, May 9, 1975, 557–61.

22. William H. Fisher, "Megadevelopment, Environmentalism, and Resistance: The Institutional Context of Kayapó Indigenous Politics in Central Brazil," *Human Organization*, 53 (1994): 220–32.

23. Foster, *Applied Anthropology*, pp. 122–23.

24. Jeannine Coreil, "Lessons from a Community Study of Oral Rehydration Therapy in Haiti," in John van Willigen, Barbara Rylko-Bauer, and Ann McElroy, eds., *Making Our Research Useful: Case Studies in the Utilization of Anthropological Knowledge* (Boulder, CO: Westview, 1989), pp. 149–50.

25. Everett M. Rogers, *Diffusion of Innovations*, 3rd ed. (New York: Free Press, 1983), pp. 321–31.

26. Carol A. Bryant and Doraine F. C. Bailey, "The Use of Focus Group Research in Program Development," in John van Willigen and Timothy L. Finan, eds., *Soundings: Rapid and Reliable Research Methods for Practicing Anthropologists, NAPA Bulletin No. 10* (Washington, DC: American Anthropological Association, 1990), pp. 24–39.

27. Niehoff, *A Casebook of Social Change*, pp. 219–24.

28. Coreil, "Lessons from a Community Study of Oral Rehydration Therapy in Haiti," p. 155.

29. Dennis M. Warren, "Utilizing Indigenous Healers in National Health Delivery Systems: The Ghanaian Experiment," in van Willigen, Rylko-Bauer, and McElroy, eds., *Making Our Research Useful*, pp. 159–78.

30. Ward H. Goodenough, *Cooperation in Change* (New York: Russell Sage Foundation, 1963), p. 416.

31. Wayne Warry, "Doing unto Others: Applied Anthropology, Collaborative Research and Native Self-Determination," *Culture*, 10 (1990): 61–62.

32. Julie Fisher, "Grassroots Organizations and Grassroots Support Organizations: Patterns of Interaction," in Emilio F. Moran, ed., *Transforming Societies, Transforming Anthropology* (Ann Arbor: University of Michigan Press, 1996), p. 57.

33. Ibid., p. 91; data from Kenya referred to in Clare Oxby, "Farmer Groups in Rural Areas of the Third World," *Community Development Journal*, 18 (1983): 50–59.

34. John Ravesloot, "Changing Native American Perceptions of Archaeology and Archaeologists," in N. Swidler et al., eds., *Native Americans and Archaeologists* (Walnut Creek, CA: Alta Mira Press), p. 174.

35. Roger Anyon and T. J. Ferguson, "Cultural Resources Management at the Pueblo of Zuni, New Mexico, USA," *Antiquity* 69 (1995): 913–30.

36. Melinda Zeder, *The American Archaeologist: A Profile* (Walnut Creek, CA: Alta Mira, 1997).

37. Mary H. Manhein, *The Bone Lady: Life as a Forensic Anthro-*

pologist (Baton Rouge: Louisiana State University Press, 1999).

38. Stanley Rhine, *Bone Voyage: A Journey in Forensic Anthropology* (Albuquerque: University of New Mexico Press, 1998), pp. 245–46.

39. "Association Business: Clyde Snow, Forensic Anthropologist, Works for Justice," *Anthropology News,* October 2000, 12.

CHAPTER 15

1. Alan H. Goodman and Thomas L. Leatherman, eds., *Building a New Biocultural Synthesis: Political-Economic Perspectives on Human Biology* (Ann Arbor: University of Michigan Press, 1998); Arthur Kleinman, Veena Das, and Margaret Lock, eds., *Social Suffering* (Berkeley: University of California Press, 1997).

2. Hans A. Baer, Merrill Singer, and Ida Susser, *Medical Anthropology and the World System: A Critical Perspective* (Westport, CT: Bergin and Garvey, 1997), p. viii.

3. Arthur J. Rubel and Michael R. Hass, in Thomas M. Johnson and Carolyn F. Sargent, *Medical Anthropology: Contemporary Theory and Method* (Westport, CT: Praeger, 1990), p. 120, rev. ed. 1996; Martha O. Loustaunau and Elisa J. Sobo, *The Cultural Context of Health, Illness, and Medicine* (Westport, CT: Bergin and Garvey, 1997), pp. 80–81.

4. Loustaunau and Sobo, *The Cultural Context of Health, Illness, and Medicine,* pp. 82–83, referring to L. Magner, *A History of Medicine* (New York: Marcel Dekker, 1992), p. 93.

5. Ibid., referring to W. Gesler, *The Cultural Geography of Health Care* (Pittsburgh: University of Pittsburgh Press, 1991), p. 16.

6. Ibid., referring to C. Leslie, "Introduction," in C. Leslie, ed., *Asian Medical Systems: A Comparative Study* (Los Angeles: University of California Press, 1976), p. 4; and G. Foster, *Hippocrates' Latin American Legacy: Humoral Medicine in the New World* (Amsterdam: Gordon and Breach, 1994), p. 11.

7. Emily M. Ahern, "Sacred and Secular Medicine in a Taiwan Village: A Study of Cosmological Disorders," in Arthur Kleinman et al., eds., *Medicine in Chinese Cultures: Comparative Studies of Health Care in Chinese and Other Societies* (Washington, DC: U.S. Department of Health, Education, and Welfare, National Institutes of Health, 1975), pp. 92–97, as appearing in the eHRAF Collection of Ethnography on the Web, 2000.

8. George Peter Murdock, *Theories of Illness: A World Survey* (Pittsburgh: University of Pittsburgh Press, 1980), p. 20.

9. Carmella Caracci Moore. "An Optimal Scaling of Murdock's Theories of Illness Data—An Approach to the Problem of Interdependence," *Behavior Science Research,* 22 (1988): 161–79.

10. Thomas Gladwin and Seymour B. Sarason, *Truk: Man in Paradise* (New York: Wenner-Gren Foundation for Anthropological Research, 1953), pp. 64–66.

11. Frank Joseph Mahony, *A Trukese Theory of Medicine* (Ann Arbor, MI: University Microfilms, 1070 [1971]), pp. 34–38, as seen in the eHRAF Collection of Ethnography on the Web, 2000.

12. Gladwin and Sarason, *Truk: Man in Paradise,* p. 65.

13. A. Irving Hallowell, "Ojibwa World View and Disease," in *Contributions to Anthropology: Selected Papers of A. Irving Hallowell* (Chicago: University of Chicago Press, 1976), pp. 410–13.

14. Jerrold E. Levy, "Hopi Shamanism: A Reappraisal," in Raymond J. DeMallie and Alfonzo Ortiz, eds., *North American Indian Anthropology: Essays on Society and Culture* (Norman: University of Oklahoma Press, 1994), p. 318.

15. Robert A. Hahn, *Sickness and Healing: An Anthropological Perspective* (New Haven, CT: Yale University Press, 1995), pp. 133–39.

16. Loustaunau and Sobo, *The Cultural Context of Health, Illness, and Medicine,* p. 115.

17. For an exhaustively documented presentation of the more universalistic approach, see Elois Ann Berlin and Brent Berlin, *Medical Ethnobiology of the Highland Maya of Chiapas, Mexico: The Gastrointestinal Diseases* (Princeton, NJ: Princeton University Press, 1996); see also Carole H. Browner, "Criteria for Selecting Herbal Remedies," *Ethnology,* 24 (1985): 13–32; and Arthur J. Rubel, Carl W. O'Nell, and Rolando Collado-Ardón, *Susto: A Folk Illness* (Berkeley: University of California Press, 1984).

18. E. A. Berlin, "General Overview of Maya Ethnomedicine," in Berlin and Berlin, *Medical Ethnobiology of the Highland Maya of Chiapas, Mexico,* pp. 52–53.

19. C. H. Browner, "Criteria for Selecting Herbal Remedies," *Ethnology,* 24 (1985): 13–32; B. R. Ortiz de Montellano and C. H. Browner, "Chemical Bases for Medicinal Plant Use in Oaxaca, Mexico," *Journal of Ethnopharmacology,* 13 (1985): 57–88.

20. Nina L. Etkin and Paul J. Ross, "Malaria, Medicine, and Meals: A Biobehavioral Perspective," in Lola Romanucci-Ross, Daniel E. Moerman, and Laurence R. Tancredi, eds., *The Anthropology of Medicine: From Culture to Method,* 3rd ed. (Westport, CT: Bergin and Garvey, 1997), pp. 169–209.

21. Daniel E. Moerman, "Physiology and Symbols: The Anthropological Implications of the Placebo Effect," in Romanucci-Ross, Moerman, and Tancredi, eds., *The Anthropology of Medicine,* pp. 240–41.

22. In Loustaunau and Sobo, *The Cultural Context of Health, Illness, and Medicine,* pp. 98–101.

23. Michael Winkelman, "Magico-Religious Practitioner Types and Socioeconomic Conditions," *Behavior Science Research,* 20 (1986): 17–46.

24. Ibid., pp. 28–29.

25. Claude Lévi-Strauss, "The Sorcerer and His Magic," in Claude Lévi-Strauss, *Structural Anthropology,* trans. Claire Jacobsen and Brooke Grundfest Schoepf (New York: Basic Books, 1963), p. 169.

26. Franz Boas, *The Religion of the Kwakiutl.* Columbia University Contributions to Anthropology, vol. 10, pt. 2 (New York: Columbia University, 1930), pp. 1–41. Reported in Lévi-Strauss, *Structural Anthropology,* pp. 169–73.

27. E. Fuller Torrey, *The Mind Game: Witchdoctors and Psychiatrists* (New York: Emerson Hall, n.d.).

28. Loustaunau and Sobo, *The Cultural Context of Health, Illness, and Medicine,* pp. 101–102; and Daniel E. Moerman, "Physiology and Symbols: The Anthropological Implications of the Placebo Effect," in Romanucci-Ross, Moerman, and Tancredi, eds., *The Anthropology of Medicine,* pp. 240–53.

29. Loustaunau and Sobo, *The Cultural Context of Health, Illness, and Medicine,* p. 102.

30. James Dow, *The Shaman's Touch: Otomi Indian Symbolic Healing* (Salt Lake City: University of Utah Press, 1986), pp. 6–9, 125.

31. Hahn, *Sickness and Healing,* pp. 131–72.

32. Ibid., p. 165.

33. For a discussion of some of the relevant research, see ibid., pp. 80–82.

34. C. G. Nicholas Mascie-Taylor, "The Biology of Social Class," in C. G. Nicholas Mascie-Taylor, ed., *Biosocial Aspects of*

Social Class (Oxford: Oxford University Press, 1990), pp. 118–21.

35. See references in Hahn, *Sickness and Healing*, pp. 82–87.

36. Alex Cohen, *The Mental Health of Indigenous Peoples: An International Overview* (Geneva: Department of Mental Health, World Health Organization, 1999).

37. As reported in Steve Jones, Robert Martin, and David Pilbeam, eds., *The Cambridge Encyclopedia of Human Evolution* (Cambridge: Cambridge University Press, 1992), p. 420.

38. Gilbert Herdt, "Sexual Cultures and Population Movement: Implications for AIDS/STDs," in Gilbert Herdt, ed., *Sexual Cultures and Migration in the Era of AIDS: Anthropological and Demographic Perspectives* (Oxford: Oxford University Press, 1997), pp. 3–22.

39. Ralph Bolton, "Introduction: The AIDS Pandemic, a Global Emergency," *Medical Anthropology*, 10 (1989): 93–104.

40. Janie Simmons, Paul Farmer, and Brooke G. Schoepf, "A Global Perspective," in Paul Farmer, Margaret Connors, and Janie Simmons, eds., *Women, Poverty, and AIDS: Sex, Drugs, and Structural Violence* (Monroe, ME: Common Courage Press, 1996), pp. 44–45.

41. Bolton, "Introduction."

42. Joseph Carrier and Ralph Bolton, "Anthropological Perspectives on Sexuality and HIV Prevention," *Annual Review of Sex Research*, 2 (1991): 49–75; B. Schoepf, "Women, AIDS, and Economic Crisis in Central Africa," *Canadian Journal of African Studies*, 22 (1988): 625, cited in Carrier and Bolton, "Anthropological Perspectives on Sexuality and HIV Prevention."

43. Simmons, Farmer, and Schoepf, "A Global Perspective," p. 64.

44. Ibid., pp. 39–57.

45. Schoepf, "Women, AIDS, and Economic Crisis in Central Africa," pp. 637–38.

46. Ralph Bolton, "AIDS and Promiscuity: Muddled in the Models of HIV Prevention," *Medical Anthropology*, 14 (1992): 145–223.

47. Paul Farmer, "Ethnography, Social Analysis, and the Prevention of Sexually Transmitted HIV Infection among Poor Women in Haiti," in Marcia C. Inhorn and Peter J. Brown, *The Anthropology of Infectious Disease: International Health Perspectives* (Amsterdam: Gordon and Breach, 1997), p. 414.

48. Douglas A. Feldman and Thomas M. Johnson, "Introduction," in Douglas A. Feldman and Thomas M. Johnson, eds., *The Social Dimensions of AIDS: Method and Theory* (New York: Praeger, 1986), p. 2.

49. Xuefei Shen and Robert F. Siliciano, "Preventing AIDS but Not HIV-1 Infection with a DNA Vaccine," *Science*, October 20, 2000, pp. 463–65.

50. John J. Honigmann, *Personality in Culture* (New York: Harper & Row, 1967), p. 406.

51. Arthur Kleinman, *Rethinking Psychiatry: From Cultural Category to Personal Experience* (New York: Macmillan, 1988), p. 3.

52. Catherine Lutz, "Depression and the Translations of Emotional Worlds," in Arthur Kleinman and Byron Good, eds., *Culture and Depression: Studies in the Anthropology and Cross-Cultural Psychiatry of Affect and Disorder* (Berkeley: University of California Press, 1985), pp. 63–100.

53. Jane Murphy, "Abnormal Behavior in Traditional Societies: Labels, Explanations, and Social Reactions," in Ruth H. Munroe, Robert L. Munroe, and Beatrice B. Whiting, eds., *Handbook of Cross-Cultural Human Development* (New York: Garland, 1981), p. 813.

54. Robert B. Edgerton, "Conceptions of Psychosis in Four East African Societies," *American Anthropologist*, 68 (1966): 408–25.

55. Robert B. Edgerton, *Sick Societies: Challenging the Myth of Primitive Harmony* (New York: Free Press, 1992), pp. 16–45.

56. J. S. Allen, A. J. Lambert, F. Y. Attah Johnson, K. Schmidt, and K. L. Nero, "Antisaccadic Eye Movements and Attentional Asymmetry in Schizophrenia in Three Pacific Populations," *Acta Psychiatrica Scandinavia*, 94 (1996): 258–65.

57. Kleinman, *Rethinking Psychiatry*, pp. 34–52; John W. Berry, Ype H. Poortinga, Marshall H. Segall, and Pierre R. Dasen, *Cross-Cultural Psychology: Research and Applications* (New York: Cambridge University Press, 1992), pp. 357–64.

58. Honigmann, *Personality in Culture*, p. 401.

59. Kleinman, *Rethinking Psychiatry*, p. 19.

60. Anthony F. C. Wallace, "Mental Illness, Biology and Culture," in F. L. K. Hsu, ed., *Psychological Anthropology*, 2nd ed. (Cambridge, MA: Schenkman, 1972), pp. 363–402.

61. Kleinman, *Rethinking Psychiatry*, pp. 167–85.

62. Rubel, Nell, and Collado-Ardón, *Susto*, pp. 8–9.

63. Ibid., pp. 15–29, 49–69.

64. Ibid., pp. 71–111.

65. William W. Dressler, *Stress and Adaptation in the Context of Culture* (Albany: State University of New York Press, 1991), pp. 11–16.

66. Ibid., pp. 66–94.

67. Ibid., pp. 165–208.

68. Sara A. Quandt, "Nutrition in Anthropology," in Carolyn F. Sargent and Thomas M. Johnson, eds., *Handbook of Medical Anthropology: Contemporary Theory and Method*, rev. ed. (Westport, CT: Greenwood Press, 1996), pp. 272–89.

69. Ann McElroy and Patricia Townsend, *Medical Anthropology in Ecological Perspective*, 3rd ed. (Boulder, CO: Westview, 1996), pp. 172, 185.

70. Daniel R. Gross and Barbara A. Underwood, "Technological Change and Caloric Costs: Sisal Agriculture in Northeastern Brazil," *American Anthropologist*, 73 (1971): 725–40.

71. McElroy and Townsend, *Medical Anthropology in Ecological Perspective*, p. 187, referring to Philip W. Harvey and Peter F. Heywood, "Twenty-five Years of Dietary Change in Simbu Province, Papua New Guinea," *Ecology of Food and Nutrition*, 13 (1983): 27–35.

72. Quandt, "Nutrition in Anthropology," p. 277.

73. Lauris McKee, "Sex Differentials in Survivorship and the Customary Treatment of Infants and Children," *Medical Anthropology*, 8 (1984): 96.

ADAMS, ROBERT McC. *Heartland of Cities: Surveys of Ancient Settlement and Land Use on the Central Floodplain of the Euphrates.* Chicago: University of Chicago Press, 1981.

ADAMS, ROBERT M. "The Origin of Cities." *Scientific American,* September 1960, 153–68.

AHERN, EMILY M. "Sacred and Secular Medicine in a Taiwan Village: A Study of Cosmological Disorders." In Arthur Kleinman et al., eds., *Medicine in Chinese Cultures: Comparative Studies of Health Care in Chinese and Other Societies.* Washington, DC: U.S. Department of Health, Education, and Welfare, National Institutes of Health, 1975, as seen in the eHRAF Collection of Ethnography on the Web, 2000.

AIELLO, L. C. "Body Size and Energy Requirements." In Jones, Martin, and Pilbeam, eds., *The Cambridge Encyclopedia of Human Evolution.*

AIELLO, LESLIE. "The Origin of the New World Monkeys." In W. George and R. Lavocat, eds., *The Africa-South America Connection.* Oxford: Clarendon Press, 1993, pp. 100–18.

AIELLO, LESLIE, AND CHRISTOPHER DEAN. *An Introduction to Human Evolutionary Anatomy.* London: Academic Press, 1990, pp. 268–74.

AITKEN, M. J. *Thermoluminescence Dating.* London: Academic Press, 1985.

ALBERTS, BRUCE, DENNIS BRAY, JULIAN LEWIS, MARTIN RAFF, KEITH ROBERTS, AND JAMES D. WATSON. *Molecular Biology of the Cell.* New York: Garland, 1983.

ALEXANDER, JOHN P. "Alas, Poor Notharctus." *Natural History,* August 1992, 55–59.

ALGAZE, GUILLERMO. *The Uruk World System: The Dynamics of Expansion of Early Mesopotamian Civilization.* Chicago: University of Chicago Press, 1993.

ALLEN, JOHN S., AND SUSAN M. CHEER. "The Non-Thrifty Genotype." *Current Anthropology,* 37 (1996): 831–42.

ALLEN, JOHN S., A. J. LAMBERT, F. Y. ATTAH JOHNSON, K. SCHMIDT, AND K. L. NERO. "Antisaccadic Eye Movements and Attentional Asymmetry in Schizophrenia in Three Pacific Populations." *Acta Psychiatrica Scandinavia,* 94 (1996): 258–65.

ANDREWS, PETER. "*Proconsul.*" In Tattersall, Delson, and van Couvering, eds., *Encyclopedia of Human Evolution and Prehistory.*

ANDREWS, PETER. "Propliopithecidae." In Tattersall, Delson, and van Couvering, eds., *Encyclopedia of Human Evolution and Prehistory.*

ANDREWS, PETER, AND CHRISTOPHER STRINGER. *Human Evolution: An Illustrated Guide.* London: British Museum, 1989.

ANYON, ROGER, AND T. J. FERGUSON. "Cultural Resources Management at the Pueblo of Zuni, New Mexico, USA." *Antiquity,* 69 (1995): 913–30.

"Appendix A: Report of the Committee on Ethics, Society for Applied Anthropology." In Fluehr-Lobban, ed., *Ethics and the Profession of Anthropology.*

"Appendix C: Statements on Ethics: Principles of Professional Responsibility, Adopted by the Council of the American Anthropological Association, May 1971." In Fluehr-Lobban, ed., *Ethics and the Profession of Anthropology.*

"Appendix F: Professional and Ethical Responsibilities, SfAA." In Fluehr-Lobban, ed., *Ethics and the Profession of Anthropology.*

"Appendix H: National Association of Practicing Anthropologists' Ethical Guidelines for Practitioners, 1988." In Fluehr-Lobban, ed., *Ethics and the Profession of Anthropology.*

"Appendix I: Revised Principles of Professional Responsibility, 1990." In Fluehr-Lobban, ed., *Ethics and the Profession of Anthropology.*

ASCH, NANCY B., AND DAVID L. ASCH. "The Economic Potential of *Iva annua* and Its Prehistoric Importance in the Lower Illinois Valley." In Ford, ed., *The Nature and Status of Ethnobotany.*

ASCHER, ROBERT. "Analogy in Archaeological Interpretation." *Southwestern Journal of Anthropology,* 17 (1961): 317–25.

ASFAW, BERHANE, TIM WHITE, OWEN LOVEJOY, BRUCE LATIMER, SCOTT SIMPSON, AND GLEN SUWA. "*Australopithecus garhi:* A New Species of Early Hominid from Ethiopia." *Science,* 284 (1999): 629–36.

"Association Business: Clyde Snow, Forensic Anthropologist, Works for Justice." *Anthropology News,* October 2000, 12.

AUSTIN, LEWIS. "Visual Symbols, Political Ideology, and Culture." *Ethos,* 5 (1977): 306–25.

AYALA, FRANCISCO J. Communication in *Science,* November 29, 1996, 1354.

AYALA, FRANCISCO J. "The Myth of Eve: Molecular Biology and Human Origins." *Science,* December 22, 1995, 1930–936.

BAER, HANS A., MERRILL SINGER, AND IDA SUSSER. *Medical Anthropology and the World System: A Critical Perspective.* Westport, CT: Bergin & Garvey, 1997.

BAHN, P. *Archaeology: A Very Short Introduction.* New York: Oxford University Press, 1996.

BAHN, PAUL. "Neanderthals Emancipated." *Nature,* 394 (1998): 719–20.

BAHN, P., AND J. VERTUT. *Images of the Ice Age.* New York: Facts on File, 1988.

BAILEY, ROBERT C., GENEVIEVE HEAD, MARK JENIKE, BRUCE OWEN, ROBERT RECTMAN, AND ELZBIETA ZECHENTER. "Hunting and Gathering in Tropical Rain Forest: Is It Possible?" *American Anthropologist,* 91 (1989): 59–82.

BALTER, MICHAEL, AND ANN GIBBONS. "A Glimpse of Humans' First Journey Out of Africa." *Science,* 288 (2000): 948–50.

BARASH, DAVID P. *Sociobiology and Behavior.* New York: Elsevier, 1977.

BARRINGER, HERBERT, GEORGE BLANKSTEIN, AND RAYMOND MACK, EDS. *Social Change in Developing Areas: A Re-Interpretation of Evolutionary Theory.* Cambridge, MA: Schenkman, 1965.

BEADLE, GEORGE, AND MURIEL BEADLE. *The Language of Life.* Garden City, NY: Doubleday, 1966.

BEARDER, SIMON K. "Lorises, Bushbabies, and Tarsiers: Diverse Societies in Solitary Foragers." In Smuts et al., eds., *Primate Societies.*

BEGUN, DAVID. "Miocene Apes." In Peregrine, Ember, and Ember, eds., *Physical Anthropology.*

BERG, PAUL, AND MAXINE SINGER. *Dealing with Genes: The Language of Heredity.* Mill Valley, CA: University Science Books, 1992.

BERGGREN, WILLIAM A., DENNIS V. KENT, JOHN D. OBRADOVICH, AND CARL C. SWISHER III. "Toward a Revised Paleogene Geochronology." In Prothero and Berggren, eds., *Eocene-Oliocene Climatic and Biotic Evolution.*

BERLIN, BRENT. *Ethnobiological Classification: Principles of Categorization of Plants and Animals in Traditional Societies.* Princeton, NJ: Princeton University Press, 1992.

BERLIN, E. A. "General Overview of Maya Ethnomedicine." In Berlin and Berlin, *Medical Ethnobiology of the Highland Maya of Chiapas, Mexico,* pp. 52–53.

BERLIN, ELOIS ANN, AND BRENT BERLIN. *Medical Ethnobiology of the Highland Maya of Chiapas, Mexico: The Gastrointestinal Diseases.* Princeton, NJ: Princeton University Press, 1996.

BERRY, JOHN W., YPE H. POORTINGA, MARSHALL H. SEGALL, AND PIERRE R. DASEN. *Cross-Cultural Psychology: Research and Applications.* New York: Cambridge University Press, 1992.

BICKERTON, DEREK. "Creole Languages." *Scientific American,* July 1983, 116–22.

BILSBOROUGH, ALAN. *Human Evolution.* New York: Blackie Academic & Professional, 1992.

BINDON, JAMES R., AND DOUGLAS E. CREWS. "Changes in Some Health Status Characteristics of American Samoan Men: Preliminary Observations from a 12-Year Follow-up Study." *American Journal of Human Biology,* 5 (1993): 31–37.

BINDON, JAMES R., AMY KNIGHT, WILLIAM W. DRESSLER, AND DOUGLAS E. CREWS. "Social Context and Psychosocial Influences on Blood Pressure among American Samoans." *American Journal of Physical Anthropology,* 103 (1997): 7–18.

BINFORD, LEWIS R. *Faunal Remains from Klasies River Mouth.* Orlando, FL: Academic Press, 1984.

BINFORD, LEWIS R. *In Pursuit of the Past: Decoding the Archaeological Record,* New York: Thames and Hudson, 1983.

BINFORD, LEWIS R. "Interassemblage Variability: The Mousterian and the 'Functional' Argument." In Renfrew, ed., *The Explanation of Culture Change.*

BINFORD, LEWIS R. "Post-Pleistocene Adaptations." In Struever, ed., *Prehistoric Agriculture.*

BINFORD, LEWIS R. "Were There Elephant Hunters at Torralba?" In Nitecki and Nitecki, eds., *The Evolution of Human Hunting.*

BINFORD, LEWIS R., AND CHUAN KUN HO. "Taphonomy at a Distance: Zhoukoudian, 'The Cave Home of Beijing Man'?" *Current Anthropology,* 26 (1985): 413–42.

BINFORD, SALLY R., AND LEWIS R. BINFORD. "Stone Tools and Human Behavior." *Scientific American,* April 1969, 70–84.

BISHOP, W. A., AND J. A. MILLER, EDS. *Calibration of Hominid Evolution.* Toronto: University of Toronto Press, 1972.

BLACK, FRANCIS L. "Why Did They Die?" *Science,* December 11, 1992, 1739–40.

BLANTON, RICHARD. *Monte Albán: Settlement Patterns at the Ancient Zapotec Capital.* New York: Academic Press, 1978.

BLANTON, RICHARD. "The Origins of Monte Albán." In Cleland, ed., *Cultural Continuity and Change.*

BLANTON, RICHARD E. "The Rise of Cities." In Sabloff, ed., *Supplement to the Handbook of Middle American Indians,* Vol. 1.

BLANTON, RICHARD E., STEPHEN A. KOWALEWSKI, GARY FEINMAN, AND JILL APPEL. *Ancient Mesoamerica: A Comparison of Change in Three Regions.* New York: Cambridge University Press, 1981.

BLANTON, RICHARD E., STEPHEN A. KOWALEWSKI, GARY M. FEINMAN, AND LAURA M. FINSTEN. *Ancient Mesoamerica: A Comparison of Change in Three Regions.* 2nd ed. Cambridge: Cambridge University Press, 1993.

BLOUNT, BEN G. "The Development of Language in Children." In Munroe, Munroe, and Whiting, eds., *Handbook of Cross-Cultural Human Development.*

BLUMLER, MARK A., AND ROGER BYRNE. "The Ecological Genetics of Domestication and the Origins of Agriculture." *Current Anthropology,* 32 (1991): 23–35.

BOAS, FRANZ. "On Grammatical Categories." In Hymes, ed., *Language in Culture and Society.* (Originally published 1911.)

BOAS, FRANZ. *The Religion of the Kwakiutl.* Columbia University Contributions to Anthropology, Vol. 10, pt. 2. New York: Columbia University, 1930.

BOAZ, N. T., AND A. J. ALMQUIST, *Biological Anthropology: A Synthetic Approach to Human Evolution.* Upper Saddle River, NJ: Prentice Hall, 1997.

BOAZ, NOEL T., AND ALAN J. ALMQUIST. *Essentials of Biological Anthropology.* Upper Saddle River, NJ: Prentice Hall, 1999.

BOGIN, BARRY. *Patterns of Human Growth.* Cambridge: Cambridge University Press, 1988.

BOLTON, RALPH. "AIDS and Promiscuity: Muddled in the Models of HIV Prevention." *Medical Anthropology,* 14 (1992): 145–223.

BOLTON, RALPH. "Introduction: The AIDS Pandemic, a Global Emergency." *Medical Anthropology,* 10 (1989): 93–104.

BORCHERT, CATHERINE, AND ADRIENNE ZIHLMAN. "The Ontogeny and Phylogeny of Symbolizing." In M. LeC. Foster and L. J. Botsharow. *The Life of Symbols.* Boulder, CO: Westview, 1990, pp. 15–44.

BORDAZ, JACQUES. *Tools of the Old and New Stone Age.* Garden City, NY: Natural History Press, 1970.

BORDES, FRANÇOIS. "Mousterian Cultures in France." *Science,* September 22, 1961, 803–10.

BORDES, FRANÇOIS. *The Old Stone Age.* New York: McGraw-Hill, 1968, pp. 51–97.

BOYD, ROBERT, AND PETER J. RICHERSON. *Culture and the Evolutionary Process.* Chicago: University of Chicago Press, 1985.

BOYD, ROBERT, AND JOAN SILK. *How Humans Evolved.* 2nd ed. New York: Norton, 2000, pp. 249–50.

BRACE, C. LORING. "A Four-Letter Word Called Race." In Larry T. Reynolds and Leonard Leiberman, eds., *Race and Other Misadventures: Essays in Honor of Ashley Montague in His Ninetieth Year.* New York: General Hall, 1996.

BRACE, C. LORING, DAVID P. TRACER, LUCIA ALLEN YAROCH, JOHN ROBB, KARI BRANDT, AND A. RUSSELL NELSON. "Clines and Clusters versus 'Race': A Test in Ancient Egypt and the Case of a Death on the Nile." *Yearbook of Physical Anthropology,* 36 (1993): 1–31.

BRAIDWOOD, ROBERT J. "The Agricultural Revolution." *Scientific American,* September 1960, 130–48.

BRAIDWOOD, ROBERT J., AND GORDON R. WILLEY. "Conclusions and Afterthoughts." In Braidwood and Willey, eds., *Courses toward Urban Life.*

BRAIDWOOD, ROBERT J., AND GORDON R. WILLEY, EDS. *Courses toward Urban Life: Archaeological Considerations of Some Cultural Alternatives.* Viking Fund Publications in Anthropology No. 32. Chicago: Aldine, 1962.

BRAIN, C. K., AND A. SILLEN. "Evidence from the Swartkrans Cave for the Earliest Use of Fire." *Nature,* December 1, 1988, 464–66.

BRANDA, RICHARD F., AND JOHN W. EATON. "Skin Color and Nutrient Photolysis: An Evolutionary Hypothesis." *Science,* August 18, 1978, 625–26.

BRANDON, ROBERT N. *Adaptation and Environment.* Princeton, NJ: Princeton University Press, 1990.

BRÄUER, GÜNTER. "A Craniological Approach to the Origin of Anatomically Modern *Homo sapiens* in Africa and Implications for the Appearance of Modern Europeans." In F. Smith and Spencer, eds., *The Origins of Modern Humans.*

BRODEY, JANE E. "Effects of Milk on Blacks Noted." *New York Times,* October 15, 1971, p. 15.

BROMAGE, TIMOTHY G. "Paleoanthropology and Life History, and Life History of a Paleoanthropologist." In C. R. Ember, Ember, and Peregrine, eds., *Research Frontiers in Anthropology,* Vol. 1; reprinted in *Physical Anthropology.*

BROMAGE, TIMOTHY G., AND M. CHRISTOPHER DEAN. "Re-evaluation of the Age at Death of Immature Fossil Hominids." *Nature,* October 10, 1985, 525–27.

BROOKS, ALISON S., FATIMAH LINDA COLLIER JACKSON, AND R. RICHARD GRINKER. "Race and Ethnicity in America." *Anthro Notes* (National Museum of Natural History Bulletin for Teachers), 15, no. 3 (Fall 1993): 1–3, 11–15.

BROOM, ROBERT. *Finding the Missing Link.* London: Watts, 1950.

BROTHWELL, DON, AND ERIC HIGGS, EDS. *Science in Archaeology.* New York: Basic Books, 1963.

BROWN, FRANK H. "Geochronometry." In Tattersall, Delson, and van Couvering, eds., *Encyclopedia of Human Evolution and Prehistory.*

BROWN, FRANK H. "Methods of Dating." In Jones, Martin, and Pilbeam, eds., *The Cambridge Encyclopedia of Human Evolution.*

BROWN, JAMES A. "Long-Term Trends to Sedentism and the Emergence of Complexity in the American Midwest." In Price and Brown, eds., pp. 201–31.

BROWN, JAMES A. "Summary." In J. L. Phillips and J. A. Brown, eds., *Archaic Hunters and Gatherers in the American Midwest.* New York: Academic Press, 1983, pp. 5–10.

BROWN, JAMES A., AND T. DOUGLAS PRICE. "Complex Hunter-Gatherers: Retrospect and Prospect." In Price and Brown, *Prehistoric Hunter-Gatherers.*

BROWN, PETER J. "Culture and the Evolution of Obesity." In Podolefsky and Brown, eds., *Applying Cultural Anthropology.*

BROWN, ROGER. "The First Sentence of Child and Chimpanzee." In Sebeok and Umiker-Sebeok, eds., *Speaking of Apes.*

BROWNER, C. H. "Criteria for Selecting Herbal Remedies." *Ethnology,* 24 (1985): 13–32.

BRUMFIEL, ELIZABETH. "Aztec State Making: Ecology, Structure, and the Origin of the State." *American Anthropologist,* 85 (1983): 261–84.

BRUMFIEL, ELIZABETH M. "Distinguished Lecture in Archeology: Breaking and Entering the Ecosystem—Gender, Class, and Faction Steal the Show." *American Anthropologist,* 94 (1992): 551–67.

BRUMFIEL, ELIZABETH M., ED. *The Economic Anthropology of the State.* Lanham, MD: University Press of America, 1994.

BRUMFIEL, ELIZABETH M. "Origins of Social Inequality." In C. R. Ember, Ember, and Peregrine, *Research Frontiers in Anthropology,* vol. 1, reprinted in Peregrine, Ember, and Ember, eds., *Archaeology.*

BRUMFIEL, ELIZABETH M. "Regional Growth in the Eastern Valley of Mexico: A Test of the 'Population Pressure' Hypothesis." In Flannery, ed., *The Early Mesoamerican Village.*

BRYANT, CAROL A., AND DORAINE F. C. BAILEY. "The Use of Focus Group Research in Program Development." In van Willigen and Finan, eds., *Soundings.*

BRYNE, RICHARD, AND ANDREW WHITEN, EDS. *Machiavellian Intelligence: Social Expertise and the Evolution of Intellect in Monkeys, Apes, and Humans.* Oxford: Clarendon Press, 1988.

BUDIANSKY, STEPHEN. *The Covenant of the Wild: Why Animals Chose Domestication.* New York: Morrow, 1992.

BUETTNER-JANUSCH, JOHN. *Physical Anthropology: A Perspective.* New York: Wiley, 1973.

BURENHULT, G., ED. *Old World Civilizations: The Rise of Cities and States.* St. Lucia, Queensland, Australia: University of Queensland Press, 1994.

BUTZER, KARL W. "Geomorphology and Sediment Stratigraphy." In Singer and Wymer, *The Middle Stone Age at Klasies River Mouth in South Africa.*

BYRNE, ROGER. "Climatic Change and the Origins of Agriculture." In Manzanilla, ed., *Studies in the Neolithic and Urban Revolutions.*

CALVIN, WILLIAM H. *The Throwing Madonna: Essays on the Brain.* New York: McGraw-Hill, 1983.

CAMPBELL, ALLAN M. "Microbes: The Laboratory and the Field." In Davis, ed., *The Genetic Revolution.*

CAMPBELL, BERNARD G. *Humankind Emerging.* 4th ed. Boston: Little, Brown, 1985.

CAMPBELL, DONALD T. "Variation and Selective Retention in Socio-Cultural Evolution." In Barringer, Blankstein, and Mack, eds., *Social Change in Developing Areas.*

CAMPBELL, JOSEPH. *The Hero with a Thousand Faces.* New York: Pantheon, 1949.

CANN, REBECCA. "DNA and Human Origins." *Annual Review of Anthropology,* 17 (1988): 127–43.

CANN, REBECCA, M. STONEKING, AND A. C. WILSON. "Mitochondrial DNA and Human Evolution." *Nature,* 325 (1987): 31–36.

CARNEIRO, ROBERT L. "The Circumscription Theory: Challenge and Response." *American Behavioral Scientist,* 31 (1988): 497–511.

CARNEIRO, ROBERT L. "A Theory of the Origin of the State." *Science,* August 21, 1970, 733–38.

CARPENTER, C. R. "A Field Study in Siam of the Behavior and Social Relations of the Gibbon *(Hylobates lar).*" *Comparative Psychology Monographs,* 16, no. 5 (1940): 1–212.

CARTMILL, MATT. "Explaining Primate Origins." In Peregrine, Ember, and Ember, eds., *Physical Anthropology.*

CARTMILL, MATT. "New Views on Primate Origins." *Evolutionary Anthropology,* 1 (1992): 105–11.

CARTMILL, MATT. "Non-Human Primates." In Jones, Martin, and Pilbeam, eds., *The Cambridge Encyclopedia of Human Evolution.*

CHAMBERS, ERVE. *Applied Anthropology: A Practical Guide.* Rev. ed. Prospect Heights, IL: Waveland, 1989.

CHANG, KWANG-CHIH. *The Archaeology of Ancient China.* New Haven, CT: Yale University Press, 1968.

CHANG, KWANG-CHIH. *Archaeology of Ancient China.* 4th ed. New Haven, CT: Yale University Press, 1986 pp. 234–94.

CHANG, KWANG-CHIH. "The Beginnings of Agriculture in the Far East." *Antiquity,* 44, no. 175 (September 1970): 175–85.

CHANG, K. C. "In Search of China's Beginnings: New Light on an Old Civilization." *American Scientist,* 69 (1981): 148–60.

CHAPMAN, JEFFERSON. *Tellico Archaeology.* Knoxville: Tennessee Valley Authority, 1985.

CHARD, CHESTER S. *Man in Prehistory.* New York: McGraw-Hill, 1969.

CHARLES-DOMINIQUE, PIERRE. *Ecology and Behaviour of Nocturnal Primates.* Trans. R. D. Martin. New York: Columbia University Press, 1977.

CHARNAIS, PETER. "Economic Factors in the Decline of the Roman Empire." *Journal of Economic History,* 13 (1953): 412–24.

CHENEY, DOROTHY, AND ROBERT SEYFARTH. *How Monkeys See the World.* Chicago: University of Chicago Press, 1990.

CHENEY, DOROTHY L., AND RICHARD W. WRANGHAM. "Predation." In Smuts et al., eds., *Primate Societies.*

CHIA, L., *The Story of Peking Man: From Archaeology to Mystery.* Oxford: Oxford University Press, 1990.

CHILDE, V. GORDON. "The Urban Revolution." *Town Planning Review,* 21 (1950): 3–17.

CHIVERS, DAVID JOHN. *The Siamang in Malaya.* Basel, Switzerland: Karger, 1974.

CHIVERS, DAVID J., ED. *Malayan Forest Primates: Ten Years' Study in Tropical Rain Forest.* New York: Plenum, 1980.

CHIVERS, DAVID J., BERNARD A. WOOD, AND ALAN BILSBOROUGH, EDS. *Food Acquisition and Processing in Primates.* New York: Plenum, 1984.

CHOMSKY, NOAM. *Reflections on Language.* New York: Pantheon, 1975.

CIOCHON, RUSSELL L., AND ROBERT S. CORRUCCINI, EDS. *New Interpretations of Ape and Human Ancestry.* New York: Plenum, 1983.

CIOCHON, RUSSELL L., AND DENNIS A. ETLER. "Reinterpreting Past Primate Diversity." In Corruccini and Ciochon, eds., *Integrative Paths to the Past.*

CIOCHON, RUSSELL L., AND JOHN G. FLEAGLE, EDS. *The Human Evolution Source Book.* Englewood Cliffs, NJ: Prentice Hall, 1993.

CIOCHON, RUSSELL, JOHN OLSEN, AND JAMIE JAMES. *Other Origins: The Search for the Giant Ape in Human Prehistory.* New York: Bantam, 1990.

CLAASSEN, CHERYL. "Gender and Archaeology." In Peregrine, Ember, and Ember, eds., *Archaeology.*

CLAASEN, CHERYL. "Gender, Shellfishing, and the Shell Mound Archaic." In Gero and Conkey, eds., *Engendering Archaeology.*

CLARK, GEOFFREY A., ED. *Perspectives on the Past: Theoretical Biases in Mediterranean Hunter-Gatherer Research.* Philadelphia: University of Pennsylvania Press, 1991.

CLARK, GRAHAME. *The Earlier Stone Age Settlement of Scandinavia.* Cambridge: Cambridge University Press, 1975.

CLARK, GRAHAME, AND STUART PIGGOTT. *Prehistoric Societies.* New York: Knopf, 1965.

CLARK, J. DESMOND. "Interpretations of Prehistoric Technology from Ancient Egyptian and Other Sources. Pt. II: Prehistoric Arrow Forms in Africa as Shown by Surviving Examples of the Traditional Arrows of the San Bushmen." *Paleorient,* 3 (1977): 127–50.

CLARK, J. DESMOND. *The Prehistory of Africa.* New York: Praeger, 1970.

CLARK, W. E. LeGROS. *The Fossil Evidence for Human Evolution.* Chicago: University of Chicago Press, 1964, p. 184.

CLARKE, RONALD J., AND P. V. TOBIAS. "Sterkfontein Member 2 Foot Bones of the Oldest South African Hominid." *Science,* 269 (1995): 521–24.

CLAYMAN, CHARLES B., ED. *American Medical Association Encyclopedia of Medicine.* New York: Random House, 1989, pp. 857–58.

CLELAND, C., ED. *Cultural Continuity and Change.* New York: Academic Press, 1976.

CLUTTON-BROCK, JULIET. "Dog." In Mason, *Evolution of Domesticated Animals.*

CLUTTON-BROCK, JULIET. "Domestication of Animals." In Jones, Martin, and Pilbeam, eds., *The Cambridge Encyclopedia of Human Evolution.*

CLUTTON-BROCK, JULIET. "Origins of the Dog: Domestication and Early History." In James Serpell, ed., *The Domestic Dog: Its Evolution, Behaviour, and Interactions with People.* Cambridge: Cambridge University Press, 1995, pp. 8–20.

CLUTTON-BROCK, T. H., AND PAUL H. HARVEY. "Primate Ecology and Social Organization." *Journal of Zoology, London,* 183 (1977): 1–39.

CLUTTON-BROCK, T. H., AND PAUL H. HARVEY. "Primates, Brains and Ecology." *Journal of Zoology, London,* 190 (1980): 309–23.

COALE, ANSLEY J. "The History of the Human Population." *Scientific American,* 1974.

COE, MICHAEL D. *The Maya.* New York: Praeger, 1966.

COHEN, ALEX. *The Mental Health of Indigenous Peoples: An International Overview.* Geneva: Department of Mental Health, World Health Organization, 1999.

COHEN, MARK N. *The Food Crisis in Prehistory: Overpopulation and the Origins of Agriculture.* New Haven, CT: Yale University Press, 1977.

COHEN, MARK NATHAN. *Health and the Rise of Civilization.* New Haven, CT: Yale University Press, 1989.

COHEN, MARK N. "Population Pressure and the Origins of Agriculture." In Reed, ed., *Origins of Agriculture.*

COHEN, MARK N. "The Significance of Long-Term Changes in Human Diet and Food Economy." In Harris and Ross, eds., *Food and Evolution.*

COHEN, MARK N. "Were Early Agriculturalists Less Healthy Than Food Collectors?" In Peregrine, Ember, and Ember, eds., *Archaeology.*

COHEN, MARK NATHAN, AND GEORGE J. ARMELAGOS. "Paleopathology at the Origins of Agriculture: Editors' Summation." In M. N. Cohen and Armelagos, eds., *Paleopathology at the Origins of Agriculture.*

COHEN, MARK NATHAN, AND GEORGE J. ARMELAGOS, EDS. *Paleopathology at the Origins of Agriculture.* Orlando, FL: Academic Press, 1984.

COHEN, RONALD, AND ELMAN R. SERVICE, EDS. *Origins of the State: The Anthropology of Political Evolution.* Philadelphia: Institute for the Study of Human Issues, 1978.

COHMAP PERSONNEL. "Climatic Changes of the Last 18,000 Years." *Science,* 241 (1988): 1043–52.

COLLIER, STEPHEN, AND J. PETER WHITE. "Get Them Young? Age and Sex Inferences on Animal Domestication in Archaeology." *American Antiquity,* 41 (1976): 96–102.

COLLINS, DESMOND. "Later Hunters in Europe." In Collins, ed., *The Origins of Europe.*

CONNAH, GRAHAM. *African Civilizations: Precolonial Cities and States in Tropical Africa, an Archaeological Perspective.* Cambridge: Cambridge University Press, 1987.

CONROY, GLENN C. *Primate Evolution.* New York: Norton, 1990.

COREIL, JEANNINE. "Lessons from a Community Study of Oral Rehydration Therapy in Haiti." In van Willigen, Rylko-Bauer, and McElroy, eds., *Making Our Research Useful.*

CORRUCCINI, ROBERT S., AND RUSSELL L. CIOCHON, EDS. *Integrative Paths to the Past: Paleoanthropological Advances in Honor of F. Clark Howell.* Englewood Cliffs, NJ: Prentice Hall, 1994.

COSTIN, CATHY LYNNE. "Cloth Production and Gender Relations in the Inka Empire." In Peregrine, Ember, and Ember, eds., *Archaeology.*

COWAN, C. WESLEY, AND PATTY JO WATSON, EDS. *The Origins of Agriculture.* Washington, DC: Smithsonian Institution Press, 1992.

CRAWFORD, GARY W. "Prehistoric Plant Domestication in East Asia." In Cowan and Watson, eds., *The Origins of Agriculture.*

CRAWFORD, R. D. "Turkey." In Mason, ed., *Evolution of Domesticated Animals.*

CROCKETT, CAROLYN, AND JOHN F. EISENBERG. "Howlers: Variations in Group Size and Demography." In Smuts et al., eds., *Primate Societies.*

CULOTTA, ELIZABETH. "New Hominid Crowds the Field." *Science,* August 18, 1995.

CURTIN, PHILIP D. *Cross-Cultural Trade in World History.* Cambridge: Cambridge University Press, 1984.

DAMON, ALBERT, ED. *Physiological Anthropology.* New York: Oxford University Press, 1975.

DANIEL, I. RANDOLPH. "Early Eastern Archaic." In P. N. Peregrine and M. Ember, eds., *Encyclopedia of Prehistory.* Vol. 6: North America (Kluwer Academic/Plenum, 2001).

DART, RAYMOND. "*Australopithecus africanus:* The Man-Ape of South Africa." *Nature,* 115 (1925): 195.

DARWIN, CHARLES. "The Origin of Species." (Originally published 1859.) In Young, ed., *Evolution of Man.*

DAVIS, BERNARD D. "The Issues: Prospects versus Perceptions." In Davis, ed., *The Genetic Revolution.*

DAVIS, BERNARD D. "Summary and Comments: The Scientific Chapters." In Davis, ed., *The Genetic Revolution.*

DAVIS, BERNARD D., ED. *The Genetic Revolution: Scientific Prospects and Public Perceptions.* Baltimore: Johns Hopkins University Press, 1991.

DAWSON, ALISTAR. *Ice Age Earth.* London: Routledge, 1992, pp. 24–71.

DAY, MICHAEL. *Guide to Fossil Man.* 4th ed. Chicago: University of Chicago Press, 1986.

DEACON, TERRENCE. "Primate Brains and Senses." In Jones, Martin, and Pilbeam, eds., *The Cambridge Encyclopedia of Human Evolution.*

DEACON, TERRENCE. *The Symbolic Species: The Co-Evolution of Language and the Brain.* New York: Norton, 1997.

DELSON, ERIC, ED. *Ancestors: The Hard Evidence.* New York: Alan R. Liss, 1985.

DE LUMLEY, HENRY. "A Paleolithic Camp at Nice." *Scientific American,* May 1969, 42–50.

DEVILLERS, CHARLES, AND JEAN CHALINE. *Evolution: An Evolving Theory.* New York: Springer Verlag, 1993.

DE VILLIERS, PETER A., AND JILL G. DE VILLIERS. *Early Language.* Cambridge, MA: Harvard University Press, 1979.

DE WAAL, FRANS, AND FRANS LANTING. *Bonobo: The Forgotten Ape.* Berkeley: University of California Press, 1997.

DIAMOND, JARED. "The Accidental Conqueror." *Discover,* December 1989, 71–76.

DIAMOND, JARED. *Guns, Germs, and Steel.* New York: Norton, 1997, pp. 205–207.

DIAMOND, JARED. "Location, Location, Location: The First Farmers." *Science,* November 14, 1997, 1243–244.

DIAMOND, JARED. "Who Are the Jews?" *Natural History,* November 1993, 12–19.

DIAMOND, STANLEY. *In Search of the Primitive: A Critique of Civilization.* New Brunswick, NJ: Transaction Books, 1974.

DIBBLE, HAROLD, P. CHASE, S. MCPHERRON, AND A. TUFREAU. "Testing the Reality of a 'Living Floor' with Archaeological Data." *American Antiquity,* 62 (1997): 629–51.

DIBBLE, H. L., AND P. MELLARS, EDS. *The Middle Paleolithic: Adap-*

tation, Behavior, and Variability. Philadelphia: University Museum, 1992.

DICKSON, D. BRUCE. *The Dawn of Belief.* Tucson: University of Arizona Press, 1990, pp. 42–44.

DILLEHAY, THOMAS. *The Settlement of the Americas.* New York: Basic Books, 2000.

DIRKS, ROBERT. "Starvation and Famine." *Cross-Cultural Research,* 27 (1993): 28–69.

DIVALE, WILLIAM, AND CLIFFORD ZIPIN. "Hunting and the Development of Sign Language: A Cross-Cultural Test." *Journal of Anthropological Research,* 33 (1977): 185–201.

DOBRES, MARCIA-ANNE. "Venus Figurines." In B. Fagan, ed., *Oxford Companion to Archaeology.* Oxford: Oxford University Press, 1998, pp. 740–41.

DOBZHANSKY, THEODOSIUS. *Mankind Evolving: The Evolution of the Human Species.* New Haven, CT: Yale University Press, 1962.

DOHLINOW, PHYLLIS JAY, AND NAOMI BISHOP. "The Development of Motor Skills and Social Relationships among Primates through Play." In Phyllis Jay Dohlinow, ed., *Primate Patterns.* New York: Holt, Rinehart & Winston, 1972.

DOW, JAMES. *The Shaman's Touch: Otomi Indian Symbolic Healing.* Salt Lake City: University of Utah Press, 1986.

DOYLE, G. A., AND R. D. MARTIN, EDS. *The Study of Prosimian Behavior.* New York: Academic Press, 1979.

DRESSLER, WILLIAM W. *Stress and Adaptation in the Context of Culture.* Albany: State University of New York Press, 1991.

DUARTE, CIDALIA, J. MAURICIO, P. B. PETTITT, P. SOUTO, E. TRINKAUS, H. VAN DER PLICHT, AND J. ZILHAO, "The Early Upper Paleolithic Human Skeleton from the Abrigo do Lagar Velho (Portugal) and Modern Human Emergence in Iberia." *Proceedings of the National Academy of Sciences of the United States,* 96 (1999): 7604–609.

DUHARD, JEAN-PIERRE. "Upper Paleolithic Figures as a Reflection of Human Morphology and Social Organization." *Antiquity,* 67 (1993): 83–91.

DUNBAR, ROBIN. *Primate Social Systems.* Ithaca, NY: Comstock, 1988, pp. 107–10.

DURHAM, WILLIAM H. *Coevolution: Genes, Culture and Human Diversity.* Stanford, CA: Stanford University Press, 1991.

EDDY, ELIZABETH M., AND WILLIAM L. PARTRIDGE, EDS. *Applied Anthropology in America.* New York: Columbia University Press, 1978.

EDDY, ELIZABETH M., AND WILLIAM L. PARTRIDGE, EDS. *Applied Anthropology in America.* 2nd ed. New York: Columbia University Press, 1987.

EDGERTON, ROBERT B. "Conceptions of Psychosis in Four East African Societies." *American Anthropologist,* 68 (1966): 408–25.

EDGERTON, ROBERT B. *Sick Societies: Challenging the Myth of Primitive Harmony.* New York: Free Press, 1992.

EISELEY, LOREN C. "The Dawn of Evolutionary Theory." In Loren C. Eiseley, *Darwin's Century: Evolution and the Men Who Discovered It.* Garden City, NY: Doubleday, 1958.

EISENBERG, JOHN F. "Comparative Ecology and Reproduction of New World Monkeys." In Devra Kleinman, ed., *The Biology and Conservation of the Callitrichidae.* Washington, DC: Smithsonian Institution, 1977.

ELDREDGE, NILES, AND IAN TATTERSALL. *The Myths of Human Evolution.* New York: Columbia University Press, 1982.

ELIOT, T. S. "The Love Song of J. Alfred Prufrock." In *Collected Poems, 1909–1962.* New York: Harcourt, Brace & World, 1963.

ELLISON, PETER T. "Natural Variation in Human Fecundity." In Peregrine, Ember, and Ember, eds., *Physical Anthropology.*

EMBER, CAROL R. "The Relative Decline in Women's Contribution to Agriculture with Intensification." *American Anthropologist,* 85 (1983): 285–304.

EMBER, CAROL R., AND MELVIN EMBER. "Resource Unpredictability, Mistrust, and War: A Cross-Cultural Study." *Journal of Conflict Resolution,* 36 (1992): 242–62.

EMBER, CAROL R., MELVIN EMBER, AND PETER N. PEREGRINE, EDS. *Research Frontiers in Anthropology.* Upper Saddle River, NJ: Prentice Hall, 1998. Prentice Hall/Simon & Schuster Custom Publishing. Three volumes.

EMBER, MELVIN, AND CAROL R. EMBER. "Male-Female Bonding: A Cross-Species Study of Mammals and Birds." *Behavior Science Research,* 14 (1979): 37–56.

EMBER, MELVIN, CAROL R. EMBER, AND DAVID LEVINSON, EDS. *Portraits of Culture: Ethnographic Originals.* Upper Saddle River, NJ: Prentice Hall, 1998. Prentice Hall/Simon & Schuster Custom Publishing.

EMENER, WILLIAM G., AND MARGARET DARROW, EDS. *Career Explorations in Human Services.* Springfield, IL: Charles C. Thomas, 1991.

ETIENNE, ROBERT. *Pompeii: The Day a City Died.* New York: Abrams, 1992.

ETKIN, NINA L., AND PAUL J. ROSS. "Malaria, Medicine, and Meals: A Biobehavioral Perspective." In Romanucci-Ross, Moerman, and Tancredi, eds., *The Anthropology of Medicine,* pp. 169–209.

EVELETH, PHYLLIS B., AND JAMES M. TANNER. *Worldwide Variation in Human Growth.* 2nd ed. Cambridge: Cambridge University Press, 1990.

FAGAN, BRIAN M. *Ancient North America: The Archaeology of a Continent.* London: Thames and Hudson, 1991.

FAGAN, BRIAN M. *In the Beginning.* Boston: Little, Brown, 1972.

FAGAN, BRIAN M. *People of the Earth: An Introduction to World Prehistory.* 6th ed. Glenview, IL: Scott, Foresman, 1989.

FAGAN, B. M. *People of the Earth: An Introduction to World Prehistory.* 9th ed. New York: HarperCollins, 1997.

FALK, DEAN. *Brain Dance.* New York: Henry Holt, 1992.

FALK, DEAN. "Cerebral Cortices of East African Early Hominids." *Science,* 221 (1983): 1072–74.

FALK, D. "Enlarged Occipital/Marginal Sinuses and Emissary Foramina: Their Significance in Hominid Evolution." In Grine, ed., *Evolutionary History of the "Robust" Australopithecines.*

FALK, DEAN. "A Good Brain Is Hard to Cool." *Natural History,* 102 (August 1993): 65–66.

FALK, DEAN. "Hominid Paleoneurology." *Annual Review of Anthropology,* 16 (1987): 13–30.

FARMER, PAUL. "Ethnography, Social Analysis, and the Prevention of Sexually Transmitted HIV Infection among Poor Women in Haiti." In Inhorn and Brown, *The Anthropology of Infectious Disease,* pp. 413–38.

FEDER, K. *Past in Perspective.* Mountain View, CA: Mayfield, 1996.

FEDIGAN, LINDA MARIE. *Primate Paradigms: Sex Roles and Social Bonds.* Montreal: Eden Press, 1982.

FEIBEL, CRAIG S., AND FRANCIS H. BROWN. "Microstratigraphy and Paleoenvironments." In Walker and Leakey, eds., *The Nariokotome Homo erectus Skeleton.*

FEINMAN, GARY M., STEPHEN A. KOWALEWSKI, LAURA FINSTEN, RICHARD E. BLANTON, AND LINDA NICHOLAS. "Long-Term Demographic Change: A Perspective from the Valley of Oaxaca, Mexico." *Journal of Field Archaeology,* 12 (1985): 333–62.

FEINMAN, GARY M., AND J. MARCUS, EDS. *Archaic States.* Santa Fe, NM: School of American Research Press, 1998.

FELDMAN, DOUGLAS A., AND THOMAS M. JOHNSON. "Introduction." In Feldman and Johnson, eds., *The Social Dimensions of AIDS.*

FELDMAN, DOUGLAS A., AND THOMAS M. JOHNSON, EDS. *The Social Dimensions of AIDS: Method and Theory.* New York: Praeger, 1986.

FELDMAN, DOUGLAS A., AND J. W. MILLER. *The AIDS Crisis: A Documentary History.* Westport, CT: Greenwood Press, 1998.

FERGUSON, R. BRIAN, AND NEIL L. WHITEHEAD. "The Violent Edge of Empire." In R. B. Ferguson and N. Whitehead, eds., *War in the Tribal Zone.* Santa Fe: School of American Research Press, 1992, pp. 1–30.

FERRARO, GARY P. *The Cultural Dimension of International Business.* 4th ed. Englewood Cliffs, NJ: Prentice Hall, 2002.

"The First Dentist." *Newsweek,* March 5, 1973, 73.

"The First Tool Kit." *Science,* January 31, 1997, 623.

FISCHMAN, JOSHUA. "Putting Our Oldest Ancestors in Their Proper Place." *Science,* September 30, 1994, 2011–12.

FISH, PAUL R. "Beyond Tools: Middle Paleolithic Debitage Analysis and Cultural Inference." *Journal of Anthropological Research,* 37 (1981): 374–86.

FISHER, JULIE. "Grassroots Organizations and Grassroots Support Organizations: Patterns of Interaction." In Moran, *Transforming Societies.*

FISHER, WILLIAM H. "Megadevelopment, Environmentalism, and Resistance: The Institutional Context of Kayapo Indigenous Politics in Central Brazil." *Human Organization,* 53 (1994): 220–32.

FLANNERY, KENT V. "Adaptation, Evolution, and Archaeological Phases: Some Implications of Reynolds' Simulation." In Flannery, ed., *Guila Naquitz,* p. 502.

FLANNERY, KENT V. "The Cultural Evolution of Civilizations." *Annual Review of Ecology and Systematics,* 3 (1972): 399–426.

FLANNERY, KENT V. "The Ecology of Early Food Production in Mesopotamia." *Science,* March 12, 1965, 1247–56.

FLANNERY, KENT V. "Guila Naquitz in Spatial, Temporal, and Cultural Context." In Flannery, ed., *Guila Naquitz,* pp. 31–42.

FLANNERY, KENT V. "The Origins of Agriculture." *Annual Review of Anthropology,* 2 (1973): 271–310.

FLANNERY, KENT V. "The Origins and Ecological Effects of Early Domestication in Iran and the Near East." In Struever, ed., *Prehistoric Agriculture.*

FLANNERY, KENT V. "The Origins of the Village as a Settlement Type in Mesoamerica and the Near East: A Comparative Study." In Tringham, ed., *Territoriality and Proxemics.*

FLANNERY, KENT V. "The Research Problem." In Flannery, ed., *Guila Naquitz.*

FLANNERY, KENT V., ED. *The Early Mesoamerican Village.* New York: Academic Press, 1976.

FLANNERY, KENT V., ED. *Guila Naquitz: Archaic Foraging and Early Agriculture in Oaxaca, Mexico.* Orlando, FL: Academic Press, 1986.

FLEAGLE, JOHN G. "Anthropoid Origins." In Corruccini and Ciochon, eds., *Integrative Paths to the Past.*

FLEAGLE, JOHN G. *Primate Adaptation and Evolution.* San Diego: Academic Press, 1988.

FLEAGLE, JOHN G. *Primate Adaptation and Evolution.* 2nd ed. San Diego: Academic Press, 1999, pp. 404–409.

FLEAGLE, JOHN G., CHARLES H. JANSON, AND KAYE E. REED, EDS. *Primate Communities.* Cambridge: Cambridge University Press, 1999.

FLEAGLE, JOHN G., AND R. F. KAY, EDS. *Anthropoid Origins.* New York: Plenum, 1994.

FLEAGLE, JOHN G., AND RICHARD F. KAY. "New Interpretations of the Phyletic Position of Oligocene Hominoids." In Ciochon and Corruccini, eds., *New Interpretations of Ape and Human Ancestry.*

FLEAGLE, JOHN G., AND RICHARD F. KAY. "The Paleobiology of Catarrhines." In Delson, ed., *Ancestors.*

FLEAGLE, JOHN G., AND R. F. KAY. "The Phyletic Position of the Parapithecidae." *Journal of Human Evolution,* 16 (1987): 483–531.

FLEISCHER, ROBERT L., AND HOWARD R. HART, JR. "Fission-Track Dating: Techniques and Problems." In Bishop and Miller, eds., *Calibration of Hominid Evolution.*

FLEISCHER, ROBERT L., P. B. PRICE, R. M. WALKER, AND L. S. B. LEAKEY. "Fission-Track Dating of Bed I, Olduvai Gorge." *Science,* April 2, 1965, 72–74.

FLUEHR-LOBBAN, CAROLYN, ED. *Ethics and the Profession of Anthropology: Dialogue for a New Era.* Philadelphia: University of Pennsylvania Press, 1991.

FOLEY, W. A. *Anthropological Linguistics: An Introduction.* Malden, MA: Blackwell, 1997.

FORD, RICHARD I., ED. *The Nature and Status of Ethnobotany.* Anthropological Papers No. 67, Museum of Anthropology. Ann Arbor: University of Michigan, 1978.

FOSSEY, DIAN. *Gorillas in the Mist.* Boston: Houghton Mifflin, 1983.

FOSTER, GEORGE M. *Applied Anthropology.* Boston: Little, Brown, 1969.

FOSTER, GEORGE M. *Hippocrates' Latin American Legacy: Humoral Medicine in the New World.* Amsterdam: Gordon and Breach, 1994.

FOWLER, BRENDA. *Iceman: Uncovering the Life and Times of a Prehistoric Man Found in an Alpine Glacier.* New York: Random House, 2000.

FOWLER, MELVIN L. "A Pre-Columbian Urban Center on the Mississippi." *Scientific American,* August 1975, 92–101.

FRANCISCUS, ROBERT G., AND ERIK TRINKAUS. "Nasal Morphology and the Emergence of *Homo erectus.*" *American Journal of Physical Anthropology,* 75 (1988): 517–27.

FRANKEL, BARBARA, AND M. G. TREND. "Principles, Pressures and Paychecks: The Anthropologist as Employee." In Fluehr-Lobban, ed., *Ethics and the Profession of Anthropology.*

FRAYER, DAVID W. "Body Size, Weapon Use, and Natural Selection in the European Upper Paleolithic and Mesolithic." *American Anthropologist,* 83 (1981): 57–73.

FRAYER, DAVID W. "Testing Theories and Hypotheses about Human Origins." In Peregrine, Ember, and Ember, eds., *Physical Anthropology.*

FRAYER, DAVID, M. WOLPOFF, A. THORNE, F. SMITH, AND G. POPE. "Theories of Modern Human Origins: The Paleontological Test." *American Anthropologist,* 95 (1993): 24–27.

FREEMAN, LESLIE G. "Torralba and Ambrona: A Review of Discoveries." In Corruccini and Ciochon, eds., *Integrative Paths to the Past.*

FRIED, MORTON H., ED. *Readings in Anthropology.* 2nd ed., Vol. 1. New York: Thomas Y. Crowell, 1968.

FRIEDMAN, J., AND M. J. ROWLANDS, EDS. *The Evolution of Social Systems.* London: Duckworth, 1977.

FRIEDMAN, SAUL S. "Holocaust." In *Academic American* [now Grolier] *Encyclopedia.* Vol. 10. Princeton, NJ: Arete, 1980.

FRISANCHO, A. ROBERTO, AND LAWRENCE P. GREKSA. "Development Responses in the Acquisition of Functional Adaptation to High Altitude." In Little and Haas, eds., *Human Population Biology.*

FRISCH, JOHN. "Individual Behavior and Intergroup Variability in Japanese Macaques." In P. C. Jay, ed., *Primates: Studies in Adaptation and Variability.* New York: Holt, Rinehart & Winston, 1968, pp. 243–52.

FRISCH, ROSE E. "Fatness, Puberty, and Fertility." *Natural History,* October 1980, 16–27.

FRUNET, MICHEL, ALAIN BEAUVILAIN, YVES COPPENS, ELILE HEINTZ, ALADJI H. E. MOUTAYE, AND DAVID PILBEAM. "The First Australopithecine 2500 Kilometers West of the Rift Valley (Chad)." *Nature,* 378 (1995): 273–75.

FUTUYMA, DOUGLAS. *Science on Trial.* New York: Pantheon, 1982.

GABUNIA, LEO, A. VEKUA, D. LORDKIPANIDZE, ET AL. "Earliest Pleistocene Hominid Cranial Remains from Dmanisi, Republic of Georgia: Taxonomy, Geological Setting, and Age." *Science,* 288 (2000): 1019–25.

GALDIKAS, BIRUTÉ M. F. "Orangutan Adaptation at Tanjung Puting Reserve: Mating and Ecology." In Hamburg and McCown, eds., *The Great Apes.*

GARDNER, BEATRICE T., AND R. ALLEN GARDNER. "Two Comparative Psychologists Look at Language Acquisition." In Nelson, ed., *Children's Language,* Vol. 2.

GARDNER, R. ALLEN, AND BEATRICE T. GARDNER. "Teaching Sign Language to a Chimpanzee." *Science,* August 15, 1969, 664–72.

GARN, STANLEY M. *Human Races.* 3rd ed. Springfield, IL: Charles C. Thomas, 1971.

GENTNER, W., AND H. J. LIPPOLT. "The Potassium-Argon Dating of Upper Tertiary and Pleistocene Deposits." In Brothwell and Higgs, eds., *Science in Archaeology.*

GERO, JOAN M., AND MARGARET W. CONKEY, EDS. *Engendering Archaeology: An Introduction to Women and Prehistory.* Oxford: Blackwell, 1991.

GESLER, W. *The Cultural Geography of Health Care.* Pittsburgh: University of Pittsburgh Press, 1991.

GIBBON, G. *Anthropological Archaeology.* New York: Columbia University Press, 1984.

GIBBONS, ANN. "First Americans: Not Mammoth Hunters, but Forest Dwellers?" *Science,* April 19, 1995, 346–47.

GINGERICH, P. D. "*Pleisiadipis* and the Delineation of the Order Primates." In B. Wood, L. Martin, and P. Andrews, eds., *Major Topics in Primate Evolution.* Cambridge: Cambridge University Press, 1986, pp. 32–46.

GLADWIN, THOMAS, AND SEYMOUR B. SARASON. *Truk: Man in Paradise.* New York: Wenner-Gren Foundation for Anthropological Research, 1953, as seen in eHRAF Collection of Ethnography on the Web, 2000.

GLEITMAN, LILA R., AND ERIC WANNER. "Language Acquisition: The State of the State of the Art." In Wanner and Gleitman, eds., *Language Acquisition.*

GOLDEN, FREDERIC, MICHAEL LEMONICK, AND DICK THOMPSON. "The Race Is Over." *Time,* July 3, 2000, 18–23.

GOLDIZEN, ANNE WILSON. "Tamarins and Marmosets: Communal Care of Offspring." In Smuts et al., eds., *Primate Societies.*

GOODALL, JANE. "My Life among Wild Chimpanzees." *National Geographic,* August 1963, 272–308.

GOODALL, JANE. *Through a Window.* Boston: Houghton Mifflin, 1990.

GOODENOUGH, WARD H. *Cooperation in Change.* New York: Russell Sage Foundation, 1963.

GOODMAN, ALAN H., AND GEORGE J. ARMELAGOS. "Disease and Death at Dr. Dickson's Mounds." *Natural History,* September 1985, 12–19.

GOODMAN, ALAN H., JOHN LALLO, GEORGE J. ARMELAGOS, AND JEROME C. ROSE. "Health Changes at Dickson Mounds, Illinois (A.D. 950–1300)." In M. N. Cohen and Armelagos, eds., *Paleopathology at the Origins of Agriculture.*

GOODMAN, ALAN H., AND THOMAS L. LEATHERMAN, EDS. *Building a New Biocultural Synthesis: Political-Economic Perspectives on Human Biology.* Ann Arbor: University of Michigan Press, 1998.

GOODMAN, MORRIS. "Reconstructing Human Evolution from Proteins." In Jones, Martin, and Pilbeam, eds., *The Cambridge Encyclopedia of Human Evolution.*

GOODRICH, L. CARRINGTON. *A Short History of the Chinese People.* 3rd ed. New York: Harper & Row, 1959.

GORMAN, CHESTER. "The Hoabinhian and After: Subsistence Patterns in Southeast Asia during the Late Pleistocene and Early Recent Periods." *World Archaeology,* 2 (1970): 315–19.

GRANT, PETER R. "Natural Selection and Darwin's Finches." *Scientific American,* October 1991, 82–87.

GRAY, J. PATRICK. *Primate Sociobiology.* New Haven, CT: HRAF Press, 1985.

GRAY, J. PATRICK, AND LINDA D. WOLFE. "Height and Sexual Dimorphism of Stature among Human Societies." *American Journal of Physical Anthropology,* 53 (1980): 446–52.

GRAY, J. PATRICK, AND LINDA WOLFE. "What Accounts for Population Variation in Height?" In Peregrine, Ember, and Ember, eds., *Physical Anthropology.*

GRAYSON, DONALD K. "Explaining Pleistocene Extinctions: Thoughts on the Structure of a Debate." In P. S. Martin and Klein, eds., *Quaternary Extinctions.*

GRAYSON, DONALD K. "Pleistocene Avifaunas and the Overkill Hypothesis." *Science,* February 18, 1977, pp. 691–92.

GREENBERG, JOSEPH H., AND MERRITT RUHLEN. "Linguistic Origins of Native Americans." *Scientific American,* November 1992, 94–99.

GREENE, L., AND F. E. JOHNSTON, EDS. *Social and Biological Predictors of Nutritional Status, Physical Growth, and Neurological Development.* New York: Academic Press, 1980.

GREENFIELD, PATRICIA MARKS, AND E. SUE SAVAGE-RUMBAUGH. "Grammatical Combination in *Pan paniscus:* Processes of Learning and Invention in the Evolution and Development of Language." In Parker and Gibson, eds., *"Language" and Intelligence in Monkeys and Apes.*

GREKSA, LAWRENCE P., AND CYNTHIA M. BEALL. "Development of Chest Size and Lung Function at High Altitude." In Little and Haas, eds., *Human Population Biology.*

GRINE, FREDERICK E. "Australopithecine Taxonomy and Phylogeny: Historical Background and Recent Interpretation." In Ciochon and Fleagle, eds., *The Human Evolution Source Book.*

GRINE, FREDERICK E. "Dental Evidence for Dietary Differences in *Australopithecus* and *Paranthropus:* A Quantitative Analysis of Permanent Molar Microwear." *Journal of Human Evolution,* 15 (1986): 783–822.

GRINE, FREDERICK E. "Evolutionary History of the 'Robust' Australopithecines: A Summary and Historical Perspective." In Grine, ed., *Evolutionary History of the "Robust" Australopithecines.*

GRINE, FREDERICK E., ED. *Evolutionary History of the "Robust" Australopithecines.* New York: Aldine, 1988.

GROSS, DANIEL R., AND BARBARA A. UNDERWOOD. "Technological Change and Caloric Costs: Sisal Agriculture in Northeastern Brazil." *American Anthropologist,* 73 (1971): 725–40.

GRUBB, HENRY J. "Intelligence at the Low End of the Curve: Where Are the Racial Differences?" *Journal of Black Psychology,* 14 (1987): 25–34.

GRUBB, HENRY J., AND ANDREA G. BARTHWELL. "Superior Intelligence and Racial Equivalence: A Look at Mensa." Paper presented at the 1996 annual meeting of the Society for Cross-Cultural Research.

GUNDERS, S., AND J. W. M. WHITING. "Mother-Infant Separation and Physical Growth." *Ethnology,* 7 (1968): 196–206.

GUTHRIE, DALE R. "Mosaics, Allelochemics, and Nutrients: An Ecological Theory of Late Pleistocene Megafaunal Extinctions." In P. S. Martin and Klein, eds., *Quaternary Extinctions.*

HABICHT, J.K.A., *Paleoclimate, Paleomagnetism, and Continental Drift.* Tulsa, OK: American Association of Petroleum Geologists, 1979.

HACKENBERG, ROBERT A. "Scientists or Survivors? The Future of Applied Anthropology under Maximum Uncertainty." In Trotter, ed., *Anthropology for Tomorrow.*

HAHN, EMILY. "Chimpanzees and Language." *New Yorker,* April 24, 1971, 54ff.

HAHN, ROBERT A. *Sickness and Healing: An Anthropological Perspective.* New Haven, CT: Yale University Press, 1995.

HALDANE, J. B. S. "Human Evolution: Past and Future." In Jepsen, Mayr, and Simpson, eds., *Genetics, Paleontology, and Evolution.*

HALL, EDWARD T. *The Hidden Dimension.* Garden City, NY: Doubleday, 1966.

HALL, K. L. R. "Social Learning in Monkeys." In P. C. Jay, ed., *Primates: Studies in Adaptation and Variability.* New York: Holt, Rinehart & Winston, 1968, pp. 383–97.

HALLOWELL, A. IRVING. "Ojibwa World View and Disease." In *Contributions to Anthropology: Selected Papers of A. Irving Hallowell.* Chicago: University of Chicago Press, 1976, pp. 410–13.

HAMBURG, DAVID A., AND ELIZABETH R. MCCOWN, EDS. *The Great Apes.* Menlo Park, CA: Benjamin/Cummings, 1979.

HANNA, JOEL M., MICHAEL A. LITTLE, AND DONALD M. AUSTIN. "Climatic Physiology." In Little and Haas, eds., *Human Population Biology.*

HANNAH, ALISON C., AND W. C. MCGREW. "Chimpanzees Using Stones to Crack Open Oil Palm Nuts in Liberia." *Primates,* 28 (1987): 31–46.

HARCOURT, A. H. "The Social Relations and Group Structure of Wild Mountain Gorillas." In Hamburg and McCown, eds., *The Great Apes.*

HARLAN, JACK R. "A Wild Wheat Harvest in Turkey." *Archaeology,* 20, no. 3 (June 1967): 197–201.

HARLOW, HARRY F., ET AL. "Maternal Behavior of Rhesus Monkeys Deprived of Mothering and Peer Association in Infancy." *Proceedings of the American Philosophical Society,* 110 (1966): 58–66.

HARRIS, DAVID R. "Settling Down: An Evolutionary Model for the Transformation of Mobile Bands into Sedentary Communities." In Friedman and Rowlands, eds., *The Evolution of Social Systems.* London: Duckworth, 1977.

HARRIS, MARVIN. *Cultural Materialism: The Struggle for a Science of Culture.* New York: Random House, 1979.

HARRIS, MARVIN, AND ERIC B. ROSS. *Food and Evolution: Toward a Theory of Human Food Habits.* Philadelphia: Temple University Press, 1987.

HARRISON, G. A., JAMES M. TANNER, DAVID R. PILBEAM, AND P. T. BAKER. *Human Biology: An Introduction to Human Evolution, Variation, Growth, and Adaptability.* 3rd ed. Oxford: Oxford University Press, 1988.

HARRISON, GAIL G. "Primary Adult Lactase Deficiency: A Problem in Anthropological Genetics." *American Anthropologist,* 77 (1975): 812–35.

HARRISON, PETER D., AND B. L. TURNER II, EDS. *Pre-Hispanic Maya Agriculture.* Albuquerque: University of New Mexico Press, 1978.

HARRISON, T. "A Reassessment of the Phylogenetic Relationships of *Oreopithecus bamboli.*" *Journal of Human Evolution,* 15 (1986): 541–84.

HARRISON, T., AND L. ROOK. "Enigmatic Anthropoid or Misunderstood Ape? The Phylogenetic Status of *Oreopithecus bamboli* Reconsidered." In D. R. Begun, C. V. Ward, and M. D. Rose, eds., *Function, Phylogeny and Fossils: Miocene Hominoid Evolution and Adaptation.* New York: Plenum, 1997, pp. 327–62.

HARTWIG, W. C. "Pattern, Puzzles and Perspectives on Platyrrhine Origins." In Corruccini and Ciochon, eds., *Integrative Paths to the Past,* pp. 69–93.

HARVEY, PHILIP W., AND PETER F. HEYWOOD. "Twenty-five Years of Dietary Change in Simbu Province, Papua New Guinea." *Ecology of Food and Nutrition,* 13 (1983): 27–35.

HASSAN, FEKRI A. *Demographic Archaeology.* New York: Academic Press, 1981.

HASTORF, CHRISTINE. "Gender, Space, and Food Prehistory." In Gero and Conkey, eds., *Engendering Archaeology.*

HAUSFATER, GLENN, JEANNE ALTMANN, AND STUART ALTMANN. "Long-Term Consistency of Dominance Relations among Female Baboons." *Science,* August 20, 1982, 752–54.

HAWKINS, ALICIA, AND M. KLEINDIENST. "Aterian." In P. N. Peregrine and M. Ember, eds., *Encyclopedia of Prehistory.* Vol. 1: Africa. New York: Kluwer Academic/Plenum, 2001, pp. 23–45.

HAYDEN, THOMAS. "A Genome Milestone." *Newsweek,* July 3, 2000, 51–52.

HAYNES, VANCE. "The Calico Site: Artifacts or Geofacts?" *Science,* 181 (1973): 305–10.

HAYS, TERENCE E. "From Ethnographer to Comparativist and Back Again." In C. R. Ember, Ember, and Peregrine, eds., *Research Frontiers in Anthropology.* Vol. 3.

HAYS, TERENCE E. "Sound Symbolism, Onomatopoeia, and New Guinea Frog Names. *Journal of Linguistic Anthropology,* 4 (1994): 153–74.

HELMS, MARY W. *Middle America.* Englewood Cliffs, NJ: Prentice Hall, 1975.

HENNIG, WILLI. *Phylogenetic Systematics.* Urbana: University of Illinois Press, 1966.

HENRY, DONALD O. *From Foraging to Agriculture: The Levant at the End of the Ice Age.* Philadelphia: University of Pennsylvania Press, 1989.

HENRY, DONALD O. "Foraging, Sedentism, and Adaptive Vigor in the Natufian: Rethinking the Linkages." In G. A. Clark, ed., *Perspectives on the Past.*

HERRNSTEIN, RICHARD J., AND CHARLES MURRAY. *The Bell Curve: Intelligence and Class Structure in American Life.* New York: Free Press, 1994.

HEWES, GORDON W. "Food Transport and the Origin of Hominid Bipedalism." *American Anthropologist,* 63 (1961): 687–710.

HIGGINS, PATRICIA J., AND J. ANTHONY PAREDES, EDS. *Classics of Practicing Anthropology: 1978–1998.* Oklahoma City, OK: Society for Applied Anthropology.

HILL, JANE H. "Apes and Language." *Annual Review of Anthropology,* 7 (1978): 89–112.

HILL, JANE H. "Do Apes Have Language?" In C. R. Ember, Ember, and Peregrine, eds., *Research Frontiers in Anthropology.* Vol. 3.

HOCKETT, C. F., AND R. ASCHER. "The Human Revolution." *Current Anthropology,* 5 (1964): 135–68.

HODDER, I. *The Domestication of Europe: Structure and Contingency in Neolithic Societies.* Oxford: Blackwell, 1990.

HOFFECKER, JOHN F., W. ROGER POWERS, AND TED GOEBEL. "The Colonization of Beringia and the Peopling of the New World." *Science,* January 1, 1993, 46–53.

HOLDAWAY, R. N., AND C. JACOMB. "Rapid Extinction of the Moas (Aves: Dinornithiformes): Model, Test, and Implications." *Science,* 287 (2000): 2250–57.

HOLDEN, CONSTANCE. "Selective Power of UV." *Science,* 289 (2000): 1461.

HOLE, FRANK. "Environmental Shock and Urban Origins." In Stein and Rothman, eds., *Chiefdoms and Early States in the Near East.*

HOLE, FRANK. "Origins of Agriculture." In Jones, Martin, and Pilbeam, eds., *The Cambridge Encyclopedia of Human Evolution.*

HOLE, FRANK, ED. *Archaeology of Western Iran.* Washington, DC: Smithsonian Institution Press, 1987.

HOLE, FRANK, KENT V. FLANNERY, AND JAMES A. NEELY. *Prehistory and Human Ecology of the Deh Luran Plain.* Memoirs of the Museum of Anthropology No. 1. Ann Arbor: University of Michigan, 1969.

HOLE, FRANK, AND ROBERT F. HEIZER. *An Introduction to Prehistoric Archeology.* 3rd ed. New York: Holt, Rinehart & Winston, 1973.

HOLLOWAY, RALPH L. "The Casts of Fossil Hominid Brains." *Scientific American,* July 1974, 106–15.

HONIGMANN, JOHN J. *Personality in Culture.* New York: Harper & Row, 1967.

HOUSTON, STEPHEN D. "The Phonetic Decipherment of Mayan Glyphs." *Antiquity,* 62 (1988): 126–35.

HOWELL, F. CLARK. "Observations on the Earlier Phases of the European Lower Paleolithic." In *Recent Studies in Paleoanthropology. American Anthropologist,* special publication, April 1966, pp. 88–200.

HOWELL, NANCY. *Demography of the Dobe !Kung.* New York: Academic Press, 1979.

HOWELLS, W. *Getting Here: The Story of Human Evolution.* 2nd ed. Washington, DC: Compass Press, 1997.

HRDY, SARAH BLAFFER. *The Langurs of Abu: Female and Male Strategies of Reproduction.* Cambridge, MA: Harvard University Press, 1977.

HSU, FRANCIS L. K., ED. *Psychological Anthropology.* 2nd ed. Cambridge, MA: Schenkman, 1972.

HUSS-ASHMORE, REBECCA, AND FRANCIS E. JOHNSTON. "Bioanthropological Research in Developing Countries." *Annual Review of Anthropology,* 14 (1985): 475–527.

HUXLEY, THOMAS H. "Man's Place in Nature." In Young, ed., *Evolution of Man.*

HYMES, DELL, ED. *Language in Culture and Society: A Reader in Linguistics and Anthropology.* New York: Harper & Row, 1964.

Inhorn, Marcia C., and Peter J. Brown. *The Anthropology of Infectious Disease: International Health Perspectives.* Amsterdam: Gordon and Breach, 1997.

Isaac, Glynn. "The Archaeology of Human Origins: Studies of the Lower Pleistocene in East Africa, 1971–1981." In Wendorf and Close, eds., *Advances in World Archaeology.*

Isaac, Glynn. "The Diet of Early Man: Aspects of Archaeological Evidence from Lower and Middle Pleistocene Sites in Africa." *World Archaeology,* 2 (1971): 277–99.

Isaac, Glynn, ed., assisted by Barbara Isaac. *Plio-Pleistocene Archaeology.* Oxford: Clarendon Press, 1997.

Itoigawa, Naosuke, Yukimaru Sugiyama, Gene P. Sackett, and Roger K. R. Thompson, eds. *Topics in Primatology.* Vol. 2. Tokyo: University of Tokyo Press, 1992.

Jablonski, Nina, and George Chaplin. "The Evolution of Human Skin Color." *Journal of Human Evolution,* 39 (2000): 57–106.

Jaeger, J., T. Thein, M. Benammi, Y. Chaimanee, A. N. Soe, T. Lwin, T. Tun, S. Wai, and S. Ducrocq. "A New Primate from the Middle Eocene of Myanmar and the Asian Early Origins of Anthropoids." *Science,* 286 (1999): 528–30.

Jayaswal, Vidula. "South Asian Upper Paleolithic." In P. N. Peregrine and M. Ember, eds., *Encyclopedia of Prehistory.* Vol. 8: *South and Southwest Asia.* New York: Kluwer Academic/Plenum, 2002.

Jelliffe, Derrick B., and E. F. Patrice Jelliffe. "Human Milk, Nutrition, and the World Resource Crisis." *Science,* May 9, 1975, 557–61.

Jennings, J. D. *Prehistory of North America.* New York: McGraw-Hill, 1968.

Jensen, Arthur. "How Much Can We Boost IQ and Scholastic Achievement?" *Harvard Educational Review,* 29 (1969): 1–123.

Jepsen, Glenn L., Ernst Mayr, and George Gaylord Simpson, eds. *Genetics, Paleontology, and Evolution.* New York: Atheneum, 1963.

Johanson, Donald C., and Maitland Edey. *Lucy: The Beginnings of Humankind.* New York: Simon & Schuster, 1981.

Johanson, Donald C., and Tim D. White. "A Systematic Assessment of Early African Hominids." *Science,* January 26, 1979, 321–30.

Johnson, Allen, and Timothy Earle. *The Evolution of Human Societies: From Foraging Group to Agrarian State.* Stanford, CA: Stanford University Press, 1987.

Johnson, Gregory A. "Aspects of Regional Analysis in Archaeology." *Annual Review of Anthropology,* 6 (1977): 479–508.

Johnson, Gregory. "The Changing Organization of Uruk Administration on the Susiana Plain." In Hole, ed., *Archaeology of Western Iran.*

Johnson, Thomas M., and Carolyn F. Sargent, eds. *Medical Anthropology: Contemporary Theory and Method.* Westport, CT: Praeger, 1990.

Jolly, Alison. *The Evolution of Primate Behavior.* 2nd ed. New York: Macmillan, 1985.

Jolly, Clifford. "The Seed-Eaters: A New Model of Hominid Differentiation Based on a Baboon Analogy." *Man,* 5 (1970): 5–28.

Jones, Steve, Robert Martin, and David Pilbeam, eds. *The Cambridge Encyclopedia of Human Evolution.* New York: Cambridge University Press, 1992.

Jordan, Ann T., ed. *Practicing Anthropology in Corporate America: Consulting on Organizational Culture.* NAPA Bulletin No. 14. Arlington, VA: American Anthropological Association, 1994.

Judge, W. James, and Jerry Dawson. "Paleo-Indian Settlement Technology in New Mexico." *Science,* June 16, 1972, 1210–16.

Jungers, William L. "New Estimates of Body Size in Australopithecines." In Grine, ed., *Evolutionary History of the "Robust" Australopithecines.*

Jungers, William L. "Relative Joint Size and Hominoid Locomotor Adaptations with Implications for the Evolution of Hominid Bipedalism." *Journal of Human Evolution,* 17 (1988): 247–65.

Kamin, Leon J. "Behind the Curve." *Scientific American,* February 1995, 99–103.

Kappelman, John. "The Attraction of Paleomagnetism." *Evolutionary Anthropology,* 2, no. 3 (1993): 89–99.

Kasarda, John D. "Economic Structure and Fertility: A Comparative Analysis." *Demography,* 8, no. 3 (August 1971): 307–18.

Kay, Richard F. "Parapithecidae." In Tattersall, Delson, and van Couvering, eds., *Encyclopedia of Human Evolution and Prehistory.*

Kay, Richard F. "Teeth." In Tattersall, Delson, and van Couvering, eds., *Encyclopedia of Human Evolution and Prehistory.*

Kay, Richard F., C. Ross, and B. A. Williams. "Anthropoid Origins." *Science,* 275 (1997): 797–804.

Keeley, Lawrence H. *Experimental Determination of Stone Tool Uses: A Microwear Analysis.* Chicago: University of Chicago Press, 1980.

Keeley, Lawrence. "The Functions of Paleolithic Flint Tools." *Scientific American,* 237 (1977): 108–26.

Kelley, Jay. "The Evolution of Apes." In Jones, Martin, and Pilbeam, eds., *The Cambridge Encyclopedia of Human Evolution.*

Kerr, Richard A. "Sea-Floor Dust Shows Drought Felled Akkadian Empire." *Science,* January 16, 1998, 325–26.

Kimbel, William H., T. D. White, and D. C. Johansen. "Cranial Morphology of *Australopithecus afarensis*: A Comparative Study Based on Composite Reconstruction of the Adult Skull." *American Journal of Physical Anthropology,* 64 (1984): 337–88.

Kingston, John D., Bruno D. Marino, and Andrew Hill. "Isotopic Evidence for Neogene Hominid Paleoenvironments in the Kenya Rift Valley." *Science,* May 13, 1994, 955–59.

Klein, Richard G. "The Ecology of Early Man in Southern Africa." *Science,* July 8, 1977, 115–26.

Klein, Richard G. *The Human Career: Human Biological and Cultural Origins.* Chicago: University of Chicago Press, 1989.

Klein, Richard G. "Ice-Age Hunters of the Ukraine." *Scientific American,* June 1974, 96–105.

Klein, Richard G. "Reconstructing How Early People Exploited Animals: Problems and Prospects." In Nitecki and Nitecki, eds., *The Evolution of Human Hunting.*

Klein, Richard G. "Southern Africa before the Ice Age." In Corruccini and Ciochon, eds., *Integrative Paths to the Past.*

Klein, Richard G. "The Stone Age Prehistory of Southern Africa." *Annual Review of Anthropology,* 12 (1983): 25–48.

Kleinberg, Jill. "Practical Implications of Organizational Culture Where Americans and Japanese Work Together." In Jordan, ed., *Practicing Anthropology in Corporate America.*

Kleinman, Arthur. *Rethinking Psychiatry: From Cultural Category to Personal Experience.* New York: Macmillan, 1988.

Kleinman, Arthur, and Byron Good, eds. *Culture and Depression: Studies in the Anthropology and Cross-Cultural Psychia-*

try of Affect and Disorder. Berkeley: University of California Press, 1985.

KLEINMAN, ARTHUR, VEENA DAS, AND MARGARET LOCK, EDS. *Social Suffering.* Berkeley: University of California Press, 1997.

KLIMA, BOHUSLAV. "The First Ground-Plan of an Upper Paleolithic Loess Settlement in Middle Europe and Its Meaning." In Braidwood and Willey, eds., *Courses toward Urban Life.*

KLINEBERG, OTTO. *Negro Intelligence and Selective Migration.* New York: Columbia University Press, 1935.

KLINEBERG, OTTO, ED. *Characteristics of the American Negro.* New York: Harper & Brothers, 1944.

KONNER, MELVIN, AND CAROL WORTHMAN. "Nursing Frequency, Gonadal Function, and Birth Spacing among !Kung Hunter-Gatherers." *Science,* February 15, 1980, 788–91.

KOZLOWSKI, S. K., ED. *The Mesolithic in Europe.* Warsaw: Warsaw University Press, 1973.

KRAMER, ANDREW. "The Natural History and Evolutionary Fate of *Homo erectus.*" In Peregrine, Ember, and Ember, eds., *Physical Anthropology.*

KRAMER, SAMUEL NOEL. *The Sumerians: Their History, Culture, and Character.* Chicago: University of Chicago Press, 1963.

KREBS, J. R., AND N. B. DAVIES. *An Introduction to Behavioural Ecology.* 2nd ed. Sunderland, MA: Sinauer, 1987.

KREBS, J. R., AND N. B. DAVIES, EDS. *Behavioural Ecology: An Evolutionary Approach.* 2nd ed. Sunderland, MA: Sinauer, 1984.

KRINGS, MATTHIAS, A. STONE, R. W. SCHMITZ, H. KRAINITZKI, M. STONEKING, AND S. PAABO. "Neandertal DNA Sequences and the Origin of Modern Humans." *Cell,* 90 (1997): 19–30.

KUEHN, STEVEN. "New Evidence for Late Paleoindian-Early Archaic Subsistence Behavior in the Western Great Lakes." *American Antiquity,* 63 (1998): 457–76.

KUSHNER, GILBERT. "Applied Anthropology." In Emener and Darrow, eds., *Career Explorations in Human Services.*

LANDAUER, THOMAS K. "Infantile Vaccination and the Secular Trend in Stature." *Ethos,* 1 (1973): 499–503.

LANDAUER, THOMAS K., AND JOHN W. M. WHITING. "Correlates and Consequences of Stress in Infancy." In Munroe, Munroe, and Whiting, eds., *Handbook of Cross-Cultural Human Development.*

LANDAUER, THOMAS K., AND JOHN W. M. WHITING. "Infantile Stimulation and Adult Stature of Human Males." *American Anthropologist,* 66 (1964): 1007–28.

LARSEN, CLARK SPENSER. "Bare Bones Anthropology: The Bioarchaeology of Human Remains." In Peregrine, Ember, and Ember, eds., *Archaeology.*

"The Last of the Cahokians." *Science,* April 19, 1996, 351.

LEAKEY, L. S. B. "Finding the World's Earliest Man." *National Geographic,* September 1960, 420–35.

LEAKEY, MARY. *Olduvai Gorge: Excavations in Beds I and II.* Cambridge: Cambridge University Press, 1971.

LEAKEY, MARY. *Olduvai Gorge: My Search for Early Man.* London: Collins, 1979; Leakey, Louis, *Olduvai Gorge.* Vol. 1: *A Preliminary Report on the Geology and Fauna.* Cambridge: Cambridge University Press, 1961.

LEAKEY, MEAVE, C. S. FEIBEL, I. McDOUGALL, AND A. WALKER. "New Four-Million-Year-Old Hominid Species from Kanapoi and Allia Bay, Kenya." *Nature,* 376 (1995): 565–71.

LEE, PHYLLIS C. "Home Range, Territory and Intergroup Encounters." In Robert A. Hinde, ed., *Primate Social Relationship: An Integrated Approach.* Sunderland, MA: Sinauer, 1983.

LEE, RICHARD B. *The !Kung San: Men, Women, and Work in a Foraging Society.* Cambridge: Cambridge University Press, 1979.

LEE, RICHARD B. "Population Growth and the Beginnings of Sedentary Life among the !Kung Bushmen." In Spooner, ed., *Population Growth.*

LESLIE, C. "Introduction." In C. Leslie, ed., *Asian Medical Systems: A Comparative Study.* Los Angeles: University of California Press, 1976.

LÉVI-STRAUSS, CLAUDE. "The Sorcerer and His Magic." In Lévi-Strauss, *Structural Anthropology.*

LÉVI-STRAUSS, CLAUDE. *Structural Anthropology.* Trans. Claire Jacobson and Brooke Grundfest Schoepf. New York: Basic Books, 1963.

LEVY, JERROLD E. "Hopi Shamanism: A Reappraisal." In Raymond J. DeMallie and Alfonzo Ortiz, eds., *North American Indian Anthropology: Essays on Society and Culture.* Norman: University of Oklahoma Press, 1994, pp. 307–27, as seen in eHRAF Collection of Ethnography on the Web, 2000.

LEWIN, ROGER. "Fossil Lucy Grows Younger, Again." *Science,* January 7, 1983, 43–44.

LEWIN, ROGER. "Is the Orangutan a Living Fossil?" *Science,* December 16, 1983, 1222–23.

LIEBERMAN, DANIEL E. "Testing Hypotheses about Recent Human Evolution from Skulls: Integrating Morphology, Function, Development, and Phylogeny." *Current Anthropology,* 36 (1995): 159–97.

LIEBERMAN, LEONARD. "Scientific Insignificance." *Anthropology Newsletter,* 40, no. 8 (1999): 11–12.

LIEBERMAN, PHILIP. *Uniquely Human: The Evolution of Speech, Thought, and Selfless Behavior.* Cambridge, MA: Harvard University Press, 1991.

LITTLE, M. A. "Growth and Development of Turkana Pastoralists." In Peregrine, Ember, and Ember, *Physical Anthropology.*

LITTLE, MICHAEL A., AND JERE D. HAAS, EDS. *Human Population Biology: A Transdisciplinary Science.* New York: Oxford University Press, 1989.

LOOMIS, W. FARNSWORTH. "Skin-Pigment Regulation of Vitamin-D Biosynthesis in Man." *Science,* August 4, 1967, 501–506.

LOUSTAUNAU, MARTHA O., AND ELISA J. SOBO. *The Cultural Context of Health, Illness, and Medicine.* Westport, CT: Bergin & Garvey, 1997.

LOVEJOY, ARTHUR O. *The Great Chain of Being: A Study of the History of an Idea.* Cambridge, MA: Harvard University Press, 1964.

LOVEJOY, C. OWEN. "Evolution of Human Walking." *Scientific American,* November 1988, 118–25.

LOVEJOY, C. OWEN. "The Origin of Man." *Science,* January 23, 1981, 341–50.

LOVEJOY, OWEN, KINGSBURY HEIPLE, AND ALBERT BERNSTEIN. "The Gait of *Australopithecus.*" *American Journal of Physical Anthropology,* 38 (1973): 757–79.

LUMBRERAS, LUIS. *The Peoples and Cultures of Ancient Peru.* Washington, DC: Smithsonian Institution Press, 1974.

LUTZ, CATHERINE. "Depression and the Translations of Emotional Worlds." In Kleinman and Good, eds., *Culture and Depression.*

MACARTHUR, R. H., AND E. O. WILSON. *Theory of Island Biogeography.* Princeton, NJ: Princeton University Press, 1967.

McCORRISTON, JOY, AND FRANK HOLE. "The Ecology of Seasonal Stress and the Origins of Agriculture in the Near East." *American Anthropologist,* 93 (1991): 46–69.

McCRACKEN, ROBERT D. "Lactase Deficiency: An Example of Dietary Evolution." *Current Anthropology,* 12 (1971): 479–500.

McDERMOTT, LEROY. "Self-representation in Female Figurines." *Cultural Anthropology,* 37 (1996): 227–75.

McDONALD, KIM A. "New Evidence Challenges Traditional Model of How the New World Was Settled." *Chronicle of Higher Education,* March 13, 1998, A22.

McELROY, ANN, AND PATRICIA TOWNSEND. *Medical Anthropology in Ecological Perspective.* 3rd ed. Boulder, CO: Westview, 1996.

McGARVEY, STEPHEN T. "The Thrifty Gene Concept and Adiposity Studies in Biological Anthropology." *Journal of the Polynesian Society,* 103 (1994): 29–42.

McGREW, W. *Chimpanzee Material Culture: Implications for Human Evolution.* Cambridge: Cambridge University Press, 1992.

McHENRY, HENRY M. "New Estimates of Body Weight in Early Hominids and Their Significance to Encephalization and Megadontia in 'Robust' Australopithecines." In Grine, ed., *Evolutionary History of the "Robust" Australopithecines.*

McHENRY, HENRY M. "The Pattern of Human Evolution: Studies on Bipedalism, Mastication, and Encephalization." *Annual Review of Anthropology,* 11 (1982): 151–73.

McHENRY, HENRY M. "'Robust' Australopithecines, Our Family Tree, and Homoplasy." In Peregrine, Ember, and Ember, eds., *Physical Anthropology.*

McKEE, LAURIS. "Sex Differentials in Survivorship and the Customary Treatment of Infants and Children." *Medical Anthropology,* 8 (1984): 91–108.

MacKINNON, JOHN, AND KATHY MacKINNON. "The Behavior of Wild Spectral Tarsiers." *International Journal of Primatology,* 1 (1980): 361–79.

MacKINTOSH, N. J. *IQ and Human Intelligence.* Oxford: Oxford University Press, 1998.

McNEILL, WILLIAM H. *Plagues and Peoples.* Garden City, NY: Doubleday/Anchor, 1976.

MacNEISH, RICHARD S. "The Evaluation of Community Patterns in the Tehuacán Valley of Mexico and Speculations about the Cultural Processes." In Tringham, ed., *Ecology and Agricultural Settlements.*

MacNEISH, RICHARD S. *The Origins of Agriculture and Settled Life.* Norman: University of Oklahoma Press, 1991.

MADIGRAL, LORENA. "Hemoglobin Genotype, Fertility, and the Malaria Hypothesis." *Human Biology,* 61 (1989): 311–25.

MAGNER, L. *A History of Medicine.* New York: Marcel Dekker, 1992.

MAHONY, FRANK JOSEPH. *A Trukese Theory of Medicine.* Ann Arbor, MI: University Microfilms, 1070 [1971]), as seen in the eHRAF Collection of Ethnography on the Web, 2000.

MANHEIN, MARY H. *The Bone Lady: Life as a Forensic Anthropologist.* Baton Rouge: Louisiana State University Press, 1999.

MANZANILLA, LINDA, ED. *Studies in the Neolithic and Urban Revolutions.* British Archaeological Reports International Series 349. Oxford, 1987.

MARCUS, JOYCE. "Maya Hieroglyphs: History or Propaganda?" In Peregrine, Ember, and Ember, eds., *Archaeology.*

MARCUS, JOYCE. "On the Nature of the Mesoamerican City." In Vogt and Leventhal, eds., *Prehistoric Settlement Patterns.*

MARCUS, JOYCE, AND KENT V. FLANNERY. *Zapotec Civilization.* London: Thames and Hudson, 1996, pp. 49–50.

MARKS, JONATHAN. "Black, White, Other: Racial Categories Are Cultural Constructs Masquerading as Biology." *Natural History,* December 1994, 32–35.

MARSHACK, ALEXANDER. *The Roots of Civilization.* New York: McGraw-Hill, 1972.

MARSHALL, ELIOT. "Rival Genome Sequencers Celebrate a Milestone Together." *Science,* June 30, 2000, 2294–295.

MARSHALL, LARRY G. "Who Killed Cock Robin? An Investigation of the Extinction Controversy." In Martin and Klein, eds., *Quaternary Extinctions.*

MARTIN, PAUL S. "The Discovery of America." *Science,* March 9, 1973, 969–74.

MARTIN, PAUL S., AND RICHARD KLEIN, EDS. *Quaternary Extinctions: A Prehistoric Revolution.* Tucson: University of Arizona Press, 1984.

MARTIN, PAUL S., AND H. E. WRIGHT, EDS. *Pleistocene Extinctions: The Search for a Cause.* New Haven, CT: Yale University Press, 1967.

MARTIN, ROBERT. "Classification and Evolutionary Relationships." In Jones, Martin, and Pilbeam, eds., *The Cambridge Encyclopedia of Human Evolution.*

MARTIN, ROBERT D. *Primate Origins and Evolution: A Phylogenetic Reconstruction.* Princeton, NJ: Princeton University Press, 1990.

MARTIN, ROBERT D. "Strategies of Reproduction." *Natural History,* November 1975, 48–57.

MARTIN, ROBERT D., AND SIMON K. BEARDER. "Radio Bush Baby." *Natural History,* October 1979, 77–81.

MARTORELL, REYNALDO. "Interrelationships between Diet, Infectious Disease and Nutritional Status." In Greene and Johnston, eds., *Social and Biological Predictors of Nutritional Status, Physical Growth and Neurological Development.*

MARTORELL, REYNALDO, JUAN RIVERA, HALEY KAPLOWITZ, AND ERNESTO POLLITT. "Long-Term Consequences of Growth Retardation during Early Childhood." Paper presented at the Sixth International Congress of Auxology, September 15–19, 1991, Madrid.

MASCIE-TAYLOR, C. G. NICHOLAS. "The Biology of Social Class." In C. G. Nicholas Mascie-Taylor, ed., *Biosocial Aspects of Social Class.* Oxford: Oxford University Press, 1990, pp. 117–42.

MASCIE-TAYLOR, C. G. N., AND G. W. LASKER. *Applications of Biological Anthropology to Human Affairs.* New York: Cambridge University Press, 1991.

MASON, IAN L. *Evolution of Domesticated Animals.* New York: Longman, 1984.

MAYR, ERNST. *The Growth of Biological Thought: Diversity, Evolution, and Inheritance.* Cambridge, MA: Belknap Press of Harvard University Press, 1982.

MAYR, ERNST. *One Long Argument: Charles Darwin and the Genesis of Modern Evolutionary Thought.* Cambridge, MA: Harvard University Press, 1993.

MAYR, ERNST. "The Nature of the Darwinian Revolution." *Science,* June 2, 1972, 981–89.

MAZESS, RICHARD B. "Human Adaptation to High Altitude." In Damon, ed., *Physiological Anthropology.*

MEAD, MARGARET. "Applied Anthropology: The State of the Art." In Wallace et al., eds., *Perspectives on Anthropology 1976.*

MEAD, MARGARET. "The Evolving Ethics of Applied Anthropology." In Eddy and Partridge, eds., *Applied Anthropology in America.*

MEGGERS, BETTY J., ED. *Anthropological Archaeology in the Americas.* Washington, DC: Anthropological Society of Washington, 1968.

MELLAART, JAMES. "A Neolithic City in Turkey." *Scientific American,* April 1964, 94–104.

MELLAART, JAMES. "Roots in the Soil." In Piggott, ed., *The Dawn of Civilization.*

MELLARS, PAUL. "The Fate of the Neanderthals." *Nature,* 395 (1998): 539–40.

MELLARS, PAUL. *The Neanderthal Legacy.* Princeton, NJ: Princeton University Press, 1996, pp. 405–19.

MELLARS, PAUL. "The Upper Paleolithic Revolution." In B. Cunliffe, ed., *The Oxford Illustrated Prehistory of Europe.* Oxford: Oxford University Press, 1994, pp. 42–78.

MELTZER, DAVID J. "Pleistocene Peopling of the Americas." *Evolutionary Anthropology.* Vol. 1. 1993.

MELTZER, DAVID J. *Search for the First Americans.* Washington, DC: Smithsonian Institution, 1993.

MELTZER, DAVID J., DON D. FOWLER, AND JEREMY A. SABLOFF, EDS. *American Archaeology Past and Future.* Washington, DC: Smithsonian Institution Press, 1986.

MERBS, CHARLES F. "A New World of Infectious Disease." *Yearbook of Physical Anthropology,* 35 (1992): 3–42.

MICHEL, R. H., McGOVERN, P. E., AND BADLER, V. R. "The First Wine and Beer: Chemical Detection of Ancient Fermented Beverages." *Analytical Chemistry,* 65 (1993): 408A–13A.

MILLER, HENRY I. "Regulation." In Davis, ed., *The Genetic Revolution.*

MILLER, NAOMI F. "The Origins of Plant Cultivation in the Near East." In Cowan and Watson, eds., *The Origins of Agriculture.*

MILLON, RENÉ. "Social Relations in Ancient Teotihuacán." In Wolf, ed., *The Valley of Mexico.*

MILLON, RENÉ. "Teotihuacán." *Scientific American,* June 1967, 38–48.

MILTON, KATHARINE. "Distribution Patterns of Tropical Plant Foods as an Evolutionary Stimulus to Primate Mental Development." *American Anthropologist,* 83 (1981): 534–48.

MILTON, KATHARINE. "The Evolution of a Physical Anthropologist." In Peregrine, Ember, and Ember, eds., *Physical Anthropology.*

MILTON, KATHARINE. "Foraging Behaviour and the Evolution of Primate Intelligence." In Byrne and Whiten, eds., *Machiavellian Intelligence.*

MINUGH-PURVIS, NANCY. "Neandertal Growth: Examining Developmental Adaptations in Earlier *Homo sapiens.*" In Peregrine, Ember, and Ember, eds., *Physical Anthropology.*

MIRACLE, ANDREW W. "A Shaman to Organizations." In C. R. Ember, Ember, and Peregrine, eds., *Research Frontiers in Anthropology.* Vol. 3.

MITTERMEIER, RUSSELL A., AND ELEANOR J. STERLING. "Conservation of Primates." In Jones, Martin, and Pilbeam, eds., *The Cambridge Encyclopedia of Human Evolution.*

MOERMAN, DANIEL E. "Physiology and Symbols: The Anthropological Implications of the Placebo Effect." In Romanucci-Ross, Moerman, and Tancredi, eds., *The Anthropology of Medicine,* pp. 240–53.

MOLNAR, STEPHEN. *Human Variation: Races, Types, and Ethnic Groups.* 4th ed. Upper Saddle River, NJ: Prentice Hall, 1998.

MONTAGU, A. *A Man's Most Dangerous Myth: The Fallacy of Race.* 6th ed. Walnut Creek, CA: Alta Mira, 1997.

MOORE, CARMELLA CARACCI. "An Optimal Scaling of Murdock's Theories of Illness Data—An Approach to the Problem of Interdependence." *Behavior Science Research,* 22 (1988): 161–179.

MORAN, EMILIO F. *Human Adaptability: An Introduction to Ecological Anthropology.* 2nd ed. Boulder, CO: Westview, 2000.

MORAN, EMILIO F., ED. *Transforming Societies, Transforming Anthropology.* Ann Arbor: University of Michigan Press, 1996.

MORELL, VIRGINIA. "The Earliest Art Becomes Older—And More Common." *Science,* March 31, 1995, 1908–1909.

MORRIS, LAURA NEWELL, ED. *Human Populations, Genetic Variation, and Evolution.* San Francisco: Chandler, 1971.

MOSER, STEPHANIE. *Ancestral Images: The Iconography of Human Origins.* Ithaca, NY: Cornell University Press, 1998.

MOTULSKY, ARNO. "Metabolic Polymorphisms and the Role of Infectious Diseases in Human Evolution." In Morris, ed., *Human Populations, Genetic Variation, and Evolution.*

MUKERJEE, MADHUSREE. "Field Notes: Interview with a Parrot." *Scientific American,* April 1996, 28.

MÜLLER-HAYE, B. "Guinea Pig or Cuy." In Mason, *Evolution of Domesticated Animals.*

MUNROE, RUTH H., ROBERT L. MUNROE, AND BEATRICE B. WHITING, EDS. *Handbook of Cross-Cultural Human Development.* New York: Garland, 1981.

MURDOCK, GEORGE PETER. *Theories of Illness: A World Survey.* Pittsburgh: University of Pittsburgh Press, 1980.

MURPHY, JANE. "Abnormal Behavior in Traditional Societies: Labels, Explanations, and Social Reactions." In Munroe, Munroe, and Whiting, eds., *Handbook of Cross-Cultural Human Development.*

MURRAY, GERALD F. "The Domestication of Wood in Haiti: A Case Study in Applied Anthropology." In Podolefsky and Brown, *Applying Cultural Anthropology.*

NAPIER, J. R. "Paleoecology and Catarrhine Evolution." In J. R. Napier and P. H. Napier, eds., *Old World Monkeys: Evolution, Systematics, and Behavior.* New York: Academic Press, 1970.

NAPIER, J. R., AND P. H. NAPIER. *A Handbook of Living Primates.* New York: Academic Press, 1967.

NEEL, JAMES V., WILLARD R. CENTERWALL, NAPOLEON A. CHAGNON, AND HELEN L. CASEY. "Notes on the Effect of Measles and Measles Vaccine in a Virgin-Soil Population of South American Indians." *American Journal of Epidemiology,* 91 (1970): 418–29.

NELSON, K. E., ED. *Children's Language.* Vol. 2. New York: Halsted Press, 1980.

NICOLSON, NANCY A. "Infants, Mothers, and Other Females." In Smuts et al., eds., *Primate Societies.*

NIEDERBERGER, CHRISTINE. "Early Sedentary Economy in the Basin of Mexico." *Science,* January 12, 1979, 131–42.

NIEHOFF, ARTHUR H. *A Casebook of Social Change.* Chicago: Aldine, 1966.

NISHIDA, TOSHISADA. "Introduction to the Conservation Symposium." In Naosuke Itoigawa, Yukimaru Sugiyama, Gene P. Sackett, and Roger K. R. Thompson, *Topics in Primatology.* Vol. 2. Tokyo: University of Tokyo Press, 1992.

NISHIDA, TOSHISADA, WILLIAM C. McGREW, PETER MARLER, MARTIN PICKFORD, AND FRANS B. M. DE WAAL, EDS. *Topics in Primatology.* Vol. 1: *Human Origins.* Tokyo: University of Tokyo Press, 1992.

NISSEN, HENRY W. "Axes of Behavioral Comparison." In Anne Roe and George Gaylord Simpson, eds., *Behavior and Evolution.* New Haven, CT: Yale University Press, 1958.

NITECKI, MATTHEW H., AND DORIS V. NITECKI, EDS. *The Evolution of Human Hunting.* New York: Plenum, 1987.

NOBLE, WILLIAM, AND IAN DAVIDSON. *Human Evolution, Language, and Mind.* Cambridge: Cambridge University Press, 1996, pp. 162–214.

NORMILE, DENNIS. "Habitat Seen Playing Larger Role in Shaping Behavior." *Science,* March 6, 1998, 1454–455.

OAKLEY, KENNETH P. "Analytical Methods of Dating Bones." In Brothwell and Higgs, eds., *Science in Archaeology.*

OAKLEY, KENNETH. "On Man's Use of Fire, with Comments on Tool-Making and Hunting." In Washburn, ed., *Social Life of Early Man.*

OLSZEWSKI, DEBORAH I. "Social Complexity in the Natufian? Assessing the Relationship of Ideas and Data." In Clark, ed., *Perspectives on the Past.*

ORTIZ DE MONTELLANO, B. R., AND C. H. BROWNER. "Chemical Bases for Medicinal Plant Use in Oaxaca, Mexico." *Journal of Ethnopharmacology,* 13 (1985): 57–88.

OXBY, CLARE. "Farmer Groups in Rural Areas of the Third World." *Community Development Journal,* 18 (1983): 50–59.

PANTER-BRICK, CATHERINE, DEBORAH S. LOTSTEIN, AND PETER T. ELLISON. "Seasonality of Reproductive Function and Weight Loss in Rural Nepali Women." *Human Reproduction,* 8 (1993): 684–90.

PARFIT, MICHAEL. "Who Were the First Americans?" *National Geographic,* December 2000, pp. 41–67.

PARKER, SUE TAYLOR. "Why Big Brains Are So Rare." In Parker and Gibson, eds., *"Language" and Intelligence in Monkeys and Apes.*

PARKER, SUE TAYLOR, AND KATHLEEN RITA GIBSON, EDS. *"Language" and Intelligence in Monkeys and Apes: Comparative Developmental Perspectives.* New York: Cambridge University Press, 1990.

PARRY, WILLIAM J. "When and How Did Humans Populate the New World?" In Peregrine, Ember, and Ember, eds., *Archaeology.*

PARTRIDGE, WILLIAM L., AND ELIZABETH M. EDDY. "The Development of Applied Anthropology in America." In Eddy and Partridge, eds., *Applied Anthropology in America,* 2nd ed.

PATTERSON, LELAND. "Criteria for Determining the Attributes of Man-Made Lithics." *Journal of Field Archaeology,* 10 (1983): 297–307.

PATTERSON, THOMAS C. "Central Peru: Its Population and Economy." *Archaeology,* 24 (1971): 316–21.

PATTERSON, THOMAS C. *The Evolution of Ancient Societies: A World Archaeology.* Englewood Cliffs, NJ: Prentice Hall, 1981.

PEACOCK, NADINE, AND ROBERT BAILEY. "Efe: Investigating Food and Fertility in the Ituri Rain Forest." In M. Ember, Ember, and Levinson, eds., *Portraits of Culture.*

PEARSALL, DEBORAH. "The Origins of Plant Cultivation in South America." In Cowan and Watson, eds., *The Origins of Agriculture.*

PEARSON, J. D., GARY D. JAMES, AND DANIEL E. BROWN. "Stress and Changing Lifestyles in the Pacific: Physiological Stress Responses of Samoans in Rural and Urban Settings." *American Journal of Human Biology,* 5 (1993): 49–60.

PENNISI, ELIZABETH. "Finally, the Book of Life and Instructions for Navigating It." *Science,* June 30, 2000, 2304–307.

PEREGRINE, PETER. *Archaeological Research: A Brief Introduction.* Upper Saddle River, NJ: Prentice Hall, 2001.

PEREGRINE, PETER N. "Cross-Cultural Approaches in Archaeology." *Annual Review of Anthropology,* 30 (2001).

PEREGRINE, PETER N. *Outline of Archaeological Traditions.* New Haven, CT: HRAF, 2001.

PEREGRINE, PETER N. "Social Change in the Woodland-Mississippian Transition: A Study of Household and Community Patterns in the American Bottom." *North American Archaeologist,* 13 (1992): 131–47.

PEREGRINE, PETER N. "Southern and Eastern Africa Later Stone Age." In Peregrine and Ember, *Encyclopedia of Prehistory.* Vol. 1, pp. 272–73.

PEREGRINE, PETER N., AND PETER BELLWOOD. "Southeast Asia Upper Paleolithic." In P. N. Peregrine and M. Ember, eds., *Encyclopedia of Prehistory.* Vol. 3: *East Asia and Oceania.* New York: Kluwer Academic/Plenum, 2001, pp. 307–09.

PEREGRINE, PETER N., C. R. EMBER, AND M. EMBER. "Teaching Critical Evaluation of Rushton." *Anthropology Newsletter,* 41, no. 2 (2000): 29–30.

PEREGRINE, PETER N., CAROL R. EMBER, AND MELVIN EMBER, EDS. *Archaeology: Original Readings in Method and Practice.* Upper Saddle River, NJ: Prentice Hall, 2002.

PEREGRINE, PETER N., CAROL R. EMBER, AND MELVIN EMBER, EDS. *Physical Anthropology: Original Readings in Method and Practice.* Upper Saddle River, NJ: Prentice Hall, 2002.

PEREGRINE, PETER N., AND MELVIN EMBER, EDS. *Encyclopedia of Prehistory.* Vol. 1: *Africa.* New York: Kluwer Academic/Plenum, 2001.

PETERSEN, ERIK B. "A Survey of the Late Paleolithic and the Mesolithic of Denmark." In Kozlowski, ed., *The Mesolithic in Europe.*

PFEIFFER, JOHN E. *The Emergence of Man.* 3rd ed. New York: Harper & Row, 1978.

PHILLIPSON, DAVID W. *African Archaeology.* 2nd ed. New York: Cambridge University Press, 1993.

PICCHI, DEBRA. "Bakairí: The Death of an Indian." In M. Ember, Ember, and Levinson, eds., *Portraits of Culture.*

PICCHI, DEBRA. "The Impact of an Industrial Agricultural Project on the Bakairí Indians of Central Brazil." *Human Organization,* 50 (1991): 26–38.

PIGGOT, STUART, ED. *The Dawn of Civilization.* London: Thames & Hudson, 1961.

PILBEAM, DAVID. *The Ascent of Man.* New York: Macmillan, 1972.

PILBEAM, DAVID, AND STEPHEN JAY GOULD. "Size and Scaling in Human Evolution." *Science,* December 6, 1974, 892–900.

PODOLEFSKY, AARON, AND PETER J. BROWN. *Applying Cultural Anthropology: An Introductory Reader.* Mountain View, CA: Mayfield, 1997.

POGGIE, JOHN J., JR., BILLIE R. DEWALT, AND WILLIAM W. DRESSLER, EDS. *Anthropological Research: Process and Application.* Albany: State University of New York Press, 1992.

POLANYI, KARL, CONRAD M. ARENSBERG, AND HARRY W. PEARSON, EDS. *Trade and Market in the Early Empires.* New York: Free Press, 1957.

POLEDNAK, ANTHONY P. "Connective Tissue Responses in Negroes in Relation to Disease." *American Journal of Physical Anthropology,* 41 (1974): 49–57.

POLGAR, STEVEN, ED. *Population, Ecology, and Social Evolution.* The Hague: Mouton, 1975.

POPE, GEOFFREY G. "Bamboo and Human Evolution." *Natural History,* October 1989, 49–57.

POST, PETER W., FARRINGTON DANIELS, JR., AND ROBERT T. BINFORD, JR. "Cold Injury and the Evolution of 'White' Skin." *Human Biology,* 47 (1975): 65–80.

POTTS, RICHARD. *Early Hominid Activities at Olduvai.* New York: Aldine, 1988.

POTTS, RICHARD. "Home Bases and Early Hominids." *American Scientist,* 72 (1984): 338–47.

PRAG, JOHN, AND RICHARD NEAVE. *Making Faces: Using Forensic and Archaeological Evidence.* College Station: Texas A&M University Press, 1997.

PREUSCHOFT, HOLGER, DAVID J. CHIVERS, WARREN Y. BROCKELMAN, AND NORMAN CREEL, EDS. *The Lesser Apes: Evolutionary and Behavioural Biology.* Edinburgh: Edinburgh University Press, 1984.

PRICE, T. DOUGLAS, AND JAMES A. BROWN. *Prehistoric Hunter-Gatherers: The Emergence of Cultural Complexity.* Orlando, FL: Academic Press, 1985.

PRICE, T. DOUGLAS, AND A. B. GEBAUER, EDS. *Last Hunters, First Farmers: New Perspectives on the Prehistoric Transition to Agriculture.* Santa Fe, NM: School of American Research Press, 1995.

PRINGLE, HEATHER. "The Slow Birth of Agriculture." *Science,* 282 (1998): 1446–50.

PROTHERO, DONALD R., AND WILLIAM A. BERGGREN, EDS. *Eocene-Oliocene Climatic and Biotic Evolution.* Princeton, NJ: Princeton University Press, 1992.

PURDY, B. *How to Do Archaeology the Right Way.* Gainesville: University Press of Florida, 1996.

QUANDT, SARA A. "Nutrition in Anthropology." In Sargent and Johnson, eds., *Handbook of Medical Anthropology,* pp. 272–89.

RADINSKY, LEONARD. "The Oldest Primate Endocast." *American Journal of Physical Anthropology,* 27 (1967): 358–88.

RASMUSSEN, D. TAB. "Primate Origins: Lessons from a Neotropical Marsupial." *American Journal of Primatology,* 22 (1990): 263–77.

RASMUSSEN, T., ED. *The Origin and Evolution of Humans and Humanness.* Boston: Jones and Bartlett, 1993.

RATHJE, WILLIAM L. "The Origin and Development of Lowland Classic Maya Civilization." *American Antiquity,* 36 (1971): 275–85.

REDMAN, CHARLES L. *The Rise of Civilization: From Early Farmers to Urban Society in the Ancient Near East.* San Francisco: W. H. Freeman, 1978.

REED, CHARLES A., ED. *Origins of Agriculture.* The Hague: Mouton, 1977.

RELETHFORD, JOHN. *The Human Species: An Introduction to Biological Anthropology.* Mountain View, CA: Mayfield, 1990.

RENFREW, COLIN. "Trade and Culture Process in European History." *Current Anthropology,* 10 (April–June 1969): 156–69.

RENFREW, COLIN, ED. *The Explanation of Culture Change: Models in Prehistory.* Pittsburgh: University of Pittsburgh Press, 1973.

RENFREW, COLIN, AND P. BAHN. *Archaeology; Theories, Methods, and Practice.* New York: Thames and Hudson, 1996.

RHINE, STANLEY. *Bone Voyage: A Journey in Forensic Anthropology.* Albuquerque: University of New Mexico Press, 1998.

RICE, PATRICIA. "Prehistoric Venuses: Symbols of Motherhood or Womanhood?" *Journal of Anthropological Research,* 37 (1981): 402–14.

RICE, PATRICIA C., AND ANN L. PATERSON. "Cave Art and Bones: Exploring the Interrelationships." *American Anthropologist,* 87 (1985): 94–100.

RICE, PATRICIA C., AND ANN L. PATERSON. "Validating the Cave Art—Archeofaunal Relationship in Cantabrian Spain." *American Anthropologist,* 88 (1986): 658–67.

RICHARD, ALISON F. "Malagasy Prosimians: Female Dominance." In Smuts et al., eds., *Primate Societies.*

RICHARD, ALISON F. *Primates in Nature.* New York: W. H. Freeman, 1985.

RIESENFELD, ALPHONSE. "The Effect of Extreme Temperatures and Starvation on the Body Proportions of the Rat." *American Journal of Physical Anthropology,* 39 (1973): 427–59.

RIGHTMIRE, G. PHILIP. *The Evolution of* Homo erectus: *Comparative Anatomical Studies of an Extinct Human Species.* Cambridge: Cambridge University Press, 1990.

RIGHTMIRE, G. PHILIP. "*Homo erectus.*" In Tattersall, Delson, and van Couvering, eds., *Encyclopedia of Human Evolution and Prehistory.*

RIGHTMIRE, G. PHILIP. "*Homo sapiens* in Sub-Saharan Africa." In F. H. Smith and Spencer, eds., *The Origins of Modern Humans.*

RIGHTMIRE, PHILIP. "Human Evolution in the Middle Pleistocene: The Role of *Homo heidelbergensis.*" *Evolutionary Anthropology,* 6 (1997): 281–27.

RIGHTMIRE, G. PHILIP. "The Tempo of Change in the Evolution of Mid-Pleistocene *Homo.*" In Delson, ed., *Ancestors.*

RIJKSEN, H. D. *A Fieldstudy on Sumatran Orang Utans (Pongo Pygmaeus Abelii Lesson 1827): Ecology, Behaviour and Conservation.* Wageningen, The Netherlands: H. Veenman and Zonen, 1978.

ROBERTS, D. F. "Body Weight, Race, and Climate." *American Journal of Physical Anthropology,* (1953): 533–58.

ROBERTS, D. F. *Climate and Human Variability.* 2nd ed. Menlo Park, CA: Cummings, 1978.

ROBINSON, JOHN G., AND CHARLES H. JANSON. "Capuchins, Squirrel Monkeys, and Atelines: Socioecological Convergence with Old World Primates." In Smuts et al., eds., *Primate Societies.*

ROBINSON, JOHN G., PATRICIA C. WRIGHT, AND WARREN G. KINZEY. "Monogamous Cebids and Their Relatives: Intergroup Calls and Spacing." In Smuts et al., eds., *Primate Societies.*

ROBINSON, ROY. "Cat." In Mason, *Evolution of Domesticated Animals.*

ROGERS, EVERETT M. *Diffusion of Innovations.* 3rd ed. New York: Free Press, 1983.

ROMANUCCI-ROSS, LOLA, DANIEL E. MOERMAN, AND LAURENCE R. TANCREDI, EDS. *The Anthropology of Medicine: From Culture to Method.* 3rd ed. Westport, CO: Bergin & Garvey, 1997.

ROMNEY, A. KIMBALL, SUSAN C. WELLER, AND WILLIAM H. BATCHELDER. "Culture as Consensus: A Theory of Culture and Informant Accuracy." *American Anthropologist,* 88 (1986): 313–38.

ROOSEVELT, ANNA CURTENIUS. "Population, Health, and the Evolution of Subsistence: Conclusions from the Conference." In Cohen and Armelagos, eds., *Paleopathology at the Origins of Agriculture.*

ROOSEVELT, ANNA CURTENIUS, ET AL. "Paleoindian Cave Dwellers in the Amazon: The Peopling of the Americas." *Science,* April 19, 1996, 373–84.

ROSE, M. D. "Food Acquisition and the Evolution of Positional Behaviour: The Case of Bipedalism." In Chivers, Wood, and Bilsborough, eds., *Food Acquisition and Processing in Primates.*

ROSENBERGER, A. L. "Cranial Anatomy and Implications of *Dolichocebus,* a Late Oligocene Ceboid Primate." *Nature,* 279 (1979): 416–18.

ROSENBLUM, L. A., ED. *Primate Behavior.* Vol. 1. New York: Academic Press, 1970.

ROSS, MARC HOWARD. "Ethnocentrism and Ethnic Conflict." In C. R. Ember, Ember, and Peregrine, eds., *Research Frontiers in Anthropology.* Vol. 3.

ROWE, N. *The Pictorial Guide to the Living Primates.* East Hampton, NY: Pogonias Press, 1996.

RUBEL, ARTHUR J., AND MICHAEL R. HASS. "Ethnomedicine." In Johnson and Sargent, *Medical Anthropology,* pp. 115–31;

reprinted in Sargent and Johnson, *Handbook of Medical Anthropology*.

RUBEL, ARTHUR J., CARL O. NELL, AND ROLANDO COLLADO-ARDÓN (with the assistance of John Krejci and Jean Krejci). *Susto: A Folk Illness*. Berkeley: University of California Press, 1984.

RUFF, CHRISTOPHER B., AND ALAN WALKER. "Body Size and Body Shape." In Walker and Leakey, eds., *The Nariokotome* Homo erectus *Skeleton*. Cambridge, MA: Harvard University Press, 1993.

RUMBAUGH, DUANE M. "Learning Skills of Anthropoids." In Rosenblum, ed., *Primate Behavior*, Vol. 1.

RUSSON, ANNE E. "The Development of Peer Social Interaction in Infant Chimpanzees: Comparative Social, Piagetian, and Brain Perspectives." In Parker and Gibson, eds., *"Language" and Intelligence in Monkeys and Apes*.

SABLOFF, JEREMY A., ED. *Supplement to the Handbook of Middle American Indians*. Vol. 1. Austin: University of Texas Press, 1981.

SADE, D. S. "Some Aspects of Parent-Offspring and Sibling Relationships in a Group of Rhesus Monkeys, with a Discussion of Grooming." *American Journal of Physical Anthropology*, 23 (1965): 1–17.

SAGAN, CARL. "A Cosmic Calendar." *Natural History*, December 1975, 70–73.

SANDERS, WILLIAM T. "Hydraulic Agriculture, Economic Symbiosis, and the Evolution of States in Central Mexico." In Meggers, ed., *Anthropological Archaeology in the Americas*.

SANDERS, WILLIAM T., JEFFREY R. PARSONS, AND ROBERT S. SANTLEY. *The Basin of Mexico: Ecological Processes in the Evolution of a Civilization*. New York: Academic Press, 1979.

SANDERS, WILLIAM T., AND BARBARA J. PRICE. *Mesoamerica*. New York: Random House, 1968.

SARGENT, CAROLYN F., AND THOMAS M. JOHNSON, EDS. *Handbook of Medical Anthropology: Contemporary Theory and Method*. Rev. ed. Westport, CT: Greenwood Press, 1996, pp. 272–89.

SARICH, VINCENT M. "The Origin of Hominids: An Immunological Approach." In Washburn and Jay, eds., *Perspectives on Human Evolution*, Vol. 1.

SARICH, VINCENT M., AND ALLAN C. WILSON. "Quantitative Immunochemistry and the Evolution of Primate Albumins: Micro-Component Fixations." *Science*, December 23, 1966, 1563–66.

SASSAMAN, KENNETH. "Early Archaic Settlement in the South Carolina Coastal Plain." In D. G. Anderson and K. E. Sassaman, eds., *The Paleoindian and Early Archaic Southeast*. Tuscaloosa: University of Alabama Press, 1996, pp. 58–83.

SAVAGE-RUMBAUGH, E. S. "Hominid Evolution: Looking to Modern Apes for Clues." In Duane Quiatt and Junichiro Itani, eds., *Hominid Culture in Primate Perspective*. Niwot: University Press of Colorado, 1994.

SAVAGE-RUMBAUGH, E. S. "Language Training of Apes." In Jones, Martin, and Pilbeam, eds., *The Cambridge Encyclopedia of Human Evolution*.

SCHALLER, GEORGE. *The Mountain Gorilla: Ecology and Behavior*. Chicago: University of Chicago Press, 1963.

SCHALLER, GEORGE B. *The Serengeti Lion: A Study of Predator-Prey Relations*. Chicago: University of Chicago Press, 1972.

SCHALLER, GEORGE. *The Year of the Gorilla*. Chicago: University of Chicago Press, 1964.

SCHICK, KATHY D., AND NICHOLAS TOTH. *Making Silent Stones Speak*. New York: Simon & Schuster, 1993.

SCHIFFER, MICHAEL B. *Formation Processes of the Archaeological Record*. Albuquerque: University of New Mexico Press, 1987.

SCHOEPF, B. "Women, AIDS and Economic Crisis in Central Africa." *Canadian Journal of African Studies*, 22 (1988): 625–44.

SCHWARCZ, HENRY P. *The Origin of Modern Humans and the Impact of Chronometric Dating*. Princeton, NJ: Princeton University Press, 1993.

SCHWARCZ, HENRY P. "Uranium-Series Dating and the Origin of Modern Man." In Schwarz, *The Origin of Modern Humans and the Impact of Chronometric Dating*.

SCUDDER, THAYER. "Opportunities, Issues and Achievements in Development Anthropology since the Mid-1960s: A Personal View." In Eddy and Partridge, eds., *Applied Anthropology in America*, 2nd ed.

SEBEOK, THOMAS A., AND JEAN UMIKER-SEBEOK, EDS. *Speaking of Apes: A Critical Anthology of Two-Way Communication with Man*. New York: Plenum, 1980.

SELIG, R. O., AND M. R. LONDON, EDS. *Anthropology Explored: The Best of Smithsonian AnthroNotes*. Washington, DC: Smithsonian Institution Press, 1998.

SEMENOV, S. A. *Prehistoric Technology*. Trans. M. W. Thompson. Bath, England: Adams & Dart, 1970.

SENNER, WAYNE M. "Theories and Myths on the Origins of Writing: A Historical Overview." In Senner, ed., *The Origins of Writing*.

SENNER, WAYNE M., ED. *The Origins of Writing*. Lincoln: University of Nebraska Press, 1989.

SERVICE, ELMAN R. *Origins of the State and Civilization: The Process of Cultural Evolution*. New York: Norton, 1975.

SEYFARTH, ROBERT M., DOROTHY L. CHENEY, AND PETER MARLER. "Monkey Response to Three Different Alarm Calls: Evidence of Predator Classification and Semantic Communication." *Science*, November 14, 1980, 801–803.

SHANKLIN, EUGENIA. *Anthropology and Race*. Belmont, CA: Wadsworth, 1994.

SHEN, XUEFEI, AND ROBERT F. SILICIANO. "Preventing AIDS but Not HIV-1 Infection with a DNA Vaccine." *Science*, October 20, 2000, 463–65.

SHIPMAN, PAT. *The Evolution of Racism: Human Differences and the Use and Abuse of Science*. New York: Simon & Schuster, 1994.

SHIPMAN, PAT. *The Man Who Found the Missing Link: Eugene Dubois and His Lifelong Quest to Prove Darwin Right*. New York: Simon & Schuster, 2001.

SHIPMAN, PAT. "Scavenging or Hunting in Early Hominids: Theoretical Framework and Tests." *American Anthropologist*, 88 (1986): 27–43.

SIMMONS, ALAN H., ILSE KÖHLER-ROLLEFSON, GARY O. ROLLEFSON, ROLFE MANDEL, AND ZEIDAN KAFAFI. "'Ain Ghazal: A Major Neolithic Settlement in Central Jordan." *Science*, April 1, 1988, 35–39.

SIMMONS, JANIE, PAUL FARMER, AND BROOKE G. SCHOEPF. "A Global Perspective." In Paul Farmer, Margaret Connors, and Janie Simmons, eds., *Women, Poverty, and AIDS: Sex, Drugs, and Structural Violence*. Monroe, ME: Common Courage Press, 1996, pp. 39–90.

SIMONS, ELWYN. "The Primate Fossil Record." In Jones, Martin, and Pilbeam, eds., *The Cambridge Encyclopedia of Human Evolution*.

SIMONS, ELWYN L. "Skulls and Anterior Teeth of *Catopithecus*

(Primates: Anthropoidea) from the Eocene Shed Light on Anthropoidean Origins." *Science,* 268 (1995): 1885–88.

SIMONS, ELWYN L., AND D. T. RASSMUSSEN. "Skull of *Catopithecus browni,* an Early Tertiary Catarrhine." *American Journal of Physical Anthropology,* 100 (1996): 261–92.

SIMPSON, GEORGE GAYLORD. *The Meaning of Evolution.* New York: Bantam, 1971.

SIMPSON, SCOTT W. "*Australopithecus afarensis* and Human Evolution." In Peregrine, Ember, and Ember, eds., *Physical Anthropology.*

SINGER, RONALD, AND JOHN WYMER. *The Middle Stone Age at Klasies River Mouth in South Africa.* Chicago: University of Chicago Press, 1982.

SINOPOLI, CARLA. "Learning about the Past through Archaeological Ceramics: An Example from Yijayanagara, India." In Peregrine, Ember, and Ember, eds., *Archaeology.*

SMITH, B. HOLLY. "Dental Development in *Australopithecus* and Early *Homo.*" *Nature,* September 25, 1986, 327–30.

SMITH, BRUCE D. *The Emergence of Agriculture.* New York: Scientific American Library, 1995.

SMITH, BRUCE D. "Prehistoric Plant Husbandry in Eastern North America." In Cowan and Watson, eds., *The Origins of Agriculture.*

SMITH, BRUCE D. *Rivers of Change.* Washington, DC: Smithsonian Institution Press, 1992.

SMITH, FRED H. "Fossil Hominids from the Upper Pleistocene of Central Europe and the Origin of Modern Humans." In F. H. Smith and Spencer, eds., *The Origins of Modern Humans.*

SMITH, FRED H., AND FRANK SPENCER, EDS. *The Origins of Modern Humans: A World Survey of the Fossil Evidence.* New York: Alan R. Liss, 1984.

SMITH, JOHN MAYNARD. *Evolutionary Genetics.* New York: Oxford University Press, 1989.

SMITH, M. W. "Alfred Binet's Remarkable Questions: A Cross-National and Cross-Temporal Analysis of the Cultural Biases Built into the Stanford-Binet Intelligence Scale and Other Binet Tests." *Genetic Psychology Monographs,* 89 (1974): 307–34.

SMUTS, BARBARA B., DOROTHY L. CHENEY, ROBERT M. SEYFARTH, RICHARD W. WRANGHAM, AND THOMAS T. STRUHSAKER, EDS. *Primate Societies.* Chicago: University of Chicago Press, 1987.

SOFFER, OLGA. "Upper Paleolithic Adaptations in Central and Eastern Europe and Man-Mammoth Interactions." In Soffer and Praslov, eds., *From Kostenki to Clovis.*

SOFFER, O. *The Upper Paleolithic of the Central Russian Plain.* Orlando, FL: Academic Press, 1985.

SOFFER, OLGA, J. M. ADOVASIO, AND D. C. HYLAND. "The 'Venus' Figurines: Textiles, Basketry, Gender, and Status in the Upper Paleolithic." *Current Anthropology,* 41 (2000): 511–37.

SOFFER, OLGA, AND N. D. PRASLOV, EDS. *From Kostenki to Clovis: Upper Paleolithic–Paleo-Indian Adaptations.* New York: Plenum, 1993.

SOUTHWORTH, FRANKLIN C., AND CHANDLER J. DASWANI. *Foundations of Linguistics.* New York: Free Press, 1974.

SPENCER, FRANK. "The Neandertals and Their Evolutionary Significance: A Brief Historical Survey." In F. H. Smith and Spencer, eds., *The Origins of Modern Humans.*

SPETH, JOHN D. "Were Our Ancestors Hunters or Scavengers?" In Peregrine, Ember, and Ember, eds., *Physical Anthropology.*

SPETH, JOHN D., AND DAVE D. DAVIS. "Seasonal Variability in Early Hominid Predation." *Science,* April 30, 1976, 441–45.

SPETH, JOHN D., AND KATHERINE A. SPIELMANN. "Energy Source, Protein Metabolism, and Hunter-Gatherer Subsistence

Strategies." *Journal of Anthropological Archaeology,* 2 (1983): 1–31.

SPOONER, BRIAN, ED. *Population Growth: Anthropological Implications.* Cambridge, MA: MIT Press, 1972.

SPRING, ANITA. *Agricultural Development and Gender Issues in Malawi.* Lanham, MD: University Press of America, 1995.

STANFORD, CRAIG. "Chimpanzee Hunting and Human Evolution." In Peregrine, Ember, and Ember, eds., *Physical Anthropology.*

STANFORD, CRAIG B. "The Social Behavior of Chimpanzees and Bonobos: Empirical Evidence and Shifting Assumptions." *Current Anthropology,* 39 (1998): 399–420.

STANFORD, CRAIG B., JANETTE WALLIS, HILALI MATAMA, AND JANE GOODALL. "Patterns of Predation by Chimpanzees on Red Colobus Monkeys in Gombe National Park, Tanzania, 1982–1991." *American Journal of Physical Anthropology,* 94 (1994): 213–29.

STEEGMAN, A. T., JR. "Human Adaptation to Cold." In Damon, ed., *Physiological Anthropology.*

STEIN, GIL, AND MITCHELL ROTHMAN, EDS. *Chiefdoms and Early States in the Near East: The Organizational Dynamics of Complexity.* Madison, WI: Prehistory Press, 1994.

STEIN, P., AND B. ROWE. *Physical Anthropology.* 7th ed. Boston: McGraw-Hill, 2000.

STEWARD, T. D. "Deformity, Trephanating, and Mutilation in South American Indian Skeletal Remains." In J. A. Steward, ed., *Handbook of South American Indians.* Vol. 6: *Physical Anthropology, Linguistics, and Cultural Geography.* Bureau of American Ethnology Bulletin 143. Washington, DC: Smithsonian Institution.

STINI, WILLIAM A. *Ecology and Human Adaptation.* Dubuque, IA: Wm. C. Brown, 1975.

STRAUSS, LAWRENCE GUY. "Comment on White." *Current Anthropology,* 23 (1982): 185–86.

STRAUSS, LAWRENCE GUY. "On Early Hominid Use of Fire." *Current Anthropology,* 30 (1989): 488–91.

STRAUSS, LAWRENCE GUY. "Solutrean Settlement of North America? A View of Reality." *American Antiquity,* 65 (2000): 219–26.

STRINGER, CHRISTOPHER. "Evolution of a Species." *Geographical Magazine,* 57 (1985): 601–607.

STRINGER, CHRISTOPHER B. "Neandertals." In Tattersall, Delson, and van Couvering, eds., *Encyclopedia of Human Evolution and Prehistory.*

STRINGER, CHRISTOPHER, AND CLIVE GAMBLE. *In Search of the Neandertals.* New York: Thames and Hudson, 1993.

STRINGER, C. B., J. J. HUBLIN, AND B. VANDERMEERSCH. "The Origin of Anatomically Modern Humans in Western Europe." In F. H. Smith and Spencer, eds., *The Origins of Modern Humans.*

STRUEVER, STUART, ED. *Prehistoric Agriculture.* Garden City, NY: Natural History Press, 1971.

SUSMAN, RANDALL L. "Fossil Evidence for Early Hominid Tool Use." *Science,* September 9, 1994, 1570–73.

SUSMAN, RANDALL L., ED. *The Pygmy Chimpanzee: Evolutionary Biology and Behavior.* New York: Plenum, 1984.

SUSMAN, RANDALL L., JACK T. STERN, JR., AND WILLIAM L. JUNGERS. "Locomotor Adaptations in the Hadar Hominids." In Delson, ed., *Ancestors.*

SUSSMAN, ROBERT. "Child Transport, Family Size, and the Increase in Human Population Size during the Neolithic." *Current Anthropology,* 13 (April 1972): 258–67.

SUSSMAN, ROBERT. "Primate Origins and the Evolution of

Angiosperms." *American Journal of Primatology,* 23 (1991): 209–23.

SUSSMAN, ROBERT W., AND W. G. KINZEY. "The Ecological Role of the Callitrichidae: A Review." *American Journal of Physical Anthropology,* 64 (1984): 419–49.

SUSSMAN, ROBERT W., AND PETER H. RAVEN. "Pollination by Lemurs and Marsupials: An Archaic Coevolutionary System." *Science,* May 19, 1978, 734–35.

SWISHER, C. C., III, G. H. CURTIS, T. JACOB, A. G. GETTY, A. SUPRIJO, AND WIDIASMORO. "Age of the Earliest Known Hominids in Java, Indonesia." *Science,* February 25, 1994, 1118–21.

SZALAY, FREDERICK S. "Hunting-Scavenging Protohominids: A Model for Hominid Origins." *Man,* 10 (1975): 420–29.

SZALAY, FREDERICK S. "Paleobiology of the Earliest Primates." In R. Tuttle, ed., *The Functional and Evolutionary Biology of the Primates.* Chicago: University of Chicago Press, 1972, pp. 3–35.

SZALAY, FREDERICK S., AND ERIC DELSON. *Evolutionary History of the Primates.* New York: Academic Press, 1979.

SZALAY, FREDERICK S., I. TATTERSALL, AND R. DECKER. "Phylogenetic Relationships of *Plesiadipis*—Postcranial Evidence." *Contributions to Primatology,* 5 (1975): 136–66.

SZATHMARY, EMÖKE J. E. "Genetics of Aboriginal North Americans." *Evolutionary Anthropology,* 1 (1993): 202–20.

TAINTER, JOSEPH. *The Collapse of Complex Societies.* Cambridge: Cambridge University Press, 1988, pp. 128–52.

TATTERSALL, IAN. *The Fossil Trail: How We Know What We Think We Know about Human Evolution.* New York: Oxford University Press, 1995.

TATTERSALL, IAN. *The Human Odyssey.* Englewood Cliffs, NJ: Prentice Hall, 1993.

TATTERSALL, IAN. *The Last Neanderthal.* Boulder, CO: Westview, 1999, pp. 115–16.

TATTERSALL, IAN. "Paleoanthropology and Evolutionary Theory." In Peregrine, Ember, and Ember, eds., *Physical Anthropology.*

TATTERSALL, IAN. *The Primates of Madagascar.* New York: Columbia University Press, 1982.

TATTERSALL, IAN, ERIC DELSON, AND JOHN VAN COUVERING, EDS. *Encyclopedia of Human Evolution and Prehistory.* New York: Garland, 1988.

TATTERSALL, IAN, AND JEFFREY SCHWARTZ. *Extinct Humans.* Boulder, CO: Westview, 2000, p. 93.

TAYLOR, R. E., AND M. J. AITKEN, EDS. *Chronometric Dating in Archaeology.* New York: Plenum, 1997.

TELEKI, GEZA. "The Omnivorous Chimpanzee." *Scientific American,* January 1973, 32–42.

TEMPLETON, ALAN R. "The 'Eve' Hypotheses: A Genetic Critique and Reanalysis." *American Anthropologist,* 95 (1993): 51–72.

TEMPLETON, ALAN R. "Gene Lineages and Human Evolution." *Science,* May 31, 1996, 1363.

TERBORGH, JOHN. *Five New World Primates: A Study in Comparative Ecology.* Princeton, NJ: Princeton University Press, 1983.

THOMPSON, ELIZABETH BARTLETT. *Africa, Past and Present.* Boston: Houghton Mifflin, 1966.

THOMPSON-HANDLER, NANCY, RICHARD K. MALENKY, AND NOEL BADRIAN. "Sexual Behavior of *Pan paniscus* under Natural Conditions in the Lomako Forest, Equateur, Zaire." In Susman, ed., *The Pygmy Chimpanzee.*

THORNE, ALAN G., AND MILFORD H. WOLPOFF. "The Multiregional Evolution of Humans." *Scientific American,* April 1992, 76–83.

TIERNEY, PATRICK. *Darkness in El Dorado.* New York: Norton, 2000.

TOBIAS, PHILIP. "The Brain of *Homo habilis:* A New Level of Organization in Cerebral Evolution." *Journal of Human Evolution,* 16 (1987): 741–61.

TOBIAS, PHILIP V. "The Craniocerebral Interface in Early Hominids: Cerebral Impressions, Cranial Thickening, Paleoneurobiology, and a New Hypothesis on Encephalization." In Corruccini and Ciochon, eds., *Integrative Paths to the Past.*

TOMASELLO, MICHAEL. "Cultural Transmission in the Tool Use and Communicatory Signaling of Chimpanzees." In Parker and Gibson, eds., *"Language" and Intelligence in Monkeys and Apes.*

TORREY, E. FULLER. *The Mind Game: Witchdoctors and Psychiatrists.* New York: Emerson Hall, n.d.

TRAVIS, JOHN. "Human Genome Work Reaches Milestone." *Science News,* July 1, 2000, 4–5.

TRIGGER, BRUCE G. *A History of Archaeological Thought.* Cambridge: Cambridge University Press, 1989.

TRINGHAM, RUTH, ED. *Ecology and Agricultural Settlements.* R2. Andover, MA: Warner Modular, 1973.

TRINGHAM, RUTH, ED. *Territoriality and Proxemics.* R1. Andover, MA: Warner Modular, 1973.

TRINKAUS, ERIK. "Bodies, Brawn, Brains and Noses: Human Ancestors and Human Predation." In Nitecki and Nitecki, eds., *The Evolution of Human Hunting.*

TRINKAUS, ERIK. "The Neandertal Face: Evolutionary and Functional Perspectives on a Recent Hominid Face." *Journal of Human Evolution,* 16 (1987): 429–43.

TRINKAUS, ERIK. "The Neandertals and Modern Human Origins." *Annual Review of Anthropology,* 15 (1986): 193–218.

TRINKAUS, ERIK. "Pathology and the Posture of the La Chapelle-aux-Saints Neandertal." *American Journal of Physical Anthropology,* 67 (1985): 19–41.

TRINKAUS, ERIK. "Western Asia." In F. H. Smith and Spencer, eds., *The Origins of Modern Humans.*

TRINKAUS, E., ED. *The Emergence of Modern Humans: Biocultural Adaptations in the Later Pleistocene.* Cambridge: Cambridge University Press, 1989.

TRINKAUS, ERIK, AND WILLIAM W. HOWELLS. "The Neanderthals." *Scientific American,* December 1979, 118–33.

TRINKAUS, ERIK, AND PAT SHIPMAN. *The Neandertals: Changing the Image of Mankind.* New York: Knopf, 1993.

TRINKAUS, ERIK, AND PAT SHIPMAN. "Neandertals: Images of Ourselves." *Evolutionary Anthropology,* 1, no. 6 (1993): 194–201.

TROTTER, ROBERT T., II, ED. *Anthropology for Tomorrow: Creating Practitioner-Oriented Applied Anthropology Programs.* Washington, DC: American Anthropological Association, 1988.

TURNER, B. L. "Population Density in the Classic Maya Lowlands: New Evidence for Old Approaches." *Geographical Review,* 66, no. 1 (January 1970): 72–82.

TURNER, CHRISTY G., II. "Teeth and Prehistory in Asia." *Scientific American,* February 1989.

TURNER, CHRISTY G., II. "Telltale Teeth." *Natural History,* January 1987.

TUTIN, CAROLINE, AND L. WHITE. "The Recent Evolutionary Past of Primate Communities: Likely Environmental Impacts during the Past Three Millennia." In J. G. Fleagle, C. Janson, and K. E. Reed, eds., *Primate Communities.* Cambridge: Cambridge University Press, 1999, pp. 230–31.

TUTTLE, RUSSELL H. *Apes of the World: Their Social Behavior,*

Communication, Mentality, and Ecology. Park Ridge, NJ: Noyes, 1986.

UCKO, PETER J., AND G. W. DIMBLEBY, EDS. *The Domestication and Exploitation of Plants and Animals.* Chicago: Aldine, 1969.

UCKO, PETER J., AND ANDRÉE ROSENFELD. *Paleolithic Cave Art.* New York: McGraw-Hill, 1967.

UCKO, PETER J., RUTH TRINGHAM, AND G. W. DIMBLEBY, EDS. *Man, Settlement, and Urbanism.* Cambridge, MA: Schenkman, 1972.

UNDERHILL, ANNE. "Investigating Craft Specialization during the Longshan Period of China." In Peregrine, Ember, and Ember, eds., *Archaeology.*

URBAN INSTITUTE. "America's Homeless. II: Populations and Services." Washington, DC: Urban Institute, February 1, 2000. Published on the Web at http://www.urban.org/housing/homeless/numbers/index.htm.

VALLADAS, H., J. L. JORON, G. VALLADAS, O. BAR-YOSEF, AND B. VANDERMEERSCH. "Thermoluminescence Dating of Mousterian 'Proto-Cro-Magnon' Remains from Israel and the Origin of Modern Man." *Nature,* February 18, 1988, 614–16.

VAN DER MERWE, N. J. "Reconstructing Prehistoric Diet." In Jones, Martin, and Pilbeam, eds., *The Cambridge Encyclopedia of Human Evolution.*

VAN LAWICK-GOODALL, JANE. *In the Shadow of Man.* Boston: Houghton Mifflin, 1971.

VAN WILLIGEN, J. *Applied Anthropology: An Introduction.* Rev. ed. Westport, CT: Bergin & Garvey, 1993.

VAN WILLIGEN, JOHN, AND TIMOTHY L. FINAN, EDS. *Soundings: Rapid and Reliable Research Methods for Practicing Anthropologists.* NAPA Bulletin No. 10. Washington, DC: American Anthropological Association, 1990.

VAN WILLIGEN, JOHN, BARBARA RYLKO-BAUER, AND ANN MCELROY. *Making Our Research Useful: Case Studies in the Utilization of Anthropological Knowledge.* Boulder, CO: Westview, 1989.

VIGILANT, LINDA, MARK STONEKING, HENRY HARPENDING, KRISTEN HAWKES, AND ALLAN C. WILSON. "African Populations and the Evolution of Human Mitochrondrial DNA." *Science,* September 27, 1991, 1503–507.

VISABERGHI, ELISABETTA, AND DOROTHY MUNKENBECK FRAGASZY. "Do Monkeys Ape?" In Parker and Gibson, eds., *"Language" and Intelligence in Monkeys and Apes.*

VOGEL, GRETCHEN. "Chimps in the Wild Show Stirrings of Culture." *Science,* 284 (1999): 2070–73.

VOGEL, JOSEPH O. "De-Mystifying the Past: Great Zimbabwe, King Solomon's Mines, and Other Tales of Old Africa." In Peregrine, Ember, and Ember, eds., *Archaeology.*

VOGT, EVON Z., AND RICHARD M. LEVANTHAL, EDS. *Prehistoric Settlement Patterns: Essays in Honor of Gordon R. Willey.* Albuquerque: University of New Mexico Press, 1983.

VRBA, ELIZABETH S. "On the Connection between Paleoclimate and Evolution." In E. S. Vrba, G. H. Denton, T. C. Partridge, and L. H. Burckle, eds., *Paleoclimate and Evolution.* New Haven, CT: Yale University Press, 1995, pp. 24–45.

WALKER, ALAN, AND R. LEAKEY. "The Evolution of *Australopithecus boisei.*" In Grine, ed., *Evolutionary History of the "Robust" Australopithecines,* pp. 247–58.

WALKER, ALAN, AND RICHARD LEAKEY, EDS. *The Nariokotome* Homo erectus *Skeleton.* Cambridge, MA: Harvard University Press, 1993.

WALKER, ALAN, AND M. PICKFORD, "New Postcranial Fossils of Proconsul Africanus and Proconsul Nyananzae." In Ciochon

and Corruccini, eds., *New Interpretation of Ape and Human Ancestry.*

WALKER, ALAN, AND PAT SHIPMAN. *The Wisdom of the Bones: In Search of Human Origins.* New York: Knopf, 1996.

WALLACE, ALFRED RUSSELL. "On the Tendency of Varieties to Depart Indefinitely from the Original Type." *Journal of the Proceedings of the Linnaean Society,* August 1858. In Young, ed., *Evolution of Man.*

WALLACE, ANTHONY. "Mental Illness, Biology and Culture." In Hsu, ed., *Psychological Anthropology.*

WALLACE, ANTHONY, J. LAWRENCE ANGEL, RICHARD FOX, SALLY MCLENDON, RACHEL SADY, AND ROBERT SHARER, EDS. *Perspectives on Anthropology 1976.* American Anthropological Association Special Publication No. 10. Washington, DC: American Anthropological Association, 1977.

WANNER, ERIC, AND LILA R. GLEITMAN, EDS. *Language Acquisition: The State of the Art.* Cambridge: Cambridge University Press, 1982.

WARD, S. "The Taxonomy and Phylogenetic Relationships of *Sivapithecus* Revisited." In *Function, Phylogeny and Fossils: Miocene Hominoid Evolution and Adaptation.* D. R. Begun, C. V. Ward, and M. D. Rose, eds. New York: Plenum, 1997, pp. 269–90.

WARD, STEVE, B. BROWN, A. HILL, J. KELLEY, AND W. DOWNS. "*Equatorius;* A New Hominoid Genus from the Middle Miocene of Kenya." *Science,* 285 (1999): 1382–86.

WARREN, DENNIS M. "Utilizing Indigenous Healers in National Health Delivery Systems: The Ghanaian Experiment." In van Willigen, Rylko-Bauer, and McElroy, eds., *Making Our Research Useful.*

WARRY, WAYNE. "Doing unto Others: Applied Anthropology, Collaborative Research and Native Self-Determination." *Culture,* 10 (1990): 61–62.

WASHBURN, S. L., ED. *Social Life of Early Man.* Chicago: Aldine, 1964.

WASHBURN, S. L., AND PHYLLIS C. JAY, EDS. *Perspectives on Human Evolution.* Vol. 1. New York: Holt, Rinehart & Winston, 1968.

WASHBURN, SHERWOOD. "Tools and Human Evolution." *Scientific American,* September 1960, 62–75.

WEAVER, MURIEL PORTER. *The Aztecs, Maya, and Their Predecessors.* 3rd ed. San Diego: Academic Press, 1993.

WEINER, JONATHAN. *Beak of the Finch.* New York: Vintage, 1994.

Weiner, J. S. "Nose Shape and Climate." *Journal of Physical Anthropology,* 4 (1954): 615–18.

WEISS, HARVEY, M. A. COURTY, W. WETTERSTROM, F. GUICHARD, L. SENIOR, R. MEADOW, AND A. CURNOW. "The Genesis and Collapse of Third Millennium North Mesopotamia Civilization." *Science,* 261 (1993): 995–1004.

WELLER, SUSAN C. "The Research Process." In C. R. Ember, Ember, and Peregrine, eds., *Research Frontiers in Anthropology.* Vol. 3.

WENDORF, FRED, AND ANGELA E. CLOSE, EDS. *Advances in World Archaeology.* Vol. 3. Orlando, FL: Academic Press, 1984.

WENKE, ROBERT J. *Patterns in Prehistory: Humankind's First Three Million Years.* 2nd ed. New York: Oxford University Press, 1984.

WENKE, ROBERT. *Patterns in Prehistory: Humankind's First Three Million Years.* 3rd ed. New York: Oxford University Press, 1990.

WHEAT, JOE B. "A Paleo-Indian Bison Kill." *Scientific American,* January 1967, 44–52.

WHEATLEY, PAUL. *The Pivot of the Four Quarters.* Chicago: Aldine, 1971.

WHEELER, PETER. "The Evolution of Bipedality and Loss of Functional Body Hair in Hominids." *Journal of Human Evolution,* 13 (1984): 91–98.

WHEELER, PETER. "The Influence of Bipedalism in the Energy and Water Budgets of Early Hominids." *Journal of Human Evolution,* 23 (1991): 379–88.

WHITE, BENJAMIN. "Demand for Labor and Population Growth in Colonial Java." *Human Ecology,* 1, no. 3 (March 1973): 217–36.

WHITE, F. J. "*Pan paniscus* 1973 to 1996: Twenty-three Years of Field Research." *Evolutionary Anthropology,* 5 (1996): 11–17.

WHITE, LESLIE A. "The Expansion of the Scope of Science." In Morton H. Fried, ed., *Readings in Anthropology.* 2nd ed. Vol. 1. New York: Thomas Y. Crowell, 1968.

WHITE, RANDALL. "Rethinking the Middle/Upper Paleolithic Transition." *Current Anthropology,* 23 (1982): 169–75.

WHITE, TIM D., DONALD C. JOHANSON, AND WILLIAM H. KIMBEL. "*Australopithecus africanus:* Its Phyletic Position Reconsidered." *South African Journal of Science,* 77 (1981): 445–70.

WHITE, TIMOTHY D., G. SUWA, AND B. ASFAW. "*Australopithecus ramidus,* a New Species of Early Hominid from Aramis, Ethiopia." *Nature,* 371 (1994): 306–33.

WHITE, TIMOTHY D., G. SUWA, AND B. ASFAW. "Corrigendum: *Australopithecus ramidus,* a New Species of Early Hominid from Aramis, Ethiopia." *Nature,* 375 (1995): 88.

WHITTAKER, JOHN C. *Flintknapping: Making and Understanding Stone Tools.* Austin: University of Texas Press, 1994.

WIENER, STEVE, Q. XI, P. GOLDBERG, J. LIU, AND O. BAR-YOUSEF. "Evidence for the Use of Fire at Zhoukoudian, China." *Science,* 281 (1998): 251–53.

WILFORD, JOHN NOBLE. "The Transforming Leap, from 4 Legs to 2." *New York Times,* September 5, 1995, p. C1ff.

WILFORD, JOHN NOBLE. "Ancient German Spears Tell of Mighty Hunters of Stone Age." *New York Times,* March 4, 1997, p. C6.

WILKINSON, ROBERT L. "Yellow Fever: Ecology, Epidemiology, and Role in the Collapse of the Classic Lowland Maya Civilization." *Medical Anthropology,* 16 (1995): 269–94.

WILLIAMS, GEORGE C. *Natural Selection: Domains, Levels, and Challenges.* New York: Oxford University Press, 1992.

WILLIAMS, MELVIN D. "Racism: The Production, Reproduction, and Obsolescence of Social Inferiority." In C. R. Ember, Ember, and Peregrine, eds., *Research Frontiers in Anthropology.* Vol. 3.

WILSON, ALLAN C, AND REBECCA L. CANN. "The Recent African Genesis of Humans." *Scientific American,* April 1992, 68–73.

WILSON, EDMUND O. *Sociobiology: The New Synthesis.* Cambridge, MA: Belknap Press of Harvard University Press, 1975.

WINKELMAN, MICHAEL JAMES. "Magico-Religious Practitioner Types and Socioeconomic Conditions." *Behavior Science Research,* 20 (1986): 17–46.

WITTFOGEL, KARL. *Oriental Despotism: A Comparative Study of Total Power.* New Haven, CT: Yale University Press, 1957.

WOLF, ERIC. "Culture: Panacea or Problem." *American Antiquity,* 49 (1984): 393–400.

WOLF, ERIC R., ED. *The Valley of Mexico: Studies in Pre-Hispanic Ecology and Society.* Albuquerque: University of New Mexico Press, 1976.

WOLF, NAOMI. *The Beauty Myth: How Images of Beauty Are Used against Women.* New York: Morrow, 1991.

WOLFF, RONALD G. *Functional Chordate Anatomy.* Lexington, MA: D. C. Heath, 1991.

WOLPOFF, MILFORD H. "*Ramapithecus* and Human Origins: An Anthropologist's Perspective of Changing Interpretations." In Ciochon and Corruccini, eds., *New Interpretations of Ape and Human Ancestry.*

WOLPOFF, MILFORD H. "Competitive Exclusion among Lower Pleistocene Hominids: The Single Species Hypothesis." *Man,* 6 (1971): 601–13.

WOLPOFF, MILFORD. *Paleoanthropology.* 2nd ed. Boston: McGraw-Hill, 1999, pp. 501–504, 727–31.

WOLPOFF, MILFORD H., AND ABEL NIKINI. "Early and Early Middle Pleistocene Hominids from Asia and Africa." In Delson, ed., *Ancestors.*

WOLPOFF, MILFORD, A. G. THORNE, J. JELINEK, AND ZHANG YINYUN. "The Case for Sinking *Homo erectus:* 100 years of *Pithecanthropus* Is Enough!" In J. L. Franzen, ed., *100 Years of* Pithecanthropus: *The* Homo Erectus *Problem. Courier Forshungsinstitut Senckenberg,* 171 (1993): 341–61.

WOOD, BERNARD A. "Evolution of Australopithecines." In Jones, Martin, and Pilbeam, eds., *The Cambridge Encyclopedia of Human Evolution.*

WOOD, BERNARD. "Hominid Paleobiology: Recent Achievements and Challenges." In Corruccini and Ciochon, eds., *Integrative Paths to the Past.*

WORLD BANK. *World Development Report 1995. Workers in an Integrating World.* Oxford: Oxford University Press, 1995.

WRANGHAM, RICHARD W. "An Ecological Model of Female-Bonded Primate Groups." *Behaviour,* 75 (1980): 262–300.

WRIGHT, GARY A. "Origins of Food Production in Southwestern Asia: A Survey of Ideas." *Current Anthropology,* 12 (1971): 447–78.

WRIGHT, HENRY T. "The Evolution of Civilizations." In Meltzer, Fowler, and Sabloff, eds., *American Archaeology Past and Future.*

WRIGHT, HENRY T., AND GREGORY A. JOHNSON. "Population, Exchange, and Early State Formation in Southwestern Iran." *American Anthropologist,* 77 (1975): 267–77.

WYNN, THOMAS. "The Intelligence of Later Acheulean Hominids." *Man,* 14 (1979): 371–91.

YAMEI, HOU, R. POTTS, Y. BAOYIN, ET AL. "Mid-Pleistocene Acheulean-like Stone Technology of the Bose Basin, South China." *Science,* 287 (2000): 1622–26.

YOUNG, LOUISE B., ED. *Evolution of Man.* New York: Oxford University Press, 1970.

YOUNG, T. CUYLER, JR. "Population Densities and Early Mesopotamian Urbanism." In Ucko, Tringham, and Dimbleby, eds., *Man, Settlement and Urbanism.*

ZEDER, MELINDA A. "After the Revolution: Post-Neolithic Subsistence in Northern Mesopotamia." *American Anthropologist,* 96 (1994): 97–126.

ZEDER, MELINDA. *The American Archaeologist: A Profile.* Walnut Creek, CA: Alta Mira, 1997.

ZEDER, MELINDA. *Feeding Cities: Specialized Animal Economy in the Ancient Near East.* Washington, DC: Smithsonian Institution Press, 1991.

ZIHLMAN, ADRIENNE L. "The Emergence of Human Locomotion: The Evolutionary Background and Environmental Context." In Nishida et al., eds., *Topics in Primatology,* Vol. 1.

ZIHLMAN, ADRIENNE. "Women's Bodies, Women's Lives: An Evolutionary Perspective." In M. E. Morbeck, A. Galloway, and A. Zihlman, eds., *The Evolving Female: A Life-History Perspec-*

tive. Princeton, NJ: Princeton University Press, 1997, pp. 185–97.

ZIMMER, CARL. "Kenyan Skeleton Shakes Ape Family Tree." *Science,* 285 (1999): 1335–337.

ZOHARY, DANIEL. "The Progenitors of Wheat and Barley in Relation to Domestication and Agriculture Dispersal in the Old World." In Ucko and Dimbleby, eds., *The Domestication and Exploitation of Plants and Animals.*

PHOTO CREDITS

INDEX

F

Facial features
eyes, forward-facing, 52–53, 74–76
Homo erectus, 122
human, evolution of, 91, 97, 114, 116
modern humans, 146
Neandertal, 140, 143
nose shape, 59, 122, 213
prognathic, 122, 143
reconstruction of, 126–27
variations in humans, 212–13
Falk, Dean, 114–15, 129
Family groups. *See also* Homesites; Primate infants
callitrichids, 59
cebids, 59
chimpanzees, 64
colobine monkeys, 60
gibbons and siamangs, 62
gorillas, 62–63
home bases, 108, 112, 113
lemurs, 57
lorises, 57–58
New World monkeys, 59
Old World monkeys, 60, 61
primates, 54
troop, 61
Fayum area, Egypt, anthropoid finds, 77, 78
Features
analysis methods, 24–25
information gained from, 24–25
types of, 17
Feet, and bipedalism, 89
Fejej, Ethiopia, hominid finds, 92
Female dominance, lemurs, 57
Fertile Crescent, domestication, 177–78, 185–86
Fertility, affecting factors, 216–17
Fertility rates
child labor related to, 188
and population growth, 188
Fijians, measles epidemic, 218
Finches, natural selection theory, 36–37
Fire, and *Homo erectus,* 125, 127–28
Fish, Paul, 144
Fish and shellfish, as food resource, 161, 165, 166, 172, 173, 174
Fishing, tools for, 158, 166, 173
Fission-track dating, method in, 29–30
Flakes, stone tool, 105–7, 125, 142, 144
Flannery, Kent, 171, 181, 182, 185
Flint tools, 179, 181
Flowering plants, emergence of, 73
Fluorine, in F-U-N trio method, 26
Fluorine, uranium, nitrogen tests. *See* F-U-N trio
Folsom point, 165
Food collection
and altitude, 173
broad-spectrum collecting, 170
Food production
Binford-Flannery model, 185–86
climate change theory, 186–87
domestication, 176–85
and health decline, 172, 188–89
meaning of, 170
Neolithic revolution, 170
origin of, 185–86
and population growth, 188
preagriculture, 171–76
and sedentarism, 170, 190
Food resources
fish and shellfish, 161, 165, 166, 167, 172, 173, 174

food carrying and bipedalism, 88
and group size, 66, 110
meat. *See* Hunting
scavenging, 107–8
sharing, 108, 112
tool use, 106–7
transporting to home base, 108, 112, 113
Footprints, hominids, 91, 92, 94
Foramen magnum, 89, 91
Forelimbs, primates, 52
Forensic anthropology, 231, 241
Formative era, civilization, 196
Fossils
analysis methods, 24
dating, 27, 30
features of, 4, 16–17
formation of, 17
indicator fossils, 25
information gained from, 24
limitations of fossil record, 17
Founder principle, 44–45
Fouts, Roger, 131
Funerals. *See* Death
F-U-N trio, method in, 25–26, 121
Fur
clothing, 125
disappearance in humans, 124
Furniture, Neolithic, 189

G

Galactosemia, 43–44
Garber, Paul, 75
Gardner, Beatrice T., 68
Gardner, R. Allen, 68
Gelada baboon, 59
Gender
anthropological study of, 7
archaeological study of, 200–201
Gender roles
division of labor, 23, 68, 200–201
as human characteristic, 68
Gene flow, 45, 210
Genes, 40–42
Genetic disorders, sickle-cell anemia, 219
Genetic drift, 44–45, 210
Genetic engineering, pros/cons of, 46–47, 228
Genetic influences
obesity, 256
race and behavior issue, 225
race and intelligence issue, 225–27
Genetics and heredity, 39–45
chromosomes, 40–41
DNA, 40–43
dominant and recessive traits, 39–40
gene flow, 45, 210
genes, 40–42
genetic drift, 44–45, 210
genetic recombination process, 43
genotype and phenotype, 40
Mendel's experiment, 39–40
mutation, 43–44
sex-linked traits, 43
Genocide, Holocaust, 223
Genotype, 40
Geographic information system (GIS), 24–25
Geomagnetic sensing, 19
Ghana, civilization of, 198, 224
Gheo-Shih, Archaic campsite, 173
Gibbons, characteristics of, 61–62

Gigantopithecus, 81, 82–83
characteristics of, 82–83
extinction of, 83
Giraffe, natural selection, 35, 38
Glaciers
and Beringia land bridge, 161–63
Last Ice Age, 154–55, 166
Glass, dating, 30
Gloger's rule, 213
Gombe Park, Tanzania, chimpanzee studies, 63, 111
Gona, Ethiopia, stone tool finds, 105
Gondwanaland, 72, 74
Gonnersdorf cave, cave art, 160
Goodall, Jane, 56, 111
Goosefoot, 184
Gorillas
characteristics of, 62–63
-human likeness, 61
Gould, Stephen Jay, 36
Gracile species, *Australopithecus,* 91–95
Grains
diet, 171, 172
domestication of, 176–77, 184
infant cereals, 176, 188
Grant, Peter, 36–37
Gray, J. Patrick, 216
Great apes. *See* Chimpanzees; Gorillas; Orangutans
Greeks, ancient
city-states, 204
medicine of, 244
theory of evolution, 33
Greenberg, Joseph, 164
Grinding tools, 167, 171
Grodin Tepe, Turkey, use-wear analysis, 22
Grooming behavior, 60, 61
and stress reduction, 110–11
Gross, Daniel, 255
Ground-living
gorillas, 62
humans, 68
Old World monkeys, 59
Ground penetrating radar (GPR), 19
Group protection, and primate groups, 66, 110
Group size, primate variations, 66
Grubb, Henry, 226–27
Guatemala
applied project, 248–49
human rights abuses, 241
Guila Naquitz cave, settlement remains, 182–83
Guinea pigs, domestication of, 184
Gunders, Shulamith, 215
Gwembe Tonga, planned change failure, 235

H

Hadar, Ethiopia, hominid finds, 92
Haiti, reforestation project, 236, 237
Half-life
carbon, 26
potassium, 27–28
Hand axes, functions of, 24, 125–26, 157, 166
Hands
hominoids, 61
humans, 66
prehensile hands, 52
primates, 52
versus claws, 75, 76
Haplorhines, 58
Harappan civilization, 199
Hard hammer method, toolmaking, 125

hysteria, 252, 254
nutritional imbalances, 257
in Paleolithic art, 159–61
status in Upper Paleolithic era, 160
Women in Agriculture Development Project, 10
Wood artifacts, 16
Wooden houses, 189
Wooden tools, uses of, 105, 106, 146
Woods, Bill, 206
Wooly spider monkeys, 59, 65
Wright, Henry, 194, 202
Wright, Sewall, 44
Wright effect, 44

Writing, early, 195–96
Wynn, Thomas, 22

Y

Yanomamö, measles epidemic, 218
Yeti, 83
Y-5 pattern, dentition, 61
Yin and *yang,* 244–45
Yuanmou, China, *Homo erectus* finds, 121

Z

Zawi Chemi Shanidar, Iraq, animal domestication, 177
Zhoukoudian, China
fire use, 127–28
Homo erectus find, 121
Zihlman, Adrienne, 89, 133
Zinjanthropus, 99
Zuni Indians, historic preservation project, 240

SINGLE PC LICENSE AGREEMENT AND LIMITED WARRANTY

READ THIS LICENSE CAREFULLY BEFORE OPENING THIS PACKAGE. BY OPENING THIS PACKAGE, YOU ARE AGREEING TO THE TERMS AND CONDITIONS OF THIS LICENSE. IF YOU DO NOT AGREE, DO NOT OPEN THE PACKAGE. PROMPTLY RETURN THE UNOPENED PACKAGE AND ALL ACCOMPANYING ITEMS TO THE PLACE YOU OBTAINED THEM.

1. GRANT OF LICENSE and OWNERSHIP: The enclosed computer programs ("Software") are licensed, not sold, to you by Prentice-Hall, Inc. ("We" or the "Company") and in consideration of your purchase or adoption of the accompanying Company textbooks and/or other materials, and your agreement to these terms. We reserve any rights not granted to you. You own only the disk(s) but we and/or our licensors own the Software itself. This license allows you to use and display your copy of the Software on a single computer (i.e., with a single CPU) at a single location for <u>academic</u> use only, so long as you comply with the terms of this Agreement. You may make one copy for back up, or transfer your copy to another CPU, provided that the Software is usable on only one computer.

2. RESTRICTIONS: You may <u>not</u> transfer or distribute the Software or documentation to anyone else. Except for backup, you may <u>not</u> copy the documentation or the Software. You may <u>not</u> network the Software or otherwise use it on more than one computer or computer terminal at the same time. You may <u>not</u> reverse engineer, disassemble, decompile, modify, adapt, translate, or create derivative works based on the Software or the Documentation. You may be held legally responsible for any copying or copyright infringement which is caused by your failure to abide by the terms of these restrictions.

3. TERMINATION: This license is effective until terminated. This license will terminate automatically without notice from the Company if you fail to comply with any provisions or limitations of this license. Upon termination, you shall destroy the Documentation and all copies of the Software. All provisions of this Agreement as to limitation and disclaimer of warranties, limitation of liability, remedies or damages, and our ownership rights shall survive termination.

4. LIMITED WARRANTY AND DISCLAIMER OF WARRANTY: Company warrants that for a period of 60 days from the date you purchase this SOFTWARE (or purchase or adopt the accompanying textbook), the Software, when properly installed and used in accordance with the Documentation, will operate in substantial conformity with the description of the Software set forth in the Documentation, and that for a period of 30 days the disk(s) on which the Software is delivered shall be free from defects in materials and workmanship under normal use. The Company does <u>not</u> warrant that the Software will meet your requirements or that the operation of the Software will be uninterrupted or error-free. Your only remedy and the Company's only obligation under these limited warranties is, at the Company's option, return of the disk for a refund of any amounts paid for it by you or replacement of the disk. THIS LIMITED WARRANTY IS THE ONLY WARRANTY PROVIDED BY THE COMPANY AND ITS LICENSORS, AND THE COMPANY AND ITS LICENSORS DISCLAIM ALL OTHER WARRANTIES, EXPRESS OR IMPLIED, INCLUDING WITHOUT LIMITATION, THE IMPLIED WARRANTIES OF MERCHANTABILITY AND FITNESS FOR A PARTICULAR PURPOSE. THE COMPANY DOES NOT WARRANT, GUARANTEE OR MAKE ANY REPRESENTATION REGARDING THE ACCURACY, RELIABILITY, CURRENTNESS, USE, OR RESULTS OF USE, OF THE SOFTWARE.

5. LIMITATION OF REMEDIES AND DAMAGES: IN NO EVENT, SHALL THE COMPANY OR ITS EMPLOYEES, AGENTS, LICENSORS, OR CONTRACTORS BE LIABLE FOR ANY INCIDENTAL, INDIRECT, SPECIAL, OR CONSEQUENTIAL DAMAGES ARISING OUT OF OR IN CONNECTION WITH THIS LICENSE OR THE SOFTWARE, INCLUDING FOR LOSS OF USE, LOSS OF DATA, LOSS OF INCOME OR PROFIT, OR OTHER LOSSES, SUSTAINED AS A RESULT OF INJURY TO ANY PERSON, OR LOSS OF OR DAMAGE TO PROPERTY, OR CLAIMS OF THIRD PARTIES, EVEN IF THE COMPANY OR AN AUTHORIZED REPRESENTATIVE OF THE COMPANY HAS BEEN ADVISED OF THE POSSIBILITY OF SUCH DAMAGES. IN NO EVENT SHALL THE LIABILITY OF THE COMPANY FOR DAMAGES WITH RESPECT TO THE SOFTWARE EXCEED THE AMOUNTS ACTUALLY PAID BY YOU, IF ANY, FOR THE SOFTWARE OR THE ACCOMPANYING TEXTBOOK. BECAUSE SOME JURISDICTIONS DO NOT ALLOW THE LIMITATION OF LIABILITY IN CERTAIN CIRCUMSTANCES, THE ABOVE LIMITATIONS MAY NOT ALWAYS APPLY TO YOU.

(continued on next page)

SINGLE PC LICENSE AGREEMENT AND LIMITED WARRANTY: (continued from previous page)

6. GENERAL: THIS AGREEMENT SHALL BE CONSTRUED IN ACCORDANCE WITH THE LAWS OF THE UNITED STATES OF AMERICA AND THE STATE OF NEW YORK, APPLICABLE TO CONTRACTS MADE IN NEW YORK, AND SHALL BENEFIT THE COMPANY, ITS AFFILIATES AND ASSIGNEES. THIS AGREEMENT IS THE COMPLETE AND EXCLUSIVE STATEMENT OF THE AGREEMENT BETWEEN YOU AND THE COMPANY AND SUPERSEDES ALL PROPOSALS OR PRIOR AGREEMENTS, ORAL, OR WRITTEN, AND ANY OTHER COMMUNICATIONS BETWEEN YOU AND THE COMPANY OR ANY REPRESENTATIVE OF THE COMPANY RELATING TO THE SUBJECT MATTER OF THIS AGREEMENT. If you are a U.S. Government user, this Software is licensed with "restricted rights" as set forth in subparagraphs (a)-(d) of the Commercial Computer-Restricted Rights clause at FAR 52.227-19 or in subparagraphs (c)(1)(ii) of the Rights in Technical Data and Computer Software clause at DFARS 252.227-7013, and similar clauses, as applicable.

Should you have any questions concerning this agreement or if you wish to contact the Company for any reason, please contact in writing: Social Sciences Media Editor, Prentice Hall, One Lake Street, Upper Saddle River, NJ 07458.